Clark Ashton Smith:
A Comprehensive Bibliography

CLARK ASHTON SMITH

A Comprehensive Bibliography

S. T. Joshi, David E. Schultz,
and Scott Connors

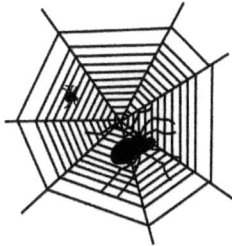

Hippocampus Press

New York

Published by Hippocampus Press
P.O. Box 641, New York, NY 10156
www.hippocampuspress.com

First Edition, 2020
3 5 7 9 8 6 4 2

ISBN 978-1-61498-242-5 (paperback)
ISBN 978-1-61498-255-5 (e-book)

Contents

Introduction

The history of the publication and dissemination of the writings of Clark Ashton Smith (1893–1961), as well as the critical analysis of his work, are governed by Smith's decision to write in genres—whether exotic and archaistic poetry or fantastic fiction—whose literary status in his own day was problematic. The result was that Smith gained little recognition for the undeniable merits of his work and was destined to remain at best a figure of local renown or an object of devotion from a small cadre of enthusiasts. The posthumous success of his tales has to some degree compensated for his lack of celebrity in his time, but he remains a specialized and cultivated taste.

Clark Ashton Smith was born on 13 January 1893, in Long Valley, California, near the town of Auburn, where he spent the bulk of his life. He was the only son of Timeus and Fanny (Gaylord) Smith. With relatively little formal schooling, Smith became a prodigious autodidact, learning Latin and also reading the entirety of Webster's Unabridged Dictionary. He began writing as early as the age of eleven, inspired by the *Arabian Nights*. In 1906, his discovery of Edgar Allan Poe proved to be a tremendous impetus to his creative faculties, and he began writing both poetry and prose soon thereafter. As early as the age of fourteen, he wrote a novel of nearly 100,000 words, *The Black Diamonds,* as well as a shorter novel, *The Sword of Zagan,* and numerous short stories. A few years later he read William Beckford's *Vathek,* and it also inspired his own nascent attempts at writing. He also read Omar Khayyam's *Rubaiyat* as translated into English verse by Edward FitzGerald (1859), and he began writing poetry based upon it. In 1907 he discovered the work of George Sterling (1869–1926), his fellow Californian, especially the fantastic poem "A Wine of Wizardry," as published in the *Cosmopolitan* (September 1907).

Smith published both poems and a few stories in the *Black Cat, Munsey's,* and other professional markets in 1910; but at this time poetry was clearly the major focus of his literary ventures. In early 1911 he wrote to Sterling, sending him some of his fantastic poetry, and Sterling immediately recognized the scintillating nature of Smith's work. Just as Ambrose Bierce had nurtured Sterling's own poetic talents—and fostered the publication of his work—a decade or so before, Sterling became Smith's poetic mentor and acted as liaison between Smith and the San Francisco publisher A. M. Robertson, who issued Smith's *The Star-Treader*

and Other Poems in August 1912. The book was an immediate sensation
on the West Coast, and a minor brouhaha erupted between Sterling and
Boutwell Dunlap as to who had actually "discovered" Smith. Bierce was
minimally involved in the tumult, as he had read and admired Smith's "Ode
to the Abyss" but objected to the extravagant praise of Smith that had been
put into his mouth by various parties. Smith had had a chance to meet
Bierce during the latter's extended stay in California in June–July 1912, but
his innate shyness caused him to decline Sterling's invitation for a gathering.
(Smith later declined to meet Sterling's close friend Jack London.)

Although *The Star-Treader* was widely reviewed in magazines and
newspapers well beyond California (including the *New York Times Book
Review*), it did not bring permanent recognition to Smith. In part this was
because Smith did not write poetry in great quantity at this time, hampered
by isolation and poor health; his next volume, *Odes and Sonnets* (1918), was
published by the prestigious Book Club of California, but was a partial
reprint of material from *The Star-Treader*. It would be another four years
before Smith published another volume, *Ebony and Crystal* (1922). The
fact that that volume was essentially self-published—printed by the *Auburn Journal* and financed by the author—was an ominous sign in terms
of Smith's long-term reputation as a poet.

For it was exactly at this time that the Modernist movement in poetry—represented by such disparate figures as T. S. Eliot, Ezra Pound,
William Carlos Williams, and Amy Lowell—were rejecting what they
came to believe were the florid extravagance of later nineteenth-century
poetry (the poetry of Swinburne, Wilde, and others, which markedly influenced Smith) and also rejecting the fantastic and the exotic as proper
subject-matter for poetry. The Modernists' emphasis on free verse, and
their scarcely disguised scorn of formal meter and rhyme, also stood in
stark contrast to Smith's poetic idiom. The result was that Smith was
doomed to achieve, at best, only local recognition as a poet. Indeed, *Ebony
and Crystal* sold so poorly that Smith had to write a column for the *Auburn Journal* as a way of reimbursing the newspaper for printing costs.

Sandalwood (1925) was another self-published volume, this time financed in part by Smith's new friend Donald Wandrei, a college student.
The volume contained some early translations of the poetry of Charles
Baudelaire. Smith had, incredibly, taught himself French to such an extent
that he produced prose translations of nearly all the poems in Baudelaire's
seminal volume, *Les Fleurs du mal;* Smith later versified some of these
prose versions, although the majority remained unpublished until long
after the author's death.

In 1922 Smith first heard from H. P. Lovecraft, who must have recognized that his own ventures into archaistic poetry—whether it be the occasional verse of the eighteenth century or weird verse in the manner of Poe—was substantially inferior to Smith's, for he essentially gave up writing poetry for nearly a decade after reading Smith's early poetry volumes. Lovecraft also waxed ecstatic over Smith's paintings, many of which were then in the possession of their mutual colleague Samuel Loveman. Smith had no formal training as an artist, but he produced paintings of striking exoticism and bizarrerie. At the time, Lovecraft was making strides in the writing of weird fiction—a tendency fostered by the establishment of the pulp magazine *Weird Tales*. Lovecraft maintained that it was through his urging that the magazine's first editor, Edwin Baird, abandoned his "no poetry" policy. Some of Smith's poems did appear in early issues of *Weird Tales,* but it was not until 1925 that he—surely inspired by Lovecraft's example, if not by Lovecraft's actual work—undertook to resume the writing of fantastic fiction himself. The result was "The Abominations of Yondo." Lovecraft praised the tale, but Smith was cut to the quick when Sterling scorned it as meaningless and outmoded. Nevertheless, Sterling engineered its publication in the *Overland Monthly,* one of the pioneering magazines on the West Coast; Sterling also arranged for the publication of an effusive article on Smith by Wandrei, "The Emperor of Dreams" (December 1926).

Sterling's suicide on November 17, 1926, essentially corresponded with Smith's shift from poetry to fiction, under the growing influence of Lovecraft. It was, however, not until 1929 that Smith began writing fiction in any great quantity—but when he did so, he went about it with remarkable diligence and prolificity. Over the next six years he wrote about 130 stories, long and short; many were published in *Weird Tales,* but as Smith explored the domains of pure fantasy as well as of science fiction, he found other markets, notably *Wonder Stories* and the short-lived *Strange Tales.*

Smith's tales, unlike those of Lovecraft and (coincidentally) like those of Robert E. Howard, tended to fall into cycles based on locality or chronological era, such as the tales of Zothique (an imagined future continent), Averoigne (an imaginary province in medieval France), Hyperborea (an imaginary polar region), Atlantis (most of the tales focused on the continent's capital, Poseidonis), and so on. Smaller cycles were set on Mars, Xiccarph (an imaginary planet), and elsewhere. Smith had his troubles with the editors of pulp magazines, notably Farnsworth Wright of *Weird Tales* (who, in the early 1930s, established a companion maga-

zine for "Orientales," *Oriental Stories* [later titled *Magic Carpet*]) and
Hugo Gernsback of *Wonder Stories*. Wright frequently rejected Smith's
work or forced him to cut or otherwise revise his stories before he would
accept them. Gernsback did the same and added insult to injury by failing
to pay Smith promptly; at one point Gernsback owed Smith nearly $1000
in back payments, and Smith hired an attorney to extract the money he
was owed. Because he had little other source of income (although at times
he did temporary work such as fruit picking and other menial tasks), and
because he was supporting two increasingly aged and enfeebled parents,
Smith felt he had no option but to accede to these editors' requests, in
order to ensure a sale and the much-needed income it generated. He also
self-published a slim volume of tales that had been rejected by the pulps,
The Double Shadow and Other Fantasies (1933), but its sales were poor and
it brought in little revenue.

Smith maintained that he would restore the tales to their original state
if they were to be gathered in a book; but he seems to have made no effort,
during the heyday of his fiction writing, to solicit publishers for a collection of his tales. But by the mid-1930s his inspiration for writing fiction
seemed to be flagging. Around 1934 he resumed the writing of poetry,
which he had all but abandoned for the past decade or so; and the next year
he took up sculpture, producing small carvings and statuettes out of local
materials, including dinosaur bone. By 1935 his fiction-writing career was
all but over, although the tales he had written earlier continued to appear
in *Thrilling Wonder Stories* and other pulp magazines of the later 1930s.

It was his association with August Derleth, begun in 1930, that led to
the next stage of Smith's career as a writer. Stunned by the death of H. P.
Lovecraft in 1937, Derleth had decided to form his own publishing
company, Arkham House, to issue the work of Lovecraft after his rather
half-hearted attempts to market Lovecraft's work with major publishers
did not yield the results he wished. After *The Outsider and Others* appeared
in 1939, Derleth decided to expand his operation to include the work of
other writers of weird and science fiction. He issued a volume of his own
tales, *Someone in the Dark* (1941), and then followed it up with one of
Smith's, *Out of Space and Time* (1942). It was the first of six volumes of
tales (the last two of them posthumous) that appeared under the Arkham
House imprint. These volumes did indeed bring some recognition to
Smith, although some mainstream critics and reviewers dismissed the
work as overwrought and verbally flamboyant. The volumes sold slowly
but steadily, but Derleth could not justify publishing a succeeding title
unless its predecessor had either sold out or fully paid its printing costs.

Smith did not make much of an attempt to publish his work in the science fiction digest magazines of the 1950s; and after the demise of *Weird Tales* in 1954, the market for weird fiction was virtually nonexistent. Smith was content to work on his poetry. At the suggestion of Donald Wandrei (co-founder of Arkham House, although after his entry into the Army he had little to do with the firm's day-to-day operations), Smith began compiling his *Selected Poems*. The job took a full five years (1944–49), and the resulting volume was so large that Derleth was unsure when he could ever find the means to issue it. Smith had taken extraordinary care in the selection of his poems and had also revised some poems extensively. He also included poems translated from French (not just those of Baudelaire, but also of Paul Verlaine, José-Maria de Heredia, and others) and also Spanish, a language he had learned in the mid-1940s. Smith had also composed original poems in French and Spanish or translated some of his English-language poems into those languages. In 1947 he took up the writing of haiku, producing more than one hundred specimens in the process.

The best that Arkham House could do in the short term was to issue two small volumes of poetry, *The Dark Chateau* (1951) and *Spells and Philtres* (1958), neither of which brought Smith much fame or revenue. Smith married Carol Jones Dorman on November 10, 1954, when he was nearly sixty-two years old. He eventually moved into Carol's house in Pacific Grove. But in spite of adjurations by his wife and by Derleth to do more writing, Smith seemed content to do the occasional carving or poem, and the even more occasional story. When Smith died on 14 August 1961, there was some doubt as to whether he would ever attain worldwide celebrity, whether as a fiction writer, a poet, or an artist.

It was therefore unsurprising that the initial attempts to reignite interest in Smith's work came from friends and colleagues. His literary executor, Roy A. Squires, issued exquisite but highly limited editions of small batches of his lesser-known poetry, beginning with *The Hill of Dionysus: A Selection* (1962). A late colleague, Donald Sidney-Fryer, assembled Smith's *Poems in Prose* (1965) for Arkham House, and that publisher at last issued *Selected Poems* in late 1971, a few months after August Derleth's own death. The publication of that long-delayed volume was largely a result of the fee that the publisher received for the television adaptation of "The Return of the Sorcerer" (on *Rod Serling's Night Gallery*), a fee larger than the totality of payments Smith received in his entire life for his own writings.

Beginning in 1970, Lin Carter edited several paperback volumes of Smith's tales—now arranged in cycles—for his Adult Fantasy series, but they sold poorly. In the later 1950s Smith himself (or, rather, his wife) had attempted to interest paperback publishers in a volume of his selected tales, *Far from Time,* with an introduction by Ray Bradbury, but found no takers; and now Carter found that Smith's recherché prose and exotic settings were indeed caviar to the general. A later series of three paperback volumes, edited by Sidney-Fryer in the early 1980s, sold somewhat better.

By this time a vigorous revival of the fantasy fandom movement, especially the part centered around Lovecraft, had made it possible for several small-press publishers to succeed with modest volumes of Smith's prose, poetry, and prose poems. Necronomicon Press initiated a more scholarly phase of the enterprise by enlisting Smith scholar Steve Behrends to edit six booklets of individual stories based on typescripts found in the Clark Ashton Smith Papers, now in the John Hay Library of Brown University. And Smith's work was regularly appearing in anthologies of weird or fantasy fiction as his status as a classic author gradually rose. Arkham House issued a fine selection of Smith's best work, *A Rendezvous in Averoigne* (1988), and Stephen Jones edited an extensive collection of Smith's stories, *The Emperor of Dreams* (2002).

Early in the new millennium, Hippocampus Press took the lead in issuing Smith's work, beginning with his juvenile novels, *The Black Diamonds* (2002) and *The Sword of Zagan* (2004). This set the stage for the monumental three-volume edition of Smith's *Complete Poetry and Translations* (2007–08). David E. Schultz had been working on the edition since the 1990s, transcribing hundreds of unpublished poems found in the Clark Ashton Smith Papers; co-editor S. T. Joshi took charge of the third volume (containing Smith's translations of French and Spanish poetry). Around the same time, Scott Connors and Ron Hilger consulted manuscripts and periodical publications to assemble an exhaustive five-volume edition of Smith's *Collected Fantasies* (2006–10), following up with a *Miscellaneous Writings* in 2011. Taken together, these editions presented the vast bulk of Smith's poetry and prose fiction in definitive, textually accurate editions. His work received canonization of a sort in Joshi's edition of *The Dark Eidolon and Other Fantasies* (2014) for Penguin Classics.

Other bodies of Smith's work soon appeared in similar editions. The discovery of a few unpublished prose poems resulted in a new edition, *Nostalgia of the Unknown* (1988). This edition was superseded by *In the Realms of Mystery and Wonder* (2017), which also included reproductions of Smith's carvings and paintings. (Some of the artwork had previously appeared in *Grotesques and Fantastiques* [1973] and *The Fantastic Art of Clark Ashton Smith* [1973].) A volume of Smith's essays—initially collected by Charles K. Wolfe in *Planets and Dimensions* (1973)—is in progress.

Smith's letters remain as one of the last frontiers in the publication of his work. A volume of his *Letters to H. P. Lovecraft* (1987) presented abridged editions of some of his correspondence with the writer from Providence. Arkham House issued a substantial volume of *Selected Letters* in 2003, while Schultz and Joshi edited *The Shadow of the Unattained* (2005), a volume of the joint correspondence of Smith and Sterling, followed by the monumental *Dawnward Spire, Lonely Hill* (2017), an annotated edition of the joint Smith–Lovecraft correspondence. More such volumes are in preparation.

The first translation of Smith's work appears to have been a translation of "The Master of the Asteroid" in a German magazine in 1933. The Spanish periodical *Narraciones Terroríficas* translated two Smith stories in 1939, and a Swedish magazine translated another story in 1945. The first book publications of Smith's work in foreign languages date to the 1970s, when volumes appeared in German, Dutch, French, Spanish, and Japanese. The great majority of these and subsequent volumes focused on Smith's fantastic fiction, and recent editions have been notably lavish and exhaustive, as witness the German *Gesammelte Erzählungen* (2011–17; 6 vols.) and a three-volume French edition under the series title "Clark Ashton Smith Intégrale" (2017). A major volume of Smith's poems, translated into French by Jean Hautepierre, has recently appeared. From at least the 1980s onward, Smith has appeared regularly in anthologies of weird fiction in nearly a dozen languages.

Criticism of Smith, exclusive of book reviews (which, in any event, tapered off after the outpouring reviews of *The Star-Treader*), has been slow in appearing until recently. His comings and goings were a subject of interest locally, as testified by numerous unsigned paragraphs on him in the "Spectator" column of the San Francisco weekly, *Town Talk*, edited by Theodore Bonnet. Wandrei's essay of 1926 was a solitary excursion into critical analysis, perhaps marred by overly effusive praise. Smith was a staple of fanzine writers during the 1930s and 1940s, but there was virtually no critical scrutiny of his work until after his death. It was then that Jack L. Chalker compiled the still valuable volume *In Memoriam: Clark Ashton Smith* (1963), with memoirs by some of Smith's friends and some attempts at criticism by Fritz Leiber, L. Sprague de Camp, and especially Donald Sidney-Fryer, who soon took the lead in fostering greater understanding of Smith's life and work.

Sidney-Fryer spent years assembling a bibliography of Smith's work; during its early stages he worked with Smith himself, querying Smith by correspondence on all manner of topics relating to Smith's various publications. Sidney-Fryer's work culminated in the landmark volume *Emperor of Dreams: A Clark Ashton Smith Bibliography* (1978), which featured letters of appreciation or recollections by a number of friends, colleagues, and critics. But Sidney-Fryer was not interested in preparing a detailed bibliography; his book could better be called a checklist. Nevertheless, his work remains a pioneering attempt to chart the totality of Smith's writings.

Steve Behrends's monograph of 1990 (substantially expanded in 2013) is a sound critical analysis, and Scott Connors's anthology *The Freedom of Fantastic Things* (2006) gathers both unpublished and previously published critical work. The Italian scholar Pietro Guarriello compiled an interesting volume, *Ombre dal cosmo* (1999), while the French scholar David Dunais published a profound study of Smith's poetry in 2013.

Aside from Sidney-Fryer's many shorter articles on Smith (some of them gathered in *The Golden State Phantasticks* [2011]), such critics as Behrends, Ron Hilger, S. T. Joshi, and Brian Stableford have taken the lead in the analysis of Smith's fiction, poetry, and other work in shorter compass. Scott Connors has established himself as the leading authority on Smith, both in his co-editing of the *Collected Fantasies* and other volumes and in his trenchant critical and biographical studies, which it is hoped will be melded into a full-length biography. Connors and Hilger edited a short-lived periodical, *Lost Worlds* (2004–08), entirely devoted to Smith, following on the heels of *Klarkash-Ton/The Dark Eidolon* (1988–93), edited by Behrends and Marc A. Michaud.

It is abundantly clear that much remains to be done in the analysis of Smith's work, especially his poetry, which many readers of fantasy fiction appear to find intimidating, even though it seems to be the pinnacle of Smith's achievement as a writer. His place in literary history, in the history of the genres he worked in, and in his historical era all remain to be specified, and it is hoped that the present volume—which charts in a reasonably exhaustive manner the full scope of his publications and the books, articles, and other matter devoted to him—will provide an impetus to that work.

Explanatory Notes

This bibliography is arranged with a view to allowing readers to locate the information they wish in the simplest possible manner, given the complex and multi-layered history of Smith's publications in books, magazines, anthologies, and the like. It is generally focused on materials in print, since material available online can be fleeting and difficult to locate if sites become defunct or otherwise unavailable. Publications have been listed through the end of 2017.

The section on book publications (I.A) lists items (books, pamphlets, and other separate publications) in strict chronological order, so far as that can be ascertained. Tables of contents and page numbers are supplied for nearly all items, and notes provide information on the nature of the edition and any other special features. As an appendix (items 89f.) selected ebook editions are listed. These are only the most notable such editions currently available. Many of Smith's tales have been published as separate ebooks.

Section I.B lists Smith's appearances (fiction, poetry [including translations of French and Spanish poetry, even if these translations are in prose], prose poems, nonfiction, published letters) in periodicals and magazines, with cross-references to their inclusion in books of Smith's writings. The works in each section are listed alphabetically by title, and the various appearances are listed in chronological order.

The section on Smith's works in translation is probably incomplete, because of the difficulty of locating or even knowing of the existence of certain items. The book publications (II.A) are grouped by language (listed alphabetically), and chronologically within a given language. (The publication in Galician was discovered very late in the preparation of this work and has been placed at the end of section II.A.) Section II.B lists translations of Smith's works in magazines and anthologies; these appearances are listed chronologically regardless of language.

The section on Smith Criticism begins with listings of news items and other informational pieces relevant to Smith or his family, followed by encyclopedias and bibliographies. Relatively few books about Smith (III.D) have so far appeared, and some of the items in this section are short pamphlets. In the section of criticism in books and periodicals (III.E), the more important introductions and other matter contained in books of Smith's writings are listed. Many items in this section are annotated, but not every item was deemed worthy of annotation. The section on book reviews (III.F) is probably incomplete, especially for more recent publications, as many reviews have appeared online. In the final section of this chapter are listed periodicals devoted to Smith, poems about Smith, media adaptations (including television shows, spoken-word recordings, musical settings, and the like), and other miscellany.

An asterisk preceding an entry means that it has not been seen or verified. Donald Sidney-Fryer pointed out, in *Emperor of Dreams,* that

Smith acknowledged in *The Dark Chateau* and *Spells and Philtres* that he work had been published in *Circle* and *Susquehanna*. No poems by Smith have been located in magazines with these or similar names.

The compilers would like to acknowledge the assistance of Marlena E. Bremseth, Eric Carlson, Pierre Comtois, Zayda Delgado (Special Collections and University Archives, University of California at Riverside), Ann Dodge of the John Hay Library, Alistair Durie, Stefan Dziemianowicz, Doug Ellis, Frank Festa, Pietro Guarriello, Ron Hilger, Derrick Hussey, Juliana Jenkins, Library Special Collections, University of California–Los Angeles, Mateusz Kopacz, Robert Lichtman, Patrice Louinet, Donovan K. Loucks, Charles Lovecraft, Christopher O'Brien, Eliot Party, Robert M. Price, Darrell Schweitzer, Jordan Douglas Smith, Darin Coelho Spring, Sybille Stahl of the Deutsche National Bibliotek, Christopher Thill, and Special Collections, Eastern New Mexico University in the preparation of this volume.

—S. T. JOSHI
DAVID E. SCHULTZ
SCOTT CONNORS

I. Works by Smith in English

A. Books and Pamphlets

1. *The Star-Treader and Other Poems.*
   a. San Francisco: A. M. Robertson, [November] 1912. 100 pp.
   b. LaVergne, TN: [Nabu Press, 2010].
   c. n.p.: Wentworth Press, 2016.

   Contents: "Nero" (1–4); "Chant to Sirius" (5); "The Star-Treader" (6–10); "The Morning Pool" (11); "The Night Forest" (12–13); "The Mad Wind" (14); "Song to Oblivion" (15); "Medusa" (16–17); "Ode to the Abyss" (18–20); "The Soul of the Sea" (21); "The Butterfly" (22–25); "The Price" (26); "The Mystic Meaning" (27); "Ode to Music" (28–30); "The Last Night" (31); "Ode on Imagination" (32–34); "The Wind and the Moon" (35); "Lament of the Stars" (36–38); "The Maze of Sleep" (39); "The Winds" (40–41); "The Masque of Forsaken Gods" (42–48); "A Sunset" (49); "The Cloud-Islands" (50–51); "The Snow-Blossoms" (52); "The Summer Moon" (53); "The Return of Hyperion" (54); "Lethe" (55); "Atlantis" (56); "The Unrevealed" (57); "The Eldritch Dark" (58); "The Cherry-Snows" (59); "Fairy Lanterns" (60); "Nirvana" (61); "The Nemesis of Suns" (62); "White Death" (63); "Retrospect and Forecast" (64); "Shadow of Nightmare" (65); "The Song of a Comet" (66–68); "The Retribution" (69); "To the Darkness" (70–71); "A Dream of Beauty" (72); "The Dream-Bridge" (73); "Pine Needles" (75); "To the Sun" (76–77); "The Fugitives" (78); "Averted Malefice" (79); "The Medusa of the Skies" (80); "A Dead City" (81); "The Song of the Stars" (82–84); "Copan" (85); "A Song of Dreams" (86–87); "The Balance" (88); "Saturn" (89–98); "Finis" (99–100).

   Notes. 2000 copies printed by the Philopolis Press in San Francisco. The edition was financed in part by CAS's mother. A photograph of CAS by Bianca Conti is laid into some copies. Several binding states exist, of which the earliest has buff boards, gold-stamped on the spine and on the front with the same design used on the dust jacket, with uncut edges. CAS's own copy was bound in brown Morocco leather with raised bands on spine. The spine lettering on the dust jacket may be printed either in gold or black. The second, later state has light blue boards with printed label on front and spine, with all edges cut, and a glassine dust jacket. Approximately half of the printed sheets were destroyed in a warehouse fire. The Nabu Press edition is a facsimile print-on-demand reprint of a.

2. *Odes and Sonnets.*
   a. San Francisco: The Book Club of California, [June] 1918. iv, 30 pp.
   b. Whitefish, MT: Kessinger, 2009.
   c. LaVergne, TN: Nabu Press, 2010.

   Contents: "Preface," by George Sterling (iii–iv); "Nero" (1–5); "Ode to the Abyss" (6–9); "To the Darkness" (10–12); "The Retribution" (13); "Satan Unrepentant" (14–18); "Alexandrines" (19); "Exotique" (20); "Ave atque Vale" (21); "The Ministers of Law" (22); "The Refuge of Beauty" (23); "The Crucifixion of Eros" (24); "The Harlot of the World" (25); "Belated Love" (26); "The Medusa of Despair" (27); "Memnon at Midnight" (28).
   Notes. Gray paper boards, linen half-binding with paper label. Limited to 300 numbered copies. Decorations by Florence Lundborg. The Kessinger and Nabu Press editions are print-on-demand facsimiles of a.

3. *Ebony and Crystal: Poems in Verse and Prose.*
   a. Auburn, CA: The Auburn Journal, [December] 1922. [ix], 154 pp.
   b. n.p.: CreateSpace, 2014 (facsimile of 1922 edition).

   Contents: "Arabesque" (1); "Beyond the Great Wall" (2); "To Omar Khayyam" (3–4); "Strangeness" (5); "The Infinite Quest" (6); "Rosa Mystica" (7); "The Nereid" (8); "In Saturn" (9); "Impression" (10); "Triple Aspect" (11); "Desolation" (12); "The Orchid" (13); "A Fragment" (14); "Crepuscle" (15); "Inferno" (16); "Mirrors" (17); "Belated Love" (18); "The Absence of the Muse" (19); "Dissonance" (20); "To Nora May French" (21–23); "In Lemuria" (24); "Recompense" (25); "Exotique" (26); "Transcendence" (27); "Satiety" (28); "The Ministers of Law" (29); "Coldness" (30); "The Desert Garden" (31); "The Crucifixion of Eros" (32); "The Exile" (33); "Ave atque Vale" (34); "Solution" (35); "The Tears of Lilith" (36); "A Precept" (37); "Remembered Light" (38); "Song" (39); "Haunting" (40); "The Hidden Paradise" (41); "Cleopatra" (42); "Ecstasy" (43); "Union" (44); "Psalm" (45–46); "In November" (47); "Symbols" (48); *The Hashish Eater; or, The Apocalypse of Evil* (49–64); "The Sorrow of the Winds" (65); "Artemis" (66); "Love Is Not Yours, Love Is Not Mine" (67); "The City in the Desert" (68); "The Melancholy Pool" (69); "The Mirrors of Beauty" (70); "Winter Moonlight" (71); "To the Beloved" (72); "Requiescat" (73); "Mirage" (74); "Inheritance" (75); "Autumnal" (76); "Chant of Autumn" (77); "Echo of Memnon" (78); "Twilight on the Snow"

(79); "Image" (80); "The Refuge of Beauty" (81); "Nightmare" (82); "The Mummy" (83); "Forgetfulness" (84); "Flamingoes" (85); "The Chimaera" (86); "Satan Unrepentant" (87–89); "The Abyss Triumphant" (90); "The Motes" (91); "The Medusa of Despair" (92); "Laus Mortis" (93); "The Ghoul and the Seraph" (94–98); "At Sunrise" (99); "The Land of Evil Stars" (100–101); "The Harlot of the World" (102); "The Hope of the Infinite" (103); "Love Malevolent" (104); "Palms" (105); "Memnon at Midnight" (106); "Eidolon" (107); "The Kingdom of Shadows" (108–9); "Requiescat in Pace" (110–11); "Alexandrines" (112); "Ashes of Sunset" (113); "November Twilight" (114); "Sepulture" (115); "Quest" (116); "Beauty Implacable" (117); "A Vision of Lucifer" (118); "Desire of Vastness" (119); "Anticipation" (120); "A Psalm to the Best Beloved" (121); "The Witch in the Graveyard" (122–24); *Poems in Prose:* "The Traveller" (127–28); "The Flower-Devil" (129); "Images" ("Tears," "The Secret Rose," "The Wind and the Garden," "Offerings," "A Coronal") (130). The Black Lake" (131); "Vignettes" ("Beyond the Mountains," "The Broken Lute," "Nostalgia of the Unknown," "Grey Sorrow," "The Hair of Circe," "The Eyes of Circe") (132–33); "A Dream of Lethe" (134); "The Caravan" (135); "The Princess Almeena" (136); "Ennui" (137–38); "The Statue of Silence" (139); "Remoteness" (140); "The Memnons of the Night" (141); "The Garden and the Tomb" (142); "In Cocaigne" (143); "The Litany of the Seven Kisses" (144); "From a Letter" (145); "From the Crypts of Memory" (146–47); "A Phantasy" (148); "The Demon, the Angel, and Beauty" (149–50); "The Shadows" (151–52).

Notes. Bound in red cloth, with title printed on front board but not on spine. Sheets are stapled and casebound. Due to a printer's error, no endpapers were included. Limited to 500 copies numbered and signed by CAS. Issued without dust jacket; one was designed by CAS, but it was not used because of cost. Terence McVicker (Glendale, CA) printed a number of copies of CAS's design for the CAS Centennial in 1993.

4.   *Sandalwood.*

    a.   Auburn, CA: The Auburn Journal Press, [October] 1925. 47 pp.

       Contents: "Semblance" (7); "The Song of Aviol" (7–8); "We Shall Meet" (I) 8–9); "Forgotten Sorrow" (9–10); "Departure" (10); "You Are Not Beautiful" (10); "Query" (10–11); "Enigma" (11); "Incognita" (11–12); "The Secret" (12); "The End of Autumn" (12–13); "The Love-Potion" (13); "The Song of Cartha" (14);

"Afterwards" (14); "Contradiction" (14–15); "The Last Oblivion" (15); "Autumn Orchards" (15–16); "Remembrance" (16); "The Wingless Archangels" (17); "Moon-Dawn" (17); "Lunar Mystery" (17–18); "Enchanted Mirrors" (18); "Duality" (18–19); "A Valediction" (19); "Selenique" (19–20); "Alienage" (20–21); "Adventure" (21–22); "Plum-Flowers" (22); "Song" (I) 22–23); "Minatory" (23–24); "Maya" (24); "Interrogation" (24–25); "Consolation" (25); "A Meeting" (25–26); "The Barrier" (27); "Apologia" (27–28); "Estrangement" (28); "Loss" (28–29); "A Catch" (29); "Don Juan Sings" (29–30); "On Reading Baudelaire" (30); "To the Chimera" (31); *Nineteen Poems from the French of Charles Pierre Baudelaire:* "Rêve Parisien" (31–33); "Semper Eadem" (33); "L'Idéal" (33–34); "La Géante" (34); "La Muse vénale" (34); "L'Examen de minuit" (35–36); "La Musique" (36); "Hymne à la beauté" (36–37); "Parfum Exotique" (37); "Mœsta et Errabunda" (37–38); "Ciel brouillé" (38–39); "La Fontaine de sang" (39); "Harmonie du soir" (39–40); "L'Aube spirituelle" (41); "Le Vin des amants" (40–41); "Obsession" (41); "Alchimie de la eouleur" (41–42); "Horreur sympathétique" [*sic*] (42); "L'Irrémédiable" (42–43).

Notes. Printed in green paper covers. Limited to 250 copies, numbered and signed by CAS.

5. *The Immortals of Mercury.*
   a. New York: Stellar Publishing Corp., 1932. 24 pp.

   Notes. Small booklet printed with white covers and saddle-bound. Science Fiction Series No. 16.

6. *The Double Shadow and Other Fantasies.*
   a. Auburn, CA: [Auburn Journal Print], [June] 1933. 30 pp.
   b. [Madison, WI: The Strange Co., 1979.]
   c. Holicong, PA: Wildside Press, 2003. 108 pp.

   Contents: "The Voyage of King Euvoran" (5–13); "The Maze of the Enchanter" (13–18); "The Double Shadow" (18–22); "A Night in Malnéant" (22–24); "The Devotee of Evil" (24–28); "The Willow Landscape" (28–30).

   Notes. Bound in gray paper; front cover has black type and an ornament (an image of a torch). Text printed in two columns. Price: 25¢. Many copies have handwritten corrections by CAS. The Strange Co. edition is a half-scale facsimile reproduction of a. issued without any identifying information as to the publisher. It was distributed through several amateur press associations and at science fiction conventions. The Wildside Press edition, printed in both hardcover and paperback, uses the Arkham House texts of the stories.

7. *The White Sybil and Men of Avalon.*
   a. Everett, PA: Fantasy Publications, 1934. 38 pp.

   Contents: "The White Sybil" (2–18); "Men of Avalon" by David H. Keller (19–38).
      Notes. Bound in white paper wrappers. The titles and authors of the two stories are printed on the front cover, with a horizontal bar dividing them.

8. *Nero and Other Poems.*
   a. Lakeport, CA: The Futile Press, [May] 1937. 24 pp.

   Contents: "Nero" (1–5); "Chant to Sirius" (6–7); "Medusa" (8–9); "The Eldritch Dark" (10); "The Winds" (11–12); "Retrospect and Forecast" (13); "The Song of a Comet" (14–17); "To the Darkness" (18–20); "A Dream of Beauty" (21); "A Song of Dreams" (22–24).
      Notes. Bound in boards with cloth-covered spine. Two inserts, printed in June 1937, were issued with many copies: "The Price of Poetry" by David Warren Ryder (3 printed sheets, one side only, unbound), and "Outlanders" (one-page broadside).

9. *Out of Space and Time.*
   a. Sauk City, WI: Arkham House, [August] 1942. xii, 370 pp.
   b. Jersey, UK: Neville Spearman, 1971.
   c.1. St. Albans, UK: Panther, 1974 (2 vols.).
   c.2. St. Albans, UK: Panther, 1974–75 (2 vols.).
   d. Lincoln: University of Nebraska Press (Bison Books), 2006.

   Contents: Clark Ashton Smith: Master of Fantasy" by August Derleth and Donald Wandrei (ix–xii); *Out of Space and Time:* "The End of the Story" (3–24); "A Rendezvous in Averoigne" (25–42); "A Night in Malnéant" (45–50); "The City of the Singing Flame" (51–99); "The Uncharted Isle" (100–112); *Judgments and Dooms:* "The Second Interment" (115–28); "The Double Shadow" (129–43); "The Chain of Aforgomon" (144–64); "The Dark Eidolon" (165–97); "The Last Hieroglyph" (198–217); "Sadastor" (218–21); "The Death of Ilalotha" (222–35); "The Return of the Sorcerer" (236–54); *Hyperborean Grotesques:* "The Testament of Athammaus" (257–79); "The Weird of Avoosl Wuthoqquan" (280–90); "Ubbo-Sathla" (291–300); *Interplanetaries:* "The Monster of the Prophecy" (303–46); "The Vaults of Yoh-Vombis" (347–366); "From the Crypts of Memory" (367–68); "The Shadows" (369–70).

Notes. Bound in black cloth; spine stamped in gold. Dust jacket art by Hannes Bok. 1054 copies of a. were printed. Both b. and d. are facsimiles of a. In d. there is a new introduction by Jeff VanderMeer.

10. *Lost Worlds.*
   a. Sauk City, WI: Arkham House, [October] 1944. 419 pp.
   b. Jersey, UK: Neville Spearman, 1971.
   c.1. St. Albans, UK: Panther, 1974 (2 vols.).
   c.2. St. Albans, UK: Panther, 1975 (2 vols.).
   d. Lincoln: University of Nebraska Press (Bison Books), 2006.

   Contents: "The Tale of Satampra Zeiros" (3–17); "The Door to Saturn" (18–41); "The Seven Geases" (42–66); "The Coming of the White Worm" (67–82); *Atlantis:* "The Last Incantation" (85–90); "A Voyage to Sfanomoë" (91–100); "The Death of Malygris" (101–15); *Averoigne:* "The Holiness of Azédarac" (119–43); "The Beast of Averoigne" (144–56); *Zothique:* "The Empire of the Necromancers" (159–70); "The Isle of the Torturers" (171–89); "Necromancy in Naat" (190–213); "Xeethra" (214–36); *Xiccarph:* "The Maze of Maal Dweb" (239–54); "The Flower-Women" (255–68); *Others:* "The Demon of the Flower" (271–82); "The Plutonian Drug" (283–95); "The Planet of the Dead" (296–310); "The Gorgon" (311–24); "The Letter from Mohaun Los" (325–65); "The Light from Beyond" (366–89); "The Hunters from Beyond" (390–409); "The Treader of the Dust" (410–19).

   Notes. Bound in black cloth; spine stamped in gold. Dust jacket art by Burt Trimpey, illustrating several of CAS's fantastic carvings. 2043 copies of a. were printed. Both b. and d. are facsimiles of a.

11. *Genius Loci and Other Tales.*
   a. Sauk City, WI: Arkham House, 1948. 228 pp.
   b. Jersey, UK: Neville Spearman, 1972.
   c. St. Albans, UK: Panther, 1974.

   Contents: "Genius Loci" (3–20); "The Willow Landscape" (21–25); "The Ninth Skeleton" (26–30); "The Phantoms of the Fire" (31–36); "The Eternal World" (37–56); "Vulthoom" (57–82); "A Star-Change" (83–102); "The Primal City" (103–9); "The Disinterment of Venus" (110–17); "The Colossus of Ylourgne" (118–55); "The Satyr" (156–61); "The Garden of Adompha" (162–71); "The Charnel God" (173–93); "The Black Abbot of Puthuum" (194–215); "The Weaver in the Vault" (216–28).

Notes. Bound in black cloth; spine stamped in gold. Dust jacket by Frank Wakefield. 3000 copies of a. were printed. The Neville Spearman edition is a facsimile of a.

12. *The Ghoul and the Seraph.*
   a.   Gargoyle Press, 1950. 6 pp.

   Notes. Green paper covers.

13. *The Dark Chateau.*
   a.   Sauk City, WI: Arkham House, 1951. 63 pp.

   Contents: "Amithaine" (3); "Seeker" (4); "The Dark Chateau" (5–6); "Lamia" (7); "Pour chercher du Nouveau" (8–9); "'O Golden-Tongued Romance'"(10–11); "Averoigne" (12–13); "Zothique" (14); "The Stylite" (15–16); "Dominium in Excelsis" (17–18); "Moly" (19); "Two Myths and a Fable" (20); "Eros of Ebony" (21); "Shapes in the Sunset" (22–23); "Not Theirs the Cypress-Arch" (24); "Don Quixote on Market Street" (25); "Malediction" (26); "Hellenic Sequel" (27); "The Cypress" [translated from José A. Calcaño] (28–29); "The Old Water-Wheel" (30); "Calenture" (31–32); "Soliloquy in an Ebon Tower" (33–36); "Sinbad, It Was Not Well to Brag" (37–38); "Sonnet for the Psychoanalysts" (39); "Surréaliste Sonnet" (40); "The Twilight of the Gods" (41); "The Poet Talks with the Biographers" (42); "Desert Dweller" (43); "Hesperian Fall" (44–46); "'Not Altogether Sleep'" (47); "Some Blind Eidolon" (48–49); "The Isle of Saturn" (50–51); "Oblivion" [translated from Jose-Maria de Heredia] (52); "Revenant" (53–54); "In Slumber" (55); "Cambion" (56); "The Witch with Eyes of Amber" (57); "The Outer Land" (58–60); "Luna Aeternalis" (61–62); "Ye Shall Return" (63).

   Notes. Bound in black cloth; spine stamped in gold. Dust jacket art by Frank Utpatel. 563 copies printed.

14. *Spells and Philtres.*
   a.   Sauk City, WI: Arkham House, 1958. xii, 54 pp.

   Contents: "Dedication: To Carol" (vii); "Didus Ineptus" (3); "Thebaid" (4); "Secret Love" (5); "The Pagan" (6); "Tired Gardener" (7–8); "Nada" (9); "High Surf" (10); "The Centaur" (11); "Said the Dreamer" (12–13); "The Nameless Wraith" (14); "The Blindness of Orion" (15–16); "Jungle Twilight" (17); "The Phoenix" (18); "The Prophet Speaks" (19–20); "Farewell to Eros" (21–22); "Alternative" (23); "Only to One Returned" (24);

"Anteros" (25); "No Stranger Dream" (26); "Do you Forget, Enchantress?" (27); "Necromancy" (28); "Dialogue" (29); "October" (30); "Dominion" (31–32); "Tolometh" (33–34); "Disillusionment" (35); "Almost Anything" (36); "Parnassus à la Mode" (37); *Distillations:* "Fence and Wall" (38); "Growth of Lichen" (38); "Cats in Winter Sunlight" (38); "Abandoned Plum-Orchard" (38); "Harvest Evening" (38); "Willow-Cutting in Autumn" (38); "Late Pear-Pruner" (39); "Geese in the Spring Night" (39); "The Sparrow's Nest" (39); "The Last Apricot" (39); *Strange Miniatures:* "Unicorn" (40); "Untold Arabian Fable" (40); "A Hunter Meets the Mantichoras" (40); "The Sciapod" (40); "The Monacle" (40); "Feast of St. Anthony" (41); "Paphnutius" (41); "Philtre" (41); "Perseus and Andromeda" (41); *Quintrains:* "Essence" (42); "Passing of an Elder God" (42); "Nightmare of the Lilliputian" (42); "Mithridates" (42); "Quiddity" (43); "'That Motley Drama'" [from "Clérigo Herrero"] (44); "Rimas XXXIII" [translated from Gustavo Adolfo Bécquer] (45); "Ecclesiastes" [translated from Charles-Marie-René Leconte de Lisle] (46); "Anterior Life" [translated from Charles Baudelaire] (47); "Song of Autumn" [translated from Charles Baudelaire] (48–49); "Lethe" [translated from Charles Baudelaire] (50); "The Metamorphoses of the Vampire" [translated from Charles Baudelaire] (51); "Epigrams and Apothegms" (52–54).

Notes. Bound in black cloth; spine stamped in gold. Dust jacket art by Frank Utpatel. 519 copies printed.

15. *The Abominations of Yondo.*
   a. Sauk City, WI: Arkham House, [February] 1960. 227 pp.
   b. Jersey, UK: Neville Spearman, 1972.
   c.1. St. Albans, UK: Panther, 1974.
   c.2. St. Albans, UK: Panther, 1974.

   Contents: "The Nameless Offspring" (3–20); "The Witchcraft of Ulua" (21–30); "The Devotee of Evil" (31–42); "The Epiphany of Death" (43–47); "A Vintage from Atlantis" (48–54); "The Abominations of Yondo" (55–61); "The White Sybil" (62–71); "The Ice-Demon" (72–87); "The Voyage of King Euvoran" (88–111); "The Master of the Crabs" (112–125); "The Enchantress of Sylaire" (126–140); "The Dweller in the Gulf" (141–160); "The Dark Age" (161–176); "The Third Episode of Vathek" (with William Beckford) (177–222); "Chinoiserie" (223); "The Mirror in the Hall of Ebony" (224); "The Passing of Aphrodite" (225–27).

Notes. Bound in black cloth; spine stamped in gold. Dust jacket designed by Ronald Clyne (from a photograph by Wynn Bullock of CAS's carving, "The High Cockalorum"). 2005 copies of a. were printed. The Neville Spearman edition is a facsimile of a.

16. *The Hill of Dionysus.*
    a. [Pacific Grove, CA: Roy A. Squires, July 1961.] [4] pp.

    Notes. Gray paper covers. Limited to 12 copies.

17. *Hesperian Fall.*
    a. [N.p.: Clyde Beck, 1961.] [7] pp.

    Notes. Tan paper covers. Limited to 12 copies.

18. *The Hill of Dionysus: A Selection.*
    a. Pacific Grove, CA: [Roy A. Squires], 1962. vii, 48 pp.

    Contents: "Bacchante" (3–4); "Wizard's Love" (5–6); "Resurrection" (7–8); "Witch Dance" (9–10); "Paean" (11); "The Knoll" (12–13); "Interim" (14–15); "Reverie in August" (16); "Ode" (17–18); "For an Antique Lyre" (19); "Silent Hour" (20); "To One Absent" (21); "Bond" (22); "Fragment" (23); "Humors of Love" (24); "Yerba Buena" (25); "Sonnet" (26); "Amor" (27); "The Sorcerer to His Love" (28); "Twilight Song" (29); "Before Dawn" (30); "Amor Hesternalis" (31–32); "Supplication" (33); "The Hill of Dionysus" (34–35); "Nocturne: Grant Avenue" (36–37); "Future Pastoral" (38); "Postlude" (39); "Midnight Beach" (40); "Illumination" (41); "Omniety" (42); "Sea Cycle" (43); "Hesperian Fall" (44–47); "'Not Altogether Sleep'" (48).
    Notes. Octavo, cloth-backed boards. Limited to 390 copies, of which 175 were bound in cloth-backed boards; 15 were bound in full smooth green cloth, with a page of typewritten manuscript, signed, and numbered limitation notice, laid in. The remainder were bound in paper.

19. *Cycles.*
    a. [Glendale, CA: Roy A. Squires, March 1963.] [4] pp.

    Notes. Broadside printing of CAS's last poem. 76 copies printed.

20. *Nero.*
    a. Pacific Grove, CA: Roy A. Squires, [September] 1964. [6] pp.

    Notes. The colophon states that 450 copies were printed, although Jack L. Chalker has stated that only 381 copies were actually produced. 50 copies were printed on Strathmore Chroma paper, numbered 1 through 50, with a photographic print of the portrait of CAS (by Bianca Conti) from *The Star-Treader and Other Poems* (A.1) laid in. The ordinary edition was printed on Warren's Old Style and sewn into salmon covers. Of the two states, copies 21 through 50 of the numbered edition and 200 copies of the ordinary edition were offered for sale.

21.   ¿*Donde Duermes, Eldorado? y Otros Poemas.* As by "Clérigo Herrero."
   a.   Glendale, CA: La Imprenta de Rojo Escuderos [Roy A. Squires], 1964. xii pp.

   Contents: "Los poetas" (iv); "¿Donde duermes, Eldorado?" (v); "La isla del naufrago" (vi); "Lo ignoto" (vii); "Dos Mitos y una fabula" (viii); "El cantar de los seres libres: (ix); "Las alquerias perdidas" (x–xi); "Memoria roja" (xii).
      Notes. A collection of CAS's poems in Spanish, although additional unpublished poems were subsequently discovered.

22.   *Tales of Science and Sorcery.*
   a.   Sauk City, WI: Arkham House, [November] 1964. 256 pp.
   b.   St. Albans, UK: Panther, 1976.

   Contents: "Clark Ashton Smith: A Memoir" by E. Hoffmann Price (3–17); "Master of the Asteroid" (18–35); "The Seed from the Sepulcher" (36–50); "The Root of Ampoi" (51–68); "The Immortals of Mercury" (69–107); "Murder in the Fourth Dimension" (108–19); "Seedling of Mars" (120–67); "The Maker of Gargoyles" (168–84); "The Great God Awto" (185–91); "Mother of Toads" (192–200); "The Tomb-Spawn" (201–12); "Schizoid Creator" (213–21); "Symposium of the Gorgon" (222–31); "The Theft of the Thirty-nine Girdles" (232–44); "Morthylla" (245–46).
      Notes. Bound in black cloth; spine stamped in gold. Dust jacket art by Frank Utpatel. 2482 copies of a. were printed. The volume consists predominantly of CAS's science fiction tales.

23.   *Poems in Prose.*
   a.   Sauk City, WI: Arkham House, [June] 1965. xxiv, 54 pp.

   Contents: "Clark Ashton Smith, Poet in Prose" by Donald S. Fryer (ix–xxiv); "The Traveller" (3–4); "The Flower-Devil" (5); "Images" ("Tears," "The Secret Rose," "The Wind and the Garden," "Offerings," "A Coronal") (6–7); "The Black Lake" (9); "Vignettes" ("Beyond the Mountains," "The Broken Lute," "Nostalgia of the Unknown," "Grey Sorrow," "The Hair of Circe," "The Eyes of Circe") (9–10); "A Dream of Lethe" (11); "The Caravan" (12); "The Princess Almeena" (13); "Ennui" (14–15); "The Statue of Silence" (16); "Remoteness" (17); "The Memnons of the Night" (18); "The Garden and the Tomb" (19); "In Cocaigne" (20); "The Litany of the Seven Kisses" (21); "From a Letter" (22); "From the Crypts of Memory" (23–24); "A Phantasy" (25); "The Demon, the Angel, and Beauty" (26–27); "The Shadows" (28–29); "The Crystals" (30); "Chinoiserie" (31); "The Mirror in the Hall of Ebony" (32); "The Muse of Hyperborea" (33); "The Lotus and the Moon" (34); "The Passing of Aphrodite" (35–37); "To the Daemon" (38); "The Forbidden Forest" (39–40); "The Mithridate" (41); "Narcissus" (42); "The Peril That Lurks among Ruins" (43); "The Abomination of Desolation" (44); "The Touchstone" (45); "The Image of Bronze and the Image of Iron" (46); "The Corpse and the Skeleton" (47–49); "The Sun and the Sepulchre" (50); "Sadastor" (51–54).

Notes. Bound in black cloth; spine stamped in gold. Dust jacket art and interior illustrations by Frank Utpatel. 1016 copies printed.

24. *Other Dimensions.*
   a. Sauk City, WI: Arkham House, [April] 1970. 329 pp.
   b. St. Albans, UK: Panther, 1977 (2 vols.).

   Contents: "Marooned in Andromeda" (3–31); "The Amazing Planet" (32–71); "An Adventure in Futurity" (72–106); "The Immeasurable Horror" (107–20); "The Invisible City" (121–40); "The Dimension of Chance" (141–63); "The Metamorphosis of Earth" (164–91); "Phoenix" (192–201); "The Necromantic Tale" (202–12); "The Venus of Azombeii" (213–37); "The Resurrection of the Rattlesnake" (238–43); "The Supernumerary Corpse" (244–51); "The Mandrakes" (252–58); "Thirteen Phantasms" (259–62); "An Offering to the Moon" (263–73); "Monsters in the Night" (274–76); "The Malay Krise" (277–79); "The Ghost of Mohammed Din" (280–86); "The Mahout" (287–92); "The Raja and the Tiger" (293–98); "Something New" (299–301); "The Justice of the Elephant" (302–5); "The Kiss of Zoraida" (306–11); "A Tale of Sir John Maundeville" (312–18); "The Ghoul" (319–23); "Told in the Desert" (324–29).

   Notes. Bound in black cloth; spine stamped in gold. Dust jacket art by Lee Brown Coye; artwork on back panel is a self-portrait drawn by CAS in his thirties. 3144 copies printed.

25. *Zothique*. Ed. Lin Carter.
   a. New York: Ballantine, [June] 1970. xiii, 273 pp.

   Contents: "About Zothique, and Clark Ashton Smith: When the World Grows Old" by Lin Carter (ix–xiii); "Zothique" (poem) (1); "Xeethra" (3–23); "Necromancy in Naat" (23–44); "The Empire of the Necromancers" (44–54); "The Master of the Crabs" (54–68); "The Death of Ilalotha" (69–80); "The Weaver in the Vault" (81–94); "The Witchcraft of Ulua" (94–104); "The Charnel God" (105–28); "The Dark Eidolon" (128–57); "Morthylla" (157–67); "The Black Abbot of Puthuum" (167–90); "The Tomb-Spawn" (190–200); "The Last Hieroglyph" (201–18); "The Isle of the Torturers" (218–34); "The Garden of Adompha" (234–45); "The Voyage of King Euvoran" (245–70); "Epilogue: The Sequence of the Zothique Tales" by Lin Carter (271–73).
   Notes. Bound in paper. Cover art by George Barr.

26. *The Fugitive Poems of Clark Ashton Smith*. 4 volumes.
   a. [Glendale, CA:] Zothique Edition [Roy A. Squires], 1970.

   Contents:

   First Fascicle: The Tartarus of the Suns (21 May 1970): "The Tartarus of the Suns" ([1]); "The Pageant of Music" ([2]); "Ode to Matter" ([3–6]); "The Power of Eld" ([7]); "Death" ([8]); "Notes" [by Squires] (11]).

   Second Fascicle: The Palace of Jewels (21 May 1970): "Morning on an Eastern Sea" ([1]); "To the Nightshade" ([2]); "The Palace of Jewels" ([3–6]); "Weavings" ([7]); "The Voice of Silence" ([8]); "Notes" [by Squires] ([11]).

   Third Fascicle: In the Ultimate Valleys (10 August 1970): "A Sierran Sunrise" ([1]); "In the Ultimate Valleys" ([2–3]); "Cloudland" ([4]); "The Eternal Snows" ([5]); "The Call of the Wind" ([6]); "The Noon of the Seasons" ([7]); "Night" ([8]); "Notes" [by Squires] ([11]).

   Fourth Fascicle: To George Sterling: Five Poems (10 August 1970): "To George Sterling: A Valediction" ([1–3]); "To George Sterling" [B.ii.881] ([4]); "To George Sterling" [B.ii.879] ([5]); "To George Sterling" [B.ii.878] ([6–7]); "To George Sterling" [B.ii.877] ([8]); "Notes" [by Squires] ([11]).
   Notes. Bound in paper. Limited to 165, 167, 160, and 180 numbered copies, respectively.

27. *Selected Poems.*
  a.   Sauk City, WI: Arkham House, 1971. xix, 403 pp.

Contents: "Clark Ashton Smith: Emperor of Shadows" by Benjamin De Casseres (3–4); *The Star-Treader and Other Poems:* "Nero" (7–9); "Chant to Sirius" (9–10); "The Star-Treader" (10–14); "The Night Forest" (14–15); "The Mad Wind" (16); "Medusa" (16–17); "Ode to the Abyss" (17–19); "The Butterfly" (19–22); "The Price" (22); "The Meaning" (23); "The Last Night" (23); "Ode on Imagination" (24–25); "The Maze of Sleep" (26); "The Winds" (26–27); "A Masque of Forsaken Gods" (27–31); "A Sunset" (32); "The Summer Moon" (32); "The Return of Hyperion" (32–33); "Lethe" (33–34); "Atlantis" (34); "The Unremembered" (34–35); "The Eldritch Dark" (35); "The Cherry-Snows" (36); "Nirvana" (36); "White Death" (37); "Retrospect and Forecast" (37–38); "Shadow of Nightmare" (38); "Song of a Comet" (38–40); "The Retribution" (40–41); "To the Darkness" (41–42); "A Dream of Beauty" (42–43); "Pine Needles" (43); "To the Sun" (43–44); "Averted Malefice" (45); "The Medusa of the Skies" (45); "A Dead City" (46); "A Song of Dreams" (46–48); "The Balance" (48); "Saturn" (48–55); "Finis" (56); *Additional Early Poems:* "The Pursuer" (57); "Said the Dreamer" (57–58); "The City of the Titans" (58–59); "In the Wind" (59); "Fire of Snow" (59–60); "To Beauty" (60–61); "Decadence" (61); "In the Desert" (61–62); "The Blindness of Orion" (62–63); "Somnus" (64); "The Nameless Wraith" (64–65); "Color of Dreams" (65); "The City of Destruction" (66–67); "Luna Aeternalis" (67–68); "To the Daemon of Sublimity" (68); *Ebony and Crystal:* "Preface" by George Sterling (71); "Arabesque" (72); "Beyond the Great Wall" (72–73); "To Omar Khayyam" (73–75); "Strangeness" (75–76); "The Infinite Quest" (76); "Rosa Mystica" (76–77); "The Nereid" (77–78); "In Saturn" (78–79); "Impression" (79); "Triple Aspect" (79–80); "Desolation" (80–81); "A Fragment" (81–82); "Crepuscule" (82); "Inferno" (82–83); "Mirrors" (83); "Belated Love" (83–84); "The Absence of the Muse" (84); "Dissonance" (85); "To Nora May French" (85–88); "In Lemuria" (88); "Recompense" (89); "Exotique" (89); "Transcendence" (90); "Satiety" (90–91); "The Ministers of Law" (91); "Coldness" (91–92); "The Crucifixion of Eros" (92–93); "The Exile" (93); "Ave Atque Vale" (93–94); "Song of Sappho's Arabian Daughter" (94–95); "Solution" (95–96); "The Tears of Lilith" (96); "A Precept" (96–97); "Remembered Light" (97–98); "Song" (98); "Haunting" (99);

"The Hidden Paradise" (99–100); "Cleopatra" (100); "Ecstasy" (101); "A Psalm to the Best Beloved" (101–2); "Symbols" (102); *The Hashish-Eater* (103–18); "The Sorrow of the Winds" (119); "Artemis" (119–20); "Love Is Not Yours, Love Is Not Mine" (120); "The City in the Desert" (120–21); "The Melancholy Pool" (121); "The Mirrors of Beauty" (122); "Winter Moonlight" (122); "To the Beloved" (123); "Requiescat" (123–24); "Mirage" (124); "Inheritance" (125); "Chant of Autumn" (125–26); "Nevermore" (126); "Echo of Memnon" (127); "Twilight on the Snow" (127–28); "Image" (128); "The Refuge of Beauty" (128–29); "Nightmare" (129); "Forgetfulness" (130); "Flamin-goes" (130); "The Chimera" (131); "The Incubus of Time" (131–32); "Satan Unrepentant" (132–34); "The Abyss Trium-phant" (135); "The Motes" (135); "The Medusa of Despair" (136); "Laus Mortis" (136–37); "Nocturne" (137); "The Ghoul and the Seraph" (137–41); "Metaphor" (142); "Sea-Memory" (142); "At Sunrise" (143); "The Land of Evil Stars" (143–44); "The Harlot of the World" (145); "Amor Aeternalis" (145–46); "The Hope of the Infinite" (146); "Palms" (146–47); "Memnon at Midnight" (147); "Eidolon" (148–48); "The Kingdom of Shadows" (148–49); "Requiescat in Pace" (149–50); "Alexan-drines" (151); "Alexandrins" (151); "Ashes of Sunset" (152); "November Twilight" (152); "Sepulture" (152–53); "Quest" (1`53–54); "Beauty Implacable" (154); "A Vision of Lucifer" (155); "Desire of Vastness" (155); "Antepast" (156); "The Witch in the Graveyard" (159); "Memorial" (159); "The Horologue" (160); "'The Last Infirmity'" (160); "The Orchid of Beauty" (160); "The Last Goddess" (161); "The Flight of Azrael" (161–62). *Sandalwood:* [epigraph] (163); "Semblance" (165); "The Song of Aviol" (166); "We Shall Meet" (167–68); "For-gotten Sorrow" (168); "You Are Not Beautiful" (168); "Lemu-rienne" (169); "Dissidence" (169); "Sestet" (169); "Change" (170); "Query" (170–71); "Enigma" (171–72); "Incognita" (172); "The Secret" (172–73); "The End of Autumn" (173–74); "The Love-Potion" (174); "The Song of Cartha" (175); "After-wards" (175); "Contradiction" (176); "The Last Oblivion" (176); "Autumn Orchards" (177); "Remembrance" (177–78); "The Wingless Archangels" (178–79); "Moon Dawn" (179); "Lunar Mystery" (179–80); "Enchanted Mirrors" (180); "Duality" (181); "A Valediction" (181); "Selenique" (182); "Alienage" (182–83); "Adventure" (183–85); "On the Canyon-Side" (185); "Song" (186); "Minatory" (187); "Maya" (187–88); "Interrogation"

(188–89); "Consolation" (189); "The Barrier" (189–90); "Apologia" (190–91); "Estrangement" (191); "Loss" (191–92); "A Catch" (192); "Don Juan Sings" (193); "On Rereading Baudelaire" (193–94); "To the Chimera" (194); *Translations and Paraphrases: From Charles P. Baudelaire:* [epigraph from Baudelaire] (195); "A Parisian Dream" (197–99); "Hymn to Beauty" (199–200); "The Ideal" (200); "Semper Eadem" (201); "The Giantess" (201–2); "Examination at Midnight" (202–3); "Doubtful Skies" (203); "The Sick Muse" (204); "Moesta et Errabunda" (204–5); "The Fountain of Blood" (205–6); "Evening Harmony" (206); "The Spiritual Dawn" (207); "The Wine of Lovers" (207–8); "The Death of Lovers" (208); "Obsession" (208–9); "Alchemy of Sorrow" (209); "Sympathetic Horror" (210); "The Owls" (210–11); "The Phantom" (211); "Mists and Rains" (211–12); "Sed non satiata" (212); "Spleen" (213); "Song of Autumn" (213–14); "Anterior Life" (215); "Lethe" (215–16); "The Irremediable" (216–17); "Beatrice" (218); "The Voice" (219); "The Poison" (219–20); "The Two Kind Sisters" (220); "The Metamorphoses of the Vampire" (220–21); *From Paul Verlaine:* "Moonlight" (221); "The Faun" (222); "En Sourdine" (222–23); "IX (Ariettes Oubliées)" (223); "Crimen Amoris" (223–26); *From Victor Hugo:* "The Wheel of Omphale" (227); *From José-Maria de Heredia:* "Oblivion" (228); *From Leconte de Lisle:* "Ecclesiastes" (229); "The Sleep of the Condor" (229–30); *From Pierre Lièvre:* "Elysian Landscape" (230–31); *From Christophe des Laurieres:* "The Pagan" (231–32); "Madrigal" (232); "The Nymph" (232–33); "Chansonette" (233–34); "An Old Theme" (234); "Classic Epigram" (234–35); "Exotic Memory" (235); "By the River" (236); "Moments" (236–37); "Tempus" (237); "Tristan to Iseult" (238–39); "Concupiscence" (239); "Heliogabalus" (239–40); "Secret Love" (240–41); "Psalm" (241–42); "In Alexandria" (242–43); "Satiety" (243); "The Whisper of the Worm" (243–44); "The Funeral Urn" (244); "Mors" (244–45); *From Gustavo Adolpho Béquer:* "Where?" (245); *From Jose A. Calcaño:* "The Cypress" (246–47); *From Clérigo Herrero:* "'That Motley Drama'" (247); *Incantations:* "La Forteresse" (251); "Outlanders" (251–52); "The Envoys" (252–53); "Shadows" (253–54); "Nyctalops" (254–55); "On a Chinese Vase" (256); "Jungle Twilight" (256–57); "The Phoenix" (257); "The Thralls of Circe Climb Parnassus" (258); "To George Sterling: A Valediction" (258–60); "To George Sterling" [B.ii.877] (260–61); "La Mare" (261); "Vaticinations" (262); "The Hill-Top" (262–63);

"The Old Water-Wheel" (263–64); "Lichens" (264); "Cumuli" (264–65); "October" (265–66); "December" (266–67); "Necromancy" (267); "The Witch With Eyes of Amber" (267–68); "Lamia" (268–69); "Dialogue" (269); "In Slumber" (270); "Warning" (271); "The Nightmare Tarn" (271–72); "Cambion" (273); "Tolometh" (274–75); "Desert Dweller" (275–76); "The Prophet Speaks" (276–77); "A Fable" (277–78); "Au bord du Léthé" (278); "L'Espoir du néant" (279); "Farewell to Eros" (279–80); "Alternative" (281); "Moly" (281–82); "Paysage païen" [*sic*] (282–83); "The Outer Land" (283–85); "A Dream of the Abyss" (285–86); "To Howard Phillips Lovecraft" (287–88); "After Armageddon" (288); "Chance" (289); "Ennui" (289); "Apostrophe" (290); "Sonnet" (290); The Saturnienne" (291); "Revenant" (292–93); "Une Vie spectrale" (293–94); "Song of the Necromancer" (294–95); "In Thessaly" (296); "Lines on a Picture" (296–97); "Hellenic Sequel" (297); "Refuge" (298); "Only to One Returned" (298); "But Grant, O Venus" (299); "Town Lights" (299–300); "Strange Girl" (300–301); "Some Blind Eidolon" (302–3); "If Winter Remain" (303–4); "Pour chercher du nouveau" (304–5); "Anteros" (306); *Quintrains:* "Attar of the Past" (307); "Passing of an Elder God" (307); "Nightmare of the Lilliputian" (307); "Poets in Hades" (308); "Mummy of the Flower" (308); "The Heron" (308); "Bird of Long Ago" (309); "Mithridates" (309); "Someone" (309); "Late November Evening" (310); "Quiddity" (310); "Epitaph for an Astronomer" (310); *Sestets:* "Copyist" (311); "Love and Death" (311); *Experiments in Haiku: Strange Miniatures:* "Unicorn" (312); "Untold Arabian Fable" (312); "A Hunter Meets the Martichoras" (312); "The Limniad" (313); "The Sciapod" (313); "The Monacle" (313); "Feast of St. Anthony" (313); "Paphnutius" (314); "Philtre" (314); "Borderland" (314); "Lethe" (314); "Perseus and Medusa" (315); "Osysseus in Eternity" (315); "The Ghost of Theseus" (315); *Distillations:* "Fence and Wall" (316); "Growth of Lichen" (316); "Cats in Winter" (316); "Abandoned Plum-Orchard" (317); "Harvest Evening" (317); "Willow-Cutting in Autumn" (317); "Declining Moon" (317); "Late Pear-Pruner" (318); "Noctournal Pines" (318); "Phallus Impudica" (318); "Stormy Afterglow" (318); "Geese in the Spring Night" (319); "Foggy Night" (319); "Reigning Empress" (319); "The Sparrow's Nest" (319); "The Last Apricot" (320); "Mushroom-Gatherers" (320); "Spring Nunnery" (320); "Nuns Walking in the Orchard" (320); "Improbable Dream" (321); "Crows in

Spring" (321); "Slaughter-House in Spring" (321); "High Mountain Juniper" (321); "Storm's End" (322); "Pool at Lobos" (322); "Poet in a Barroom" (322); "Fallen Grape-Leaf" (322); "Slaughter-House Pasture" (323); "Gopher-Hole in an Orchard" (323); "Basin in Boulder" (323); "Indian Acorn-Mortar" (323); "Old Limestone Kiln" (324); "Love in Dreams" (324); "Night of Miletus" (324); "Tryst at Lobos" (324); "Prisoner in Vain" (325); "Mountain Trail" (325); "Future Meeting" (325); "Classic Reminiscence" (325); "Goats and Manzanita-Boughs" (326);

"Picture by Piero di Cosimo" (326); "Garden of Priapus" (326); "Bed of Mint" (326); "Chainless Captive" (327); "January Willow" (327); "Snowfall on Acacia" (327); "Flight of the Yellow-Hammer" (328); "Sunset Over Farm-Land" (328); "Flora" (328); "Windows at Lamplighting Time" (328); "Old Hydraulic Diggings" (329); "Hearth on Old Cabin-Site" (329); "Builder of Deserted Hearth" (330); "Aftermath of Mining Days" (330); "River-Canyon" (330–31); *Childhood:* "School-Room Pastime" (332); "Boys Telling Bawdy Tales" (332); "Water-Flight" (332); "Boys Rob a Yellow-Hammer's Nest" (332); "Grammar-School Vixen" (333); "Girl of Six" (333); *Mortal Essences:* "Snake, Owl, Cat or Hawk" (333); "Cattle Salute the Psychopomp" (334); "Field Behind the Abatoir" (334); "Plague from the Abatoir" (334); "La Mort des Amants" (334); "Vultures Come to the Ambarvalia" (335); "For the Dance of Death" (335); "Berries of the Deadly Nightshade" (335); "Water-Hemlock" (335); "Felo-de-se of the Parasite" (336); *Satires and Travesties:* "Disillusionment" (337); "Almost Anything" (337–38); "To Whom it May Concern" (338); "Tin Can on the Mountain-Top" (339–40); "Surrealist Sonnet" (340); "Sonnet for the Psychoanalysts" (340–41); "Parnassus à la Mode" (341); *The Jasmine Girdle:* Epigraph from Christophe des Laurières (343); "The Nevermore-to-be" (345); "Fantaisie d'antan" (345–46); "One Evening" (347); "Trope" (347); "Canticle" (348); "Venus" (348–49); "November" (349); "Le Miroir des blanches fleurs" (349–50); "Les Marées" (351); "The Autumn Lake" (351); "Winter Moonlight" (352); "To Antares" (352–53); "Connaissance" (353); "Exorcism" (353–54); "Calendar" (354–55); "Madrigal of Evanescence" (355); "September" (356); "Indian Summer" (356–57); "The Dragon-Fly" (357); "Touch" (357–58); "Sufficiency" (358); "Ineffability" (359); "Mystery" (359–60); "Dominion" (360–61); *The Hill of Dionysus:* "Dancer" (365); "Bacchante" (365–66); "Wizard's Love" (366–67); "Resurrection" (368); "Witch Dance" (369–70); "Paean" (370); "The Knoll" (370–71); "Interim" (372–73); "Reverie in August" (373); "Wine of Summer" (374); "Ode" (374–75); "For an Antique Lyre" (375–76); "Silent Hour" (376–77); "To One Absent" (377–78); "Bond" (378); "The Mime of Sleep" (379); "Madrigal of Memory" (379–80); "Fragment" (380–81); "Humors of Love" (381); "Grecian Yesterday" (381–82); "Yerba Buena" (382–83); "Sonnet" (383); "'All Is Dross That Is Not Helena'" (383–84); "Amor" (384); "The Sorcerer to His Love" (385); "Twilight Song" (385–86); "Before Dawn" (386); "Amor Hesternalis" (387); "Supplication" (388); "Erato" (388–89); "The Hill of Dionysus" (389–91); "Anodyne of Autumn" (391); "Nocturne: Grant Avenue" (392); "Future Pastoral" (393); "Postlude" (394); "Midnight Beach" (394–95); "Even in Slumber" (395); "De Profundis" (396); "Illumination" (397); "Omniety" (397–98); "From Arcady" (398–99); "Sea Cycle" (399–400); "Did You Forget, Enchantress?" (400); "No Stranger Dream" (400–401); "On the Mount of Stone" (401); "Calenture" (402–3); "Avowal" (403).

Notes. Bound in black cloth; spine stamped in gold. Portrait painting of CAS (1946) by Natalae Bixby Carter. Dust jacket designed by Gary Gore. The book was compiled in 1944–49, as CAS made many revisions of his earlier poems and added many previously unpublished poems. Financial strains on Arkham House prevented the volume from appearing until years after CAS's death.

28. *The Mortuary.*
   a. [Glendale, CA: Roy A. Squires,] 1971. [4] pp.

   Notes. Bound in paper. Limited to 199 copies.

29. *Hyperborea.* Ed. Lin Carter.
   a. New York: Ballantine, [April] 1971. xvi, 205 pp.

   Contents: "About Hyperborea, and Clark Ashton Smith: Behind the North Wind" by Lin Carter (ix–xvi); "The Muse of Hyperborea" (3); "The Seven Geases" (4–29); "The Weird of Avoosl Wuthoqquan" (30–40); "The White Sybil" (41–52); "The Testament of Athammaus" (53–76); "The Coming of the White Worm" (77–93); "Ubbo-Sathla" (94–103); "The Door to Saturn" (104–27); "The Ice-Demon" (128–47); "The Tale of Satampra Zeiros" (148–63); "The Theft of the Thirty-nine Girdles" (164–77) "The World's Rim" by Lin Carter (179); "The Abominations of Yondo" (181–89); "The Desolation of Soom" by Lin Carter (190–91); "The Passing of Aphrodite" (192–94); "The

Memnons of the Night" (195–96); "Notes on the Commoriom Myth-Cycle" by Lin Carter (197–205).

Notes. Bound in paper. Cover art by Bill Martin.

30.   *Xiccarph.* Ed. Lin Carter.
     a.   New York: Ballantine, [February] 1972. 247 pp.

       Contents: "About Xiccarph, and Clark Ashton Smith: Other Stars and Skies" by Lin Carter (3–8); "To the Daemon: An Invocation" (prose poem) (9–10); *Xiccarph:* editor's note (13–14); "The Maze of Maal Dweb" (15–36); "The Flower-Women" (37–53); *Aihai:* editor's note (57); "Vulthoom" (58–93); "The Dweller in the Gulf" (94–120); "The Vaults of Yoh-Vombis" (121–44); *Phandiom:* "The Doom of Antarion" (i.e. "The Planet of the Dead") (147–63); *Lophai:* editor's note (167); "The Demon of the Flower" (168–81); *Satabbor:* "The Monster of the Prophecy" (185–235); *Beyond the Stars:* "Sadastor" (239–43); "From the Crypts of Memory" (244–46); editor's note (247).

       Notes. Bound in paper. Cover art by Gervasio Gallardo.

31.   *Sadastor.*
     a.   [Glendale, CA: Roy A. Squires, 1 September] 1972. [12] pp.

       Notes. Bound in paper, with rice paper dust wrapper bearing the title. Limited to 108 numbered copies.

32.   *Grotesques and Fantastiques.*
     a.   Saddle River, NJ: Gerry de la Ree, 1973. 40 pp.
     b.   Saddle River, NJ: Gerry de la Ree, 1975 (abridged; as *Clark Ashton Smith—Poet*). 16 pp.

       Contents: "Clark Ashton Smith—Artist" by de la Ree (3–8); assorted drawings by CAS ([9–32]); "Poems Till Now Unpublished" [by de la Ree] (33); "L'Irreparable" [not identified as translation from Baudelaire] (34–35); "Reclamation" (35); "The Sphinx of the Infinite" (35); "Poplars" (36); "Dream-Mystery" (36); "Epigrams" (37); "A Prayer" (37); "Offering" (prose poem) (37); "The Garden of Dreams" (38); "Dead Love" (38); "Ode to Beauty" (39); "The Days" (39); "L'Amour Supreme" (39); "Nocturne" (40); "Suggestion" (40); "Fawn-Lilies" (40).

       Notes. Limited to 600 numbered copies, 50 of which were bound in black buckram with gold leaf stamping on the spine and front board, with the remainder being saddle-bound in tan leatherette. Artwork by CAS on the front, inside rear, and back covers.

The inside front cover is a portrait of CAS drawn by Anne M. Bremer during the 1915 Panama-Pacific International Exposition. A collection of previously unpublished poems and artwork by CAS from the de la Ree collection. De la Ree's essay draws heavily upon CAS's correspondence with Samuel Loveman, which de la Ree had bought from Loveman. The abridged edition includes only the poems, although excluding "L'Irreparable," "Reclamation," and "The Sphinx of the Infinite" and adding "The Ennuye," "Spectral Life," and "Psalm to the Desert." With interior illustrations by Stephen Fabian and CAS.

33. *Planets and Dimensions: Collected Essays of Clark Ashton Smith*. Ed. Charles K. Wolfe.

    a.   Baltimore: Mirage Press, 1973. xii, 87 pp.

Contents: "Acknowledgements" by Wolfe (v); "Introduction" by Wolfe (ix–xii); "George Sterling—An Appreciation" (3–8); "[Where Fantasy Meets Science Fiction]" (9–10); "Beyond the Singing Flame" [introductory note] (11); "[On Garbage-Mongering]" (12–13); "[Fantasy and Human Experience]" (14–17); "[The Tale of Macrocosmic Horror]" (18–19); "[Realism and Fantasy]" (20–22); "[The Validity of Weird Stories]" (23); "Horror, Fantasy, and Science" (24–28); "[On the Forbidden Books]" (29); "The Weird Works of M. R. James" (30–33); "[The Psychology of the Horror Story]" (33); "The Family Tree of the Gods" (34–36); "Clark Ashton Smith/An Autobiographette" (37); "On Fantasy" (38–39); "The Demonian Face" (40); "The Favorite Weird Stories of C. A. Smith" (41); "An Autobiography of Clark Ashton Smith" (42–43); "Story-Writing Hints" [not by CAS] (44–45); "In Appreciation of William Hope Hodgson" (46–47); "In Memoriam: H. P. Lovecraft" (48); "[On H. P. Lovecraft—I]" (49); "[On H. P. Lovecraft—II]" (50); "Atmosphere in Weird Fiction" (51–54); "The Decline of Civilization: A Note on 'The Dark Age'" (55); "Planets and Dimensions" (56–57); "George Sterling: Poet and Friend" (58–65); "The Philosophy of the Weird Tale" (66); "Review of Marianne Moore's *Nevertheless*" (67); "[On Grotesque Carvings]" (68); "A Cosmic Novel: *The Web of Easter Island*"(69–70); "[On Science Fiction History]" (71–72); "Why I Selected: *The Uncharted Isle*" (73); "[About 'The Plutonian Drug']" (74); "[On Tales about the Cthulhu Mythos]" (75); "Appendix: Notes" (77–87).

Notes. 1250 copies printed, 500 of which were numbered and bound in black cloth with gold leaf stamping on the spine; the remainder were bound in paper. Cover art by Joseph Wehrle. A compilation of CAS's relatively small number of essays, including published letters and other brief notes. "Story-Writing Hints" (first published in *Tesseract*, January 1937) is in fact by C. Hamilton Bloomer.

34. *Poseidonis: Tales of Lost Atlantis.* Ed. Lin Carter.
 a. New York: Ballantine, [July] 1973. 210 pp.

 Contents: "About Poseidonis, and Clark Ashton Smith: The Mage of Atlantis" by Lin Carter (1–6); editor's note (9–10); "The Muse of Atlantis" (11); "The Last Incantation" (12–17); "The Death of Malygris" (18–32); "Tolometh" (33–34); "The Double Shadow" (35–49); "A Voyage to Sfanomoë" (50–58); "A Vintage from Atlantis" (59–66); "Atlantis" (67); *Lemuria:* editor's note (71); "In Lemuria" (73); "An Offering to the Moon" (75–87); "The Uncharted Isle" (88–100); "Lemurienne" (101); *Ptolemides:* editor's note (105); "The Epiphany of Death" (107–22); *Other Realms:* editor's note (115); "In Cocaigne" (116); "Symposium of the Gorgon" (117–26); "The Venus of Azombeii" (127–57); "The Isle of Saturn" (158–59); "The Root of Ampoi" (160–76); "The Invisible City" (177–201); "Amithaine" (202); "The Willow Landscape" (203–8); "The Shadows" (209–10).
 Notes. Bound in paper. Cover art by Gervasio Gallardo.

35. *From the Crypts of Memory: A Prose Poem; Illustrated by the Author.*
 a. [Glendale, CA: Roy A. Squires, 8 August] 1973. [9] pp.

 Contents: "From the Crypts of Memory" ([3–6]); photograph of watercolor and ink painting by CAS (tipped in on p. [9]).
 Notes. Bound in paper, with rice paper dust jacket bearing the title. Limited to 198 copies. A companion to *Sadastor* (A.31).

36. *The Fantastic Art of Clark Ashton Smith.* Ed. Dennis Rickard.
 a. Baltimore: Mirage Press, September 1973. 25 + [35] pp.

 Contents: "Foreword" by Rickard (v); "Introduction" by Gahan Wilson (1–2); "The Fantastic Art of Clark Ashton Smith" by Rickard: "Chapter 1—The Artist" (5–6); "Chapter 2—Paintings and Drawings" (7–9); photo of Kilaga Mine and Pit (10); "Chapter 3—The Carvings" (11–16); "Chapter 4—Checklist: Carvings" (17–20); "Other Carvings" (21–22); "Paintings" (23–24). Black-and-white photos of paintings, drawings, and carvings by CAS compose the remainder of the book.

Notes. Bound in paper. Cover photo by Wayne Bullock. 1500 copies printed. A pioneering study of CAS's graphic work.

37. *Klarkash-Ton and Monstro Ligriv.*
    a. Saddle River, NJ: Gerry de la Ree, 1974. [28] pp.

Contents: "Preface" by de la Ree [3–4]; "Smith and Parents" (photograph sent to Samuel Loveman by CAS) [5]; letter to Virgil Finlay (15 May 1937) [6–7]; letter to Virgil Finlay (13 June 1937); [8–10]; drawing by Virgil Finlay [11]; letter to Virgil Finlay (27 September 1937) [12–14]; drawing by Finlay [15]; "Maenad" (poem) by Finlay [16]; "So Deep a Dream" (poem) by Finlay [17]; "Finlay with First Cover" (photo) [18]; "Dimitri" (sketch) by Finlay [19]; "Marescha" (sketch) by Finlay [20]; drawing by CAS [21]; "The Ennuye" [22]; "February" [23]; "Temporality" [24]; "Spectral Life" [25]; "Psalm to the Desert" [26–27]; "Helen" (sketch) by Finlay.

Notes. Limited to 500 numbered copies, 50 of which were bound in black buckram with gold leaf stamping on the spine and front board, with the remainder being saddle-bound in tan leatherette. Cover artwork by Virgil Finlay. Another collection of miscellaneous items related to CAS and Virgil Finlay centered on their brief correspondence in the aftermath of H. P. Lovecraft's death.

38. *The Fugitive Poems of Clark Ashton Smith: Second Series.* 6 volumes.
    a. Glendale, CA: Roy A. Squires, 1974–77.

Contents:

Volume 1: The Titans in Tartarus (1974): "Ode to Light" ([5–6]); "The Titans in Tartarus" ([7–10]); "The Suns and the Void" ([11–12]).

Volume 2: A Song from Hell (1975): "The Song of the Worlds" ([5–7]); "The Ancient Quest" ([8]); "A Song from Hell" ([9–11]); "The Burning-Ghauts at Benares" ([12]).

Volume 3: The Potion of Dreams (1975): "A Dream of Oblivion" ([5]); "The Dream-God's Realm" ([6]); "The Years Restored" ([7]); "The Potion of Dreams" ([8]); "A Phantasy of Twilight" ([9]); "Sphinx and Medusa" ([10]); "Beyond the Door" ([11]); "The Castle of Dreams" ([12]).

Volume 4: The Fanes of Dawn (1976): "Winter Midnight" ([5]); "The Twilight Woods" ([6]); "The Waning Moon" ([7]); "The Throne of Winter" ([8]); "The Fanes of Dawn" ([9]); "To the

Morning Star" ([10]); "Temporality" ([11]); "Wings of Perfume" ([12]).

Volume 5: Seer of the Cycles (1976): "Seer of the Cycles" ([5]); "A Madrigal" ([6]); "Souvenance" ([7]); "High Surf: Monterey Bay" ([8]); "Lawn-Mower" ([8]); "Adjuration" ([9]); "Harmony" ([9]); "Immortelle" ([10]); "To a Mariposa Lily" ([10]); "A Sunset" ([11]); "Saturnian Cinema" ([12]).

Volume 6: The Burden of the Suns (1977): "The Sea-Gods" ([5]); "Sonnet" ([6]); "The Burden of the Suns" ([7]); "The Wind-Threnody" ([8]); "Amor Autumnalis" ([9]); "The Harbour of the Past" ([10]); "The Unmerciful Mistress" ([11]); "The Unfinished Quest" ([12]).

Notes. Bound in paper. Limited to 320, 296, 296, 303, 325, and 295 numbered copies, respectively. Out of the total print run for each volume, there are at least 52 copies bearing roman enumeration that are printed on oversize folio paper, as opposed to octavo for the regular numbered edition. Each set of these oversize folios were accompanied by a seventh, uniformly sized folio containing one of the manuscripts or typescripts used in the preparation of the edition.

39. *The Black Book of Clark Ashton Smith.* [Ed. Donald Sidney-Fryer and Rah Hoffman.]
a.   Sauk City, WI: Arkham House, 1979. 143 pp.

Contents: "Foreword" by Marvin R. Hiemstra (v–vi); *The Black Book of Clark Ashton Smith:* "A Note on the Text" by Donald Sidney-Fryer (ix–xi); "Explanation of Editorial Devices" (xii); "Index by Title" (xiii–xv); *The Black Book* of Clark Ashton Smith (1–74); "Excerpts from *The Black Book*" (75–82); *Appendix of Finished Poems:* [note] (85); "Song of the Necromancer" (86); "Dominium in Excelsis" (87); "Shapes in the Sunset" (88); "Don Quixote on Market Street" (89); "Soliloquy in an Ebon Tower" (90–92); "The Isle of Saturn" (93–94); "The Centaur" (95); "Ye Shall Return" (96); "Thebaid" (97); "Appendix of Published Epigrams and Pensées" (99–106); *Two Memoirs of Smith by George F. Haas:* "As I Remember Klarkash-Ton" (109–30); "Memories of Klarkash-Ton" (131–41); "Cycles" ([143]).

Notes. Bound in paper (the first Arkham House paperback edition); cover contains a small illustration in gold. With interior illustrations by Andrew Smith. The edition of CAS's commonplace book was completed in 1962 (the "Note on the Text" is dated

March 1962). The ms. is now at the University of Nevada–Reno
Special Collections.

40.   *The City of the Singing Flame.* [Ed. Donald Sidney-Fryer.]
  a.   New York: Pocket/Timescape, August 1981. 240 pp.

   Contents: "Introduction" by Donald Sidney-Fryer (9–12); "The
   City of the Singing Flame" (13–54); *Hyperborea:* "The White
   Sibyl" (56–65); "The Tale of Satampra Zeiros" (66–78); "The
   Theft of the Thirty-nine Girdles" (79–89); "The Door to Saturn"
   (90–108); *Zothique:* "The Dark Eidolon" (110–36); "The Black
   Abbot of Puthuum" (137–58); "The Garden of Adompha"
   (159–68); *Xiccarph:* "The Maze of Maal Dweb" (170–83); "The
   Flower-Women" (184–95); *Averoigne & Elsewhere:* "The Enchantress of Sylaire" (198–213); "The Beast of Averoigne"
   (214–24); "The Hunters from Beyond" (225–40).
   Notes. Bound in paper; cover art by Rowena Morrill. The first
   of three mass-market paperback editions of CAS's best fantasy and
   horror tales.

41.   *The Last Incantation.* [Ed. Donald Sidney-Fryer.]
  a.   New York: Pocket/Timescape, August 1982. 262 pp.

   Contents: "Introduction" by Donald Sidney-Fryer (1–4); "The
   Double Shadow" (7–18); "The Last Incantation" (19–23); "The
   Death of Malygris" (24–36); "Seedling of Mars" (39–77); "The
   Ice-Demon" (81–96); "Ubbo-Sathla" (97–104); "The Plutonian
   Drug" (107–17); "The Colossus of Ylourgne" (121–57); "The
   Holiness of Azédarac" (158–77); "The End of the Story"
   (178–95); "The Vaults of Yoh-Vombis" (199–215); "The Devo-
   tee of Evil" (219–30); "The Root of Ampoi" (231–45); "Genius
   Loci" (246–62).
   Notes. Bound in paper; cover art by Rowena Morrill.

42.   *The Monster of the Prophecy.* [Ed. Donald Sidney-Fryer.]
  a.   New York: Pocket/Timescape, April 1983. 238 pp.

   Contents: "Introduction" by Donald Sidney-Fryer (7–10); "The
   Monster of the Prophecy" (13–47); "Xeethra" (5169); "The Empire
   of the Necromancers" (70–79); "The Charnel God" (80–101);
   "The Witchcraft of Ulua" (102–11); "Vulthoom" (112–36); "The
   Weird of Avoosl Wuthoqquan" (139–47); "The Seven Geases"
   (148–67); "The Coming of the White Worm" (168–81); "The
   Master of the Asteroid" (185–99); "The Immeasurable Horror"

(200–214); "Monsters in the Night" (215–18); "The Gorgon" (219–30); "A Voyage to Sfanomoë" (231–38).

Notes. Bound in paper; cover art by Rowena Morrill.

43. *Letters to H. P. Lovecraft.* Ed. Steve Behrends.
   a. West Warwick, RI: Necronomicon Press, July 1987. 70 pp.

   Contents: "Abbreviations" (iii); "Chronology" (iv); "Introduction" by Behrends (v–viii); letters (1–53); "Appendix I: Letters to August Derleth, March–May 1937" (54–67); "Appendix II: Relation to Lovecraft's *Selected Letters*" (68); "To Klarkash-Ton, Lord of Averoigne" by H. P. Lovecraft (79); "To Howard Phillips Lovecraft" (70).

   Notes. Bound in paper; cover art by Robert H. Knox. Reproduced from typewritten copy. The letters are abridged but extensively annotated. Appendix I contains letters by CAS to Derleth discussing Lovecraft's pseudomythology and Derleth's purported additions to it.

44. *Mother of Toads.* Ed. Steve Behrends.
   a.1. West Warwick, RI: Necronomicon Press, December 1987. 15 pp.
   a.2. West Warwick, RI: Necronomicon Press, June 1988.
   b. West Warwick, RI: Necronomicon Press, January 1993. 12 pp.

   Contents: "Foreword" by Behrends (5–8); "Mother of Toads" (9–15).

   Notes. Bound in paper; cover art by Robert H. Knox. The Unexpurgated Clark Ashton Smith. The first of a series of pamphlets printing unabridged texts of CAS's stories derived from mss. The 1993 edition is reset (text printed in two columns per page) with new cover art by Knox. The foreword is now titled "Introduction."

45. *The Dweller in the Gulf.* Ed. Steve Behrends.
   a.1. West Warwick, RI: Necronomicon Press, December 1987. 18 pp.
   a.2. West Warwick, RI: Necronomicon Press, June 1988.
   b. West Warwick, RI: Necronomicon Press, January 1993. 14 pp.

   Contents: "Foreword" by Behrends (5–7); "The Dweller in the Gulf" (17); "Appendix: Conclusion of the *Wonder Stories* Appearance" (18).

   Notes. Bound in paper; cover art by Robert H. Knox. The Unexpurgated Clark Ashton Smith. The 1993 edition is reset (text printed in two columns per page) with new cover art by Knox. The foreword is now titled "Introduction."

46. *The Vaults of Yoh-Vombis.* Ed. Steve Behrends.
    a.1. West Warwick, RI: Necronomicon Press, March 1988. 10 pp.
    a.2. West Warwick, RI: Necronomicon Press, June 1988.
    b. West Warwick, RI: Necronomicon Press, January 1993. 16 pp.

    Contents: "Foreword" by Behrends (v–vi); "The Vaults of
    Yoh-Vombis" (1–9); "Appendix: Synopsis" (10).
         Notes. Bound in paper; cover art by Robert H. Knox. The
    Unexpurgated Clark Ashton Smith. The 1993 edition is reset (text
    printed in two columns per page) with new cover art by Knox. The
    foreword is now titled "Introduction."

47. *A Rendezvous in Averoigne: The Best Fantastic Tales of Clark Ashton
    Smith.*
    a.1. Sauk City, WI: Arkham House, 1988. 472 pp.
    a.2. Sauk City, WI: Arkham House, [May] 2003.

    Contents: "The Sorcerer Departs" (v); "Introduction" by Ray
    Bradbury (ix–x); *Averoigne:* "The Holiness of Azédarac" (3–21);
    "The Colossus of Ylourgne" (22–56); "The End of the Story"
    (57–75); "A Rendezvous in Averoigne" (76–89); *Atlantis:* "The
    Last Incantation" (93–97); "The Death of Malygris" (98–111); "A
    Voyage to Sfanomoë" (112–19); *Hyperborea:* "The Weird of
    Avoosl Wuthoqquan" (123–30); "The Seven Geases" (131–49);
    "The Tale of Satampra Zeiros" (150–63); "The Coming of the
    White Worm" (164–76); *Lost Worlds:* "The City of the Singing
    Flame" (179–94); "The Dweller in the Gulf" (195–212); "The
    Chain of Aforgomon" (213–30); "Genius Loci" (231–46); "The
    Maze of Maal Dweb" (247–58); "The Vaults of Yoh-Vombis"
    (259–76); "The Uncharted Isle" (277–86); "The Planet of the
    Dead" (287–98); "Master of the Asteroid" (299–312); *Zothique:*
    "The Empire of the Necromancers" (313–25); "The Charnel God"
    (326–46); "Xeethra" (347–64); "The Dark Eidolon" (365–91);
    "The Death of Ilalotha" (392–402); "The Last Hieroglyph"
    (403–18); "Necromancy in Naat" (419–36); "The Garden of
    Adompha" (437–48); "The Isle of the Torturers" (449–63);
    "Morthylla" (464–72).
         Notes. Bound in black cloth; spine stamped in gold. Dust jacket
    of a.1 is by J. K. Potter; that of a.2 is by Dariusz Jasiczak. A se-
    lection of what, in the opinion of silent editor James Turner,
    constitutes the best of CAS's stories. Some texts presented in
    corrected texts based on mss., others not.

48. *The Monster of the Prophecy.* Ed. Steve Behrends.
    a. West Warwick, RI: Necronomicon Press, July 1988. 28 pp.

    Contents: "Introduction" by Behrends (5–6); "The Monster of the Prophecy" (7–27); "Appendix: Vizaphmal in Ophiuchus (synopsis)" (28).

    Notes. Bound in paper; cover art by Robert H. Knox. The Unexpurgated Clark Ashton Smith.

49. *Nostalgia of the Unknown: The Complete Prose Poetry of Clark Ashton Smith.* Ed. Marc and Susan Michaud, Steve Behrends, and S. T. Joshi.
    a. West Warwick, RI: Necronomicon Press, July 1988. 32 pp.
    b. West Warwick, RI: Necronomicon Press, January 1993. 32 pp.

    Contents: "Introduction" by the editors (vi–viii); *From Ebony and Crystal:* "The Traveller" (1); "The Flower-Devil" (2); "Images" ("Tears," "The Secret Rose," "The Wind and the Garden," "Offerings," "A Coronal") (2–3); "The Black Lake" (3–4); "Vignettes" ("Beyond the Mountains," "The Broken Lute," "Nostalgia of the Unknown," "Grey Sorrow," "The Hair of Circe," "The Eyes of Circe") (4–5); "A Dream of Lethe" (5–6); "The Caravan" (6); "The Princess Almeena" (6); "Ennui" (7); "The Statue of Silence" (8); "Remoteness" (8); "The Memnons of the Night" (8–9); "The Garden and the Tomb" (9); "In Cocaigne" (9–10); "The Litany of the Seven Kisses" (10); "From a Letter" (11); "From the Crypts of Memory" [text taken from original manuscripts] (11–12); "From the Crypts of Memory" [text taken from *Ebony and Crystal*] (12–13); "A Phantasy" (13); "The Demon, the Angel, and Beauty" (14–15); "The Shadows" (15–16); *December 1929:*"The Mirror in the Hall of Ebony" (17); "To the Daemon" (17–18); "The Abomination of Desolation" (18); "The Touch-stone" (19); "The Lotus and the Moon" (19); "The Osprey and the Shark" (20); "The Forbidden Forest" (20–21); "The Mithridate" (21); "The Muse of Hyperborea" (21–22); "Chinoiserie" (22); *Additional Prose Poems:* "The City of Destruction" [fragment] (23–24); "The Image of Bronze and the Image of Iron" [fragment] (24); "The Crystals" (24–25); "The Lake of Enchanted Silence" (25); "The Mortuary" (25–26); "The Corpse and the Skeleton" (26–27); "The Sun and the Sepulchre" (27); "The Frozen Waterfall" (27–28); "Preference" (28); "The Passing of Aphrodite" (28–29); "The Days" (30); "Offering" (30); "Narcissus" (30); "The Peril That Lurks among Ruins" [text taken from original manuscript] (31); "The Peril That Lurks among Ruins" [text taken from a later manuscript] (31–32); [Untitled] (32).

   Notes. Bound in paper; cover art by Robert H. Knox. The second edition is reset. For a French translation, see II.A.iii.12.

50. *Xeethra.* Ed. Steve Behrends.
   a. West Warwick, RI: Necronomicon Press, October 1988. 16 pp.

   Contents: "Foreword" by Behrends (5–6); "Xeethra" (7–16).
   Notes. Bound in paper; cover art by Robert H. Knox. The Unexpurgated Clark Ashton Smith.

51. *The Witchcraft of Ulua.* Ed. Steve Behrends.
   a. West Warwick, RI: Necronomicon Press, October 1988. 12 pp.

   Contents: "Foreword" by Behrends (5–6); "The Witchcraft of Ulua" (7–11); "Appendix: First version of the 'temptation scene'" (12).
   Notes. Bound in paper; cover art by Robert H. Knox. The Unexpurgated Clark Ashton Smith.

52. *Strange Shadows: The Uncollected Fiction and Essays of Clark Ashton Smith.* Ed. Steve Behrends, Donald Sidney-Fryer, and Rah Hoffman.
   a. Westport, CT: Greenwood Press, 1989. 281 pp.

   Contents: "Acknowledgments" (xiii); "Introduction" by Robert Bloch (xv–xix); "A Note on the Contents" by Behrends (xxi–xxiv); FANTASTIC FICTION: *Completed Stories:* "A Good Embalmer" (3–6); "Double Cosmos" (7–15); "Strange Shadows"/"I Am Your Shadow" (16–35); "Nemesis of the Unfinished" (36–43); "The Dart of Rasafa" (44–49); *Variant Versions of Published Stories:* "The Beast of Averoigne" (51–62); "The Coming of the White Worm" (63–76); "In the Book of Vergama" (77); *Fragmentary Stories with Accompanying Synopses:* "The Ocean-World of Alioth" (79–81); "Ascharia" (82–85); "The Master of Destruction" (86–90); "Slaves of the Black Pillar" (91–94); "The Music of Death" (95–100); *Fragmentary Stories:* "In a Hashish Dream" (101–3); "The Eggs from Saturn" (104–6); "The Lord of Lunacy" (106); "The Infernal Star" (106–28); "The House of Haon-Dor" (128–31); "Shapes of Adamant" (131–32); "Eviction by Night" (132–34); "Mandor's Enemy" (134–35); "Mnemoka" (135–39); "The Point of the Jest" (139–40); "Chincharrero" (140–41); "Unquiet Boundary" (141–42); "Wingless Phoenix" (142); "Djinn without a Bottle" (142); *Synopses:* "Vizaphmal in Ophiuchus" (143–44); "The Sorceress of Averoigne/The Tower of Istarelle" (144–46); "The Atmospheric

Entity" (146); "The Minotaur's Brother" (146–47); "Offspring of the Grave" (147); "I Am a Witch" (147–48); "The Feet of Sidavia" (148); "The Crabs of Iribos" (148–50); "Beyond the Rose-Arbor" (150–51); "Maker of Prodigies" (151–52); "Queen of the Sabbat" (152–53); "The Pilgrim of Eternity" (153); "The Menace of the Dust" (153); "The Galley from Atlantis" (153); "The Trilithon" (154); "The Transformation of Athanor" (154); "A Gift from the Beloved" (154); "The Double Dream" (154); "The Youngest Vampire" (154–55); "The God of the Asteroid" (155); "Poseidon" (155); "The Mummy-Case of Hammen-Tha" (155); "Dead Assassins" (155); "From a Lost World" (155); "Prisoners of the Black Dimension" (155); "The Entity of the Sands" (156); "Hecate" (156); "The Ghoul from Mercury" (156); "The Moon-Spectre" (156); "The Thing from the Antarctic" (156); "The Conquest of Mercury" (156); "A Misadventure of Don Juan" (157); "Neria" (157); "The Hyperborean City" (157); "The Devotee of Evil" (157); "The Testament of Athammaus" (157–58); "The Mechanical Murder" (158); "Between Two Worlds" (158); "The Planet of the Dead" (158); "The Dome in the Ice" (158); "The Empire of the Necromancers" (short synopsis) (158); "The Invisible City" (short synopsis) (158–59); "The Re-union" (159); "A Star-Change" (159); "A Good Embalmer" (159); "The World- Maker" (159); "The Supernumerary Corpse" (159); "The Cypress" (160); "A Sojourn in Mercury" (160); "An Excursion in Time" (160); "The Elder Manor" (160); "The Moraine" (160); "Men of the Macrocosm" (161); "The Lunar Path" (161); "(titles)" (161–62); "The Other Entity" (162); "The Vapor from the Void" (162); "The Vaults of Yoh-Vombis" (162–63); "The Burial-Place of the Unknown" (163); "The Arm from the Fig-Tree" (163); "The Scarab" (163); "The Spectral Tarn" (163–64); "The Vestibule of the Past" (164); "The Nameless Offsrping" (164); "The Mysterious Poison" (164); "The Invisible Satellite" (165); "The Protean People" (165); "The Destination of Gideon Balcoth" (165); "The After-Men" (165); "A Tale of Gnydron" (165); "The Invisible Devourer" (166); "The Weird of Avoosl Wuthoqquan" (166); "The Demon from Alphard" (166); "The Werewolf of Averoigne" (166); "The Disinternment of Venus" (166–67); "[The Gargoyle of Vyones]" (167); "The Maker of Gargoyles" (167); "A Bottle on the Orinoco" (167); "A Vintage from Atlantis" (168); "The Cairn" (168–69); "(titles)" (169); "The Cairn" (new ending) (170); "(titles)" (170); "The Empire of the Necromancers" (long synopsis) (170); "The River of Mystery" (170–71); "The Rebirth of the Flame" (171–72); "Across the Time-Stream" (172); "The Invisible City" (long synopsis) (172–73); "The Immortals of Mercury" (173); "The Lunar Brain" (173); "Prisoners of the Black Dimension" (title only) (173); "The Beast of Averoigne" (short synopsis) (173); "The Inverse Avatar" (173); "The Double Shadow" (174); "The Cosmic Sequel" (174); "The Embassy to Tiirath" (174); "Ubbo-Sathla" (174); "The Beast of Averoigne" (long synopsis) (174–75); "The Flower-Women" (175); "Vulthoom" (175–76); *Fantastic Titles* (177–87); *Fantastic Names* (189–93); NON-FANTASTIC FICTION: "The Flirt" (197–98); "The Perfect Woman" (198–99); "Gossip" (fragment) (199); "A Platonic Entanglement" (199–201); "The Expert Lover" (201–8); "The Parrot" (208–10); "A Copy of Burns" (211–12); "Checkmate" (212–17); *Prose-Poems and Plays:* "The City of Destruction" (fragment) (221–22); "The Lake of Enchanted Silence" (222); "Preference" (222–23); "The Days" (223); "Offering" (223); "The Mortuary" (223–24); "The Frozen Waterfall" (224); "The Osprey and the Shark" (224–25); "[The Land of Fruitful Palms]" (225); *The Fugitives* (fragment) (225–26); "Venus and the Priest" (fragment) (226); *The Dead Will Cuckold You* (227–42); *Miscellaneous and Non-fiction Prose:* "Account of an Actual Dream—1912" (245); "Argument of 'The Hashish-Eater'" (245–46); "Introduction to *Shadows of Wings*" (246); "Cigarette Characterization" (246); "[On the Art of Ephraim Doner]" (247); "Introduction to *Wine of Wonder*" (247); "Notes to the Text" (251–65); "Appendix I: The Lost Worlds of Clark Ashton Smith" (269–72); "Appendix II: Don Carter's Outline for 'Nemesis of the Unfinished'" (273–75); "Appendix III: *The Black Book:* Addenda" (276–81).

Notes. Bound in green boards; spine stamped in white; no dust jacket. Contributions to the Study of Science Fiction and Fantasy, No. 36. Valuable collection of previously unpublished documents pertaining to CAS's fiction.

53. *The Hashish-Eater; or, The Apocalypse of Evil.*

a. West Warwick, RI: Necronomicon Press, September 1989. 22 pp.

Notes. Bound in paper. Cover art and numerous full-page interior illustrations by Robert H. Knox. First separate printing of CAS's longest poem. The "Argument of 'The Hashish-Eater'" is printed on the copyright page.

54. *The Devil's Notebook: Collected Epigrams and Pensées of Clark Ashton Smith.* Compiled by Donald Sidney-Fryer. Edited by Don Herron.
   a. Mercer Island, WA: Starmont House, 1990. 82 pp.

> *Contents:* "Introduction" by Herron (v–x); "By Way of Preface: Epigrams and Paragraphs Selected by Clark Ashton Smith" (epigrams by Remy de Gourmont, Anatole France, Honoré de Balzac, and other writers) (xi–xv); "The Devil's Notebook" (1–22); "Cocktails and Crème de Menthe" (23–47); "New Teeth for Old Saws" (49–50); "Points for the Pious" (51–54); "Unpopular Sayings" (55–56); "Paradox and Persiflage" (57–68); "The Epigrams of Alastor" (69–71); "Epigrams and Apothegms" (73–79); "A Note on the Text" (81–82).
>
> *Notes.* Bound in both hardcover and paperback (paperback cover art by Bruce Timm).

55. *The Hashish-Eater; or, The Apocalypse of Evil.* Ed. Donald Sidney-Fryer.
   a. Sacramento, CA: Innervisions Group Design Firm, 1990. 48 pp.

> *Contents:* "About Clark Ashton Smith and *The Hashish-Eater*" by Sidney-Fryer (5–13); "Materials by Smith Related to the Poem, the Sustaining Mind-set, and the Final Stage" by Sidney-Fryer (15–19) (includes "The Crystals" [17], "Argument of *The Hashish-Eater*" [17]; "The Face from Infinity" [extract from *The Black Book*] [18]; "Excerpt from a Letter by Smith, Summer 1950" [19]); *The Hashish-Eater; or, The Apocalypse of Evil* (21–35); "Glossary of Unusual Words, &c." by Sidney-Fryer (37–47).
>
> *Notes.* Comb-bound with clear cover and back. Issued as a private publication on the occasion of Sidney-Fryer's dramatic reading of the poem at Webbers Bookstore in Sacramento, 24 November 1990. The text of CAS's poem is the 1922 version.

56. *Tales of Zothique.* Ed. Will Murray and Steve Behrends.
   a. West Warwick, RI: Necronomicon Press, June 1995. 224 pp.

> *Contents:* "Textual Note" (6); "Introduction" by Murray (7–12); *Book I:* "The Empire of the Necromancers" (13–19); "The Isle of the Torturers" (20–31); "The Charnel God" (31–48); "The Dark Eidolon" (48–68); "The Voyage of King Euvoran" (69–86); "The Weaver in the Vault" (86–96); "The Tomb-Spawn" (96–103); "The Witchcraft of Ulua" (103–10); "Xeethra" (111–26); "In the Book of Vergama" [excised preface to "The Last Hieroglyph"] (126); "The Last Hieroglyph" (127–39); *Book II:* "Shapes of Adamant" [fragment] (140–41); "Necromancy in Naat" (141–55); "The

Black Abbot of Puthuum" (156–72); "The Death of Ilalotha" (172–80); "The Garden of Adompha" (180–87); *Book III:* "Zothique" [poem] (188); "The Master of the Crabs" (189–98); "Mandor's Enemy" [fragment] (199); "Morthylla" (199–206); *The Dead Will Cuckold You* (207–21); "Postscript" by Murray (222–24).

Notes. Bound in paper; cover art by Jason C. Eckhardt and Homer D. Eckhardt; frontispiece by Robert H. Knox. First complete publication of all of CAS's writings (stories and poems) about Zothique, in corrected texts.

57. *A Prophecy of Monsters.* Ed. Les Thomas.
    a. N.p.: 13th Hour Books, 1995. iv, 3 pp.

    Contents: "Clark Ashton Smith" by Paul A. Roales (iii–iv); "A Prophecy of Monsters" (1–3).

    Notes. Bound in paper; cover art by Stanley Sargent. Limited to 100 numbered copies.

58. *The Book of Hyperborea.* Ed. Will Murray.
    a. West Warwick, RI: Necronomicon Press, July 1996. 173 pp.

    Contents: "Textual Note" (6); "Introduction" (7–14); "The Tale of Satampra Zeiros" (15–26); "The Muse of Hyperborea" (27); "The Door to Saturn" (28–45); "The Testament of Athammaus" (46–62); "The Weird of Avoosl Wuthoqquan" (63–70); "Ubbo-Sathla" (71–78); "The Ice-Demon" (79–93); "The White Sybil" (94–102); "The House of Haon-Dor" [fragment] (103–6); "The Coming of the White Worm" (107–23); "The Seven Geases" (124–42); "Lament for Vixeela" (143); "The Theft of the Thirty-nine Girdles" (144–53); "Appendix: The Coming of the White Worm" (abridged) (154–68); "Postscript" by Will Murray (167–73).

    Notes. Bound in paper; cover art by Robert H. Knox; frontispiece by Jason C. Eckhardt. First complete publication of all of CAS's writings (stories, poems, and fragments) about Hyperborea, in corrected texts.

59. *The Emperor of Dreams.* Ed. Stephen Jones.
    a. London: Gollancz, [January] 2002. 580 pp.

    Contents: "On Fantasy" [essay] (1–2); "Song of the Necromancer" [poem] (3–4); "The Abominations of Yondo" (5–11); "The Ninth Skeleton" (12–16); "The Last Incantation" (17–21); "A Rendezvous in Averoigne" (22–37); "The Return of the Sorcerer" (39–54); "The Tale of Satampra Zeiros" (55–67); ""The Door to Saturn"

(68–87); "The Gorgon" (88–99); "The Weird of Avoosl Wuth-oqquan" (100–108); "The Nameless Offspring" (109–27); "The Empire of the Necromancers" (128–37); "The Hunters from Beyond" (138–54); "The Isle of the Torturers" (155–70); "The Beast of Averoigne" (171–81); "Genius Loci" (182–99); "Ub-bo-Sathla" (200–207); "The Kiss of Zoraida" (208–13); "The Seed from the Sepulcher" (214–26); "The Weaver in the Vault" (227–39); "The Ghoul" (240–45); "The Charnel God" (246–68); "The Death of Malygris" (269–81); "The Tomb-Spawn" (282–91); "The Seven Geases" (292–312); "Xeethra" (313–32); "The Dark Eidolon" (333–60); "The Flower-Women" (361–72); "The Treader of the Dust" (373–81); "The Black Abbot of Puthuum" (383–404); "Necromancy in Naat" (405–25); "The Death of Ila-lotha" (426–37); "The Garden of Adompha" (438–48); "Mother of Toads" (449–56); "The Double Shadow" (457–69); "The Coming of the White Worm" (470–83); "The Root of Ampoi" (484–98); "Morthylla" (499–508); "An Offering to the Moon" (509–20); "The Theft of Thirty-Nine [*sic*] Girdles" (521–31); "Symposium of the Gorgon" (532–40); "Told in the Desert" (541–47); "Prince Alcouz and the Magician" (548–49); "A Good Embalmer" (550–54); "The Mortuary" [prose poem] (555); "Afterword: The Lost Worlds of Klarkash-Ton" by Jones (556–80).

Notes. Bound in paper; cover art by J. K. Potter. Volume 26 in Gollancz's "Fantasy Masterworks" series.

60.   *The Black Diamonds.* Ed. S. T. Joshi.
   a.   New York: Hippocampus Press, [March] 2002. 181 pp.
   b.   New York: Hippocampus Press, n.d. 184 pp.

     Contents: "Introduction" by Joshi (5–6); *The Black Diamonds* (9–184).

     Notes. Bound in paper; cover and interior art by Jason C. Eck-hardt; cover design by Barbara Briggs Silbert. First publication of CAS's juvenile novel (written c. 1909). Shortly after publication, some missing leaves (constituting the end of ch. 17) were discovered by W. C. Farmer; an undated reprint includes the missing text. (The text was first published in *The Sword of Zagan* [item 64 below]).

61.   *The Last Oblivion: Best Fantastic Poems of Clark Ashton Smith.* Ed. S. T. Joshi and David E. Schultz.
   a.   New York: Hippocampus Press, [November] 2002. 194 pp.

     Contents: "Introduction" (9–11) by Joshi and Schultz; "A Note on the Text" (12); "Acknowledgments" (12); *The Hashish-Eater; or,*

The Apocalypse of Evil (15–29); *I. The Star-Treader:* "The Star-Treader" (30–33); "Ode to the Abyss" (33–35); "Nirvana" (35–36); "The Song of a Comet" (36–37); "Lament of the Stars" (38–40); "In Saturn" (40); "Triple Aspect" (40–41); "The Abyss Triumphant" (41); "The Motes" (41–42); "Desire of Vastness" (42); "Shadows" (42–43); "A Dream of the Abyss" (43–44); "After Armageddon" (44–45); "The Ancient Quest" (45); "A Dream of Oblivion" (45–46); "Ode to Light" (46–47); "Ode to Matter" (47–48); *II. Medusa and Other Horrors:* "Nero" (49–51); "Medusa" (51–52); "Averted Malefice" (52–53); "The Medusa of the Skies" (53); "Saturn" (53–60); "In Lemuria" (60); "Satan Unrepentant" (60–63); "The Ghoul and the Seraph" (63–67); "The Medusa of Despair" (67); "A Vision of Lucifer" (67); "The Witch in the Graveyard" (68–70); "The Flight of Azrael" (70–71); "The Mummy" (71–72); "Minatory" (72); "To the Chimera" (72–73); "The Whisper of the Worm" (73); "The Envoys" (73–74); "Nyctalops" (74–75); "Jungle Twilight" (76); "Necromancy" (76); "The Witch with Eyes of Amber" (77); "Cambion" (77–78); "The Saturnienne" (78–79); "Chance" (79); "Revenant" (79–80); "Song of the Necromancer" (81); "Pour chercher du nouveau" (82); "Witch-Dance" (83); "Not Theirs the Cypress-Arch" (84); *III. The Eldritch Dark*: "A Song from Hell" (85–86); "The Titans in Tartarus" (86–88); "The Twilight Woods" (88); "Lethe" (89); "Atlantis" (89); "The Eldritch Dark" (89–90); "White Death" (90); "A Dead City" (90–91); "The Cloud-Islands" (91); "The City of the Titans" (92); "The City of Destruction" (92–93); "Beyond the Great Wall" (93); "Solution" (94); "Rosa Mystica" (94–95); "Symbols" (95); "The City in the Desert" (95–96); "The Melancholy Pool" (96); "Twilight on the Snow" (96–97); "The Land of Evil Stars" (97–98); "Memnon at Midnight" (98); "The Kingdom of Shadows" (98–99); "Moon-Dawn" (100); "Outlanders" (100); "Warning" (100–101); "The Nightmare Tarn" (101–2); "The Prophet Speaks" (102–3); "The Outer Land" (103–5); "In Thessaly" (105–6); "Le Miroir des blanches fleurs" (106–7); "The Moonlight Desert" (107); "Ougabalys" (107–8); "Desert Dweller" (108–9); "Amithaine" (109–10); "The Dark Chateau" (110–11); "Averoigne" (111–12); "Zothique" (112–13); *IV. Said the Dreamer:* "The Castle of Dreams" (114); "The Dream-God's Realm" (114–15); "Imagination" (115–18); "The Last Night" (118); "Shadow of Nightmare" (118); "A Song of Dreams" (119–20); "The Dream-Bridge" (120); "Said the Dreamer" (120–21); "Dolor of Dreams" (121–22); "Luna Aeternalis"

(122–23); "Echo of Memnon" (123); "Nightmare" (123–24); "The Last Goddess" (124); "Love Malevolent" (124–25); "The Wingless Archangels" (125); "Enchanted Mirrors" (125–26); "Selenique" (126); "Maya" (126–27); "Fantaisie d'antan" (127–28); "In Slumber" (128); *V. The Refuge of Beauty:* "The Power of Eld" (129); "Strangeness" (129–30); "The Nereid" (130–31); "Exotique" (131); "Transcendence" (131–32); "The Tears of Lilith" (132); "Cleopatra" (132–33); "The Refuge of Beauty" (133); "Sandalwood" (133–34); "The Last Oblivion" (134); "Alienage" (135–36); "Adventure" (136–37); "Interrogation" (137); "Canticle" (138); "To Antares" (138–39); "Connaissance" (139); "Exorcism" (139–40); "Lamia" (140); "Farewell to Eros" (141); "Some Blind Eidolon" (142–43); "Bacchante" (143–44); "Resurrection" (144–45); "The Sorcerer to His Love" (145); "The Hill of Dionysus" (145–46); "Midnight Beach" (147); "Omniety" (147–48); *VI. To the Darkness:* "Ode on Imagination" (149–50); "Retrospect and Forecast" (151); "To the Darkness" (151–52); "A Dream of Beauty" (152–53); "The Pursuer" (153); "In the Desert" (153–54); "The Nameless Wraith" (154–55); "To the Daemon of Sublimity" (155); "Desolation" (155); "Inferno" (156); "Dissonance" (156); "Remembered Light" (156–57); "The Incubus of Time" (157–58); "Laus Mortis" (158); "The Hope of the Infinite" (158–59); "Antepast" (159); "Forgotten Sorrow" (159); "Lunar Mystery" (160); "The Funeral Urn" (160–61); "Mors" (161); "September" (161–62); "Ennui" (162); *VII. The Sorcerer Departs:* "To Omar Khayyam" (163–65); "To Nora May French" (165–67); "On Re-reading Baudelaire" (167–68); "To George Sterling: A Valediction" (168–70); "To Howard Phillips Lovecraft" (170–71); "H. P. L." (171); "Soliloquy in an Ebon Tower" (171–74); "Cycles" (174); "Glossary" (175–78); "Bibliography" (179–85); "Index of Titles" (187–90); "Index of First Lines" (191–94).

Notes. Bound in paper; cover art by CAS; cover design by Barbara Briggs Silbert. The poems are arranged in broad thematic categories. CAS's drawing "An Afreet" appears on the title page. Between pp. 128 and 129 is a sheet containing color reproductions of two paintings by CAS.

62. *The Red World of Polaris: The Adventures of Captain Volmar.* Ed. Ronald S. Hilger and Scott Connors.
a. San Francisco: Night Shade Books, 2003. 115 pp.
b. San Francisco: Night Shade Books, 2003.

Contents: "The Magellan of the Constellations" (introduction) by Hilger and Connors (1–8); "Marooned in Andromeda" (11–36); "A Captivity in Serpens" (39–77); "The Red World of Polaris" (79–107); "The Ocean-World of Alioth" (109–11); "Captain Volmar and Crew: An Afterword" by Donald Sidney-Fryer (113–15).

Notes. Bound in black cloth; spine stamped in white. Just jacket illustration by Jason Van Hollander, who has also contributed a frontispiece and interior illustrations. First publication of CAS's three stories about Captain Volmar, triggered by the discovery of the ms. of "The Red World of Polaris," previously thought to be lost. There are four states of this book. The first edition was limited to 500 copies signed by Hilger and Sidney-Fryer (Connors was unable to sign the limitation sheets at the time, due to injury); this edition sold for $35.00. A special lettered edition was bound in red leather and came in a slipcase covered with greenish-gray cloth. The 26-copy lettered edition added two color plates of paintings by CAS and "A Chinese Fable" (prose poem). Ten Greek-lettered copies are identical to the lettered edition, except that the binding is green leather; these copies were presentation copies to the editors. A regular trade edition consisting of 2000 copies was sold for $27.00. This state corrects a transposition error in the introduction on p. 2.

63.   *Selected Letters of Clark Ashton Smith.* Ed. David E. Schultz and Scott Connors.

a.   Sauk City, WI: Arkham House, 2003. xxvii, 417 pp.

Contents: "Introduction" by Connors and Schultz (xv–xxiv); "Editorial Practices" (xxv); "Acknowledgments" (xxvi); "Abbreviations" (xxvi–xxvii); 1. To George Sterling (21 May 1911) (3–4); 2. To George Sterling (6 October 1911) (4–5); 3. To George Sterling (24 March 1912) (6–8); 4. To George Sterling (12 April 1912) (8–10); 5. To George Sterling (28 April 1912) (10–12); 6. To George Sterling (26 May 1912) (12–14); 7. To George Sterling (18 August 1912) (14–15); 8. To George Sterling (11 September 1912) (15–16); 9. To George Sterling (26 September 1912) (16–17); 10. To George Sterling (13 November 1912) (17–18); 11. To Herbert Bashford (15 January 1913) (18–19); 12. To George Sterling (3 February 1913) (19–20); 13. To George Sterling (11 May 1913) (20–21); 14. To George Sterling (1 July 1913) (21–22); 15. To George Sterling (27 January 1914) (22); 16. To George Sterling (27 July 1914) (23–24); 17. To George Sterling (16 October 1914) (24); 18. To George Sterling

(11 March 1915) (25–26); 19. To George Sterling (23 April 1915) (26–27); 20. To George Sterling (16 August 1915) (27–28); 21. To Albert M. Bender (6 November 1915) (28); 22. To Albert M. Bender (9 February 1916) (29); 23. To George Sterling (5 April 1916) (29–30); 24. To George Sterling (15 June 1916) (30–31); 25. To George Sterling (11 October 1916) (31–32); 26. To Samuel Loveman (24 October 1916) (32–33); 27. To Albert M. Bender (19 January 1917) (33); 28. To George Sterling (28 February 1917) (34–35); 29. To George Sterling (3 March 1917) (35–36); 30. To George Sterling (14 April 1917) (36–37); 31. To Albert A. Bender (15 January 1918) (37); 32. To George Sterling (25 February 1918) (37–38); 33. To George Sterling (8 April 1918) (38–39); 34. To George Sterling (10 August 1918) (39–40); 35. To George Sterling (31 August 1918) (40–41); 36. To George Sterling (13 October 1918) (41–42); 37. To George Sterling (16 November 1918) (42–43); 38. To Samuel Loveman (1 April 1919) (43–45); 39. To George Sterling (10 June 1919) (45–46); 40. To George Sterling (28 August 1919) (46–47); 41. To George Sterling (1 November 1919) (47–48); 42. To George Sterling (29 January 1920) (49–50); 43. To George Sterling (29 March 1920) (50–52); 44. To George Sterling (10 July 1920) (52–53); 45. To George Kirk (16 September 1920) (54); 46. To George Kirk (3 October 1920) (54–55); 47. To George Sterling (19 October 1920) (55–56); 48. To Samuel Loveman (6 December 1920) (56–57); 49. To George Kirk (4 February 1921) (57–58); 50. To George Kirk (1 September 1921) (58–59); 51. To George Sterling (5 September 1921) (59–60); 52. To George Sterling (17 December 1921) (60–61); 53. To George Kirk (11 April 1922) (61); 54. To George Sterling (11 April 1922) (62); 55. To George Sterling (25 June 1922) (62–63); 56. To George Sterling (29 September 1922) (63–64); 57. To George Sterling (23 November 1922) (64–65); 58. To George Sterling (13 December 1922) (65–66); 59. To George Sterling (17 December 1922) (66–67); 60. To George Sterling (9 February 1923) (67–68); 61. To George Sterling (23 June 1923) (68–69); 62. To Frank Belknap Long (7 July 1923) (69–70); 63. To George Sterling (4 November 1923) (70–71); 64. To George Sterling (21 July 1924) (71–72); 65. To George Sterling (20 January 1925) (72); 66. To Ina Coolbrith (12 March 1925) (73); 67. To George Sterling (15 March 1925) (73–74); 68. To H. P. Lovecraft (20 March 1925) (75–76); 69. To George Sterling (21 May 1925) (76–77); 70. To George Sterling (1 July 1925)

(77–78); 71. To Donald Wandrei (10 July 1925) (78–79); 72. To Donald Wandrei (25 August 1925) (80–81); 73. To Donald Wandrei (12 September 1925) (81–83); 74. To George Sterling (14 September 1925) (83); 75. To George Sterling (1 December 1925) (84); 76. To George Sterling (8 May 1926) (85–86); 77. To H. P. Lovecraft (9 May 1926) (86–87); 78. To Benjamin De Casseres (22 May 1926) (87–88); 79. To Donald Wandrei (4 July 1926) (88); 80. To Donald Wandrei (27 September 1926) (89); 81. To George Sterling (28 September 1926) (90); 82. To William Whittingham Lyman (10 October 1926) (90–91); 83. To George Sterling (11 October 1926) (91–92); 84. To Donald Wandrei (26 October 1926) (92); 85. To William Whittingham Lyman (26 October 1926) (93); 86. To George Sterling (27 October 1926) (93–94); 87. To George Sterling (November 4, 1926) (94–95); 88. To Helen Hoyt (7 November 1926) (95–96); 89. To James D. Phelan (19 November 1926) (96); 90. To Donald Wandrei (6 December 1926) (97–98); 91. To Donald Wandrei (7 May 1927) (98–99); 92. To Donald Wandrei (9 July 1927) (99); 93. To Donald Wandrei (18 September 1927) (99–100); 94. To Donald Wandrei (20 April 1928) (101); 95. To Donald Wandrei (21\ October 1928) (102); 96. To Donald Wandrei (20 March 1928) (102–3); 97. To H. P. Lovecraft (26 November 1929) (103–5); 98. To H. P. Lovecraft (10 December 1929) (105–7); 99. To H. P. Lovecraft (9 January 1930) (107–8); 100. To H. P. Lovecraft (27 January 1930) (108–11); 101. To H. P. Lovecraft (2 April 1930) (111–13); 102. To H. P. Lovecraft (23 April 1930) (113–14); 103. To Helen Hoyt (16 May 1930) (114–15); 104. To H. P. Lovecraft (30 July 1930) (115–16); 105. To H. P. Lovecraft (22 August 1930) (117–18); 106. To H. P. Lovecraft ([mid-September 1930]) (118–21); 107. To H. P. Lovecraft ([late October 1930]) (121–24); 108. To Donald Wandrei (9 October 1930) (124–25); 109. To H. P. Lovecraft (24 October 1930) (125–31); 110. To August Derleth (2 November 1930) (131); 111. To H. P. Lovecraft (10 November 1930) (132–33); 112. To H. P. Lovecraft (16 November 1930) (133–39); 113. To August Derleth (1 December 1930) (139–40); 114. To Albert M. Bender (14 December 1930) (140–41); 115. To H. P. Lovecraft ([early January 1931]) (141–43); 116. To H. P. Lovecraft (27 January 1931) (143–47); 117. To H. P. Lovecraft ([15–23 February 1931]) (147–50); 118. To August Derleth (9 April 1931) (150–51); 119. To William Whittingham Lyman (4 May 1931) (151–52); 120. To August Derleth (8 May 1931)

(152–53); 121. To August Derleth (June 15, 1931) (153–54); 122. To August Derleth (9 July 1931) (155–57); 123. To August Derleth (20 July 1931) (157–58); 124. To H. P. Lovecraft ([early August 1931]) (158–60); 125. To August Derleth (18 August 1931) (160–61); 126. To August Derleth (28 August 1931) (161–62); 127. To August Derleth (6 September 1931) (162–63); 128. To August Derleth (26 September 1931) (163–64); 129. To August Derleth (3 November 1931) (164–65); 130. To H. P. Lovecraft ([early November 1931]) (165–67); 131. To August Derleth (31 December 1931) (167–68); 132. To August Derleth (16 February 1932) (168–69); 133. To Donald Wandrei (17 February 1932) (169–70); 134. To Donald Wandrei ([c. March 1932]) (170–71); 135. To H. P. Lovecraft ([March 1932]) (171–73); 136. To August Derleth (15 March 1932) (173–74); 137. To H. P. Lovecraft ([early April 1932]) (174–75); 138. To Lester Anderson (4 May 1932) (175–76); 139. To Lester Anderson (14 May 1932) (176); 140. To August Derleth (15 May 1932) (176–78); 141. To Lester Anderson (22 May 1932) (178); 142. To Lester Anderson (4 June 1932) (178–79); 143. To Lester Anderson (4 July 1932) (179–80); 144. To August Derleth (10 July 1932) (180–81); 145. To Genevieve K. Sully (18 July 1932) (181–82); 146. To Genevieve K. Sully (23 July 1932) (183); 147. To Genevieve K. Sully (August 5, 1932) (183–85); 148. To August Derleth (11 August 1932) (185–86); 149. To Genevieve K. Sully (12 August 1932) (186–87); 150. To Lester Anderson (1 September 1932) (187); 151. To August Derleth (11 September 1932) (188–89); 152. To H. P. Lovecraft (15 September 1932) (189–90); 153. To August Derleth (20 September 1932) (190–91); 154. To August Derleth (28 September 1932) (191–93); 155. To Lester Anderson (6 October 1932) (193); 156. To August Derleth (8 October 1932) (193–94); 157. To Donald Wandrei (10 November 1932) (195–96); 158. To August Derleth (24 November 1932) (196–97); 159. To August Derleth (24 December 1932) (197–99); 160. To August Derleth (1 February 1933) (199–200); 161. To August Derleth (9 February 1933) (200–202); 162. To H. P. Lovecraft (1 March 1933) (202–4); 163. To August Derleth (12 May 1933) (204–5); 164. To August Derleth (23 May 1933) (205–7); 165. To Margaret and Ray St. Clair (23 May 1933) (207–9); 166. To Albert M. Bender (11 June 1933) (209); 167. To August Derleth (18 June 1933) (209–10); 168. To Lester Anderson (20 June 1932) (210–11); 169. To August Derleth (12 July 1933) (211–12); 170.

To August Derleth (22 July 1933) (213); 171. To August Derleth (4 August 1933) (214–15); 172. To R. H. Barlow (6 August 1933) (215–16); 173. To Donald Wandrei (6 August 1933) (216–18); 174. To August Derleth (29 August 1933) (218–20); 175. To August Derleth (14 September 1933) (220–21); 176. To R. H. Barlow (19 September 1933) (222–23); 177. To August Derleth (26 September 1933) (223–24); 178. To H. P. Lovecraft [late September 1933] (224–27); 179. To H. P. Lovecraft ([mid-October 1933]) (227–31); 180. To August Derleth (19 October 1933) (232); 181. To R. H. Barlow (25 October 1933) (233–34); 182. To H. P. Lovecraft ([early November 1933]) (235–38); 183. To H. P. Lovecraft (4 December 1933) (238–43); 184. To Lester Anderson (31 December 1933) (243–44); 185. To H. P. Lovecraft ([late January 1934]) (244–49); 186. To Donald Wandrei (23 January 1934) (249–50); 187. To H. P. Lovecraft ([late February–early March 1934]) (250–54); 188. To R. H. Barlow (21 May 1934) (254–56); 189. To R. H. Barlow (16 June 1934) (256–57); 190. To H. P. Lovecraft (16 June 1934) (258–59); 191. To Lester Anderson (31 July 1934) (259–60); 192. To Lester Anderson (30 September 1934) (260–61); 193. To Donald Wandrei (28 February 1935) (261–63); 194. To August Derleth (28 May 1935) (263–64); 195. To H. P. Lovecraft ([June 1935]) (264–66); 196. To Donald Wandrei (24 June 1935) (266–68); 197. To Ethel Heipel ([13 September 1935]) (269); 198. To R. H. Barlow ([November 1935]) (269–71); 199. To Albert M. Bender (4 December 1935) (271–72); 200. To R. H. Barlow ([c. January 1936]) (272–73); 201. To Donald Wandrei (17 November 1936) (273–74); 202. To R. H. Barlow (23 November 1936) (274–76); 203. To H. P. Lovecraft (27 November 1936) (276–79); 204. To Albert M. Bender (12 December 1936) (279–80); 205. To Margaret and Ray St. Clair (20 January 1937) (280–82); 206. To August Derleth (23 March 1937) (282–83); 207. To August Derleth (30 March 1937) (283–85); 208. To Donald Wandrei (3 April 1937) (285–86); 209. To August Derleth (13 April 1937) (286–90); 210. To August Derleth (21 April 1937) (290–92); 211. To August Derleth (28 April 1937) (293–95); 212. To August Derleth (13 May 1937) (296–97); 213. To Virgil Finlay (15 May 1937) (297–99); 214. To R. H. Barlow (16 May 1937) (299–303); 215. To Donald Wandrei (17 May 1937) (303–4); 216. To Virgil Finlay (13 June 1937) (304–7); 217. To R. H. Barlow (12 July 1937) (308–11); 218. To R. H. Barlow (9 September 1937) (311–14);

219. To Virgil Finlay (27 September 1937) (314–18); 220. To Claire Beck (10 May 1938) (318–19); 221. To R. H. Barlow (10 May 1938) (319–20); 222. To R. H. Barlow (5 July 1938) (320–23); 223. To Donald Wandrei (30 September 1938) (323–24); 224. To Donald Wandrei (10 December 1938) (325–26); 225. To Albert M. Bender (29 April 1939) (326–27); 226. To Albert M. Bender (4 November 1939) (327); 227. To Margaret St. Clair (22 February 1940) (328–29); 228. To Albert M. Bender (4 April 1940) (329–30); 229. To Margaret and Ray St. Clair (21 April 1940) (330–31); 230. To August Derleth (13 July 1941) (331–32); 231. To August Derleth (5 September 1941) (332–33); 232. To August Derleth (19 October 1941) (333–34); 233. To August Derleth (22 October 1941) (334); 234. To Rudolph Blatterer (25 October 1941) (335); 235. To August Derleth (29 October 1941) (335–36); 236. To August Derleth (22 December 1941) (337–38); 237. To August Derleth (16 April 1942) (338); 238. To August Derleth (9 May 1942) (339); 239. To August Derleth (31 [*sic*] April 1943) (339–40); 240. To August Derleth (18 July 1943) (340); 241. To Robert A. Hoffman (14 September 1943) (340–41); 242. To August Derleth (30 November 1943) (341–42); 243. To August Derleth (9 June 1944) (343); 244. To August Derleth (26 July 1944) (344–45); 245. To Donald Wandrei (13 August 1944) (345–46); 246. To Robert A. Hoffman (9 September 1944) (346–48); 247. To August Derleth (10 June 1945) (348); 248. To August Derleth (April 14, 1947) (349); 249. To August Derleth (3 July 1947) (349–50); 250. To August Derleth (9 July 1947) (350–51); 251. To Samuel J. Sackett (13 May 1948) (351–52); 252. To Donald Wandrei (27 October 1948) (352–55); 253. To August Derleth (6 November 1948) (355); 254. To Robert A. Hoffman (31 January 1949) (355–56); 255. To August Derleth (11 February 1949) (356–59); 256. To Samuel J. Sackett (30 June 1949) (359–62); 257. To Samuel J. Sackett (1 December 1949) (363); 258. To August Derleth (31 March 1950) (363–64); 259. To Samuel J. Sackett (11 July 1950) (364–66); 260. To L. Sprague de Camp (24 October 1950) (367); 261. To August Derleth (16 June 1951) (367–68); 262. To August Derleth (7 October 1953) (368–70); 263. To L. Sprague de Camp (21 October 1953) (370–73); 264. To L. Sprague de Camp (3 November 1953) (374–75); 265. To George Haas (1 February 1954) (375–76); 266. To George Haas (11 April 1955) (376–78); 267. To Donald Wandrei (12 August 1956) (378–79); 268. To August Derleth (12 May 1956)

(379–80); 269. To August Derleth (3 July 1956) (380–81); 270. To August Derleth (7 September 1957) (381); 271. To August Derleth ([c. 5 February 1958]) (381–82); 272. To George Haas (16 June 1959) (382–83); 273. To August Derleth (8 February 1960) (383); 274. To George Haas (27 April 1961) (383–84); 275. To Donald Sidney-Fryer (5 June 1961) (384); 276. To T. G. L. Cockcroft [28 July 1961] (384–85); "Selected Bibliography" (387–93); "Index" (395–417).

 Notes. Bound in black cloth; spine stamped in gold. Dust jacket design by JenGraph—Jennifer Niles, consisting of reproductions of CAS's fantasy sculptures from the Arkham House collection. An extensive selection of CAS's letters, meticulously annotated. Most of the letters are abridged.

64. *The Sword of Zagan and Other Writings.* Ed. W. C. Farmer.
 a.   New York: Hippocampus Press, 2004. 181 pp.

 Contents: "Introduction" by S. T. Joshi (7–9); "A Note on the Text" by Farmer (9); "Acknowledgments" by Farmer (9–10); *The Sword of Zagan* (11–100); *Poems:* "The River of Life" (103); "The World" (103–4); "The Departed City" (104); "Bedouin Song" (104–5); "Zuleika: An Oriental Song" (105–6); "Benares" (106–7); "Rubaiyat of Saiyed" (107); "The Isle of Saturn" (108–9); "Temporality" (109); "Shapes in the Sunset" (109–10); "Epitaph for the Earth" (110–11); "Night" (111–12); "Rêve Parisien" (112–14); "Averiogne" (114); *Short Stories:* "The Emir's Captive" (117–23); "Fakhreddin" (123–27); "Prince Alcorez and the Magician" (127–28); "The Haunted Gong" (128–31); "The Malay Creese" (132–33); "The Shah's Messenger" (134–38); "The Bronze Image" (138–41); "The Fulfilled Prophecy" (141–43); "The Haunted Chamber" (143–47); *Fragments:* "When the Earth Trembled" (151); "Oriental Tales: The Yogi's Ring" (151); "The Opal of Delhi [I]" (152–55); "The Opal of Delhi [II]" (155–56); "The Guardian of the Temple" (156–61); "The Emerald Eye" (161); "[Untitled]" (161–64); "[Fragment of an essay]" (164–65); [Letter to Munsey's] (167); "Lost Pages from *The Black Diamonds*" (169–71); "Clark Ashton Smith: A Memoir" by Farmer (173–81).

 Notes. Bound in paper; cover art by Jason C. Eckhardt. First publication of a second juvenile novel by CAS, along with other works from mss. in Farmer's possession. *The Sword of Zagan* includes some interior illustrations by Eckhardt.

65. *The Lure of the Grotesque and Monstrous: Three Letters.* Ed. D. S. Black.
   a. [Berkeley, CA:] Bancroft Library Press, 2004. [10] pp.

> *Contents:* "Introduction" by D. S. Black ([3–4]); Letter to Samuel Loveman (19 June 1915) ([5–6]); Letter to Samuel Loveman (16 February 1921) ([7–8]); Letter to Samuel Loveman (12 May 1930) ([9–10]).
>
> *Notes.* Printed by letterpress and sewn into paper covers. Limited to 50 copies. Laid in is a frontispiece photograph of CAS's carving "The Bird of Wisdom."

66. *Star Changes.* Ed. Scott Connors and Ronald S. Hilger.
   a. Seattle: Darkside Press, 2005. 234 pp.

> *Contents:* "Introduction: The Non-Human Equation" by Connors and Hilger (9–24); *Dreads and Drolls:* "The Monster of the Prophecy" (25–53); "The Letter from Mohaun Los" (55–80); "The Plutonian Drug" (81–89); "The Immortals of Mercury" (91–115); *Alien Epochs:* "The Eternal World" (117–31); "The Demon of the Flower" (133–41); "A Star-Change" (143–57); "The Secret of the Cairn" (159–73); *Martian Oddities:* "The Vaults of Yoh-Vombis" (175–89); "The Dweller in the Gulf" (191–203); "Vulthoom" (205–24); "Phoenix" (225–32); "A Note on the Text" [by Connors and Hilger] (233–34).
>
> *Notes.* Bound in light brown cloth; spine and front cover stamped in gold. Dust jacket illustration by Allen Koszowski. Limited to 500 copies. A collection of CAS's science fiction stories (a subtitle printed only on the dust jacket reads: "the science fiction of Clark Ashton Smith").

67. *The Maker of Gargoyles and Other Stories.*
   a.1. Holicong, PA: Wildside Press, 2004 (hardcover). 152 pp.
   a.2. Holicong, PA: Wildside Press, 2004 (paperback).

> *Contents:* "Klarkash-Ton, Sorcerer-Poet" by Darrell Schweitzer (7–9); "The Abominations of Yondo" (10–17); "The Testament of Athammaus" (18–41); "The Third Episode of Vathek" (with William Beckford) (42–99); "Thirteen Phantasms" (100–104); "The Resurrection of the Rattlesnake" (105–11); "The Nameless Offspring" (112–34); "The Maker of Gargoyles" (135–52).
>
> *Notes.* Bound in both paper and black cloth. Cover artwork by Rich DiSilvio.

68. *The White Sybil and Other Stories.*
    a. Holicong, PA: Wildside Press, 2005. 143 pp.

    Contents: "The White Sybil" (7–18); "Chinoiserie" (19); "The Raja and the Tiger" (20–27); "The Justice of the Elephant" (28–32); "The Kiss of Zoraida" (33–39); "The Ghoul" (40–46); "Something New" (47–49); "The Malay Krise" (50–52); "The Ghost of Mohammed Din" (53–61); "The Mirror in the Hall of Ebony" (62–63); "The Mahout" (64–71); "The Primal City" (72–79); "The Hunters from Beyond" (80–99); "The Satyr" (100–106); "The Passing of Aphrodite" [prose poem] (107–9); "The Tale of Sir John Maundeville" (110–19); "The Light from Beyond" (120–43).

    Notes. Bound in both paper and dark gray cloth. Cover art by Rich DeSilvio.

69. *The Shadow of the Unattained: The Letters of George Sterling and Clark Ashton Smith.* Ed. David E. Schultz and S. T. Joshi.
    a. New York: Hippocampus Press, 2005. 342 pp.

    Contents: "Introduction" by S. T. Joshi and David E. Schultz (7–15); "A Note on This Edition" [by Schultz and Joshi] (15–16); "The Shadow of the Unattained" (extract) (17); letters of Clark Ashton Smith and George Sterling, 1911–26 (19–285); Appendix: "To George Sterling" [B.ii.878] (287); "To George Sterling" [B.ii.881] (287–88); "To George Sterling" [B.ii.879] (288); "To the Editor of *Town Talk*" by Ambrose Bierce (288–89); "The Coming Singer" by George Sterling (289); "Preface to *Odes and Sonnets*" by George Sterling (289–90); "Preface to *Ebony and Crystal*" by George Sterling (290); "Recent Books of Fact and Fiction" by George Douglas (i.e., George Sterling) (290–91); "Poetry of the Pacific Coast—California" by George Sterling (extract) (291–92); "To George Sterling: A Valediction" (292–93); "George Sterling: An Appreciation" (294–98); "George Sterling: Poet and Friend" (298–302); "To George Sterling" [B.ii.877] (303); "Glossary of Names" (305–6); "List of Extant Enclosures" (307–11); "Bibliography" (313–27); "Index" (329–42).

    Notes. Bound in paper; covert art by Thomas S. Brown. The first unabridged publication of the joint correspondence of CAS and Sterling, with extensive annotations by the editors. The book also contains numerous reproductions of artwork by CAS.

70. *The Collected Fantasies of Clark Ashton Smith*. Ed. Scott Connors and Ronald S. Hilger.
   a. San Francisco: Night Shade Books, 2006–10. 5 vols. (hardcover).
   b. San Francisco: Night Shade Books, 2015–17. 5 vols. (paperback).

   Contents:

   Volume 1 (The End of the Story [2006]): "Introduction" by Ramsey Campbell (vii–x); "A Note on the Texts" [by Connors and Hilger] (xi–xii); "To the Daemon" (1); "The Abominations of Yondo" (3–8); "Sadastor" (9–11); "The Ninth Skeleton" (13–16); "The Last Incantation" (17–20); "The End of the Story" (21–34); "The Phantoms of the Fire" (35–39); "A Night in Malnéant" (41–46); "The Resurrection of the Rattlesnake" (47–51); "Thirteen Phantasms" (53–56); "The Venus of Azombeii" (57–76); "The Tale of Satampra Zeiros" (77–86); "The Monster of the Prophecy" (87–116); "The Metamorphosis of the World" (117–40); "The Epiphany of Death" (141–44); "A Murder in the Fourth Dimension" (145–52); "The Devotee of Evil" (153–62); "The Satyr" (163–67); "The Planet of the Dead" (169–78); "The Uncharted Isle" (179–87); "Marooned in Andromeda" (189–212); "The Root of Ampoi" (213–24); "The Necromantic Tale" (225–33); "The Immeasurable Horror" (235–45); "A Voyage to Sfanomoë" (247–53); *Appendixes:* "Story Notes" [by Connors and Hilger] (255–78); "The Satyr: Alternate Conclusion" (279); "From the Crypts of Memory" (281–82); "Bibliography" (283–84); "About the Editors" (285).

   Volume 2 (The Door to Saturn [2007]): "Introduction" by Tim Powers (vii–ix); "A Notes on the Texts" [by Connors and Hilger] (xi–xv); "The Door to Saturn" (1–15); "The Red World of Polaris" (17–43); "Told in the Desert" (45–49); "The Willow Landscape" (51–54); "A Rendezvous in Averoigne" (55–66); "The Gorgon" (67–75); "An Offering to the Moon" (77–85); "The Kiss of Zoraida" (87–91); "The Face by the River" (93–98); "The Ghoul" (99–103); "The Kingdom of the Worm" (105–10); "An Adventure in Futurity" (111–39); "The Justice of the Elephant" (141–44); "The Return of the Sorcerer" (145–56); "The City of the Singing Flame" (157–70); "A Good Embalmer" (171–74); "The Testament of Athammaus" (175–89); "A Captivity in Serpens" (191–224); "The Letter from Mohaun Los" (225–50); "The Hunters from Beyond" (251–63); *Appendixes:* "Story Notes" [by Connors and Hilger] (265–93); "Alternate Ending to 'The Return of the Sorcerer'" (295–96); "Bibliography" (297–98); "About the Editors" (299).

Volume 3 (*A Vintage from Atlantis* [2007]): "Introduction" by Michael Dirda (vii–x); "A Note on the Texts" [by Connors and Hilger] (xi–xiv); "The Holiness of Azédarac" (1–16); "The Maker of Gargoyles" (17–28); "Beyond the Singing Flame" (29–46); "Seedling of Mars" (47–77); "The Vaults of Yoh-Vombis" (79–93); "The Eternal World" (95–109); "The Demon of the Flower" (111–19); "The Nameless Offspring" (121–34); "A Vintage from Atlantis" (135–40); "The Weird of Avoosl Wuthoqquan" (141–47); "The Invisible City" (149–65); "The Immortals of Mercury" (167–91); "The Empire of the Necromancers" (193–200); "The Seed from the Sepulcher" (201–11); "The Second Interment" (213–21); "Ubbo-Sathla" (223–28); "The Double Shadow" (229–38); "The Plutonian Drug" (239–47); "The Supernumerary Corpse" (249–55); "The Colossus of Ylourgne" (257–85); "The God of the Asteroid" (287–98); *Appendixes:* "Story Notes" [by Connors and Hilger] (299–331); "The Flower-Devil" (333); "Bibliography" (335–36).

Volume 4 (*The Maze of the Enchanter* [2009]): "Introduction" by Gahan Wilson (vii–ix); "A Note on the Texts" [by Connors and Hilger] (xi–xiv); "The Mandrakes" (1–6);" The Beast of Averoigne" (7–18); "A Star-Change" (19–34); "The Disinterment of Venus" (35–42); "The White Sybil" (43–50); "The Ice-Demon" (51–62); "The Isle of the Torturers" (63–74); "The Dimension of Chance" (75–94); "The Dweller in the Gulf" (95–108); "The Maze of the Enchanter" (109–20); "The Third Episode of Vathek" (with William Beckford) (121–56); "Genius Loci" (157–70); "The Secret of the Cairn" (171–86); "The Charnel God" (187–204); "The Dark Eidolon" (205–26); "The Voyage of King Euvoran" (227–44); "Vulthoom" (245–64); "The Weaver in the Vault" (265–74); "The Flower-Women" (275–83); *Appendixes:* "Story Notes" [by Connors and Hilger] (285–318); "Alternate Ending to 'The White Sybil'" (319); "The Muse of Hyperborea" (321); "The Dweller in the Gulf: Added Material" (323–25); "Bibliography" (327–28).

Volume 5 (*The Last Hieroglyph* [2010]): "Introduction" by Richard A. Lupoff (vii–xii); "A Note on the Texts" [by Connors and Hilger] (xiii–xvi); "The Dark Age" (1–12); "The Death of Malygris" (13–22); "The Tomb-Spawn" (23–30); "The Witchcraft of Ulua" (31–38); "The Coming of the White Worm" (39–52); "The Seven Geases" (53–68); "The Chain of Aforgomon" (69–81); "The Primal City" (83–88); "Xeethra" (89–104); "The Last Hieroglyph" (105–17); "Necromancy in Naat" (119–36);

"The Treader of the Dust" (137–43); "The Black Abbot of Pu-thuum" (145–61); "The Death of Ilalotha" (163–71); "Mother of Toads" (173–79); "The Garden of Adompha" (181–88); "The Great God Awto" (189–93); "Strange Shadows" (195–206); "The Enchantress of Sylaire" (207–18); "Double Cosmos" (219–26); "Nemesis of the Unfinished" (with Don Carter) (227–31); "The Master of the Crabs" (233–43); "Morthylla" (245–52); "Schizoid Creator" (253–58); "Monsters in the Night" (259–61); "Phoenix" (263–71); "The Theft of the Thirty-nine Girdles" (273–81); "Symposium of the Gorgon" (283–89); "The Dart of Rasasfa" (291–96); *Appendixes:* "Story Notes" [by Connors and Hilger] (299–339); "Variant Temptation Scenes from 'The Witchcraft of Ulua'" (341–42); "The Traveller" (343–44); "Material Removed from 'The Black Abbot of Puthuum'" (345–47); "Alternate End-ing to 'I Am Your Shadow'" (349–53); "Alternate Ending to 'Nemesis of the Unfinished'" (355–58); "Bibliography" (359–60).

Notes. Bound in brown cloth; spine and front cover stamped in gold. Dust jacket art (different for each volume) by Jason Van Hollander; jacket design by Claudia Noble. Collected edition of CAS's short fiction, based on manuscripts and first appearances, with extensive notes to each story.

71.   *Shadows Seen and Unseen: Poetry from the Shadows.* Ed. Raymond L. F. Johnson and Ardath W. Winterowd.

a.   San Jose, CA: HIH Art Studio, 2007. 93 pp.

Contents: "Dedication" and "Acknowledgments" (3); CAS's illus-tration for H. P. Lovecraft's "The Haunter of the Dark" (6); "Foreword" by Raymond L. F. Johnson; photograph of CAS's sculpture "Young Ghoul" (8); "An Autobiography of Clark Ash-ton Smith" (9); CAS's painting "Spring Clouds" (10); "Flamin-gos" (biography of CAS) by Hal Rubin (11–13); "Clark Ashton Smith's Auburn/'Old Auburn'" (map) (14); photograph of CAS's home in Long Valley (15); letter by Wilma Yount (8 April 1997) authenticating CAS's painting "The Spy" (16); "The Spy" (17); photograph of the Joss House in Auburn's Chinatown (18); "The Devotee of Evil" (19–25); photograph of Happy Hour Club, Auburn (26); "A Conversation with Bud Procissi" (27–28); CAS's painting "Plants" (30); *Original Signed Poems (Group I):* "Desert Dweller" (32–33); "Lamia" (34); "Omniety" (35); "To George Sterling" [B.ii.877] (36); "Los sátiros son decornados" (37); "¿Que sueñas, Musa?" and "What Dreamest Thou, Muse?" (38);

"Lichens" (39); "The Prophet Speaks" (40–41); "On a Chinese Vase" (42); "The Thralls of Circe Climb Parnassus" (43); "Song of Autumn" [translated from Baudelaire] (44–45); "Nyctalops" (46–47); "The Old Water-Wheel" (48); CAS's illustration to "Genius Loci" (50); "Genius Loci" (51–60); CAS's painting "The Basilisk" (61); photograph of Poet Smith Drive in Long Valley (62); *Original Signed Poems (Group II):* "Dominion" (64); "Averoigne" (65); "Ecclesiastes" [translated from Leconte de Lisle] (66); "El eros de ébano" and "Eros of Ebony" (67); "Dice el soñador" and "Says the Dreamer" (68–69); "Strange Girl" (70); "Zothique" (71); "For an Antique Lyre" (72); "Dos mitos y una fabula" and "Two Myths and a Fable" (73); "Spleen (LXXX)" [translated from Baudelaire] (74); "¿Dónde duermes, Eldorado?" (75); "Anteros" (76); "Seeker" (77); "Hesperian Fall" (78–79); "Malediction" (80); "La isla de Circe" and "The Isle of Circe" (80–81); "Cantar" and "Song" (81); CAS's painting "Moonlight on Boulder Ridge" (82); "The Horizon" (83); CAS's painting for "The Sorcerer Departs" (84); "The Sorcerer Departs" (85); CAS's painting "Communing Spirits" (86); "Keeper of the Pulps" by Ray Johnson (87–89); fractal image by Ardath Winterowd (90); "Bogies" (poem) by Alan Hines (91); "The Spectral Moonlight" (poem) by Alan Hines (92); "Index of Artwork" (93).

Notes. Bound in red cloth; spine printed in white and black type; dust jacket art (also reproduced on the front cover) by Ardath Winterowd. All poems in the volume save "The Horizon" and "The Sorcerer Departs" are facsimile reprints of CAS's TMSs.

72.   *The Black Abbot of Puthuum.*
   a.   Glendale, CA: The RAS Press, 2007. 43 pp.

   Contents: "Song of King Horaph's Bowmen" ([1]); frontispiece by Virgil Finlay ([5]); "The Black Abbot of Puthuum" (7–40); [afterword by Terence McVicker] ([43]).

   Notes. Exquisite hand-printed edition limited to 250 copies of the original version of this story rejected by *Weird Tales* editor Farnsworth Wright. Virgil Finlay's frontispiece is tipped in and reproduced from the original drawing he did to illustrate this story when it appeared in the March 1936 issue.

73.   *The Complete Poetry and Translations.* Ed. S. T. Joshi and David E. Schultz.
   a.   New York: Hippocampus Press, 2007–08. 3 vols. (hardcover).
   b.   New York: Hippocampus Press, 2012. 3 vols. (paperback).

Contents:

Volume 1 (The Abyss Triumphant [2008]): "Introduction" by the editors (xxxi–xxxix); *The Voice of Silence (1910–1911):* "Cloudland" (3); "The Fountain of Youth" (3); "The Road of Pain" (3); "Reincarnation" (4); "Lethe" (4); "A White Rose" (4); "Death" (4); "Companionship" (4–5); "Illusion" (5); "The Call of the Wind" (5); "The Expanding Ideal" (5–6); "Imagination" (6–8); "The Sunrise" (9); "Night" (9); "To a Yellow Pine" (9–10); "A Sierran Sunrise" (10); "The Sierras" (11); "The Wind and the Moon" (11); "Moonlight" (12); "The Altars of Sunset" (12); "To George Sterling" [B.ii.878] (12–13); "The Voice of Silence" (13); "Weavings" (13–14); "The West Wind" (14); "Before Sunrise" (14–15); "At Nadir" (15); "The Besieging Billows" (15); "The Butterfly" (15–18); "The Meaning" (18); "To the Nightshade" (18–19); "The Garden of Dreams" (19); "Ode to Matter" (19–21); "Ode to Poetry" (21); "The Pageant of Music" (22); "Autumn Dew" (22); "The Eclipse" (22); "The Falling Leaves" (23); "The Freedom of the Hills" (23); "The Hosts of Heaven" (23–24); "Ode on the Future of Song" (24); "The Suns and the Void" (24–25); "To George Sterling" [B.ii.879] (25–26); "Moods of the Sea" (26); "Sonnets of the Seasons" (26–27); "The Storm" (27–28); "To the Morning Star" (28); "The Flower of the Night" (28); "A Sunset" (28); "War" (29); "Wings of Perfume" (29); "The Island of a Dream" (30); "Autumn's Pall" (30); "The Music of the Gods" (30); "The Night of Despair" (31); "Somnus" (31); "At Midnight" (31–32); "The Fanes of Dawn" (32); "The Summer Hills" (32); "To George Sterling" [B.ii.880] (33); "The Wind-Threnody" (33); "The Voice in the Pines" (33–34); "Black Enchantment" (34); "The Burden of the Suns" (35); "The Castle of Dreams" (35); "A Dream of Oblivion" (36); "A Dream of Darkness" (36); "The Revelation" (36–37); "The Dream-God's Realm" (37); "Ephemera" (37); "The Eternal Gleam" (37–38); "Evening" (38); "The Harbour of the Past" (38); "In Extremis" (39); "Lost Beauty" (39); "Nature's Orchestra" (39–40); "The Past" (40); "The Present" (40); "The Future" (40); "Time the Wonder" (40); "The Palace of Jewels" (40); "The Past" (41); "The Potion of Dreams" (41–42); "The Power of Eld" (42); "Romance" (42–43); "The Song of the Worlds" (43–44); "Sonnet on Music" (44–45); "Sonnet on Oblivion" (45); "Sonnet to the Sphinx" (45); "Sphinx and Medusa" (46); "The Sphinx of the Infinite" (46); "The Tartarus of the Suns" (46–47); "The Temple of Night" (47); "The Throne of Winter" (47–48); "Time" (48); "To a Cloud" (48–49); "To a Mariposa Lily" (49–50); "To a Snow-drop" (50); "To Ambition" (50); "To the Crescent Moon" (50); "To the Morning Star" (51); "To Thomas Paine" (51); "To Thomas Paine" (51–52); "Twilight" (52); "The Twilight Woods" (52); "The Vampire Night" (53–54); "The Waning Moon" (54); *The Abyss Triumphant (1911–1912):* "Antony to Cleopatra" (57); "Poetry" (57); "The Last Night" (58); "The Eternal Snows" (58); "The Moonlight Desert" (58–59); "Nocturne" (59); "Ode to Music" (59–61); "The Dream-Weaver" (61–62); "Ode to the Abyss" (62–64); "Medusa" (64); "The Messengers" (65); "Chant to Sirius" (65–66); "The Horizon" (66); "A Dream of Beauty" (66–67); "A Live-Oak Leaf" (67); "Wind-Ripples" (67); "A Song from Hell" (67–68); "The Palace of Jewels" (69–70); "The Star-Treader" (70–74); "To George Sterling" [B.ii.881] (74); "The Dream-Bridge" (74); "The Nemesis of Suns" (75); "Retrospect and Forecast" (75); "The Song of a Comet" (75–77); "Said the Dreamer" (77–78); "Saturn" (78–85); "The Shadow of the Unattained" (85–88); "The Pursuer" (88–89); "Echo of Memnon" (89); "Nero" (89–91); "The Mad Wind" (92); "Finis" (92–93); "Ode to Light" (93–94); "In the Desert" (94); "The Return of Hyperion" (95); "To the Daemon Sublimity" (95–96); "Atlantis" (96); "Averted Malefice" (96); "The Balance" (97); "The Cherry-Snows" (97); "Copan" (97–98); "A Dead City" (98); "The Eldritch Dark" (98); "Epitaph for the Earth" (99); "Fairy Lanterns" (99); "The Fugitives" (100); "Lament of the Stars" (100–102); "Lethe" (102); "The Masque of Forsaken Gods" (102–6); "The Maze of Sleep" (106); "The Medusa of the Skies" (107); "The Night Forest" (107–8); "Nirvana" (108); "Ode on Imagination" (109–10); "Pine Needles" (110–11); "The Price" (111); "The Retribution" (111); "Shadow of Nightmare" (111–12); "The Snow-Blossoms" (112); "A Song of Dreams" (112–13); "The Song of the Stars" (113–15); "Song to Oblivion" (115); "The Soul of the Sea" (115–16); "The Summer Moon" (116); "To the Darkness" (116–17); "To the Sun" (117–18); "The Unremembered" (118–19); "White Death" (119); "The Winds" (119–20); "The Morning Pool" (120); "The Abyss Triumphant" (120); "The Last Goddess" (121); "Satan Unrepentant" (121–23); "The Titans in Tartarus" (124–25); "The Cloud-Islands" (125–26); "Remembered Light" (126–27); "The Sorrow of the Winds" (127); "Luna Aeternalis" (127–28); "[In the Ultimate Valleys]" (129); "The Nereid" (129–30); *A Phantasy at Twilight (1913–1917):* "The Ghoul" (133); "The Land of Evil

Stars" (133–34); "The Clouds" (134–35); "The Doom of America" (135–37); "Nightmare" (138); "The City of the Titans" (138); "Desire of Vastness" (138–39); "The Medusa of Despair" (139); "The Refuge of Beauty" (139–40); "The Years Restored" (140); "The Witch in the Graveyard" (140–42); "The Sea-Gods" (142–43); "The Ministers of Law" (143); "Decadence" (144); "Somnus" (144); "To Beauty" (144–45); "The City of Destruction" (145–46); "The Orchid of Beauty" (146); "A Phantasy of Twilight" (146–47); "Beauty Implacable" (147); "The Nameless Wraith" (147–48); "The Ancient Quest" (148); "Aspect of Iron" (149); "Beyond the Door" (149); "The Harlot of the World" (149–50); "Psalm to the Desert" (150–51); "Inheritance" (151); "Memnon at Midnight" (151); "The City in the Desert" (152); "The Blindness of Orion" (152–53); "The Mirrors of Beauty" (153); "The Flight of Azrael" (154); "Duality" (155); "Love Malevolent" (155); "Exotique" (155–56); "Alien Memory" (156); "Fire of Snow" (156–57); "In the Wind" (157); "Lunar Mystery" (157); "Moon-Dawn" (158); "The Mummy" (158); "Morning on an Eastern Sea" (158); "Reclamation" (159); "Afterglow" (159); "Nocturne" (159); "The Crucifixion of Eros" (159–60); "Suggestion" (160); "Arabesque" (160); "Belated Love" (161); "November Twilight" (161); "Desolation" (161–62); "Coldness" (162); "The Kingdom of Shadows" (162–63); "Give Me Your Lips" (164); "Strangeness" (164–65); "Impression" (165); "The Exile" (165–66); "Ave atque Vale" (166); "The Tears of Lilith" (166); "Alexandrines" (167); "Autumnal" (167); *The Whisper of the Worm (1918–1920):* "A Vision of Lucifer" (171); "Sepulture" (171); "Palms" (171–72); "Mors" (172); "Dissonance" (172); "Eidolon" (173); "Haunting" (173); "Image" (173–74); "In November" (174); "Memorial" (174–75); "A Precept" (175); "Requiescat in Pace" (175–76); "In Saturn" (176); "Winter Moonlight" (176–77); "Inferno" (177); "The Whisper of the Worm" (177–78); "The Chimera" (178); "Autumn Orchards" (178); "Disillusionment" (178–79); "Ode to Peace" (179); "Antepast" (179); "Ashes of Sunset" (180); "At Sunrise" (180); "Crepuscule" (180); "The Melancholy Pool" (180–81); "Mirage" (181); "Mirrors" (181–82); "The Motes" (182); "Recompense" (182); "Satiety" (182); "Triple Aspect" (183); "Twilight on the Snow" (183–84); "Fantasie" (184); "Song of Sappho's Arabian Daughter" (184); "Forgetfulness" (185); "Transcendence" (185); "To the Beloved" (185–86); "Laus Mortis" (186); "The Traveller" (186); "Ombos" (187); "The Absence of the Muse" (187);

"Quest" (187–88); "Symbols" (188); "Heliogabalus" (189); "The Hope of the Infinite" (189–90); "Flamingoes" (190); "Rosa Mystica" (190); "For a Wine-Jar" (191); "To Omar Khayyam" (191–92); "Beyond the Great Wall" (193); "Ennui" (193); "In Lemuria" (194); "Solution" (194–95); "The Ghoul and the Seraph" (195–98); "Tempus" (199); "The Dials" (199); "Silhouette" (199); "To Whom It May Concern" (199–200); "Speculation" (200); "Ode to Aphrodite" (200); "The Oracle" (200); "A Memory" (201); "To a Northern Venus" (201–2); "In Alexandria" (202); "The Incubus of Time" (202–3); "Amor Aeternalis" (203); *The Hashish-Eater; or, The Apocalypse of Evil* (207–21); *The Infinite Quest (1920–1922):* "The Dream" (225); "Requiescat" (226); "To Nora May French" (226–29); "Psalm" (229–30); "A Psalm to the Best Beloved" (230); "Cleopatra" (230–31); "Nightfall" (231); "Ecstasy" (232); "Secret Love" (232); "The Hidden Paradise" (233); "The Infinite Quest" (233); "Exotic Memory" (233–34); "Satiety" (234); "Fawn-Lilies" (234–35); "Artemis" (235); "Plum-Flowers" (235–36); "Chance" (236); "Union" (236); "Song" (236–37); "Love Is Not Yours, Love Is Not Mine" (237); "Poplars" (237); "The Fugitives" (238–40) [includes "The Song of Aviol" (238), "Song" (238–39), "The Love-Potion" (239), "The Song of Cartha" (240)]; "Chant of Autumn" (240); "A Fragment" (241); *Enchanted Mirrors (1923–1926):* "Selenique" (245); "Semblance" (245–46); "Change" (246); "Don Juan Sings" (246–47); "The Nymph" (247); "By the River" (247–48); "Fashion" (248); "The Witch with Eyes of Amber" (248); "On the Canyon-Side" (249); "We Shall Meet" (249–50); "The Secret" (250–51); "Contradiction" (251); "Alienage" (251–52); "Moments" (252–53); "Exchange" (253); "Metaphor" (253); "The Wingless Archangels" (253–54); "A Valediction" (254); "Cocaigne" (254); "Forgotten Sorrow" (255); "Septembral" (255); "Afterwards" (255–56); "The Barrier" (256); "The Funeral Urn" (256–57); "Dolor of Dreams" (257); "Brumal" (257); "Autumn Orchards" (257–58); "Remembrance" (258); "Departure" (259); "Diversity" (259); "The End of Autumn" (259); "On Re-reading Baudelaire" (260); "Lemurienne" (260); "You Are Not Beautiful" (260); "December" (260–61); "The Pagan" (261); "A Meeting" (261–62); "Adventure" (262–63); "Transmutation" (263); "The Last Oblivion" (264); "To the Chimera" (264); "Immortelle" (264–65); "In Autumn" (265); "Estrangement" (265); "A Catch" (266); "Consolation" (266); "The Temptation" (266–68); "Apologia" (268–69);

"Incognita" (269); "Enigma" (269); "Query" (270); "Loss" (270–71); "Concupiscence" (271); "Maya" (271–72); "Dead Love" (272); "A Prayer" (272); "Enchanted Mirrors" (273); "Minatory" (273); "Interrogation" (274); "Madrigal" (274); "Sandalwood" (275); "October" (275–76); "The Envoys" (276–77); "Ode" (277); "Un Couchant" (278); "A Sunset" (278–79); "Un Madrigal" (279); "A Madrigal" (279); "The Saturnienne" (280); "Apostrophe" (280–81); "Chansonette" (281); "Idylle païenne" (281–82); "Idylle païenne" (282); "Retrospect and Forecast" (283); "Sonnet lunaire" (283–84); "Sonnet lunaire" (284); "À Mi-Chemin" [French] (284); "À Mi-Chemin" [English] (285); "L'Abîme" (285); "Le Cauchemar" (286); "Chanson de rêve" (286); "Le Cheveu" (286–87); "Éloignement" (287); "Exotique" (287); "La Méduse des cieux" (288); "To George Sterling: A Valediction" (288–90); "After Armageddon" (290); *Juvenilia:* "[Untitled]" (293); "[Fragment 1]" (293–94); "[Fragment 2]" (294–95); "[Fragment 3]" (295–96); "[Fragment 4]" (296); "[Fragment 5]" (297–98); "[Fragment 6]" (298); "Benares" (298–300); "The Prayer Rug" (300–301); "The Rubaiyat of Seyyid" (301–3); "Sunrise" (303); "The Skull" (303–4); "The Orient" (304–5); "Time" (305); "To an Eastern City" (306); "Fortune" (306–7); "The Ocean" (307); "Allah" (307–8); "Arab Song" (308); "Arabian Love-Song" (308–9); "Bedouin Song" (309–10); "The City of the Djinn" (310–11); "The Desert" (311–12); "A Dream of Vathek" (313–23); "A Dream of Zanoni" (324); "Eblis Repentant" (325–26); "From the Persian" (327); "From the Persian" (327); "From the Persian" (327–28); "Haroun Al-Raschid" (328); "The Inscription" (328); "Jewel of the Orient" (328–30); "Jewel of the Orient" (330–31); "Kismet" (331); "Mohammed" (331–32); "The Muezzin" (332); "Ode from the Persian" (332); "Odes of Alnaschar" (333); "Omar's Philosophy" (333–34); "The Palace of the Jinn" (334–35); "The Prayer Rug" (335–36); "The Prince and the Peri" (336–39); "Quatrain" (339); "Quatrains" (340); "Quatrains" (340) [includes "The Snare" and "Song"]; "Quatrains on Jewels" (341) [includes "The Diamond," "The Pearl," "The Turquoise," "The Ruby," and "The Opal"]; "Rubaiyat" (341–42); "Rubaiyat" (342–43); "Rubaiyat of Saiyed" (343); "The Seekers" (343–44); "Some Maxims from the Persian" (344); "Stamboul" (344–45); "Suleyman Jan ben Jan" (345); "The Temple" (346–47); "The World" (347–48); "Youth and Age" (348–49); "Zuleika" (349–50); "Asia" (350); "Aurungzeb's Mosque" (350–51); "The

Burning Ghauts" (351); "The Burning-Ghauts at Benares" (351–52); "Dawn" (352); "Delhi" (352–53); "A Dream of India" (353–55); "The Ganges" (355–56); "Alchemy" (356); "The Book of Years" (356); "Courage" (356–57); "The Days of Time" (357); "The Departed City" (357–58); "A Dream" (358–59); "Fear" (360); "The Fear of Death" (360); "The Feast" (360–61); "Hate and Love" (362); "Hope" (362); "The Land o' Dreams" (362–63); "The Leveler" (364); "Love" (364); "The Lure of Gold" (365); "Mercy" (365–66); "The Moon" (366); "Perseverance" (366–67); "Poem [?]" (367); "Resignation" (368); "The River" (368); "The River of Life" (368); "Sea-Lure" (369); "The Sea-Shell" (369); "Silence" (369); "Solitude" (370); "Summer Idleness" (370); "To the Best Beloved" (370); "The World" (371); "[Fragment 7]" (371);

Volume 2: *The Wine of Summer* (2008): *Spectral Life (1927–1929):* "Les Violons" (375); "Au bord du Léthé" (375); "The Nevermore-to-Be" (375–76); "Fantaisie d'antan" (376–77); "Canticle" (377–78); "A Fable" (378); "De Consolation" (378); "De Consolation" (378–79); "Simile" (379); "Trope" (379); "Venus" (379–80); "One Evening" (380); "Tristan to Iseult" (380–81); "Souvenance" (381); "To Antares" (381–82); "Song" (382); "Amor Autumnalis" (382); "Warning" (383); "Temporality" (383); "Chansonette" (384); "Chansonette" (384); "Credo" (385); "The Autumn Lake" (385); "Le Lac d'automne" (385); "On a Chinese Vase" (385–86); "November" (386); "Chanson de Novembre" [French] (386–87); "Chanson de Novembre" [English] (387); "Exorcism" (387); "Winter Moonlight" (388); "Connaissance" (388); "Harmony" (389); "Moon-Sight" (389); "Sonnet" (390); "Similitudes" (390); "Calendar" (391); "February" (391–92); "Variations" (392); "Sufficiency" (392); "Lichens" (393); "Vaticinations" (393); "Nyctalops" (393–94); "The Hill-Top" (395); "L'Amour suprême" [French] (395–96); "L'Amour suprême" [English] (396); "Alexandrins" (396); "Absence" (397); "Une Vie spectrale" (397–98); "Spectral Life" (398–99); "Seins" (399); "Les Marées" (399); "Paysage païen" (400); "Le Souvenir" (400–401); "Rêvasserie" (401–2); "La Mare" (402); "Le Miroir des blanches fleurs" [French] (402–3); "Le Miroir des blanches fleurs" [English] (403–4); "The Dragon-Fly" (404); "September" (404–5); "Shadows" (405–6); "Evanescence" (406); "Fellowship" (406–7); "Ougabalys" (407–8); "Ineffability" (408); "The Nightmare Tarn" (408–9); "Cumuli" (409–10); "Refuge" (410); *Some Older Bourn (1930–1938):*

"Answer" (449); "Song at Evenfall" (449); "Jungle Twilight" (450); "Madrigal of Evanescence" (450); "Solicitation" (451); "An Old Theme" (451); "Psalm" (452); "The Pool" (453); "Revenant" (453–54); "A Dream of the Abyss" (454–55); "In Slumber" (455–56); "Necromancy" (456); "Outlanders" (457); "Dominion" (457–58); "In Thessaly" (458); "The Phoenix" (458–59); "The Outer Land" (459–61); "Day-Dream" (461–62); "Contra Mortem" (462); "The Cycle" (462–63); "Kin" (463); "Sanctuary" (463); "Simile" (463); "Le Refuge" [French] (464); "Le Refuge" [English] (464); "La Forteresse" (465); "The Fortress" (465); "Sonnet" (466); "Ennui" (466); "Adjuration" (466–67); "Song of the Necromancer" (467–68); "Rêves printaniers" [French] (468); "Rêves printaniers" [English (468–69); "Amour bizarre" (469); "L'Ensorcellement" (469–70); "Le Fabliau d'un dieu" (470–71); "Orgueil" (471); "Sea-Memory" (471); "Farewell to Eros" (471–72); "Indian Summer" (472); "Mystery" (473); "Touch" (473); "To Howard Phillips Lovecraft" (474); "The Prophet Speaks" (475); "Desert Dweller" (476); "Requiescat" (476–77); "Wizard's Love" (477–78); *The Last and Utmost Land (1939–1947)*: "From Arcady" (481); "Ode" (481–82); "Sestet" (482); "Bacchante" (482–83); "Resurrection" (483–84); "Witch-Dance" (484–85); "Song of the Bacchic Bards" (485–86); "Anteros" (486); "Lamia" (486–87); "Interim" (487–88); "Sonnet" (488); "To One Absent" (488–89); "Silent Hour" (489); "Grecian Yesterday" (490); "But Grant, O Venus" (490); "Bond" (491); "Madrigal of Memory" (491–92); "'That Last Infirmity'" (492); "The Thralls of Circe Climb Parnassus" (492); "Dialogue" (492–93); "The Mime of Sleep" (493); "The Old Water-Wheel" (493–94); "Fragment" (494); "Yerba Buena" (494–95); "Consummation" (495); "Humors of Love" (495–96); "Town Lights" (496–97); "The Sorcerer to His Love" (497); "To George Sterling" [B.ii.877] (497); "L'Espoir du néant" (498); "Amor Hesternalis" (498–99); "'All Is Dross That Is Not Helena'" (499); "Future Pastoral" (499–500); "Wine of Summer" (500–501); "In Another August" (501); "Nocturne: Grant Avenue" (501–2); "Classic Epigram" (502); "Twilight Song" (503); "Supplication" (503); "Erato" (504); "Anodyne of Autumn" (504–5); "The Hill of Dionysus" (505–6); "Before Dawn" (506–7); "Amor" (507); "Interval" (507); "Postlude" (508); "Strange Girl" (508–9); "De Profundis" (509–10); "Midnight Beach" (510); "Illumination" (511); "Omniety" (511); "Even in Slumber" (511–12); "Moly" (512); "Cambion" (512–13); "The

Knoll" (513–14); "For an Antique Lyre" (514); "On Trying to Read *Four Quartets*" (514); "Greek Epigram" (515); "Lines on a Picture" (515); "Alternative" (515); "Hymn" (516); "The Sorcerer Departs" (516–17); "Surréalist Sonnet" (517); "Paean" (517); "Do You Forget, Enchantress?" (518); "The Horologe" (518); "Parnassus à la Mode" (518); "Sea Cycle" (518–19); "Dancer" (519); "Nevermore" (519–20); "Reverie in August" (520); "Tin Can on the Mountain-Top" (520–21); "Some Blind Eidolon" (521–22); "The Pursuer" (523); "To Bacchante" (523); "Calenture" (523–24); "Copyist" (525); "Love and Death" (525); *Quintrains:* "Essence" (525); "Epitaph for an Astronomer" (525); "The Heron" (525); "Bird of Long Ago" (526); "Late November Evening" (526); "Mithridates" (526); "Mummy of the Flower" (526); "Nightmare of the Lilliputian" (526); "Passing of an Elder God" (527); "Poets in Hades" (527); "Quiddity" (527); "Someone" (527); "Dying Prospector" (527); *Experiments in Haiku (1947):* "Strange Miniatures" (531); "Unicorn" (531); "Untold Arabian Fable" (531); "A Hunter Meets the Martichoras" (531); "The Limniad" (531); "The Sciapod" (531); "The Monacle" (531); "Feast of St. Anthony" (531); "Paphnutius" (532); "Philtre" (532); "Borderland" (532); "Lethe" (532); "Empusa Waylays a Traveller" (532); "Perseus and Medusa" (532); "Odysseus in Eternity" (532); "The Ghost of Theseus" (533); "Distillations" (533); "Fence and Wall" (533); "Growth of Lichen" (533); "Cats in Winter Sunlight" (533); "Abandoned Plum-Orchard" (533); "Harvest Evening" (533); "Willow-Cutting in Autumn" (533); "Declining Moon" (534); "Late Pear-Pruner" (534); "Nocturnal Pines" (534); "Phallus Impudica" (534); "Stormy Afterglow" (534); "Geese in the Spring Night" (534); "Foggy Night" (534); "Reigning Empress" (535); "The Sparrow's Nest" (535); "The Last Apricot" (535); "Mushroom-Gatherers" (535); "Spring Nunnery" (535); "Nuns Walking in the Orchard" (535); "Improbable Dream" (535); "Crows in Spring" (536); "High Mountain Juniper" (536); "Storm's End" (536); "Pool at Lobos" (536); "Poet in a Barroom" (536); "Fallen Grape-Leaf" (536); "Gopher-Hole in Orchard" (536); "Basin in Boulder" (537); "Indian Acorn-Mortar" (537); "Old Limestone Kiln" (537); "Love in Dreams" (537); "Night of Miletus" (537); "Tryst at Lobos" (537); "Mountain Trail" (537); "Future Meeting" (538); "Classic Reminiscence" (538); "Goats and Manzanita-Boughs" (538); "Bed of Mint" (538); "Chainless Captive" (538); "California Winter" (538); "January Willow" (538);

"Snowfall on Acacia" (539); "Flight of the Yellow-Hammer" (539); "Sunset over Farm-Land" (539); "Flora" (539); "Windows at Lamplighting Time" (539); "Old Hydraulic Diggings" (540); "Hearth on Old Cabin-Site" (540); "Builder of Deserted Hearth" (540); "Aftermath of Mining Days" (540); "River-Canyon" (541–42); "Childhood" (542); "School-Room Pastime" (542); "Boys Telling Bawdy Tales" (542); "Fight on the Play-Ground" (542); "Water-Fight" (542); "Boys Rob a Yellow-Hammer's Nest" (543); "Nest of the Screech-Owl" (543); "Grammar-School Vixen" (543); "Girl of Six" (543); "Mortal Essences" (543); "Snake, Owl, Cat or Hawk" (543); "Slaughter-House in Spring" (543); "Cattle Salute the Psychopomp" (543); "Slaughter-House Pasture" (544); "Field Behind the Abatoir" (544); "Plague from the Abatoir" (544); "La Mort des amants" (544); "Vultures Come to the Ambarvalia" (544); "For the Dance of Death" (544); "Berries of the Deadly Nightshade" (544); "Water-Hemlock" (545); "Felo-de-se of the Parasite" (545); "Pagans Old and New" (545); "Initiate of Dionysus" (545); "Bacchic Orgy" (545); "Abstainer" (545); "Picture by Piero di Cosimo" (545); "Bacchants and Bacchante" (545); "Garden of Priapus" (546); "Morning Star of the Mountains" (546); "Bygone Interlude" (546); "Prisoner in Vain" (546); "Epitaphs" (546); "Braggart" (546); "Slaughtered Cattle" (546); "The Earth" (546); *Miscellaneous Haiku:* "Illuminatus" (547); "Limestone Cavern" (547); "Maternal Prostitute" (547); "Ocean Twilight" (547); "Radio" (547); "Tule-Mists" (547); *If Winter Remain (1948–1950):* "Hellenic Sequel" (551); "No Stranger Dream" (551); "On the Mount of Stone" (552); "Only to One Returned" (552); "Sonnet for the Psychoanalysts" (552–53); "Avowal" (553); "Tolometh" (553–54); "If Winter Remain" (554–55); "Almost Anything" (555–56); "'That Motley Drama'" (556); "Pour chercher du nouveau" (556–57); "Dans l'univers lointain" (557–58); "In a Distant Universe" (558–59); "High Surf: Monterey Bay" (559); "Isaac Newton" (559–60); "La Muse moderne" (560); "The Mystical Number" (560); "Pantheistic Dream" (561); "Rêve panthéistique" (562); "Poèmes d'amour" (563); "Sandalwood and Onions" (563); "The Dark Chateau" (563–64); "Don Quixote on Market Street" (565); "The Isle of Saturn" (566–67); "'O Golden-Tongued Romance'" (567–68); "Averoigne" (568–69); "Zothique" (569); "Le Poéte parle avec ses biographes" (569–70); "The Poet Talks with the Biographers" (570–71); "Beauty" (571); "La Hermosura" (571); "Las Poetas del optimismo" (571); "The Poets of Optimism"

(571–72); "El Cantar de los seres libres" (572); "Song of the Free Beings" (572); "¿Donde duermes, Eldorado?" (573); "Where Sleepest Thou, O Eldorado?" (573); "Los Dueños" (574); "Dominium in Excelsis" (574–75); "Parnaso" (575); "Parnassus" (576); "Las Alquerías perdidas" (576–77); "Lost Farmsteads" (577–78); "Cantar" (578); "Song" (578–79); "Eros in the Desert" (579); "Dice el soñador" (579–80); "Says the Dreamer" (580–81); "Memoria roja" (581); "Red Memory" (581–82); "Dos Mitos y una fábula" (582); "Two Myths and a Fable" (582); "La Nereida" (583); "La isla de Circe" (584); "The Isle of Circe" (584); "Lo Ignoto" (585); "The Unknown" (585); "Leteo" (585–86); "[Lethe]" (586); "Añoranza" (586–87); "Melancholia" (587); "El Vendaval" [Spanish] (587–88); "El Vendaval" [English] (588–89); "Farmyard Fugue" (589–90); "Didus Ineptus" (590); "Amithaine" (591); "Malediction" (591–92); "Shapes in the Sunset" (592–93); "Sinbad, It Was Not Well to Brag" (593–94); "El Eros de ébano" (595); "Eros of Ebony" (595); *The Dead Will Cuckold You* (599–615); *The Sorcerer Departs (1951– 1961):* "The Stylite" (619); "Two on a Pillar" (620); "Not Theirs the Cypress-Arch" (620); "Alpine Climber" (620–21); "Hesperian Fall" (621–23); "'Not Altogether Sleep'" (623–24); "Seeker" (624); "Soliloquy in a Ebon Tower" (624–27); "The Twilight of the Gods" (627–28); "Qu'Importe?" (628); "¿Qué sueñas, Musa?" (628); "What Dreamest Thou, Muse?" (629); "Que songes-tu, Muse?" (629–30); "Ye Shall Return" (630); "Lives of the Saints" (630); "Secret Worship" (631); "The Song of Songs" (631); "STYES WITH SPIRES" (632); "In Time of Absence" (632); "Nada" (632–33); "Seer of the Cycles" (633); "I Shall Not Greatly Grieve" (633–34); "Geometries" (634); "Alchemy" (635); "Sacraments" (635–36); "Delay" (636); "Verity" (636); "La isla del náufrago" (636–37); "Isle of the Shipwrecked" (637); "Thebaid" (637–38); "Saturnian Cinema" (638); "Dedication: To Carol" (639); "The Centaur" (639); "Lawn-Mower" (640); "Tired Gardener" (640–41); "High Surf" (641); "H. P. L." (641–42); "Cycles" (642); *Fragments and Untitled Poems:* "Al borde del Leteo" (645); "Ballad of a Lost Soul" (645–46); "The Brook" (646–47); [Christmas card verses] (647); "Demogorgon" (647–48); "Despondency" (648); "The Flight of the Seraphim" (648); "For Iris" (648–49); "Haunting" (649); "The Milky Way" (649–50); "Night" (650); "The Night Wind" (650–51); "No-Man's-Land" (651); "Ode on Matter" (651–52); "The Regained Past" (652–53); "The Saturnienne" (653); "Sonnets of the

Desert" (653–54); "The Temptation" (654); "To a Comet" (654–55); "To Iris" (655); "To Iris" (655); "To the Sun" (656); "The Vampire Night" (656); [untitled fragments] (656–71); "Broceliande" (671); [untitled fragments] (671); "Twilight Pilgrimage" (672); [untitled fragments] (673–75); "Limericks" (675–77) [includes "Ripe Mulberries" (675) and other untitled limericks]; "From 'Ode to Antares'" (677); "From 'The Song of Xeethra'" (677–78); "From 'Song of the Galley Slaves'" (678); "From 'Song of King Hoaraph's Bowmen'" (678); "From 'Ludar's Litany to Thasaidon'" (678); "From 'Ludar's Litany to Thasaidon'" (679); *Appendix:* Prospective Tables of Contents: "The Jasmine Girdle" (681–82); "The Jasmine Girdle and Other Poems" (682); "Incantations" (683–84); "The Abalone Song" (685–86); Translations: "Le Désir d'Aimer" [by Hélène Picard] (686–87); "The Desire of Loving" [translation of the preceding] (687); "[Sandalwood]" [stanza from Baudelaire and translation] (688); "Voices" (688–89); Notes (691–799); Index of Titles (801–22); Index of First Lines (823–46).

Volume 3: *The Flowers of Evil and Others* (2007): "Introduction" by the editors (19–26); LES FLEURS DU MAL, BY CHARLES BAUDELAIRE: "Préface/"Preface" (28–29); *Spleen et Idéal:* I. "Bénédiction"/"Bénédiction" (30–34); II. "L'Albatros"/"The Albatross" (34–35); III. "Elévation"/"Elevation" (34–37); IV. "Correspondances"/"Correspondences" (36–37); V. [Untitled] (38–39); VI. "Les Phares"/"The Beacons" (40–43); VII. "La Muse malade"/"The Sick Muse" (42–43); VIII. "La Muse vénale"/"The Venal Muse" (42–45); IX. "Le Mauvais Moine"/"The Evil Monk" (44–45); X. "L'Ennemi" (44–45); XI. "Le Guignon" (46–47); XII. "La Vie antérieure"/"Anterior Life" (46–47); XIII. "Bohémiens en voyage"/"Travelling Gypsies" (48–49); XIV. "L'Homme et la mer" (48–49); XV. "Don Juan aux enfers" (50–51); XVI. "A Theodore de Banville"/"To Theodore de Banville" (50–52); XVII. "Châtiment de l'orgueil"/"Chastisement of Pride" (52–53); XVIII. "La Beauté"/"Beauty" (54–55); XIX. "L'Idéal"/"The Ideal" (54–55);; XX. "Le Géante"/"The Giantess" (56–57); XXI. "Le Masque" (56–59); XXII. "Hymne à la beauté"/"Hymn to Beauty" (58–61); XXIII. "Parfum exotique"/"Exotic Perfume" (60–61); XXIV. "La Chevelure"/"The Chevelure" (60–63); XXV. [Untitled] (62–63); XXVI. [Untitled] (64–65); XXVII. *"Sed non satiata"* (64–65); XXVIII. [Untitled] (66–67); XXIX. "Le Serpent qui danse" (66–69); XXX. "Une Charogne" (68–71); XXXI. *"De profundis clamavi"* (72–73); XXXII. "Le Vampire"/"The Vampire"

(72–73); XXXIII. [Untitled] 974–75); XXXIV. "Remords posthume"/"The Remorse of the Dead" (74–77); XXXV. "Le Chat"/"The Cat" (76–77); XXXVI. *Duellum*"/"The Duel" (76–78); XXXVII. "Le Balcon"/"The Balcony" (78–79); XXXVIII. "Le Possédé"/"The Possessed" (80–81); XXXIX. "Un Fantôme" (80–85); XL. [Untitled] (84–85); XLI. "Semper Eadem" (86–87); XLII. "Tout entière" (86–88); XLIII. [Untitled] (88–89); XLIV. "Le Flambeau vivant" (88–89); XLV. "Réversibilité" (90–91); XLVI. "Confession" (90–93); XLVII. "L'Aube spirituelle"/"The Spiritual Dawn" (94–95); XLVIII. "L'Harmonie du soir"/"Evening Harmony" (94–95); XLIX. "Le Flacon" (96–97); L. "Le Poison"/"The Poison" (98–99); LI. "Ciel brouillé"/"Doubtful Skies" (98–101); LII. "Le Chat" (100–103); LIII. "Le Beau Navire" (102–5); LIV. "L'Invitation au voyage" (104–7); LV. "L'Irréparable"/"The Irreparable" (108–11); LVI. "Causerie" (110–11); LVII. "Chant d'automne"/"Song of Autumn" (112–13); LVIII. "A une Madone" (114–17); LIX. "Chanson d'après-midi" (116–19); LX. "Sisina" (118–19); LXI. "Vers pour le portrait d'Honoré Daumier" (120–21); LXII. "Franciscæ Meæ Laudes" (120, 122; Baudelaire text only); LXIII. "A une Dame créole"/"To a Creole Lady" (122–23); LXIV. "Mœsta et Errabunda" (124–25); LXV. "Le Revenant"/"The Phantom" (126–27); LXVI. "Sonnet d'automne" (126–27); LXVII. "Tristesses de la lune" (128–29); LXVIII. "Les Chats"/"The Cats" (128–29); LXIX. "Les Hiboux"/"The Owls" (130–31); LXX. "La Pipe" (130–31); LXXI. "La Musique"/"Music" (132–33); LXXII. "Sépulture" (132; Baudelaire text only); LXXIII. "Une Gravure fantastique" (134–35); LXXIV. "Le Mort joyeux" (134–35); LXXV. "Le Tonneau de la haine"/"The Barrel of Hate" (136–37); LXXVI. "La Cloche fêlée" (136–37); LXXVII. "Spleen" (138–39); LXXVIII. "Spleen" (138–40); LXXIX. "Spleen" (140–41); LXXX. "Spleen" (140–43); LXXXI. "Obsession" (142–43); LXXXII. "Le Goût du néant" (142, 144; Baudelaire text only); LXXXIII. "Alchimie de la douleur"/"Alchemy of Sorrow" (144–45); LXXXIV. "Horreur sympathique"/"Sympathetic Horror" (144–45); LXXXV. "Le Calumet de paix" (146–50); LXXXVI. "La Prière d'un païen"/"A Pagan's Prayer" (152–53); LXXXVII. "Le Couvercle"/"The Cover" (152–53); LXXXVIII. "L'Imprévu" (154–57); LXXXIX. "L'Examen de minuit"/"Examination at Midnight" (156–59); XC. "Madrigal triste"/"Madrigal of Sorrow" (158–61); XCI. "L'Avertisseur"/"The Adviser" (160–62); XCII. "A une Malabaraise"/"To a Malabaress" (162–63); XCIII. "La

Voix"/"The Voice" (164–65); XCIV. "Hymne"/"Hymn" (165–67); XCV. "Le Rebelle"/"The Rebel" (166–67); XCVI. "Les Yeux de Berthe"/"The Eyes of Bertha" (166–69); XCVII. "Le Jet d'eau"/"The Fountain" (168–71); XCVIII. "La Rançon" (170–71); XCIX. "Bien loin d'ici"/"Very Far from Here" (172–73); C. "Le Coucher du Soleil romantique" (172–73); CI. "Sur *Le Tasse en Prison* d'Eugène Delacroix"/"On 'Tasso in Prison' by Eugène Delacroix" (174–75); CII. "Le Gouffre"/"The Gulf" (174–75); CIII. "Les Plaintes d'un Icare"/"The Lament of Icarus" (176–77); CIV. "Receuillement"/"Contemplation" (176–77); CV. "*L'Héautontimorouménos*" (178–79); CVI. "L'Irrémédiable"/"The Irremediable" (180–83); CVII. "L'Horloge"/"The Clock" (182–83); *Tableaux Parisiens:* CVIII. "Paysage" (184–85); CIX. "Le Soleil"/ "The Sun" (186–87); CX. "Lola de Valence" (186–87); CXI. "La Lune offensée" (188–89); CXII. "A une Mendiante rousse" (188–91); CXIII. "Le Cygne" (182–95); CXIV. "Les Sept Vieillards" (196–99); CXV. "Les Petites Vieilles" (198–203); CXVI. "Les Aveugles"/"The Blind" (204–5); CXVII. "A une Passante"/"To a Passer-by" (204–5); CXVIII. "Le Squelette laboureur"/"The Toiling Skeleton" (206–7); CXIX. "Le Crépuscule du soir"/"Evening Twilight" (208–9); CXX. "Le Jeu"/"The Game" (210–11); CXXI. "Danse macabre"/"The Dance of Death" (210–15); CXXII. "L'Amour du mensonge"/"The Love of Falsehood" (214–17); CXXIII. [Untitled] (216–17); CXXIV. [Untitled] (216–17); CXXV. "Brumes et pluies"/"Mists and Rains" (218–19); CXXVI. "Rêve parisien"/"Parisian Dream" (218–23); CXXVII. "Le Crépuscule du matin" (222–23); *Le Vin:* CXXVIII. "L'Ame du vin" (224–25); CXXIX. "Le Vin de chiffonniers"/"The Wine of the Rag-Pickers" (226–27); CXXX. "Le Vin de l'assassin"/"The Wine of the Assassin" (228–31); CXXXI. "Le Vin du solitaire"/"The Wine of the Solitary" (230–31); CXXXII. "Le Vin des amants"/"The Wine of Lovers" (232–33); *Fleurs du Mal:* CXXXIII. "Epigraphe pour un livre condamné"/ "Epigraph for a Condemned Book" (234–35); CXXXIV. "La Destruction"/"Destruction" (234–35); CXXXV. "Une Martyre" (236–39); CXXXVI. "Femmes damnées" (240–41); CXXXVII. "Les Deux Bonnes Sœurs"/"The Two Kind Sisters" (242–43); CXXXVIII. "La Fontaine de sang"/"The Fountain of Blood" (242–43); CXXXIX. "Allégorie" (244–45); CXL. "La Béatrice"/ "Beatrice" (244–47); CXLI. "Un voyage à Cythère" (247–51); CXLII. "L'Amour et la crâne"/"Love and the Cranium" (150–51); *Révolte:* CXLIII. "Le Reniement de Saint Pierre"/"The Denial of

St. Peter" (252–53); CXLIV. "Abel et Caïn" (254–57); CXLV. "Les Litanies de Satan"/"Litany to Satan" (256–59); *La Mort:* CXLVI. "La Mort des amants"/"The Death of Lovers" (260–61); CXLVII. "La Mort des pauvres" (260–61); CXLVIII. "La Mort des artistes" (262–63); CXLIX. "La Fin de la journée" (262–63); CL. "La Rêve d'un curieux" (264–65); CLI. "Le Voyage"/"The Voyage" (264–73); [*Jetsam*]: I. "Les Bijoux" (274–75); II. "La Léthe"/"Lethe" (276–77); III. "A celle qui est trop gaie"/"To Her Who Is Too Gay" (278–79); IV. "Lesbos" (280–83); V. "Femmes damnées: Delphine et Hippolyte" (284–89); VI. "Les Métamorphoses du vampire"/"The Metamorphoses of the Vampire" (290–91); TRANSLATIONS FROM THE FRENCH: *Marie Dauguet:* "Epilogue"/[Untitled] (294–95); *Théophile Gautier:* "Le Pot de fleurs"/"The Flower-Pot" (296–97); "L'Impassible"/"The Impassible" (296–97); "Pastel" (298–99); *Gérard de Nerval:* "Artémis"/"Artemis" (300–301); "Vers dorés"/"Golden Verses" (300–301); *José-Maria de Heredia:* "Antoine et Cléopatre"/"Antony and Cleopatra" (302–3); "Le Récif de corail"/"The Coral Reef" (302–3); "La Dogaresse" (304–5); "Némée"/"Nemea" (304–5); "L'Oubli"/"Oblivion" (306–7); "Sur un Marbre brisé"/"On a Broken Statue" (306–7); "Le Samouraï"/"The Samurai" (308–9); "Soleil couchant"/"A Setting Sun" (308–9); "Vitrail"/"The Stained Window" (310–11); *Victor Hugo:* "Crépuscule"/"Twilight" (312–13); "Ce qu'on entend sur la montagne"/"What One Hears on the Mountain" (314–19); "Le Rouet d'Omphale"/"The Wheel of Omphale" (318–19); *Tristan Klingsor:* "Plaisir d'Amour" (320–21); *Alphonse Louis Marie de Lamartine:* "Le Lac"/"The Lake" (322–25); *Charles Marie René Leconte de Lisle:* "La Panthère noire"/"The Black Panther" (326–29); "L'Ecclésiaste"/"Ecclesiastes" (329–29); "Les Montreurs"/"The Exhibitionists" (328–31); "Les Hurleurs"/"The Howlers" (330–33); "Le Sommeil du condor"/ "The Sleep of the Condor" (332–35); "Solvet seclum" (334–35); *Charles van Lerberghe:* "[Chanson]"/"Song" (336–37); *Pierre Li-èvre:* "Paysage Elyséen"/"Elysian Landscape" (339; French text not printed); "The End of Supper" (339; French text not printed); *Stuart Merrill:* "Celle qui prie"/"A Woman at Prayer" (340–41); *Alfred de Musset:* "Rappelle-toi"/"Remember Thee" (342–43); "Chanson"/"Song" (344–45); *Sully-Prudhomme:* "Sieste"/"Siesta" (346–47); *Albert Samain:* [Untitled]/"I Dream" (348–49); "Myrtil et Palémone"/"Myrtil and Palemone" (350–51); *Fernand Severin:* "Bois sacré"/"Sonnet" (352–55); *Paul Verlaine:* "Ariettes Oubliées IX"/"XI (Ariettes Oubliées)" (356–57); "Il Bacio" (356–57); "La

Bonne Chanson" (358–63); "Crimen Amoris" (364–69); "En Sourdine" (370–71); "Le Faune"/"The Faun" (370–71); "Green" (372–73); "Claire de lune"/"Moonlight" (372–73); "[Song from] *Les Uns et les autres*"/"Song from *Les Uns et les autres*" (372–75); "Spleen" (376–77); "A une femme"/"To a Woman" (376–77); TRANSLATIONS FROM THE SPANISH: *Gustavo Adolfo Bécquer:* "Rimas LII"/"Invocation" (378–79); "Rimas LX"/"The Sower" (378–79); "Rimas XXXVIII"/"Where?" (378–79); "Rimas I (Libro de los gorriones)"/"The World Rolls On" (380–81); *José A. Calcaño:* "Le ciprés"/"The Cypress" (382–83); *José Santos Chocano:* "El sueño del caimán"/"The Sleep of the Cayman" (384–85); *Rubén Darío:* "El Cantar de los Cantares"/"The Song of Songs" (386–87); *Juana de Ibarbourou:* "Vida aldeana"/"Rustic Life" (388–89); *Jorge Isaacs:* "Luminar"/"Luminary" (390–91); *Juan Lozano y Lozano:* "Ritmo"/"Rhythm" (392–93); *Amado Nervo:* "Noche"/"Night" (394–95); Appendix: XXVII. *"Sed non satiata"* (poetic version) (397); LV. "L'Irréparable" (prose version) (397–98); CXLI. "Un Voyage à Cythère" (poetic version; fragment) (398); "The Peace-Pipe" by Henry Wadsworth Long-fellow (399–403); "Notes" [by Joshi and Schultz] (405–24); "Index of Titles" (425–32); "Index of First Lines" (433–42).

Notes. Bound in black cloth; dust jacket art by Jack Newton (volume 1) and Anastasia Damianakos (volumes 2 and 3). The volume of translations was published first. Three of Baudelaire's poems from *Les Fleurs du mal* either were not translated by CAS, or the translations have been lost. Most of the translations are in prose; CAS customarily prepared fairly literal prose translations prior to setting them in verse. The French or Spanish texts have been printed on the versos, CAS translations on the rectos. The poems in French by Pierre Lièvre had not been located when the book went to press; they were subsequently found and printed in a paperback reissue of the three-volume set. In Volume 2, a computer error resulted in the apparent skipping of pages 413–48; no poems were omitted. The editors learned after publication that some of the untitled poems and fragments in the appendix are actually poems by others that CAS had merely copied by hand. CAS's translation of a poem by Hélène Picard and by Baudelaire (the epigraph to *Sandalwood*) were discovered only after Volume 3 had gone to press; they were transferred to Volume 3 in the paperback edition. Two newly discovered poems, "The Canyon" and "The Invisible Host," were added to Volume 1.

74. *The Klarkash-Ton Cycle: The Lovecraftian Fiction of Clark Ashton Smith*. Ed. Robert M. Price.
   a. N.p.: Chaosium, 2008. x, 212 pp.

   Contents: "The Smythos" by Price (v–x); "The Ghoul" (1–7); "A Rendering from the Arabic" (8–24); "The Hunters from Beyond" (25–43); "The Vaults of Abomi" (44–66); "The Nameless Offspring" (67–87); "Ubbo-Sathla" (88–97); "The Werewolf of Averoigne" (98–114); "The Eidolon of the Blind" (115–32); "Vulthoom" (133–61); "The Treader of the Dust" (162–71); "The Infernal Star" (172–202); "Story Introductions: Notes on Each Tale" [by Price] (203–12).

   Notes. Bound in paper. Cover art by Stephen Gilberts. A collection of CAS's fiction thought by Price to have been influenced or inspired by H. P. Lovecraft's Cthulhu Mythos. Price uses several variant texts: for instance, "A Rendering from the Arabic" was the original title for "The Return of the Sorcerer," and this edition uses the original, more gory ending. Likewise, "The Vaults of Abomi" was the first title for what became "The Vaults of Yoh-Vombis," and "The Werewolf of Averoigne" is an extrapolation from a note for what became "The Beast of Averoigne." Price here uses the version originally rejected by *Weird Tales* editor Farnsworth Wright.

75. *The Hashish-Eater*. Edited by Donald Sidney-Fryer.
   a. New York: Hippocampus Press, 2008. 85 pp.

   Contents. "A Wind from the Unknown" by Ron Hilger (7–9); "About Clark Ashton Smith and *The Hashish-Eater*: by Sidney-Fryer (11–20); "The Crystals" (21); "Argument of *The Hashish-Eater*" (21–22); "The Face from Infinity" [extract from *The Black Book*] (22–23); "Excerpt from a letter by Smith, summer 1950" (23); *The Hashish-Eater; or, The Apocalypse of Evil* (25–69); *Commentary:* "Glossary" (71–83); "The Final Image" (83); "Suggested Interpretation" (83–84); "Conclusion" (84–85).

   Notes. Cover illustration by CAS. Expanded from the editor's privately printed booklet (1990; See A.55). Audio CD contains hidden tracks of Sidney-Fryer reading a selection of other poems by CAS.

   A thoroughly annotated edition of CAS's longest poem (581 lines). The text of the poem comprises the original appearance in *Ebony and Crystal* (1922) on verso pages and CAS's revised version (dating to the 1940s) from his *Selected Poems* (1971) on facing recto pages.

76. *The Return of the Sorcerer.* Ed. Robert Weinberg.
    a. Holicong, PA: Prime Books, 2009. 349 pp.
    b. Holicong, PA: Prime Books/Science Fiction Book Club, 2012.

> *Contents:* "Introduction" by Gene Wolfe (7–10); "The Return of the Sorcerer" (11–28); "The City of Singing Flame" [*sic*] (29–48); "Beyond the Singing Flame" (49–74); "The Vaults of Yoh-Vombis" (75–93); "The Double Shadow" (94–107); "The Monster of the Prophecy" (108–47); "The Hunters from Beyond" (148–65); "The Isle of the Torturers" (166–81); "A Night in Malnéant" (182–89); "The Chain of Aforgomon" (190–208); "The Dark Eidolon" (209–38); "The Seven Geases" (239–61); "The Holiness of Azédarac" (262–84); "The Beast of Averoigne" (285–96); "The Empire of the Necromancers" (297–307); "The Disinterment of Venus" (308–16); "The Devotee of Evil" (317–29); "The Enchantress of Sylaire" (330–46); "Publication History" (347–48); "About the Author" (349).
>
> *Notes.* Bound in paper; cover art by Peter Bergting. Subtitled "The Best of CLARK ASHTON SMITH" on the cover only. Robert Weinberg selected the original pulp magazine appearances for his texts. A projected cloth limited edition never appeared.

77. *A Phantasy and Other Prose Poems.*
    a. London: Dodo Press, 2009. 34 pp.

> *Contents:* "A Phantasy" (1); "From the Crypts of Memory" (2–4); "The Memnons of the Night" (5–6); "Ennui" (7–8); "The Princess Almeena" (9); "The Black Lake" (10–11); "The Caravan" (12); "The Demon, the Angel, and Beauty" (13–15); "A Dream of Lethe" (16–17); "The Flower-Devil" (18–19); "From a Letter" (20); "The Garden and the Tomb" (21); "In Cocaigne" (22); "The Lake of Enchanted Silence" (23); "The Litany of Seven Kisses" (24–25); "Remoteness" (26); "The Shadows" (27–29); "The Statue of Silence" (30); "To the Daemon" (31–32); "The Traveller" (33–34).
>
> *Notes.* Bound in paper.

78. *Moonlight and Other Poems.*
    a. London: Dodo Press, 2009. 167 pp.

> *Contents:* "Moonlight" (1); "Autumn's Pall" (2); "Before Sunrise" (3); "A Dream of Beauty" (4); "A Live-Oak Leaf" (5); "Medusa" (6–7); "Ode to the Abyss" (8–9); "The Horizon" (10); "The Abyss Triumphant" (11); "Atlantis" (12); "Averted Malefice"

(13); "The Balance" (14); "The Butterfly" (15–17); "Chant to Sirius" (18); "The Cherry-Snows" (19); "The Cloud-Islands" (20); "Copan" (21); "A Dead City" (22); "The Dream-Bridge" (23); "Fairy Lanterns" (24); "Finis" (25); "The Fugitives" (26); "Lament of the Stars" (27–28); "The Last Night" (29); "The Mad Wind" (30); "The Masque of Forsaken Gods" (31–35); "The Maze of Sleep" (36); "The Medusa of the Skies" (37); "The Morning Pool" (38); "The Nemesis of Suns" (39); "Nero" (40–42); "The Night Forest" (43–44); "Nirvana" (45); "Ode on Imagination" (46–47); "Ode to Music" (48–49); "Pine Needles" (50); "The Price" (51); "Remembered Light" (52); "The Retribution" (53); "Retrospect and Forecast" (54); "The Return of Hyperion" (55); "Saturn" (56–62); "Shadow of Nightmare" (63); "The Snow-Blossoms" (64); "A Song of Dreams" (65–66); "Song to Oblivion" (67); "A Song of the Stars" (68–69); "The Sorrow of the Winds" (70); "The Star-Treader" (71–74); "The Summer Moon" (75); "A Sunset" (76); "To the Darkness" (77–78); "To the Sun" (79); "White Death" (80); "The Wind and the Moon" (81); "The Winds" (82); "The Medusa of Despair" (83); "The Nereid" (84); "Dream Mystery" (85); "The Harlot of the World" (86); "Psalm to the Desert" (87–88); "Strangeness" (89); "The Tears of Lilith" (90); "Alexandrines" (91); "Ave Atque Vale" (92); "Belated Love" (93); "The Crucifixion of Eros" (94); "Exotique" (95); "Inferno" (96); "Memnon at Midnight" (97); "The Ministers of Law" (98); "The Refuge of Beauty" (99); "Satan Unrepentant" (100–102); "Sepulture" (103); "Palms" (104); "Resquiescat in Pace" (105–6); "The Absence of the Muse" (107); "Laus Mortis" (108); "Antepast" (109); "Arabesque" (110); "Artemis" (111); "Ashes of Sunset" (112); "At Sunrise" (113); "Autumnal" (114); "Beauty Implacable" (115); "Chant of Autumn" (116); "The City in the Desert" (117); "Desire of Vastness" (118); "Desolation" (119); "Echo of Memnon" (120); "Ecstacy" (121); "Eidolon" (122); "The Exile" (123); "The Ghoul and the Seraph" (124–27); "Haunting" (128); "The Hidden Paradise" (129); "The Hope of the Infinite" (130); "Impression" (131); "Inheritance" (132); "The Infinite Quest" (133); "The Kingdom of Shadows" (134–35); "The Land of Evil Stars" (136–37); "Love Is Not Yours, Love Is Not Mine" (138); "Love Malevolent" (139); "The Melancholy Pool" (140); "Mirage" (141); "Mirrors" (142); "The Mirrors of Beauty" (143); "The Motes" (144); "Nightmare" (145); "November Twilight" (146); "The Orchid of Beauty" (147); "A Precept" (148); "Psalm" (149); "A Psalm to the Best

Beloved" (150); "Quest" (151); "Recompense" (152); "Rosa
Mystica" (153); "Solution" (154); "Song" [from *Ebony and
Crystal*] (155); "Symbols" (156); "To Omar Khayyam" (157–58);
"To the Beloved" (159); "Transcendence" (160); "Triple Aspect"
(161); "Twilight on the Snow" (162); "Union" (163); "Winter
Moonlight" (164); "The Witch in the Graveyard" (165–67).

Notes. Bound in paper. Some of the texts were taken from Internet sources such as Wikisources.

79. *The Colossus of Ylourgne and Three Others.*
   a. Holicong, PA: Wildside Press, 2009. 87 pp.

   Contents: "The Abominations of Yondo" (7–12); "The Dark Eidolon" (13–35); "The Charnel God" (36–54); "The Colossus of
   Ylourgne" (55–87).

   Notes. Bound in paper.

80. *The Empire of the Necromancers and Three Others.*
   a. Holicong, PA: Wildside Press, 2009. 58 pp.

   Contents: "The Empire of the Necromancers" (7–15); "The Enchantress of Sylaire" (16–30); "The Invisible City" (31–50);
   "Mother of Toads" (51–58).

   Notes. Bound in paper.

81. *The Song of the Necromancer and Others: The Complete Poems from
   Weird Tales.* Ed. Stephen Jones.
   a. Hornsea, UK: Stanza, 2010. xiv, 45 pp.

   Contents: "Introduction" by Jones (xi–xiv); "The Garden of Evil"
   (3); "The Red Moon" (3); "Solution" (4); "The Melancholy Pool"
   (5); "A Fable" (5); "Interrogation" (6); "The Saturnienne" (7–8);
   "Warning" (8); "Sonnet" (9); "Nyctalops" (10–11); "The Night-
   mare Tarn" (12–13); *"Fantaisie d'antan"* (14–15); "Ougabalys"
   (16); "Shadows" (17); "Fellowship" (18); "In Slumber" (19);
   "Dominion" (20–21); "In Thessaly" (21); "Ennui" (22); "Song of
   the Necromancer" (23); "To Howard Phillips Lovecraft" (24–25);
   "Outlanders" (26); "Farewell to Eros" (27–28); "The Prophet
   Speaks" (28–29); "Bacchante" (30–31); "The Phoenix" (31);
   "Witch Dance" (32–33); "Necromancy" (34); "Dialogue" (34);
   "Desert Dweller" (35); "The Sorcerer to His Love" (36); "Resur-
   rection" (37); "To the Chimera" (38); "Do You Forget, Enchant-
   ress?" (39); "Luna Aeternalis" (40–41); "'Not Altogether Sleep'"

(42); "Sonnet for the Psychoanalysts" (42); "'O Golden-Tongued Romance'" (43–44); "Don Quixote on Market Street" (45).

    Notes. Bound in decorated paper-covered boards. Cover and frontispiece art by CAS. End papers designed by Ann Muir Marbling.

82.   *The Miscellaneous Writings of Clark Ashton Smith.* Ed. Scott Connors and Ron Hilger.

   a.   San Francisco: Night Shade Books, 2011. xviii, 233 pp.

    Contents: "Foreword" by Connors and Hilger (vii–xviii); "Introduction: The Sorcerer Departs" by Donald Sidney-Fryer (1–42); "The Animated Sword" (45–50); "The Red Turban" (51–55); "Prince Alcouz and the Magician" (57–58); "The Malay Krise" (59–61); "The Ghost of Mohammed Din" (63–69); "The Mahout" (71–74); "The Rajah and the Tiger" (77–82); "Something New" (83–85); "The Flirt" (87–88); "The Perfect Woman" (89–90); "A Platonic Entanglement" (91–93); "The Expert Lover" (95–103); "The Parrot" (105–8); "A Copy of Burns" (109–11); "Checkmate" (113–18); "The Infernal Star" (119–44); "Dawn of Discord" (145–61); "House of the Monoceros" (163–78); *The Dead Will Cuckold You* (179–202); *The Hashish-Eater; or, The Apocalypse of Evil* (203–19); "Bibliography" (220–21); "O Amor atque Realitas! Clark Ashton Smith's First Adult Fiction" by Donald Sidney-Fryer (225–33).

    Notes. Bound in brown cloth; spine and front cover stamped in gold; dust jacket art by Jason Von Hollander. A collection of miscellaneous tales (fantasy, mainstream, etc.) and other matter, meant as a kind of sixth volume to the *Collected Fantasies* edition (A.71).

83.   *The City of the Singing Flame.*

   a.   Rockville, MD: Wildside Press, 2011. 62 pp.

    Contents: "The City of the Singing Flame" (with "Beyond the Singing Flame").

    Notes. Bound in paper.

84.   *The Dark Eidolon and Other Fantasies.* Ed. S. T. Joshi.

   a.   New York: Penguin Classics, [February] 2014. xxvii, 370 pp.

    Contents: "Introduction" by S. T. Joshi (ix–xxii); "Suggestions for Further Reading" [by Joshi] (xxiii–xxvi); "A Note on the Texts" [by Joshi] (xxvii); *Short Stories:* "The Tale of Satampra Zeiros"

(3–15); "The Last Incantation" (16–20); "The Devotee of Evil" (21–33); "The Uncharted Isle" (34–44); "The Face by the River" (45–51); "The City of the Singing Flame" (52–69); "The Holiness of Azédarac" (70–90); "The Vaults of Yoh-Vombis" (91–111); "Ubbo-Sathla" (112–19); "The Double Shadow" (120–32); "The Maze of the Enchanter" (133–48); "Genius Loci" (149–66); "The Dark Eidolon" (167–94); "The Weaver in the Vault" (195–207); "Xeethra" (208–28); "The Treader of the Dust" (229–37); "Mother of Toads" (238–46); "Phoenix" (247–57); *Prose Poems:* "The Image of Bronze and the Image of Iron" (261); "The Memnons of the Night" (262); "The Demon, the Angel, and Beauty" (263–64); "The Corpse and the Skeleton" (264–66); "A Dream of Lethe" (266–67); "From the Crypts of Memory" (267–68); "Ennui" (268–69); "The Litany of the Seven Kisses" (270–71); "In Cocaigne" (271); "The Flower-Devil" (272); "The Shadows" (273–74); "The Passing of Aphrodite" (274–76); "To the Daemon" (276–77); "The Abomination of Desolation" (277–78); "The Mirror in the Hall of Ebony" (278–79); "The Touch-Stone" (279–80); "The Muse of Hyperborea" (280); *Poetry:* "The Last Night" (283); "Ode to the Abyss" (283–85); "A Dream of Beauty" (285–86); "The Star-Treader" (286–89); "Retrospect and Forecast" (290); "Nero" (290–93); "To the Daemon Sublimity" (293); "Averted Malefice" (293–94); "The Eldritch Dark" (294); "Shadow of Nightmare" (294–95); "Satan Unrepentant" (295–97); "The Ghoul" (297–98); "Desire of Vastness" (298); "The Medusa of Despair" (298–99); "The Refuge of Beauty" (299); "The Harlot of the World" (299–300); "Memnon at Midnight" (300); "Love Malevolent" (300–301); "The Crucifixion of Eros" (301); "The Tears of Lilith" (302); "Requiescat in Pace" (302–3); "The Motes" (303); *The Hashish-Eater* (304–19); "A Psalm to the Best Beloved" (319–20); "The Witch with Eyes of Amber" (320); "We Shall Meet" (320–21); "On Re-reading Baudelaire" (322); "To George Sterling: A Valediction" (322–24); "Anterior Life" (324–25); "Hymn to Beauty" (325–26); "The Remorse of the Dead" (326); "Exorcism" (326–27); "Nyctalops" (327–28); "Outlanders" (328–29); "Song of the Necromancer" (329–30); "To Howard Phillips Lovecraft" (330–31); "Madrigal of Memory" (331–32); "The Old Water-Wheel" (332); "The Hill of Dionysus" (333–34); "If Winter Remain" (334–35); "Amithaine" (335–36); "Cycles" (336–37); "Explanatory Notes" (339–70).

Notes. Bound in paper; cover art CAS. Major selection of CAS's fiction, prose poetry, and poetry, with biographical-critical introduction and notes by Joshi. An important landmark in CAS's literary recognition.

85. *The Averoigne Chronicles.* Ed. Ron Hilger.
   a. Lakewood, CO: Centipede Press, April 2016. 256 pp.

Contents: "Introduction" by Gahan Wilson ([9]–13); "A Note on the Text" by Ronald S. Hilger ([15]–19); "Averoigne" ([22–23]); "A Night in Malnéant" ([25]–32); "The Nevermore-to-Be" ([33]); "The Maker of Gargoyles" ([35]–49); "The Broken Lute" ([51]); "The Holiness of Azédarac" ([53]–72); "In Cocaigne" ([73]); "The Colossus of Ylourgne" ([75]–110); "Necromancy" ([111]); "The Enchantress of Sylaire" ([113]–28); "Amithaine" ([130–31]); "The Beast of Averoigne" ([133]–47); "Song of the Necromancer" ([148–49]); "Mother of Toads" ([151]–60); "The Witch with Eyes of Amber" ([161]); "A Rendezvous in Averoigne" ([163]–78); "The Dark Chateau" ([180–81]); "The Mandrakes" ([183]–91); "Canticle" ([193]); "The Satyr" ([195]–202); "Cambion" ([203]); "The Disinterment of Venus" ([205]–13); "'O Golden-Tongued Romance'" ([214–15]); "The End of the Story" ([217]–34); "To Klarkash-Ton, Lord of Averoigne" by H. P. Lovecraft ([235]); "Averoigne: An Afterword" by Donald Sidney-Fryer ([237]–52); [acknowledgments] ([255–56]).

Notes. Bound in black cloth; spine stamped in gold; dust jacket art and interior illustrations by David Ho. A book long in the works, originally scheduled to have been published decades ago by Donald M. Grant. The editor appears as "Ron Hilger" on the title page and as "Ronald S. Hilger" at the end of the introduction.

86. *Dawnward Spire, Lonely Hill: The Letters of H. P. Lovecraft and Clark Ashton Smith.* Ed. David E. Schultz and S. T. Joshi.
   a. New York: Hippocampus Press, [August] 2017. 799 pp.

Contents: "Introduction" by the editors (7–29); "Epithets for Friends and Associates" (30–31); "[Letters]" (35–666); *Appendix:* Postcard to CAS by Annie E. P. Gamwell (667); "[Review of *Ebony and Crystal*]" by Lovecraft (667–68); "From 'Supernatural Horror in Literature'" by Lovecraft (668–69); "[Fantasy and Human Experience]" by CAS (669–71); "[On 'GarbageMongering']" by CAS (672); "[Realism and Fantasy]" by CAS (673–74); "[On the Forbidden Books]" by CAS (674–75); "[The Tale of Macrocosmic Horror]" by CAS (675); "[Crossword Puzzles]" by CAS (676–87);

"Treader of Obscure Stars" by Clifford Gessler (687); *Various:* "In re exhibitions of Smith's artwork" (687–88); "The Boiling Point" (689–98); "Chronology" (699–710); "Glossary of Frequently Mentioned Names" (711–16); "Bibliography" (717–69); "Index" (771–99).

Notes. Bound in black cloth; spine stamped in orange; dust jacket art by David Verba. Complete publication of the joint correspondence of Lovecraft and CAS, exhaustively annotated—the result of decades of work, mostly by Schultz. Two postcards by CAS to Lovecraft will be included in a future reprinting.

87. *In the Realms of Mystery and Wonder: Collected Prose Poems and Artwork of Clark Ashton Smith.* Ed. Scott Connors.

a. Lakewood, CO: Centipede Press, [November] 2017. 440 pp.

Contents: "Introduction" by Connors (9–53); *The Sculptures* (55–110); *The Paintings and Drawings* (111–242); *The Prose Poems* (243–322): "A Note on the Texts" by Connors ([245–46]); "The Traveller" ([247–48]); "The Flower Devil" ([249–50]); "Images" ("Tears" [251], "The Secret Rose" [251], "The Wind and the Garden" [251], "Offerings" [252], "A Coronal" [252]); "The Black Lake" ([253]); "Vignettes" ("Beyond the Mountains" [254], "The Broken Lute" [254], "Nostalgia of the Unknown" [255], "Grey Sorrow" [255], "The Hair of Circe" [256], "The Eyes of Circe" [256]); "A Dream of Lethe" ([257–58]); "The Caravan" ([259]); "The Princess Almeena" ([260]); "Ennui" ([261–62]); "The Statue of Silence" ([263]); "Remoteness" ([264]); "The Memnons of the Night" ([265–66]); "The Garden and the Tomb" ([267]); "In Cocaigne" ([268]); "From a Letter" ([269]); "The Litany of the Seven Kisses" ([270–71]); "From the Crypts of Memory" ([272–74]); "A Phantasy" ([275]); "The Demon, the Angel, and Beauty" ([276–78]); "The Shadows" ([279–80]); "Prose Pastels" ("To the Daemon" [281], "The Abomination of Desolation" [281–82], "The Mirror in the Hall of Ebony" [284–85]); "The Lotus and the Moon" ([286]); "The Shark and the Osprey" ([287]); "The Touch-Stone" ([288–89]); "The Forbidden Forest" ([290–92]); "The Mithridate" ([293]); "The Muse of Hyperborea" ([294]); "Narcissus" ([295]); "Chinoiserie" ([296–97]); "The Peril That Lurks among Ruins" ([298]); "The Passing of Aphrodite" ([299–302]); "The Crystals" ([303–4]); "The Corpse and the Skeleton" ([305–7]); "The Image of Bronze and the Image of Iron" ([308–9]); "The Sun and the Sepulchre" ([310]); "The Mortuary" ([311–12]); "The Frozen Waterfall"

([313]); "The Lake of Enchanted Silence" ([314]); "The City of Destruction" ([315–16]); "The Days" ([317]); "Offering" ([318]); "Preference" ([319]); "[Untitled]" ([320]); "A Chinese Fable" ([321]); *Memoirs:* "Clark Ashton Smith, Poet in Prose" by Donald Sidney-Fryer (325–42); "Recollections of Clark Ashton Smith" by Samuel J. Sackett (434–48); "Clark Ashton Smith: An Appreciation" by Fritz Leiber (349–52); "Clark Ashton Smith" by William Whittingham Lyman (353–62); "The Man in the Mist" by Emil Petaja (363–70); "As I Remember Klarkash-Ton" by George F. Haas (371–402); "Memories of Klarkash-Ton by George F. Haas (403–18); "Clark Ashton Smith: In Memory of a Great Friendship" by Eric Barker (419–24); "A Letter" by Rah Hoffman (425–32); "Reminiscences" by Ethel Heiple (433–39).

Notes. Bound in black cloth; spine stamped in yellow and white; dust jacket designed by Jacob McMurray (contains a photograph of a carving by CAS); with slipcase. Limited to 600 copies (200 copies signed by the editor). A substantial reproduction of CAS's paintings and sculptures, as well as a new, complete edition of his prose poems. Of the three "prose pastels" labeled so, only "To the Daemon" and "The Mirror in the Hall of Ebony" were published under that heading in the *Fantasy Fan* and *Acolyte;* but one ms. of "The Abomination of Desolation" bears that designation.

88. *Zothique Prism.*
 a. Olympia, WA: Pegana Press, 2017. 17 pp.

   Contains: "The Empire of the Necromancers."
   Notes. Chapbook. Illustrated by Robert H. Knox. Limited to 55 hand-numbered copies.

Appendix: Ebooks

89. *The Ultimate Weird Tales Collection.*
 a. n.p.: Trilogus Books, 2011.

   Contents: "A Copy of Burns"; "A Good Embalmer"; "A Night in Malnéant"; "A Platonic Entanglement"; "A Star-Change"; "A Vintage from Atlantis"; "A Voyage to Sfanomoë"; "An Adventure in Futurity"; "An Offering to the Moon"; "Checkmate"; "Double Cosmos"; "Fakhreddin"; "Genius Loci"; "Marooned in Andromeda"; "Monsters in the Night"; "Morthylla"; "Mother of Toads"; "Murder in the Fourth Dimension"; "Necromancy in Naat"; "Nemesis of the Unfinished" (with Don Carter); "Phoenix";

"Prince Alcorez and the Magician"; "Prince Alcouz and the Magician"; "Puthuum"; "Quest of the Gazolba"; "Sadastor"; "Schizoid Creator"; "Seedling of Mars"; "Something New"; "Strange Shadows, or I Am Your Shadow"; "Symposium of the Gorgon"; "The Abominations of Yondo"; "The Beast of Averoigne"; "The Bronze Image"; "The Chain of Aforgomon"; "The Charnel God"; "The City of the Singing Flame"; "The Colossus of Ylourgne"; "The Coming of the White Worm"; "The Dark Age"; "The Dark Eidolon"; "The Dart of Rasasfa"; "The Death of Ilalotha"; "The Death of Malygris"; "The Demon of the Flower"; "The Devotee of Evil"; "The Dimension of Chance"; "The Disinterment of Venus"; "The Door to Saturn"; "The Double Shadow"; "The Emir's Captive"; "The Empire of the Necromancers"; "The Enchantress of Sylaire"; "The End of the Story"; "The Epiphany of Death"; "The Eternal World"; "The Expert Lover"; "The Flirt"; "The Flower-Women"; "The Fulfilled Prophecy"; "The Garden of Adompha"; "The Ghost of Mohammed Din"; "The Ghoul"; "The Gorgon"; "The Great God Awto"; "The Haunted Chamber"; "The Haunted Gong"; "The Holiness of Azédarac"; "The Hunters from Beyond"; "The Ice-Demon"; "The Immeasurable Horror"; "The Immortals of Mercury"; "The Invisible City"; "The Isle of the Torturers"; "The Justice of the Elephant"; "The Kiss of Zoraida"; "The Last Hieroglyph"; "The Last Incantation"; "The Letter from Mohaun Los"; "The Light from Beyond"; "The Light from the Pole" [by Lin Carter]; "The Mahout"; "The Maker of Gargoyles"; "The Malay Krise"; "The Mandrakes"; "The Master of the Crabs"; "The Maze of Maal Dweb"; "The Maze of the Enchanter"; "The Metamorphosis of Earth"; "The Monster of the Prophecy"; "The Nameless Offspring"; "The Necromantic Tale"; "The Ninth Skeleton"; "The Parrot"; "The Perfect Woman"; "The Phantoms of the Fire"; "The Planet of the Dead"; "The Plutonian Drug"; "The Raja and the Tiger"; "The Resurrection of the Rattlesnake"; "The Return of the Sorcerer"; "The Root of Ampoi"; "The Satyr"; "The Second Interment"; "The Seed from the Sepulcher"; "The Seven Geases"; "The Shah's Messenger"; "The Stairs in the Crypt" [by Lin Carter]; "The Supernumerary Corpse"; "The Tale of Satampra Zeiros"; "The Tale of Sir John Maundeville"; "The Testament of Athammaus"; "The Theft of the Thirty-nine Girdles"; "The Tomb-Spawn"; "The Treader of the Dust"; "The Uncharted Isle"; "The Vaults of Yoh-Vombis (Abridged)"; "The Venus of Azombeii"; "The Voyage of King Euvoran"; "The Weaver in the Vault"; "The Weird of Avoosl Wuthuqquan"; "The White Sybil";

"The Willow Landscape"; "The Witchcraft of Ulua"; "Thirteen Phantasms"; "Told in the Desert"; "Ubbo-Sathla"; "Vulthoom"; "Xeethra."

90. *Clark Ashton Smith's Works.*
   a. n.p.: Seng Books, 2014.

   Contents: "Clark Ashton Smith" by [Unsigned]; "The Ghost of Mohammed Din"; "The Mahout"; "Prince Alcouz and the Magician"; "The Raja and the Tiger"; "Something New"; "The Double Shadow"; "The Chain of Aforgomon"; "The Black Abbot of Puthuum"; "The Garden of Adompha"; "The Memnons of the Night"; "The Flower-Devil"; "The Traveller"; "The Shadows."

91. *The Golden Age of Weird Fiction Megapack, Volume 6.*
   a. Rockville, MD: Wildside Press, 2015.

   Contents: "The Abominations of Yondo"; "The Third Episode of Vathek" (with William Beckford); "Thirteen Phantasms"; "The Charnel God"; "The Colossus of Ylourgne"; "The Chain of Aforgomon"; "The Black Abbot of Puthuum"; "The Voyage of King Euvoran"; "The Maze of the Enchanter"; "The Double Shadow"; "A Night in Malnéant"; "The Devotee of Evil"; "The Willow Landscape"; "The Empire of the Necromancers"; "The Enchantress of Sylaire"; "The Invisible City"; "Mother of Toads."

B. Contributions to Books and Periodicals

i. Fiction

1. "The Abominations of Yondo."
    a. *Overland Monthly* 84, No. 4 (April 1926): 100–101, 114, 126.
    b. *Celephais* 1, No. 1 (March 1944): 4–7.
    c. In *The Abominations of Yondo* (A.15).
    d. In *Hyperborea* (A.29).
    e. In *The Emperor of Dreams* (A.59).
    f. In *The Maker of Gargoyles* (A.67).
    g. In *Collected Fantasies,* Volume 1 (A.70).
    h. In *The Colossus of Ylournge* (A.79).
    i. In *The Ultimate Weird Tales Collection* (A.89).
    j. In *Clark Ashton Smith's Works* (A.90).

2. "An Adventure in Futurity."
    a. *Wonder Stories* 2, No. 11 (April 1931): 1230–51, 1328.
    b. In *Other Dimensions* (A.24).
    c. In *Collected Fantasies,* Volume 2 (A.70).
    d. In *The Ultimate Weird Tales Collection* (A.89).
    e. *High Adventure* No. 153 (2017): 94–116 (facsimile a.).

3. "The Animated Sword."
    a. In *The Miscellaneous Writings of Clark Ashton Smith* (A.82).

4. "Asharia."
    a. *Crypt of Cthulhu* No. 27 (Hallowmas 1984 [special issue: *Untold Tales*]): 25–27.
    b. In *Strange Shadows* (A.52).

5. "The Beast of Averoigne."
    a. *Weird Tales* 21, No. 5 (May 1933): 628–35.
    b. *Weird Terror Tales* 1, No. 1 (Winter 1969/70): 66–76.
    c. In *Lost Worlds* (A.10).
    d. In *The City of the Singing Flame* (A.40).
    e. In *Strange Shadows* (A.52).
    f. In *The Emperor of Dreams* (A.59).
    g. In *Collected Fantasies,* Volume 4 (A.70).

h. In *The Klarkash-Ton Cycle* (A.74) (as "The Werewolf of Averoigne").
i. In *The Return of the Sorcerer* (A.76).
j. In *The Averoigne Chronicles* (A.85).
k. In *The Ultimate Weird Tales Collection* (A.89).
l. In S. T. Joshi, ed. *The Red Brain: Great Tales of the Cthulhu Mythos.* Portland, OR: Dark Regions Press, 2017. 27–42.

Written in June 1932. CAS cut 1400 words from the story to satisfy editorial requirements; this version is published in a.–d, f., and i. The original version may be found in e. and h., while g. and j. represent an editorial reconstruction based upon both versions.

6. "Beyond the Singing Flame."
   a. *Wonder Stories* 3, No. 6 (November 1931): 752–61.
   b. *Tales of Wonder* No. 10 (Spring 1940): 6–31 (combined with and published as "The City of the Singing Flame").
   c. In *Out of Space and Time* (A.9) (combined with and published as "The City of the Singing Flame").
   d. *Startling Stories* 11, No. 1 (Summer 1944): 90–99.
   e. In August Derleth, ed. *The Other Side of the Moon.* New York: Pellegrini & Cudahy, 1949. 79–129.
   f. In Leo Margulies and Oscar J. Friend, ed. *From Off This World.* New York: Merlin Press, 1949. 186–216.
   g. In August Derleth, ed. *The Other Side of the Moon.* [Abridged edition.] London: Grayson & Grayson, 1956. 10–51 (combined with and published as "The City of the Singing Flame").
   h. In August Derleth, ed. *The Other Side of the Moon.* [Abridged edition.] London: Mayflower, 1966. 48–80 (combined with and published as "The City of the Singing Flame").
   i. *Famous Science Fiction* 1, No. 3 (Summer 1967): 8–29.
   j. In Garyn G. Roberts, ed. *The Prentice Hall Anthology of Science Fiction and Fantasy.* Upper Saddle River, NJ: Prentice Hall, 2000. 232–56 (combined with and published as "The City of the Singing Flame").
   k. In *Collected Fantasies*, Volume 3 (A.70).
   l. In *The Return of the Sorcerer* (A.76).

Written 30 June 1931. Original title: "The Secret of the Flame." In d. the paragraphing and some of the prose has been changed by Walter Gillings. When CAS was preparing *Out of Space and Time* for Arkham House, he could find neither the *Wonder Stories* appearance nor the original typescript, so he sent tearsheets of the *Tales of Wonder* appearance instead. See Gillings to Donald S. Fryer (26 April 1964; ms, California State Library, Sacramento).

7.   "The Black Abbot of Puthuum."
   a.   *Weird Tales* 27, No. 3 (March 1936): 308–22.
   b.   In *Genius Loci* (A.11).
   c.   In *Zothique* (A.25).
   d.   In *The City of the Singing Flame* (A.40).
   e.   In *Tales of Zothique* (A.56).
   f.   In *The Emperor of Dreams* (A.59).
   g.   In *Collected Fantasies*, Volume 5 (A.70).
   h.   A.72.
   i.   In *The Ultimate Weird Tales Collection* (A.89) (as "Puthuum").
   j.   In *Clark Ashton Smith's Works* (A.90).

8.   *The Black Diamonds.*
   a.   A.60.
   b.   In *The Sword of Zagan and Other Writings* (A.64) (fragment).

   The appearance in b. represents pages from ch. 17 that were believed to have been lost and that did not appear in the first printing of A.60. The text was included in the revised edition of A.60.

9.   "The Bronze Image."
   a.   In *The Sword of Zagan and Other Writings* (A.64).
   b.   In *The Ultimate Weird Tales Collection* (A.89).

10.   "A Captivity in Serpens."
   a.   *Wonder Stories Quarterly* 2, No. 4 (Summer 1931): 534–51, 569 (as "The Amazing Planet").
   b.   *Fantastic Story Quarterly* 2, No. 1 (Winter 1951): 86–108 (as "The Amazing Planet").
   c.   In *Other Dimensions* (A.24).
   d.   In *The Red World of Polaris* (A.62).
   e.   In *Collected Fantasies*, Volume 2 (A.70).

   A sequel to "Marooned in Andromeda."

11.   "The Chain of Aforgomon."
   a.   *Weird Tales* 26, No. 6 (December 1935): 695–706.
   b.   In *Out of Space and Time* (A.9).

   c. In Donald A. Wollheim, ed. *Avon Fantasy Reader No. 12*. New York: Avon, 1950. 34–47.

   d. *Weird Tales* 47, No. 4 (Summer 1974): 46–55.

   e. In *A Rendezvous in Averoigne* (A.47).

   f. In *Collected Fantasies,* Volume 5 (A.70).

   g. In *The Return of the Sorcerer* (A.76).

   h. In *The Ultimate Weird Tales Collection* (A.89).

   i. In *Clark Ashton Smith's Works* (A.90).

Begun April 1933; completed January 1934.

12. "The Charnel God."

   a. *Weird Tales* 23, No. 3 (March 1934): 316–30.

   b. In *Genius Loci* (A.11).

   c. In *Zothique* (A.25).

   d. In *The Monster of the Prophecy* (A.42).

   e. In *A Rendezvous in Averoigne* (A.47).

   f. In Martin H. Greenberg and Charles G. Waugh, ed. *Back from the Dead*. New York: DAW, 1991. 267–91.

   g. In *Tales of Zothique* (A.56).

   h. In *Emperor of Dreams* (A.59).

   i. In *Collected Fantasies,* Volume 4 (A.70).

   j. In *The Colossus of Ylourgne* (A.79).

   k. In *The Ultimate Weird Tales Collection* (A.89).

   l. In *Clark Ashton Smith's Works* (A.90).

13. "Checkmate."

   a. In *Strange Shadows* (A.52).

   b. In *The Miscellaneous Writings of Clark Ashton Smith* (A.82).

   c. In *The Ultimate Weird Tales Collection* (A.89).

14. "Chincharrero."

   a. In *Strange Shadows* (A.52).

15. "Cigarette Characterizations."

   a. *Fantasy Magazine* 3, No. 4 (June 1934): 15–16, 32 (CAS contribution on p. 16).

   b. In *Strange Shadows* (A.52) (as "Cigarette Characterization").

16. "The City of the Singing Flame."

   a. *Wonder Stories* 3, No. 2 (July 1931): 202–13.

b. *Tales of Wonder* No. 10 (Spring 1940): 6–31 (combined with "Beyond the Singing Flame").

c. *Startling Stories* 5, No. 1 (January 1941): 98–106.

d. In *Out of Space and Time* (A.9) (combined with "Beyond the Singing Flame").

e. In August Derleth, ed. *The Other Side of the Moon.* New York: Pellegrini & Cudahy, 1949. 79–129 (combined with "Beyond the Singing Flame").

f. In Leo Margulies, ed. *From Off This World.* New York: Merlin Press, 1949. 163–85.

g. In August Derleth, ed. *The Other Side of the Moon.* [Abridged edition.] London: Grayson & Grayson, 1956. 10–51 (combined with "Beyond the Singing Flame").

h. In August Derleth, ed. *The Other Side of the Moon.* [Abridged edition.] London: Mayflower, 1966. 48–80 (combined with "Beyond the Singing Flame").

i. *Famous Science Fiction* 1, No. 1 (Winter 1966/67): 61–78 (as "The City of Singing Flame").

j. In Robert Silverberg, ed. *Lost Worlds, Unknown Horizons.* New York: Thomas Nelson, 1978. 45–65.

k. In *The City of the Singing Flame* (A.40).

l. In *A Rendezvous in Averoigne* (A.47).

m. In Garyn G. Roberts, ed. *The Prentice Hall Anthology of Science Fiction and Fantasy.* Upper Saddle River, NJ: Prentice Hall, 2003. 232–56 (combined with "Beyond the Singing Flame").

n. In *Collected Fantasies,* Volume 2 (A.70).

o. In *The Return of the Sorcerer* (A.76) (as "The City of Singing Flame").

p. A.83.

q. In *The Dark Eidolon and Other Fantasies* (A.84).

r. In *The Ultimate Weird Tales Collection* (A.89).

   Written 15 January 1931. Original title: "The Journal of Giles Angarth."

17. "The Colossus of Ylourgne."

a. *Weird Tales* 23, No. 6 (June 1934): 696–720.

b. In *Genius Loci* (A.11).

c. *Magazine of Horror* 4, No. 2 (January 1969): 80–113.

d. In Michel Parry, ed. *The Rivals of Frankenstein.* London: Corgi, 1977; New York: Barnes & Noble, 1980. 17–55.

e. In *The Last Incantation* (A.41).
f. In Isaac Asimov, Martin H. Greenberg, and Charles G. Waugh, ed. *Isaac Asimov's Magical Worlds of Fantasy #5: Giants*. New York: Signet, 1985. 312–51.
g. In *A Rendezvous in Averoigne* (A.47).
h. In *Collected Fantasies,* Volume 3 (A.70).
i. In *The Colossus of Ylourgne* (A.79).
j. In *The Averoigne Chronicles* (A.85).
k. In *The Ultimate Weird Tales Collection* (A.89).
l. In *Clark Ashton Smith's Works* (A.90).

Begun April 1932; completed 1 May 1932.

18. "The Coming of the White Worm."
a. *Stirring Science Stories* 1, No. 2 (April 1941): 105–14.
b. *Uncanny Tales* 2. No. 11 (December 1941): 10–17.
c. In *Lost Worlds* (A.10).
d. In *Hyperborea* (A.29).
e. In Terry Carr and Martin H. Greenberg, ed. *A Treasury of Modern Fantasy*. New York: Avon, 1981; New York: Galahad, 1992 (abridged; as *Masters of Fantasy*). 85–95.
f. In *The Monster of the Prophecy* (A.42).
g. In *A Rendezvous in Averoigne* (A.47).
h. In *Strange Shadows* (A.52).
i. In *The Book of Hyperborea* (A.58).
j. In *The Emperor of Dreams* (A.59).
k. In Robert M. Price, ed. *The Book of Eibon*. Oakland, CA: Chaosium, 2002. 97–114.
l. In *Collected Fantasies,* Volume 5 (A.70).
m. In *The Ultimate Weird Tales Collection* (A.89).

Written August–September 1933. A purported translation of chapter IX of *The Book of Eibon*.

19. "A Copy of Burns."
a. In *Strange Shadows* (A.52).
b. In *The Miscellaneous Writings of Clark Ashton Smith* (A.82).
c. In *The Ultimate Weird Tales Collection* (A.89).

20. "The Dark Age."
a. *Thrilling Wonder Stories* 11, No. 2 (April 1938): 95–103.
b. In *The Abominations of Yondo* (A.15).

   c. In *Collected Fantasies,* Volume 5 (A.70).
   d. In *The Ultimate Weird Tales Collection* (A.89).

   Written April 1933.

21. "The Dark Eidolon."
   a. *Weird Tales* 25, No. 1 (January 1935): 93–111.
   b. In *Out of Space and Time* (A.9).
   c. In L. Sprague de Camp, ed. *The Spell of Seven.* New York: Pyramid, 1965. 41–67.
   d. In *Zothique* (A.25).
   e. In *The City of the Singing Flame* (A.40).
   f. In *A Rendezvous in Averoigne* (A.47).
   g. In *Tales of Zothique* (A.56).
   h. In *The Emperor of Dreams* (A.59).
   i. In *Collected Fantasies,* Volume 4 (A.70).
   j. In *The Return of the Sorcerer* (A.76).
   k. In *The Colossus of Ylourgne* (A.79).
   l. In *The Dark Eidolon and Other Fantasies* (A.84).
   m. In *The Ultimate Weird Tales Collection* (A.89).

   Written November–December 1932.

22. "The Dart of Rasasfa."
   a. *Crypt of Cthulhu* No. 27 (Hallowmas 1984 [special issue: *Untold Tales*]): 5–8.
   b. In *Strange Shadows* (A.52).
   c. In *Collected Fantasies,* Volume 5 (A.70).
   d. In *The Ultimate Weird Tales Collection* (A.89).

   Written July 1961. CAS's last story.

23. "Dawn of Discord" (with E. Hoffmann Price).
   a. *Spicy Mystery Stories* 9, No. 4 (October 1940): 30–41, 106–14 (as by E. Hoffmann Price).
   b. In *The Miscellaneous Writings of Clark Ashton Smith* (A.82).

   The story (like "House of the Monoceros") was originally written by CAS and accepted by *Weird Tales* but later rejected when *Weird Tales* had a change of ownership. CAS sent the two stories to Price, and Price rewrote them and sold them to *Spicy.*

24. "The Death of Ilalotha."
   a. *Weird Tales* 30, No. 3 (September 1937): 323–30.

b.   In *Out of Space and Time* (A.9).
c.   In *Zothique* (A.25).
d.   In James Dickie, ed. *The Undead*. Jersey, UK: Neville Spearman, 1971; London: Pan, 1973; New York: Pocket, 1976. 79–91.
e.   In *A Rendezvous in Averoigne* (A.47).
f.   In *Tales of Zothique* (A.56).
g.   In *The Emperor of Dreams* (A.59).
h.   In *Collected Fantasies,* Volume 5 (A.70).
i.   In *The Ultimate Weird Tales Collection* (A.89).
j.   In [Unsigned, ed.] *Weird Tales Super Pack #2.* n.p.: Positronic Publishing, 2016. 283–91.

Written c. March 1937.

25.   "The Death of Malygris."
a.   *Weird Tales* 30, No. 3 (April 1934): 488–96.
b.   In *Lost Worlds* (A.10).
c.   In Lin Carter, ed. *The Magic of Atlantis*. New York: Lancer, 1970. 139–56.
d.   In *Poseidonis* (A.34).
e.   In *The Last Incantation* (A.41).
f.   In *A Rendezvous in Averoigne* (A.47).
g.   In *The Emperor of Dreams* (A.59).
h.   In *Collected Fantasies,* Volume 5 (A.70).
i.   In Farnsworth Wright, ed. *Weird Tales, Volume 30, Number 3 (April 1934)*. Mississauga, ON: Girasol Collectables, 2014. 488–95 (facsimile of a.).
j.   In *The Ultimate Weird Tales Collection* (A.89).

26.   "The Demon of the Flower."
a.   *Astounding Stories* 12, No. 4 (December 1933): 131–38.
b.   In *Lost Worlds* (A.10).
c.   In *Xiccarph* (A.30).
d.   In Robert Weinberg, Stefan Dziemianowicz, and Martin H. Greenberg, ed. *100 Astounding Little Alien Stories*. New York: Barnes & Noble, 1996. 99–108.
e.   In *Star Changes* (A.66).
f.   In *Collected Fantasies,* Volume 3 (A.70).
g.   In *The Ultimate Weird Tales Collection* (A.89).

Written October 1931. Elaborated from a prose poem, "The Flower-Devil" (iv.13).

27. "The Devotee of Evil."
   a. In *The Double Shadow and Other Fantasies* (A.6).
   b. *Stirring Science Stories* 1, No. 1 (February 1941): 109–17.
   c. In *The Abominations of Yondo* (A.15).
   d. In *The Last Incantation* (A.41).
   e. In *Collected Fantasies,* Volume 1 (A.70).
   f. In *Shadows Seen and Unseen* (A.71).
   g. In *The Return of the Sorcerer* (A.76).
   h. In *The Dark Eidolon and Other Fantasies* (A.84).
   i. In *The Ultimate Weird Tales Collection* (A.89).
   j. In *Clark Ashton Smith's Works* (A.90).

   Written 9 March 1930. b. and c. represent a version revised to eliminate many of CAS's stylistic signifiers.

28. "The Dimension of Chance."
   a. *Wonder Stories* 4, No. 6 (November 1932): 521–29.
   b. *Tales of Wonder and Super-Science* No. 13 (Winter 1941): 61–73.
   c. *Startling Stories* 13, No. 3 (Spring 1946): 72–83.
   d. In *Other Dimensions* (A.24).
   e. In *Collected Fantasies,* Volume 4 (A.70).
   f. In *The Ultimate Weird Tales Collection* (A.89).

   Written August 1932.

29. "The Disinterment of Venus."
   a. *Weird Tales* 24, No. 1 (July 1934): 112–17.
   b. In *Genius Loci* (A.11).
   c. In Robert Weinberg, Stefan R. Dziemianowicz, and Martin H. Greenberg, ed. *100 Wild Little Weird Tales.* New York: Barnes & Noble, 1994. 131–38.
   d. In *Collected Fantasies,* Volume 4 (A.70).
   e. In *The Return of the Sorcerer* (A.76).
   f. In *The Averoigne Chronicles* (A.85).
   g. In *The Ultimate Weird Tales Collection* (A.89).

   Written July 1932.

30. "Djinn without a Bottle."
   a. In *Strange Shadows* (A.52).

31. "The Door to Saturn."
a. *Strange Tales of Mystery and Terror* 1, No. 3 (January 1932): 390–403.
b. In *Lost Worlds* (A.10).
c. *Magazine of Horror* 1, No. 6 (November 1964): 103–21.
d. In *Hyperborea* (A.29).
e. In William H. Desmond, Diane Howard, John R. Howard, and Robert K. Weiner, ed. *Strange Tales.* Melrose Highlands, MA: Odyssey Publications, 1976. 69–82.
f. In *The City of the Singing Flame* (A.40).
g. In *The Book of Hyperborea* (A.58).
h. In *The Emperor of Dreams* (A.59).
i. In Robert M. Price, ed. *The Book of Eibon.* Oakland, CA: Chaosium, 2002. 236–54.
j. In *Collected Fantasies,* Volume 2 (A.70).
k. In *The Ultimate Weird Tales Collection* (A.89).

Written 25 July 1930.

32. "Double Cosmos."
a. *Crypt of Cthulhu* No. 17 (Michaelmas 1983): 35–41.
b. In *Strange Shadows* (A.52).
c. In *Collected Fantasies,* Volume 5 (A.70).
d. In *The Ultimate Weird Tales Collection* (A.89).

33. "The Double Shadow."
a. In *The Double Shadow and Other Fantasies* (A.6).
b. *Weird Tales* 33, No. 2 (February 1939): 47–55.
c. In *Out of Space and Time* (A.9).
d. In August Derleth, ed. *The Sleeping and the Dead: Thirty Uncanny Tales.* New York: Pellegrini & Cudahy, 1947; Toronto: George J. McLeod, 1947. 173–86.
e. In August Derleth, ed. *The Unquiet Grave.* London: New English Library, 1964. 55–68.
f. In *Poseidonis* (A.34).
g. In Isaac Asimov, Martin H. Greenberg, and Charles G. Waugh, ed. *Atlantis.* New York: Signet, 1988. 77–94.
h. In Stephen Jones and Dave Carson, ed. *H. P. Lovecraft's Book of Horror.* London: Robinson, 1993; New York: Barnes & Noble, 1998. 295–305.
i. In *The Emperor of Dreams* (A.59).

    j. In Mike Ashley, ed. *The Mammoth Book of Sorcerers' Tales.* New York: Carroll & Graf, 2004. 150–62.

    k. In *Collected Fantasies,* Volume 3 (A.70).

    l. In *The Return of the Sorcerer* (A.76).

    m. In *The Dark Eidolon and Other Fantasies* (A.84).

    n. In *The Ultimate Weird Tales Collection* (A.89).

    o. In *Clark Ashton Smith's Works* (A.90).

    p. *Exterus* 1 (2015): 111–24.

    Written 13 March 1932. CAS revised the text published in b. in order to satisfy editorial requirements. All subsequent reprints use this text except for k. and m.

34. "The Dweller in the Gulf."

    a. *Wonder Stories* 4, No. 10 (March 1933): 768–75 (as "The Dweller in Martian Depths").

    b. In *The Abominations of Yondo* (A.15).

    c. In *Xiccarph* (A.30).

    d. A.45.

    e. In *A Rendezvous in Averoigne* (A.47).

    f. In *Star Changes* (A.66).

    g. In *Collected Fantasies,* Volume 4 (A.70).

    h. In *The Klarkash-Ton Cycle* (A.74) (as "The Eidolon of the Blind").

    Written August 1932. Original title: "The Eidolon of the Blind." The editor of *Wonder Stories* required changes before accepting the story, which CAS made, but then changed CAS's ending without consulting him. CAS restored the altered ending in b., but did not eliminate the other changes that he had made. c. and e. follow b. d., f., g., and h are all based upon CAS's original submission to *Wonder Stories,* eliminating the changes required by the magazine's editors but incorporate certain alterations in word choice made in the final submitted version.

35. "The Eggs from Saturn."

    a. In *Strange Shadows* (A.52).

36. "The Emerald Eye."

    a. In *The Sword of Zagan and Other Writings* (A.64).

    Fragment.

37. "The Emir's Captive."

    a. In *The Sword of Zagan and Other Writings* (A.64).

b. In *The Ultimate Weird Tales Collection* (A.89).

38. "The Empire of the Necromancers."
   a. *Weird Tales* 20, No. 3 (September 1932): 338–44.
   b. In *Lost Worlds* (A.10).
   c. In Donald A. Wollheim, ed. *Avon Fantasy Reader No. 7.* New York: Avon, 1948. 85–93.
   d. In *Zothique* (A.25).
   e. In *The Monster of the Prophecy* (A.42).
   f. In *A Rendezvous in Averoigne* (A.47).
   g. In *Tales of Zothique* (A.56).
   h. In *The Emperor of Dreams* (A.59).
   i. In *Collected Fantasies,* Volume 3 (A.70).
   j. In *The Return of the Sorcerer* (A.76).
   k. In *The Empire of the Necromancers* (A.80).
   l. In *The Ultimate Weird Tales Collection* (A.89).
   m. In *Clark Ashton Smith's Works* (A.90).

39. "The Enchantress of Sylaire."
   a. *Weird Tales* 35, No. 10 (July 1941): 25–34.
   b. In *The Abominations of Yondo* (A.15).
   c. In Robert H. Boyer and Kenneth J. Zahorski, ed. *Dark Imaginings.* New York: Dell, 1978. 111–28.
   d. In *The City of the Singing Flame* (A.40).
   e. In *Collected Fantasies,* Volume 5 (A.70).
   f. In *The Return of the Sorcerer* (A.76).
   g. In *The Empire of the Necromancers* (A.80).
   h. In *The Averoigne Chronicles* (A.85).
   i. In *The Ultimate Weird Tales Collection* (A.89).
   j. In *Clark Ashton Smith's Works* (A.90).

40. "The End of the Story."
   a. *Weird Tales* 15, No. 5 (May 1930): 637–48.
   b. In *Out of Space and Time* (A.9).
   c. In James Dickie, ed. *The Undead.* London: Neville Spearman, 1971; London: Pan, 1973. 59–78. New York: Pocket, 1976. 59–79.
   d. In *The Last Incantation* (A.41).
   e. In *A Rendezvous in Averoigne* (A.47).

f.   In Stefan Dziemianowicz, Robert Weinberg, and Martin H. Greenberg, ed. *Girls' Night Out: Twenty-one Female Vampire Stories.* New York: Barnes & Noble, 1997. 436–52.
g.   In *Collected Fantasies,* Volume 1 (A.70).
h.   In *The Averoigne Chronicles* (A.85).
i.   In *The Ultimate Weird Tales Collection* (A.89).

Written 1 October 1929.

41.   "The Epiphany of Death."
a.   *Fantasy Fan* 1, No. 11 (July 1934): 165–68.
b.   *Weird Tales* 32, No. 3 (September 1942): 71–74 (as "Who Are the Living?").
c.   In *The Abominations of Yondo* (A.15).
d.   In *Poseidonis* (A.34).
e.   In Robert Weinberg, Stefan R. Dziemianowicz, and Martin H. Greenberg, ed. *100 Tiny Tales of Terror.* New York: Barnes & Noble, 1996. 102–5.
f.   In *Collected Fantasies,* Volume 1 (A.70).
g.   In *The Ultimate Weird Tales Collection* (A.89).
h.   In Charles D. Hornig, ed. *The Fantasy Fan: September, 1933–February, 1935.* [n.p.: Lance Thingmaker, 2010.] 165–68 (facsimile of a.).

Written 25 January 1930. Dedicated to H. P. Lovecraft.

42.   "The Eternal World."
a.   *Wonder Stories* 3, No. 10 (March 1932): 1130–37.
b.   In *Genius Loci* (A.11).
c.   In *Star Changes* (A.66).
d.   In *Collected Fantasies,* Volume 3 (A.70).
e.   In *The Ultimate Weird Tales Collection* (A.89).

Written September 1931.

43.   "Eviction by Night."
a.   In *Strange Shadows* (A.52).

44.   "The Expert Lover."
a.   In *Strange Shadows* (A.52).
b.   In *The Miscellaneous Writings of Clark Ashton Smith* (A.82).
c.   In *The Ultimate Weird Tales Collection* (A.89).

45.   "The Face by the River."
  a.   *Lost Worlds* No. 1 (2004): 3–7.
  b.   *Weird Tales* 61, No. 1 (July 2005): 52–55.
  c.   In Douglas A. Anderson, ed. *Seekers of Dream: Masterpieces of Fantasy.* Cold Spring Harbor, NY: Cold Spring Press, 2005. 146–51.
  d.   In *Collected Fantasies,* Volume 2 (A.70).
  e.   In *The Dark Eidolon and Other Fantasies* (A.84).

  Written 29 October 1930.

46.   "Fakhreddin."
  a.   In *The Sword of Zagan and Other Writings* (A.64).
  b.   In *The Ultimate Weird Tales Collection* (A.89).

47.   "The Flirt."
  a.   *Live Stories* 36, No. 1 (March 1923): 98.
  b.   In *Strange Shadows* (A.52).
  c.   In *The Miscellaneous Writings of Clark Ashton Smith* (A.82).
  d.   In *The Ultimate Weird Tales Collection* (A.89).

48.   "The Flower-Women."
  a.   *Weird Tales* 25, No. 5 (May 1935): 624–32.
  b.   In *Lost Worlds* (A.10).
  c.   In Donald A. Wollheim, ed. *Avon Fantasy Reader No. 9.* New York: Avon, 1949. 3–11.
  d.   In *Xiccarph* (A.30).
  e.   In *The City of the Singing Flame* (A.40).
  f.   In *The Emperor of Dreams* (A.59).
  g.   In *Collected Fantasies,* Volume 4 (A.70).
  h.   In *The Ultimate Weird Tales Collection* (A.89).

  Written October 1932–March 1933. Original title: "Maal Dweb and the Flower-Women."

49.   "The Fulfilled Prophecy."
  a.   In *The Sword of Zagan and Other Writings* (A.64).
  b.   In *The Ultimate Weird Tales Collection* (A.89).

50.   "The Garden of Adompha."
  a.   *Weird Tales* 31, No. 6 (June 1938): 393–400.
  b.   In *Genius Loci* (A.11).
  c.   In *Zothique* (A.25).

d   In Peter Haining, ed. *Weird Tales*. Jersey, UK: Neville Spearman, 1976. London: Xanadu Publications, 1990. New York: Carroll & Graff, 1990. 87–94 (facsimile of a.).

e. In Peter Haining, ed. *Weird Tales: Volume 1*. London: Sphere, 1978. 151–64.

f. In *The City of the Singing Flame* (A.40).

g. In *A Rendezvous in Averoigne* (A.47).

h. In *Tales of Zothique* (A.56).

i. In *The Emperor of Dreams* (A.59).

j. In *Collected Fantasies*, Volume 5 (A.70).

k. In *The Ultimate Weird Tales Collection* (A.89).

l. In *Clark Ashton Smith's Works* (A.90).

m. *Exterus* No. 5 (2017): 123–32.

Written July–August 1937.

51. "Genius Loci."

a. *Weird Tales* 21, No. 6 (June 1933): 747–58.

b. In *Genius Loci* (A.11).

c. In *The Last Incantation* (A.41).

d. In *A Rendezvous in Averoigne* (A.47).

e. In *Collected Fantasies*, Volume 4 (A.70).

f. In *Shadows Seen and Unseen* (A.71).

g. In Peter Straub, ed. *American Fantastic Tales: Terror and the Uncanny from Poe to the Pulps*. New York: Library of America, 2009. 681–97.

h. In Farnsworth Wright, ed. *Weird Tales, Volume 21, Number 6 (June 1933)*. Mississauga, ON: Girasol Collectables, 2012. 747–58 (facsimile of a.).

i. In *The Dark Eidolon and Other Fantasies* (A.84).

j. In *The Ultimate Weird Tales Collection* (A.89).

Written September 1932.

52. "The Ghost of Mohammed Din."

a. *Overland Monthly* 51, No. 5 (November 1910): 519–22.

b. In *Other Dimensions* (A.24).

c. In *The White Sybil* (A.68).

d. In *The Miscellaneous Writings of Clark Ashton Smith* (A.82).

e. In *The Ultimate Weird Tales Collection* (A.89).

f. In *Clark Ashton Smith's Works* (A.90).

53. "The Ghoul."
    a. *Fantasy Fan* 1, No. 5 (January 1934): 69–72.
    b. In *Other Dimensions* (A.24).
    c. In *The Emperor of Dreams* (A.59).
    d. In *The White Sybil* (A.68).
    e. In *Collected Fantasies,* Volume 2 (A.70).
    f. In *The Klarkash-Ton Cycle* (A.74).
    g. In *The Ultimate Weird Tales Collection* (A.89).
    h. In Charles D. Hornig, ed. *The Fantasy Fan: September, 1933–February, 1935.* [n.p.: Lance Thingmaker, 2010.] 69–72 (facsimile of a.).

    Written 12 November 1930.

54. "God of the Asteroid."
    a. *Wonder Stories* 4, No. 5 (October 1932): 435–39, 469.
    b. *Tales of Wonder* No. 11 (Summer 1940): 46–55.
    c. In August Derleth, ed. *Strange Ports of Call.* New York: Pellegrini & Cudahy, 1948. 244–58.
    d. In August Derleth, ed. *Strange Ports of Call.* [Abridged edition.] New York: Berkley, 1958. 5–20.
    e. In *Tales of Science and Sorcery* (A.22).
    f. In *The Monster of the Prophecy* (A.42).
    g. In *A Rendezvous in Averoigne* (A.47).
    h. In *Collected Fantasies,* Volume 3 (A.70).

    Written June 1932. All appearances as "Master of the Asteroid." The title change was made by Hugo Gernsback, editor of *Wonder Stories.*

55. "A Good Embalmer."
    a. In *Strange Shadows* (A.52).
    b. In *The Emperor of Dreams* (A.59).
    c. In *Collected Fantasies,* Volume 2 (A.70).
    d. In *The Ultimate Weird Tales Collection* (A.89).

56. "The Gorgon."
    a. *Weird Tales* 19, No. 4 (April 1932): 551–58.
    b. In *Lost Worlds* (A.10).
    c. In Michel Parry and Christopher Lee, ed. *Christopher Lee's X Certificate.* London: Star, 1975; London: W. H. Allen, 1976. 84–96. New York: Warner, 1976 (as *From the Archives of Evil*). 98–110.
    d. In *The Monster of the Prophecy* (A.42).
    e. In Stefan Dziemianowicz, Robert Weinberg, and Martin H.

Greenberg, ed. *100 Fiendish Little Frightmares*. New York: Barnes & Noble, 1997. 220–28.

  f. In *The Emperor of Dreams* (A.59).

  g. In *Collected Fantasies*, Volume 2 (A.70).

  h. In *The Ultimate Weird Tales Collection* (A.89).

Written 2 October 1930. Original titles: "Medusa" or "Medusa's Head."

57. "Gossip."

  a. In *Strange Shadows* (A.52).

58. "The Great God Awto."

  a. *Thrilling Wonder Stories* 15, No. 2 (February 1940): 111–14.

  b. In *Tales of Science and Sorcery* (A.22).

  c. In Robert Weinberg, Stefan Dziemianowicz, and Martin H. Greenberg, ed. *100 Astounding Little Alien Stories*. New York: Barnes & Noble, 1996. 193–99.

  d. In *Collected Fantasies*, Volume 5 (A.70).

  e. In *The Ultimate Weird Tales Collection* (A.89).

59. "The Guardian of the Temple."

  a. In *The Sword of Zagan and Other Writings* (A.64).

Fragment.

60. "The Haunted Chamber."

  a. In *The Sword of Zagan and Other Writings* (A.64).

  b. In *The Ultimate Weird Tales Collection* (A.89).

61. "The Haunted Gong."

  a. In *The Sword of Zagan and Other Writings* (A.64).

  b. In *The Ultimate Weird Tales Collection* (A.89).

62. "The Holiness of Azédarac."

  a. *Weird Tales* 22, No. 5 (November 1933): 594–607.

  b. In *Lost Worlds* (A.10).

  c. *Bizarre Fantasy Tales* 1, No. 2 (March 1971): 84–102.

  d. In *The Last Incantation* (A.41).

  e. In *A Rendezvous in Averoigne* (A.47).

  f. In *Collected Fantasies*, Volume 3 (A.70).

  g. In *The Return of the Sorcerer* (A.76).

  h. In *The Dark Eidolon and Other Fantasies* (A.84).

    i.   In *The Averoigne Chronicles* (A.85).

    j.   In *The Ultimate Weird Tales Collection* (A.89).

    Written 19 May 1931.

63.   "The House of Haon-Dor."
  a. *Crypt of Cthulhu* No. 27 (Hallowmas 1984 [special issue: *Untold Tales*]): 12–14.
  b. In *Strange Shadows* (A.52).
  c. In *The Book of Hyperborea* (A.58).

64.   "House of the Monoceros."
  a. *Spicy Mystery Stories* 10, No. 1 (February 1941): 18–29 (as "The Old Gods Eat"; as by E. Hoffmann Price).
  b. In E. Hoffmann Price. *Far Lands, Other Days.* Chapel Hill, NC: Carcosa, 1975. 463–77.
  c. In *The Miscellaneous Writings of Clark Ashton Smith* (A.82).

    See note on "Dawn of Discord."

65.   "The Hunters from Beyond."
  a. *Strange Tales of Mystery and Terror* 2, No. 3 (October 1932): 292–303.
  b. In *Lost Worlds* (A.10).
  c. In [Walter H. Gillings, ed.] *Strange Tales: First Selection.* London: Utopian Publications, 1946. 43–54.
  d. In Donald A. Wollheim, ed. *The Macabre Reader.* New York: Ace, 1959. 134–52. London: Brown, Watson (Digit Books), [1960]. 113–28.
  e. *A Book of Weird Tales* 1, No. 1 (1960): 91–103.
  f. *Magazine of Horror* 6, No. 2 (May 1970): 8–26.
  g. In *The City of the Singing Flame* (A.40).
  h. In *The Emperor of Dreams* (A.59).
  i. In *The White Sybil* (A.68).
  j. In *Collected Fantasies,* Volume 2 (A.70).
  k. In *The Klarkash-Ton Cycle* (A.74).
  l. In *The Return of the Sorcerer* (A.76).
  m. In H. P. Lovecraft [et al.]. *Lovecraft Short Stories: Anthology of Classic Tales.* London: Flame Tree Publishing, 2017. 316-25.
  n. In *The Ultimate Weird Tales Collection* (A.89).

66.   "I Am Your Shadow."
  a. *Crypt of Cthulhu* No. 29 (Candlemas 1985): 37–44.

b. In *Strange Shadows* (A.52) (included in "Strange Shadows/I Am Your Shadow").

c. In *Collected Fantasies*, Volume 5 (A.70) (as "Alternate Ending to 'I Am Your Shadow'").

67. "The Ice-Demon."
   a. *Weird Tales* 21, No. 4 (April 1933): 484–94.
   b. In *The Abominations of Yondo* (A.15).
   c. In *Hyperborea* (A.29).
   d. In *The Last Incantation* (A.41).
   e. In *The Book of Hyperborea* (A.58).
   f. In *Collected Fantasies*, Volume 4 (A.70).
   g. In *The Ultimate Weird Tales Collection* (A.89).

   Written July 1932.

68. "The Immeasurable Horror."
   a. *Weird Tales* 18, No. 2 (September 1931): 233–42.
   b. *Tales of Wonder* No. 8 (Autumn 1939): 92–101 (as "World of Horror").
   c. In Donald A. Wollheim, ed. *Avon Science-Fiction Reader No. 1*. New York: Avon, 1951. 34–44.
   d. In *Other Dimensions* (A.24).
   e. In *The Monster of the Prophecy* (A.42).
   f. In *Collected Fantasies*, Volume 1 (A.70).
   g. In *The Ultimate Weird Tales Collection* (A.89).

   Written 13 July 1930.

69. "The Immortals of Mercury."
   a. A.5.
   b. In *Tales of Science and Sorcery* (A.22).
   c. In *Star Changes* (A.66).
   d. In *Collected Fantasies*, Volume 3 (A.70).
   e. In *The Ultimate Weird Tales Collection* (A.89).

   Written December 1931–February 1932.

70. "In a Hashish-Dream."
   a. *Crypt of Cthulhu* No. 27 (Hallowmas 1984 [special issue: *Untold Tales*]): 15–16.
   b. In *Strange Shadows* (A.52).

71. "In the Book of Vergama."
    a. In *Strange Shadows* (A.52).
    b. In *Tales of Zothique* (A.56).

    A foreword to "The Last Hieroglyph."

72. "The Infernal Star."
    a. In *Strange Shadows* (A.52).
    b. In *The Klarkash-Ton Cycle* (A.74).
    c. In *The Miscellaneous Writings of Clark Ashton Smith* (A.82).

    Begun February 1933. An unfinished novel.

73. "The Invisible City."
    a. *Wonder Stories* 4, No. 1 (June 1932): 6–13.
    b. *Tales of Wonder* No. 9 (Winter 1939): 50–63.
    c. In *Other Dimensions* (A.24).
    d. In *Poseidonis* (A.34).
    e. In *Collected Fantasies*, Volume 3 (A.70).
    f. In *The Empire of the Necromancers* (A.80).
    g. In *The Ultimate Weird Tales Collection* (A.89).
    h. In *Clark Ashton Smith's Works* (A.90).

    Written December 1931–February 1932.

74. "The Isle of the Torturers."
    a. *Weird Tales* 21, No. 3 (March 1933): 362–72.
    b. In Christine Campbell Thomson, ed. *Keep On the Light!* London: Selwyn & Blount, 1933. 237–54.
    c. In *Lost Worlds* (A.10).
    d. In *Zothique* (A.25).
    e. In *A Rendezvous in Averoigne* (A.47).
    f. In Stefan R. Dziemianowicz, Robert Weinberg, and Martin H. Greenberg, ed. *Weird Tales: 32 Unearthed Terrors*. New York: Bonanza, 1988. 187–98.
    g. In *Tales of Zothique* (A.56).
    h. In *The Emperor of Dreams* (A.59).
    i. In *Collected Fantasies*, Volume 4 (A.70).
    j. In *The Return of the Sorcerer* (A.76).
    k. In Farnsworth Wright, ed. *Weird Tales, Volume 21, Number 3 (March 1933)*. Mississauga, ON: Girasol Collectables, 2014. 362–72 (facsimile of a.).
    l. In *The Ultimate Weird Tales Collection* (A.89).

Written July–August 1932.

75. "The Justice of the Elephant."
    a. *Oriental Stories* 1, No. 6 (Autumn 1931): 856, 858, 863–64.
    b. In *Other Dimensions* (A.24).
    c. In *The White Sybil* (A.68).
    d. In Farnsworth Wright, ed. *Oriental Stories, Volume 1, Number 6 (Autumn 1931)*. Mississauga, ON: Girasol Collectables, 2006. 856, 858, 863–64 (facsimile of a.).
    e. In *Collected Fantasies*, Volume 2 (A.70).
    f. In *The Ultimate Weird Tales Collection* (A.89).

76. "The Kingdom of the Worm."
    a. *Fantasy Fan* 1, No. 2 (October 1933): 17–22.
    b. In *Other Dimensions* (A.24) (as "A Tale of Sir John Maundeville").
    c. In *The White Sybil* (A.68) (as "A Tale of Sir John Maundeville").
    d. In *Collected Fantasies*, Volume 2 (A.70).
    e. In *The Ultimate Weird Tales Collection* (A.89) (as "The Tale of Sir John Maundeville").
    f. In Charles D. Hornig, ed. *The Fantasy Fan: September, 1933–February, 1935.* [n.p.: Lance Thingmaker, 2010.] 17–22 (facsimile of a.).

77. "The Kiss of Zoraida."
    a. *Magic Carpet Magazine* 3, No. 3 (July 1933): 373–76.
    b. In *Other Dimensions* (A.24).
    c. In William H. Desmond, John R. Howard, Diane M. Howard, and Robert K. Weiner, ed. *The Magic Carpet Magazine.* Newton, MA: Odyssey, 1977. 42–45.
    d. In *The Emperor of Dreams* (A.59).
    e. In *The White Sybil and Other Stories* (A.68).
    f. In Farnsworth Wright, ed. *Magic Carpet Magazine, Volume 3, Number 3 (July 1933)*. Mississauga, ON: Girasol Collectables, 2007. 373–76 (facsimile of a.).
    g. In *Collected Fantasies*, Volume 2 (A.70).
    h. In *The Ultimate Weird Tales Collection* (A.89).

78. "The Last Hieroglyph."
    a. *Weird Tales* 25, No. 4 (April 1935): 466–77.
    b. In *Out of Space and Time* (A.9).

c. In *Zothique* (A.25).
d. In *A Rendezvous in Averoigne* (A.47).
e. In *Tales of Zothique* (A.56).
f. In Mike Ashley, ed. *The Mammoth Book of Fantasy*. London: Constable & Robinson, 2001; New York: Carroll & Graf, 2001. 120–36.
g. In *Collected Fantasies,* Volume 5 (A.70).
h. In *The Ultimate Weird Tales Collection* (A.89).

Written March–May 1934. Original title: "The Last Hieroglyph; or, In the Book of Agoma"; second title: "In the Book of Vergama."

79. "The Last Incantation."
a. *Weird Tales* 15, No. 6 (June 1930): 783–86.
b. In *Lost Worlds* (A.10).
c. In *Poseidonis* (A.34).
d. In *The Last Incantation* (A.41).
e. In *A Rendezvous in Averoigne* (A.47).
f. In Robert Weinberg, Stefan R. Dziemianowicz, and Martin H. Greenberg, ed. *100 Wild Little Weird Tales*. New York: Barnes & Noble, 1994. 293–97.
g. In *The Emperor of Dreams* (A.59).
h. In *Collected Fantasies,* Volume 1 (A.70).
i. In *The Dark Eidolon and Other Fantasies* (A.84).
j. In *The Ultimate Weird Tales Collection* (A.89).

Written 23 September 1929.

80. "The Letter from Mohaun Los."
a. *Wonder Stories* 4, No. 3 (August 1932): 218–29 (as "Flight into Super-Time").
b. *Tales of Wonder* No. 16 (Spring 1942): 54–72 (as "Flight through Time").
c. In *Lost Worlds* (A.10).
d. In *Star Changes* (A.66).
e. In *Collected Fantasies,* Volume 2 (A.70).
f. In *The Ultimate Weird Tales Collection* (A.89).

81. "The Lord of Lunacy."
a. In *Strange Shadows* (A.52).

82. "The Mahout."
    a. *Black Cat* 16, No. 11 (August 1911): 25–30.
    b. *Houston Post* (11 November 1923): 31.
    c. In *Other Dimensions* (A.24).
    d. In *The White Sybil* (A.68).
    e. In *The Miscellaneous Writings of Clark Ashton Smith* (A.82).
    f. In *The Ultimate Weird Tales Collection* (A.89).

    CAS later reworked this story into "The Justice of the Elephant."

83. "The Maker of Gargoyles."
    a. *Weird Tales* 20, No. 2 (August 1932): 198–207.
    b. In *Tales of Science and Sorcery* (A.22).
    c. In *The Maker of Gargoyles* (A.67).
    d. In *Collected Fantasies,* Volume 3 (A.70).
    e. In *The Averoigne Chronicles* (A.85).
    f. In *The Ultimate Weird Tales Collection* (A.89).

    Written June–August 1931.

84. "The Malay Krise."
    a. *Overland Monthly* 51, No. 4 (October 1910): 354–55.
    b. In *Other Dimensions* (A.24).
    c. In *The Sword of Zagan and Other Writings* (A.64) (as "The Malay Creese").
    d. In *The Maker of Gargoyles and Other Stories* (A.67).
    e. In *The White Sybil* (A.68).
    f. In *The Miscellaneous Writings of Clark Ashton Smith* (A.82).
    g. In *The Ultimate Weird Tales Collection* (A.89).

    CAS's first published story.

85. "Mandor's Enemy."
    a. *Crypt of Cthulhu* No. 27 (Hallowmas 1984 [special issue: *Untold Tales*]): 24.
    b. In *Strange Shadows* (A.52).
    c. In *Tales of Zothique* (A.56).

86. "The Mandrakes."
    a. *Weird Tales* 21, No. 2 (February 1933): 254–59.
    b. In *Other Dimensions* (A.24).

   c. In Stefan Dziemianowicz, Robert Weinberg, and Martin H. Greenberg, ed. *100 Wicked Little Witch Stories.* New York: Barnes & Noble, 1995. 61–67.

   d. In *Collected Fantasies,* Volume 4 (A.70).

   e. In *The Averoigne Chronicles* (A.85).

   f. In *The Ultimate Weird Tales Collection* (A.89).

Written 15 May 1932.

87. "Marooned in Andromeda."

   a. *Wonder Stories* 2, No. 5 (October 1930): 390–401, 465.

   b. In *Other Dimensions* (A.24).

   c. In *The Red World of Polaris* (A.62).

   d. In *Collected Fantasies,* Volume 1 (A.70).

   e. In *The Ultimate Weird Tales Collection* (A.89).

Written 14 May 1930. See "The Amazing Planet."

88. "The Master of Destruction."

   a. *Crypt of Cthulhu* No. 27 (Hallowmas 1984 [special issue: *Untold Tales*]): 28–31.

   b. In *Strange Shadows* (A.52).

Fragment.

89. "The Master of the Crabs."

   a. *Weird Tales* 40, No. 3 (March 1948): 64–71.

   b. In *The Abominations of Yondo* (A.15).

   c. In L. Sprague de Camp, ed. *Warlocks and Warriors.* New York: G. P. Putnam's Sons, 1970; New York: Berkley, 1971. 206–22.

   d. In *Zothique* (A.25).

   e. In *Tales of Zothique* (A.56).

   f. In *Collected Fantasies,* Volume 5 (A.70).

   g. In *The Ultimate Weird Tales Collection* (A.89).

Written c. September–October 1947.

90. "The Maze of the Enchanter."

   a. In *The Double Shadow and Other Fantasies* (A.6).

   b. In Dudley Chadwick Gordon, Vernon Rupert King, and William Whittingham Lyman, ed. *Today's Literature.* New York: American Book Co., 1935. 222–32.

   c. *Weird Tales* 32, No. 4 (October 1938): 475–83 (as "The Maze of Maal Dweb").
   d. In *Lost Worlds* (A.10). (as "The Maze of Maal Dweb")
   e. In Lin Carter, ed. *The Young Magicians*. New York: Ballantine, 1969. 104–20. (as "The Maze of Maal Dweb")
   f. In *Xiccarph* (A.30) (as "The Maze of Maal Dweb").
   g. In *The City of the Singing Flame* (A.40). (as "The Maze of Maal Dweb")
   h. In *A Rendezvous in Averoigne* (A.47).
   i. In *Collected Fantasies,* Volume 4 (A.70).
   j. In *The Dark Eidolon and Other Fantasies* (A.84).
   k. In *The Ultimate Weird Tales Collection* (A.89).
   l. In *Clark Ashton Smith's Works* (A.90).

Written c. September 1932. Original title: "The Maze of Mool Dweb." c., d., and h. represent a simplified version that CAS prepared to satisfy editorial requirements. a. represents the preferred text and is reprinted in b., e., f., i., j., and k.

91. "The Metamorphosis of the World."
   a. *Weird Tales* 43, No. 6 (September 1951): 62–79.
   b. In August Derleth, ed. *Beachheads in Space: Stories on a Theme in Science Fiction*. New York: Pellegrini & Cudahy, 1952. 253–80. London: Weidenfeld & Nicolson, 1954. 192–224.
   c. In August Derleth, ed. *From Other Worlds*. London: Four Square, 1964. 125–58. [Abridged edition of *Beachheads in Space.*]
   d. In *Other Dimensions* (A.24).
   e. In *Collected Fantasies,* Volume 1 (A.70).
   f. In *The Ultimate Weird Tales Collection* (A.89).

Written late 1929. All appearances except e. as "The Metamorphosis of Earth."

92. "Mnemoka."
   a. *Astro-Adventures* No. 1 (January 1987): 32–38.
   b. In *Strange Shadows* (A.52).

93. "Mohammed's Tomb."
   a. Unpublished.

Variant title: "Like Mohammed's Tomb." CAS sold the only copy of the ms. to Michael DeAngelis of Brooklyn, N.Y., sometime in the early 1950s; the whereabouts of both DeAngelis and the manuscript are now unknown.

94. "The Monster of the Prophecy."
    a. *Weird Tales* 19, No. 1 (January 1932): 8–31.
    b. In *Out of Space and Time* (A.9).
    c. *Magazine of Horror* 3, No. 4 (Summer 1967): 82–117.
    d. In *Xiccarph* (A.30).
    e. In *The Monster of the Prophecy* (A.42).
    f. A.48.
    g. In *Star Changes* (A.66).
    h. In *Collected Fantasies*, Volume 1 (A.70).
    i. In *The Return of the Sorcerer* (A.76).
    j. In *The Ultimate Weird Tales Collection* (A.89).

    Written early 1930.

95. "Monsters in the Night."
    a. *Magazine of Fantasy and Science Fiction* 7, No. 4 (October 1954): 119–21.
    b. In Alden H. Norton, ed. *Hauntings and Horrors*. New York: Berkley, 1969. 127–29.
    c. In *Other Dimensions* (A.24).
    d. In Bill Pronzini, ed. *Werewolf!* New York: Arbor House, 1979. 183–86. New York: Perennial Library, 1980. 208–10.
    e. In Isaac Asimov, Terry Carr, and Martin H. Greenberg, ed. *100 Great Fantasy Short Short Stories*. Garden City, NY: Doubleday, 1984. 20–22.
    f. In *The Monster of the Prophecy* (A.42).
    g. In Stefan R. Dziemianowicz, Robert Weinberg, and Martin H. Greenberg, ed. *100 Creepy Little Creature Stories*. New York: Barnes & Noble, 1994. 321–24.
    h. A.57.
    i. In Greg Cox and T. K. F. Weisskopf, ed. *Tomorrow Bites*. Riverdale, NY: Baen, 1995. 193–96.
    j. In *Collected Fantasies*, Volume 5 (A.70).
    k. In *The Ultimate Weird Tales Collection* (A.89).

    Written 11 April 1953. All texts except c., f., j., and k. as "A Prophecy of Monsters."

96. "Morthylla."
    a. *Weird Tales* 45, No. 2 (May 1953): 41–46.

b. In *Tales of Science and Sorcery* (A.22).
c. In *Zothique* (A.25).
d. In *A Rendezvous in Averoigne* (A.47).
e. In *Tales of Zothique* (A.56).
f. In *The Emperor of Dreams* (A.59).
g. In *Collected Fantasies,* Volume 5 (A.70).
h. In *The Ultimate Weird Tales Collection* (A.89).

97. "Mother of Toads."
a. *Weird Tales* 32, No. 1 (July 1938): 86–90.
b. In *Tales of Science and Sorcery* (A.22).
c. In Leo Margulies, ed. *Worlds of Weird.* New York: Pyramid, 1965. 127–34.
d. A.45.
e. In Stefan R. Dziemianowicz, Robert Weinberg, and Martin H. Greenberg, ed. *100 Creepy Little Creature Stories.* New York: Barnes & Noble, 1994. 328–34.
f. In Scott Allie, ed. *The Dark Horse Book of Witchcraft.* Milwaukie, OR: Dark Horse Books, 2004. 23–34.
g. In Scott Allie, ed. *The Dark Horse Book of Horror.* Milwaukie, OR: Dark Horse Books, 2007. 113–51.
h. In *Collected Fantasies,* Volume 5 (A.70).
i. In *The Empire of the Necromancers* (A.80).
j. In *The Dark Eidolon and Other Fantasies* (A.84).
k. In *The Averoigne Chronicles* (A.85).
l. In *The Ultimate Weird Tales Collection* (A.89).
m. In *Clark Ashton Smith's Works* (A.90).

98. "Murder in the Fourth Dimension."
a. *Amazing Detective Tales* 1, No. 10 (October 1930): 908–37.
b. *Tales of Wonder* No. 14 (Spring 1941): 40–45.
c. In *Tales of Science and Sorcery* (A.22).
d. In Robert Weinberg, Stefan Dziemianowicz, and Martin H. Greenberg, ed. *100 Menacing Little Murder Stories.* New York: Barnes & Noble, 1998. 348–57.
e. In *Collected Fantasies,* Volume 1 (A.70).
f. In *The Ultimate Weird Tales Collection* (A.89).

Written 30 January 1930. Original title: "A Murder in the Fourth Dimension."

99.   "The Music of Death."
    a. In *Strange Shadows* (A.52).

100. "The Nameless Offspring."
    a. *Strange Tales of Mystery and Terror* 2, No. 2 (June 1932): 264–76.
    b. *Strange Tales of the Mysterious and Supernatural* No. 2 ([February 1946]): 16–27.
    c. In *The Abominations of Yondo* (A.15).
    d. *Magazine of Horror* 6, No. 3 (Summer 1970): 60–80.
    e. In *The Emperor of Dreams* (A.59).
    f. In *The Maker of Gargoyles* (A.67).
    g. In *Collected Fantasies,* Volume 3 (A.70).
    h. In *The Klarkash-Ton Cycle* (A.74).
    i. In Harry Bates, ed. *Strange Tales, Volume 2, Number 2 (July 1932).* Mississauga, ON: Girasol Collectables, 2008. 264–76 (facsimile of a.).
    k. In *The Ultimate Weird Tales Collection* (A.89).
    k. *Strange Tales #5.* Rockville, MD: Wildside Press, 2017: 264–76 (facsimile of a.).

      Written October–November 1931.

101. "Necromancy in Naat."
    a. *Weird Tales* 28, No. 1 (July 1936): 2–15.
    b. In *Lost Worlds* (A.10).
    c. In *Zothique* (A.25).
    d. In Eric Pendragon [i.e. Michel Parry], ed. *Savage Heroes.* London: Star, 1975; New York: Taplinger, 1980 (as edited by Michel Parry). 70–90.
    e. In *A Rendezvous in Averoigne* (A.47).
    f. In *Tales of Zothique* (A.56).
    g. In *The Emperor of Dreams* (A.59).
    h. *Lost Worlds* No. 4 (2006): 5–22 (with variant readings).
    i. In *Collected Fantasies,* Volume 5 (A.70).
    j. In Farnsworth Wright, ed. *Weird Tales, Volume 28, Number 1 (July 1936).* Mississauga, ON: Girasol Collectables, 2013. 2–15 (facsimile of a.).
    k. In *The Ultimate Weird Tales Collection* (A.89).

102. "The Necromantic Tale."
    a. *Weird Tales* 17, No. 1 (January 1931): 54–61.
    b. In *Other Dimensions* (A.24).

    c. In Vic Ghidalia, ed. *Wizards and Warlocks.* New York: Manor, 1972. 47–60.

    d. In *Collected Fantasies,* Volume 1 (A.70).

    e. In *The Ultimate Weird Tales Collection* (A.89).

103. "Nemesis of the Unfinished" (with Don Carter).

    a. *Crypt of Cthulhu* No. 27 (Hallowmas 1984 [special issue: *Untold Tales*]): 1–4.

    b. *Crypt of Cthulhu* No. 31 (Roodmas 1985): 31–35 (with alternate ending).

    c. In *Strange Shadows* (A.52).

    d. In *Collected Fantasies,* Volume 5 (A.70).

    e. In *The Ultimate Weird Tales Collection* (A.89).

104. "A Night in Malnéant."

    a. In *The Double Shadow and Other Fantasies* (A.6).

    b. *Weird Tales* 34, No. 3 (September 1939): 102–5.

    c. In *Out of Space and Time* (A.9).

    d. In Robert Hoskins, ed. *The Edge of Never.* Greenwich, CT: Fawcett Premier, 1973. 97–104.

    e. In *Collected Fantasies,* Volume 1 (A.70).

    f. In *The Return of the Sorcerer* (A.76).

    g. In *The Averoigne Chronicles* (A.85).

    h. In [Unsigned, ed.] *H. P. Lovecraft Selects: Classic Horror Stories.* New York: Fall River Press, 2016. 751–56.

    i. In *The Ultimate Weird Tales Collection* (A.89).

    j. In *Clark Ashton Smith's Works* (A.90).

    Written 14 October 1929. b., c., and d. represent a revised version that CAS pruned of certain atmospheric touches and exotic diction, while a., e., and g. print CAS's original, preferred text.

105. "The Ninth Skeleton."

    a. *Weird Tales* 12, No. 3 (September 1928): 363–66.

    b. In *Genius Loci* (A.11).

    c. In *The Emperor of Dreams* (A.59).

    d. In *Collected Fantasies,* Volume 1 (A.70).

    e. In *The Ultimate Weird Tales Collection* (A.89).

106. "An Offering to the Moon."

    a. *Weird Tales* 45, No. 4 (September 1953): 54–61.

    b. In *Other Dimensions* (A.24).

   c. In *Poseidonis* (A.34).
   d. In Peter Haining, ed. *The Ancient Mysteries Reader.* Garden City, NY: Doubleday, 1975; London: Gollancz, 1976. 222–31.
   e. In Peter Haining, ed. *The Ancient Mysteries Reader: Book 2.* London: Sphere, 1978. 63–74.
   f. In *Collected Fantasies,* Volume 2 (A.70).
   g. In *The Ultimate Weird Tales Collection* (A.89).

107. "The Opal of Delhi" [I].
   a. In *The Sword of Zagan and Other Writings* (A.64).

   Fragment.

108. "The Opal of Delhi" [II].
   a. In *The Sword of Zagan and Other Writings* (A.64).

   Fragment.

109. "Oriental Tales: The Yogi's Ring."
   a. In *The Sword of Zagan and Other Writings* (A.64).

   Fragment.

110. "The Parrot."
   a. In *Strange Shadows* (A.52).
   b. In *The Miscellaneous Writings of Clark Ashton Smith* (A.82).
   c. In *The Ultimate Weird Tales Collection* (A.89).

   Alternate title: "The Pawnbroker's Parrot."

111. "The Perfect Woman."
   a. In *Strange Shadows* (A.52).
   b. In *The Miscellaneous Writings of Clark Ashton Smith* (A.82).
   c. In *The Ultimate Weird Tales Collection* (A.89).

112. "The Phantoms of the Fire."
   a. *Weird Tales* 16, No. 3 (September 1930): 363–66.
   b. In *Genius Loci* (A.11).
   c. In *Collected Fantasies,* Volume 1 (A.70).
   d. In *The Ultimate Weird Tales Collection* (A.89).

   Written 7 October 1929.

113. "Phoenix."
    a. In August Derleth, ed. *Time to Come: Science-Fiction Stories of Tomorrow*. New York: Farrar, Straus & Young, 1954, pp. 285–98. New York: Tower, 1965. 209–21.
    b. In August Derleth, ed. *Time to Come: Science Fiction Stories of Tomorrow*. [Abridged edition.] New York: Berkley, 1958. 18–28.
    d. In Richard J. Hurley, ed. *Beyond Belief.* New York: Scholastic Book Services, 1966. 118–34.
    e. In *Other Dimensions* (A.24).
    g. In Isaac Asimov, Martin H. Greenberg, and Charles G. Waugh, ed. *Catastrophes!* New York: Fawcett Crest, 1981. 86–95.
    h. In *Star Changes* (A.66).
    h. In *Collected Fantasies,* Volume 5 (A.70).
    i. In *The Dark Eidolon and Other Fantasies* (A.84).
    j. In *The Ultimate Weird Tales Collection* (A.89).

114. "The Planet of the Dead."
    a. *Weird Tales* 19, No. 3 (March 1932): 364–72.
    b. In *Lost Worlds* (A.10).
    c. In Donald A. Wollheim, ed. *Avon Fantasy Reader No. 4.* New York: Avon, 1947. 101–11.
    d. In *Xiccarph* (A.30) (as "The Doom of Antarion").
    e. In *A Rendezvous in Averoigne* (A.47).
    f. In *Collected Fantasies,* Volume 1 (A.70).
    g. In *The Ultimate Weird Tales Collection* (A.89).

    Variant title: "The Doom of Antarion." Elaborated from a prose poem, "From the Crypts of Memory" (I.B.iv.16).

115. "A Platonic Entanglement."
    a. In *Strange Shadows* (A.52).
    b. In *The Miscellaneous Writings of Clark Ashton Smith* (A.82).
    c. In *The Ultimate Weird Tales Collection* (A.89).

116. "The Plutonian Drug."
    a. *Amazing Stories* 9, No. 5 (September 1934): 41–48.
    b. In *Lost Worlds* (A.10).
    c. In August Derleth, ed. *The Outer Reaches: Favorite Science Fiction Tales Chosen by Their Authors.* New York: Pellegrini & Cudahy, 1951. 240–51.
    d. In August Derleth, ed. *The Outer Reaches.* [Abridged edition.] New York: Berkley, 1958. 144–57.

   e. In August Derleth, ed. *The Time of Infinity*. London: World Distributors/Consul, 1963. 110–14. [Abridged edition of *The Outer Reaches*.]

   f. *Amazing Stories* 40, No. 4 (February 1966): 149–59.

   g. In Michel Parry, ed. *Strange Ecstasies*. St. Albans, UK: Panther, 1973. 9–22.

   h. In *The Last Incantation* (A.41).

   i. In Martin H. Greenberg, ed. *Amazing Science Fiction Anthology: The Wonder Years 1926–1935*. Lake Geneva, WI: TSR, 1987. 241–56.

   j. In *Star Changes* (A.66).

   k. In *Collected Fantasies*, Volume 3 (A.70).

   l. In *The Ultimate Weird Tales Collection* (A.89).

Written February 1932.

117. "The Point of the Jest."
   a. *Crypt of Cthulhu* No. 27 (Hallowmas 1984 [special issue: *Untold Tales*]): 20–21.

   b. In *Strange Shadows* (A.52).

118. "The Primal City."
   a. *Fantasy Fan* 2, No. 3 (November 1934): 41–45.

   b. *Comet Stories* 1, No. 1 (December 1940): 102–6.

   c. In *Genius Loci* (A.11).

   d. In *The White Sybil* (A.68).

   e. In *Collected Fantasies*, Volume 5 (A.70).

   f. In Charles D. Hornig, ed. *The Fantasy Fan: September, 1933–February, 1935*. [n.p.: Lance Thingmaker, 2010.] [Part 2,] 41–45 (facsimile of a.).

Original title: "The Cloud-Things"; second title: "The Clouds."

119. "Prince Alcouz and the Magician."
   a. In Peter Ruber, ed. *Arkham's Masters of Horror*. Sauk City, WI: Arkham House, 2000. 62–63.

   b. In *The Emperor of Dreams* (A.59).

   c. In *The Sword of Zagan and Other Writings* (A.64) (as "Prince Alcorez and the Magician").

   d. In *The Miscellaneous Writings of Clark Ashton Smith* (A.82).

   e. In *The Ultimate Weird Tales Collection* (A.89) (also as "Prince Alcorez and the Magician").

f. In *Clark Ashton Smith's Works* (A.90).

120. "The Raja and the Tiger.'"
   a. *Black Cat* 17, No. 5 (February 1912): 12–18.
   b. In *Other Dimensions* (A.24).
   c. In *The White Sybil* (A.68).
   d. In *The Miscellaneous Writings of Clark Ashton Smith* (A.82).
   e. In *The Ultimate Weird Tales Collection* (A.89).
   f. In *Clark Ashton Smith's Works* (A.90).

121. "The Red Turban."
   a. In *The Miscellaneous Writings of Clark Ashton Smith* (A.82).

122. "The Red World of Polaris."
   a. In *The Red World of Polaris* (A.62).
   b. In *Collected Fantasies,* Volume 2 (A.70).

123. "A Rendezvous in Averoigne."
   a. *Weird Tales* 17, No. 3 (April–May 1931): 364–74.
   b. *Weird Tales* 33, No. 1 (January 1939): 112–22.
   c. In *Out of Space and Time* (A.9).
   d. In Charles M. Collins, ed. *A Feast of Blood.* New York: Avon, 1967. 160–73.
   e. *Magazine of Horror* 6, No. 5 (February 1971): 74–87.
   f. *Tales of Voodoo* 4, No. 6 (November 1971): 21–28 (as "The Vampires").
   g. In Alan Ryan, ed. *Vampires.* New York: Doubleday, 1987; London: Penguin, 1988 (as *The Penguin Book of Vampire Stories*); London: Bloomsbury, 1991 (as *The Penguin Book of Vampire Stories*). 241–54.
   h. In *A Rendezvous in Averoigne* (A.47).
   i. In Chris Baldick, ed. *The Oxford Book of Gothic Tales.* London: Oxford University Press, 1992. 331–43.
   j. In Robert Weinberg, Stefan R. Dziemianowicz, and Martin H. Greenberg, ed. *Weird Vampire Tales.* New York: Gramercy, 1992. 75–86.
   k. In *The Emperor of Dreams* (A.59).
   l. In *Collected Fantasies,* Volume 2 (A.70).
   m. In *The Averoigne Chronicles* (A.85).

   Written 12 September 1930.

124. "The Resurrection of the Rattlesnake."
   a. *Weird Tales* 18, No. 3 (October 1931): 387–90.
   b. In *Other Dimensions* (A.24).
   c. In *The Maker of Gargoyles* (A.67).
   d. In *Collected Fantasies*, Volume 1 (A.70).
   e. In *The Ultimate Weird Tales Collection* (A.89).

   Written 9–10 October 1929.

125. "The Return of the Sorcerer."
   a. *Strange Tales of Mystery and Terror* 1, No. 1 (September 1931): 99–109.
   b. In *Out of Space and Time* (A.9).
   c. In August Derleth, ed. *Sleep No More! Twenty Masterpieces of Horror for the Connoisseur*. New York: Farrar & Rinehart, 1944. 73–89. New York: Editions for the Armed Services, 1944. 85–104. St. Albans, UK: Panther, 1964, 1966. 56–69.
   d. In August Derleth, ed. *Sleep No More*. [Abridged edition.] New York: Bantam, 1967. 67–76.
   e. *Startling Mystery Stories* 2, No. 2 (Spring 1968): 76–89.
   f. In August Derleth, ed. *Tales of the Cthulhu Mythos*. Sauk City, WI: Arkham House, 1969. 31–44.
   g. In August Derleth, ed. *Tales of the Cthulhu Mythos: Volume 1*. New York: Ballantine, 1971. 35–51. St. Albans, UK: Panther, 1975. 35–51.
   h. In Michel Parry, ed. *The 2nd Mayflower Book of Black Magic Stories*. London: Mayflower, 1974. 46–63.
   i. In Carol Serling, Martin H. Greenberg, and Charles G. Waugh, ed. *Rod Serling's Night Gallery Reader*. New York: Dembner, 1987. 261–78.
   j. In August Derleth, ed. *Tales of the Cthulhu Mythos*. [Rev. ed. by James Turner.] Sauk City, WI: Arkham House, 1990; New York: Del Rey, 1998. 33–47.
   k. In Robert Weinberg, Stefan R. Dziemianowicz, and Martin H. Greenberg, ed. *Rivals of Weird Tales*. New York: Bonanza, 1990. 9–21.
   l. In *The Emperor of Dreams* (A.59).
   m. In Harry Bates, ed. *Strange Tales, Volume 1, No. 1 (September 1931)*. Mississauga, ON: Girasol Collectables, 2002. 99–109 (facsimile of a.).
   n. In *Collected Fantasies*, Volume 2 (A.70).

o. In *The Klarkash-Ton Cycle* (A.74) (as "A Rendering from the Arabic").

p. In *The Return of the Sorcerer* (A.76).

q. In *The Ultimate Weird Tales Collection* (A.89).

r. In Gregory Luce, ed. *Horror Gems, Volume Thirteen.* n.p.: Armchair Books, 2017. 43–59.

Written 4 January 1931. Original title: "Helman Carnby"; later as "The Return of Helman Carnby."

126. "The Root of Ampoi."

a. *Arkham Sampler* 2, No. 2 (Spring 1949): 3–16.

b. *Fantastic Stories of Imagination* 10, No. 8 (August 1961): 31–46.

c. In *Tales of Science and Sorcery* (A.22).

d. In Peter Haining, ed. *The Freak Show.* London: Rapp & Whiting, 1970; London: Corgi, 1971. 59–72. New York: Thomas Nelson, 1972. 53–66 (as "The Ampoi Giant").

e. In *Poseidonis* (A.34).

f. In *The Last Incantation* (A.41).

g. In *The Emperor of Dreams* (A.59).

h. In *Collected Fantasies*, Volume 1 (A.70).

i. In *The Ultimate Weird Tales Collection* (A.89).

Original title: "Jim Knox and the Giantess."

127. "Sadastor."

a. *Weird Tales* 16, No. 1 (July 1930): 133–35.

b. In *Out of Space and Time* (A.9).

c. In *Poems in Prose* (A.23).

d. In *Xiccarph* (A.30).

e. A.31.

f. In Lin Carter, ed. *Kingdoms of Sorcery.* Garden City, NY: Doubleday, 1976. 115–16 (as "Fables from the Edge of Night," Part III).

g. In *Collected Fantasies*, Volume 1 (A.70).

h. In *The Ultimate Weird Tales Collection* (A.89).

i. In *Autres mondes* (II.A.iii.16).

Written 1925.

128. "The Satyr."

a. *La Paree Stories* 2, No. 5 (July 1931): 9–11, 48.

b. In *Genius Loci* (A.11).

c. In *The White Sybil* (A.68).
d. In *Collected Fantasies,* Volume 1 (A.70).
e. In *The Averoigne Chronicles* (A.85).
f. In *The Ultimate Weird Tales Collection* (A.89).

Written 31 March 1930. d. restores CAS's original ending, but also includes the published ending as an appendix.

129. "Schizoid Creator."
a. *Fantasy Fiction* 1, No. 4 (November 1953): 78–85.
b. In *Tales of Science and Sorcery* (A.22).
c. In *Collected Fantasies,* Volume 5 (A.70).
d. In *The Ultimate Weird Tales Collection* (A.89).

130. "The Second Interment."
a. *Strange Tales of Mystery and Terror* 3, No. 1 (January 1933): 8–16.
b. In *Out of Space and Time* (A.9).
c. In Vic Ghidalia, ed. *Eight Strange Tales.* Greenwich, CT: Fawcett, 1972. 83–93.
d. In *Collected Fantasies,* Volume 3 (A.70).
e. In *The Ultimate Weird Tales Collection* (A.89).

131. "The Secret of the Cairn."
a. *Wonder Stories* 4, No. 11 (April 1933): 823–29 (as "The Light from Beyond").
b. In *Lost Worlds* (A.10) (as "The Light from Beyond").
c. In *Star Changes* (A.66).
d. In *The White Sybil* (A.68) (as "The Light from Beyond").
e. In *Collected Fantasies,* Volume 4 (A.70).
f. In *The Ultimate Weird Tales Collection* (A.89) (as "The Light from Beyond").

Written October–December 1932. The title was changed by the editors of *Wonder Stories* without CAS's consultation.

132. "The Seed from the Sepulcher."
a. *Weird Tales* 22, No. 4 (October 1933): 497–505.
b. In Elinor Blaisdell, ed. *Tales of the Undead.* New York: Thomas Y. Crowell Co., 1947. 234–45.
c. In August Derleth, ed. *When Evil Wakes.* London: Souvenir Press, 1963; Toronto: Ryerson Press, 1963. 223–35. London: Corgi, 1965. 173–82. London: Sphere, 1977. 196–206.

    d. In *Tales of Science and Sorcery* (A.22).

    e. In Marvin Allen Karp, ed. *The Unhumans.* New York: Popular Library, 1965. 66–77.

    f. In Tony Goodstone, ed. *The Pulps.* New York: Bonanza, 1970; New York: Chelsea House, 1976. 196–200. [Not included in 1980 ed. (New York: Chelsea House).]

    g. In Vic Ghidalia, ed. *Gooseflesh!* New York: Berkley Medallion, 1974. 61–75.

    h. In Carlos Cassaba [i.e. Michel Parry], ed. *Roots of Evil.* London: Corgi, 1976. 13–24.

    i. In Rick Ferreira, ed. *A Chill to the Sunlight.* London: William Kimber, 1978. 33–45.

    j. In Eric Protter, ed. *A Harvest of Horrors.* New York: Vanguard Press, 1980. 61–75.

    k. In Mark Ronson, ed. *The Beaver Book of Horror Stories.* London: Hamlyn, 1981. 136–49.

    l. In Mary Danby, ed. *65 Great Spine Chillers.* London: Octopus, 1982. 563–72.

    m. In John Betancourt and Robert Weinberg, ed. *Weird Tales: Seven Decades of Terror.* New York: Barnes & Noble, 1997. 77–90.

    n. In *The Emperor of Dreams* (A.59).

    o. In Farnsworth Wright, ed. *Weird Tales, Volume 22, Number 4 (October 1933).* Mississauga, ON: Girasol Collectables, 2005. 497–505 (facsimile of a.).

    p. *Lost Sanctum* No. 2 (2006): 45–53.

    q. In *Collected Fantasies,* Volume 3 (A.70).

    r. In *The Ultimate Weird Tales Collection* (A.89).

    Written January–February 1932.

133. "Seedling of Mars."

    a. *Wonder Stories Quarterly* 3, No. 1 (Fall 1931): 110–25, 136 (as "The Planet Entity").

    b. In *Tales of Science and Sorcery* (A.22).

    c. In *The Last Incantation* (A.41).

    d. In August Derleth, ed. *New Horizons: Yesterday's Portraits of Tomorrow.* Sauk City, WI: Arkham House, 1998. 261–98 (as "The Planet Entity").

    e. In *Collected Fantasies,* Volume 3 (A.70).

    f. In *The Ultimate Weird Tales Collection* (A.89).

Based on a plot by E. M. Johnston. CAS's original title was "The Martian."

134. "The Seven Geases."
   a. *Weird Tales* 24, No. 4 (October 1934): 422–35.
   b. In *Lost Worlds* (A.10).
   c. In *Hyperborea* (A.29).
   d. In *The Monster of the Prophecy* (A.42).
   e. In *A Rendezvous in Averoigne* (A.47).
   f. In Robert M. Price, ed. *Tales of the Lovecraft Mythos*. Minneapolis, MN: Fedogan & Bremer, 1992. 28–46.
   g. In *The Book of Hyperborea* (A.58).
   h. In *The Emperor of Dreams* (A.59).
   i. In Robert M. Price, ed. *The Tsathoggua Cycle*. Oakland, CA: Chaosium, 2005. 9–32.
   j. In *Collected Fantasies*, Volume 5 (A.70).
   k. In *The Return of the Sorcerer* (A.76).
   l. In Farnsworth Wright, ed. *Weird Tales, Volume 24, Number 4 (October 1934)*. Mississauga, ON: Girasol Collectables, 2014. 422–35 (facsimile of a.).
   m. In *The Ultimate Weird Tales Collection* (A.89).

Written September–October 1933.

135. "The Shah's Messenger."
   a. In *The Sword of Zagan and Other Writings* (A.64).
   b. In *The Ultimate Weird Tales Collection* (A.89).

136. "Shapes of Adamant."
   a. *Crypt of Cthulhu* No. 27 (Hallowmas 1984 [special issue: *Untold Tales*]): 23.
   b. In *Strange Shadows* (A.52).
   c. In *Tales of Zothique* (A.56).

137. "Slaves of the Black Pillar."
   a. *Crypt of Cthulhu* No. 27 (Hallowmas 1984 [special issue: *Untold Tales*]): 17–18 (synopsis on p. 19).
   b. In *Strange Shadows* (A.52).

138. "Something New."
   a. *10 Story Book* 23, No. 9 (August 1924): 36–37.
   b. *10 Story Book* 25, No. 9 (September 1927): 40–41.

   c. In *Other Dimensions* (A.24).
   d. In *The White Sybil* (A.68).
   e. In *The Miscellaneous Writings of Clark Ashton Smith* (A.82).
   f. In *The Ultimate Weird Tales Collection* (A.89).
   g. In *Clark Ashton Smith's Works* (A.90).

139. "A Star-Change."
   a. *Wonder Stories* 4, No. 12 (May 1933): 962–69 (as "The Visitors from Mlok").
   b. *Tales of Wonder and Super-Science* No. 15 (Autumn 1941): 57–67 (as "Escape to Mlok").
   c. In *Genius Loci* (A.11).
   d. In *Star Changes* (A.66).
   e. In *Collected Fantasies,* Volume 4 (A.70).
   f. In *The Ultimate Weird Tales Collection* (A.89).

Written July 1932.

140. "Strange Shadows."
   a. *Crypt of Cthulhu* No. 25 (Michaelmas 1984): 22–31.
   b. In Arthur W. Saha, ed. *The Year's Best Fantasy Stories: 11.* New York: DAW, 1985. 161–78.
   c. In *Strange Shadows* (A.52) (as part of "Strange Shadows/I Am Your Shadow").
   d. In *Collected Fantasies,* Volume 5 (A.70).
   e. In *The Ultimate Weird Tales Collection* (A.89) (as "Strange Shadows, or I Am Your Shadow").

141. "The Supernumerary Corpse."
   a. *Weird Tales* 20, No. 5 (November 1932): 693–98.
   b. In *Other Dimensions* (A.24).
   c. In *Collected Fantasies,* Volume 3 (A.70).
   d. In Farnsworth Wright, ed. *Weird Tales, Volume 20, Number 5 (November 1932).* Mississauga, ON: Girasol Collectables, 2012. 693–98 (facsimile of a.).
   e. In *The Ultimate Weird Tales Collection* (A.89).

Written c. April 1932.

142. *The Sword of Zagan.*
   a. In *The Sword of Zagan and Other Writings* (A.64).

143. "Symposium of the Gorgon."
    a. *Fantastic Universe Science Fiction* 10, No. 4 (October 1958): 49–56.
    b. In *Tales of Science and Sorcery* (A.22).
    c. In *Poseidonis* (A.34).
    d. In *The Emperor of Dreams* (A.59).
    e. In *Collected Fantasies,* Volume 5 (A.70).
    f. In *The Ultimate Weird Tales Collection* (A.89).

144. "The Tale of Satampra Zeiros."
    a. *Weird Tales* 18, No. 4 (November 1931): 491–99.
    b. In *Lost Worlds* (A.10).
    c. In *Hyperborea* (A.29).
    d. In Lin Carter, ed. *The Spawn of Cthulhu.* New York: Ballantine, 1971. 195–209.
    e. In *The City of the Singing Flame* (A.40).
    f. In *A Rendezvous in Averoigne* (A.47).
    g. In *The Book of Hyperborea* (A.58).
    h. In *The Emperor of Dreams* (A.59).
    i. In Robert M. Price, ed. *The Tsathoggua Cycle.* Oakland, CA: Chaosium, 2005. 57–70.
    j. In *Collected Fantasies,* Volume 1 (A.70).
    k. In *The Dark Eidolon and Other Fantasies* (A.84).
    l. In *The Ultimate Weird Tales Collection* (A.89).

    Written 16 November 1929.

145. "The Testament of Athammaus."
    a. *Weird Tales* 20, No. 4 (October 1932): 509–21.
    b. In *Out of Space and Time* (A.9).
    c. In L. Sprague de Camp, ed. *Swords and Sorcery: Stories of Heroic Fantasy.* New York: Pyramid, 1963. 169–86.
    d. In *Hyperborea* (A.29).
    e. *Magazine of Horror* 6, No. 6 (April 1971): 26–43.
    f. In *The Book of Hyperborea* (A.58).
    g. In *The Emperor of Dreams* (A.59).
    h. In *The Maker of Gargoyles* (A.67).
    i. In Robert M. Price, ed. *The Tsathoggua Cycle.* Oakland, CA: Chaosium, 2005. 34–55.
    j. In *Collected Fantasies,* Volume 2 (A.70).
    k. In *The Ultimate Weird Tales Collection* (A.89).

    Written 22 February 1931.

146. "The Theft of the Thirty-nine Girdles."
   a. *Saturn Science Fiction and Fantasy* 1, No. 5 (March 1958): 52–62 (as "The Powder of Hyperborea").
   b. In *Tales of Science and Sorcery* (A.22).
   c. In *Hyperborea* (A.29).
   d. In *The City of the Singing Flame* (A.40).
   e. In *The Book of Hyperborea* (A.58).
   f. In *The Emperor of Dreams* (A.59).
   g. In Robert M. Price, ed. *The Tsathoggua Cycle*. Oakland, CA: Chaosium, 2005. 72–83.
   h. In *Collected Fantasies*, Volume 5 (A.70).
   i. In *The Ultimate Weird Tales Collection* (A.89).

   Completed in April 1957.

147. "The Third Episode of Vathek" (with William Beckford).
   a. *Leaves* No. 1 (Summer 1937): 1–24.
   b. In *The Abominations of Yondo* (A.15).
   c. In Lin Carter, ed. *New Worlds for Old*. New York: Ballantine, 1971. 3–55 (as "The Story of the Princess Zulkais and the Prince Kalilah").
   d. In *The Maker of Gargoyles* (A.67).
   e. In *Collected Fantasies*, Volume 4 (A.70).
   f. In *Clark Ashton Smith's Works* (A.90).

   Written 16 September 1932. c. incorrectly lists CAS as translator.

148. "Thirteen Phantasms."
   a. *Fantasy Magazine* 6, No. 2 (March 1936): 37–41, 68.
   b. In *Other Dimensions* (A.24).
   c. In Stefan R. Dziemianowicz, Robert Weinberg, and Martin H. Greenberg, ed. *100 Ghastly Little Ghost Stories*. New York: Barnes & Noble, 1993. 487–90.
   d. In *The Maker of Gargoyles* (A.67).
   e. In *Collected Fantasies*, Volume 1 (A.70).
   f. In *The Ultimate Weird Tales Collection* (A.89).
   g. In *Clark Ashton Smith's Works* (A.90).

   Original title: "Twenty-nine Phantasms."

149. "Told in the Desert."
    a. In August Derleth, ed. *Over the Edge: New Stories of the Macabre.* Sauk City, WI: Arkham House, 1964; London: Victor Gollancz, 1967. 88–95. London: Arrow, 1976. 78–84.
    b. In *Other Dimensions* (A.24).
    c. In Stefan Dziemianowicz, Robert Weinberg, and Martin H. Greenberg, ed. *100 Twisted Little Tales of Torment.* New York: Barnes & Noble, 1998. 542–47.
    d. In *Collected Fantasies,* Volume 2 (A.70).
    e. In *The Ultimate Weird Tales Collection* (A.89).

150. "The Tomb-Spawn."
    a. *Weird Tales* 23, No. 5 (May 1934): 634–40.
    b. In *Tales of Science and Sorcery* (A.22).
    c. In *Zothique* (A.25).
    d. In *Tales of Zothique* (A.56).
    e. In *The Emperor of Dreams* (A.59).
    f. In *Collected Fantasies,* Volume 5 (A.70).
    g. In Farnsworth Wright, ed. *Weird Tales, Volume 23, Number 5 (May 1934).* Mississauga, ON: Girasol Collectables, 2012. 634–40 (facsimile of a.).
    h. In *The Ultimate Weird Tales Collection* (A.89).

    Written c. July 1933.

151. "The Treader of the Dust."
    a. *Weird Tales* 26, No. 2 (August 1935): 241–46.
    b. In *Lost Worlds* (A.10).
    c. In Gahan Wilson, ed. *Favorite Tales of Horror.* New York: Tempo, 1976. 22–31.
    d. In *The Emperor of Dreams* (A.59).
    e. In *Collected Fantasies,* Volume 5 (A.70).
    f. In *The Klarkash-Ton Cycle* (A.74).
    g. In *The Dark Eidolon and Other Fantasies* (A.84).
    h. In *The Ultimate Weird Tales Collection* (A.89).

152. "Ubbo-Sathla."
    a. *Weird Tales* 22, No. 1 (July 1933): 112–16.
    b. In *Out of Space and Time* (A.9).
    c. In Donald A. Wollheim, ed. *Avon Fantasy Reader No. 15.* New York: Avon, 1951. 109–14.

d.   In August Derleth, ed. *Tales of the Cthulhu Mythos*. Sauk City, WI: Arkham House, 1969. 45–52.

e.   In Donald A. Wollheim and George Ernsberger, ed. *The 2nd Avon Fantasy Reader*. New York: Avon, 1969. 91–98.

f.   In *Hyperborea* (A.29).

g.   In August Derleth, ed. *Tales of the Cthulhu Mythos: Volume 1*. New York: Ballantine, 1971; St. Albans, UK: Panther, 1975. 53–61.

h.   In *The Last Incantation* (A.41).

i.   In August Derleth, ed. *Tales of the Cthulhu Mythos*. [Rev. ed. by James Turner.] Sauk City, WI: Arkham House, 1990; New York: Del Rey, 1998. 48–55.

j.   In Stefan R. Dziemianowicz, Robert Weinberg and Martin H. Greenberg, ed. *To Sleep, Perchance to Dream . . . Nightmare*. New York: Barnes & Noble, 1993. 141–47.

k.   In *The Book of Hyperborea* (A.58).

l.   In *The Emperor of Dreams* (A.59).

m. In *Collected Fantasies,* Volume 3 (A.70).

n.   In *The Klarkash-Ton Cycle* (A.74).

o.   In *The Dark Eidolon and Other Fantasies* (A.84).

p.   In Farnsworth Wright, ed. *Weird Tales, Volume 22, Number 1 (July 1933)*. Mississauga, ON: Girasol Collectables, 2014. 112–16 (facsimile of a.).

q.   In *The Ultimate Weird Tales Collection* (A.89).

Written February 1932.

153. "The Uncharted Isle."

a.   *Weird Tales* 16, No. 5 (November 1930): 605–8, 710–14.

b.   In *Out of Space and Time* (A.9).

c.   In Leo Margulies and Oscar J. Friend, ed. *My Best Science Fiction Story*. New York: Merlin Press, 1949. 403–16.

d.   In Seon Manley and Gogo Lewis, ed. *Shapes of the Supernatural*. Garden City, NY: Doubleday, 1969. 90–100.

e.   In *Poseidonis* (A.34).

f.   In *A Rendezvous in Averoigne* (A.47).

g.   In *Collected Fantasies,* Volume 1 (A.70).

h.   In *The Dark Eidolon and Other Fantasies* (A.84).

i.   In *The Ultimate Weird Tales Collection* (A.89).

Written 21 April 1930.

154. "Unquiet Boundary."
   a. *Crypt of Cthulhu* No. 27 (Hallowmas 1984 [special issue: *Untold Tales*]): 22.
   b. In *Strange Shadows* (A.52).

155. "The Vaults of Yoh-Vombis."
   a. *Weird Tales* 19, No. 5 (May 1932): 599–610.
   b. In *Out of Space and Time* (A.9).
   c. In Donald A. Wollheim, ed. *Avon Fantasy Reader No. 1.* New York: Avon, 1947. 101–14.
   d. *Startling Mystery Stories* 3, No. 5 (Fall 1970): 32–50.
   e. In *Xiccarph* (A.30).
   f. In *The Last Incantation* (A.41).
   g. A.46.
   h. In *A Rendezvous in Averoigne* (A.47).
   i. In Robert Weinberg, Stefan Dziemianowicz, and Martin H. Greenberg, ed. *Between Time and Terror.* New York: Roc, 1995. 65–80.
   j. In *Star Changes* (A.66).
   k. In *Collected Fantasies,* Volume 3 (A.70).
   l. In S. T. Joshi, ed. *American Supernatural Tales.* New York: Penguin, 2007. 153–73.
   m. In *The Klarkash-Ton Cycle* (A.74) (as "The Vaults of Abomi").
   n. In *The Return of the Sorcerer* (A.76).
   o. In *The Ultimate Weird Tales Collection* (A.89).

   Written August–September 1931. a.–f., h.–i., and o. use a revised version that CAS rewrote to meet editorial requirements; g. and j.-m. use CAS's original, preferred text.

156. "Venus and the Priest."
   a. In *Strange Shadows* (A.52).

157. "The Venus of Azombeii."
   a. *Weird Tales* 17, No. 4 (June–July 1931): 496–514.
   b. In *Other Dimensions* (A.24).
   c. In *Poseidonis* (A.34).
   d. In *Collected Fantasies,* Volume 1 (A.70).
   e. In *The Ultimate Weird Tales Collection* (A.89).

   Written 4 November 1929.

158. "A Vintage from Atlantis."
   a. *Weird Tales* 22, No. 3 (September 1933): 394–99.
   b. In *The Abominations of Yondo* (A.15).
   c. In *Poseidonis* (A.34).
   d. In Frank D. McSherry, Jr., Martin H. Greenberg, and Charles G. Waugh, ed. *Pirate Ghosts of the American Coast: Stories of Hauntings at Sea*. Little Rock, AK: August House, 1988; New York: Barnes & Noble, 2007 (as *Pirate Ghosts: Tales of Hauntings at Sea*). 158–65.
   e. In T. Liam McDonald, Stefan Dziemianowicz, and Martin H. Greenberg, ed. *Sea-Cursed*. New York: Barnes & Noble, 1994. 319–24.
   f. In *Collected Fantasies,* Volume 3 (A.70).
   g. In Farnsworth Wright, ed. *Weird Tales, Volume 22, Number 3 (September 1933)*. Mississauga, ON: Girasol Collectables, 2009. 394–99 (facsimile of a.).
   h. In *The Ultimate Weird Tales Collection* (A.89).

   Written November 1931.

159. "The Voyage of King Euvoran."
   a. In *The Double Shadow and Other Fantasies* (A.6).
   b. *Weird Tales* 39, No. 12 (September 1947): 4–13 (as "Quest of the Gazolba"; abridged).
   c. In *The Abominations of Yondo* (A.15).
   d. In *Zothique* (A.25).
   e. In *Tales of Zothique* (A.56).
   f. In *Collected Fantasies,* Volume 4 (A.70).
   g. In *The Ultimate Weird Tales Collection* (A.89) (as "Quest of the Gazolba"; also printed under proper title).
   h. In *Clark Ashton Smith's Works* (A.90).

   Written January 1933.

160. "A Voyage to Sfanomoë."
   a. *Weird Tales* 18, No. 1 (August 1931): 111–15.
   b. In *Lost Worlds* (A.10).
   c. In August Derleth, ed. *Beyond Time and Space: A Compendium of Science-Fiction through the Ages*. New York: Pellegrini & Cudahy, 1950; Toronto: George J. McLeod, 1950. 387–94.

   d. In August Derleth, ed. *Beyond Time and Space: A Compendium of Science-Fiction through the Ages.* [Abridged ed.] New York: Berkley, 1958. 96–104.
   e. In *Poseidonis* (A.34).
   f. In *The Monster of the Prophecy* (A.42).
   g. In *A Rendezvous in Averoigne* (A.47).
   h. In *Collected Fantasies,* Volume 1 (A.70).
   i. In *The Ultimate Weird Tales Collection* (A.89).

161. "Vulthoom."
   a. *Weird Tales* 26, No. 3 (September 1935): 336–52.
   b. In *Genius Loci* (A.11).
   c. In Donald A. Wollheim, ed. *Avon Science Fiction Reader No. 2.* New York: Avon, 1951. 70–88.
   d. In *Xiccarph* (A.30).
   e. In *The Monster of the Prophecy* (A.42).
   f. In *Star Changes* (A.66).
   g. In *Collected Fantasies,* Volume 4 (A.70).
   h. In *The Klarkash-Ton Cycle* (A.74).
   i. In *The Ultimate Weird Tales Collection* (A.89).

Written October 1932–February 1933.

162. "The Weaver in the Vault."
   a. *Weird Tales* 23, No. 1 (January 1934): 85–93.
   b. In *Genius Loci* (A.11).
   c. In *Zothique* (A.25).
   d. In *Tales of Zothique* (A.56).
   e. In *The Emperor of Dreams* (A.59).
   f. In *Collected Fantasies,* Volume 4 (A.70).
   g. In *The Dark Eidolon and Other Fantasies* (A.84).
   h. In *The Ultimate Weird Tales Collection* (A.89).

Written February–March 1933.

163. "The Weird of Avoosl Wuthoqquan."
   a. *Weird Tales* 19, No. 6 (June 1932): 835–40.
   b. In *Out of Space and Time* (A.9).
   c. In Boris Karloff, ed. *And the Darkness Falls.* Cleveland: World Publishing Co., 1946. 516–23.
   d. In *In Memoriam: Clark Ashton Smith* (III.D.4).
   e. In *Hyperborea* (A.29).
   f. In *The Monster of the Prophecy* (A.42).

   g. In Robert Silverberg and Martin H. Greenberg, ed. *The Fantasy Hall of Fame*. New York: Arbor House, 1983; London: Robinson, 1988, 1990 (as *The Mammoth Book of Fantasy All-Time Greats*); Brookvale, NSW: Book Co., 1997 (as *The Giant Book of Fantasy All-Time Greats*); New York: HarperPrism, 1998. 76–85.

   h. In *A Rendezvous in Averoigne* (A.47).

   i. In Marvin Kaye and Saralee Kaye, ed. *Weird Tales: The Magazine That Never Dies*. New York: Science Fiction Book Club, 1988; New York: Barnes & Noble, 1996 (as *Weird Tales*). 499–508.

   j. In *The Book of Hyperborea* (A.58).

   k. In *The Emperor of Dreams* (A.59).

   l. In *Collected Fantasies*, Volume 3 (A.70).

   m. In *The Ultimate Weird Tales Collection* (A.89).

Written November 1931.

164. "When the Earth Trembled."

   a. In *The Sword of Zagan and Other Writings* (A.64).

Fragment.

165. "The White Sybil."

   a. In *The White Sybil and Men of Avalon* (A.7).

   b. In *The Abominations of Yondo* (A.15).

   c. In *Hyperborea* (A.29).

   d. In *The City of the Singing Flame* (A.40).

   e. In *The Book of Hyperborea* (A.58).

   f. In *The White Sybil* (A.68).

   g. In *Collected Fantasies*, Volume 4 (A.70).

   h. In *The Ultimate Weird Tales Collection* (A.89).

Written July 1932. Original title: "The White Sybil of Polarion." g. prints CAS's original ending for the first time, but includes the published ending as an appendix.

166. "The Willow Landscape."

   a. *Philippine Magazine* 27, No. 12 (May 1931): 728, 752, 756.

   b. In *The Double Shadow and Other Fantasies* (A.6).

   c. *Weird Tales* 34, No. 1 (June–July 1939): 87–90.

   d. In *Genius Loci* (A.11).

   e. In *Poseidonis* (A.34).

   f. In *Collected Fantasies*, Volume 2 (A.70).

   g. In *The Ultimate Weird Tales Collection* (A.89).

h. In *Clark Ashton Smith's Works* (A.90).

Written 8 September 1930.

167. "Wingless Phoenix."
a. In *Strange Shadows* (A.52).

168. "The Witchcraft of Ulua."
a. *Weird Tales* 23, No. 2 (February 1934): 253–59.
b. In *The Abominations of Yondo* (A.15).
c. In *Zothique* (A.25).
d. In *The Monster of the Prophecy* (A.42).
e. A.51.
f. In *Tales of Zothique* (A.56).
g. In *Collected Fantasies,* Volume 5 (A.70).
h. In *The Ultimate Weird Tales Collection* (A.89).

Written August 1933.

169. "Xeethra."
a. *Weird Tales* 24, No. 6 (December 1934): 726–38.
b. In *Lost Worlds* (A.10).
c. In *Zothique* (A.25).
d. In *The Monster of the Prophecy* (A.42).
e. In *A Rendezvous in Averoigne* (A.47).
f. A.50.
g. In Tom Shippey, ed. *The Oxford Book of Fantasy Stories.* London: Oxford University Press, 1994. 88–104.
h. In *Tales of Zothique* (A.56).
i. In *The Emperor of Dreams* (A.59).
j. In *Collected Fantasies,* Volume 5 (A.70).
k. In Farnsworth Wright, ed. *Weird Tales, Volume 24, Number 6 (December 1934).* Mississauga, ON: Girasol Collectables, 2013. 726–38 (facsimile of a.).
l. In *The Dark Eidolon and Other Fantasies* (A.84).
m. In *The Ultimate Weird Tales Collection* (A.89).

Written February–March 1934. e., g., and h. represent CAS's original, preferred text.

170. [Untitled.]
a. In *The Sword of Zagan and Other Writings* (A.64).
Fragment.

Synopses

171. "The Feet of Sidaiva."
    a. *Crypt of Cthulhu* No. 27 (Hallowmas 1984 [special issue: *Untold Tales*]): 34.
    b. In *Strange Shadows* (A.52).

172. "The Ocean-World of Alioth."
    a. *Crypt of Cthulhu* No. 27 (Hallowmas 1984 [special issue: *Untold Tales*]): 32–33.
    b. In *Strange Shadows* (A.52).
    c. In *The Red World of Polaris* (A.62).

173. "Queen of the Sabbat."
    a. *Crypt of Cthulhu* No. 27 (Hallowmas 1984 [special issue: *Untold Tales*]): 36.
    b. In *Strange Shadows* (A.52).

174. "The Rebirth of the Flame."
    a. *Crypt of Cthulhu* No. 27 (Hallowmas 1984 [special issue: *Untold Tales*]): 37.
    b. In *Strange Shadows* (A.52).

175. "The Sorceress of Averoigne/The Tower of Istarelle."
    a. *Crypt of Cthulhu* No. 27 (Hallowmas 1984 [special issue: *Untold Tales*]): 34–36.
    b. In *Strange Shadows* (A.52).

176. "Vizaphmal in Ophiuchus."
    a. *Crypt of Cthulhu* No. 27 (Hallowmas 1984 [special issue: *Untold Tales*]): 33–34.
    b. In *Strange Shadows* (A.52).

177. "The Werewolf of Averoigne."
    a. *Crypt of Cthulhu* No. 27 (Hallowmas 1984 [special issue: *Untold Tales*]): 37.
    b. In *Strange Shadows* (A.52).

ii. Poetry

1. "À Mi-Chemin." [English]
    a. In *The Complete Poetry and Translations*, Volume 1 (A.73).

    14 lines. For CAS's French version, see item 2.

2. "À Mi-Chemin." [French]
    a. In *The Complete Poetry and Translations*, Volume 1 (A.73).

    14 lines. For CAS's English version, see item 1.

3. "The Abalone Song" [with others].
    a. In *The Complete Poetry and Translations*, Volume 2 (A.73).
    b. In *Anno Klarkash-Ton* (III.D.1).

    60 lines. A collective effort among CAS's colleagues, including George Sterling and others. It is not possible to identify which stanzas are by CAS.

4. "Abandoned Plum-Orchard."
    a. In *Spells and Philtres* (A.14).
    b. In *Selected Poems* (A.27).
    c. In *The Complete Poetry and Translations*, Volume 2 (A.73).

    Haiku.

5. "L'Abîme."
    a. In *The Complete Poetry and Translations*, Volume 1 (A.73).

    20 lines. In French.

6. "Absence."
    a. In *The Complete Poetry and Translations*, Volume 2 (A.73).

    8 lines. In French. Dated 28 May 1929.

7. "The Absence of the Muse."
    a. *Lyric West* 1, No. 6 (October 1921): 14.
    b. In *Ebony and Crystal* (A.3).
    c. In *Selected Poems* (A.27).
    d. *Adventure Tales* No. 3 (Summer 2006): 22.
    e. In *The Complete Poetry and Translations*, Volume 1 (A.73).
    f. In *Moonlight and Other Poems* (A.78).

Sonnet. Written before 4 June 1919. First title: "To an Absent Muse."

8. "Abstainer."
    a. In *The Complete Poetry and Translations,* Volume 2 (A.73).

    Haiku.

9. "The Abyss Triumphant."
    a. *Town Talk* No. 1041 (3 August 1912): 8.
    b. *Current Literature* 53, No. 4 (October 1912): 473.
    c. In *Ebony and Crystal* (A.3).
    d. In *Selected Poems* (A.27).
    e. In *The Last Oblivion* (A.61).
    f. In *The Complete Poetry and Translations,* Volume 1 (A.73).
    g. In *Moonlight and Other Poems* (A.78).

    16 lines.

10. "Adjuration."
    a. In *The Complete Poetry and Translations,* Volume 2 (A.73).

    16 lines.

11. "Adventure."
    a. *Auburn Journal* 24, No. 18 (14 February 1924): 6. [30 lines only.]
    b. In *Sandalwood* (A.4).
    c. In Dudley Chadwick Gordon, Vernon Rupert King, and William Whittingham Lyman, ed. *Today's Literature.* New York: American Book Co., 1935. 448–49.
    d. In *Selected Poems* (A.27).
    e. In *The Last Oblivion* (A.61).
    f. *Adventure Tales* No. 4 (Spring 2007): 21.
    g. In *The Complete Poetry and Translations,* Volume 1 (A.73).

    42 lines. Dated 21 January 1924.

12. "After Armageddon."
    a. *Recluse* (1927): 15.
    b. In *Selected Poems* (A.27).
    c. In *The Last Oblivion* (A.61).
    d. In *The Complete Poetry and Translations,* Volume 1 (A.73).

    20 lines. Dated 19 December 1926.

13.   "Afterglow."
      a.   In *The Complete Poetry and Translations*, Volume 1 (A.73).

           8 lines.

14.   "Aftermath of Mining Days."
      a.   In *Selected Poems* (A.27).
      b.   In *The Complete Poetry and Translations*, Volume 2 (A.73).

           Haiku.

15.   "Afterwards."
      a.   *Auburn Journal* 23, No. 44 (16 August 1923): 6.
      b.   In *Sandalwood* (A.4).
      c.   In *Selected Poems* (A.27).
      d.   *Strange Tales of Mystery and Terror* 4, No. 2 (2005): 26.
      e.   In *The Complete Poetry and Translations*, Volume 1 (A.73).
      f.   *Adventure Tales* No. 6 (Winter 2010): 74.

           12 lines.

16.   "Al borde del Leteo."
      a.   In *The Complete Poetry and Translations*, Volume 2 (A.73).

           8 lines. In Spanish. A fragment (not a translation of the French
           poem "Au bord du Léthé").

17.   "Alchemy." [In smoke, in tapered darkness, and in mist,]
      a.   In *The Complete Poetry and Translations*, Volume 2 (A.73).

           11 lines. Dated 12 September 1952. The last line is illegible in the ms.

18.   "Alchemy." [The rain poured down in torrents fast]
      a.   In *The Complete Poetry and Translations*, Volume 1 (A.73).

           8 lines. Juvenilia.

19.   "Alexandrines."
      a.   In *Odes and Sonnets* (A.2).
      b.   In *Ebony and Crystal* (A.3).
      c.   In *Selected Poems* (A.27).
      d.   In *The Complete Poetry and Translations*, Volume 1 (A.73).
      e.   In *Moonlight and Other Poems* (A.78).
      f.   *Adventure Tales* No. 7 (Summer 2014): 123,

           12 lines. Written May 1917. For CAS's French version, see "Al-
           exandrins" (item 20).

20. "Alexandrins."
  a. In *Selected Poems* (A.27).
  b. In *The Complete Poetry and Translations*, Volume 2 (A.73).

  12 lines. Dated 14 April 1929. A French translation of "Alexandrines" (item 19).

21. "Alien Memory."
  a. In *The Complete Poetry and Translations*, Volume 1 (A.73).

  Sonnet. Later rewritten as "Exotic Memory" (item 263).

22. "Alienage."
  a. *Auburn Journal* 23, No. 38 (5 July 1923): 6.
  b. *Wanderer* 1, No. 6 (November 1923): 4–5.
  c. In *Sandalwood* (A.4).
  d. In *Selected Poems* (A.27).
  e. In *The Last Oblivion* (A.61).
  f. In *The Complete Poetry and Translations*, Volume 1 (A.73).
  g. In *Celui qui marchait parmi les étoiles* (II.A.iii.17).

  41 lines. First title: "Iris." The first draft was written on 18 April 1923; the final draft was completed in June 1923.

23. "'All Is Dross That Is Not Helena.'"
  a. In *Selected Poems* (A.27).
  b. In *The Complete Poetry and Translations*, Volume 2 (A.73).

  Sonnet. Dated 9 February 1942.

24. "Allah."
  a. In *The Complete Poetry and Translations*, Volume 1 (A.73).

  10 lines. Juvenilia.

25. "Almost Anything."
  a. In *Spells and Philtres* (A.14).
  b. In *Selected Poems* (A.27).
  c. In *The Complete Poetry and Translations*, Volume 2 (A.73).

  27 lines. Dated 15 February 1949.

26. "Alpine Climber."
  a. In *The Complete Poetry and Translations*, Volume 2 (A.73).

  18 lines. Dated 13 January 1951.

27. "Las alquerías perdidas."
    a. In *¿Donde Duermes, Eldorado? y Otros Poemas* (A.21).
    b. In *The Complete Poetry and Translations,* Volume 2 (A.73).

       35 lines. In Spanish. Written 12 April 195[0?] (ms. mutilated). For CAS's English version, see "Lost Farmsteads" (item 465).

28. "The Altars of Sunset."
    a. In *The Complete Poetry and Translations,* Volume 1 (A.73).

       8 lines.

29. "Alternative."
    a. *Raven* 2, No. 2 (Summer 1944): 13.
    b. In *Spells and Philtres* (A.14).
    c. In *Selected Poems* (A.27).
    d. In *The Complete Poetry and Translations,* Volume 2 (A.73).

       Sonnet. Dated 5 January 1944.

30. "Amithaine."
    a. *Different* 7, No. 3 (Autumn 1951): 9.
    b. In *The Dark Chateau* (A.13).
    c. In *Poseidonis* (A.34).
    d. In *The Last Oblivion* (A.61).
    e. In *The Complete Poetry and Translations,* Volume 2 (A.73).
    f. In *The Dark Eidolon and Other Fantasies* (A.84).
    g. In *The Averoigne Chronicles* (A.85).

       30 lines. Dated 21 October 1950.

31. "Amor."
    a. *Acolyte* 2, No 2 (Spring 1944): 7.
    b. In *The Hill of Dionysus* (A.18).
    c. In *Selected Poems* (A.27).
    d. *Nyctalops* No. 7 (August 1972): 83.
    e. In *The Complete Poetry and Translations,* Volume 2 (A.73).

       Sonnet. Dated 25 February 1943.

32. "Amor Aeternalis."
    a. In August Derleth, ed. *Fire and Sleet and Candlelight.* Sauk City, WI: Arkham House, 1961. 186.
    b. In *Selected Poems* (A.27).
    c. In *The Complete Poetry and Translations,* Volume 1 (A.73).

Sonnet. Dated 1 January 1920. First title: "To Love."

33. "Amor Autumnalis."
 a. In *The Fugitive Poems of Clark Ashton Smith: Second Series* (A.38).
 b. In *The Complete Poetry and Translations*, Volume 2 (A.73).

 17 lines. Dated 28 December 1927.

34. "Amor Hesternalis."
 a. *Wings* 5, No. 7 (Autumn 1942): 17.
 b. In *The Hill of Dionysus* (A.18).
 c. In *Selected Poems* (A.27).
 d. In *The Complete Poetry and Translations*, Volume 2 (A.73).

 30 lines. Dated 5 January 1942.

35. "Amour bizarre."
 a. In *The Complete Poetry and Translations*, Volume 2 (A.73).

 20 lines. In French.

36. "L'Amour suprême." [English]
 a. In *Grotesques and Fantastiques* (A.32).
 b. In Jonathan Bacon and Steve Troyanovich, ed. *Omniumgathum: An Anthology of Verse by Top Authors in the Field of Fantasy.* Lamoni, IA: Stygian Isle Press, 1976. 51.
 c. In *The Complete Poetry and Translations*, Volume 2 (A.73).

 Sonnet. Dated 25 March 1929. For CAS's French version of the same title, see item 37.

37. "L'Amour suprême." [French]
 a. In *The Complete Poetry and Translations*, Volume 2 (A.73).

 Sonnet. For CAS's English version, see item 36.

38. "The Ancient Quest."
 a. In *The Fugitive Poems of Clark Ashton Smith: Second Series* (A.38).
 b. In *The Last Oblivion* (A.61).
 c. In *The Complete Poetry and Translations*, Volume 1 (A.73).

 20 lines.

39. "Anodyne of Autumn."
 a. In *Selected Poems* (A.27).
 b. In *The Complete Poetry and Translations*, Volume 2 (A.73).

24 lines. Dated 18 October 1942.

40. "Añoranza."
   a. In *The Complete Poetry and Translations,* Volume 2 (A.73).

      24 lines. In Spanish. For CAS's English version, see "Melancholia" (item 494).

41. "Answer."
   a. In *The Complete Poetry and Translations,* Volume 2 (A.73).

      25 lines.

42. "Antepast."
   a. In *Ebony and Crystal* (A.3) (as "Anticipation").
   b. In *Selected Poems* (A.27).
   c. In *The Last Oblivion* (A.61).
   d. In *The Complete Poetry and Translations,* Volume 1 (A.73).
   e. In *Moonlight and Other Poems* (A.78).

      8 lines.

43. "Anteros."
   a. In *Spells and Philtres* (A.14).
   b. In *Selected Poems* (A.27).
   c. In *Shadows Seen and Unseen* (A.71).
   d. In *The Complete Poetry and Translations,* Volume 2 (A.73).

      18 lines.

44. "Antony to Cleopatra."
   a. In *The Complete Poetry and Translations,* Volume 1 (A.73).

      29 lines.

45. "Apologia."
   a. *Auburn Journal* 25, No. 1 (16 October 1924): 6.
   b. *Step Ladder* 10, No. 3 (February 1925): 49.
   c. *United Amateur* 24, No. 1 (July 1925): [1].
   d. In *Sandalwood* (A.4).
   e. In *Selected Poems* (A.27).
   f. In *The Complete Poetry and Translations,* Volume 1 (A.73).

      24 lines.

46. "Apostrophe."
 a. In *Selected Poems* (A.27).
 b. In *The Complete Poetry and Translations*, Volume 1 (A.73).

   6 lines. First title: "Sempiternal"; one ms. Titled "Bâillement."
   Dated 20 January 1926.

47. "Arab Song."
 a. In *The Complete Poetry and Translations*, Volume 1 (A.73).

   10 lines. Juvenilia.

48. "Arabesque."
 a. In *Ebony and Crystal* (A.3).
 b. In *Selected Poems* (A.27).
 c. In *One Hundred Years of Klarkash-Ton* (III.D.10).
 d. In *The Complete Poetry and Translations*, Volume 1 (A.73).
 e. In *Moonlight and Other Poems* (A.78).

   12 lines. Written before 15 June 1916. CAS said *Art World* pur-
   chased the poem, but it did not appear there.

49. "Arabian Love-Song."
 a. In *The Complete Poetry and Translations*, Volume 1 (A.73).

   54 lines. Juvenilia.

50. "Artemis."
 a. In *Ebony and Crystal* (A.3).
 b. In *Selected Poems* (A.27).
 c. In *The Complete Poetry and Translations*, Volume 1 (A.73).
 d. In *Moonlight and Other Poems* (A.78).

   16 lines. Dated 16 May 1922.

51. "Ashes of Sunset."
 a. In *Ebony and Crystal* (A.3).
 b. In *Selected Poems* (A.27).
 c. In *The Complete Poetry and Translations*, Volume 1 (A.73).
 d. In *Moonlight and Other Poems* (A.78).

   8 lines.

52. "Asia."
 a. In *The Complete Poetry and Translations*, Volume 1 (A.73).

   14 lines. Juvenilia.

53. "Aspect of Iron."
   a. In *The Complete Poetry and Translations*, Volume 1 (A.73).
   12 lines.

54. "At Midnight."
   a. In *The Complete Poetry and Translations*, Volume 1 (A.73).
   13 lines.

55. "At Nadir."
   a. In *The Complete Poetry and Translations*, Volume 1 (A.73).
   8 lines.

56. "At Sunrise."
   a. In *Ebony and Crystal* (A.3).
   b. In *Selected Poems* (A.27).
   c. In *The Complete Poetry and Translations*, Volume 1 (A.73).
   d. In *Moonlight and Other Poems* (A.78).
   12 lines.

57. "Atlantis."
   a. In *The Star-Treader and Other Poems* (A.1).
   b. *California News* 1 (January 1913): 1.
   c. *Tesseract* 2, No. 5 (May 1937): 9.
   d. *Tesseract Annual* 1, No. 1 (1939): 11.
   e. In *Selected Poems* (A.27).
   f. In *The Last Oblivion* (A.61).
   g. In *The Complete Poetry and Translations*, Volume 1 (A.73).
   h. In *Moonlight and Other Poems* (A.78).
   i. In *Mondes premiers* (II.A.iii.15).
   j. In *Celui qui marchait parmi les étoiles* (II.A.iii.17).
   k. In *Atlantide e i mondi perduti* (II.A.vi.13).
   Sonnet.

58. "Au bord du Léthé."
   a. In *Selected Poems* (A.27).
   b. In *The Complete Poetry and Translations*, Volume 2 (A.73).
   16 lines. In French. Dated 7 January 1927.

59. "Aurungzeb's Mosque."
   a. In *The Complete Poetry and Translations*, Volume 1 (A.73).

15 lines. Juvenilia.

60. "Autumn Dew."
    a. In *The Complete Poetry and Translations*, Volume 1 (A.73).
    4 lines.

61. "The Autumn Lake."
    a. In *Selected Poems* (A.27).
    b. In *The Complete Poetry and Translations*, Volume 2 (A.73).
    8 lines. Dated 29 October 1928. See CAS's French translation, "Le Lac d'automne" (item 436).

62. "Autumn Orchards." [Templed beneath unmoving skies,]
    a. In *The Complete Poetry and Translations*, Volume 1 (A.73).
    8 lines.

63. "Autumn Orchards." [Walled with far azures of the wintering year,]
    a. *Auburn Journal* 24, No. 5 (15 November 1923): 6.
    b. *Buccaneer* 1, No. 2 (October 1924): 3.
    c. In *Sandalwood* (A.4).
    d. In Henry Meade Bland, ed. *A Day in the Hills*. San Francisco: Taylor & Taylor, 1926. 69.
    e. In Edwin Markham, ed. *Songs and Stories*. Los Angeles: Powell Publishing Company, 1931; Freeport, NY: Books for Libraries Press, 1974. 424–25.
    f. In [Helen Hoyt, ed.] *California Poets: An Anthology of 224 Contemporaries*. New York: Henry Harrison, 1932. 665–66.
    g. In *Selected Poems* (A.27).
    h. In *The Complete Poetry and Translations*, Volume 1 (A.73).
    16 lines. Dated 5 November 1923.

64. "Autumnal."
    a. In *Ebony and Crystal* (A.3).
    b. In *The Complete Poetry and Translations*, Volume 1 (A.73).
    c. In *Moonlight and Other Poems* (A.78).
    12 lines. Written before 23 July 1917.

65. "Autumn's Pall."
    a. In *The Complete Poetry and Translations*, Volume 1 (A.73).
    b. In *Moonlight and Other Poems* (A.78).

8 lines. First title: "The Wizardry of Winter."

66. "Ave atque Vale."
    a. In *Odes and Sonnets* (A.2).
    b. In *Ebony and Crystal* (A.3).
    c. *Step Ladder* 13, No. 5 (May 1927): 136.
    d. In *Selected Poems* (A.27).
    e. In *The Complete Poetry and Translations*, Volume 1 (A.73).
    f. In *Moonlight and Other Poems* (A.78).

    Sonnet. Written before 29 April 1917.

67. "Averoigne."
    a. *Challenge* 1, No. 4 (Spring 1951): 6.
    b. In *The Dark Chateau* (A.13).
    c. In *The Last Oblivion* (A.61).
    d. In *The Sword of Zagan and Other Writings* (A.64).
    e. In *Shadows Seen and Unseen* (A.71).
    f. In *The Complete Poetry and Translations*, Volume 2 (A.73).
    g. In *The Averoigne Chronicles* (A.85).
    h. In *Mondes derniers* (II.A.iii.14).
    i. In *Atlantide e i mondi perduti* (II.A.vi.13).

    36 lines. The appearance in A.64 is an early draft.

68. "Averted Malefice."
    a. In *The Star-Treader and Other Poems* (A.1).
    b. In *Selected Poems* (A.27).
    c. In *The Last Oblivion* (A.61).
    d. In *The Complete Poetry and Translations*, Volume 1 (A.73).
    e. In *Moonlight and Other Poems* (A.78).
    f. In *The Dark Eidolon and Other Fantasies* (A.84).

    Sonnet.

69. "Avowal."
    a. *Arkham Sampler* 2, No. 1 (Winter 1949): 31.
    b. In *Selected Poems* (A.27).
    c. In *The Complete Poetry and Translations*, Volume 2 (A.73).

    Sonnet. Written 15 October 1948.

70. "Bacchante."
    a. *Weird Tales* 34, No. 6 (December 1939): 84.

b. In *The Hill of Dionysus* (A.18).

c. In *Selected Poems* (A.27).

d. In *The Last Oblivion* (A.61).

e. In *The Complete Poetry and Translations,* Volume 2 (A.73).

f. In *The Song of the Necromancer and Others* (A.81).

35 lines. Written before 29 April 1939.

71. "Bacchants and Bacchante."

a. In *The Complete Poetry and Translations,* Volume 2 (A.73).

Haiku.

72. "Bacchic Orgy."

a. In *The Complete Poetry and Translations,* Volume 2 (A.73).

Haiku.

73. "The Balance."

a. In *The Star-Treader and Other Poems* (A.1).

b. In *Selected Poems* (A.27).

c. In *The Complete Poetry and Translations,* Volume 1 (A.73).

d. In *Moonlight and Other Poems* (A.78).

Sonnet.

74. "Ballad of a Lost Soul."

a. In *The Complete Poetry and Translations,* Volume 2 (A.73).

39 lines. A fragment.

75. "The Barrier."

a. *Auburn Journal* 23, No. 48 (13 September 1923): 6.

b. In *Sandalwood* (A.4).

c. *Step Ladder* 13, No. 5 (May 1927): 130.

d. In *Selected Poems* (A.27).

e. In *In Memoriam: Clark Ashton Smith* (III.D.4).

f. In *The Complete Poetry and Translations,* Volume 1 (A.73).

20 lines. Dated 22 August 1923. First title: "Fear."

76. "Basin in Boulder."

a. In *Selected Poems* (A.27).

b. In *The Complete Poetry and Translations,* Volume 2 (A.73).

Haiku.

77. "Beauty."
    a. In *The Complete Poetry and Translations*, Volume 2 (A.73).

       4 lines. For CAS's Spanish version, see "La Hermosura" (item 363).

78. "Beauty Implacable."
    a. *Auburn Journal* 1, No. 141 (23 December 1914): 1.
    b. In *Ebony and Crystal* (A.3).
    c. *Step Ladder* 13, No. 5 (May 1927): 136.
    d. In *Selected Poems* (A.27).
    e. In *The Fugitive Poems of Clark Ashton Smith: Second Series* (A.38) (as "The Unmerciful Mistress").
    f. In *The Complete Poetry and Translations*, Volume 1 (A.73).
    g. In *Moonlight and Other Poems* (A.78).

       Sonnet. First title: "The Unmerciful Mistress."

79. "Bed of Mint."
    a. In *Selected Poems* (A.27).
    b. In *The Complete Poetry and Translations*, Volume 2 (A.73).

       Haiku.

80. "Bedouin Song."
    a. In *The Sword of Zagan and Other Writings* (A.64).
    b. In *The Complete Poetry and Translations*, Volume 1 (A.73).

       24 lines. Juvenilia.

81. "Before Dawn."
    a. *Carmel Pine Cone* 42, No. 9 (1 March 1956): 6.
    b. In *The Hill of Dionysus* (A.18).
    c. In *Selected Poems* (A.27).
    d. In *The Complete Poetry and Translations*, Volume 2 (A.73).

       16 lines. Dated 7 November 1942. First title: "Now, Ere the Morning Break."

82. "Before Sunrise."
    a. In *The Complete Poetry and Translations*, Volume 1 (A.73).
    b. In *Moonlight and Other Poems* (A.78).

       16 lines. Written 1910.

83. "Belated Love."
    a. In *Odes and Sonnets* (A.2).
    b. In *Ebony and Crystal* (A.3).
    c. *Step Ladder* 13, No. 5 (May 1927): 132.
    d. In *Selected Poems* (A.27).
    e. In *The Complete Poetry and Translations*, Volume 1 (A.73).
    f. In *Moonlight and Other Poems* (A.78).

    Sonnet. CAS first sent the sonnet to George Sterling on 15 June 1916.

84. "Benares."
    a. In *The Sword of Zagan and Other Writings* (A.64).
    b. In *The Complete Poetry and Translations*, Volume 1 (A.73).

    44 lines. Juvenilia.

85. "Berries of the Deadly Nightshade."
    a. In *Selected Poems* (A.27).
    b. In *The Complete Poetry and Translations*, Volume 2 (A.73).

    Haiku.

86. "The Besieging Billows."
    a. In *The Complete Poetry and Translations*, Volume 1 (A.73).

    12 lines.

87. "Beyond the Door."
    a. In *The Fugitive Poems of Clark Ashton Smith: Second Series* (A.38).
    b. In *The Complete Poetry and Translations*, Volume 1 (A.73).

    Sonnet.

88. "Beyond the Great Wall."
    a. In *Ebony and Crystal* (A.3).
    b. *Asia* 24, No. 5 (May 1924): 359.
    c. *Greensboro* [NC] *Record* (22 June 1924): 20.
    d. In *Selected Poems* (A.27).
    e. In *The Last Oblivion* (A.61).
    f. In *The Complete Poetry and Translations*, Volume 1 (A.73).
    g. In *Celui qui marchait parmi les étoiles* (II.A.iii.17).

    20 lines. Dated 21 December 1919.

89. "Bird of Long Ago."
    a. In *Selected Poems* (A.27).
    b. In *The Complete Poetry and Translations*, Volume 2 (A.73).
       5 lines.

90. "Black Enchantment."
    a. In *The Complete Poetry and Translations*, Volume 1 (A.73).
       26 lines.

91. "The Blindness of Orion."
    a. *Arkham Sampler* 1, No. 2 (Spring 1948): 20.
    b. In *Spells and Philtres* (A.14).
    c. In *Selected Poems* (A.27).
    d. In *The Complete Poetry and Translations*, Volume 1 (A.73).
       35 lines.

92. "Bond."
    a. In *The Hill of Dionysus* (A.18).
    b. In *Selected Poems* (A.27).
    c. 'n *The Complete Poetry and Translations*, Volume 2 (A.73).
       19 lines. Dated 17 March 1941.

93. "The Book of Years."
    a. In *The Complete Poetry and Translations*, Volume 1 (A.73).
       8 lines. Juvenilia.

94. "Borderland."
    a. In *Selected Poems* (A.27).
    b. In *The Complete Poetry and Translations*, Volume 2 (A.73).
       Haiku.

95. "Boys Rob a Yellow-Hammer's Nest."
    a. In *Selected Poems* (A.27).
    b. In *The Complete Poetry and Translations*, Volume 2 (A.73).
       Haiku.

96. "Boys Telling Bawdy Tales."
    a. In *Selected Poems* (A.27).
    b. In *The Complete Poetry and Translations*, Volume 2 (A.73).
       Haiku.

97. "Braggart."
    a. In *The Complete Poetry and Translations*, Volume 2 (A.73).
    Haiku. [First line only is extant.]

98. "Broceliande."
    a. In *The Complete Poetry and Translations*, Volume 2 (A.73).
    14 lines. A fragment.

99. "The Brook."
    a. In *The Complete Poetry and Translations*, Volume 2 (A.73).
    27 lines. A fragment.

100. "Brumal."
    a. *Auburn Journal* 24, No. 3 (1 November 1923): 6.
    b. In *The Complete Poetry and Translations*, Volume 1 (A.73).
    12 lines. Variant title: "Winter Song."

101. "Builder of Deserted Hearth."
    a. In *Selected Poems* (A.27).
    b. In *The Complete Poetry and Translations*, Volume 2 (A.73).
    Haiku.

102. "The Burden of the Suns."
    a. In *The Fugitive Poems of Clark Ashton Smith: Second Series* (A.38).
    b. In *The Complete Poetry and Translations*, Volume 1 (A.73).
    Sonnet.

103. "The Burning Ghauts."
    a. In *The Complete Poetry and Translations*, Volume 1 (A.73).
    16 lines. Juvenilia. A fragment.

104. "The Burning-Ghauts at Benares."
    a. In *The Fugitive Poems of Clark Ashton Smith: Second Series* (A.38).
    b. In *The Complete Poetry and Translations*, Volume 1 (A.73).
    12 lines. Juvenilia.

105. "But Grant, O Venus."
    a. In *Selected Poems* (A.27).
    b. In *The Complete Poetry and Translations*, Volume 2 (A.73).

Sonnet. Dated 20 February 1941. First title: "Sonnet."

106. "The Butterfly."
    a. In *The Star-Treader and Other Poems* (A.1).
    b. In *Selected Poems* (A.27).
    c. In *The Complete Poetry and Translations*, Volume 1 (A.73).
    d. In *Moonlight and Other Poems* (A.78).

    80 lines.

107. "By the River."
    a. *Auburn Journal* 23, No. 49 (20 September 1923): 6.
    b. *Fresno Bee* (17 November 1923): 13.
    c. In *Selected Poems* (A.27) (as a translation from "Christophe des Laurières").
    d. In *The Complete Poetry and Translations*, Volume 1 (A.73).

    15 lines. Dated 9 March 1923.

108. "Bygone Interlude."
    a. In *The Complete Poetry and Translations*, Volume 2 (A.73).

    Haiku.

109. "Calendar."
    a. *Troubadour* 2, No. 6 (February 1930): 11.
    b. In *Selected Poems* (A.27).
    c. In *The Complete Poetry and Translations*, Volume 2 (A.73).

    24 lines. Dated 2 February 1929.

110. "Calenture."
    a. *Arkham Sampler* 2, No. 4 (Autumn 1949): 17–18.
    b. In *The Dark Chateau* (A.13).
    c. In *Selected Poems* (A.27).
    d. In *The Complete Poetry and Translations*, Volume 2 (A.73).

    50 lines. Written 1947.

111. "Californian Winter."
    a. In *The Complete Poetry and Translations*, Volume 2 (A.73).

    Haiku. First version of "January Willow" (item 428).

112. "The Call of the Wind."
    a. In *In the Ultimate Valleys* (A.26).

b. In *The Complete Poetry and Translations,* Volume 1 (A.73).

10 lines. Written 1910.

113. "Cambion."
   a. In *The Dark Chateau* (A.13).
   b. In *Selected Poems* (A.27).
   c. In *The Last Oblivion* (A.61).
   d. In *The Complete Poetry and Translations,* Volume 2 (A.73).
   e. In *The Averoigne Chronicles* (A.85).

   24 lines. Dated 5 December 1943. First title: "The Unnamed."

114. "Cantar."
   a. In *Shadows Seen and Unseen* (A.71).
   b. In *The Complete Poetry and Translations,* Volume 2 (A.73).

   16 lines. In Spanish. For CAS's English version, see "Song" (item 786).

115. "El cantar de los seres libres."
   a. In *¿Donde Duermes, Eldorado? y Otros Poemas* (A.21).
   b. In *The Complete Poetry and Translations,* Volume 2 (A.73).

   12 lines. For CAS's English version, see "Song of the Free Beings" (item 796).

116. "Canticle."
   a. *Troubadour* 3, No. 8 (July 1931): 26.
   b. In *Selected Poems* (A.27).
   c. In *The Last Oblivion* (A.61).
   d. In *The Complete Poetry and Translations,* Volume 2 (A.73).
   e. In *The Averoigne Chronicles* (A.85).
   f. In *Celui qui marchait parmi les étoiles* (II.A.iii.17).

   24 lines. Dated 22 May 1927.

117. "The Canyon."
   a. *Rosary Magazine* 40, No. 2 (February 1912): 204.
   b. In *The Complete Poetry and Translations,* Volume 1 (A.73.b).

   4 lines.

118. "The Castle of Dreams."
   a. In *The Fugitive Poems of Clark Ashton Smith: Second Series* (A.38).
   b. In *The Last Oblivion* (A.61).

  c. In *The Complete Poetry and Translations*, Volume 1 (A.73).

   21 lines.

119. "A Catch."
  a. *Auburn Journal* 24, No. 51 (2 October 1924): 6 (as "Song").
  b. In *Sandalwood* (A.4).
  c. In *Selected Poems* (A.27).
  d. In *The Complete Poetry and Translations*, Volume 1 (A.73).

   8 lines. Dated 12 September 1924.

120. "Cats in Winter Sunlight."
  a. In *Spells and Philtres* (A.14).
  b. In *Selected Poems* (A.27).
  c. In *The Complete Poetry and Translations*, Volume 2 (A.73).

   Haiku.

121. "Cattle Salute the Psychopomp."
  a. In *Selected Poems* (A.27).
  b. In *In Memoriam: Clark Ashton Smith* (III.D.4).
  c. In *The Complete Poetry and Translations*, Volume 2 (A.73).

   Haiku.

122. "Le Cauchemar."
  a. In *The Complete Poetry and Translations*, Volume 2 (A.73).

   8 lines. In French.

123. "The Centaur."
  a. In *Spells and Philtres* (A.14).
  b. In *The Black Book of Clark Ashton Smith* (A.39).
  c. In *Freedom of Fantastic Things* (III.D.5).
  d. In *The Complete Poetry and Translations*, Volume 2 (A.73).

   18 lines.

124. "Chainless Captive."
  a. In *Selected Poems* (A.27).
  b. In *The Complete Poetry and Translations*, Volume 2 (A.73).

   Haiku.

125. "Chance."
  a. *Auburn Journal* 23, No. 35 (14 June 1923): 6.

b. *Bloodstone* 1, No. 2 (November 1937): [4].
c. In *Selected Poems* (A.27).
d. In *The Last Oblivion* (A.61).
e. In *The Complete Poetry and Translations,* Volume 1 (A.73).
f. In *Celui qui marchait parmi les étoiles* (II.A.iii.17).

Sonnet. Dated 19 May 1922.

126. "Change."
a. *Auburn Journal* 23, No. 39 (12 July 1923): 6.
b. In *Selected Poems* (A.27).
c. In *The Complete Poetry and Translations,* Volume 1 (A.73).

20 lines. Dated 7 March 1923.

127. "Chanson de Novembre." [English]
a. In *The Complete Poetry and Translations,* Volume 2 (A.73).

12 lines. Dated 16 November 1928. The original title was "Chant de Novembre." For CAS's French version, see item 127.

128. "Chanson de Novembre." [French]
a. In *The Complete Poetry and Translations,* Volume 2 (A.73).

12 lines. For CAS's English version, see item 126.

129. "Chanson de rêve."
a. In *The Complete Poetry and Translations,* Volume 1 (A.73).

18 lines. In French.

130. "Chansonette." [English]
a. In *Selected Poems* (A.27) (as a translation from "Christophe des Laurières").
b. In *The Complete Poetry and Translations,* Volume 2 (A.73).

18 lines. For CAS's French version, see item 132.

131. "Chansonette." [French: Mon amour, la chair des roses]
a. In *The Complete Poetry and Translations,* Volume 1 (A.73).

25 lines. In French.

132. "Chansonette." [French: Mon coeur n'a trouvé point de valeur, par delà]
a. In *The Complete Poetry and Translations,* Volume 2 (A.73).

18 lines. Written 1928? For CAS's English version, see item 130.

133. "Chant of Autumn."
    a. *Lyric West* 2, No. 6 (October 1922): 3.
    b. In *Ebony and Crystal* (A.3).
    c. In *Selected Poems* (A.27).
    d. In *The Complete Poetry and Translations*, Volume 1 (A.73).
    e. In *Moonlight and Other Poems* (A.78).

    24 lines.

134. "Chant to Sirius."
    a. In *The Star-Treader and Other Poems* (A.1).
    b. In *Nero and Other Poems* (A.8).
    c. In *Selected Poems* (A.27).
    d. In *The Complete Poetry and Translations*, Volume 1 (A.73).
    e. In *Moonlight and Other Poems* (A.78).

    27 lines. The ms. is dated 12 July 1911.

135. "The Cherry-Snows."
    a. In *The Star-Treader and Other Poems* (A.1).
    b. In LeRoy E. Armstrong, ed. *California State Series: Sixth Year Literature Reader*. Sacramento: Robert L. Telfer, Superintendent State Publishing, 1916 (11th ed. 1928). 86.
    c. In *Selected Poems* (A.27).
    d. In *The Complete Poetry and Translations*, Volume 1 (A.73).
    e. In *Moonlight and Other Poems* (A.78).

    8 lines.

136. "The Cheveu."
    a. In *The Complete Poetry and Translations*, Volume 1 (A.73).

    8 lines. In French.

137. "The Chimera."
    a. In *Ebony and Crystal* (A.3) (as "The Chimaera").
    b. In *Selected Poems* (A.27).
    c. In *The Complete Poetry and Translations*, Volume 1 (A.73).

    Sonnet.

138. "[Christmas card verses]."
    a. In *The Complete Poetry and Translations*, Volume 2 (A.73).

Three separate poems (6, 4, and 4 lines). Written in 1931 and entered by Ethel Heiple (with three verses of her own) in a Christmas card verse contest.

139. "The City in the Desert."
   a. In *Ebony and Crystal* (A.3).
   b. In *Selected Poems* (A.27).
   c. In *The Last Oblivion* (A.61).
   d. In *The Complete Poetry and Translations,* Volume 1 (A.73).
   e. In *Moonlight and Other Poems* (A.78).

   16 lines. CAS noted that "The lines entitled 'The City in the Desert' were remembered out of a dream. They're a bit disordered, but seem to present a sort of picture" (letter to SL, 22 April 1915; ms., BL).

140. "The City of Destruction."
   a. *Arkham Sampler* 1, No. 1 (Winter 1948): 22.
   b. In *Selected Poems* (A.27).
   c. In *The Complete Poetry and Translations,* Volume 1 (A.73).
   d. In *Celui qui marchait parmi les étoiles* (II.A.iii.17).

   22 lines. Begun 13 May 1914.

141. "The City of the Djinn."
   a. In *The Complete Poetry and Translations,* Volume 1 (A.73).

   48 lines. Juvenilia.

142. "The City of the Titans."
   a. *Challenge* 1, No. 2 (Fall 1950): [12].
   b. In *Selected Poems* (A.27).
   c. In G. Randal Rau and M. Bruce Farr, ed. *World Tales.* Tempe, AZ: World Fantasy Convention, 1985. 62.
   d. In *The Last Oblivion* (A.61).
   e. In *The Complete Poetry and Translations,* Volume 1 (A.73).
   f. In *Celui qui marchait parmi les étoiles* (II.A.iii.17).

   16 lines. Written 12 May 1913.

143. "Classic Epigram."
   a. In *Selected Poems* (A.27) (as a translation from "Christophe des Laurières").
   b. In *The Fugitive Poems of Clark Ashton Smith: Second Series* (A.38) (as "Adjuration").

c. In *The Complete Poetry and Translations,* Volume 2 (A.73).

    8 lines. Dated 29 September 1942. Alternate title: "To Lesbia."

144. "Classic Reminiscence."
a. In *Selected Poems* (A.27).
b. In *The Complete Poetry and Translations,* Volume 2 (A.73).

    Haiku. First title: "Reminiscence."

145. "Cleopatra."
a. In *Ebony and Crystal* (A.3).
b. In *Selected Poems* (A.27).
c. In *The Last Oblivion* (A.61).
d. In *The Complete Poetry and Translations,* Volume 1 (A.73).
e. In *Celui qui marchait parmi les étoiles* (II.A.iii.17).

    25 lines. Dated 18 May 1921.

146. "The Cloud-Islands."
a. In *The Star-Treader and Other Poems* (A.1).
b. *San Francisco Call* (1 December 1912): 6.
c. *Current Opinion* 54, No. 2 (February 1913): 150 (as "Cloud Islands").
d. In *The Last Oblivion* (A.61).
e. In *The Complete Poetry and Translations,* Volume 1 (A.73).
f. In *Moonlight and Other Poems* (A.78).
g. In *Celui qui marchait parmi les étoiles* (II.A.iii.17).

    25 lines. First title: "The Sunset Islands."

147. "Cloudland."
a. In *In the Ultimate Valleys* (A.26).
b. In *The Complete Poetry and Translations,* Volume 1 (A.73).

    Sonnet. Written c. 1910. L. 13 appears to be deficient.

148. "The Clouds."
a. In *The Complete Poetry and Translations,* Volume 1 (A.73).

    24 lines.

149. "Cocaigne."
a. *Auburn Journal* 23, No. 40 (19 July 1923): 6.
b. In *The Complete Poetry and Translations,* Volume 1 (A.73).

    15 lines.

150. "The Cohorts of the Storm."
   a. *Rosary Magazine* 42, No. 2 (February 1913): 182.
   b. In *The Complete Poetry and Translations,* Volume 1 (A.73) (as "The Storm").

   20 lines.

151. "Coldness."
   a. In *Ebony and Crystal* (A.3).
   b. In *Selected Poems* (A.27).
   c. In *The Complete Poetry and Translations,* Volume 1 (A.73).

   12 lines. Written c. June 1916.

152. "Companionship."
   a. In *The Complete Poetry and Translations,* Volume 1 (A.73).

   12 lines. Written 1910.

153. "Concupiscence."
   a. In *Selected Poems* (A.27) (as a translation from "Christophe des Laurières").
   b. In *The Complete Poetry and Translations,* Volume 1 (A.73).

   Sonnet. Written c. March 1925.

154. "Connaissance."
   a. In *Selected Poems* (A.27).
   b. In *The Last Oblivion* (A.61).
   c. In *The Complete Poetry and Translations,* Volume 2 (A.73).
   d. In *Celui qui marchait parmi les étoiles* (II.A.iii.17).

   19 lines. Written 26 January 1929. First title: "Knowledge."

155. "Consolation."
   a. In *Sandalwood* (A.4).
   b. *Step Ladder* 13, No. 5 (May 1927): 130.
   c. In [Helen Hoyt, ed.] *California Poets: An Anthology of 224 Contemporaries.* New York: Henry Harrison, 1932. 666.
   d. In Dudley Chadwick Gordon, Vernon Rupert King, and William Whittingham Lyman, ed. *Today's Literature.* New York: American Book Co., 1935. 449.
   d. In *Selected Poems* (A.27).
   e. In *The Complete Poetry and Translations,* Volume 1 (A.73).

   10 lines. First title: "Éloignement."

156. "Consummation."
    a. In *The Complete Poetry and Translations*, Volume 2 (A.73).

    Sonnet. Dated 15 October 1941.

157. "Contra Mortem."
    a. In *The Black Book of Clark Ashton Smith* (A.39).
    b. In *The Complete Poetry and Translations*, Volume 2 (A.73).

    17 lines. The first appearance contains early versions of several passages.

158. "Contradiction."
    a. *Auburn Journal* 23, No. 31 (17 May 1923): 6.
    b. In *Sandalwood* (A.4).
    c. In *Selected Poems* (A.27).
    d. In *The Complete Poetry and Translations*, Volume 1 (A.73).

    9 lines.

159. "Copan."
    a. In *The Star-Treader and Other Poems* (A.1).
    b. *Romantist* Nos. 9–10 (1985–86): 26.
    c. In *The Complete Poetry and Translations*, Volume 1 (A.73).
    d. In *Moonlight and Other Poems* (A.78).

    Sonnet.

160. "Copyist."
    a. In *Selected Poems* (A.27).
    b. In *The Complete Poetry and Translations*, Volume 2 (A.73).

    6 lines.

161. "Un Couchant."
    a. In *The Complete Poetry and Translations*, Volume 1 (A.73).

    18 lines. In French. Written c. December 1925. On a typescript of a poem sent to Albert Bender, CAS wrote: "My first attempt in French!" See CAS's translation into English, "A Sunset" (item 842).

162. "Courage."
    a. In *The Complete Poetry and Translations*, Volume 1 (A.73).

    25 lines. Juvenilia: written c. 24 December 1906.

163. "Credo."
     a. In *The Complete Poetry and Translations,* Volume 2 (A.73).
         8 lines. Dated 28 October 1928.

164. "Crepuscule."
     a. In *Ebony and Crystal* (A.3) (as "Crepuscle").
     b. In *Selected Poems* (A.27).
     c. In *The Complete Poetry and Translations,* Volume 1 (A.73).
         8 lines. Accepted by the *Thrill Book,* but the magazine folded before
         the poem could be published.

165. "Crows in Spring."
     a. In *Selected Poems* (A.27).
     b. In *The Complete Poetry and Translations,* Volume 2 (A.73).
         Haiku. Alternate title: "Crows in March."

166. "The Crucifixion of Eros."
     a. In *Odes and Sonnets* (A.2).
     b. In *Ebony and Crystal* (A.3).
     c. *Step Ladder* 13, No. 5 (May 1927): 132.
     d. *Golden Atom* 1, No. 10 (Winter 1943): 23.
     e. In *Selected Poems* (A.27).
     f. In *The Complete Poetry and Translations,* Volume 1 (A.73).
     g. In *Moonlight and Other Poems* (A.78).
     h. In *The Dark Eidolon and Other Fantasies* (A.84).
         Sonnet. Written c. June 1916.

167. "Cumuli."
     a. *Interludes* 8, No. 1 (Spring 1931): 11.
     b. In *Selected Poems* (A.27).
     c. In *The Complete Poetry and Translations,* Volume 2 (A.73).
         16 lines. Dated 12 December 1929.

168. "The Cycle."
     a. In *The Complete Poetry and Translations,* Volume 2 (A.73).
         11 lines.

169. "Cycles."
     a. A.19.
     b. In *In Memoriam: Clark Ashton Smith* (III.D.4).

    c. In *The Black Book of Clark Ashton Smith* (A.39).

    d. In *One Hundred Years of Klarkash-Ton* (III.D.10).

    e. In *Clark Ashton Smith: The Sorcerer Departs* (III.D.14).

    f. In *The Last Oblivion* (A.61).

    g. In *The Complete Poetry and Translations*, Volume 2 (A.73).

    h. In *The Dark Eidolon and Other Fantasies* (A.84).

    i. In *Celui qui marchait parmi les étoiles* (II.A.iii.17).

    Sonnet. Dated 4 June 1961. CAS's last poem.

170. "Dancer."

    a. In *Selected Poems* (A.27).

    b. In *The Complete Poetry and Translations*, Volume 2 (A.73).

    8 lines.

171. "Dans l'univers lointain."

    a. In *The Complete Poetry and Translations*, Volume 2 (A.73).

    35 lines. In French. Written before 7 December 1949. For CAS's English translation, see "In a Distant Universe" (item 393).

172. "The Dark Chateau."

    a. In *The Dark Chateau* (A.13).

    b. In *The Last Oblivion* (A.61).

    c. In *The Complete Poetry and Translations*, Volume 2 (A.73).

    d. In *The Averoigne Chronicles* (A.85).

    e. In *Celui qui marchait parmi les étoiles* (II.A.iii.17).

    48 lines. Written c. 1950.

173. "Dawn."

    a. In *The Complete Poetry and Translations*, Volume 1 (A.73).

    12 lines. Juvenilia.

174. "Day-Dream."

    a. In *The Complete Poetry and Translations*, Volume 2 (A.73).

    36 lines. Written c. November 1935. An English translation of "Rêvasserie" (item 704).

175. "The Days of Time."

    a. In *The Complete Poetry and Translations*, Volume 1 (A.73).

    8 lines. Juvenilia.

176. "De Consolation." [English]
   a. In *The Complete Poetry and Translations,* Volume 2 (A.73).

   8 lines. For CAS's French version, see item 177.

177. "De Consolation." [French]
   a. In *The Complete Poetry and Translations,* Volume 2 (A.73).

   8 lines. Written August 1927. For CAS's English version, see item 176.

178. "De Profundis."
   a. In *Selected Poems* (A.27).
   b. In *The Complete Poetry and Translations,* Volume 2 (A.73).

   24 lines. Dated 4 September 1943.

179. "A Dead City."
   a. In *The Star-Treader and Other Poems* (A.1).
   b. In *Selected Poems* (A.27).
   c. In *The Last Oblivion* (A.61).
   d. In *The Complete Poetry and Translations,* Volume 1 (A.73).
   e. In *Moonlight and Other Poems* (A.78).

   Sonnet.

180. "Dead Love."
   a. In *Grotesques and Fantastiques* (A.32).
   b. In Jonathan Bacon and Steve Troyanovich, ed. *Omniumgathum: An Anthology of Verse by Top Authors in the Field of Fantasy.* Lamoni, IA: Stygian Isle Press, 1976. 51.
   b. In *The Complete Poetry and Translations,* Volume 1 (A.73).

   Sonnet.

181. *The Dead Will Cuckold You.*
   a. In *In Memoriam: Clark Ashton Smith* (III.D.4).
   b. In *Strange Shadows* (A.52).
   c. In *Tales of Zothique* (A.56).
   d. In *The Complete Poetry and Translations,* Volume 2 (A.73).
   e. In *The Miscellaneous Writings of Clark Ashton Smith* (A.82).

   466 lines. Written c. 1950/51. A verse drama.

182. "Death."
    a. In *The Fugitive Poems of Clark Ashton Smith* (A.26).
    b. In *The Complete Poetry and Translations*, Volume 2 (A.73).
        Sonnet.

183. "Decadence."
    a. In *Selected Poems* (A.27).
    b. In *The Complete Poetry and Translations*, Volume 1 (A.73).
        Sonnet.

184. "December."
    a. *Auburn Journal* 24, No. 8 (6 December 1923): 6.
    b. *Poetry* 33, No. 3 (December 1928): 123.
    c. *Oakland Tribune* (1 December 1928): 42.
    d. *Kansas City Star* (2 December 1928): 18.
    e. *Amarillo* [TX] *Daily News* (4 December 1928): 5.
    f. *Pantagraph* (Bloomington, IL) (6 December 1928): 4.
    g. *Kingsport* [TN] *Times* (9 December 1929): 6.
    h. In *Selected Poems* (A.27).
    i. In *The Complete Poetry and Translations*, Volume 1 (A.73).
        20 lines.

185. "Declining Moon."
    a. In *Selected Poems* (A.27).
    b. In *The Complete Poetry and Translations*, Volume 2 (A.73).
        Haiku.

186. "Dedication: To Carol."
    a. In *Spells and Philtres* (A.14).
    b. In *The Complete Poetry and Translations*, Volume 2 (A.73).
        Sonnet. Dated 19 February 1955.

187. "Delay."
    a. In *The Complete Poetry and Translations*, Volume 2 (A.73).
        10 lines. Dated 12 September 1952.

188. "Delhi."
    a. In *The Complete Poetry and Translations*, Volume 1 (A.73).
        28 lines. Juvenilia.

189. "Demogorgon."
   a. In *The Complete Poetry and Translations,* Volume 2 (A.73).

   27 lines. Written c. September 1913. A fragment.

190. "The Departed City."
   a. In *The Sword of Zagan and Other Writings* (A.64).
   b. In *The Complete Poetry and Translations,* Volume 1 (A.73).

   12 lines. Juvenilia.

191. "Departure."
   a. *Auburn Journal* 24, No. 7 (29 November 1923): 6.
   b. In *Sandalwood* (A.4).
   c. In *The Complete Poetry and Translations,* Volume 1 (A.73).

   4 lines. Dated 16 November 1923.

192. "The Desert."
   a. In *The Complete Poetry and Translations,* Volume 1 (A.73).

   40 lines. Juvenilia.

193. "Desert Dweller."
   a. *Weird Tales* 36, No. 12 (July 1943): 71.
   b. In *The Dark Chateau* (A.13).
   c. In *Selected Poems* (A.27).
   d. In *The Last Oblivion* (A.61).
   e. In *Shadows Seen and Unseen* (A.71).
   f. In *The Complete Poetry and Translations,* Volume 2 (A.73).
   g. In *The Song of the Necromancer and Others* (A.81).

   28 lines. Dated 13 August 1937.

194. "Desire of Vastness."
   a. In *Ebony and Crystal* (A.3).
   b. In *Selected Poems* (A.27).
   c. In *The Last Oblivion* (A.61).
   d. In *The Complete Poetry and Translations,* Volume 1 (A.73).
   e. In *Moonlight and Other Poems* (A.78).
   f. In *The Dark Eidolon and Other Fantasies* (A.84).

   Sonnet. Written c. June 1913.

195. "Desolation."
   a. In *Ebony and Crystal* (A.3).

    b. In *Selected Poems* (A.27).
    c. In *The Last Oblivion* (A.61).
    d. In *The Complete Poetry and Translations*, Volume 1 (A.73).
    e. In *Moonlight and Other Poems* (A.78).
    f. In *Celui qui marchait parmi les étoiles* (II.A.iii.17).

    Sonnet. Written c. June 1916.

196. "Despondency."
    a. In *The Complete Poetry and Translations*, Volume 2 (A.73).

    7 lines. A fragment (ms. also mutilated).

197. "Dialogue."
    a. *Weird Tales* 36, No. 11 (May 1943): 67 (as by "Timeus Gay-lord").
    b. In *Spells and Philtres* (A.14).
    c. In *Selected Poems* (A.27).
    d. In *The Complete Poetry and Translations*, Volume 2 (A.73).
    e. In *The Song of the Necromancer and Others* (A.81).

    Sonnet. Dated 28 July 1941.

198. "The Dials."
    a. In *The Complete Poetry and Translations*, Volume 1 (A.73).

    3 lines.

199. "Dice el soñador."
    a. In *Shadows Seen and Unseen* (A.71).
    b. In *The Complete Poetry and Translations*, Volume 2 (A.73).

    28 lines. In Spanish. Written c. 1950. For CAS's English version, see "Says the Dreamer" (item 733).

200. "Didus Ineptus."
    a. In *Spells and Philtres* (A.14).
    b. In *The Complete Poetry and Translations*, Volume 2 (A.73).

    31 lines. Dated 10 October 1950.

201. "Disillusionment."
    a. In *Spells and Philtres* (A.14).
    b. In *Selected Poems* (A.27).
    c. In *The Complete Poetry and Translations*, Volume 1 (A.73).

11 lines. First title: "Disenchantment."

202. "Dissonance."
   a. *Thrill Book* 2, No. 6 (15 September 1919): 149.
   b. In *Ebony and Crystal* (A.3).
   c. In *Selected Poems* (A.27).
   d. In *The Last Oblivion* (A.61).
   e. In *The Complete Poetry and Translations*, Volume 1 (A.73).
   f. In *Celui qui marchait parmi les étoiles* (II.A.iii.17).

   Sonnet. Written before 24 April 1918.

203. "Diversity."
   a. *Auburn Journal* 24, No. 7 (29 November 1923): 6.
   b. In *Selected Poems* (A.27) (as "Dissidence").
   c. In *The Complete Poetry and Translations*, Volume 1 (A.73).

   4 lines. Dated 16 November 1923. The title "Diversity" is found on a revised ms. of *Sandalwood* (c. 1952), hence presumably represents CAS's final wishes.

204. "Do You Forget, Enchantress?"
   a. *Weird Tales* 42, No. 3 (March 1950): 29.
   b. In *Spells and Philtres* (A.14).
   c. In *Selected Poems* (A.27).
   d. In *The Complete Poetry and Translations*, Volume 2 (A.73).
   e. In *The Song of the Necromancer and Others* (A.81).

   15 lines. Dated 9 July 1946.

205. "Dolor of Dreams."
   a. *Auburn Journal* 23, No. 46 (30 August 1923): 6.
   b. In *Selected Poems* (A.27).
   c. In *The Last Oblivion* (A.61).
   d. In *The Complete Poetry and Translations*, Volume 1 (A.73).

   12 lines.

206. "Dominion."
   a. *Weird Tales* 25, No. 6 (June 1935): 724.
   b. In *Spells and Philtres* (A.14).
   c. In *Selected Poems* (A.27).
   d. In *Shadows Seen and Unseen* (A.71).
   e. In *The Complete Poetry and Translations*, Volume 2 (A.73).

f.   In *The Song of the Necromancer and Others* (A.81).

30 lines. Dated 26 January 1935.

207. "Dominium in Excelsis."
   a.   In *The Dark Chateau* (A.13).
   b.   In *In Memoriam: Clark Ashton Smith* (III.D.4) (first six stanzas only).
   c.   In *The Black Book of Clark Ashton Smith* (A.39).
   d.   In *The Complete Poetry and Translations,* Volume 2 (A.73).

31 lines. Dated 13 February 1950.

208. "Don Juan Sings."
   a.   *Auburn Journal* 23, No. 30 (10 May 1923): 6.
   b.   *Wanderer* 2, No. 3 (March 1924): 30.
   c.   In *Sandalwood* (A.4).
   d.   In *Selected Poems* (A.27).
   e.   In *The Complete Poetry and Translations,* Volume 1 (A.73).

16 lines. Dated 7 March 1923.

209. "Don Quixote on Market Street."
   a.   In *The Dark Chateau* (A.13).
   b.   *Weird Tales* 45, No. 1 (March 1953): 11.
   c.   In *The Black Book of Clark Ashton Smith* (A.39).
   d.   In *The Complete Poetry and Translations,* Volume 2 (A.73).
   e.   In *The Song of the Necromancer and Others* (A.81).

33 lines. Written 1950.

210. "¿Donde duermes, Eldorado?"
   a.   In *¿Donde Duermes, Eldorado? y Otros Poemas* (A.21).
   b.   In *Shadows Seen and Unseen* (A.71).
   c.   In *The Complete Poetry and Translations,* Volume 2 (A.73).

12 lines. Alternate title: "Súplica." In Spanish. For CAS's English version, see "Where Sleepest Thou, Eldorado?" (item 952).

211. "The Doom of America."
   a.   In *The Complete Poetry and Translations,* Volume 1 (A.73).

48 lines (biblical verses). Written c. May 1913.

212. "Dos mitos y una fábula."
   a.   In *¿Donde Duermes, Eldorado? y Otros Poemas* (A.21).

b. In *Shadows Seen and Unseen* (A.71).

c. In *The Complete Poetry and Translations,* Volume 2 (A.73).

> 12 lines. In Spanish. For CAS's English version, see "Two Myths and a Fable" (item 920).

213. "The Dragon-Fly."
    a. In *Selected Poems* (A.27).
    b. In *The Complete Poetry and Translations,* Volume 2 (A.73).

> 10 lines. Dated 11 September 1929.

214. "A Dream."
    a. In *The Complete Poetry and Translations,* Volume 1 (A.73).

> 72 lines. Juvenilia.

215. "The Dream."
    a. In *The Complete Poetry and Translations,* Volume 1 (A.73).

> 32 lines.

216. "The Dream-Bridge."
    a. In *The Star-Treader and Other Poems* (A.1).
    b. In *The Last Oblivion* (A.61).
    c. In *The Complete Poetry and Translations,* Volume 1 (A.73).
    d. In *Moonlight and Other Poems* (A.78).
    e. In *Celui qui marchait parmi les étoiles* (II.A.iii.17).

> 8 lines. Written c. 1911.

217. "The Dream-God's Realm."
    a. In *The Fugitive Poems of Clark Ashton Smith: Second Series* (A.38).
    b. In *The Last Oblivion* (A.61).
    c. In *The Complete Poetry and Translations,* Volume 1 (A.73).
    d. In *Celui qui marchait parmi les étoiles* (II.A.iii.17).

> Sonnet. Alternate title: "Sonnets on Dreams."

218. "A Dream of Beauty."
    a. *Academy* 81 (12 August 1911): 196.
    b. In *The Star-Treader and Other Poems* (A.1).
    c. In Augustin S. Macdonald, ed. *A Collection of Verse by California Poets: From 1849 to 1915.* San Francisco: A. M. Robertson, 1914. 54.
    d. In *Nero and Other Poems* (A.8).

e. *Golden Atom* 1, No. 8 (May 1940): 3.
f. In Stanton A. Coblentz, ed. *Unseen Wings: The Living Poetry of Man's Immortality*. New York: Beechhurst Press, 1949. 261–62.
g. In *Selected Poems* (A.27).
h. In *The Last Oblivion* (A.61).
i. In *The Complete Poetry and Translations,* Volume 1 (A.73).
j. In *Moonlight and Other Poems* (A.78).
k. In *The Dark Eidolon and Other Fantasies* (A.84).
l. In *Celui qui marchait parmi les étoiles* (II.A.iii.17).

Sonnet.

219. "A Dream of Darkness."
a. In *The Complete Poetry and Translations,* Volume 1 (A.73).

7 lines.

220. "A Dream of India."
a. In *The Complete Poetry and Translations,* Volume 1 (A.73).

95 lines. Juvenilia.

221. "A Dream of Oblivion."
a. In *The Fugitive Poems of Clark Ashton Smith: Second Series* (A.38).
b. In *The Last Oblivion* (A.61).
c. In *The Complete Poetry and Translations,* Volume 1 (A.73).
d. In *Celui qui marchait parmi les étoiles* (II.A.iii.17).

19 lines.

222. "A Dream of the Abyss."
a. *Fantasy Fan* 1, No. 3 (November 1933): 41.
b. In *Selected Poems* (A.27).
c. In *The Last Oblivion* (A.61).
d. In *The Complete Poetry and Translations,* Volume 2 (A.73).
e. In Charles D. Hornig, ed. *The Fantasy Fan: September, 1933–February, 1935.* [n.p.: Lance Thingmaker, 2010.] 41 (facsimile of a.).

36 lines.

223. *A Dream of Vathek.*
a. In *The Complete Poetry and Translations,* Volume 1 (A.73).

386 lines. Juvenilia. A verse drama.

224. "A Dream of Zanoni."
   a. In *The Complete Poetry and Translations*, Volume 1 (A.73).
   40 lines. Juvenilia.

225. "The Dream-Weaver."
   a. In *The Complete Poetry and Translations*, Volume 1 (A.73).
   30 lines. Dated 3 April 1911.

226. "Duality."
   a. *Weird Tales* 2, No. 1 (July–August 1923): 69 (as "The Garden of Evil").
   b. *Auburn Journal* 24, No. 20 (28 February 1924): 6.
   c. In *Sandalwood* (A.4).
   d. In *Selected Poems* (A.27).
   e. In *The Complete Poetry and Translations*, Volume 1 (A.73).
   f. In *The Song of the Necromancer and Others* (A.81) (as "The Garden of Evil").
   g. In Farnsworth Wright, ed. *Weird Tales, Volume 2, Number 1 (July–August 1923)*. Mississauga, ON: Girasol Collectables, 2014. 69 (as "The Garden of Evil"; facsimile of a.).
   Sonnet. First title: "Sonnet."

227. "Los Dueños."
   a. In *The Complete Poetry and Translations*, Volume 2 (A.73).
   20 lines. In Spanish. Dated 30 January 1950.

228. "Dying Prospector."
   a. In *The Complete Poetry and Translations*, Volume 2 (A.73).
   5 lines.

229. "The Earth."
   a. In *The Complete Poetry and Translations*, Volume 2 (A.73).
   Haiku. [First line only extant.]

230. "Eblis Repentant."
   a. In *The Complete Poetry and Translations*, Volume 1 (A.73).
   76 lines. Juvenilia.

231. "Echo of Memnon."
   a. In *Ebony and Crystal* (A.3).

b. In *Selected Poems* (A.27).
c. In *The Last Oblivion* (A.61).
d. In *The Complete Poetry and Translations,* Volume 1 (A.73).
e. In *Moonlight and Other Poems* (A.78).
f. In *Celui qui marchait parmi les étoiles* (II.A.iii.17).

16 lines. Written before 27 May 1912.

232. "The Eclipse."
a. In *The Complete Poetry and Translations,* Volume 1 (A.73).

11 lines.

233. "Ecstasy."
a. *Pearson's Magazine* 48, No. 10 (October 1922): 32.
b. In *Ebony and Crystal* (A.3).
c. In *Selected Poems* (A.27).
d. In *The Complete Poetry and Translations,* Volume 1 (A.73).
e. In *Moonlight and Other Poems* (A.78).

20 lines. Dated 19 May 1921.

234. "Eidolon."
a. In *Ebony and Crystal* (A.3).
b. In *Selected Poems* (A.27).
c. In *The Complete Poetry and Translations,* Volume 1 (A.73).
d. In *Moonlight and Other Poems* (A.78).

Sonnet. Written before 24 April 1918.

235. "The Eldritch Dark."
a. In *The Star-Treader and Other Poems* (A.1).
b. *Berkeley Daily Gazette* (27 September 1932): 14.
c. In *Nero and Other Poems* (A.8).
d. In August Derleth, ed. *Dark of the Moon: Poems of Fantasy and the Macabre.* Sauk City, WI: Arkham House, 1947; Freeport, NY: Books for Libraries Press, 1969; Miami, FL: Granger, 1976. 319–20.
e. In *Selected Poems* (A.27).
f. In Edward Foster, ed. *Decadents, Symbolists, and Aesthetes in America: Fin-de-Siècle American Poetry: An Anthology.* Jersey City, NJ: Talisman House, 2000. 139.
g. In *The Last Oblivion* (A.61).
h. In *The Complete Poetry and Translations,* Volume 1 (A.73).
i. In *The Dark Eidolon and Other Fantasies* (A.84).

    j. In *Celui qui marchait parmi les étoiles* (II.A.iii.17).
    k. *Deciduous: Tales of Darkness and Horror* 1, No. 1 (Fall/Winter 2017): 117.

    Sonnet.

236. "Éloignement."
    a. In *The Complete Poetry and Translations*, Volume 1 (A.73).

    Sonnet. In French.

237. "Empusa Waylays a Traveller."
    a. In *The Complete Poetry and Translations*, Volume 2 (A.73).

    Haiku.

238. "Enchanted Mirrors."
    a. In *Sandalwood* (A.4).
    b. *Auburn Journal* 26, No. 4 (5 November 1925): 4.
    c. *Overland Monthly* 83, No. 11 (November 1925): 407.
    d. In *Selected Poems* (A.27).
    e. In *The Last Oblivion* (A.61).
    f. In *The Complete Poetry and Translations*, Volume 1 (A.73).

    Sonnet. Dated 16 March 1925.

239. "The End of Autumn."
    a. *Auburn Journal* 24, No. 7 (29 November 1923): 6.
    b. *Fresno Bee* (2 February 1924): 24.
    c. *Wanderer* 2, No. 11 (November 1924): 153.
    d. In *Sandalwood* (A.4).
    e. In *Selected Poems* (A.27).
    f. In *The Complete Poetry and Translations*, Volume 1 (A.73).

    20 lines. Written c. September 1924.

240. "Enigma."
    a. *Auburn Journal* 25, No. 18 (12 February 1925): 4.
    b. In *Sandalwood* (A.4).
    c. In *Selected Poems* (A.27).
    d. In *The Complete Poetry and Translations*, Volume 1 (A.73).

    10 lines. Written before 20 January 1925.

241. "Ennui." [My days are as a garden, where the dust]
    a. *Auburn Journal* 25, No. 14 (15 January 1925): 5.

b. *Soma* No. 2 (May 1953): 2.
c. In *Clark Ashton Smith—Poet* (A.32.b) (as "The Ennuye").
d. In *Klarkash-Ton and Monstro Ligriv* (A.37) (as "The Ennuye").
e. In *The Complete Poetry and Translations,* Volume 1 (A.73).

Sonnet. Dated 22 December 1919.

242. "Ennui." [Thou art immured in some sad garden sown with dust]
a. *Weird Tales* 27, No. 5 (May 1936): 547.
b. In *Selected Poems* (A.27).
c. In *The Last Oblivion* (A.61).
d. In *The Complete Poetry and Translations,* Volume 2 (A.73).
e. In *The Song of the Necromancer and Others* (A.81).

Sonnet. Written before 11 December 1935. A recasting of the sonnet "Ennui" in alexandrines.

243. "L'Ensorcellement."
a. In *The Complete Poetry and Translations,* Volume 2 (A.73).

15 lines. In French.

244. "The Envoys."
a. *Auburn Journal* 26, No. 13 (7 January 1926): 4.
b. *Overland Monthly* 84, No. 6 (June 1926): frontispiece.
c. *Overland Monthly* 84, No. 7 (July 1926): 230 (corrected version).
d. In August Derleth, ed. *Dark of the Moon: Poems of Fantasy and the Macabre.* Sauk City, WI: Arkham House, 1947; Freeport, NY: Books for Libraries Press, 1969; Miami, FL: Granger, 1976. 342–43.
e. In *Selected Poems* (A.27).
f. In *The Last Oblivion* (A.61).
g. In *The Complete Poetry and Translations,* Volume 1 (A.73).
h. In *Celui qui marchait parmi les étoiles* (II.A.iii.17).

42 lines. Dated 1 December 1925.

245. "Ephemera."
a. In *The Complete Poetry and Translations,* Volume 1 (A.73).

4 lines.

246. "Epitaph for an Astronomer."
a. In *Selected Poems* (A.27).
b. In *The Complete Poetry and Translations,* Volume 2 (A.73).

5 lines.

247. "Epitaph for the Earth."
  a. In *The Sword of Zagan and Other Writings* (A.64).
  b. In *The Complete Poetry and Translations*, Volume 1 (A.73).

  27 lines. Written c. January 1912.

248. "Erato."
  a. In *Selected Poems* (A.27).
  b. In *The Complete Poetry and Translations*, Volume 2 (A.73).

  23 lines. Dated 2 October 1942.

249. "El Eros de ébano."
  a. In *Shadows Seen and Unseen* (A.71).
  b. In *The Complete Poetry and Translations*, Volume 2 (A.73).

  14 lines. In Spanish. Written c. 1950. For CAS's English version, see "Eros of Ebony" (item 251).

250. "Eros in the Desert."
  a. In *The Complete Poetry and Translations*, Volume 2 (A.73).

  10 lines.

251. "Eros of Ebony."
  a. In *The Dark Chateau* (A.13).
  b. In *Shadows Seen and Unseen* (A.71).
  c. In *The Complete Poetry and Translations*, Volume 2 (A.73).

  14 lines. For CAS's Spanish version, see "El Eros de ébano" (item 249).

252. "L'Espoir du néant."
  a. In *Selected Poems* (A.27).
  b. In *The Complete Poetry and Translations*, Volume 2 (A.73).

  21 lines. In French. Dedicated to George Sterling.

253. "Essence."
  a. In *Spells and Philtres* (A.14).
  b. In *Selected Poems* (A.27).
  c. In *The Complete Poetry and Translations*, Volume 2 (A.73).

  5 lines.

254. "Estrangement."
  a. *Auburn Journal* 24, No. 50 (25 September 1924): 6.

b. *Step Ladder* 10, No. 4 (March 1925): 80.
c. In *Sandalwood* (A.4).
d. In *Selected Poems* (A.27).
e. In *The Complete Poetry and Translations*, Volume 1 (A.73).

16 lines. Dated 9 September 1924.

255. "The Eternal Gleam."
a. In *The Complete Poetry and Translations*, Volume 1 (A.73).

20 lines.

256. "The Eternal Snows."
*a. Publication in 1911–12 not found.
b. In *In the Ultimate Valleys* (A.26).
c. In *The Complete Poetry and Translations*, Volume 1 (A.73).

Sonnet. Written c. January 1911?

257. "Evanescence."
a. In *The Complete Poetry and Translations*, Volume 2 (A.73).

18 lines. Dated 15 September 1929.

258. "Even in Slumber."
a. In *Selected Poems* (A.27).
b. In *The Complete Poetry and Translations*, Volume 2 (A.73).

8 lines. Dated 11 November 1943.

259. "Evening."
a. In *The Complete Poetry and Translations*, Volume 1 (A.73).

10 lines.

260. "Exchange."
a. *Auburn Journal* 23, No. 34 (7 June 1923): 6.
b. *Buccaneer* 1, No. 5 (January 1925): 17.
c. In *The Complete Poetry and Translations*, Volume 2 (A.73).

8 lines.

261. "The Exile."
a. *Bohemia* 2, No. 2 (March 1917): 20.
b. In *Ebony and Crystal* (A.3).
c. *Stars* (June–July 1940): [2].
d. In *Selected Poems* (A.27).

e. In *The Complete Poetry and Translations,* Volume 1 (A.73).
f. In *Moonlight and Other Poems* (A.78).

12 lines.

262. "Exorcism."
a. *Troubadour* 3, No. 5 and 6 (February–March 1931): 6.
b. In *Selected Poems* (A.27).
c. In *The Last Oblivion* (A.61).
d. In *The Complete Poetry and Translations,* Volume 2 (A.73).
e. In *The Dark Eidolon and Other Fantasies* (A.84).

21 lines. Dated 14 January 1929.

263. "Exotic Memory."
a. In *Selected Poems* (A.27) (as a translation from "Christophe des Laurières").
b. In *The Complete Poetry and Translations,* Volume 1 (A.73).

Sonnet. First version: "Alien Memory" (item 21).

264. "Exotique." [English]
a. In *Odes and Sonnets* (A.2).
b. In *Ebony and Crystal* (A.3).
c. In *Selected Poems* (A.27).
d. In *The Last Oblivion* (A.61).
e. In *The Complete Poetry and Translations,* Volume 1 (A.73).
f. In *Moonlight and Other Poems* (A.78).

Sonnet. dated 14 June 1915. Variant title: "Exotic." See CAS's French translation of the same title (item 273).

265. "Exotique." [French]
a. In *The Complete Poetry and Translations,* Volume 1 (A.73).

Sonnet. A French translation of an English poem of the same title (item 272).

266. "The Expanding Ideal."
a. In *The Complete Poetry and Translations,* Volume 1 (A.73).

Sonnet. First draft titled "The Unattainable."

267. "A Fable."
a. *Weird Tales* 10, No. 1 (July 1927): 76.
b. In *Selected Poems* (A.27).

 c. In *The Complete Poetry and Translations,* Volume 2 (A.73).
 d. In *The Song of the Necromancer and Others* (A.81).

  13 lines.

268. "Le Fabliau d'un dieu."
 a. In *The Complete Poetry and Translations,* Volume 2 (A.73).

  27 lines. In French.

269. "Fairy Lanterns."
 a. In *The Star-Treader and Other Poems* (A.1).
 b. In *The Complete Poetry and Translations,* Volume 1 (A.73).
 c. In *Moonlight and Other Poems* (A.78).

  8 lines.

270. "Fallen Grape-Leaf."
 a. In *Selected Poems* (A.27).
 b. In *The Complete Poetry and Translations,* Volume 2 (A.73).

  Haiku.

271. "The Falling Leaves."
 a. In *The Complete Poetry and Translations,* Volume 1 (A.73).

  4 lines.

272. "The Fanes of Dawn."
 a. In *The Fugitive Poems of Clark Ashton Smith: Second Series* (A.38).
 b. In *The Complete Poetry and Translations,* Volume 1 (A.73).

  Sonnet.

273. "Fantasie."
 a. In *The Complete Poetry and Translations,* Volume 1 (A.73).

  8 lines.

274. "Fantaisie d'antan."
 a. *Weird Tales* 14, No. 6 (December 1929): 724.
 b. In August Derleth, ed. *Dark of the Moon: Poems of Fantasy and the Macabre.* Sauk City, WI: Arkham House, 1947; Freeport, NY: Books for Libraries Press, 1969; Miami, FL: Granger, 1976. 343–44.
 c. In *Selected Poems* (A.27).
 d. In *The Last Oblivion* (A.61).
 e. In *The Complete Poetry and Translations,* Volume 2 (A.73).

f. In *The Song of the Necromancer and Others* (A.81).

40 lines. Dated 1 April 1927.

275. "Farewell to Eros."
  a. *Weird Tales* 31, No. 6 (June 1938): 759.
  b. In *Spells and Philtres* (A.14).
  c. In *Selected Poems* (A.27).
  d. In *The Last Oblivion* (A.61).
  e. In *The Complete Poetry and Translations,* Volume 2 (A.73).
  f. In *The Song of the Necromancer and Others* (A.81).
  g. In Farnsworth Wright, ed. *Weird Tales, Volume 31, Number 6 (June 1938)*. Mississauga, ON: Girasol Collectables, 2011. 759 (facsimile of a.).

32 lines. Written c. March 1937.

276. "Farmyard Fugue."
  a. In *The Complete Poetry and Translations,* Volume 2 (A.73).

28 lines. Written c. 1 October 1950.

277. "Fashion."
  a. In *The Complete Poetry and Translations,* Volume 1 (A.73).

8 lines. Dated 9 March 1923.

278. "Fawn-Lilies."
  a. In *Grotesques and Fantastiques* (A.32).
  b. In *The Complete Poetry and Translations,* Volume 1 (A.73).

20 lines. Dated 19 April 1922.

279. "Fear."
  a. In *The Complete Poetry and Translations,* Volume 1 (A.73).

12 lines. Juvenilia.

280. "The Fear of Death."
  a. In *The Complete Poetry and Translations,* Volume 1 (A.73).

18 lines. Juvenilia.

281. "The Feast."
  a. In *The Complete Poetry and Translations,* Volume 1 (A.73).

40 lines. Juvenilia.

282. "Feast of St. Anthony."
   a.   In *Spells and Philtres* (A.14).
   b.   In *Selected Poems* (A.27).
   c.   In *The Complete Poetry and Translations*, Volume 2 (A.73).

   Haiku.

283. "February."
   a.   In *Klarkash-Ton and Monstro Ligriv* (A.37).
   b.   In *The Complete Poetry and Translations*, Volume 2 (A.73).

   16 lines. Dated 2 February 1929.

284. "Fellowship."
   a.   *Decatur* [TX] *Wise County Messenger* (18 September 1930): 8
        (lines 1–4 and 13–16 only).
   b.   *Weird Tales* 16, No. 4 (October 1930): 550.
   c.   In *The Complete Poetry and Translations*, Volume 2 (A.73).
   d.   In *The Song of the Necromancer and Others* (A.81).

   16 lines. Dated 15 September 1929.

285. "Felo-de-se of the Parasite."
   a.   In *Selected Poems* (A.27).
   b.   In *The Complete Poetry and Translations*, Volume 2 (A.73).

   Haiku.

286. "Fence and Wall."
   a.   In *Spells and Philtres* (A.14).
   b.   In *Selected Poems* (A.27).
   c.   In *The Complete Poetry and Translations*, Volume 2 (A.73).

   Haiku.

287. "Field Behind the Abatoir."
   a.   In *In Memoriam: Clark Ashton Smith* (III.D.4) (as "Behind the
        Abattoir").
   b.   In *Selected Poems* (A.27).
   c.   In *The Complete Poetry and Translations*, Volume 2 (A.73).

   Haiku.

288. "Fight on the Play-Ground."
   a.   In *Selected Poems* (A.27).
   b.   In *The Complete Poetry and Translations*, Volume 2 (A.73).

   Haiku.

289. "Finis."
    a. In *The Star-Treader and Other Poems* (A.1).
    b. In Ella Sterling Mighels, ed. *Literary California*. San Francisco: Harr Wagner Publishing Co., 1918. 381.
    c. *Tesseract* 2, No. 3 (March 1937): 9.
    d. In *Selected Poems* (A.27).
    e. In *The Complete Poetry and Translations*, Volume 1 (A.73).
    f. In *Moonlight and Other Poems* (A.78).

    36 lines. Written 1912.

290. "Fire of Snow."
    a. *Poetry* 6, No. 4 (July 1915): 178.
    b. In *Selected Poems* (A.27).
    c. In *The Complete Poetry and Translations*, Volume 1 (A.73).

    Sonnet.

291. "Flamingoes."
    a. *Asia* 19, No. 11 (November 1919): 1134.
    b. *Denver Rocky Mountain News* (4 January 1920): 22.
    c. In *Ebony and Crystal* (A.3).
    d. In *Selected Poems* (A.27).
    e. In *The Complete Poetry and Translations*, Volume 1 (A.73).

    8 lines.

292. "The Flight of Azrael."
    a. *Fantastic Worlds* 1, No. 1 (Summer 1952): 15.
    b. In *Selected Poems* (A.27).
    c. In *The Last Oblivion* (A.61).
    d. In *The Complete Poetry and Translations*, Volume 1 (A.73).
    e. In *Celui qui marchait parmi les étoiles* (II.A.iii.17).

    33 lines. Written before 10 May 1915.

293. "The Flight of the Seraphim."
    a. In *The Complete Poetry and Translations*, Volume 2 (A.73).

    2 lines. A fragment.

294. "Flight of the Yellow-Hammer."
    a. In *Selected Poems* (A.27).
    b. In *The Complete Poetry and Translations*, Volume 2 (A.73).

    Haiku.

295. "Flora."
    a. In *Selected Poems* (A.27).
    b. In *The Complete Poetry and Translations*, Volume 2 (A.73).
       Haiku.

296. "The Flower of the Night."
    a. In *The Complete Poetry and Translations*, Volume 1 (A.73).
       4 lines.

297. "Foggy Night."
    a. In *Selected Poems* (A.27).
    b. In *The Complete Poetry and Translations*, Volume 2 (A.73).
       Haiku.

298. "For a Wine-Jar."
    a. In *The Complete Poetry and Translations*, Volume 1 (A.73).
       4 lines. Written c. 1919.

299. "For an Antique Lyre."
    a. *Agenbite of Inwit* 3, No. 1 (January 1946): 2.
    b. In *The Hill of Dionysus* (A.18).
    c. In *Selected Poems* (A.27).
    d. In *Shadows Seen and Unseen* (A.71).
    e. In *The Complete Poetry and Translations*, Volume 2 (A.73).
       16 lines.

300. "For Iris."
    a. In *The Complete Poetry and Translations*, Volume 2 (A.73).
       17 lines. A fragment.

301. "For the Dance of Death."
    a. In *Selected Poems* (A.27).
    b. In *The Complete Poetry and Translations*, Volume 2 (A.73).
       Haiku.

302. "Forgetfulness."
    a. *Sonnet* 4, No. 2 (May–June 1919): 2.
    b. In *Ebony and Crystal* (A.3).
    c. In *Selected Poems* (A.27).
    d. In *The Complete Poetry and Translations*, Volume 1 (A.73).

e. In *Celui qui marchait parmi les étoiles* (II.A.iii.17).

Sonnet. Written c. January 1919.

303. "Forgotten Sorrow."
a. *Auburn Journal* 23, No. 42 (2 August 1923): 6.
b. In *Sandalwood* (A.4).
c. In *Selected Poems* (A.27).
d. In *The Last Oblivion* (A.61).
e. In *The Complete Poetry and Translations,* Volume 1 (A.73).

Sonnet.

304. "La Forteresse."
a. In *The Complete Poetry and Translations,* Volume 2 (A.73).

Sonnet. In French. Written 25–26 November 1935. Revised version of "Le Refuge." For CAS's English version, see item 305.

305. "The Fortress."
a. In *The Complete Poetry and Translations,* Volume 2 (A.73).

Sonnet. For CAS's French version, see item 304.

306. "Fortune."
a. In *The Complete Poetry and Translations,* Volume 1 (A.73).

18 lines. Juvenilia.

307. "The Fountain of Youth."
a. In *The Complete Poetry and Translations,* Volume 1 (A.73).

4 lines.

308. "Fragment."
a. *Wings* 5, No. 5 (Spring 1942): 6.
b. *Niagara Falls Gazette* (27 June 1942): 5.
c. In Stanton A. Coblentz, ed. *Unseen Wings: The Living Poetry of Man's Immortality.* New York: Beechhurst Press, 1949. 210–11.
d. In *The Hill of Dionysus* (A.18).
e. In *Selected Poems* (A.27).
f. In *The Complete Poetry and Translations,* Volume 2 (A.73).

16 lines. Dated 11 September 1941.

309. "A Fragment."
a. In *Ebony and Crystal* (A.3).

b. *Step Ladder* 13, No. 5 (May 1927): 134.
c. In *Selected Poems* (A.27).
d. In *The Complete Poetry and Translations*, Volume 1 (A.73).
   24 lines.

310. "[Fragment 1]."
   a. In *The Complete Poetry and Translations*, Volume 1 (A.73).
      24 lines. Juvenilia.

311. "[Fragment 2]."
   a. In *The Complete Poetry and Translations*, Volume 1 (A.73).
      54 lines. Juvenilia.

312. "[Fragment 3]."
   a. In *The Complete Poetry and Translations*, Volume 1 (A.73).
      14 lines. Juvenilia.

313. "[Fragment 4]."
   a. In *The Complete Poetry and Translations*, Volume 1 (A.73).
      14 lines. Juvenilia.

314. "[Fragment 5]."
   a. In *The Complete Poetry and Translations*, Volume 1 (A.73).
      46 lines. Juvenilia.

315. "[Fragment 6]."
   a. In *The Complete Poetry and Translations*, Volume 1 (A.73).
      8 lines. Juvenilia. Identified as "Heading for Chapter II" of "The Afghan Knife."

316. "[Fragment 7]."
   a. In *The Complete Poetry and Translations*, Volume 1 (A.73).
      14 lines. Juvenilia.

317. "The Freedom of the Hills."
   a. In *The Complete Poetry and Translations*, Volume 1 (A.73).
      20 lines.

318. "From Arcady."
    a. In *Selected Poems* (A.27).
    b. In *The Complete Poetry and Translations*, Volume 2 (A.73).

    28 lines.

319. "From 'Ludar's Litany to Thasaidon'" [I].
    a. In *The Complete Poetry and Translations*, Volume 2 (A.73).

    13 lines. The epigraph to the story "The Death of Ilalotha" (written 16 March 1937).

320. "From 'Ludar's Litany to Thasaidon'" [II].
    a. In *The Complete Poetry and Translations*, Volume 2 (A.73).

    11 lines. The epigraph to the story "The Garden of Adompha" (written 31 July 1937).

321. "From 'Ode to Antares.'"
    a. In *The Complete Poetry and Translations*, Volume 2 (A.73).

    4 lines. Included in the story "The Monster of the Prophecy" (written 3 December 1929).

322. "From 'Song of King Hoaraph's Bowmen.'"
    a. In *The Complete Poetry and Translations*, Volume 2 (A.73).

    4 lines. Designed as an epigraph to the story "The Black Abbot of Puthuum" (written 1935–36).

323. "From 'Song of the Galley Slaves.'"
    a. In *The Complete Poetry and Translations*, Volume 2 (A.73).

    4 lines. Designed as an epigraph to the story "Necromancy in Naat" (written 6 February 1935).

324. "From 'The Song of Xeethra.'"
    a. In *The Complete Poetry and Translations*, Volume 2 (A.73).

    10 lines. Designed as an epigraph to the story "The Dark Eidolon" (written 23 December 1932).

325. "From the Persian." [I read upon a gate in letters bold:]
    a. In *The Complete Poetry and Translations*, Volume 1 (A.73).

    2 lines. Juvenilia.

326. "From the Persian." [I stood amid the ruins of a city great]
    a. In *The Complete Poetry and Translations*, Volume 1 (A.73).

    16 lines. Juvenilia.

327. "From the Persian." [Out of the Great Bazaar there came a cry]
    a. In *The Complete Poetry and Translations*, Volume 1 (A.73).

    16 lines. Juvenilia.

328. "The Fugitives."
    a. In *The Star-Treader and Other Poems* (A.1).
    b. In *The Complete Poetry and Translations*, Volume 1 (A.73).
    c. In *Moonlight and Other Poems* (A.78).

    12 lines.

329. *The Fugitives.*
    a. In *Strange Shadows* (A.52) [includes "The Song of Aviol" only (as "Song")].
    a. In *The Complete Poetry and Translations*, Volume 1 (A.73).

    An unfinished drama. See "The Song of Aviol," "Song" (item 785), "The Love-Potion," and "The Song of Cartha."

330. "The Funeral Urn."
    a. *Auburn Journal* 23, No. 45 (23 August 1923): 6.
    b. In *Selected Poems* (A.27) (as a translation from "Christophe des Laurières").
    c. In *The Last Oblivion* (A.61).
    d. In *The Complete Poetry and Translations*, Volume 1 (A.73).

    12 lines.

331. "The Future."
    a. In *The Complete Poetry and Translations*, Volume 1 (A.73).

    4 lines.

332. "Future Meeting."
    a. In *Selected Poems* (A.27).
    b. In *The Complete Poetry and Translations*, Volume 2 (A.73).

    Haiku.

333. "Future Pastoral."
    a. *Wings* 6, No. 1 (Spring 1943): 20.

    b. *Garrett: Where Poets Meet* 5, No. 3 (October 1943): 28.

    c. In *The Hill of Dionysus* (A.18).

    d. In *Selected Poems* (A.27).

    e. In *The Complete Poetry and Translations*, Volume 2 (A.73).

    24 lines. Dated 28 February 1942. First title: "Prescience"; variant title: "Foreknowledge."

334. "The Ganges."
    a. In *The Complete Poetry and Translations*, Volume 1 (A.73).

    16 lines. Juvenilia.

335. "The Garden of Dreams."
    a. In *Grotesques and Fantastiques* (A.32).

    b. In *The Complete Poetry and Translations*, Volume 1 (A.73).

    25 lines. Written 1911.

336. "Garden of Priapus."
    a. In *Selected Poems* (A.27).

    b. In *The Complete Poetry and Translations*, Volume 2 (A.73).

    Haiku.

337. "Geese in the Spring Night."
    a. In *Spells and Philtres* (A.14).

    b. In *Selected Poems* (A.27).

    c. In *The Complete Poetry and Translations*, Volume 2 (A.73).

    Haiku.

338. "Geometries."
    a. *Risqué Stories* No. 1 (March 1984): 41.

    a. In *The Complete Poetry and Translations*, Volume 2 (A.73).

    32 lines. Dated 9 August 1952.

339. "The Ghost of Theseus."
    a. In *Selected Poems* (A.27).

    b. In *The Complete Poetry and Translations*, Volume 2 (A.73).

    Haiku.

340. "The Ghoul."
    a. In *The Complete Poetry and Translations*, Volume 1 (A.73).

    b. In *The Dark Eidolon and Other Fantasies* (A.84).

Sonnet. Dated 16 February 1913.

341. "The Ghoul and the Seraph."
   a. In *Ebony and Crystal* (A.3).
   b. A.12.
   c. In *Selected Poems* (A.27).
   d. In *One Hundred Years of Klarkash-Ton* (III.D.10) (first dialogue only).
   e. In *The Last Oblivion* (A.61).
   f. In *The Complete Poetry and Translations*, Volume 1 (A.73).
   g. In *Moonlight and Other Poems* (A.78).
   h. In *Celui qui marchait parmi les étoiles* (II.A.iii.17).

   132 lines.

342. "Girl of Six."
   a. In *Selected Poems* (A.27).
   b. In *The Complete Poetry and Translations*, Volume 2 (A.73).

   Haiku.

343. "Give Me Your Lips."
   a. *Live Stories* 10, No. 1 (February 1917): 48.
   b. In *The Complete Poetry and Translations*, Volume 1 (A.73).

   22 lines. Dated 3 October 1916.

344. "Goats and Manzanita-Boughs."
   a. In *Selected Poems* (A.27).
   b. In *The Complete Poetry and Translations*, Volume 2 (A.73).

   Haiku.

345. "Gopher-Hole in Orchard."
   a. In *Selected Poems* (A.27).
   b. In *The Complete Poetry and Translations*, Volume 2 (A.73).

   Haiku.

346. "Grammar-School Vixen."
   a. In *Selected Poems* (A.27).
   b. In *The Complete Poetry and Translations*, Volume 2 (A.73).

   Haiku.

347. "Grecian Yesterday."
    a. In *Selected Poems* (A.27).
    b. In *The Complete Poetry and Translations*, Volume 2 (A.73).

    18 lines. Dated 17 February 1941.

348. "Greek Epigram."
    a. In *The Complete Poetry and Translations*, Volume 2 (A.73).

    4 lines.

349. "Growth of Lichen."
    a. In *Spells and Philtres* (A.14).
    b. In *Selected Poems* (A.27).
    c. In *The Complete Poetry and Translations*, Volume 2 (A.73).

    Haiku.

350. "H. P. L."
    a. In H. P. Lovecraft and others. *The Shuttered Room and Other Pieces*. Ed. August Derleth. Sauk City, WI: Arkham House, 1959. 204.
    b. In Scott Connors, ed. *A Century Less a Dream: Selected Criticism of H. P. Lovecraft*. Holicong, PA: Wildside Press, 2002. 253.
    b. In *The Last Oblivion* (A.61).
    c. In *The Complete Poetry and Translations*, Volume 2 (A.73).
    d. In *Celui qui marchait parmi les étoiles* (II.A.iii.17).

    Sonnet. Dated 17 June 1959. A poem in memory of H. P. Lovecraft.

351. "The Harbour of the Past."
    a. In *The Fugitive Poems of Clark Ashton Smith: Second Series* (A.38).
    b. In *The Complete Poetry and Translations*, Volume 1 (A.73).

    Sonnet.

352. "The Harlot of the World."
    a. *Town Talk* No. 1115 (27 March 1915): 5.
    b. In *Odes and Sonnets* (A.2).
    c. *Town Talk* No. 1361 (21 September 1918 ["Golden Gate Literary Number"]): [15].
    d. In *Ebony and Crystal* (A.3).
    e. In *Selected Poems* (A.27).
    f. In *The Complete Poetry and Translations*, Volume 1 (A.73).

g. In *Moonlight and Other Poems* (A.78).
h. In *The Dark Eidolon and Other Fantasies* (A.84).

Sonnet. Written c. January 1915. Variant title: "To Life."

353. "Harmony."
a. In *The Fugitive Poems of Clark Ashton Smith: Second Series* (A.38).
b. In *The Complete Poetry and Translations*, Volume 2 (A.73).

8 lines. Dated 29 January 1929. First title: "Harmony," changed to "Similitude" but ultimately back to "Harmony."

354. "Haroun Al-Raschid."
a. In *The Complete Poetry and Translations*, Volume 1 (A.73).

18 lines. Juvenilia. See item 824.

355. "Harvest Evening."
a. In *Spells and Philtres* (A.14).
b. In *Selected Poems* (A.27).
c. In *The Complete Poetry and Translations*, Volume 2 (A.73).

Haiku. First title: "Buckeyes."

356. *The Hashish-Eater; or, The Apocalypse of Evil.*
a. In *Ebony and Crystal* (A.3).
b. In August Derleth, ed. *Dark of the Moon: Poems of Fantasy and the Macabre.* Sauk City, WI: Arkham House, 1947; Freeport, NY: Books for Libraries Press, 1969; Miami, FL: Granger, 1976. 321–38.
c. In *Selected Poems* (A.27).
d. In Lin Carter, ed. *New Worlds for Old.* New York: Ballantine, 1971. 279–95.
e. A.53.
f. A.55.
g. In *The Last Oblivion* (A.61).
h. In *The Complete Poetry and Translations*, Volume 1 (A.73).
i. In *The Hashish-Eater* (A.75).
j. In *The Miscellaneous Writings of Clark Ashton Smith* (A.82).
k. In Charles Lovecraft, ed. *Avatars of Wizardry.* Sydney, Australia: P'rea Press, 2012. 27–43.
l. In *The Dark Eidolon and Other Fantasies* (A.84).
m. In *Celui qui marchait parmi les étoiles* (II.A.iii.17).

581 lines. Written January–February 1920.

357. "Hate and Love."
    a. In *The Complete Poetry and Translations,* Volume 1 (A.73).

       25 lines. Juvenilia.

358. "Haunting." [All things incomprehensible, unseen,]
    a. In *The Complete Poetry and Translations,* Volume 1 (A.73).

       12 lines. Dated 12 December 1912. A fragment (probably intended to be a sonnet).

359. "Haunting." [There is no peace amid the moonlight and the pines;]
    a. *Lyric West* 1, No. 10 (February 1922): 6.
    b. In *Ebony and Crystal* (A.3).
    c. In *Selected Poems* (A.27).
    d. In *The Complete Poetry and Translations,* Volume 1 (A.73).
    e. In *Moonlight and Other Poems* (A.78).

       12 lines. Written before 24 April 1918.

360. "Hearth on Old Cabin-Site."
    a. In *Selected Poems* (A.27).
    b. In *The Complete Poetry and Translations,* Volume 2 (A.73).

       Haiku.

361. "Heliogabalus."
    a. In *Selected Poems* (A.27) (as a translation from "Christophe des Laurières").
    b. In *The Complete Poetry and Translations,* Volume 1 (A.73).

       Two sonnets. Written c. August 1919.

362. "Hellenic Sequel."
    a. *Arkham Sampler* 1, No. 2 (Spring 1948): 12.
    b. In *The Dark Chateau* (A.13).
    c. In *Selected Poems* (A.27).
    d. In *The Complete Poetry and Translations,* Volume 2 (A.73).

       17 lines.

363. "La Hermosura."
    a. In *The Complete Poetry and Translations,* Volume 2 (A.73).

       4 lines. In Spanish (possibly CAS's first Spanish poem). For CAS's English version, see "Beauty" (item 77).

364. "The Heron."
   a. In *The Complete Poetry and Translations*, Volume 2 (A.73).

   5 lines.

365. "Hesperian Fall."
   a. In *The Dark Chateau* (A.13).
   b. A.17.
   c. In *The Hill of Dionysus* (A.18).
   d. In *Shadows Seen and Unseen* (A.71).
   e. In *The Complete Poetry and Translations*, Volume 2 (A.73).

   95 lines. Written before 22 February 1951. Alternate title: "Hesperian Autumn."

366. "The Hidden Paradise."
   a. In *Ebony and Crystal* (A.3).
   b. In *Selected Poems* (A.27).
   c. In *The Complete Poetry and Translations*, Volume 1 (A.73).
   d. In *Moonlight and Other Poems* (A.78).

   Sonnet. Dated 24 May 1921.

367. "High Mountain Juniper."
   a. In *Selected Poems* (A.27).
   b. In *The Complete Poetry and Translations*, Volume 2 (A.73).

   Haiku.

368. "High Surf."
   a. *Lyric* 37, No. 2 (Spring 1957): 42.
   b. In *Spells and Philtres* (A.14).
   c. In *The Complete Poetry and Translations*, Volume 2 (A.73).

   19 lines.

369. "High Surf: Monterey Bay."
   a. In *The Fugitive Poems of Clark Ashton Smith: Second Series* (A.38).
   b. In *The Complete Poetry and Translations*, Volume 2 (A.73).

   8 lines.

370. "The Hill of Dionysus."
   a. A.16.
   b. In *The Hill of Dionysus* (A.18).
   c. In *Selected Poems* (A.27).

d. In *The Last Oblivion* (A.61).

e. In *The Complete Poetry and Translations,* Volume 2 (A.73).

f. In *The Dark Eidolon and Other Fantasies* (A.84).

g. In *Celui qui marchait parmi les étoiles* (II.A.iii.17).

> 47 lines. Dated 5 November 1942. Alternate title: "Hill of Dionysus."

371. "The Hill-Top."

a. In The Edwin Markham Poetry Society, ed. *The Laureate's Wreath: An Anthology in Honor of Dr. Henry Meade Bland, Poet Laureate of California.* San Jose: The Edwin Markham Poetry Society, 1934. 108.

b. In Rufus Rockwell Wilson, ed. *The Golden Year: A Calendar of the Poets.* New York: Wilson-Erickson, 1936. 15.

c. In Stanton A. Coblentz, ed. *The Music Makers.* New York: Bernard Ackerman, 1945. 225–26.

d. In *Selected Poems* (A.27).

e. In *The Complete Poetry and Translations,* Volume 2 (A.73).

> 24 lines. Dated 21 March 1929.

372. "Hope."

a. In *The Complete Poetry and Translations,* Volume 1 (A.73).

> 6 lines. Juvenilia.

373. "The Hope of the Infinite."

a. In *Ebony and Crystal* (A.3).

b. In *Selected Poems* (A.27).

c. In *The Last Oblivion* (A.61).

d. In *The Complete Poetry and Translations,* Volume 1 (A.73).

e. In *Moonlight and Other Poems* (A.78).

f. In *Celui qui marchait parmi les étoiles* (II.A.iii.17).

> Sonnet. Dated 17 September 1919. First title: "Esperance."

374. "The Horizon."

a. *Overland Monthly* 58, No. 2 (August 1911): 119 (as by C. Ashton Smith).

b. In *Shadows Seen and Unseen* (A.71).

c. In *The Complete Poetry and Translations,* Volume 1 (A.73).

d. In *Moonlight and Other Poems* (A.78).

> 12 lines. Alternate title: "The Horizon Line."

375. "The Horologe."
   a. In August Derleth, ed. *Fire and Sleet and Candlelight*. Sauk City, WI: Arkham House, 1961. 186.
   b. In *Selected Poems* (A.27).
   c. In *The Complete Poetry and Translations*, Volume 2 (A.73).
   4 lines.

376. "The Hosts of Heaven."
   a. In *The Complete Poetry and Translations*, Volume 1 (A.73).
   Sonnet.

377. "Humors of Love."
   a. *Saturday Review of Literature* 29, No. 33 (17 August 1946): 11.
   b. In *The Hill of Dionysus* (A.18).
   c. In *Selected Poems* (A.27).
   d. In *The Complete Poetry and Translations*, Volume 2 (A.73).
   Sonnet. Written before 29 October 1941.

378. "A Hunter Meets the Martichoras."
   a. In *Spells and Philtres* (A.14).
   b. In *Selected Poems* (A.27).
   c. In *The Complete Poetry and Translations*, Volume 2 (A.73).
   Haiku.

379. "Hymn."
   a. In *The Complete Poetry and Translations*, Volume 2 (A.73).
   24 lines.

380. "I Shall Not Greatly Grieve."
   a. In *The Complete Poetry and Translations*, Volume 2 (A.73).
   16 lines. Dated 5 August 1952. Alternate title: "Haply I Shall Not Greatly Grieve."

381. "Idylle païenne." [English]
   a. In *The Complete Poetry and Translations*, Volume 1 (A.73).
   28 lines. See CAS's French version of the same title (item 381).

382. "Idylle païenne." [French]
   a. In *The Complete Poetry and Translations*, Volume 1 (A.73).

28 lines. See CAS's English version of the same title (item 280).

383. "If Winter Remain."
   a. In *Selected Poems* (A.27).
   b. In *The Complete Poetry and Translations*, Volume 2 (A.73).
   c. In *The Dark Eidolon and Other Fantasies* (A.84).

   41 lines. Dated 26 January 1949.

384. "Lo Ignoto."
   a. In *¿Donde Duermes, Eldorado? y Otros Poemas* (A.21).
   b. In *The Complete Poetry and Translations*, Volume 2 (A.73).

   14 lines. In Spanish. Dated 22 May 1950. For CAS's English version, see "The Unknown" (item 924).

385. "Illumination."
   a. In *The Hill of Dionysus* (A.18).
   b. In *Selected Poems* (A.27).
   c. In *The Complete Poetry and Translations*, Volume 2 (A.73).

   Sonnet. Dated 9 September 1943.

386. "Illuminatus."
   a. In *The Complete Poetry and Translations*, Volume 2 (A.73).

   Haiku.

387. "Illusion."
   a. In *The Complete Poetry and Translations*, Volume 1 (A.73).

   8 lines. Written c. 1910.

388. "Image."
   a. In *Ebony and Crystal* (A.3).
   b. In *Selected Poems* (A.27).
   c. In *The Complete Poetry and Translations*, Volume 1 (A.73).

   16 lines. Written before 24 April 1918.

389. "Imagination."
   a. In *The Last Oblivion* (A.61).
   b. In *The Complete Poetry and Translations*, Volume 1 (A.73).
   c. In *Celui qui marchait parmi les étoiles* (II.A.iii.17).

   108 lines.

390. "Immortelle."
   a. *Auburn Journal* 25, No. 10 (18 December 1924): 14.
   b. In *The Fugitive Poems of Clark Ashton Smith: Second Series* (A.38).
   c. In *The Complete Poetry and Translations,* Volume 1 (A.73).

   10 lines. Dated 2 September 1924.

391. "Impression."
   a. In *Ebony and Crystal* (A.3).
   b. In Wallace Alvin Briggs, ed. *Great Poems of the English Language.* New York: Robert M. McBride, 1927; London: George C. Harrap & Co., 1928. 1338. Rev. ed. New York: Tudor Publishing Co., 1936. 1338.
   c. *Ottumwa* [IA] *Daily Courier* (5 September 1934): 4.
   d. *Dispatch* (Moline, IL) (6 September 1934): 6.
   e. *San Bernardino Sun* (10 September 1934): 8.
   f. *Wilkes-Barre* [PA] *Record* (10 September 1934): 14.
   g. *Oshkosh* [WI] *Northwestern* (12 September 1934): 12.
   h. In *Selected Poems* (A.27).
   i. In *The Complete Poetry and Translations,* Volume 1 (A.73).
   j. In *Moonlight and Other Poems* (A.78).

   12 lines. Dated 20 November 1916.

392. "Improbable Dream."
   a. In *Selected Poems* (A.27).
   b. In *The Complete Poetry and Translations,* Volume 2 (A.73).

   Haiku.

393. "In a Distant Universe."
   a. In *The Complete Poetry and Translations,* Volume 2 (A.73).

   35 lines. Written before 7 December 1949. For CAS's French version, see "Dans l'univers lointain" (item 171).

394. "In Alexandria."
   a. In *Selected Poems* (A.27) (as a translation from "Christophe des Laurières").
   b. In *The Complete Poetry and Translations,* Volume 1 (A.73).

   13 lines.

395. "In Another August."
   a. In *The Complete Poetry and Translations,* Volume 2 (A.73).

20 lines. Dated 11 September 1942.

396. "In Autumn."
  a. In *The Complete Poetry and Translations*, Volume 1 (A.73).
  8 lines. Dated 9 September 1924.

397. "In Extremis."
  a. In *The Complete Poetry and Translations*, Volume 1 (A.73).
  8 lines.

398. "In Lemuria."
  a. *Lyric West* 1, No. 4 (July–August 1921): 6.
  b. In *Ebony and Crystal* (A.3).
  c. *Outré* No. 3 (c. 1956): 24.
  d. In *Selected Poems* (A.27).
  e. In *Poseidonis* (A.34).
  f. In *The Last Oblivion* (A.61).
  g. In *The Complete Poetry and Translations*, Volume 1 (A.73).
  Sonnet. Dated 24 December 1919.

399. "In November."
  a. *Ainslee's* 44, No. 5 (December 1919): 121.
  b. In *Ebony and Crystal* (A.3).
  c. In *The Complete Poetry and Translations*, Volume 1 (A.73).
  12 lines. Written before 24 April 1918.

400. "In Saturn."
  a. *Sonnet* 2, No. 2 (January–February 1919): 2.
  b. In *Ebony and Crystal* (A.3).
  c. In *Selected Poems* (A.27).
  d. In *The Last Oblivion* (A.61).
  e. In *The Complete Poetry and Translations*, Volume 1 (A.73).
  Sonnet. Written before 24 April 1918. First title: "Upon the Seas of Saturn."

401. "In Slumber."
  a. *Weird Tales* 24, No. 2 (August 1934): 253.
  b. In *The Dark Chateau* (A.13).
  c. In *Selected Poems* (A.27).

d. In Farnsworth Wright, ed. *Weird Tales, Volume 24, Number 2 (August 1934)*. Mississauga, ON: Girasol Collectables, 2007. 253 (facsimile of a.).
e. In *The Complete Poetry and Translations*, Volume 2 (A.73).
f. In *The Song of the Necromancer and Others* (A.81).

30 lines. Written before 21 January 1934.

402. "In the Desert."
a. In *Selected Poems* (A.27).
b. In *The Last Oblivion* (A.61).
c. In *The Complete Poetry and Translations*, Volume 1 (A.73).

28 lines.

403. "In the Ultimate Valleys."
a. In *In the Ultimate Valleys* (A.26).
b. In *The Complete Poetry and Translations*, Volume 1 (A.73).

16 lines. Written 17 December 1912.

404. "In the Wind."
a. *Poetry* 6, No. 4 (July 1915): 178.
b. In *Selected Poems* (A.27).
c. In *The Complete Poetry and Translations*, Volume 1 (A.73).

4 lines.

405. "In Thessaly."
a. *Weird Tales* 26, No. 5 (November 1935): 551.
b. In August Derleth, ed. *Dark of the Moon: Poems of Fantasy and the Macabre*. Sauk City, WI: Arkham House, 1947; Freeport, NY: Books for Libraries Press, 1969; Miami, FL: Granger, 1976. 344–45.
c. In *Selected Poems* (A.27).
d. In *The Last Oblivion* (A.61).
e. In *The Complete Poetry and Translations*, Volume 2 (A.73).
f. In Farnsworth Wright, ed. *Weird Tales, Volume 26, Number 5 (November 1935)*. Mississauga, ON: Girasol Collectables, 2009. 551 (facsimile of a.).
g. In *The Song of the Necromancer and Others* (A.81).

18 lines. Dated 24 May 1935.

406. "In Time of Absence."
a. In *The Complete Poetry and Translations*, Volume 2 (A.73).

16 lines. The ms. is dated 20 June 1952.

407. "Incognita."
   a. *Auburn Journal* 25 No. 25 (2 April 1925): 12.
   b. In *Sandalwood* (A.4).
   c. *Step Ladder* 13, No. 5 (May 1927): 137.
   d. In *Selected Poems* (A.27).
   e. In *The Complete Poetry and Translations*, Volume 1 (A.73).

   Sonnet. Dated 15 January 1925. Variant title: "Unique."

408. "The Incubus of Time."
   a. In August Derleth, ed. *Fire and Sleet and Candlelight*. Sauk City, WI: Arkham House, 1961. 184–85.
   b. In *Selected Poems* (A.27).
   c. In *The Last Oblivion* (A.61).
   d. In *The Complete Poetry and Translations*, Volume 1 (A.73).

   Sonnet.

409. "Indian Acorn-Mortar."
   a. In *Selected Poems* (A.27).
   b. In *The Complete Poetry and Translations*, Volume 2 (A.73).

   Haiku.

410. "Indian Summer."
   a. In *Selected Poems* (A.27).
   b. In *The Complete Poetry and Translations*, Volume 2 (A.73).

   11 lines.

411. "Ineffability."
   a. In *In Memoriam: Clark Ashton Smith* (III.D.4).
   b. In *Selected Poems* (A.27).
   c. In *The Complete Poetry and Translations*, Volume 2 (A.73).

   12 lines. Dated 18 September 1929. First title: "Ineffabilité."

412. "Inferno."
   a. In *Ebony and Crystal* (A.3).
   b. In *Selected Poems* (A.27).
   c. In *The Complete Poetry and Translations*, Volume 1 (A.73).
   d. In *Moonlight and Other Poems* (A.78).

   Sonnet. Dated 24 April 1918.

413. "The Infinite Quest."
   a. *Lyric West* 1, No. 4 (July–August 1921): 6.
   b. In *Ebony and Crystal* (A.3).
   c. In *Selected Poems* (A.27).
   d. In *The Fugitive Poems of Clark Ashton Smith: Second Series* (A.38) (as "The Unfinished Quest").
   e. In *The Complete Poetry and Translations,* Volume 1 (A.73).
   f. In *Moonlight and Other Poems* (A.78).
   g. In *Celui qui marchait parmi les étoiles* (II.A.iii.17).

   12 lines. Alternate title: "The Unfinished Quest."

414. "Inheritance."
   a. In *Ebony and Crystal* (A.3).
   b. In *Selected Poems* (A.27).
   c. In *The Complete Poetry and Translations,* Volume 1 (A.73).
   d. In *Moonlight and Other Poems* (A.78).

   16 lines. Written c. March 1915.

415. "Initiate of Dionysus."
   a. In *The Complete Poetry and Translations,* Volume 2 (A.73).

   Haiku. Alternate title: "Initiate."

416. "The Inscription."
   a. In *The Complete Poetry and Translations,* Volume 1 (A.73).

   2 lines. Juvenilia.

417. "Interim."
   a. *Scienti-Snaps* 3, No. 1 (February 1940): 14.
   b. *Auburn Journal* 69, No 100 (13 November 1941): 5 (last 10 lines omitted).
   c. *Wings* 5, No. 3 (Autumn 1941): 12.
   d. In *The Hill of Dionysus* (A.18).
   e. In *Selected Poems* (A.27).
   f. In *The Complete Poetry and Translations,* Volume 2 (A.73).

   39 lines. Written c. September 1934.

418. "Interrogation."
   a. In *Sandalwood* (A.4).
   b. *Weird Tales* 10, No. 3 (September 1927): 414.

    c. In [Unsigned, ed.] *Principal Poets of the World: Volume 1: 1930–1931*. London: Mitre Press, 1932. 182.

    d. In *Selected Poems* (A.27).

    e. In *The Last Oblivion* (A.61).

    f. In *The Complete Poetry and Translations*, Volume 1 (A.73).

    g. In *The Song of the Necromancer and Others* (A.81).

    25 lines. Dated 14 September 1925.

419. "Interval."

    a. In *The Complete Poetry and Translations*, Volume 2 (A.73).

    15 lines. Dated 20 April 1943.

420. "The Invisible Host."

    a. *Farm Journal* 25, No. 5 (November 1911): 546.

    b. In *The Complete Poetry and Translations*, Volume 1 (A.73.b).

    16 lines.

421. "Isaac Newton."

    a. In *The Complete Poetry and Translations*, Volume 2 (A.73).

    16 lines.

422. "La isla de Circe."

    a. In *Shadows Seen and Unseen* (A.71).

    b. In *The Complete Poetry and Translations*, Volume 2 (A.73).

    16 lines. In Spanish. Written 24 September 1950. For CAS's Spanish version, see "The Isle of Circe" (item 425).

423. "La isla del náufrago."

    a. In *¿Donde Duermes, Eldorado? y Otros Poemas* (A.21).

    b. In *The Complete Poetry and Translations*, Volume 2 (A.73).

    18 lines. In Spanish. Dated 18 December 1953. For CAS's English version, see "Isle of the Shipwrecked" (item 427).

424. "The Island of a Dream."

    a. In *The Complete Poetry and Translations*, Volume 1 (A.73).

    12 lines.

425. "The Isle of Circe."

    a. In *Shadows Seen and Unseen* (A.71).

    b. In *The Complete Poetry and Translations*, Volume 2 (A.73).

16 lines. Written 1950. For CAS's Spanish version, see "La isla de Circe" (item 422).

426. "The Isle of Saturn."
   a.   In *The Dark Chateau* (A.13).
   b.   In *Poseidonis* (A.34).
   c.   In *The Black Book of Clark Ashton Smith* (A.39).
   d.   In *The Sword of Zagan and Other Writings* (A.64).
   e.   In *The Complete Poetry and Translations*, Volume 2 (A.73).

   40 lines. Written 1950.

427. "Isle of the Shipwrecked."
   a.   In *The Complete Poetry and Translations*, Volume 2 (A.73).

   18 lines. For CAS's Spanish version, see "La isla del náufrago" (item 423).

428. "January Willow."
   a.   In *Selected Poems* (A.27).
   b.   In *The Complete Poetry and Translations*, Volume 2 (A.73).

   Haiku. Later version of "Californian Winter" (item 111).

429. "Jewel of the Orient." [Amid palm groves and almond trees,]
   a.   In *The Complete Poetry and Translations*, Volume 1 (A.73).

   68 lines. Juvenilia. Possibly a fragment.

430. "Jewel of the Orient." [In Bagdad, capital of the caliphate,]
   a.   In *The Complete Poetry and Translations*, Volume 1 (A.73).

   39 lines. Juvenilia. Apparently a fragment.

431. "Jungle Twilight."
   a.   *Oriental Stories* 2, No. 3 (Summer 1932): 420 (15 lines only).
   b.   In *Spells and Philtres* (A.14).
   c.   In *Selected Poems* (A.27).
   d.   In *The Last Oblivion* (A.61).
   e.   In Farnsworth Wright, ed. *Oriental Stories, Volume 2, Number 3 (Summer 1932)*. Mississauga, ON: Girasol Collectables, 2007. 420 (facsimile of a.).
   f.   In *The Complete Poetry and Translations*, Volume 2 (A.73).

   20 lines. Written early September 1930.

432. "Kin."
   a. In *The Complete Poetry and Translations,* Volume 2 (A.73).
      8 lines.

433. "The Kingdom of Shadows."
   a. In *Ebony and Crystal* (A.3).
   b. In *Selected Poems* (A.27).
   c. In *The Last Oblivion* (A.61).
   d. In *The Complete Poetry and Translations,* Volume 1 (A.73).
   e. In *Moonlight and Other Poems* (A.78).
   f. In *Celui qui marchait parmi les étoiles* (II.A.iii.17).
      40 lines.

434. "Kismet."
   a. In *The Complete Poetry and Translations,* Volume 1 (A.73).
      9 lines. Juvenilia.

435. "The Knoll."
   a. *Kansas City Poetry Magazine* 4, No. 4 (January 1944): 4.
   b. In *The Hill of Dionysus* (A.18).
   c. In *Selected Poems* (A.27).
   d. In *The Complete Poetry and Translations,* Volume 2 (A.73).
      30 lines.

436. "Le Lac d'automne."
   a. In *The Complete Poetry and Translations,* Volume 2 (A.73).
      8 lines. Written c. 1928. See CAS's English version, "The Autumn Lake" (item 61).

437. "Lament of the Stars."
   a. In *The Star-Treader and Other Poems* (A.1).
   b. In *The Complete Poetry and Translations,* Volume 1 (A.73).
   c. In *Moonlight and Other Poems* (A.78).
      77 lines.

438. "Lamia."
   a. *Arkham Sampler* 1, No. 1 (Winter 1948): 20.
   b. In *The Dark Chateau* (A.13).
   c. In *Selected Poems* (A.27).
   d. In *The Last Oblivion* (A.61).

    e. In *Shadows Seen and Unseen* (A.71).

    f. In *The Complete Poetry and Translations*, Volume 2 (A.73).

    g. In *Celui qui marchait parmi les étoiles* (II.A.iii.17).

      19 lines. Dated 24 January 1940.

439. "The Land o' Dreams."

    a. In *The Complete Poetry and Translations*, Volume 1 (A.73).

      40 lines. Juvenilia.

440. "The Land of Evil Stars."

    a. In *Ebony and Crystal* (A.3).

    b. In *Selected Poems* (A.27).

    c. In *The Last Oblivion* (A.61).

    d. In *The Complete Poetry and Translations*, Volume 1 (A.73).

    e. In *Moonlight and Other Poems* (A.78).

      43 lines. Written c. February 1913.

441. "The Last Apricot."

    a. In *Spells and Philtres* (A.14).

    b. In *Selected Poems* (A.27).

    c. In *The Complete Poetry and Translations*, Volume 2 (A.73).

      Haiku.

442. "The Last Goddess (A Fragment)."

    a. In *Selected Poems* (A.27).

    b. In *The Last Oblivion* (A.61).

    c. In *The Complete Poetry and Translations*, Volume 1 (A.73).

      18 lines. Written c. September 1912. Alternate title: "A Fragment."

443. "The Last Night."

    a. In *The Star-Treader and Other Poems* (A.1).

    b. *Strange Fantasy* (Winter 1940): 44.

    c. In *Selected Poems* (A.27).

    d. In *The Last Oblivion* (A.61).

    e. In *The Complete Poetry and Translations*, Volume 1 (A.73).

    f. In *Moonlight and Other Poems* (A.78).

    g. In *The Dark Eidolon and Other Fantasies* (A.84).

    h. In *Celui qui marchait parmi les étoiles* (II.A.iii.17).

Sonnet. Written c. February 1911. Quoted in full in III.A.33, prior to its appearance in *The Star-Treader.*.

444. "The Last Oblivion."
   a. *Auburn Journal* 24, No. 17 (7 February 1924): 6.
   b. In *Sandalwood* (A.4).
   c. In *Selected Poems* (A.27).
   d. In *The Last Oblivion* (A.61).
   e. In *The Complete Poetry and Translations,* Volume 1 (A.73).

   Sonnet. First title: "Oblivion."

445. "Late November Evening."
   a. In *Selected Poems* (A.27).
   b. In *The Complete Poetry and Translations,* Volume 2 (A.73).

   5 lines.

446. "Late Pear-Pruner."
   a. In *Spells and Philtres* (A.14).
   b. In *Selected Poems* (A.27).
   c. In *The Complete Poetry and Translations,* Volume 2 (A.73).

   Haiku.

447. "Laus Mortis."
   a. *Pearson's Magazine* 47, No. 3 (September 1921): 100.
   b. In *Ebony and Crystal* (A.3).
   c. In *Selected Poems* (A.27).
   d. In *The Last Oblivion* (A.61).
   e. In *The Complete Poetry and Translations,* Volume 1 (A.73).
   f. In *Moonlight and Other Poems* (A.78).
   g. In *Celui qui marchait parmi les étoiles* (II.A.iii.17).

   Sonnet. Written February 1919.

448. "Lawn-Mower."
   a. In *The Fugitive Poems of Clark Ashton Smith: Second Series* (A.38).
   b. In *The Complete Poetry and Translations,* Volume 2 (A.73).

   7 lines. Written c. 1954–55.

449. "Lemurienne."
   a. *Auburn Journal* 24, No. 10 (20 December 1923): 6 (as "The Lemurienne").

b. *Arkham Collector* No. 3 (Summer 1968): 57 (as "The Lemurienne").
c. In *Selected Poems* (A.27).
d. In *Poseidonis* (A.34).
e. In *The Complete Poetry and Translations*, Volume 1 (A.73).

4 lines.

450. "Leteo."
a. In *The Complete Poetry and Translations*, Volume 2 (A.73).

8 lines. In Spanish. For CAS's English version, see "[Lethe]" (item 454).

451. "Lethe." [From the nameless dark distilled,]
a. In *The Complete Poetry and Translations*, Volume 2 (A.73).

Haiku. Alternate title: "Oblivion."

452. "Lethe." [I flow beneath the columns that upbear]
a. In *The Star-Treader and Other Poems* (A.1).
b. In *Selected Poems* (A.27).
c. In *The Last Oblivion* (A.61).
d. In *The Complete Poetry and Translations*, Volume 1 (A.73).

Sonnet.

453. "Lethe." [Seekst thou that Lethe of whose depths profound]
a. *Rosary Magazine* 39, No. 5 (November 1911): 555.
b. In *The Complete Poetry and Translations*, Volume 1 (A.73).

4 lines.

454. "[Lethe.]" [Somber and waveless on the waters]
a. In *The Complete Poetry and Translations*, Volume 2 (A.73).

8 lines. For CAS's Spanish version, see "Leteo" (item 450).

455. "The Leveler."
a. In *The Complete Poetry and Translations*, Volume 1 (A.73).

16 lines. Juvenilia.

456. "Lichens."
a. *Wings* 1, No. 2 (Summer 1933): 7.
b. *Virginian-Pilot and the Norfolk Landmark* (10 September 1933): 6.
c. *Dallas Morning News* (18 September 1933): 1.

   d. *Daily Press* [Newport News, VA] (19 September 1933): 3.
   e. *News and Observer* [Raleigh, NC] (24 September 1933): 13.
   f. *Berkeley Daily Gazette* (30 October 1933): 17.
   g. *Berkeley Daily Gazette* (13 April 1934): 9.
   h. *Charleston News and Courier* (3 June 1934): 4.
   i. *Stars* (December 1940–January 1941): 2.
   j. In *Selected Poems* (A.27).
   k. In *Shadows Seen and Unseen* (A.71).
   l. In *The Complete Poetry and Translations,* Volume 2 (A.73).

   17 lines. Dated 8 February 1929.

457. "Limericks."
   a. In *The Complete Poetry and Translations,* Volume 2 (A.73).

   17 limericks (16 of 5 lines, 1 of 4 lines; one titled "Ripe Mulberries").

458. "Limestone Cavern."
   a. In *The Complete Poetry and Translations,* Volume 2 (A.73).

   Haiku.

459. "The Limniad."
   a. In *Selected Poems* (A.27).
   b. In *The Complete Poetry and Translations,* Volume 2 (A.73).

   Haiku.

460. "Lines on a Picture."
   a. *Raven* 2, No. 1 (Spring 1944): 22.
   b. In *Selected Poems* (A.27).
   c. In *The Complete Poetry and Translations,* Volume 2 (A.73).

   12 lines. Dated 3 January 1944. First title: "To Lilith." Suggested by a photograph of Lilith Lorraine.

461. "A Live-Oak Leaf."
   a. In *The Star-Treader and Other Poems* (A.1).
   b. In *The Complete Poetry and Translations,* Volume 2 (A.73).
   c. In *Moonlight and Other Poems* (A.78).

   8 lines. Written c. October 1911

462. "Lives of the Saints."
   a. In *The Complete Poetry and Translations,* Volume 2 (A.73).

4 lines. Early draft titled "Censored." A poem imitating the style of Ogden Nash.

463. "Loss."
   a. In *Sandalwood* (A.4).
   b. *United Amateur* 25, No. 2 (May 1926): 8.
   c. In *Selected Poems* (A.27).
   d. In *The Complete Poetry and Translations*, Volume 1 (A.73).

   20 lines. Dated 30 January 1925.

464. "Lost Beauty."
   a. In *The Complete Poetry and Translations*, Volume 1 (A.73).

   Sonnet.

465. "Lost Farmsteads."
   a. In *The Complete Poetry and Translations*, Volume 2 (A.73).

   35 lines. For CAS's Spanish version, see "Los alquerías perdidas" (item 27).

466. "Love."
   a. In *The Complete Poetry and Translations*, Volume 1 (A.73).

   20 lines. Juvenilia.

467. "Love and Death."
   a. In *Selected Poems* (A.27).
   b. In *The Complete Poetry and Translations*, Volume 2 (A.73).

   6 lines.

468. "Love in Dreams."
   a. In *Selected Poems* (A.27).
   b. In *The Complete Poetry and Translations*, Volume 2 (A.73).

   Haiku.

469. "Love Is Not Yours, Love Is Not Mine."
   a. In *Ebony and Crystal* (A.3).
   b. *Step Ladder* 13, No. 5 (May 1927): 134–5.
   c. In *Selected Poems* (A.27).
   d. In *The Complete Poetry and Translations*, Volume 1 (A.73).
   e. In *Moonlight and Other Poems* (A.78).

   8 lines. Dated 25 June 1922. First title: "Song."

470. "Love Malevolent."
   a. *Live Stories* 8, No. 3 (October 1916): 122.
   b. *Medical World* 35, No. 3 (March 1917): 102.
   c. In *Ebony and Crystal* (A.3).
   d. *Step Ladder* 13, No. 5 (May 1927): 134.
   e. In *The Last Oblivion* (A.61).
   f. In *The Complete Poetry and Translations*, Volume 1 (A.73).
   g. In *Moonlight and Other Poems* (A.78).
   h. In *The Dark Eidolon and Other Fantasies* (A.84).

   Sonnet.

471. "The Love-Potion."
   a. *Auburn Journal* 23, No. 29 (3 May 1923): 6.
   b. In *Sandalwood* (A.4).
   c. *Step Ladder* 13, No. 5 (May 1927): 135.
   d. In *Selected Poems* (A.27).
   e. In *The Complete Poetry and Translations*, Volume 1 (A.73).

   12 lines. Written before 10 May 1923. Part of an unfinished play, *The Fugitives* (item 329).

472. "Luna Aeternalis."
   a. *Weird Tales* 42, No. 4 (May 1950): 43.
   b. In *The Dark Chateau* (A.13).
   c. In *Selected Poems* (A.27).
   d. In *The Last Oblivion* (A.61).
   e. In *The Complete Poetry and Translations*, Volume 1 (A.73).
   f. In *The Song of the Necromancer and Others* (A.81).

   44 lines. Written 12 December 1912; rev. 1948.

473. "Lunar Mystery."
   a. In *Sandalwood* (A.4).
   b. In *Selected Poems* (A.27).
   c. In *Grotesques and Fantastiques* (A.32) (as "Dream-Mystery").
   d. In *The Last Oblivion* (A.61).
   e. In *The Complete Poetry and Translations*, Volume 1 (A.73).
   f. In *Moonlight and Other Poems* (A.78) (as "Dream Mystery").

   21 lines. Dated 5 July 1915 in c. First title: "Dream-Mystery."

474. "The Lure of Gold."
   a. In *The Complete Poetry and Translations*, Volume 1 (A.73).

22 lines. Juvenilia.

475. "The Mad Wind."
 a. *San Francisco Call* (2 August 1912): 2.
 b. In *The Star-Treader and Other Poems* (A.1).
 c. In *Selected Poems* (A.27).
 d. In *The Complete Poetry and Translations*, Volume 1 (A.73).
 e. In *Moonlight and Other Poems* (A.78).

 10 lines.

476. "Madrigal."
 a. In *Selected Poems* (A.27) (as a translation from "Christophe des Laurières").
 b. In *The Complete Poetry and Translations*, Volume 1 (A.73).

 10 lines. Written c. 14 September 1925.

477. "A Madrigal."
 a. In *The Fugitive Poems of Clark Ashton Smith: Second Series* (A.38).
 b. In *The Complete Poetry and Translations*, Volume 1 (A.73).

 15 lines. An English translation of "Un Madrigal" (item 478).

478. "Un Madrigal."
 a. In *The Complete Poetry and Translations*, Volume 1 (A.73).

 15 lines. In French. Alternate title: "Madrical." See CAS's English translation, "A Madrigal" (item 477).

479. "Madrigal of Evanescence."
 a. *Kaleidoscope* 2, No. 11 (March 1931): 3.
 b. In *Selected Poems* (A.27).
 c. In *The Complete Poetry and Translations*, Volume 2 (A.73).

 15 lines.

480. "Madrigal of Memory."
 a. *Kaleidograph* 13, No. 9 (January 1942): 7.
 b. In *Selected Poems* (A.27).
 c. In *The Complete Poetry and Translations*, Volume 2 (A.73).
 d. In *The Dark Eidolon and Other Fantasies* (A.84).

 25 lines. Written 15 July 1941.

481. "Malediction."
   a. In *The Dark Chateau* (A.13).
   b. In *Shadows Seen and Unseen* (A.71).
   c. In *The Complete Poetry and Translations*, Volume 2 (A.73).
      19 lines.

482. "La Mare."
   a. In *Selected Poems* (A.27).
   b. In *The Complete Poetry and Translations*, Volume 2 (A.73).
      16 lines. In French. Dated 3 August 1929.

483. "Les Marées."
   a. In *Selected Poems* (A.27).
   b. In *The Complete Poetry and Translations*, Volume 2 (A.73).
      14 lines. In French. Dated 24 July 1929.

484. "The Masque of Forsaken Gods."
   a. In *The Star-Treader and Other Poems* (A.1).
   b. In *Selected Poems* (A.27).
   c. In *The Complete Poetry and Translations*, Volume 1 (A.73).
   d. In *Moonlight and Other Poems* (A.78).
   e. *Fungi* No. 21 (Summer 2013): 346–47.
      139 lines.

485. "Maternal Prostitute."
   a. In *The Complete Poetry and Translations*, Volume 2 (A.73).
      Haiku.

486. "Maya."
   a. *Auburn Journal* 25, No. 23 (19 March 1925): 4.
   b. In *Sandalwood* (A.4).
   c. *Step-Ladder* 13, No. 5 (May 1927): 135.
   d. *Helios* 1, No. 3 (October–November–December 1937): 11.
   e. *Fantasy Times* 1, No. 10 (December 1945): 8.
   f. *Inside* No. 2 (June 1963): 11.
   g. In *Selected Poems* (A.27).
   h. In *The Last Oblivion* (A.61).
   i. In *The Complete Poetry and Translations*, Volume 1 (A.73).
      Sonnet. Written c. March 1925.

487. "The Maze of Sleep."
   a. In *The Star-Treader and Other Poems* (A.1).
   b. In *Selected Poems* (A.27).
   c. In *The Complete Poetry and Translations,* Volume 1 (A.73).
   d. In *Moonlight and Other Poems* (A.78).

   4 lines.

488. "The Meaning."
   a. In *The Star-Treader and Other Poems* (A.1) (as "The Mystic Meaning").
   b. *Los Angeles Science Fantasy Society Newsletter* No. 22 (February 1964): 2 (as "The Mystic Meaning").
   c. In *Selected Poems* (A.27).

   12 lines. Written c. 1911.

489. "Medusa."
   a. In *The Star-Treader and Other Poems* (A.1).
   b. *Fantasy Fan* 2, No. 3 (November 1934): 46–47.
   c. In *Nero and Other Poems* (A.8).
   d. In *Selected Poems* (A.27).
   e. In *The Last Oblivion* (A.61).
   f. In *The Complete Poetry and Translations,* Volume 1 (A.73).
   g. In *Moonlight and Other Poems* (A.78).
   h. In Charles D. Hornig, ed. *The Fantasy Fan: September, 1933–February, 1935.* [n.p.: Lance Thingmaker, 2010.] [Part 2,] 46–47 (facsimile of b.).
   i. In *Celui qui marchait parmi les étoiles* (II.A.iii.17).

   39 lines. Dated 17 May 1911.

490. "The Medusa of Despair."
   a. *Town Talk* No. 1113 (20 December 1913): 8.
   b. In *Odes and Sonnets* (A.2).
   c. In *Ebony and Crystal* (A.3).
   d. In *Selected Poems* (A.27).
   e. In *The Last Oblivion* (A.61).
   f. In *The Complete Poetry and Translations,* Volume 1 (A.73).
   g. In *Moonlight and Other Poems* (A.78).
   h. In *The Dark Eidolon and Other Fantasies* (A.84).

   Sonnet. Written c. June 1913.

491. "The Medusa of the Skies."
   a. In *The Star-Treader and Other Poems* (A.1).
   b. In *Selected Poems* (A.27).
   c. In *The Last Oblivion* (A.61).
   d. In *The Complete Poetry and Translations*, Volume 1 (A.73).
   e. In *Moonlight and Other Poems* (A.78).

   Sonnet. For CAS's French translation, see "La Méduse des cieux" (item 492).

492. "La Méduse des cieux."
   a. In *The Complete Poetry and Translations*, Volume 1 (A.73).

   Sonnet. Alternate title: "The Medusa of the Skies." A French translation of "The Medusa of the Skies" (item 491).

493. "A Meeting."
   a. *Auburn Journal* 24, No. 12 (3 January 1924): 6.
   b. *Fresno Bee* (1 March 1924): 28.
   c. In *Sandalwood* (A.4).
   d. In *The Complete Poetry and Translations*, Volume 1 (A.73).

   39 lines. First title: "To Columbine."

494. "Melancholia."
   a. In *The Complete Poetry and Translations*, Volume 2 (A.73).

   24 lines. The last two stanzas are mutilated in the ms. For CAS's Spanish version, see "Añoranza" (item 40).

495. "The Melancholy Pool."
   a. In *Ebony and Crystal* (A.3).
   b. *Weird Tales* 3, No. 3 (March 1924): 21.
   c. *Manitoba Literary Supplement* (4 November 1927): 3 (as "Melancholy Pool").
   d. In *Selected Poems* (A.27).
   e. In *The Last Oblivion* (A.61).
   f. In *The Complete Poetry and Translations*, Volume 1 (A.73).
   g. In *Moonlight and Other Poems* (A.78).
   h. In *The Song of the Necromancer and Others* (A.81).

   Sonnet.

496. "Memnon at Midnight."
   a. In *Odes and Sonnets* (A.2).

b. In *Ebony and Crystal* (A.3).
c. In Edwin Markham, ed. *Songs and Stories*. Los Angeles: Powell Publishing Company, 1931; Freeport, NY: Books for Libraries Press, 1974. 425.
d. In *Selected Poems* (A.27).
e. In *The Last Oblivion* (A.61).
f. In *The Complete Poetry and Translations*, Volume 1 (A.73).
g. In *Moonlight and Other Poems* (A.78).
h. In *The Dark Eidolon and Other Fantasies* (A.84).
i. In *Celui qui marchait parmi les étoiles* (II.A.iii.17).

Sonnet. Written before 11 March 1915.

497. "Memoria roja."
a. In *¿Donde Duermes, Eldorado? y Otros Poemas* (A.21).
b. In *The Complete Poetry and Translations*, Volume 2 (A.73).
c. *Vórtice en Línea* No. 3 (2005): 4.
d. *Weird Tales de Lhork* No. 29 (2008): 18.

18 lines. In Spanish. Written 20 May 1950. For CAS's English version, see "Red Memory" (item 684).

498. "Memorial."
a. In August Derleth, ed. *Fire and Sleet and Candlelight*. Sauk City, WI: Arkham House, 1961. 185–86.
b. In *Selected Poems* (A.27).
c. In *The Complete Poetry and Translations*, Volume 1 (A.73).

Sonnet. Written before 24 April 1918.

499. "A Memory."
a. In *The Complete Poetry and Translations*, Volume 1 (A.73).
26 lines.

500. "Mercy."
a. In *The Complete Poetry and Translations*, Volume 1 (A.73).
19 lines. Juvenilia.

501. "The Messengers."
a. In *The Complete Poetry and Translations*, Volume 1 (A.73).
8 lines. Written c. 21 May 1911

502. "Metaphor."
   a. *Auburn Journal* 23, No. 34 (7 June 1923): 6.
   b. In August Derleth, ed. *Fire and Sleet and Candlelight*. Sauk City, WI: Arkham House, 1961. 185.
   c. In *Selected Poems* (A.27).
   d. In *The Complete Poetry and Translations*, Volume 1 (A.73).

   12 lines.

503. "Midnight Beach."
   a. *Wings* 6, No. 7 (Autumn 1944): 14 (25 lines only).
   b. In *The Hill of Dionysus* (A.18).
   c. In *Selected Poems* (A.27).
   d. In *The Last Oblivion* (A.61).
   e. In *The Complete Poetry and Translations*, Volume 2 (A.73).

   25 lines. The ms. is dated 5 September 1943.

504. "The Milky Way."
   a. In *The Complete Poetry and Translations*, Volume 2 (A.73).

   9 lines. A fragment.

505. "The Mime of Sleep."
   a. *Acolyte* 1, No. 3 (Spring 1943): 6.
   b. In *Selected Poems* (A.27).
   c. *Nyctalops* No. 7 (August 1972): 83.
   d. In *The Complete Poetry and Translations*, Volume 2 (A.73).

   Sonnet. The ms. is dated 28 July 1941.

506. "Minatory."
   a. *Auburn Journal* 25, No. 29 (30 April 1925): 6 (16 lines only).
   b. In *Sandalwood* (A.4) (16 lines only).
   c. *Raven* 2, No. 3 (Autumn 1944): 17.
   d. In *Selected Poems* (A.27).
   e. In *The Last Oblivion* (A.61).
   f. In *The Complete Poetry and Translations*, Volume 1 (A.73).

   20 lines.

507. "The Ministers of Law."
   a. In *Odes and Sonnets* (A.2).
   b. In *Ebony and Crystal* (A.3).
   c. In *Selected Poems* (A.27).

    d. In *The Complete Poetry and Translations*, Volume 1 (A.73).
    e. In *Moonlight and Other Poems* (A.78).

    13 lines. Written 7 August 1913.

508. "Mirage."
    a. In *Ebony and Crystal* (A.3).
    b. In *Selected Poems* (A.27).
    c. In *The Complete Poetry and Translations*, Volume 1 (A.73).
    d. In *Moonlight and Other Poems* (A.78).

    16 lines.

509. "Le Miroir des blanches fleurs." [English]
    a. In *The Last Oblivion* (A.61).
    b. In *The Complete Poetry and Translations*, Volume 2 (A.73).

    30 lines. Dated 9 August 1929. For CAS's French version, see item 510.

510. "Le Miroir des blanches fleurs." [French]
    a. In *The Complete Poetry and Translations*, Volume 2 (A.73).

    30 lines. For CAS's English version, see item 509.

511. "Mirrors."
    a. In *Ebony and Crystal* (A.3).
    b. In *Selected Poems* (A.27).
    c. In *The Complete Poetry and Translations*, Volume 1 (A.73).
    d. In *Moonlight and Other Poems* (A.78).

    Sonnet.

512. "The Mirrors of Beauty."
    a. In *Ebony and Crystal* (A.3).
    b. In *Selected Poems* (A.27).
    c. In *The Complete Poetry and Translations*, Volume 1 (A.73).
    d. In *Moonlight and Other Poems* (A.78).

    Sonnet. Dated 23 April 1915.

513. "Mithridates."
    a. In *Spells and Philtres* (A.14).
    b. In *Selected Poems* (A.27).
    c. In *The Complete Poetry and Translations*, Volume 2 (A.73).
    5 lines.

514. "Mohammed."
   a. In *The Complete Poetry and Translations*, Volume 1 (A.73).

   Sonnet. Juvenilia.

515. "Moly."
   a. *New Atheneum* (Fall 1950): [25].
   b. In *The Dark Chateau* (A.13).
   c. In *Selected Poems* (A.27).
   d. In *The Complete Poetry and Translations*, Volume 2 (A.73).

   20 lines. Dated 2 December 1943.

516. "Moments."
   a. In *Selected Poems* (A.27) (as a translation from "Christophe des Laurières").
   b. In *The Complete Poetry and Translations*, Volume 1 (A.73).

   24 lines. Written c. June 1923.

517. "The Monacle."
   a. In *Spells and Philtres* (A.14).
   b. In *Selected Poems* (A.27).
   c. In *The Complete Poetry and Translations*, Volume 2 (A.73).

   Haiku.

518. "Moods of the Sea."
   a. In *The Complete Poetry and Translations*, Volume 1 (A.73).

   12 lines.

519. "The Moon."
   a. In *The Complete Poetry and Translations*, Volume 1 (A.73).

   24 lines. Juvenilia.

520. "Moon-Dawn."
   a. *Weird Tales* 2, No. 1 (July–August 1923): 48 (as "The Red Moon").
   b. *Auburn Journal* 24, No. 15 (24 January 1924): 6 (as "The Red Moon").
   c. In *Sandalwood* (A.4).
   d. *Golden Atom* 1, No. 9 (December 1940): 25.
   e. In *Selected Poems* (A.27).
   f. In *The Last Oblivion* (A.61).

g. In *The Complete Poetry and Translations*, Volume 1 (A.73).

h. In *The Song of the Necromancer and Others* (A.81) (as "The Red Moon").

i. In Farnsworth Wright, ed. *Weird Tales, Volume 2, Number 1 (July–August 1923)*. Mississauga, ON: Girasol Collectables, 2014. 48 (as "The Red Moon"; facsimile of a.).

8 lines. Written c. September 1915.

521. "Moon-Sight."

a. In *The Complete Poetry and Translations*, Volume 2 (A.73).

25 lines. Written 30 January 1929.

522. "Moonlight."

a. *Overland Monthly* 56, No. 2 (August 1910): 229.

b. In *The Complete Poetry and Translations*, Volume 1 (A.73).

c. In *Moonlight and Other Poems* (A.78).

15 lines. First title: "The Moon." CAS's first published poem.

523. "The Moonlight Desert."

a. In *The Last Oblivion* (A.61).

b. In *The Complete Poetry and Translations*, Volume 1 (A.73).

Sonnet. Written before 2 February 1911.

524. "Morning on an Eastern Sea."

a. In *The Fugitive Poems of Clark Ashton Smith* (A.26).

b. In *The Complete Poetry and Translations*, Volume 1 (A.73).

9 lines. Written in 1915

525. "The Morning Pool."

a. In *The Star-Treader and Other Poems* (A.1).

b. In *The Complete Poetry and Translations*, Volume 1 (A.73).

c. In *Moonlight and Other Poems* (A.78).

8 lines. Written c. 1912. Quoted in full in III.A.57.a.

526. "Morning Star of the Mountains."

a. In *The Complete Poetry and Translations*, Volume 2 (A.73).

Haiku.

527. "Mors."
   a. In *Selected Poems* (A.27) (as a translation from "Christophe des Laurières").
   b. In *The Complete Poetry and Translations*, Volume 1 (A.73).

   16 lines. Dated 12 April 1918. First title: "Anodyne."

528. "La Mort des amants."
   a. In *Selected Poems* (A.27).
   b. In *The Complete Poetry and Translations*, Volume 2 (A.73).

   Haiku.

529. "The Motes."
   a. In *Ebony and Crystal* (A.3).
   b. In *Selected Poems* (A.27).
   c. In *One Hundred Years of Klarkash-Ton* (III.D.10).
   d. In *The Last Oblivion* (A.61).
   e. In *The Complete Poetry and Translations*, Volume 1 (A.73).
   f. In *Moonlight and Other Poems* (A.78).
   g. In *The Dark Eidolon and Other Fantasies* (A.84).

   8 lines.

530. "Mountain Trail."
   a. In *Selected Poems* (A.27).
   b. In *The Complete Poetry and Translations*, Volume 2 (A.73).

   Haiku.

531. "The Muezzin."
   a. In *The Complete Poetry and Translations*, Volume 1 (A.73).

   18 lines. Juvenilia.

532. "The Mummy."
   a. *Sonnet* 4, No. 2 (May–June 1919): 3.
   b. *Fresno Bee* (10 March 1923): 7.
   c. In *Ebony and Crystal* (A.3).
   d. In *The Last Oblivion* (A.61).
   e. In *The Complete Poetry and Translations*, Volume 1 (A.73).
   f. In *Celui qui marchait parmi les étoiles* (II.A.iii.17).

   Sonnet. Written in 1915.

533. "Mummy of the Flower."
    a. In *Selected Poems* (A.27).
    b. In *The Complete Poetry and Translations*, Volume 2 (A.73).
       5 lines.

534. "La Muse moderne."
    a. In *The Complete Poetry and Translations*, Volume 2 (A.73).
       4 lines.

535. "Mushroom-Gatherers."
    a. In *Selected Poems* (A.27).
    b. In *The Complete Poetry and Translations*, Volume 2 (A.73).
       Haiku.

536. "The Music of the Gods."
    a. In *The Complete Poetry and Translations*, Volume 1 (A.73).
       Sonnet.

537. "Mystery."
    a. In *Selected Poems* (A.27).
    b. In *The Complete Poetry and Translations*, Volume 2 (A.73).
       24 lines.

538. "The Mystical Number."
    a. In *The Complete Poetry and Translations*, Volume 2 (A.73).
       15 lines.

539. "Nada."
    a. *Lyric* 37, No. 2 (Spring 1957): 42.
    b. In *Spells and Philtres* (A.14).
    c. In *The Complete Poetry and Translations*, Volume 2 (A.73).
       Sonnet. Dated 23 June 1952.

540. "The Nameless Wraith."
    a. *Arkham Sampler* 1, No. 1 (Winter 1948): 21.
    b. In *Spells and Philtres* (A.14).
    c. In *Selected Poems* (A.27).
    d. In *The Last Oblivion* (A.61).
    e. In *The Complete Poetry and Translations*, Volume 1 (A.73).
    f. In *Celui qui marchait parmi les étoiles* (II.A.iii.17).

20 lines. First title: "The Wraith of Beauty."

541. "Nature's Orchestra."
   a. In *The Complete Poetry and Translations,* Volume 2 (A.73).
   18 lines.

542. "Necromancy."
   a. *Fantasy Fan* 1, No. 12 (August 1934): 188.
   b. *Weird Tales* 36, No. 10 (March 1943): 105.
   c. In *Spells and Philtres* (A.14).
   d. In *Selected Poems* (A.27).
   e. In *The Last Oblivion* (A.61).
   f. In *The Complete Poetry and Translations,* Volume 2 (A.73).
   g. In *The Song of the Necromancer and Others* (A.81).
   h. In Charles D. Hornig, ed. *The Fantasy Fan: September, 1933–February, 1935.* [n.p.: Lance Thingmaker, 2010.] 188 (facsimile of a.).
   i. In *The Averoigne Chronicles* (A.85).

   Sonnet. Written before 21 January 1934.

543. "The Nemesis of Suns."
   a. In *The Star-Treader and Other Poems* (A.1).
   b. In *The Complete Poetry and Translations,* Volume 1 (A.73).
   c. In *Moonlight and Other Poems* (A.78).

   Sonnet. Dated 10 January 1912.

544. "The Nereid."
   a. *Yale Review* 2, No. 4 (July 1913): 685–86.
   b. *Fresno Bee* (23 December 1922): 15.
   c. In *Ebony and Crystal* (A.3).
   d. In [Helen Hoyt, ed.] *California Poets: An Anthology of 224 Contemporaries.* New York: Henry Harrison, 1932. 665.
   e. In *Selected Poems* (A.27).
   f. In *The Last Oblivion* (A.61).
   g. In *The Complete Poetry and Translations,* Volume 1 (A.73).
   h. In *Moonlight and Other Poems* (A.78).
   i. In *Celui qui marchait parmi les étoiles* (II.A.iii.17).

   32 lines. Written c. December 1912. For CAS's Spanish translation, see "La Nereida" (item 545).

545. "La Nereida."
    a. In *The Complete Poetry and Translations*, Volume 2 (A.73).

    32 lines. In Spanish. Dated 27 June 1950. A translation of "The Nereid" (item 544).

546. "Nero."
    a. In *The Star-Treader and Other Poems* (A.1).
    b. In Marguerite Wilkinson, ed. *Golden Songs of the Golden State.* Chicago: A. C. McClurg & Co., 1917; Greak Neck, NY: Granger Book Co., 1979. 116–20.
    c. In *Odes and Sonnets* (A.2).
    d. In Edwin Markham, ed. *The Book of Poetry.* New York: William H. Wise & Co., 1926 [3 vols.], 1927 [2 vols.], 1928 [10 vols.], 1948 [6 vols.] [as *Anthology of the World's Best Poems*]). 749–50 (extracts; as "From Nero").
    e. In *Nero and Other Poems* (A.8).
    f. A.20.
    g. In *Selected Poems* (A.27).
    h. In *The Last Oblivion* (A.61).
    i. In *The Complete Poetry and Translations*, Volume 1 (A.73).
    j. In *Moonlight and Other Poems* (A.78).
    k. In *The Dark Eidolon and Other Fantasies* (A.84).
    l. In *Celui qui marchait parmi les étoiles* (II.A.iii.17).

    96 lines. Written c. April 1912. The poem was quoted in its entirety in III.A.57.

547. "Nest of the Screech-Owl."
    a. In *The Complete Poetry and Translations*, Volume 2 (A.73).
    Haiku.

548. "Nevermore."
    a. In *Selected Poems* (A.27).
    b. In *The Complete Poetry and Translations*, Volume 2 (A.73).
    14 lines. Alternate title: "Song."

549. "The Nevermore-to-Be."
    a. In *Selected Poems* (A.27).
    b. In *The Complete Poetry and Translations*, Volume 2 (A.73).
    c. In *The Averoigne Chronicles* (A.85).

    24 lines. Dated 25 March 1927. Alternate title: "Chatelaine."

550. "Night." [The fires of sunset die reluctantly]
   a. In *In the Ultimate Valleys* (A.26).
   b. In *The Complete Poetry and Translations,* Volume 1 (A.73).

   8 lines. Written c. 1910.

551. "Night." [Twilight dim and gray,]
   a. In *The Sword of Zagan and Other Writings* (A.64).
   b. In *The Complete Poetry and Translations,* Volume 2 (A.73).

   26 lines. A fragment.

552. "The Night Forest."
   a. In *The Star-Treader and Other Poems* (A.1).
   b. In *Selected Poems* (A.27).
   c. In *The Complete Poetry and Translations,* Volume 1 (A.73).
   d. In *Moonlight and Other Poems* (A.78).

   43 lines.

553. "The Night of Despair."
   a. In *The Complete Poetry and Translations,* Volume 1 (A.73).

   Sonnet.

554. "Night of Miletus."
   a. In *Selected Poems* (A.27).
   b. In *The Complete Poetry and Translations,* Volume 2 (A.73).

   Haiku.

555. "The Night Wind."
   a. In *The Complete Poetry and Translations,* Volume 2 (A.73).

   8 lines. A fragment.

556. "Nightfall."
   a. *Home Brew* 3, No. 2 (March 1923): 23.
   b. *Auburn Journal* 24, No. 13 (10 January 1924): 13.
   c. In *The Complete Poetry and Translations,* Volume 1 (A.73).

   20 lines. Dated 18 May 1921.

557. "Nightmare."
   a. In *Ebony and Crystal* (A.3).
   b. In August Derleth, ed. *Dark of the Moon: Poems of Fantasy and the Macabre.* Sauk City, WI: Arkham House, 1947; Freeport, NY:

Books for Libraries Press, 1969; Miami, FL: Granger, 1976. 338.

c. In *Selected Poems* (A.27).

d. In *The Last Oblivion* (A.61).

e. In *The Complete Poetry and Translations*, Volume 1 (A.73).

f. In *Moonlight and Other Poems* (A.78).

12 lines. In a letter to George Sterling (11 May 1913) CAS referred to the poem as "Gothic Nightmare."

558. "Nightmare of the Lilliputian."

a. In *Spells and Philtres* (A.14).

b. In *Selected Poems* (A.27).

c. In *The Complete Poetry and Translations*, Volume 2 (A.73).

5 lines.

559. "The Nightmare Tarn."

a. *Weird Tales* 14, No. 5 (November 1929): 624.

b. In *Selected Poems* (A.27).

c. In *The Last Oblivion* (A.61).

d. In *The Complete Poetry and Translations*, Volume 2 (A.73).

e. In *The Song of the Necromancer and Others* (A.81).

f. In *Celui qui marchait parmi les étoiles* (II.A.iii.17).

40 lines.

560. "Nirvana."

a. In *The Star-Treader and Other Poems* (A.1).

b. In *Selected Poems* (A.27).

c. In *The Last Oblivion* (A.61).

d. In *The Complete Poetry and Translations*, Volume 1 (A.73).

e. In *Moonlight and Other Poems* (A.78).

Sonnet.

561. "No-Man's-Land."

a. In *The Complete Poetry and Translations*, Volume 2 (A.73).

15 lines. A fragment.

562. "No Stranger Dream."

a. *Arkham Sampler* 1, No. 3 (Summer 1948): 20.

b. In *Spells and Philtres* (A.14).

c. In *Selected Poems* (A.27).

   d. In *The Complete Poetry and Translations*, Volume 2 (A.73).

   Sonnet.

563. "Nocturnal Pines."
   a. In *Selected Poems* (A.27).
   b. In *The Complete Poetry and Translations*, Volume 2 (A.73).
   Haiku.

564. "Nocturne." [A silver sleep is on the vale;]
   a. In *Selected Poems* (A.27).
   b. In *Grotesques and Fantastiques* (A.32).
   c. In *The Complete Poetry and Translations*, Volume 1 (A.73).
   8 lines. Dated 13 March 1916.

565. "Nocturne." [Intensified and re-enforced with clouds,]
   a. *International* 6, No. 4 (September 1912): 76 (as "Nocturn").
   b. In *The Complete Poetry and Translations*, Volume 1 (A.73).
   Sonnet. Written c. January 1911.

566. "Nocturne: Grant Avenue."
   a. *Wings* 6, No. 5 (Spring 1944): 15.
   b. In *The Hill of Dionysus* (A.18).
   c. In *Selected Poems* (A.27).
   d. In *The Complete Poetry and Translations*, Volume 2 (A.73).
   30 lines. Dated 29 September 1942. First title: "City Nocturne."

567. "'Not Altogether Sleep.'"
   a. In *The Dark Chateau* (A.13).
   b. *Weird Tales* 44, No. 2 (January 1952): 73.
   c. In *The Hill of Dionysus* (A.18).
   d. In *The Complete Poetry and Translations*, Volume 2 (A.73).
   e. In *The Song of the Necromancer and Others* (A.81).
   Sonnet.

568. "Not Theirs the Cypress-Arch."
   a. In *The Dark Chateau* (A.13).
   b. *Wings* 10, No. 4 (Winter 1952): 13.
   c. In *The Last Oblivion* (A.61).
   d. In *The Complete Poetry and Translations*, Volume 2 (A.73).

18 lines. Dated 12 January 1951. First title: "Resurgam" (Latin for "I shall rise up"); alternate title: "Ellos Resurgen."

569. "November."
   a. In *Selected Poems* (A.27).
   b. In *The Complete Poetry and Translations,* Volume 2 (A.73).

   15 lines.

570. "November Twilight."
   a. In *Ebony and Crystal* (A.3).
   b. In *Selected Poems* (A.27).
   c. In *The Complete Poetry and Translations,* Volume 1 (A.73).
   d. In *Moonlight and Other Poems* (A.78).

   8 lines. Written before 15 June 1916. First title: "Autumn Twilight."

571. "Nuns Walking in the Orchard."
   a. In *Selected Poems* (A.27).
   b. In *The Complete Poetry and Translations,* Volume 2 (A.73).

   Haiku.

572. "Nyctalops."
   a. *Weird Tales* 14, No. 4 (October 1929): 516.
   b. In The Edwin Markham Poetry Society, ed. *The Laureate's Wreath: An Anthology in Honor of Dr. Henry Meade Bland, Poet Laureate of California.* San Jose: The Edwin Markham Poetry Society, 1934. 109.
   c. In Dudley Chadwick Gordon, Vernon Rupert King, and William Whittingham Lyman, ed. *Today's Literature.* New York: American Book Co., 1935. 449.
   d. In August Derleth, ed. *Dark of the Moon: Poems of Fantasy and the Macabre.* Sauk City, WI: Arkham House, 1947; Freeport, NY: Books for Libraries Press, 1969; Miami, FL: Granger, 1976. 339–40.
   e. In *Selected Poems* (A.27).
   f. *Nyctalops* No. 7 (August 1972): 4.
   f. In *The Last Oblivion* (A.61).
   h. In *Shadows Seen and Unseen* (A.71).
   i. In *The Complete Poetry and Translations,* Volume 2 (A.73).
   j. In *The Song of the Necromancer and Others* (A.81).
   k. In *The Dark Eidolon and Other Fantasies* (A.84).

   42 lines. Dated 21 March 1929.

573. "The Nymph."
    a. In *Selected Poems* (A.27) (as a translation from "Christophe des Laurières").
    b. In *The Complete Poetry and Translations,* Volume 1 (A.73).

    20 lines. Dated 8–9 March 1923. First title: "Dream."

574. "'O Golden-Tongued Romance.'"
    a. In *The Dark Chateau* (A.13).
    b. *Weird Tales* 44, No. 3 (March 1952): [33] (as "O Golden-Tongued Romance").
    c. In *One Hundred Years of Klarkash-Ton* (III.D.10).
    d. In *The Complete Poetry and Translations,* Volume 2 (A.73).
    e. In *The Song of the Necromancer and Others* (A.81).
    f. In *The Averoigne Chronicles* (A.85).

    36 lines. Written 1950.

575. "The Ocean."
    a. In *The Complete Poetry and Translations,* Volume 1 (A.73).

    24 lines. Juvenilia.

576. "Ocean Twilight."
    a. In *The Complete Poetry and Translations,* Volume 2 (A.73).

    Haiku.

577. "October."
    a. *Westward* 4, No. 5 (May 1935): 5.
    b. In Hans A. Hoffmann, ed. *Poets of the Western Scene.* San Leandro, CA: Greater West Publishing Company, 1937. 89.
    c. In *Spells and Philtres* (A.14).
    d. In *Selected Poems* (A.27).
    e. In *The Complete Poetry and Translations,* Volume 1 (A.73).

    24 lines. Dated 11 October 1925.

578. "Ode." [O young and dear and tender sorceress!]
    a. *Agenbite of Inwit* 2, No. 4 (September 1945): [6].
    b. In *The Hill of Dionysus* (A.18).
    c. In *Selected Poems* (A.27).
    d. In *The Complete Poetry and Translations,* Volume 2 (A.73).

    31 lines.

579. "Ode." [Your name is like the opening of a flow'r]
 a. *Auburn Journal* 26, No. 8 (3 December 1925): 14.
 b. In *The Complete Poetry and Translations*, Volume 1 (A.73).

 16 lines.

580. "Ode from the Persian."
 a. In *The Complete Poetry and Translations*, Volume 1 (A.73).

 3 lines. Juvenilia. A fragment.

581. "Ode on Imagination."
 a. In *The Star-Treader and Other Poems* (A.1).
 b. In *Selected Poems* (A.27).
 c. In *The Last Oblivion* (A.61).
 d. In *The Complete Poetry and Translations*, Volume 1 (A.73).
 e. In *Moonlight and Other Poems* (A.78).
 f. In *Celui qui marchait parmi les étoiles* (II.A.iii.17).

 72 lines.

582. "Ode on Matter."
 a. In *The Complete Poetry and Translations*, Volume 2 (A.73).

 46 lines. Written 1912. A fragment.

583. "Ode on the Future of Song."
 a. In *The Complete Poetry and Translations*, Volume 1 (A.73).

 26 lines.

584. "Ode to Aphrodite."
 a. In *The Complete Poetry and Translations*, Volume 1 (A.73).

 19 lines. Variant title: "To Aphrodite."

585. "Ode to Light."
 a. In *The Fugitive Poems of Clark Ashton Smith: Second Series* (A.38).
 b. In *The Last Oblivion* (A.61).
 c. In *The Complete Poetry and Translations*, Volume 1 (A.73).

 39 lines. Written 1912. Unfinished.

586. "Ode to Matter."
 a. In *The Fugitive Poems of Clark Ashton Smith* (A.26).
 b. In *The Last Oblivion* (A.61).
 c. In *The Complete Poetry and Translations*, Volume 1 (A.73).

d. In *Celui qui marchait parmi les étoiles* (II.A.iii.17).

56 lines. Written 1911.

587. "Ode to Music."
a. *Placer County Republican* 42, No. 23 (26 September 1912): 1.
b. In *The Star-Treader and Other Poems* (A.1).
c. In *The Complete Poetry and Translations*, Volume 1 (A.73).
d. In *Moonlight and Other Poems* (A.78).

81 lines. Written c. March 1911.

588. "Ode to Peace."
a. In *The Complete Poetry and Translations*, Volume 1 (A.73).

21 lines. Written c. November 1918.

589. "Ode to Poetry."
a. In *The Complete Poetry and Translations*, Volume 1 (A.73).

26 lines. Written 1911. First draft: "To Poetry."

590. "Ode to the Abyss."
a. In *The Star-Treader and Other Poems* (A.1).
b. In *Odes and Sonnets* (A.2).
c. *Tesseract* 2, No. 3 (March 1937): 9–10.
d. In *Selected Poems* (A.27).
e. In *The Last Oblivion* (A.61).
f. In *The Complete Poetry and Translations*, Volume 1 (A.73).
g. In *Moonlight and Other Poems* (A.78).
h. In *The Dark Eidolon and Other Fantasies* (A.84).
i. In *Celui qui marchait parmi les étoiles* (II.A.iii.17).

75 lines. Written 3 May 1911.

591. "Odes of Alnaschar."
a. In *The Complete Poetry and Translations*, Volume 1 (A.73).

25 lines. Juvenilia.

592. "Odysseus in Eternity."
a. In *Selected Poems* (A.27).
b. In *The Complete Poetry and Translations*, Volume 2 (A.73).

Haiku.

593. "Old Hydraulic Diggings."
   a. In *Selected Poems* (A.27).
   b. In *The Complete Poetry and Translations,* Volume 2 (A.73).
      Four haiku.

594. "Old Limestone Kiln."
   a. In *Selected Poems* (A.27).
   b. In *The Complete Poetry and Translations,* Volume 2 (A.73).
      Haiku.

595. "An Old Theme."
   a. In *Selected Poems* (A.27) (as a translation from "Christophe des Laurières").
   b. In *The Complete Poetry and Translations,* Volume 2 (A.73).
      13 lines.

596. "The Old Water-Wheel."
   a. *Poetry* 61, No. 3 (December 1942): 492.
   b. *Kansas City Star* (24 January 1943): 10D.
   c. In *The Dark Chateau* (A.13).
   d. In *In Memoriam: Clark Ashton Smith* (III.D.4).
   e. In *Selected Poems* (A.27).
   f. In *One Hundred Years of Klarkash-Ton* (III.D.10).
   g. In *Shadows Seen and Unseen* (A.71).
   h. In *The Complete Poetry and Translations,* Volume 2 (A.73).
      20 lines. Dated 2 August 1941.

597. "Omar's Philosophy."
   a. In *The Complete Poetry and Translations,* Volume 1 (A.73).
      20 lines. Juvenilia. Variant title: "Quatrains."

598. "Ombos."
   a. In *The Complete Poetry and Translations,* Volume 1 (A.73).
      9 lines.

599. "Omniety."
   a. *Raven* 1, No. 4 (Winter 1944): 21.
   b. In *The Hill of Dionysus* (A.18).
   c. In *Selected Poems* (A.27).
   d. In *The Last Oblivion* (A.61).

    e. In *Shadows Seen and Unseen* (A.71).

    f. In *The Complete Poetry and Translations,* Volume 2 (A.73).

    16 lines. Dated 14 September 1943.

600. "On a Chinese Vase."

    a. *Oriental Stories* 2, No. 2 (Spring 1932): 174.

    b. In *Selected Poems* (A.27).

    c. In Farnsworth Wright, ed. *Oriental Stories, Volume 2, Number 2 (Spring 1932).* Mississauga, ON: Girasol Collectables, 2006. 174 (facsimile of a.).

    d. In *Shadows Seen and Unseen* (A.71).

    e. In *The Complete Poetry and Translations,* Volume 2 (A.73).

    15 lines. Dated 2 November 1928.

601. "On Re-reading Baudelaire."

    a. *Auburn Journal* 24, No. 9 (13 December 1923): 6 (as "On Reading Baudelaire").

    b. In *Sandalwood* (A.4) (as "On Reading Baudelaire").

    c. In *Selected Poems* (A.27).

    d. In *The Last Oblivion* (A.61).

    e. In *The Complete Poetry and Translations,* Volume 1 (A.73).

    f. In *The Dark Eidolon and Other Fantasies* (A.84).

    Sonnet.

602. "On the Canyon-Side."

    a. *Auburn Journal* 23, No. 50 (27 September 1923): 6.

    b. In George Sterling, Genevieve Taggard, and James Rorty, ed. *Continent's End: An Anthology of Contemporary California Poets.* San Francisco: Book Club of California, 1925. 54.

    c. In *Selected Poems* (A.27).

    d. In *The Complete Poetry and Translations,* Volume 1 (A.73).

    24 lines. Dated 4–12 March 1923.

603. "On the Mount of Stone."

    a. *Arkham Sampler* 1, No. 3 (Summer 1948): 31.

    b. In *Selected Poems* (A.27).

    c. In *The Complete Poetry and Translations,* Volume 2 (A.73).

    13 lines.

604. "On Trying to Read *Four Quartets*."
   a. In *The Complete Poetry and Translations*, Volume 2 (A.73).

   8 lines. The manuscript is mutilated, so that the ends of some lines are illegible.

605. "One Evening."
   a. In *Selected Poems* (A.27).
   b. In *The Complete Poetry and Translations*, Volume 2 (A.73).

   12 lines.

606. "Only to One Returned."
   a. *Arkham Sampler* 1, No. 4 (Autumn 1948): 13.
   b. In *Spells and Philtres* (A.14).
   c. In *Selected Poems* (A.27).
   d. In *The Complete Poetry and Translations*, Volume 2 (A.73).

   Sonnet.

607. "The Oracle."
   a. In *The Complete Poetry and Translations*, Volume 1 (A.73).

   4 lines.

608. "The Orchid of Beauty."
   a. In *Ebony and Crystal* (A.3) (as "The Orchid").
   b. In *Selected Poems* (A.27).
   c. In *The Complete Poetry and Translations*, Volume 1 (A.73).
   d. In *Moonlight and Other Poems* (A.78).

   Sonnet. Dated 21 May 1914.

609. "Orgueil."
   a. In *The Complete Poetry and Translations*, Volume 2 (A.73).

   12 lines. In French. Dedicated to Benjamin De Casseres.

610. "The Orient."
   a. In *The Complete Poetry and Translations*, Volume 1 (A.73).

   40 lines. Juvenilia.

611. "Ougabalys."
   a. *Weird Tales* 15, No. 1 (January 1930): 135.
   b. In *The Last Oblivion* (A.61).
   c. In *The Complete Poetry and Translations*, Volume 2 (A.73).

    d. In *The Song of the Necromancer and Others* (A.81).
    e. In *Celui qui marchait parmi les étoiles* (II.A.iii.17).

    30 lines. Dated 15 September 1929. The poem was later revised as "Tolometh."

612. "The Outer Land."
    a. *Supramundane Stories Quarerly* 1, No. 2 (Spring 1937): 3–4 (as "Alienation").
    b. *Spearhead* 2, No. 2 (Spring 1951): 3–5.
    c. In *The Dark Chateau* (A.13).
    d. In *Selected Poems* (A.27).
    e. In *The Last Oblivion* (A.61).
    f. In *The Complete Poetry and Translations,* Volume 2 (A.73).

    72 lines. Dated 26 May 1935.

613. "Outlanders."
    a. In *Nero and Other Poems* (A.8).
    b. *Weird Tales* 31, No. 6 (June 1938): 746.
    c. In August Derleth, ed. *Dark of the Moon: Poems of Fantasy and the Macabre.* Sauk City, WI: Arkham House, 1947; Freeport, NY: Books for Libraries Press, 1969; Miami, FL: Granger, 1976. 339.
    d. In *Selected Poems* (A.27).
    e. In *The Last Oblivion* (A.61).
    f. In *The Complete Poetry and Translations,* Volume 2 (A.73).
    g. In *The Song of the Necromancer and Others* (A.81).
    h. In Farnsworth Wright, ed. *Weird Tales, Volume 31, Number 6 (June 1938).* Mississauga, ON: Girasol Collectables, 2011. 746 (facsimile of b.).
    i. In *The Dark Eidolon and Other Fantasies* (A.84).

    Sonnet. Dated 26 June 1934.

614. "Paean."
    a. *Wings* 7, No. 6 (Summer 1946): 14.
    b. In *The Hill of Dionysus* (A.18).
    c. In *Selected Poems* (A.27).
    d. In *The Complete Poetry and Translations,* Volume 2 (A.73).

    15 lines.

615. "The Pagan."
    a. In *Spells and Philtres* (A.14).

b. In *Selected Poems* (A.27) (as a translation from "Christophe des Laurières").

c. In *The Complete Poetry and Translations*, Volume 1 (A.73).

Sonnet. Written 1923.

616. "The Pageant of Music."
   a. In *The Fugitive Poems of Clark Ashton Smith* (A.26).
   b. In *The Complete Poetry and Translations*, Volume 1 (A.73).

   Sonnet. Written c. 1910–11.

617. "The Palace of Jewels." [Fronting the sea's blue chambers fluctuant—]
   a. In *The Fugitive Poems of Clark Ashton Smith* (A.26).
   b. In *The Complete Poetry and Translations*, Volume 1 (A.73).

   64 lines. Written c. June 1913.

618. "The Palace of Jewels." [It rears beside the cliff-confronted sea,]
   a. In *The Complete Poetry and Translations*, Volume 1 (A.73).

   20 lines. Presumably the first version of the above, a poem later expanded into 16 stanzas.

619. "The Palace of the Jinn."
   a. In *The Complete Poetry and Translations*, Volume 1 (A.73).

   28 lines. Juvenilia. A fragment.

620. "Palms."
   a. *Asia* 20, No. 3 (April 1920): 330.
   b. *Orlando* [FL] *Sentinel* (13 April 1920): 2.
   c. In *Ebony and Crystal* (A.3).
   d. In Edwin Markham, ed. *Songs and Stories*. Los Angeles: Powell Publishing Co., 1931; Freeport, NY: Books for Libraries Press, 1974. 424.
   e. In *Selected Poems* (A.27).
   f. In *The Complete Poetry and Translations*, Volume 1 (A.73).
   g. In *Moonlight and Other Poems* (A.78).

   8 lines. Dated 10 April 1918.

621. "Pantheistic Dream."
   a. In *The Complete Poetry and Translations*, Volume 2 (A.73).

36 lines. For CAS's French version, see "Rêve panthéistique" (item 704).

622. "Paphnutius."
   a. In *Spells and Philtres* (A.14).
   b. In *Selected Poems* (A.27).
   c. In *The Complete Poetry and Translations*, Volume 2 (A.73).
   Haiku.

623. "Parnaso."
   a. In *The Complete Poetry and Translations*, Volume 2 (A.73).
   17 lines. In Spanish. For CAS's English version (one line shorter), see "Parnassus" (item 624).

624. "Parnassus."
   a. *Asmodeus* 1, No. 1 (Summer 1950): 21.
   b. In *The Complete Poetry and Translations*, Volume 2 (A.73).
   16 lines. Dated 24 March 1950. For CAS's Spanish version, see "Parnaso" (item 623).

625. "Parnassus à la Mode."
   a. In *Spells and Philtres* (A.14).
   b. In *Selected Poems* (A.27).
   c. In *The Complete Poetry and Translations*, Volume 2 (A.73).
   4 lines.

626. "Passing of an Elder God."
   a. In *Spells and Philtres* (A.14).
   b. In *Selected Poems* (A.27).
   c. In *The Complete Poetry and Translations*, Volume 2 (A.73).
   5 lines.

627. "The Past." [Drawn hither by the tides of change and chance]
   a. In *The Complete Poetry and Translations*, Volume 1 (A.73).
   Sonnet.

628. "The Past." [Naught of the Past is left but memories—]
   a. In *The Complete Poetry and Translations*, Volume 1 (A.73).
   4 lines.

629. "Paysage païen."
   a. In *Selected Poems* (A.27).
   b. In *The Complete Poetry and Translations*, Volume 2 (A.73).

   30 lines. In French. Dated 28 July 1929.

630. "Perseus and Medusa."
   a. In *Spells and Philtres* (A.14).
   b. In *Selected Poems* (A.27).
   c. In *The Complete Poetry and Translations*, Volume 2 (A.73).

   Haiku.

631. "Perseverance."
   a. In *The Complete Poetry and Translations*, Volume 1 (A.73).

   20 lines. Juvenilia.

632. "Phallus Impudica."
   a. In *Selected Poems* (A.27).
   b. In *The Complete Poetry and Translations*, Volume 2 (A.73).

   Haiku.

633. "A Phantasy of Twilight."
   a. In *The Fugitive Poems of Clark Ashton Smith: Second Series* (A.38).
   b. In *The Complete Poetry and Translations*, Volume 1 (A.73).

   20 lines. Written before 23 June 1914.

634. "Philtre."
   a. In *Spells and Philtres* (A.14).
   b. In *Selected Poems* (A.27).
   c. In *The Complete Poetry and Translations*, Volume 2 (A.73).

   Haiku.

635.   "The Phoenix."
   a. *Weird Tales* 35, No. 3 (May 1940): 94.
   b. In *Spells and Philtres* (A.14).
   c. In *Selected Poems* (A.27).
   d. In *The Complete Poetry and Translations*, Volume 2 (A.73).
   e. In *The Song of the Necromancer and Others* (A.81).

   18 lines. Dated 24 May 1935.

636. "Picture by Piero di Cosimo."
    a. In *Selected Poems* (A.27).
    b. In *The Complete Poetry and Translations*, Volume 2 (A.73).
    Haiku.

637. "Pine Needles."
    a. In *The Star-Treader and Other Poems* (A.1).
    b. In *Selected Poems* (A.27).
    c. In *The Complete Poetry and Translations*, Volume 1 (A.73).
    d. In *Moonlight and Other Poems* (A.78).
    8 lines.

638. "Plague from the Abatoir."
    a. In *Selected Poems* (A.27).
    b. In *The Complete Poetry and Translations*, Volume 2 (A.73).
    Haiku.

639. "Plum-Flowers."
    a. *L'Alouette* 1, No. 2 (March 1924): 44.
    b. In *Sandalwood* (A.4).
    c. In *The Complete Poetry and Translations*, Volume 1 (A.73).
    9 lines. Dated 17 May 1922.

640. "[Poem.]"
    a. In *The Complete Poetry and Translations*, Volume 1 (A.73).
    20 lines. Juvenilia. The title and the first three lines are mutilated; all that can be read of the title is "Poem."

641. "Poèmes d'amour."
    a. In *The Complete Poetry and Translations*, Volume 2 (A.73).
    16 lines.

642. "Poet in a Barroom."
    a. In *Selected Poems* (A.27).
    b. In *The Complete Poetry and Translations*, Volume 2 (A.73).
    Haiku.

643. "The Poet Talks with the Biographers."
    a. In *The Dark Chateau* (A.13).
    b. In *The Complete Poetry and Translations*, Volume 2 (A.73).

25 lines. Alternate title: "The Poet Speaks with the Ghouls." For CAS's French version, see "Le Poéte parle avec ses biographes" (item 645).

644. "Las poetas del optimismo."
   a.   In *¿Donde Duermes, Eldorado? y Otros Poemas* (A.18) (as "Los Poetas").
   b.   In *The Complete Poetry and Translations*, Volume 2 (A.73).

   9 lines. In Spanish. For CAS's English version, see "The Poets of Optimism" (item 648)..

645. "Le Poéte parle avec ses biographes."
   a.   In *The Complete Poetry and Translations*, Volume 2 (A.73).

   25 lines. In French. Alternate title: "Le Poète parle avec les goules." For CAS's English version, see "The Poet Talks with the Biographers" (item 643).

646. "Poetry."
   a.   In *The Complete Poetry and Translations*, Volume 1 (A.73).
   8 lines.

647. "Poets in Hades."
   a.   In *Selected Poems* (A.27).
   b.   In *The Complete Poetry and Translations*, Volume 2 (A.73).
   5 lines.

648. "The Poets of Optimism."
   a.   In *The Complete Poetry and Translations*, Volume 2 (A.73).

   9 lines. For CAS's Spanish version, see "Las Poetas del optimismo" (item 644).

649. "The Pool."
   a.   In *The Complete Poetry and Translations*, Volume 2 (A.73).
   16 lines.

650. "Pool at Lobos."
   a.   In *Selected Poems* (A.27).
   b.   In *The Complete Poetry and Translations*, Volume 2 (A.73).
   Haiku.

651. "Poplars."
   a. *Snappy Stories* 70, No. 2 (5 November 1922): 46.
   b. In *Grotesques and Fantastiques* (A.32).
   c. In *The Complete Poetry and Translations,* Volume 1 (A.73).

   13 lines. Written c. July 1922.

652. "Postlude."
   a. In *Selected Poems* (A.27).
   b. *Carmel Pine Cone* 42, No. 1 (5 January 1956): 6.
   c. In *The Hill of Dionysus* (A.18).
   d. In *The Complete Poetry and Translations,* Volume 2 (A.73).

   12 lines. Dated 22 April 1943. First title: "Éloignement"; second title: "Any Shadow, Any Dream."

653. "The Potion of Dreams."
   a. In *The Fugitive Poems of Clark Ashton Smith: Second Series* (A.38).
   b. In *The Complete Poetry and Translations,* Volume 1 (A.73).

   Sonnet.

654. "Pour chercher du nouveau."
   a. *Arkham Sampler* 2, No. 4 (Autumn 1949): 28–29.
   b. In *The Dark Chateau* (A.13).
   c. In *Selected Poems* (A.27).
   d. In *The Last Oblivion* (A.61).
   e. In *The Complete Poetry and Translations,* Volume 2 (A.73).
   f. In *Celui qui marchait parmi les étoiles* (II.A.iii.17).

   33 lines. In French.

655. "The Power of Eld."
   a. In *The Fugitive Poems of Clark Ashton Smith* (A.26).
   b. In *The Last Oblivion* (A.61).
   c. In *The Complete Poetry and Translations,* Volume 1 (A.73).

   Sonnet.

656. "A Prayer."
   a. *Snappy Stories* 24, No. 3 (4 February 1917): 23.
   b. In *Grotesques and Fantastiques* (A.32).
   c. In *The Complete Poetry and Translations,* Volume 1 (A.73).

   12 lines.

657. "The Prayer Rug." [How calm, O Rug of Persian loom]
   a. In *The Complete Poetry and Translations*, Volume 1 (A.73).

   36 lines. Juvenilia.

658. "The Prayer Rug." [Out of the past thou comest, rug of Persian loom,]
   a. In *The Complete Poetry and Translations*, Volume 1 (A.73).

   24 lines. Juvenilia.

659. "A Precept."
   a. In *Ebony and Crystal* (A.3).
   b. *Lyric West* 3, No. 9 (January 1924): 4.
   c. *Fresno Bee* (26 January 1924): 24.
   d. *Berkeley Daily Gazette* (3 November 1931): 7.
   e. In *Selected Poems* (A.27).
   f. In *The Complete Poetry and Translations*, Volume 1 (A.73).
   g. In *Moonlight and Other Poems* (A.78).

   12 lines. Written before 24 April 1918.

660. "The Present."
   a. In *The Complete Poetry and Translations*, Volume 1 (A.73).

   4 lines.

661. "The Price."
   a. In *The Star-Treader and Other Poems* (A.1).
   b. In Ella Sterling Mighels, ed. *Literary California*. San Francisco: Harr Wagner Publishing Co., 1918. 326 (as "Behind Each Thing a Shadow Lies").
   c. In *Selected Poems* (A.27).
   d. In *The Complete Poetry and Translations*, Volume 1 (A.73).
   e. In *Moonlight and Other Poems* (A.78).

   4 lines.

662. "The Prince and the Peri."
   a. In *The Complete Poetry and Translations*, Volume 1 (A.73).

   124 lines. Juvenilia.

663. "Prisoner in Vain."
   a. In *Selected Poems* (A.27).
   b. In *The Complete Poetry and Translations*, Volume 2 (A.73).

Haiku.

664. "The Prophet Speaks."
   a. *Weird Tales* 32, No. 3 (September 1938): 348–49.
   b. In *Spells and Philtres* (A.14).
   c. In *Selected Poems* (A.27).
   d. In *The Last Oblivion* (A.61).
   e. In *Shadows Seen and Unseen* (A.71).
   f. In *The Complete Poetry and Translations*, Volume 2 (A.73).
   g. In *The Song of the Necromancer and Others* (A.81).

   34 lines. Written August 1937.

665. "Psalm." [I have sealed my desire upon thee]
   a. In *Selected Poems* (A.27) (as a translation from "Christophe des Laurières").
   b. In *The Complete Poetry and Translations*, Volume 2 (A.73).

   34 lines.

666. "Psalm." [My beloved is a well of clear waters,]
   a. In *Ebony and Crystal* (A.3).
   b. In *The Complete Poetry and Translations*, Volume 1 (A.73).
   c. In *Moonlight and Other Poems* (A.78).

   35 lines. Dated 28 April 1921.

667. "A Psalm to the Best Beloved."
   a. In *Ebony and Crystal* (A.3).
   b. In *Selected Poems* (A.27).
   c. In *The Complete Poetry and Translations*, Volume 1 (A.73).
   d. In *Moonlight and Other Poems* (A.78).
   e. In *The Dark Eidolon and Other Fantasies* (A.84).

   21 lines. Written 29 April 1921.

668. "Psalm to the Desert."
   a. In *Klarkash-Ton and Monstro Ligriv* (A.37).
   b. In *Clark Ashton Smith—Poet* (A.32.b).
   c. In *The Complete Poetry and Translations*, Volume 1 (A.73).
   d. In *Moonlight and Other Poems* (A.78).
   e. In *Celui qui marchait parmi les étoiles* (II.A.iii.17).

   19 lines (biblical verses). Written c. February 1915.

669. "The Pursuer." [Ascendant from what dead profundity,]
    a. In *The Complete Poetry and Translations,* Volume 1 (A.73).

    Sonnet. Dated 15 May 1912.

670. "The Pursuer." [Climbing from out what nadir-fountained sea,]
    a. *Portals* 1, No. 1 (November 1957): 7–9.
    b. In *Selected Poems* (A.27).
    c. In *The Last Oblivion* (A.61).
    d. In *The Complete Poetry and Translations,* Volume 2 (A.73).

    Sonnet. A radical revision of the early poem of the same title.

671. "Quatrain."
    a. In *The Complete Poetry and Translations,* Volume 1 (A.73).

    4 lines. Juvenilia.

672. "Quatrains."
    a. In *The Complete Poetry and Translations,* Volume 1 (A.73).

    Two poems, "The Snare" and "Song" [Over the desert I forward ride,] each of 8 lines. Juvenilia.

673. "Quatrains." [Think not of the past,]
    a. In *The Complete Poetry and Translations,* Volume 1 (A.73).

    16 lines. Juvenilia.

674. "Quatrains on Jewels."
    a. In *The Complete Poetry and Translations,* Volume 1 (A.73).

    Four quatrains: "The Diamond," "The Pearl," "Turquoise," and "The Ruby." A fifth quatrain exists only as a title: "The Opal."

675. "Que songes-tu, Muse?"
    a. In *The Complete Poetry and Translations,* Volume 2 (A.73).

    20 lines. In French. For CAS's Spanish version, see "¿Que sueñas, Musa?" (item 676). For CAS's English version, see "What Dreamest Thou, Muse?" (item 951).

676. "¿Qué sueñas, Musa?"
    a. In *The Complete Poetry and Translations,* Volume 2 (A.73).

    20 lines. In Spanish. For CAS's French version, see "Que songes-tu, Muse?" (item 675). For CAS's English version, see "What Dreamest Thou, Muse?" (item 951).

677. "Query."
   a. *Auburn Journal* 25, No. 26 (9 April 1925): 4.
   b. In *Sandalwood* (A.4).
   c. *United Amateur* 25, No. 2 (May 1926): 7.
   d. *Step Ladder* 13, No. 5 (May 1927): 131.
   e. In *Selected Poems* (A.27).
   f. In *The Complete Poetry and Translations,* Volume 1 (A.73).

   30 lines. Dated 20 January 1925. First title: "To a Friend."

678. "Quest."
   a. *Auburn Journal* 22, No. 10 (22 December 1921): 4.
   b. In *Ebony and Crystal* (A.3).
   c. *Step Ladder* 13, No. 5 (May 1927): 133.
   d. *Stars* (June–July 1940): [2].
   e. In *Selected Poems* (A.27).
   f. In *The Complete Poetry and Translations,* Volume 1 (A.73).
   g. In *Moonlight and Other Poems* (A.78).

   33 lines.

679. "Quiddity."
   a. In *Spells and Philtres* (A.14).
   b. In *Selected Poems* (A.27).
   c. In *The Complete Poetry and Translations,* Volume 2 (A.73).

   5 lines.

680. "Qu'Importe?"
   a. In *The Complete Poetry and Translations,* Volume 2 (A.73).

   5 lines.

681. "Radio."
   a. In *The Complete Poetry and Translations,* Volume 2 (A.73).

   Haiku.

682. "Reclamation."
   a. In *Grotesques and Fantastiques* (A.32.a).
   b. In *The Complete Poetry and Translations,* Volume 1 (A.73).

   8 lines. Written c. 1915.

683. "Recompense."
   a. In *Ebony and Crystal* (A.3).

    b. In Wallace Alvin Briggs, ed. *Great Poems of the English Language.* New York: Robert M. McBride, 1927; London: George C. Harrap & Co., 1928. 1338. Rev. ed. New York: Tudor Publishing Co., 1936. 1338.

    c. *Ottumwa* [IA] *Daily Courier* (14 September 1934): 4.

    d. *Beckley* [WV] *Post Herald* (19 September 1934): 2.

    e. In *Selected Poems* (A.27).

    f. In *The Complete Poetry and Translations,* Volume 1 (A.73).

    g. In *Moonlight and Other Poems* (A.78).

    8 lines.

684. "Red Memory."

    a. In *The Complete Poetry and Translations,* Volume 2 (A.73).

    18 lines. For CAS's Spanish version, see "Memoria roja" (item 497).

685. "Refuge."

    a. In *Selected Poems* (A.27).

    b. In *The Complete Poetry and Translations,* Volume 2 (A.73).

    9 lines.

686. "Le Refuge." [English]

    a. In *The Complete Poetry and Translations,* Volume 2 (A.73).

    Sonnet. Written before 25 November 1935. For CAS's French version, see item 687.

687. "Le Refuge." [French]

    a. In *The Complete Poetry and Translations,* Volume 2 (A.73).

    Sonnet. For CAS's English version, see item 686.

688. "The Refuge of Beauty."

    a. In *Odes and Sonnets* (A.2).

    b. In *Ebony and Crystal* (A.3).

    c. *L'Alouette* 1, No. 3 (May 1924): 66.

    d. In *Selected Poems* (A.27).

    e. In *The Last Oblivion* (A.61).

    f. In *The Complete Poetry and Translations,* Volume 1 (A.73).

    g. In *Moonlight and Other Poems* (A.78).

    h. In *The Dark Eidolon and Other Fantasies* (A.84).

    Sonnet. Written c. June 1913.

689. "The Regained Past."
    a. In *The Complete Poetry and Translations,* Volume 2 (A.73).
    Sonnet.

690. "Reigning Empress."
    a. In *Selected Poems* (A.27).
    b. In *The Complete Poetry and Translations,* Volume 2 (A.73).
    Haiku.

691. "Reincarnation."
    a. In *The Complete Poetry and Translations,* Volume 1 (A.73).
    4 lines.

692. "Remembered Light."
    a. *Poetry* 1, No. 3 (December 1912): 78.
    b. In *Ebony and Crystal* (A.3).
    c. In *Selected Poems* (A.27).
    d. In *The Last Oblivion* (A.61).
    e. In *The Complete Poetry and Translations,* Volume 1 (A.73).
    f. In *Moonlight and Other Poems* (A.78).
    35 lines.

693. "Remembrance."
    a. *Auburn Journal* 24, No. 14 (17 January 1924): 6.
    b. In *Sandalwood* (A.4).
    c. In *Selected Poems* (A.27).
    d. In *The Complete Poetry and Translations,* Volume 1 (A.73).
    12 lines. Dated 5 November 1923. First title: "Song."

694. "Requiescat." [What was Love's worth,]
    a. *Smart Set* 68, No. 4 (August 1922): 102.
    b. In *Ebony and Crystal* (A.3).
    c. In *Selected Poems* (A.27).
    d. In *The Complete Poetry and Translations,* Volume 1 (A.73).
    20 lines. Dated 4 February 1920. First title: "Dirge."

695. "Requiescat." [Whither, on soft and soundless feet,]
    a. In *The Complete Poetry and Translations,* Volume 2 (A.73).
    16 lines. Dated 9 November 1938.

696. "Requiescat in Pace."
    a. In *Ebony and Crystal* (A.3).
    b. In *Selected Poems* (A.27).
    c. In *The Complete Poetry and Translations*, Volume 1 (A.73).
    d. In *Moonlight and Other Poems* (A.78).
    e. In *The Dark Eidolon and Other Fantasies* (A.84).

    32 lines. Written before 24 April 1918. b. and c. bear a dedication to "M.L.M." (Mamie Lowe Miller).

697. "Resignation."
    a. In *The Complete Poetry and Translations*, Volume 1 (A.73).

    4 lines. Juvenilia.

698. "Resurrection."
    a. *Weird Tales* 39, No. 11 (July 1947): 85.
    b. In August Derleth, ed. *Dark of the Moon: Poems of Fantasy and the Macabre*. Sauk City, WI: Arkham House, 1947; Freeport, NY: Books for Libraries Press, 1969; Miami, FL: Granger, 1976. 345–46.
    c. In *The Hill of Dionysus* (A.18).
    d. In *Selected Poems* (A.27).
    e. In *The Last Oblivion* (A.61).
    f. In *The Complete Poetry and Translations*, Volume 2 (A.73).
    g. In *The Song of the Necromancer and Others* (A.81).
    h. In *Celui qui marchait parmi les étoiles* (II.A.iii.17).

    32 lines. Written before 29 April 1939.

699. "The Retribution."
    a. In *The Star-Treader and Other Poems* (A.1).
    b. In *Odes and Sonnets* (A.2).
    c. In *Selected Poems* (A.27).
    d. In *The Complete Poetry and Translations*, Volume 1 (A.73).
    e. In *Moonlight and Other Poems* (A.78).

    Sonnet.

700. "Retrospect and Forecast." [English]
    a. In *The Star-Treader and Other Poems* (A.1).
    b. *Current Opinion* 54, No. 2 (February 1913): 150.
    c. *Los Angeles Times* (12 February 1913): 22.
    d. In *Nero and Other Poems* (A.8).

  e. In *Selected Poems* (A.27).
  f. In *The Last Oblivion* (A.61).
  g. In *The Complete Poetry and Translations*, Volume 1 (A.73).
  h. In *Moonlight and Other Poems* (A.78).
  i. In *The Dark Eidolon and Other Fantasies* (A.84).

  Sonnet. Dated 11 January 1912. See CAS's French translation of
  the same title (item 701).

701. "Retrospect and Forecast." [French]
  a. In *The Complete Poetry and Translations*, Volume 1 (A.73).

  Sonnet. A French translation of a sonnet of the same title (item
  700).

702. "The Return of Hyperion."
  a. In *The Star-Treader and Other Poems* (A.1).
  b. In *Selected Poems* (A.27).
  c. In *The Last Oblivion* (A.61).
  d. In *The Complete Poetry and Translations*, Volume 1 (A.73).
  e. In *Moonlight and Other Poems* (A.78).

  26 lines. Written c. 1912.

703. "Rêvasserie."
  a. In *The Complete Poetry and Translations*, Volume 2 (A.73).

  36 lines. In French. Dated 30 July 1929. For CAS's English version, see item 174.

704. "Rêve panthéistique."
  a. In *The Complete Poetry and Translations*, Volume 2 (A.73).

  36 lines. In French. The ms. is mutilated, rendering the second
  stanza largely illegible. For CAS's English version, see "Pantheistic
  Dream" (item 621).

705. "The Revelation."
  a. In *The Complete Poetry and Translations*, Volume 1 (A.73).
  Sonnet.

706. "Revenant."
  a. *Fantasy Fan* 1, No. 7 (March 1934): 106–7.
  b. In *The Dark Chateau* (A.13).
  c. In *Selected Poems* (A.27).

d. In *The Last Oblivion* (A.61).
e. In *The Complete Poetry and Translations*, Volume 2 (A.73).
f. In Charles D. Hornig, ed. *The Fantasy Fan: September, 1933–February, 1935*. [n.p.: Lance Thingmaker, 2010.] 106–7 (facsimile of a.).

54 lines. Written before 22 July 1933.

707. "Reverie in August."
a. In *The Hill of Dionysus* (A.18).
b. In *Selected Poems* (A.27).
c. In *The Complete Poetry and Translations*, Volume 2 (A.73).

20 lines.

708. "Rêves printaniers." [English]
a. In *The Complete Poetry and Translations*, Volume 2 (A.73).

Sonnet. For CAS's French version, see item 709.

709. "Rêves printaniers." [French]
a. In *The Complete Poetry and Translations*, Volume 2 (A.73).

Sonnet. For CAS's English version, see item 708.

710. "Ripe Mulberries."
a. In *The Complete Poetry and Translations*, Volume 2 (A.73).

Limerick (5 lines).

711. "The River."
a. In *The Complete Poetry and Translations*, Volume 1 (A.73).

16 lines. Juvenilia. A fragment.

712. "River-Canyon."
a. In *Selected Poems* (A.27).
b. In *The Complete Poetry and Translations*, Volume 2 (A.73).

Ten haiku. Written 7 February 1947. First title: "Canyon-Side."

713. "The River of Life."
a. In *The Sword of Zagan and Other Writings* (A.64).
b. In *The Complete Poetry and Translations*, Volume 1 (A.73).

12 lines. Juvenilia.

714. "The Road of Pain."
   a. In *The Complete Poetry and Translations*, Volume 1 (A.73).
      10 lines.

715. "Romance."
   a. In *The Complete Poetry and Translations*, Volume 1 (A.73).
      Sonnet.

716. "Rosa Mystica."
   a. *Lyric West* 1, No. 8 (December 1921): 7.
   b. In *Ebony and Crystal* (A.3).
   c. In *Selected Poems* (A.27).
   d. In *The Last Oblivion* (A.61).
   e. In *The Complete Poetry and Translations*, Volume 1 (A.73).
   f. In *Moonlight and Other Poems* (A.78).
   g. In *Celui qui marchait parmi les étoiles* (II.A.iii.17).
      Sonnet. Dated 5 November 1919.

717. "Rubaiyat." [I sought in wingèd flight from star to star]
   a. In *The Complete Poetry and Translations*, Volume 1 (A.73).
      16 lines. Juvenilia. A fragment.

718. "Rubaiyat." [Some talk of paradise and some of Hell,]
   a. In *The Complete Poetry and Translations*, Volume 1 (A.73).
      16 lines. Juvenilia.

719. "Rubaiyat of Saiyed."
   a. In *The Sword of Zagan and Other Writings* (A.64).
   b. In *The Complete Poetry and Translations*, Volume 1 (A.73).
      8 lines. Juvenilia. A fragment.

720. "The Rubaiyat of Seyyid."
   b. In *The Complete Poetry and Translations*, Volume 1 (A.73).
      48 lines. Juvenilia. Fragmentary: only stanzas 1–4 and 17–24 survive.

721. "Sacraments."
   a. In *The Complete Poetry and Translations*, Volume 2 (A.73).
      25 lines. Dated 5 August 1952.

722. "Said the Dreamer."
   a. *Vortex* No. 2 (1947): 25–26.
   b. In *Spells and Philtres* (A.14).
   c. In *Selected Poems* (A.27).
   d. In *The Last Oblivion* (A.61).
   e. In *The Complete Poetry and Translations*, Volume 1 (A.73).

   32 lines. Dated 5 March 1912; rev. 1944. First title: "In the Grip of Dreams."

723. "Sanctuary."
   a. In *The Complete Poetry and Translations*, Volume 2 (A.73).

   10 lines.

724. "Sandalwood."
   a. *Leaves* No. 1 (Summer 1937): 49.
   b. In *The Last Oblivion* (A.61).
   c. In *The Complete Poetry and Translations*, Volume 1 (A.73).
   d. In *Celui qui marchait parmi les étoiles* (II.A.iii.17).

   30 lines. Written before October 1925. CAS's original proem to *S*, but not included in *Sandalwood* (A.4).

725. "Sandalwood and Onions."
   a. In *The Complete Poetry and Translations*, Volume 2 (A.73).

   10 lines.

726. "Satan Unrepentant."
   a. In *Odes and Sonnets* (A.2).
   b. In *Ebony and Crystal* (A.3).
   c. In *Selected Poems* (A.27).
   d. In *The Last Oblivion* (A.61).
   e. In *The Complete Poetry and Translations*, Volume 1 (A.73).
   f. In *Moonlight and Other Poems* (A.78).
   g. In *The Dark Eidolon and Other Fantasies* (A.84).
   h. In *Celui qui marchait parmi les étoiles* (II.A.iii.17).

   96 lines. Written c. September 1912.

727. "Satiety." [A weary Juan, smothered in boudoirs,]
   a. In *Selected Poems* (A.27) (as a translation from "Christophe des Laurières").
   b. In *The Complete Poetry and Translations*, Volume 1 (A.73).

4 lines.

728. "Satiety." [Dear you were as is the tree of Being]
   a. In *Ebony and Crystal* (A.3).
   b. In *Selected Poems* (A.27).
   c. In *The Complete Poetry and Translations,* Volume 1 (A.73).

   16 lines. Dated 5 March 1922.

729. "Saturn."
   a. In *The Star-Treader and Other Poems* (A.1).
   b. In *Selected Poems* (A.27).
   c. In *The Last Oblivion* (A.61).
   d. In *The Complete Poetry and Translations,* Volume 1 (A.73).
   e. In *Moonlight and Other Poems* (A.78).
   f. In *Celui qui marchait parmi les étoiles* (II.A.iii.17).

   295 lines. Lines 254f. in d are found in a separate ms. (ms, John
   Hay Library, Brown University) under the title (or instruction)
   "Concluding Lines for 'Saturnian Epic'."

730. "Saturnian Cinema."
   a. In *The Fugitive Poems of Clark Ashton Smith: Second Series* (A.38).
   b. In *The Complete Poetry and Translations,* Volume 2 (A.73).

   16 lines. Written 13 September 1954.

731. "The Saturnienne." [Beneath the skies of Saturn, pale and many-
   mooned,]
   a. *Weird Tales* 10, No. 6 (December 1927): 728.
   b. In *Selected Poems* (A.27).
   c. In *The Last Oblivion* (A.61).
   d. In *The Complete Poetry and Translations,* Volume 1 (A.73).
   e. In *The Song of the Necromancer and Others* (A.81).

   32 lines. Written c. December 1925.

732. "The Saturnienne." [Emblazoned by vast flames of cycle-grounded
   snow,]
   a. In *The Complete Poetry and Translations,* Volume 2 (A.73).

   4 lines. A fragment.

733. "Says the Dreamer."
   a. In *Shadows Seen and Unseen* (A.71).

b. In *The Complete Poetry and Translations*, Volume 2 (A.73).

28 lines. Written c. 1950. For CAS's Spanish version, see "Dice el soñador" (item 199).

734. "School-Room Pastime."
a. In *Selected Poems* (A.27).
b. In *The Complete Poetry and Translations*, Volume 2 (A.73).

Haiku.

735. "The Sciapod."
a. In *Spells and Philtres* (A.14).
b. In *Selected Poems* (A.27).
c. In *The Complete Poetry and Translations*, Volume 2 (A.73).

Haiku.

736. "Sea Cycle."
a. *Wings* 8, No. 1 (Spring 1947): 11.
b. In *The Hill of Dionysus* (A.18).
c. In *Selected Poems* (A.27).
d. In *The Complete Poetry and Translations*, Volume 2 (A.73).

26 lines.

737. "The Sea-Gods."
a. *Auburn Journal* 23, No. 36 (21 June 1923): 6.
b. In *The Fugitive Poems of Clark Ashton Smith: Second Series* (A.38).
c. In Lin Carter, ed. *Weird Tales #4*. New York: Zebra, 1983. 215–16.
d. In *The Complete Poetry and Translations*, Volume 2 (A.73).

24 lines. Written c. July 1913.

738. "Sea-Lure."
a. In *The Complete Poetry and Translations*, Volume 1 (A.73).

12 lines. Juvenilia.

739. "Sea-Memory."
a. In *Selected Poems* (A.27).
b. In *The Complete Poetry and Translations*, Volume 2 (A.73).

8 lines.

740. "The Sea-Shell."
   a. In *The Complete Poetry and Translations*, Volume 1 (A.73).

   8 lines. Juvenilia.

741. "The Secret."
   a. *Auburn Journal* 23, No. 27 (19 April 1923): 6.
   b. In *Sandalwood* (A.4).
   c. *San Francisco Chronicle* (10 January 1926): 42.
   d. In Dudley Chadwick Gordon, Vernon Rupert King, and William Whittingham Lyman, ed. *Today's Literature*. New York: American Book Company, 1935. 448.
   e. In *Selected Poems* (A.27).
   f. In *The Complete Poetry and Translations*, Volume 1 (A.73).

   16 lines. Dated 13 March 1923.

742. "Secret Love."
   a. *Sinisterra* 1, No. 2 (Summer 1950): gatefold inserted between pages 4 and 5 (as a translation from "Christophe des Laurières").
   b. In *Spells and Philtres* (A.14).
   c. In *Selected Poems* (A.27) (as a translation from "Christophe des Laurières").
   d. In *The Complete Poetry and Translations*, Volume 1 (A.73).

   Sonnet. Dated 22 May 1921.

743. "Secret Worship."
   a. In *The Complete Poetry and Translations*, Volume 2 (A.73).

   16 lines.

744. "Seeker."
   a. In *The Dark Chateau* (A.13).
   b. In *Shadows Seen and Unseen* (A.71).
   c. In *The Complete Poetry and Translations*, Volume 2 (A.73).

   20 lines. Written before 22 February 1951.

745. "The Seekers."
   a. In *The Complete Poetry and Translations*, Volume 1 (A.73).

   28 lines. Juvenilia. Original title: "Song."

746. "Seer of the Cycles."
   a. *Epos* 8, No. 1 (Fall 1956): 9.

b. In *The Fugitive Poems of Clark Ashton Smith: Second Series* (A.38).
c. In *The Complete Poetry and Translations*, Volume 2 (A.73).

> Sonnet. Written 23 June 1952. An early version is titled "Seer."

747. "Seins."
a. In *The Complete Poetry and Translations*, Volume 2 (A.73).

> 10 lines. In French. Dated 20 July 1929.

748. "Selenique."
a. *Auburn Journal* 23, No. 41 (26 July 1923): 6 (as "Simile").
b. In *Sandalwood* (A.4).
c. In *Selected Poems* (A.27).
d. In *The Last Oblivion* (A.61).
e. In *The Complete Poetry and Translations*, Volume 1 (A.73).

> 15 lines. Dated 3 March 1923.

749. "Semblance."
a. *Auburn Journal* 23, No. 26 (12 April 1923): 6.
b. *Auburn Journal* 23, No. 27 (19 April 1923): 6 (with corrections).
c. *Wanderer* 1, No. 2 (July 1923): 7.
d. In *Sandalwood* (A.4).
e. *Outré* 1, No. 4 (November 1939): 8. (This entire issue was included in and attached to *Golden Atom* 1, No. 7 (April 1940): [25].)
f. In *Selected Poems* (A.27).
g. In *The Complete Poetry and Translations*, Volume 1 (A.73).

> 25 lines. Dated 4 March 1923.

750. "September."
a. In *In Memoriam: Clark Ashton Smith* (III.D.2).
b. In *Selected Poems* (A.27).
c. In *The Last Oblivion* (A.61).
d. In *The Complete Poetry and Translations*, Volume 2 (A.73).

> 24 lines. dated 11 September 1929.

751. "Septembral."
a. *Auburn Journal* 23, No. 47 (6 September 1923): 6.
b. In *The Complete Poetry and Translations*, Volume 1 (A.73).

> 12 lines. Written c. 1923. First title: "August."

752. "Sepulture."
    a. *Smart Set* 57, No. 2 (October 1922): 122.
    b. In *Ebony and Crystal* (A.3).
    c. In [Unsigned, ed.] *California Poets: An Anthology of 224 Contemporaries.* New York: Henry Harrison, 1932. 664.
    d. In *Selected Poems* (A.27).
    e. In *The Complete Poetry and Translations*, Volume 1 (A.73).
    f. In *Moonlight and Other Poems* (A.78).

    Sonnet. Written c. April 1918.

753. "Sestet."
    a. In *Selected Poems* (A.27).
    b. In *The Complete Poetry and Translations*, Volume 2 (A.73).

    6 lines.

754. "Shadow of Nightmare."
    a. In *The Star-Treader and Other Poems* (A.1).
    b. *Challenge* 1, No. 3 (Winter 1950): 3.
    c. In *Selected Poems* (A.27).
    d. In *The Last Oblivion* (A.61).
    e. In *The Complete Poetry and Translations*, Volume 1 (A.73).
    f. In *Moonlight and Other Poems* (A.78).
    g. In *The Dark Eidolon and Other Fantasies* (A.84).

    Sonnet.

755. "The Shadow of the Unattained."
    a. In *The Shadow of the Unattained* (A.69) (extract only).
    b. *Lost Worlds* No. 3 (2006): 5–8.
    c. In *The Complete Poetry and Translations*, Volume 1 (A.73).

    108 lines. Written c. April 1912.

756. "Shadows."
    a. *Weird Tales* 15, No. 2 (February 1930): 154.
    b. In August Derleth, ed. *Dark of the Moon: Poems of Fantasy and the Macabre.* Sauk City, WI: Arkham House, 1947; Freeport, NY: Books for Libraries Press, 1969; Miami, FL: Granger, 1976. 341.
    c. In *Selected Poems* (A.27).
    d. In *The Last Oblivion* (A.61).
    e. In *The Complete Poetry and Translations*, Volume 2 (A.73).

    f. In *The Song of the Necromancer and Others* (A.81).
    g. In *Autres mondes* (II.A.iii.16).
    h. In *Celui qui marchait parmi les étoiles* (II.A.iii.17).

    32 lines. Dated 12 September 1929.

757. "Shapes in the Sunset."
    a. In *The Dark Chateau* (A.13).
    b. In *The Black Book of Clark Ashton Smith* (A.39).
    c. In *The Sword of Zagan and Other Writings* (A.64).
    d. In *The Complete Poetry and Translations,* Volume 2 (A.73).

    32 lines.

758. "A Sierran Sunrise."
    a. In *In the Ultimate Valleys* (A.26).
    b. In *The Complete Poetry and Translations,* Volume 1 (A.73).

    16 lines. Written c. 1910.

759. "The Sierras."
    a. *Munsey's* 43, No. 6 (September 1910): 781 (as by "C. Ashton Smith").
    b. In Mrs. P. T. Smith, Mrs. Earl Lukens, and Mrs. D. W. Lubeck, ed. *Auburn Blue Book.* Auburn, CA: Privately printed, 1913. 11.
    c. In *The Complete Poetry and Translations,* Volume 1 (A.73).

    8 lines.

760. "Silence."
    a. In *The Complete Poetry and Translations,* Volume 1 (A.73).

    12 lines. Juvenilia.

761. "Silent Hour."
    a. *Wings* 5, No. 2 (Summer 1941): 15.
    b. In *The Hill of Dionysus* (A.18).
    c. In *Selected Poems* (A.27).
    d. In *The Complete Poetry and Translations,* Volume 2 (A.73).

    22 lines. Dated 30 January 1941.

762. "Silhouette."
    a. In *The Complete Poetry and Translations,* Volume 1 (A.73).
    8 lines.

763. "Simile." [Ah! chide me not for silence, or that I,]
  a. In *The Complete Poetry and Translations*, Volume 2 (A.73).

      8 lines. The ms. is dated 12 August 1927. Originally titled "Metaphor."

764. "Simile." [Truth is a soundless gong]
  a. In *The Complete Poetry and Translations*, Volume 2 (A.73).

      6 lines.

765. "Similitudes."
  a. In *The Complete Poetry and Translations*, Volume 2 (A.73).

      18 lines. Dated 1 February 1929. Variant title: "Similes."

766. "Sinbad, It Was Not Well to Brag."
  a. In *The Dark Chateau* (A.13).
  b. In *The Complete Poetry and Translations*, Volume 2 (A.73).

      64 lines.

767. "The Skull."
  a. In *The Complete Poetry and Translations*, Volume 1 (A.73).

      23 lines. Juvenilia.

768. "Slaughtered Cattle."
  a. In *The Complete Poetry and Translations*, Volume 2 (A.73).

      Haiku. [First line only extant.]

769. "Slaughter-House in Spring."
  a. In *In Memoriam: Clark Ashton Smith* (III.D.4).
  b. In *Selected Poems* (A.27).
  c. In *The Complete Poetry and Translations*, Volume 2 (A.73).

      Haiku.

770. "Slaughter-House Pasture."
  a. In *In Memoriam: Clark Ashton Smith* (III.D.4).
  b. In *Selected Poems* (A.27).
  c. In *The Complete Poetry and Translations*, Volume 2 (A.73).

      Haiku.

771. "Snake, Owl, Cat or Hawk."
  a. In *Selected Poems* (A.27).

b. In *The Complete Poetry and Translations*, Volume 2 (A.73).
    Haiku.

772. "The Snow-Blossoms."
    a. In *The Star-Treader and Other Poems* (A.1).
    b. In *The Complete Poetry and Translations*, Volume 1 (A.73).
    c. In *Moonlight and Other Poems* (A.78).

    8 lines.

773. "Snowfall on Acacia."
    a. In *Selected Poems* (A.27).
    b. In *The Complete Poetry and Translations*, Volume 2 (A.73).

    Two haiku.

774. "Solicitation."
    a. *Golden Atom* (August 1959 [Twentieth Anniversary Issue]): 5.
    b. In *The Complete Poetry and Translations*, Volume 2 (A.73).

    20 lines. The ms. is dated 14 September 1932.

775. "Soliloquy in a Ebon Tower."
    a. In *The Dark Chateau* (A.13).
    b. In *The Black Book of Clark Ashton Smith* (A.39).
    c. *Chronicles of the Cthulhu Codex* No. 17 (Winter 2000): 46–49.
    d. In *The Last Oblivion* (A.61).
    e. In *The Complete Poetry and Translations*, Volume 2 (A.73).
    f. In *Celui qui marchait parmi les étoiles* (II.A.iii.17).

    100 lines. Written before 15 April 1951.

776. "Solitude."
    a. In *The Complete Poetry and Translations*, Volume 1 (A.73).

    8 lines. Juvenilia.

777. "Solution."
    a. In *Ebony and Crystal* (A.3).
    b. *Weird Tales* 3, No. 1 (January 1924): 32.
    c. In *Selected Poems* (A.27).
    d. In *The Last Oblivion* (A.61).
    e. In *The Complete Poetry and Translations*, Volume 1 (A.73).
    f. In *Moonlight and Other Poems* (A.78).
    g. In *The Song of the Necromancer and Others* (A.81).

30 lines. Dated 25 December 1919.

778. "Some Blind Eidolon."
    a. *Kaleidograph* 19, No. 2 (June 1947): 2–3.
    b. In *The Dark Chateau* (A.13).
    c. In *Selected Poems* (A.27).
    d. In *The Last Oblivion* (A.61).
    e. In *The Complete Poetry and Translations*, Volume 2 (A.73).

    41 lines. Dated 23 March 1947. First title: "The Shadow."

779. "Some Maxims from the Persian."
    a. In *The Complete Poetry and Translations*, Volume 1 (A.73).

    8 lines. Juvenilia.

780. "Someone."
    a. In *Selected Poems* (A.27).
    b. In *The Complete Poetry and Translations*, Volume 2 (A.73).

    5 lines.

781. "Somnus."
    a. In *The Complete Poetry and Translations*, Volume 1 (A.73).

    Sonnet.

782. "Somnus (A Fragment)."
    a. In *Selected Poems* (A.27).
    b. In *The Complete Poetry and Translations*, Volume 1 (A.73).

    13 lines.

783. "Song." [I am grown tired of suffering,]
    a. In *The Complete Poetry and Translations*, Volume 2 (A.73).

    10 lines. Written 19 December 1927.

784. "Song." [I bring my weariness to thee,]
    a. In *Ebony and Crystal* (A.3).
    b. In *Selected Poems* (A.27).
    c. In *The Complete Poetry and Translations*, Volume 1 (A.73).
    d. In *Moonlight and Other Poems* (A.78).

    10 lines. Written before 25 June 1922.

785. "Song." [Vagrant from the realms of rose,]
    a. *Auburn Journal* 23, No. 33 (31 May 1923): 6.
    b. *Wanderer* 2, No. 1 (January 1924): 1 (as "The Fugitive").
    c. In *Sandalwood* (A.4).
    d. In *Selected Poems* (A.27).
    e. In *The Complete Poetry and Translations*, Volume 1 (A.73).

       30 lines. Written before 7 March 1923. Part of an unfinished play, *The Fugitives* (item 329).

786. "Song." [When in the desert]
    a. In *Shadows Seen and Unseen* (A.71).
    b. In *The Complete Poetry and Translations*, Volume 2 (A.73).

       16 lines. For CAS's Spanish version, see "Cantar" (item 114).

787. "Song at Evenfall."
    a. *Overland Monthly* 88, No. 5 (May 1930): 149.
    b. In *The Complete Poetry and Translations*, Volume 2 (A.73).

       10 lines.

788. "A Song from Hell."
    a. In *The Fugitive Poems of Clark Ashton Smith: Second Series* (A.38).
    b. In *The Last Oblivion* (A.61).
    c. In *The Complete Poetry and Translations*, Volume 1 (A.73).
    d. In *Celui qui marchait parmi les étoiles* (II.A.iii.17).

       50 lines. Written c. October 1911.

789. "The Song of a Comet."
    a. In *The Star-Treader and Other Poems* (A.1).
    b. In *Nero and Other Poems* (A.8).
    c. In *Selected Poems* (A.27).
    d. In *The Last Oblivion* (A.61).
    e. In *The Complete Poetry and Translations*, Volume 1 (A.73).

       70 lines. Written c. January 1912.

790. "The Song of Aviol."
    a. *Auburn Journal* 23, No. 25 (5 April 1923): 6.
    b. *Lyric West* 3, No. 11 (March 1924): 28.
    c. In *Sandalwood* (A.4).
    d. In *Selected Poems* (A.27).
    e. In *Strange Shadows* (A.52) (as "Song").

f. In *The Complete Poetry and Translations*, Volume 1 (A.73).

24 lines. Dated 17 September 1922. Part of an unfinished play, *The Fugitives* (item 329).

791. "The Song of Cartha."
   a. *Auburn Journal* 23, No. 29 (3 May 1923): 6.
   b. *Wanderer* 2, No. 8 (August 1924): 103.
   c. In *Sandalwood* (A.4).
   d. In *Selected Poems* (A.27).
   e. In *The Complete Poetry and Translations*, Volume 1 (A.73).

12 lines. Written before 10 May 1923. Part of an unfinished play, *The Fugitives* (item 329).

792. "A Song of Dreams."
   a. In *The Star-Treader and Other Poems* (A.1).
   b. In *Nero and Other Poems* (A.8).
   c. In *Selected Poems* (A.27).
   d. In *The Last Oblivion* (A.61).
   e. In *The Complete Poetry and Translations*, Volume 1 (A.73).
   f. In *Moonlight and Other Poems* (A.78).

54 lines.

793. "Song of Sappho's Arabian Daughter."
   a. *Ainslee's* 43, No. 1 (February 1919): 80 (as "The Desert Garden").
   b. In *Ebony and Crystal* (A.3) (as "The Desert Garden").
   c. In *Selected Poems* (A.27).
   d. In *The Complete Poetry and Translations*, Volume 1 (A.73).

20 lines.

794. "The Song of Songs."
   a. In *The Complete Poetry and Translations*, Volume 2 (A.73).

14 lines.

795. "Song of the Bacchic Bards."
   a. In *The Complete Poetry and Translations*, Volume 2 (A.73).

24 lines.

796. "Song of the Free Beings."
   a. In *The Complete Poetry and Translations*, Volume 2 (A.73).

12 lines. First title: "Song of the Free Creatures." For CAS's Spanish version, see "El Cantar de los seres libres" (item 115).

797. "Song of the Necromancer."
  a. *Weird Tales* 29, No. 2 (February 1937): 220.
  b. In *Selected Poems* (A.27).
  c. In *The Black Book of Clark Ashton Smith* (A.39).
  d. In *The Emperor of Dreams* (A.59).
  e. In *The Last Oblivion* (A.61).
  f. In *The Complete Poetry and Translations*, Volume 2 (A.73).
  g. In *The Song of the Necromancer and Others* (A.81).
  h. In *The Dark Eidolon and Other Fantasies* (A.84).
  i. In *The Averoigne Chronicles* (A.85).
  j. In *Celui qui marchait parmi les étoiles* (II.A.iii.17).

  35 lines.

798. "The Song of the Stars."
  a. In *The Star-Treader and Other Poems* (A.1).
  b. In *The Complete Poetry and Translations*, Volume 1 (A.73).
  c. In *Moonlight and Other Poems* (A.78).

  57 lines.

799. "The Song of the Worlds."
  a. In *The Fugitive Poems of Clark Ashton Smith: Second Series* (A.38).
  b. In *The Complete Poetry and Translations*, Volume 1 (A.73).

  60 lines.

800. "Song to Oblivion."
  a. In *The Star-Treader and Other Poems* (A.1).
  b. *Berkeley Daily Gazette* (27 September 1932): 14.
  c. *Berkeley Daily Gazette* (25 September 1936): 21.
  d. In *The Complete Poetry and Translations*, Volume 1 (A.73).
  e. In *Moonlight and Other Poems* (A.78).

  15 lines.

801. "Sonnet." [Empress with eyes more sad and aureate]
  a. *Weird Tales* 13, No. 4 (April 1929): 542.
  b. In *Selected Poems* (A.27).
  c. In *The Complete Poetry and Translations*, Volume 2 (A.73).
  d. In *The Song of the Necromancer and Others* (A.81).

Sonnet.

802. "Sonnet." [How shall our hearts, those fragile shrines of thee,]
   a. In *The Hill of Dionysus* (A.18).
   b. In *Selected Poems* (A.27).
   c. In *The Complete Poetry and Translations*, Volume 2 (A.73).

   Sonnet. Written before 22 February 1940.

803. "Sonnet." [Slowly, sweetly, from the fear that folds or breaks,]
   a. In *The Complete Poetry and Translations*, Volume 2 (A.73).

   Sonnet.

804. "Sonnet for the Psychoanalysts."
   a. In *The Dark Chateau* (A.13).
   b. *Weird Tales* 44, No. 2 (January 1952): 73.
   c. In *Selected Poems* (A.27).
   d. In *The Complete Poetry and Translations*, Volume 2 (A.73).
   e. In *The Song of the Necromancer and Others* (A.81).

   Sonnet. Written October 1948. First title: "Surréaliste Sonnet 2."

805. "Sonnet lunaire." [English]
   a. In *The Complete Poetry and Translations*, Volume 1 (A.73).

   Sonnet. See CAS's French version of the same title (item 806).

806. "Sonnet lunaire." [French]
   a. In *The Complete Poetry and Translations*, Volume 1 (A.73).

   Sonnet. See CAS's English version of the same title (item 805).

807. "Sonnet on Music."
   a. In *The Complete Poetry and Translations*, Volume 1 (A.73).

   Sonnet.

808. "Sonnet on Oblivion."
   a. In *The Complete Poetry and Translations*, Volume 1 (A.73).

   Sonnet.

809. "Sonnet to the Sphinx."
   a. In *The Complete Poetry and Translations*, Volume 1 (A.73).

   Sonnet.

810. "Sonnets of the Desert."
    a. In *The Complete Poetry and Translations,* Volume 2 (A.73).

    Two sonnets, one complete, the other not (10 lines only).

811. "Sonnets of the Seasons."
    a. In *In the Ultimate Valleys* (A.26) ("Summer" only; as "The Noon of the Seasons").
    b. In *The Complete Poetry and Translations,* Volume 2 (A.73).

    Three sonnets: "Spring," "Summer," "The Wizardry of Winter." If CAS wrote a sonnet for autumn, it is non-extant.

812. "The Sorcerer Departs."
    a. *Acolyte* 2, No. 2 (Spring 1944): 15.
    b. In *Clark Ashton Smith: The Sorcerer Departs* (III.D.14).
    c. In *A Rendezvous in Averoigne* (A.47).
    d. In *Shadows Seen and Unseen* (A.71).
    e. In *The Complete Poetry and Translations,* Volume 2 (A.73).

    10 lines.

813. "The Sorcerer to His Love."
    a. *Weird Tales* 39, No. 1 (September 1945): 63.
    b. In *The Hill of Dionysus* (A.18).
    c. In *Selected Poems* (A.27).
    d. In *The Last Oblivion* (A.61).
    e. In *The Complete Poetry and Translations,* Volume 2 (A.73).
    f. In *The Song of the Necromancer and Others* (A.81).

    16 lines. Dated 16 November 1941.

814. "The Sorrow of the Winds."
    a. *Poetry* 1, No. 3 (December 1912): 80 (as "Sorrowing of Winds").
    b. In *Ebony and Crystal* (A.3).
    c. In *Selected Poems* (A.27).
    d. In *The Complete Poetry and Translations,* Volume 1 (A.73).
    e. In *Moonlight and Other Poems* (A.78).

    16 lines.

815. "The Soul of the Sea."
    a. In *The Star-Treader and Other Poems* (A.1).
    b. In *The Complete Poetry and Translations,* Volume 1 (A.73).

    15 lines.

816. "Souvenance."
   a. In *The Fugitive Poems of Clark Ashton Smith: Second Series* (A.38).
   b. In *The Complete Poetry and Translations*, Volume 2 (A.73).

   12 lines. Dated 25 August 1927. First title: "Verses."

817. "Le Souvenir."
   a. In *The Complete Poetry and Translations*, Volume 2 (A.73).

   16 lines. In French. Dated 28 July 1929.

818. "The Sparrow's Nest."
   a. In *Spells and Philtres* (A.14).
   b. In *Selected Poems* (A.27).
   c. In *The Complete Poetry and Translations*, Volume 2 (A.73).

   Haiku.

819. "Spectral Life."
   a. In *Klarkash-Ton and Monstro Ligriv* (A.37).
   b. In *Clark Ashton Smith—Poet* (A.32.b).
   c. In *The Complete Poetry and Translations*, Volume 2 (A.73).

   36 lines. For CAS's French version, see "Une Vie spectrale" (item 936).

820. "Speculation."
   a. In *The Complete Poetry and Translations*, Volume 1 (A.73).

   5 lines.

821. "Sphinx and Medusa."
   a. In *The Fugitive Poems of Clark Ashton Smith: Second Series* (A.38).
   b. In *The Complete Poetry and Translations*, Volume 1 (A.73).

   Sonnet.

822. "The Sphinx of the Infinite."
   a. In *Grotesques and Fantastiques* (A.32.a).
   b. In Jonathan Bacon and Steve Troyanovich, ed. *Omniumgathum: An Anthology of Verse by Top Authors in the Field of Fantasy.* Lamoni, IA: Stygian Isle Press, 1976. 29.
   c. In *The Complete Poetry and Translations*, Volume 1 (A.73).

   16 lines.

823. "Spring Nunnery."
    a. In *Selected Poems* (A.27).
    b. In *The Complete Poetry and Translations*, Volume 2 (A.73).
    Haiku.

824. "Stamboul."
    a. In *The Complete Poetry and Translations*, Volume 1 (A.73).
    22 lines. Juvenilia. Revision of "Haroun Al-Raschid" (item 354).

825. "The Star-Treader."
    a. In *The Star-Treader and Other Poems* (A.1).
    b. In *Selected Poems* (A.27).
    c. In *The Last Oblivion* (A.61).
    d. In *The Complete Poetry and Translations*, Volume 1 (A.73).
    e. In *Moonlight and Other Poems* (A.78).
    f. In *The Dark Eidolon and Other Fantasies* (A.84).
    g. In *Celui qui marchait parmi les étoiles* (II.A.iii.17).

    130 lines. Written before 6 October 1911. First title: "The Sun-Treader."

826. "Storm's End."
    a. In *Selected Poems* (A.27).
    b. In *The Complete Poetry and Translations*, Volume 2 (A.73).
    Haiku.

827. "Stormy Afterglow."
    a. In *Selected Poems* (A.27).
    b. In *The Complete Poetry and Translations*, Volume 2 (A.73).
    Haiku. First title: "Stormy Sunset."

828. "Strange Girl."
    a. *Wings* 6, No. 3 (Autumn 1943): 12–13.
    b. In Stanton A. Coblentz, ed. *The Music Makers*. New York: Bernard Ackerman, 1945. 224–25.
    c. In *Selected Poems* (A.27).
    d. In *Shadows Seen and Unseen* (A.71).
    e. In *The Complete Poetry and Translations*, Volume 2 (A.73).

    40 lines. Written c. May 1943.

829. "Strangeness."
   a. *Bohemia* 2, No. 4 ([May] 1917): 3.
   b. In *Ebony and Crystal* (A.3).
   c. In *Selected Poems* (A.27) (20 lines).
   d. In *The Last Oblivion* (A.61).
   e. In *The Complete Poetry and Translations*, Volume 1 (A.73).
   f. In *Moonlight and Other Poems* (A.78).

   28 lines. Dated 3 October 1916. The TMS of *Selected Poems* has 24 lines, four of which had been added in pen.

830. "STYES WITH SPIRES."
   a. In *The Complete Poetry and Translations*, Volume 2 (A.73).

   8 lines. The entire ms. is typed in all capitals.

831. "The Stylite."
   a. In *The Dark Chateau* (A.13).
   b. In *The Complete Poetry and Translations*, Volume 2 (A.73).

   35 lines. Dated 10 January 1951.

832. "Sufficiency."
   a. In *Selected Poems* (A.27).
   b. In *The Complete Poetry and Translations*, Volume 2 (A.73).

   17 lines. Dated 5 February 1929.

833. "Suggestion."
   a. In *Grotesques and Fantastiques* (A.32).
   b. In *The Complete Poetry and Translations*, Volume 1 (A.73).

   10 lines.

834. "Suleyman Jan ben Jan."
   a. In *The Complete Poetry and Translations*, Volume 1 (A.73).

   16 lines. Juvenilia.

835. "The Summer Hills."
   a. In *The Complete Poetry and Translations*, Volume 1 (A.73).

   12 lines.

836. "Summer Idleness."
   a. In *The Complete Poetry and Translations*, Volume 1 (A.73).

   22 lines. Juvenilia.

837. "The Summer Moon."
   a. In *The Star-Treader and Other Poems* (A.1).
   b. In *Selected Poems* (A.27).
   c. In *Moonlight and Other Poems* (A.78).

   14 lines.

838. "Sunrise."
   a. In *The Complete Poetry and Translations*, Volume 1 (A.73).

   12 lines. Juvenilia.

839. "The Sunrise."
   a. *Rosary Magazine* 42, No. 1 (January 1913): 96 (last quatrain only; as "Dawn").
   b. In *The Complete Poetry and Translations*, Volume 1 (A.73).

   16 lines.

840. "The Suns and the Void."
   a. In *The Fugitive Poems of Clark Ashton Smith: Second Series* (A.38).
   b. In *The Complete Poetry and Translations*, Volume 1 (A.73).

   31 lines.

841. "A Sunset." [As blood from some enormous hurt]
   a. In *The Star-Treader and Other Poems* (A.1).
   b. In *Selected Poems* (A.27).
   c. In *The Complete Poetry and Translations*, Volume 1 (A.73).
   d. In *Moonlight and Other Poems* (A.78).

   4 lines.

842. "A Sunset." [Far-falling from a wounded heaven,]
   a. In *The Fugitive Poems of Clark Ashton Smith: Second Series* (A.38).
   b. In *The Complete Poetry and Translations*, Volume 1 (A.73).

   18 lines. Written before 15 November 1925. A translation of "Un Couchant" (item 161).

843. "Sunset Over Farm-Land."
   a. In *Selected Poems* (A.27).
   b. In *The Complete Poetry and Translations*, Volume 2 (A.73).

   Haiku.

844. "Supplication."
   a. In *The Hill of Dionysus* (A.18).
   b. In *Selected Poems* (A.27).

   18 lines. Dated 30 September 1942. First title: "Prayer."

845. "Surréalist Sonnet."
   a. In *The Dark Chateau* (A.13).
   b. In *Selected Poems* (A.27).
   c. In *The Complete Poetry and Translations,* Volume 2 (A.73).

   Sonnet. Written 29 December 1945.

846. "Symbols."
   a. *London Mercury* No. 33 (July 1922): 245 (as by "A. Clark Ashton Smith").
   b. In *Ebony and Crystal* (A.3).
   c. In [Helen Hoyt, ed.] *California Poets: An Anthology of 224 Contemporaries.* New York: Henry Harrison, 1932. 664.
   d. In *Selected Poems* (A.27).
   e. In *The Last Oblivion* (A.61).
   f. In *The Complete Poetry and Translations,* Volume 1 (A.73).
   g. In *Moonlight and Other Poems* (A.78).

   Sonnet. Dated 13 August 1919.

847. "The Tartarus of the Suns."
   a. In *The Fugitive Poems of Clark Ashton Smith* (A.26).
   b. In *The Complete Poetry and Translations,* Volume 1 (A.73).

   Sonnet.

848. "The Tears of Lilith."
   a. In *Ebony and Crystal* (A.3).
   b. In *Selected Poems* (A.27).
   c. In *The Last Oblivion* (A.61).
   d. In *The Complete Poetry and Translations,* Volume 1 (A.73).
   e. In *Moonlight and Other Poems* (A.78).
   f. In *The Dark Eidolon and Other Fantasies* (A.84).

   12 lines. The ms. is dated 26 April 1917.

849. "The Temple."
   a. In *The Complete Poetry and Translations,* Volume 1 (A.73).

   39 lines. Juvenilia. A fragment.

850. "The Temple of Night."
   a. In *The Complete Poetry and Translations*, Volume 1 (A.73).

   Sonnet.

851. "Temporality."
   a. In *Klarkash-Ton and Monstro Ligriv* (A.37).
   b. In *The Fugitive Poems of Clark Ashton Smith: Second Series* (A.38).
   c. In *The Sword of Zagan and Other Writings* (A.64).
   d. In *The Complete Poetry and Translations*, Volume 2 (A.73).

   12 lines. Dated 13 April 1928.

852. "The Temptation." [In the close and clinging night,]
   a. In *The Complete Poetry and Translations*, Volume 1 (A.73).

   78 lines. Begun 23 September 1924; completed 27 October 1924.
   First title: "To Lilith."

853. "The Temptation." [Lilith, queen of all delight,]
   a. In *The Complete Poetry and Translations*, Volume 2 (A.73).

   11 lines. A fragment. Quoted in its entirety in Fritz Leiber, "On
   Fantasy," *Fantasy Newsletter* No. 33 (February 1981): 4, prior to
   its appearance in I.A.73.

854. "Tempus."
   a. In *Selected Poems* (A.27) (as a translation from "Christophe des
       Laurières").
   b. In *The Complete Poetry and Translations*, Volume 1 (A.73).

   8 lines.

855. "'That Last Infirmity.'"
   a. *Wings* 5, No. 1 (Spring 1941): 18 (as "Fame").
   b. In *Selected Poems* (A.27).
   c. In *The Complete Poetry and Translations*, Volume 2 (A.73).

   4 lines.

856. "'That Motley Drama.'"
   a. In *Spells and Philtres* (A.14) (as a translation of "Clérigo Herrero").
   b. In *Selected Poems* (A.27).

   8 lines. Written 21 October 1949.

857. "Thebaid."
  a. In *Spells and Philtres* (A.14).
  b. In *The Black Book of Clark Ashton Smith* (A.39).
  c. In *The Complete Poetry and Translations*, Volume 2 (A.73).

  25 lines. Dated 14 February 1954. Variant titles: "Arctica Deserta" and "Ultima Thule."

858. "The Thralls of Circe Climb Parnassus."
  a. In *Selected Poems* (A.27).
  b. In *Shadows Seen and Unseen* (A.71).
  c. In *The Complete Poetry and Translations*, Volume 2 (A.73).

  Sonnet. Dated 16 July 1941. First title: "Swine and Azaleas."

859. "The Throne of Winter."
  a. In *The Fugitive Poems of Clark Ashton Smith: Second Series* (A.38).
  b. In *The Complete Poetry and Translations*, Volume 1 (A.73).

  Sonnet.

860. "Time." [O Time, great satrap of Eternity,]
  a. In *The Complete Poetry and Translations*, Volume 1 (A.73).

  Sonnet.

861. "Time." [O who can stem its tide,]
  a. In *The Complete Poetry and Translations*, Volume 1 (A.73).

  18 lines. Juvenilia.

862. "Time the Wonder."
  a. In *The Complete Poetry and Translations*, Volume 1 (A.73).

  4 lines.

863. "Tin Can on the Mountain-Top."
  a. In *Selected Poems* (A.27).
  b. In *The Complete Poetry and Translations*, Volume 2 (A.73).

  39 lines. First title: "Tomato-Can on the Mountain-Top."

864. "Tired Gardener."
  a. *Epos* 9, No. 1 (Fall 1957): 16–17.
  b. In *Spells and Philtres* (A.14).
  c. In *The Complete Poetry and Translations*, Volume 2 (A.73).

37 lines. Dated 5 August 1955.

865. "The Titans in Tartarus."
    a. In *The Fugitive Poems of Clark Ashton Smith: Second Series* (A.38).
    b. In *The Last Oblivion* (A.61).
    c. In *The Complete Poetry and Translations*, Volume 1 (A.73).
    d. In *Celui qui marchait parmi les étoiles* (II.A.iii.17).

    71 lines. Written before 29 October 1912.

866. "To a Cloud."
    a. In *The Complete Poetry and Translations*, Volume 1 (A.73).
    51 lines.

867. "To a Comet."
    a. In *The Complete Poetry and Translations*, Volume 2 (A.73).
    13 lines. A fragment (probably intended to be a sonnet).

868. "To a Mariposa Lily."
    a. In *The Fugitive Poems of Clark Ashton Smith: Second Series* (A.38).
    b. In *The Complete Poetry and Translations*, Volume 1 (A.73).
    8 lines.

869. "To a Northern Venus."
    a. In *The Complete Poetry and Translations*, Volume 1 (A.73).
    24 lines.

870. "To a Snowdrop."
    a. In *The Complete Poetry and Translations*, Volume 1 (A.73).
    8 lines. First titles: "To a Fairy-Lantern" and "A Snowdrop."

871. "To a Yellow Pine."
    a. In *The Complete Poetry and Translations*, Volume 1 (A.73).
    30 lines. Written c. 1910.

872. "To Ambition."
    a. In *The Complete Poetry and Translations*, Volume 1 (A.73).
    12 lines.

873. "To an Eastern City."
    a. In *The Complete Poetry and Translations*, Volume 1 (A.73).

20 lines. Juvenilia.

874. "To Antares."
   a. In *Selected Poems* (A.27).
   b. In *The Last Oblivion* (A.61).
   c. In *The Complete Poetry and Translations,* Volume 2 (A.73).

   14 lines. Dated 25 August 1927.

875. "To Bacchante."
   a. In *The Hill of Dionysus* (A.18).
   b. In *Selected Poems* (A.27) (without title).
   c. In *The Complete Poetry and Translations,* Volume 2 (A.73).

   7 lines. The last two lines are a quotation from J. W. Mackail's translation of a poem from *The Greek Anthology.*

876. "To Beauty (A Fragment)."
   a. In *Selected Poems* (A.27).
   b. In *Grotesques and Fantastiques* (A.32) (as "Ode to Beauty"; called "unfinished").
   c. In *The Complete Poetry and Translations,* Volume 1 (A.73).

   22 lines. Written c. 1914.

877. "To George Sterling." [Deep are the chasmal years and lustrums long]
   a. In *To George Sterling: Five Poems* (A.26).
   b. In *Selected Poems* (A.27).
   c. In *The Shadow of the Unattained* (A.69).
   d. In *Shadows Seen and Unseen* (A.71).
   e. In *The Complete Poetry and Translations,* Volume 1 (A.73).

   Sonnet. Dated 20 November 1941.

878. "To George Sterling." [High priest of this our latter Song,]
   a. In *To George Sterling: Five Poems* (A.26).
   b. In *The Shadow of the Unattained* (A.69).
   c. In *The Complete Poetry and Translations,* Volume 1 (A.73).

   24 lines. Written 1910.

879. "To George Sterling." [His song shall waken the dull-sleeping throng,]
   a. In *To George Sterling: Five Poems* (A.26).
   b. In *The Shadow of the Unattained* (A.69).

c. In *The Complete Poetry and Translations,* Volume 1 (A.73).

Sonnet.

880. "To George Sterling." [O Beauty, goddess known and sung of old]
  a. In *The Complete Poetry and Translations,* Volume 1 (A.73).

Sonnet.

881. "To George Sterling." [What questioners have met the gaze of Time,]
  a. In *To George Sterling: Five Poems* (A.26).
  b. In *The Shadow of the Unattained* (A.69).
  c. In *The Complete Poetry and Translations,* Volume 1 (A.73).

Sonnet. Written c. December 1911

882. "To George Sterling: A Valediction."
  a. *Overland Monthly* 85, No. 11 (November 1927): 338.
  b. In *To George Sterling: Five Poems* (A.26).
  c. In *Selected Poems* (A.27).
  d. In *The Last Oblivion* (A.61).
  e. In *The Shadow of the Unattained* (A.69).
  f. In *The Complete Poetry and Translations,* Volume 1 (A.73).
  g. In *The Dark Eidolon and Other Fantasies* (A.84).
  h. In *Celui qui marchait parmi les étoiles* (II.A.iii.17).

60 lines. Written December 1926. All published appearances except e. and f. as "A Valediction to George Sterling." A poem written after the death of Sterling.

883. "To Howard Phillips Lovecraft."
  a. *Weird Tales* 30, No. 1 (July 1937): 48.
  b. In H. P. Lovecraft [et al.]. *Marginalia.* Ed. August Derleth and Donald Wandrei. Sauk City, WI: Arkham House, 1944. 370–71.
  c. In *Selected Poems* (A.27).
  d. In S. T. Joshi, ed. *H. P. Lovecraft: Four Decades of Criticism.* Athens: Ohio University Press, 1980. 227–28.
  e. In *Letters to H. P. Lovecraft* (A.43).
  f. In *The Last Oblivion* (A.61).
  g. In *The Complete Poetry and Translations,* Volume 2 (A.73).
  h. In *The Song of the Necromancer and Others* (A.81).
  i. In *The Dark Eidolon and Other Fantasies* (A.84).

j. In *Celui qui marchait parmi les étoiles* (II.A.iii.17).

   40 lines. Dated 31 March 1937.

884. "To Iris." [Nymph of the harvest-coloured hair,]
   a. In *The Complete Poetry and Translations,* Volume 2 (A.73).

   19 lines. Apparently a fragment.

885. "To Iris." [Hidden within thy heart, as in some]
   a. In *The Complete Poetry and Translations,* Volume 2 (A.73).

   4 lines. A fragment.

886. "To Nora May French."
   a. In *Ebony and Crystal* (A.3).
   b. In *Selected Poems* (A.27).
   c. In *The Last Oblivion* (A.61).
   d. In *The Complete Poetry and Translations,* Volume 1 (A.73).
   e. In *Celui qui marchait parmi les étoiles* (II.A.iii.17).

   99 lines. Begun c. June 1916, completed before 10 July 1920.

887. "To Omar Khayyam."
   a. In *Ebony and Crystal* (A.3).
   b. *Lyric West* 5, No. 8 (May–June 1926): 216–17.
   c. In *Selected Poems* (A.27).
   d. In *The Last Oblivion* (A.61).
   e. In *The Complete Poetry and Translations,* Volume 1 (A.73).
   f. In *Moonlight and Other Poems* (A.78).
   g. In *Celui qui marchait parmi les étoiles* (II.A.iii.17).

   72 lines. Dated 13 December 1919. First title: "To Omar."

888. "To One Absent."
   a. In *The Hill of Dionysus* (A.18).
   b. In *Selected Poems* (A.27).
   c. In *The Complete Poetry and Translations,* Volume 2 (A.73).

   24 lines. Written 29 January 1941; revised 1943.

889. "To the Beloved."
   a. In *Ebony and Crystal* (A.3).
   b. In *Selected Poems* (A.27).
   c. In *The Fugitive Poems of Clark Ashton Smith: Second Series* (A.38)
       (as "Sonnet").

d. In *The Complete Poetry and Translations*, Volume 1 (A.73).
e. In *Moonlight and Other Poems* (A.78).

Sonnet. Written February 1919. First title: "Sonnet."

890. "To the Best Beloved."
a. In *The Complete Poetry and Translations*, Volume 1 (A.73).

5 lines. Juvenilia.

891. "To the Chimera."
a. *Auburn Journal* 24, No. 25 (3 April 1924): 6.
b. *United Amateur* 23, No. 1 (May 1924): 7.
c. In *Sandalwood* (A.4).
d. *Helios* 1, No. 3 (August–September 1937): 10.
e. *Weird Tales* 40, No. 6 (September 1948): 79.
f. In *Selected Poems* (A.27).
g. In Peter Haining, ed. *Weird Tales*. Jersey, UK: Neville Spearman, 1976. 220.
h. In Peter Haining, ed. *More Weird Tales*. London: Sphere, 1978. 179.
i. In *The Last Oblivion* (A.61).
j. In *The Complete Poetry and Translations*, Volume 1 (A.73).
k. In *The Song of the Necromancer and Others* (A.81).

Sonnet.

892. "To the Crescent Moon."
a. In *The Complete Poetry and Translations*, Volume 1 (A.73).

8 lines.

893. "To the Daemon Sublimity."
a. In August Derleth, ed. *Fire and Sleet and Candlelight*. Sauk City, WI: Arkham House, 1961. 184.
b. In *Selected Poems* (A.27).
c. In *The Last Oblivion* (A.61).
d. In *The Complete Poetry and Translations*, Volume 1 (A.73).
e. In *The Dark Eidolon and Other Fantasies* (A.84).

Sonnet. Written 1912. First title: "To the Spirit of Sublimity."

894. "To the Darkness."
a. In *The Star-Treader and Other Poems* (A.1).
b. In *Odes and Sonnets* (A.2).
c. In *Nero and Other Poems* (A.8).

  d. In *Selected Poems* (A.27).
  e. In *The Last Oblivion* (A.61).
  f. In *The Complete Poetry and Translations*, Volume 1 (A.73).
  g. In *Moonlight and Other Poems* (A.78).
  h. In *Celui qui marchait parmi les étoiles* (II.A.iii.17).

  49 lines.

895. "To the Morning Star." [Thou art the star of hope that 'fore the dawn]
  a. In *The Complete Poetry and Translations*, Volume 1 (A.73).

  8 lines.

896. "To the Morning Star." [Triumphant rise, O star, on pinions fleet,]
  a. In *The Fugitive Poems of Clark Ashton Smith: Second Series* (A.38).
  b. In *The Complete Poetry and Translations*, Volume 1 (A.73).

  Sonnet.

897. "To the Nightshade."
  a. In *The Fugitive Poems of Clark Ashton Smith* (A.26).
  b. In Lin Carter, ed. *Weird Tales #3*. New York: Zebra, 1981. 83.
  c. In *The Complete Poetry and Translations*, Volume 1 (A.73).

  14 lines. Written c. 1910.

898. "To the Sun." [Thou most august and everlasting one]
  a. In *The Complete Poetry and Translations*, Volume 2 (A.73).

  2 lines. A fragment.

899. "To the Sun." [Thy light is as an eminence unto thee,]
  a. In *The Star-Treader and Other Poems* (A.1).
  b. In *Selected Poems* (A.27).
  c. In *The Complete Poetry and Translations*, Volume 1 (A.73).
  d. In *Moonlight and Other Poems* (A.78).

  39 lines.

900. "To Thomas Paine." [O priest of Truth and herald of the light,]
  a. In *The Complete Poetry and Translations*, Volume 1 (A.73).

  11 lines.

901. "To Thomas Paine." [O thou who dared the sacred truth proclaim]
  a. In *The Complete Poetry and Translations*, Volume 1 (A.73).

Sonnet.

902. "To Whom It May Concern."
    a. In *Selected Poems* (A.27).
    b. In *The Complete Poetry and Translations*, Volume 1 (A.73).

    13 lines.

903. "Tolometh."
    a. In *Spells and Philtres* (A.14).
    b. In *Selected Poems* (A.27).
    c. In *Poseidonis* (A.34).
    d. In *The Complete Poetry and Translations*, Volume 2 (A.73).
    e. In *Mondes premiers* (II.A.iii.15).
    f. In *Atlantide e i mondi perduti* (II.A.vi.13).

    36 lines. A revised version of "Ougabalys."

904. "Touch."
    a. In *Selected Poems* (A.27).
    b. In *The Complete Poetry and Translations*, Volume 2 (A.73).

    11 lines.

905. "Town Lights."
    a. *Wings* 5, No. 8 (Winter 1943): 15.
    b. In Stanton A. Coblentz, ed. *The Music Makers*. New York: Bernard Ackerman, 1945. 223–24.
    c. In *In Memoriam: Clark Ashton Smith* (III.D.4).
    d. In *Selected Poems* (A.27).
    e. In *The Complete Poetry and Translations*, Volume 2 (A.73).

    28 lines. Dated 15 November 1941.

906. "Transcendence."
    a. In *Ebony and Crystal* (A.3).
    b. In George Sterling, Genevieve Taggard, and James Rorty, ed. *Continent's End: An Anthology of Contemporary California Poets*. San Francisco: Book Club of California, 1925. 195.
    c. In Wallace Alvin Briggs, ed. *Great Poems of the English Language*. New York: Robert M. McBride, 1927; London: George C. Harrap & Co., 1928. 1338–39. Rev. ed. New York: Tudor Publishing Co., 1936. 1338–39.
    d. In *Selected Poems* (A.27).

e. In *The Last Oblivion* (A.61).
f. In *The Complete Poetry and Translations,* Volume 1 (A.73).
g. In *Moonlight and Other Poems* (A.78).
h. In *Celui qui marchait parmi les étoiles* (II.A.iii.17).

Sonnet. Written c. February 1919.

907. "Transmutation."
a. *Auburn Journal* 24, No. 16 (31 January 1924): 6.
b. In *The Complete Poetry and Translations,* Volume 1 (A.73).

4 lines.

908. "The Traveller."
a. In *The Complete Poetry and Translations,* Volume 1 (A.73).

10 lines. Dated 21 April 1919.

909. "Triple Aspect."
a. In *Ebony and Crystal* (A.3).
b. In *Selected Poems* (A.27).
c. In *The Last Oblivion* (A.61).
d. In *The Complete Poetry and Translations,* Volume 1 (A.73).
e. In *Moonlight and Other Poems* (A.78).
f. In *Celui qui marchait parmi les étoiles* (II.A.iii.17).

24 lines.

910. "Tristan to Iseult."
a. *Westward* 4, No. 4 (April 1935): 7.
b. In *Selected Poems* (A.27) (as a translation from "Christophe des Laurières").
c. In *The Complete Poetry and Translations,* Volume 2 (A.73).

35 lines. Dated 13–15 August 1927.

911. "Trope."
a. In *Selected Poems* (A.27).
b. In *The Complete Poetry and Translations,* Volume 2 (A.73).

12 lines. Dated 12 August 1927.

912. "Tryst at Lobos."
a. In *Selected Poems* (A.27).
b. In *The Complete Poetry and Translations,* Volume 2 (A.73).

Haiku.

913. "Tule-Mists."
   a. In *The Complete Poetry and Translations*, Volume 2 (A.73).
   Haiku.

914. "Twilight."
   a. In *The Complete Poetry and Translations*, Volume 1 (A.73).
   Sonnet.

915. "The Twilight of the Gods."
   a. *Short Stories* 211, No. 5 (May 1951): 65.
   b. In *The Dark Chateau* (A.13).
   c. In *Shadows Seen and Unseen* (A.71) (as "Los Sátiros son decor-
       nados" ["The Satyrs Are Dehorned"]).

       28 lines. First title: "Los Sátiros son mochos" ("The Satyrs Are
       Hornless").

916. "Twilight on the Snow."
   a. In *Ebony and Crystal* (A.3).
   b. In *Selected Poems* (A.27).
   c. In *The Last Oblivion* (A.61).
   d. In *The Complete Poetry and Translations*, Volume 1 (A.73).
   e. In *Moonlight and Other Poems* (A.78).

       12 lines.

917. "Twilight Pilgrimage."
   a. In *The Black Book of Clark Ashton Smith* (A.39).
   b. In *The Complete Poetry and Translations*, Volume 2 (A.73).

       3 lines. A fragment.

918. "Twilight Song."
   a. *Wings* 7, No. 1 (Spring 1945): 18.
   b. In *The Hill of Dionysus* (A.18).
   c. In *Selected Poems* (A.27).
   d. In *The Complete Poetry and Translations*, Volume 2 (A.73).

       16 lines. Dated 29 September 1942.

919. "The Twilight Woods."
   a. In *The Fugitive Poems of Clark Ashton Smith: Second Series* (A.38).

b. In *The Last Oblivion* (A.61).

c. In *The Complete Poetry and Translations*, Volume 1 (A.73).

Sonnet.

920. "Two Myths and a Fable."

a. In *The Dark Chateau* (A.13).

b. In *Shadows Seen and Unseen* (A.71).

c. In *The Complete Poetry and Translations*, Volume 2 (A.73).

12 lines. Dated 20 June 1950. For CAS's Spanish version, see "Dos mitos y una fábula" (item 212).

921. "Two on a Pillar."

a. In *The Complete Poetry and Translations*, Volume 2 (A.73).

12 lines.

922. "Unicorn."

a. In *Spells and Philtres* (A.14).

b. In *Selected Poems* (A.27).

c. In *The Complete Poetry and Translations*, Volume 2 (A.73).

Haiku.

923. "Union."

a. In *Ebony and Crystal* (A.3).

b. In *The Complete Poetry and Translations*, Volume 1 (A.73).

c. In *Moonlight and Other Poems* (A.78).

13 lines.

924. "The Unknown."

a. In *The Complete Poetry and Translations*, Volume 2 (A.73).

14 lines. For CAS's Spanish version, see "Lo Ignoto" (item 324).

925. "The Unremembered."

a. In *The Star-Treader and Other Poems* (A.1) (as "The Unrevealed").

b. In *Selected Poems* (A.27).

c. In *The Complete Poetry and Translations*, Volume 1 (A.73).

Sonnet.

926. "Untold Arabian Fable."

a. In *Spells and Philtres* (A.14).

b. In *Selected Poems* (A.27).

c. In *The Complete Poetry and Translations*, Volume 2 (A.73).

   Haiku.

927. "A Valediction."
a. *Auburn Journal* 23, No. 43 (9 August 1923): 6.
b. *Buccanneer* 1, No. 1 (September 1924): 12.
c. In *Sandalwood* (A.4).
d. In *Selected Poems* (A.27).
e. In *The Complete Poetry and Translations*, Volume 1 (A.73).

   8 lines. Dated 16 July 1923.

928. "The Vampire Night." [Sunset as of the world's concluding day:]
a. In *The Complete Poetry and Translations*, Volume 1 (A.73).

   41 lines.

929. "The Vampire Night." [The darkness falls like some great, silent doom,]
a. In *The Complete Poetry and Translations*, Volume 2 (A.73).

   25 lines. A fragment.

930. "Variations."
a. In *The Complete Poetry and Translations*, Volume 2 (A.73).

   10 lines. Dated 4 February 1929. First title: "Three Similes."

931. "Vaticinations."
a. In *Selected Poems* (A.27).
b. In *The Complete Poetry and Translations*, Volume 2 (A.73).

   8 lines. Dated 9 February 1929.

932. "El Vendaval." [English]
a. In *The Complete Poetry and Translations*, Volume 2 (A.73).

   28 lines. For CAS's Spanish version, see item 933.

933. "El Vendaval." [Spanish]
a. In *The Complete Poetry and Translations*, Volume 2 (A.73).

   28 lines. For CAS's English version, see item 932.

934. "Venus."
a. In *Selected Poems* (A.27).
b. In *The Complete Poetry and Translations*, Volume 2 (A.73).

8 lines. Dated 13 August 1927.

935. "Verity."
   a. In *The Complete Poetry and Translations*, Volume 2 (A.73).

   12 lines. Dated 14 September 1952.

936. "Une Vie spectrale."
   a. In *Selected Poems* (A.27).
   b. In *The Complete Poetry and Translations*, Volume 2 (A.73).

   36 lines. In French. Dated 29 May 1929. For CAS's English version, see "Spectral Life" (item 819).

937. "Les Violons."
   a. In *The Complete Poetry and Translations*, Volume 2 (A.73).

   10 lines. In French. Dated 4 January 1927.

938. "A Vision of Lucifer."
   a. In *Ebony and Crystal* (A.3).
   b. In *Selected Poems* (A.27).
   c. In *The Last Oblivion* (A.61).
   d. In *The Complete Poetry and Translations*, Volume 1 (A.73).

   Sonnet.

939. "The Voice in the Pines."
   a. In *In Memoriam: Clark Ashton Smith* (III.D.4).
   b. In *The Complete Poetry and Translations*, Volume 1 (A.73).

   12 lines. Written c. 1911.

940. "The Voice of Silence."
   a. In *The Fugitive Poems of Clark Ashton Smith* (A.26).
   b. In *The Complete Poetry and Translations*, Volume 1 (A.73).

   12 lines. Written c. 1910.

941. "Voices."
   a. In *The Complete Poetry and Translations*, Volume 2 (A.73).

   58 lines. The poem is signed "José Velasco (trans. by Clark Ashton Smith)." No Spanish-language poet of this name has been identified.

942. "Vultures Come to the Ambarvalia."
   a. In *Selected Poems* (A.27).

    b. In *The Complete Poetry and Translations*, Volume 2 (A.73).

    Haiku.

943. "The Waning Moon."
    a. In *The Fugitive Poems of Clark Ashton Smith: Second Series* (A.38).
    b. In *The Complete Poetry and Translations*, Volume 1 (A.73).

    Sonnet.

944. "War."
    a. In *The Complete Poetry and Translations*, Volume 1 (A.73).

    Sonnet.

945. "Warning."
    a. *Weird Tales* 12, No. 4 (October 1928): 525.
    b. In August Derleth, ed. *Dark of the Moon: Poems of Fantasy and the Macabre*. Sauk City, WI: Arkham House, 1947; Freeport, NY: Books for Libraries Press, 1969; Miami, FL: Granger, 1976. 320–21.
    c. In *Selected Poems* (A.27).
    d. In *The Last Oblivion* (A.61).
    e. In *The Complete Poetry and Translations*, Volume 2 (A.73).
    f. In *The Song of the Necromancer and Others* (A.81).

    21 lines. Written 3 March 1928.

946. "Water-Fight."
    a. In *Selected Poems* (A.27).
    b. In *The Complete Poetry and Translations*, Volume 2 (A.73).

    Haiku.

947. "Water-Hemlock."
    a. In *Selected Poems* (A.27).
    b. In *The Complete Poetry and Translations*, Volume 2 (A.73).

    Haiku.

948. "We Shall Meet."
    a. *Auburn Journal* 23, No. 28 (26 April 1923): 6.
    b. *Wanderer* 2, No. 5 (May 1924): 60–61.
    c. In *Sandalwood* (A.4).
    d. In *Selected Poems* (A.27).
    e. In *The Complete Poetry and Translations*, Volume 1 (A.73).
    f. In *The Dark Eidolon and Other Fantasies* (A.84).

36 lines. Dated 10 March 1923. First title: "At the Last."

949. "Weavings."
    a. In *The Fugitive Poems of Clark Ashton Smith* (A.26).
    b. In *The Complete Poetry and Translations*, Volume 1 (A.73).

    12 lines. Written c. 1910.

950. "The West Wind."
    a. *Overland Monthly* 56, No. 6 (December 1910): 575 (as by "C. Ashton Smith").
    b. In *The Complete Poetry and Translations*, Volume 1 (A.73).

    20 lines. First title: "To the West Wind."

951. "What Dreamest Thou, Muse?"
    a. *Asmodeus* No. 2 (Fall 1951): 32.
    b. In *Shadows Seen and Unseen* (A.71).
    c. In *The Complete Poetry and Translations*, Volume 2 (A.73).

    20 lines. For CAS's Spanish version, see "¿Que sueñas, Musa?" (item 676). For CAS's French version, see "Que songes-tu, Muse?" (item 675).

952. "Where Sleepest Thou, O Eldorado?"
    a. In *The Complete Poetry and Translations*, Volume 2 (A.73).

    12 lines. For CAS's Spanish version, see "¿Donde duermes, Eldorado?" (item 210).

953. "The Whisper of the Worm."
    a. In *Selected Poems* (A.27) (as a translation from "Christophe des Laurières").
    b. In *The Last Oblivion* (A.61).
    c. In *The Complete Poetry and Translations*, Volume 1 (A.73).

    Sonnet. Written 9 September 1918.

954. "White Death."
    a. In *The Star-Treader and Other Poems* (A.1).
    b. *Tesseract* 2, No. 4 (April 1937): 6.
    c. *Tesseract Annual* 1, No. 1 (1939): 12.
    d. In *Selected Poems* (A.27).
    e. *Fantasy Commentator* 7, No. 1 (Fall 1990): 11.

f. In Edward Foster, ed. *Decadents, Symbolists, and Aesthetes in America: Fin-de-Siècle American Poetry: An Anthology.* Jersey City, NJ: Talisman House, 2000. 139–40.
g. In *The Last Oblivion* (A.61).
h. In *The Complete Poetry and Translations*, Volume 1 (A.73).
i. In *Moonlight and Other Poems* (A.78).

Sonnet.

955. "A White Rose."
a. In *The Complete Poetry and Translations*, Volume 1 (A.73).

4 lines.

956. "Willow-Cutting in Autumn."
a. In *Spells and Philtres* (A.14).
b. In *Selected Poems* (A.27).
c. In *The Complete Poetry and Translations*, Volume 2 (A.73).

Haiku.

957. "The Wind and the Moon."
a. In *The Star-Treader and Other Poems* (A.1).
b. In *The Complete Poetry and Translations*, Volume 1 (A.73).
c. In *Moonlight and Other Poems* (A.78).

26 lines.

958. "Wind-Ripples."
a. In *The Complete Poetry and Translations*, Volume 1 (A.73).

4 lines. Written c. October 1911.

959. "The Wind-Threnody."
a. In *The Fugitive Poems of Clark Ashton Smith: Second Series* (A.38).
b. In *The Complete Poetry and Translations*, Volume 1 (A.73).

12 lines.

960. "The Windows at Lamplighting Time."
a. In *Selected Poems* (A.27).
b. In *The Complete Poetry and Translations*, Volume 2 (A.73).

Haiku.

961. "The Winds."
a. In *The Star-Treader and Other Poems* (A.1).

   b. In *Nero and Other Poems* (A.8).
   c. In *Selected Poems* (A.27).
   d. In *The Complete Poetry and Translations*, Volume 1 (A.73).
   e. In *Moonlight and Other Poems* (A.78).

   24 lines.

962. "Wine of Summer."
   a. *Wings* 5, No. 6 (Summer 1942): 9.
   b. In *Selected Poems* (A.27).
   c. In *The Complete Poetry and Translations*, Volume 2 (A.73).

   24 lines.

963. "The Wingless Archangels."
   a. *Auburn Journal* 23, No. 37 (28 June 1923): 6.
   b. In *Sandalwood* (A.4).
   c. In *Selected Poems* (A.27).
   d. In *The Last Oblivion* (A.61).
   e. In *The Complete Poetry and Translations*, Volume 1 (A.73).

   Sonnet.

964. "Wings of Perfume."
   a. In *The Fugitive Poems of Clark Ashton Smith: Second Series* (A.38).
   b. In *The Complete Poetry and Translations*, Volume 1 (A.73).

   22 lines.

965. "Winter Moonlight." [After our fond, reiterate farewells]
   a. In *Selected Poems* (A.27).
   b. In *The Fugitive Poems of ClarkAshton Smith: Second Series* (A.38) (as "Winter Midnight").
   c. In *The Complete Poetry and Translations*, Volume 2 (A.73).

   19 lines. Dated 23 January 1929. Variant title: "Winter Midnight."

966. "Winter Moonlight." [The silence of the silver night]
   a. In *Ebony and Crystal* (A.3).
   b. In *Selected Poems* (A.27).
   c. In *The Complete Poetry and Translations*, Volume 1 (A.73).
   d. In *Moonlight and Other Poems* (A.78).

   12 lines. Written before 24 April 1918.

967. "Witch-Dance."
  a. *Weird Tales* 36, No. 1 (September 1941): 104–5.
  b. In *The Hill of Dionysus* (A.18).
  c. In *Selected Poems* (A.27).
  d. In *The Last Oblivion* (A.61).
  e. In *The Complete Poetry and Translations*, Volume 2 (A.73).
  f. In *The Song of the Necromancer and Others* (A.81).

  32 lines. Written before 29 April 1939.

968. "The Witch in the Graveyard."
  a. In *Ebony and Crystal* (A.3).
  b. In *Selected Poems* (A.27).
  c. In *The Last Oblivion* (A.61).
  d. In *The Complete Poetry and Translations*, Volume 1 (A.73).
  e. In *Moonlight and Other Poems* (A.78).

  67 lines. Dated 26–27 June 1913. Alternate title: "The Witch in the Churchyard."

969. "The Witch with Eyes of Amber."
  a. *Auburn Journal* 23, No. 32 (24 May 1923): 6.
  b. *Agenbite of Inwit* 2, No. 5 (November 1945): [16].
  c. *Epos* 1, No. 4 (Summer 1950): 14.
  d. In *The Dark Chateau* (A.13).
  e. In *Selected Poems* (A.27).
  f. In *The Last Oblivion* (A.61).
  g. In *The Complete Poetry and Translations*, Volume 1 (A.73).
  h. In *The Dark Eidolon and Other Fantasies* (A.84).
  i. In *The Averoigne Chronicles* (A.85).

  16 lines. Dated 11 March 1923. Alternate titles: "The Witch" and "The Witch with the Heart of Amber."

970. "Wizard's Love."
  a. *Denventioneer Alchemist* (July 1941): 5.
  b. *Golden Atom* No. 11 (1954–55): 91.
  c. In *The Hill of Dionysus* (A.18).
  d. In *Selected Poems* (A.27).
  e. In *The Complete Poetry and Translations*, Volume 2 (A.73).

  41 lines. Written before 20 December 1938. *Denventioner Alchemist* (a special issue of *Alchemist*) was part of a "combozine," i.e., a publication that bound several fanzines together.

971. "The World." [Life is but a fleeting shadow,]
   a. In *The Sword of Zagan and Other Writings* (A.64).
   b. In *The Complete Poetry and Translations*, Volume 1 (A.73).

   42 lines. Juvenilia.

972. "The World." [The world is world of ups and downs,]
   a. In *The Complete Poetry and Translations*, Volume 1 (A.73).

   22 lines. Juvenilia.

973. "Ye Shall Return."
   a. In *The Dark Chateau* (A.13).
   b. In *The Black Book of Clark Ashton Smith* (A.39).
   c. In *The Complete Poetry and Translations*, Volume 2 (A.73).

   20 lines. Dated 30 September 1951.

974. "The Years Restored."
   a. In *The Fugitive Poems of Clark Ashton Smith: Second Series* (A.38).
   b. In *The Complete Poetry and Translations*, Volume 1 (A.73).

   Sonnet. Written c. June 1913.

975. "Yerba Buena."
   a. *Wings* 7, No. 4 (Winter 1946): 14.
   b. In *The Hill of Dionysus* (A.18).
   c. In *Selected Poems* (A.27).
   d. In *The Complete Poetry and Translations*, Volume 2 (A.73).

   24 lines. Dated 11 September 1941.

976. "You Are Not Beautiful."
   a. *Auburn Journal* 24, No. 10 (20 December 1923): 6.
   b. In *Sandalwood* (A.4).
   c. In *Selected Poems* (A.27).
   d. In *The Complete Poetry and Translations*, Volume 1 (A.73).

   4 lines.

977. "Youth and Age."
   a. In *The Complete Poetry and Translations*, Volume 1 (A.73).

   48 lines. Juvenilia.

978. "Zothique."
   a. In *The Dark Chateau* (A.13).

b. In *Zothique* (A.22).
c. *Zothique* No. 1 (1985): 3 (with French translation).
d. In *Tales of Zothique* (A.56).
e. In *The Last Oblivion* (A.61).
f. In *Shadows Seen and Unseen* (A.71).
g. In *The Complete Poetry and Translations*, Volume 2 (A.73).
h. In *Mondes derniers* (II.A.iii.14).
i. In *Celui qui marchait parmi les étoiles* (II.A.iii.17).
j. In *Atlantide e i mondi perduti* (II.A.vi.13).

24 lines.

979. "Zuleika: An Oriental Song."
a. In *The Sword of Zagan and Other Writings* (A.64).
b. In *The Complete Poetry and Translations*, Volume 1 (A.73).

24 lines. Juvenilia.

980. [Untitled poem.]
a. *Auburn Journal* 2, No. 62 (27 March 1915): 1.
b. In *The Complete Poetry and Translations*, Volume 1 (A.73).

3 lines. CAS's first poem, written when "he was a very little lad" (i.e., c. 1900?).

981. [Untitled poems and fragments.]
a. In *Selected Poems* (A.27) [fragment 32; as epigraph to "The Jasmine Girdle").
b. In *The Book of Hyperborea* (A.58) [fragment 120; as "Lament for Vixeela"].
c. In *The Complete Poetry and Translations*, Volume 2 (A.73).

98 poems (4, 4, 2, 6, 4, 8, 8, 4, 5, 5, 11, 7 [in French], 4, 15 [in French], 10, 4, 10, 10, 7, sonnet, 5, 4, 19, 12, 3, sonnet, 13, 27, 4, 7, 4, 5, 4, 6, 28, 4, 2, 4, 8 [in French], 4, 10, 5, 3, 4, 3, sonnet, 17, 3, 5, 4, 2, 2, 2, 3, 2, 2, 2, 1, 2, 1, 4, 2, 2 [in Spanish], 2, 3, 1, 2, 1, 4, 4, 2, 1, 1, 4, 5, 2, 1, 3, 3, 4, 2, 6, 3, 2, 4, 4, 1, 5, 2, 5, 1, 2, 2, 8, 5, 6, 11, 4 lines).

iii. Translations of Poems

a. **From French**

Charles Baudelaire

1. "A une Madone." [LVIII]
    a. In *The Complete Poetry and Translations*, Volume 3 (A.73).
        In prose.

2. "A une Mendiante rousse." [CXII]
    a. In *The Complete Poetry and Translations*, Volume 3 (A.73).
        In prose.

3. "Abel et Caïn." [CXLIV]
    a. In *The Complete Poetry and Translations*, Volume 3 (A.73).
        16 lines.

4. "The Adviser." [XCI]
    a. In *The Complete Poetry and Translations*, Volume 3 (A.73).
        Translation of "L'Avertisseur." In prose.

5. "The Albatross." [II]
    a. In *The Complete Poetry and Translations*, Volume 3 (A.73).
        Translation of "L'Albatros." In prose.

6. "Alchemy of Sorrow." [LXXXIII]
    a. *Auburn Journal* 25, No. 49 (17 September 1925): 4 (as "Al-chimie de la Douleur").
    b. In *Sandalwood* (A.4) (as "Alchimie de la Douleur").
    c. *Step Ladder* 13, No. 5 (May 1927): 138 (as "Alchimie de la Douleur").
    d. *Bacon's Essays* 2, No. 2 (Summer 1929): 7 (as "Alchimie de la Dou-leur").
    e. In *Selected Poems* (A.27).
    f. In *The Complete Poetry and Translations*, Volume 3 (A.73).
    g. In *L'Art étrange de Clark Ashton Smith* (III.D.7) (as "Al-chimidue de la douleur").
        Translation of "Alchimie de la douleur." Sonnet.

7.   "Allégorie." [CXXXIX]
     a.   In *The Complete Poetry and Translations*, Volume 3 (A.73).
          In prose.

8.   "L'Ame du vin." [CXXVIII]
     a.   In *The Complete Poetry and Translations*, Volume 3 (A.73).
          In prose.

9.   "Anterior Life." [XII]
     a.   *Arkham Sampler* 1, No. 4 (Autumn 1948): 81.
     b.   In *Spells and Philtres* (A.14).
     c.   In *Selected Poems* (A.27).
     d.   In *The Complete Poetry and Translations*, Volume 3 (A.73).
     e.   In *The Dark Eidolon and Other Fantasies* (A.84).

          Translation of "La Vie antérieure." Sonnet.

10. "The Balcony." [XXXVII]
     a.   *Auburn Journal* 25, No. 50 (24 September 1925): 4 (as "Le
          Balcon").
     b.   *Bacon's Essays* 2, No. 1 (Spring 1929): [1] (as "Le Balcon").
     c.   In *The Complete Poetry and Translations*, Volume 3 (A.73).

          Translation of "Le Balcon." 30 lines.

11. "The Barrel of Hate." [LXXV]
     a.   In *The Complete Poetry and Translations*, Volume 3 (A.73).

          Translation of "Le Tonneau de la haine." In prose.

12. "The Beacons." [VI]
     a.   In *The Complete Poetry and Translations*, Volume 3 (A.73).

          Translation of "Les Phares." In prose.

13. "Beatrice." [CXL]
     a.   In *Selected Poems* (A.27).
     b.   In *The Complete Poetry and Translations*, Volume 3 (A.73).
     c.   In *L'Art étrange de Clark Ashton Smith* (III.D.7) (as "La Béatrice").

          Translation of "La Béatrice." 30 lines.

14. "Le Beau Navire." [LIII]
     a.   In *The Complete Poetry and Translations*, Volume 3 (A.73).
          In prose.

15. "Beauty." [XVIII]
     a. *Auburn Journal* 25, No. 22 (12 March 1925): 4.
     b. In *The Complete Poetry and Translations*, Volume 3 (A.73).
         Translation of "La Beauté." Sonnet.

16. "Bénédiction." [I]
     a. In *The Complete Poetry and Translations*, Volume 3 (A.73).
         Translation of "Bénédiction." In prose.

17. "Les Bijoux." [Jetsam I]
     a. In *The Complete Poetry and Translations*, Volume 3 (A.73).
         In prose.

18. "The Blind." [CXVI]
     a. In *The Complete Poetry and Translations*, Volume 3 (A.73).
         Translation of "Les Aveugles." In prose.

19. "Le Calumet de paix." [LXXXV]
     a. In *The Complete Poetry and Translations*, Volume 3 (A.73).
         In prose; apparently incomplete. Baudelaire's poem is an imitation
         of a section of Longfellow's *Hiawatha*.

20. "The Cat." [XXV]
     a. In *The Complete Poetry and Translations*, Volume 3 (A.73).
         Translation of "Le Chat." In prose.

21. "The Cats." [LXVIII]
     a. In *The Complete Poetry and Translations*, Volume 3 (A.73).
         Translation of "Les Chats." In prose.

22. "Causerie." [LVI]
     a. *Auburn Journal* 25, No. 30 (7 May 1925): 4.
     b. In *The Complete Poetry and Translations*, Volume 3 (A.73).
         Sonnet.

23. "Chanson d'après-midi." [LIX]
     a. In *The Complete Poetry and Translations*, Volume 3 (A.73).
         In prose.

24. "Une Charogne." [XXX]
     a. In *The Complete Poetry and Translations*, Volume 3 (A.73).
         In prose.

25. "Chastisement of Pride." [XVII]
     a. In *The Complete Poetry and Translations*, Volume 3 (A.73).
         Translation of "Châtiment de l'orgueil." In prose.

26. "Le Chat." [LII]
     a. In *The Complete Poetry and Translations*, Volume 3 (A.73).
         In prose.

27. "The Chevelure." [XXIV]
     a. In *The Complete Poetry and Translations*, Volume 3 (A.73).
         Translation of "La Chevelure." In prose.

28. "La Cloche fêlée." [LXXVI]
     a. In *The Complete Poetry and Translations*, Volume 3 (A.73).
         In prose.

29. "The Clock." [CVII]
     a. In *The Complete Poetry and Translations*, Volume 3 (A.73).
         Translation of "L'Horloge." In prose.

30. "Confession." [XLVI]
     a. In *The Complete Poetry and Translations*, Volume 3 (A.73).
         In prose.

31. "Contemplation." [CIV]
     a. In *The Complete Poetry and Translations*, Volume 3 (A.73).
         Translation of "Recuillement." In prose.

32. "Correspondences." [IV]
     a. In *The Complete Poetry and Translations*, Volume 3 (A.73).
         Translation of "Correspondances." In prose.

33. "Le Coucher du soleil romantique." [C]
     a. *United Amateur* 25, No. 2 (May 1926): 6.
     b. In *The Complete Poetry and Translations*, Volume 3 (A.73).
         Sonnet.

34. "The Cover." [LXXXVII]
 a. In *The Complete Poetry and Translations,* Volume 3 (A.73).
 Translation of "Le Couvercle." In prose.

35. "Le Crépuscule du matin." [CXXVII]
 a. In *The Complete Poetry and Translations,* Volume 3 (A.73).
 In prose.

36. "Le Cygne." [CXIII]
 a. In *The Complete Poetry and Translations,* Volume 3 (A.73).
 In prose.

37. "The Dance of Death." [CXXI]
 a. In *The Complete Poetry and Translations,* Volume 3 (A.73).
 Translation of "Danse macabre." In prose.

38. "*De profundis clamavi.*" [XXXI]
 a. In *The Complete Poetry and Translations,* Volume 3 (A.73).
 In prose.

39. "The Death of Lovers." [CXLVI]
 a. *Auburn Journal* 25, No. 42 (30 July 1925): 4 (as "La Mort des Amants").
 b. *United Amateur* 25, No. 3 (July 1926): 6 (as "La Mort des Amants").
 c. *Arkham Sampler* 2, No. 4 (Autumn 1949): 80.
 d. In *Selected Poems* (A.27).
 e. In *The Complete Poetry and Translations,* Volume 3 (A.73).
 Translation of "La Mort des amants." Sonnet.

40. "The Denial of St. Peter." [CXLIII]
 a. In *The Complete Poetry and Translations,* Volume 3 (A.73).
 Translation of "Le Reniement de Saint Pierre." In prose.

41. "Destruction." [CXXXIV]
 a. In *The Complete Poetry and Translations,* Volume 3 (A.73).
 Translation of "La Destruction." In prose.

42. "Don Juan aux enfers." [XV]
 a. In *The Complete Poetry and Translations,* Volume 3 (A.73).
 20 lines.

43. "Doubtful Skies." [LI]
   a. *Auburn Journal* 25, No. 34 (4 June 1925): 9 (as "Ciel Brouillé").
   b. In *Sandalwood* (A.4) (as "Ciel Brouillé").
   c. In *Selected Poems* (A.27).
   d. In *The Complete Poetry and Translations*, Volume 3 (A.73).

   Translation of "Ciel brouillé." 16 lines.

44. "The Duel." [XXXVI]
   a. In *The Complete Poetry and Translations*, Volume 3 (A.73).

   Translation of *"Duellum."* In prose.

45. "Elevation." [III]
   a. In *The Complete Poetry and Translations*, Volume 3 (A.73).

   Translation of "Élévation." In prose.

46. "L'Ennemi." [X]
   a. In *The Complete Poetry and Translations*, Volume 3 (A.73).

   In prose.

47. "Epigraph for a Condemned Book." [CXXXIII]
   a. *Weird Tales* 11, No. 3 (March 1928): 385 (as "Epigraphe pour un Livre Condamné").
   b. In *The Complete Poetry and Translations*, Volume 3 (A.73).

   Translation of "Epigraphe pour un livre condamné." Sonnet.

48. "Evening Harmony." [XLVIII]
   a. *Auburn Journal* 25, No. 47 (3 September 1925): 6 (as "Harmonie du Soir").
   b. In *Sandalwood* (A.4) (as "Harmonie du Soir").
   c. In *Selected Poems* (A.27).
   d. In *The Complete Poetry and Translations*, Volume 3 (A.73).

   Translation of "L'Harmonie du soir." 16 lines.

49. "Evening Twilight." [CXIX]
   a. In *The Complete Poetry and Translations*, Volume 3 (A.73).

   Translation of "Le Crépuscule du soir." In prose.

50. "The Evil Monk." [IX]
   a. *Auburn Journal* 26, No. 9 (10 December 1925): 13 (as "Le Mauvais Moine").

b. In *The Complete Poetry and Translations,* Volume 3 (A.73).

Translation of "Le Mauvais Moine." Sonnet.

51. "Examination at Midnight." [LXXXIX]
   a. *Auburn Journal* 25, No. 40 (16 July 1925): 2 (as "L'Examen de Minuit").
   b. In *Sandalwood* (A.4) (as "L'Examen de Minuit").
   c. In Charles Baudelaire. *Flowers of Evil.* Ed. James Laver. London: Limited Editions Club/Fanfare Press, 1940. 147–48 (as "Self-Questioning at Midnight").
   d. In *Selected Poems* (A.27).
   e. In *The Complete Poetry and Translations,* Volume 3 (A.73).

   Translation of "L'Examen de minuit." 38 lines.

52. "Exotic Perfume." [XXIII]
   a. *Measure* No. 50 (April 1925): 9 (as "Parfum Exotique").
   b. In *Sandalwood* (A.4) (as "Parfum Exotique").
   c. In *The Complete Poetry and Translations,* Volume 3 (A.73).

   Translation of "Parfum exotique." Sonnet.

53. "The Eyes of Bertha." [XCVI]
   a. In *The Complete Poetry and Translations,* Volume 3 (A.73).

   "Les Yeux de Berthe." In prose.

54. "Un Fantôme." [XXXIX]
   a. In *The Complete Poetry and Translations,* Volume 3 (A.73).

   In prose.

55. "Femmes damnées." [CXXXVI]
   a. In *The Complete Poetry and Translations,* Volume 3 (A.73).

   In prose.

56. "Femmes damnées: Delphine et Hippolyte." [Jetsam V]
   a. In *The Complete Poetry and Translations,* Volume 3 (A.73).

   In prose.

57. "Le Fin de la journée." [CXLIX]
   a. In *The Complete Poetry and Translations,* Volume 3 (A.73).

   In prose.

58. "Le Flacon." [XLIX]
    a. In *The Complete Poetry and Translations*, Volume 3 (A.73).
    In prose. Apparently incomplete.

59. "Le Flambeau vivant." [XLIV]
    a. In *The Complete Poetry and Translations*, Volume 3 (A.73).
    In prose.

60. "The Fountain." [XCVII]
    a. In *The Complete Poetry and Translations*, Volume 3 (A.73).
    Translation of "Le Jet d'eau." In prose.

61. "The Fountain of Blood." [CXXXVIII]
    a. In *Sandalwood* (A.4) (as "La Fontaine de Sang").
    b. In *Selected Poems* (A.27).
    c. In *The Complete Poetry and Translations*, Volume 3 (A.73).
    Translation of "La Fontaine de sang." Sonnet.

62. "The Game." [CXX]
    a. In *The Complete Poetry and Translations*, Volume 3 (A.73).
    Translation of "Le Jeu." In prose.

63. "The Giantess." [X]
    a. In *Sandalwood* (A.4) (as "La Géante").
    b. *Arkham Sampler* 2, No. 3 (Summer 1949): 82.
    c. In *Selected Poems* (A.27).
    d. In *The Complete Poetry and Translations*, Volume 3 (A.73).
    Translation of "La Géante." Sonnet.

64. "Une Gravure fantastique." [LXXIII]
    a. In *The Complete Poetry and Translations*, Volume 3 (A.73).
    In prose.

65. "Le Guignon." [XI]
    a. In *The Complete Poetry and Translations*, Volume 3 (A.73).
    In prose.

66. "The Gulf." [CII]
    a. In *The Complete Poetry and Translations*, Volume 3 (A.73).
    Translation of "Le Gouffre." In prose.

67. *"L'Héautontimorouménos."* [CV]
    a. In *The Complete Poetry and Translations,* Volume 3 (A.73).

    In prose.

68. "L'Homme et la mer." [XIV]
    a. In *The Complete Poetry and Translations,* Volume 3 (A.73).

    In prose.

69. "Hymn." [XCIV]
    a. In *Selected Poems* (A.27) (untitled; partial verse translation).
    b. In *The Complete Poetry and Translations,* Volume 3 (A.73) (prose translation).
    c. In *The Complete Poetry and Translations,* Volume 2 (A.73) (partial verse translation; as "[Sandalwood]").

    Translation of "Hymne." In prose. In a., the translation (4 lines) is presented as a two-stanza verse epigraph to the "Sandalwood" section of *Selected Poems.* Inadvertently included in first edition of Volume 2, as not recognized of a translation of Baudelaire.

70. "Hymn to Beauty." [XXII]
    a. *Auburn Journal* 25, No. 48 (10 September 1925): 8 (as "Hymne à la Beauté").
    b. In *Sandalwood* (A.4) (as "Hymne à la Beauté").
    c. *Weird Tales* 29, No. 6 (June 1937): 719.
    d. In *Selected Poems* (A.27).
    e. In *The Complete Poetry and Translations,* Volume 3 (A.73).
    f. In *The Dark Eidolon and Other Fantasies* (A.84).

    Translation of "Hymne à la beauté." 28 lines.

71. "The Ideal." [XIX]
    a. *Auburn Journal* 25, No. 39 (9 July 1925): 10 (as "L'Idéal").
    b. In *Sandalwood* (A.4) (as "L'Idéal").
    c. In *Selected Poems* (A.27).
    d. In *The Complete Poetry and Translations,* Volume 3 (A.73).

    Translation of "L'Idéal." Sonnet.

72. "L'Imprévu." [LXXXVIII]
    a. In *The Complete Poetry and Translations,* Volume 3 (A.73).

    In prose.

73. "L'Invitation au voyage." [LIV]
   a. In *The Complete Poetry and Translations*, Volume 3 (A.73).

   In prose.

74. "The Irremediable." [CVI]
   a. *Auburn Journal* 25, No. 41 (23 July 1925): 3 (as "L'Irrémédiable").
   b. In *Sandalwood* (A.4) (as "L'Irrémédiable").
   c. In Charles Baudelaire. *Flowers of Evil*. Ed. James Laver. London: Limited Editions Club/Fanfare Press, 1940. 172–74.
   d. In *Selected Poems* (A.27).
   e. In *The Complete Poetry and Translations*, Volume 3 (A.73).

   Translation of "L'Irrémédiable." 40 lines.

75. "The Irreparable." [LV]
   a. *Weird Tales* 12, No. 2 (August 1928): 261 (prose; as "L'Irreparable"; as one of "Three Poems in Prose").
   b. In *Grotesques and Fantastiques* (A.32.a) (verse; as "L'Irreparable").
   c. In *The Complete Poetry and Translations*, Volume 3 (A.73) (both verse and prose versions).

   Translation of "L'Irréparable." Verse version is 50 lines.

76. "The Lament of Icarus." [CIII]
   a. In *The Complete Poetry and Translations*, Volume 3 (A.73).

   Translation of "Les Plaintes d'un Icare." In prose.

77. "Lesbos." [Jetsam IV]
   a. In *The Complete Poetry and Translations*, Volume 3 (A.73).

   In prose.

78. "Lethe." [Jetsam II]
   a. *Arkham Sampler* 2, No. 3 (Summer 1949): 83.
   b. In *Spells and Philtres* (A.14).
   c. In *Selected Poems* (A.27).
   d. In *The Complete Poetry and Translations*, Volume 3 (A.73).

   Translation of "La Léthé." 24 lines.

79. "Litany to Satan." [CXLV]
   a. In *The Complete Poetry and Translations*, Volume 3 (A.73).

Translation of "Les Litanies de Satan." In prose.

80. "Lola de Valence." [CX]
   a. In *The Complete Poetry and Translations*, Volume 3 (A.73).
   In prose.

81. "Love and the Cranium." [CXLII]
   a. In *The Complete Poetry and Translations*, Volume 3 (A.73).
   Translation of "L'Amour et la crâne." In prose.

82. "The Love of Falsehood." [CXXII]
   a. In *The Complete Poetry and Translations*, Volume 3 (A.73).
   Translation of "L'Amour du mensonge." In prose.

83. "La Lune Offensée." [CXI]
   a. In *The Complete Poetry and Translations*, Volume 3 (A.73).
   In prose.

84. "Madrigal of Sorrow." [XC]
   a. In *The Complete Poetry and Translations*, Volume 3 (A.73).
   Translation of "Madrigal triste." In prose.

85. "Une Martyre." [CXXXV]
   a. In *The Complete Poetry and Translations*, Volume 3 (A.73).
   In prose.

86. "Le Masque." [XXI]
   a. In *The Complete Poetry and Translations*, Volume 3 (A.73).
   In prose.

87. "The Metamorphoses of the Vampire." [Jetsam VI]
   a. In *Spells and Philtres* (A.14).
   b. In *Selected Poems* (A.27).
   c. In *The Complete Poetry and Translations*, Volume 3 (A.73).
   d. In *L'Art étrange de Clark Ashton Smith* (III.D.7) (as "Les Métamorphoses du vampire").
   Translation of "Les Métamorphoses du vampire." In prose.

88. "Mists and Rains." [CXXV]
   a. *Auburn Journal* 26, No. 6 (19 November 1925): 5 (as "Brumes et Pluies").
   b. *Recluse* No. 1 (1927): 60.
   c. In *Selected Poems* (A.27).
   d. In *The Complete Poetry and Translations*, Volume 3 (A.73).
   e. In *L'Art étrange de Clark Ashton Smith* (III.D.7) (as "Brumes et pluies").

   Translation of "Brumes et pluies." Sonnet.

89. "Moesta et Errabunda." [LXIV]
   a. *Auburn Journal* 25, No. 44 (13 August 1925): 4.
   b. In *Sandalwood* (A.4).
   c. *Step Ladder* 13, No. 5 (May 1927): 140.
   d. In *Selected Poems* (A.27).
   e. In *The Complete Poetry and Translations*, Volume 3 (A.73).
   30 lines.

90. "La Mort des artistes." [CXLVIII]
   a. *Auburn Journal* 25, No. 43 (6 August 1925): 6 (as "Le Vin des Amants").
   b. In *The Complete Poetry and Translations*, Volume 3 (A.73).

   Sonnet.

91. "La Mort des pauvres." [CXLVII]
   a. In *The Complete Poetry and Translations*, Volume 3 (A.73).

   In prose.

92. "Le Mort joyeux." [LXXIV]
   a. In *The Complete Poetry and Translations*, Volume 3 (A.73).

   In prose.

93. "Music." [LXXI]
   a. *Auburn Journal* 25, No. 38 (2 July 1925): 3 (as "La Musique").
   b. In *Sandalwood* (A.4) (as "La Musique").
   c. In *The Complete Poetry and Translations*, Volume 3 (A.73).

   Translation of "La Musique." Sonnet.

94. "Obsession." [LXXXI]
   a. In *Sandalwood* (A.4).

    b. *Step Ladder* 13, No. 5 (May 1927): 139.
    c. In *Selected Poems* (A.27).
    d. In *The Complete Poetry and Translations,* Volume 3 (A.73).

    Sonnet.

95. "On 'Tasso in Prison' by Eugène Delacroix." [CI]
    a. In *The Complete Poetry and Translations,* Volume 3 (A.73).

    Translation of "Sur *Le Tasse en Prison* d'Eugène Delacroix." In prose.

96. "The Owls." [LXIX]
    a. *Auburn Journal* 25, No. 51 (1 October 1925): 4 (as "Les Hiboux").
    b. *Step Ladder* 13, No. 5 (May 1927): 138 (as "Les Hiboux").
    c. *Weird Tales* 36, No. 2 (November 1941): 120 (as translated by "Timeus Gaylord").
    d. In August Derleth, ed. *Dark of the Moon: Poems of Fantasy and the Macabre.* Sauk City, WI: Arkham House, 1947; Freeport, NY: Books for Libraries Press, 1969; Miami, FL: Granger, 1976. 346–47 (as by "Timeus Gaylord").
    e. In *Selected Poems* (A.27).
    f. In *The Complete Poetry and Translations,* Volume 3 (A.73).

    Translation of "Les Hiboux." Sonnet.

97. "A Pagan's Prayer." [LXXXVI]
    a. In *The Complete Poetry and Translations,* Volume 3 (A.73).

    Translation of "Le Prière d'un païen." In prose.

98. "Parisian Dream." [CXXVI]
    a. In *Sandalwood* (A.4) (as "Rêve Parisien").
    b. In *Selected Poems* (A.27) (as "A Parisian Dream").
    c. In *The Complete Poetry and Translations,* Volume 3 (A.73).

    Translation of "Rêve parisien." 60 lines.

99. "Paysage." [CVIII]
    a. In *The Complete Poetry and Translations,* Volume 3 (A.73).

    In prose.

100. "Les Petites Vieilles." [CXV]
    a. In *The Complete Poetry and Translations,* Volume 3 (A.73).

    In prose. Apparently incomplete.

101. "The Phantom." [LXV]
     a. *Weird Tales* 13, No. 5 (May 1929): 720 (as "Le Revenant").
     b. In *Selected Poems* (A.27).
     c. In *The Complete Poetry and Translations*, Volume 3 (A.73).

     Translation of "Le Revenant." Sonnet.

102. "Le Pipe." [LXX]
     a. In *The Complete Poetry and Translations*, Volume 3 (A.73).

     In prose.

103. "The Poison." [L]
     a. In *Selected Poems* (A.27).
     b. In *The Complete Poetry and Translations*, Volume 3 (A.73).

     Translation of "Le Poison." In prose.

104. "The Possessed." [XXXVIII]
     a. In *The Complete Poetry and Translations*, Volume 3 (A.73).

     Translation of "Le Possédé." In prose.

105. "Preface."
     a. In *The Complete Poetry and Translations*, Volume 3 (A.73).

     Translation of "[Préface]: Au lecteur." In prose.

106. "Le Rançon." [XCVIII]
     a. In *The Complete Poetry and Translations*, Volume 3 (A.73).

     In prose.

107. "The Rebel." [XCV]
     a. In *The Complete Poetry and Translations*, Volume 3 (A.73).

     Translation of "Le Rebelle." In prose.

108. "The Remorse of the Dead." [XXXIV]
     a. *Measure* No. 50 (April 1925): 9 (as by CAS).
     b. In *The Complete Poetry and Translations*, Volume 3 (A.73).
     c. In *The Dark Eidolon and Other Fantasies* (A.84).

     Translation of "Remords posthume." Sonnet.

109. "Le Rêve d'un curieux." [CL]
     a. In *The Complete Poetry and Translations*, Volume 3 (A.73).

     In prose.

110. "Réversibilité." [XLV]
   a. In *The Complete Poetry and Translations*, Volume 3 (A.73).

   In prose.

111. "Sed non satiata." [XXVII]
   a. *Arkham Sampler* 2, No. 2 (Spring 1949): 24.
   b. In *Selected Poems* (A.27).
   c. In *The Complete Poetry and Translations*, Volume 3 (2 different verse versions).

   Sonnet. In c., the second version (previously unpublished) derives from a manuscript in private hands.

112. "Semper Eadem." [XLI]
   a. *Auburn Journal* 25, No. 36 (18 June 1925): 8.
   b. In *Sandalwood* (A.4).
   c. *Step Ladder* 13, No. 5 (May 1927): 137.
   d. In *Selected Poems* (A.27).
   e. In *The Complete Poetry and Translations*, Volume 3 (A.73).

   Sonnet.

113. "Les Sept Viellards." [CXIV]
   a. *Weird Tales* 12, No. 2 (August 1928): 261–62 (as one of "Three Poems in Prose").
   b. In *The Complete Poetry and Translations*, Volume 3 (A.73).

   In prose.

114. "Le Serpent qui danse." [XXIX]
   a. In *The Complete Poetry and Translations*, Volume 3 (A.73).

   In prose.

115. "The Sick Muse." [VII]
   a. *Auburn Journal* 25, No. 37 (25 June 1925): 10 (as "La Muse Malade").
   b. *Weird Tales* 27, No. 4 (April 1936): 485.
   c. In *Selected Poems* (A.27).
   d. In *The Complete Poetry and Translations*, Volume 3 (A.73).

   Translation of "La Muse malade." Sonnet.

116. "Sisina." [LX]
   a. In *The Complete Poetry and Translations*, Volume 3 (A.73).

   In prose.

117. "Song of Autumn." [LVII]
    a. *Weird Tales* 26, No. 4 (October 1935): 506.
    b. In *Spells and Philtres* (A.14).
    c. In *Selected Poems* (A.27).
    d. In *Shadows Seen and Unseen* (A.71).
    e. In *The Complete Poetry and Translations*, Volume 3 (A.73).
    f. In *L'Art étrange de Clark Ashton Smith* (III.D.7) (as "Chant d'automne").

    Translation of "Chant d'automne." 28 lines.

118. "Sonnet d'automne." [LXVI]
    a. In *The Complete Poetry and Translations*, Volume 3 (A.73).

    In prose.

119. "The Spiritual Dawn." [XLVII]
    a. *Auburn Journal* 25, No. 53 (15 October 1925): 4 (as "L'Aube Spirituelle").
    b. In *Sandalwood* (A.4) (as "L'Aube Spirituelle").
    c. In *Selected Poems* (A.27).
    d. In *The Complete Poetry and Translations*, Volume 3 (A.73).
    e. In *L'Art étrange de Clark Ashton Smith* (III.D.7) (as "L'Aube spirituelle").

    Translation of "L'Aube spirituelle." Sonnet.

120. "Spleen." [LXXVII]
    a. In *The Complete Poetry and Translations*, Volume 3 (A.73).

    In prose.

121. "Spleen." [LXXVIII]
    a. In *The Complete Poetry and Translations*, Volume 3 (A.73).

    In prose.

122. "Spleen." [LXXIX]
    a. In *The Complete Poetry and Translations*, Volume 3 (A.73).

    In prose.

123. "Spleen." [LXXX]
    a. *Weird Tales* 7, No. 2 (February 1926): 254.
    b. In *Selected Poems* (A.27).
    c. In *Shadows Seen and Unseen* (A.71).

    d. In *The Complete Poetry and Translations,* Volume 3 (A.73).

       20 lines.

124. "The Sun." [CIX]

    a. In *The Complete Poetry and Translations,* Volume 3 (A.73).

       Translation of "Le Soleil." In prose.

125. "Sympathetic Horror." [LXXXIV]

    a. *Auburn Journal* 25, No. 46 (27 August 1925): 6 (as "Horreur Sympathétique").

    b. In *Sandalwood* (A.4) (as "Horreur Sympathétique").

    c. *Weird Tales* 7, No. 5 (May 1926): 664 (as "Horreur Sympathique").

    d. In Charles Baudelaire. *Flowers of Evil.* Ed. James Laver. London: Limited Editions Club/Fanfare Press, 1940. 134 (as "Magnetic Horror").

    e. In *Selected Poems* (A.27).

    f. In *The Complete Poetry and Translations,* Volume 3 (A.73).

       Translation of "Horreur sympathique." Sonnet.

126. "To a Creole Lady." [LXIII]

    a. In *The Complete Poetry and Translations,* Volume 3 (A.73).

       Translation of "A une Dame créole." In prose.

127. "To a Malabaress." [XCII]

    a. In *The Complete Poetry and Translations,* Volume 3 (A.73).

       Translation of "À une Malabaraise." In prose.

128. "To a Passer-by." [CXVII]

    a. In *The Complete Poetry and Translations,* Volume 3 (A.73).

       Translation of "A une Passante." In prose.

129. "To Her Who Is Too Gay." [Jetsam III]

    a. In *The Complete Poetry and Translations,* Volume 3 (A.73).

       Translation of "À celle qui est trop gaie." In prose.

130. "To Theodore de Banville." [XVI]

    a. In *The Complete Poetry and Translations,* Volume 3 (A.73).

       Translation of "À Theodore de Banville." In prose.

131. "The Toiling Skeleton." [CXVIII]
   a. In *The Complete Poetry and Translations*, Volume 3 (A.73).

   Translation of "Le Squelette laboureur." In prose.

132. "Tout entière." [XLII]
   a. In *The Complete Poetry and Translations*, Volume 3 (A.73).

   In prose.

133. "Travelling Gypsies." [XIII]
   a. In *The Complete Poetry and Translations*, Volume 3 (A.73).

   Translation of "Bohémiens en voyage." In prose.

134. "Tristesses de la lune." [LXVII]
   a. In *The Complete Poetry and Translations*, Volume 3 (A.73).

   In prose.

135. "The Two Kind Sisters." [CXXXVII]
   a. *Sinisterra* 2, No. 2 (Autumn 1954): 36.
   b. In *Selected Poems* (A.27).
   c. In *The Complete Poetry and Translations*, Volume 3 (A.73).
   d. In *L'Art étrange de Clark Ashton Smith* (III.D.7) (as "Les Deux Bonnes Soeurs").

   Translation of "Les Deux Bonnes Soeurs." In prose.

136. "The Vampire." [XXXII]
   a. In *The Complete Poetry and Translations*, Volume 3 (A.73).

   Translation of "Le Vampire." In prose.

137. "The Venal Muse." [VIII]
   a. In *Sandalwood* (A.4) (as "La Muse Vénale").
   b. In *The Complete Poetry and Translations*, Volume 3 (A.73).

   Translation of "La Muse vénale." Sonnet.

138. "Vers pour le portrait d'Honoré Daumier." [LXI]
   a. In *The Complete Poetry and Translations*, Volume 3 (A.73).

   In prose.

139. "Very Far from Here." [XCIX]
   a. In *The Complete Poetry and Translations*, Volume 3 (A.73).

Translation of "Bien loin d'ici." In prose.

140. "The Voice." [XCIII]
   a. In *Selected Poems* (A.27).
   b. In *The Complete Poetry and Translations*, Volume 3 (A.73).

Translation of "La Voix." In prose.

141. "Le Voyage." [CLI]
   a. In *The Complete Poetry and Translations*, Volume 3 (A.73).

Translation of "Le Voyage." In prose.

142. "Un Voyage à Cythère." [CXLI]
   a. In *The Complete Poetry and Translations*, Volume 3 (both verse and prose versions).

The verse version, apparently a fragment, is 20 lines.

143. "The Wine of Lovers." [CXXXII]
   a. *Auburn Journal* 25, No. 42 (30 July 1925): 4 (as "Le Vin des Amants").
   b. In *Sandalwood* (A.4) (as "Le Vin des Amants").
   c. *United Amateur* 25, No. 3 (July 1926): 6 (a "Le Vin des Amants").
   d. *Step Ladder* 13, No. 5 (May 1927): 139 (as "Le Vin des Amants").
   e. In *Selected Poems* (A.27).
   f. In *The Complete Poetry and Translations*, Volume 3 (A.73).

Translation of "Le Vin des amants." Sonnet.

144. "The Wine of the Assassin." [CXXX]
   a. In *The Complete Poetry and Translations*, Volume 3 (A.73).

Translation of "Le Vin de l'assassin." In prose.

145. "The Wine of the Rag-Pickers." [CXXIX]
   a. In *The Complete Poetry and Translations*, Volume 3 (A.73).

Translation of "Le Vin de chiffoniers." In prose.

146. "The Wine of the Solitary." [CXXXI]
   a. In *The Complete Poetry and Translations*, Volume 3 (A.73).

Translation of "Le Vin du solitaire." In prose.

147. [Untitled.] [V]
   a. In *The Complete Poetry and Translations*, Volume 3 (A.73).

In prose.

148. [Untitled.] [XXV]
  a.   In *The Complete Poetry and Translations*, Volume 3 (A.73).
  In prose.

149. [Untitled.] [XXVI]
  a.   In *The Complete Poetry and Translations*, Volume 3 (A.73).
  In prose.

150. [Untitled.] [XXVIII]
  a.   In *The Complete Poetry and Translations*, Volume 3 (A.73).
  In prose.

151. [Untitled.] [XXXIII]
  a.   In *The Complete Poetry and Translations*, Volume 3 (A.73).
  In prose.

152. [Untitled.] [XL]
  a.   In *The Complete Poetry and Translations*, Volume 3 (A.73).
  In prose.

153. [Untitled.] [XLIII]
  a.   In *The Complete Poetry and Translations*, Volume 3 (A.73).
  In prose.

154. [Untitled.] [CXXIII]
  a.   In *The Complete Poetry and Translations*, Volume 3 (A.73).
  In prose.

155. [Untitled.] [CXXIV]
  a.   In *The Complete Poetry and Translations*, Volume 3 (A.73).
  In prose.

Marie Dauguet

156. [Untitled.]
  a.   In *The Complete Poetry and Translations*, Volume 3 (A.73).
  Translation of "Epilogue." 16 lines. CAS has translated only a portion of the poem.

Théophile Gautier

157. "The Flower Pot."
   a. In *The Complete Poetry and Translations*, Volume 3 (A.73).
   Translation of "Le Pot de fleurs." 15 lines.

158. "The Impassable."
   a. In *The Complete Poetry and Translations*, Volume 3 (A.73).
   Translation of "L'Impassable." Sonnet.

159. "Pastel."
   a. In *The Complete Poetry and Translations*, Volume 3 (A.73).
   15 lines.

Gérard de Nerval

160. "Artemis."
   a. In *The Complete Poetry and Translations*, Volume 3 (A.73).
   Sonnet.

161. "Golden Verses."
   a. In *The Complete Poetry and Translations*, Volume 3 (A.73).
   Translation of "Vers dorés." Sonnet.

José-Maria de Heredia

162. "Antony and Cleopatra."
   a. In *The Complete Poetry and Translations*, Volume 3 (A.73).
   Translation of "Antoine et Cléopâtre." Sonnet.

163. "The Coral Reef."
   a. In *The Complete Poetry and Translations*, Volume 3 (A.73).
   Translation of "Le Récif de corail." Sonnet.

164. "La Dogaresse."
   a. In *The Complete Poetry and Translations*, Volume 3 (A.73).
   Sonnet.

165. "Nemea."
   a. In *The Complete Poetry and Translations*, Volume 3 (A.73).

Translation of "Némée." Sonnet.

166. "Oblivion."
    a. *Arkham Sampler* 2, No. 3 (Summer 1949): 73.
    b. In *The Dark Chateau* (A.13).
    c. In *Selected Poems* (A.27).
    d. In *The Complete Poetry and Translations*, Volume 3 (A.73).
    Translation of "L'Oubli." Sonnet.

167. "On a Broken Statue."
    a. In *The Complete Poetry and Translations*, Volume 3 (A.73).
    Translation of "Sur un Marbre brisé." Sonnet.

168. "The Samurai."
    a. In *The Complete Poetry and Translations*, Volume 3 (A.73).
    Translation of "Le Samouraï." Sonnet.

169. "A Setting Sun."
    a. In *The Complete Poetry and Translations*, Volume 3 (A.73).
    Translation of "Soleil couchant." Sonnet.

170. "The Stained Window."
    a. In *The Complete Poetry and Translations*, Volume 3 (A.73).
    Translation of "Vitrail." Sonnet.

Victor Hugo

171. "Twilight."
    a. In *The Complete Poetry and Translations*, Volume 3 (A.73).
    Translation of "Crépuscule." 28 lines.

172. "What One Hears on the Mountain."
    a. In *The Complete Poetry and Translations*, Volume 3 (A.73).
    Translation of "Ce qu'on entend sur la montagne." 82 lines.

173. "The Wheel of Omphale."
    a. In *Selected Poems* (A.27).
    b. In *The Complete Poetry and Translations*, Volume 3 (A.73).
    Translation of "Le Rouet d'Omphale." 24 lines.

Tristan Klingsor

174. "Plaisir d'amour."
   a. In *The Complete Poetry and Translations*, Volume 3 (A.73).
   12 lines.

Alphonse Louis Marie de Lamartine

175.   "The Lake."
   a. In *The Complete Poetry and Translations*, Volume 3 (A.73).
   Translation of "Le Lac." 64 lines.

Charles-Marie René Leconte de Lisle

176. "The Black Panther."
   a. In *The Complete Poetry and Translations*, Volume 3 (A.73).
   Translation of "La Panthère noire." 44 lines.

177. "Ecclesiastes."
   a. *Epos* 8, No. 2 (Winter 1956): 15.
   b. *Daily Press* (Newport News, VA) (24 January 1957): 6.
   c. In *Spells and Philtres* (A.14).
   d. In *Selected Poems* (A.27).
   e. In *Shadows Seen and Unseen* (A.71).
   f. In *The Complete Poetry and Translations*, Volume 3 (A.73).
   Translation of "L'Ecclésiaste." Sonnet.

178. "The Exhibitionists."
   a. In *The Complete Poetry and Translations*, Volume 3 (A.73).
   Translation of "Les Montreurs." Sonnet.

179. "The Howlers."
   a. In *The Complete Poetry and Translations*, Volume 3 (A.73).
   Translation of "Les Hurleurs." 36 lines.

180. "The Sleep of the Condor."
   a. In *Selected Poems* (A.27).
   b. In *The Complete Poetry and Translations*, Volume 3 (A.73).
   Translation of "Le Sommeil du condor." 28 lines.

181. "Solvet Seclum."
   a. In *The Complete Poetry and Translations*, Volume 3 (A.73).
       28 lines.

Charles van Lerberghe

182.   "Song."
   a. In *The Complete Poetry and Translations*, Volume 3 (A.73).
       Translation of "[Chanson]." 12 lines.

Pierre Lièvre

183. "Elysian Landscape."
   a. In *Selected Poems* (A.27).
   b. In *The Complete Poetry and Translations*, Volume 3 (A.73).
       Translation of "Paysage Elyséen." 20 lines.

184. "The End of Supper."
   a. In *The Complete Poetry and Translations*, Volume 3 (A.73).
       Translation of "Fin de souper." 12 lines.

Stuart Merrill

185.   "A Woman at Prayer."
   a. In *The Complete Poetry and Translations*, Volume 3 (A.73).
       Translation of "Celle qui prie." Sonnet.

Alfred de Musset

186.   "Remember Thee."
   a. In *The Complete Poetry and Translations*, Volume 3 (A.73).
       Translation of "Rappelle-toi." 27 lines.

187.   "Song."
   a. In *The Complete Poetry and Translations*, Volume 3 (A.73).
       Translation of "Chanson." 16 lines.

Hélène Picard

188. "The Desire of Loving."
   a. In *The Complete Poems and Translations*, Volume 2 (A.73).

Translation of "Le Désir d'aimer." 20 lines. Erroneously placed in Vol. 2 of of first edition of *The Complete Poetry and Translations*, as the poem was not recognized as a translation.

Albert Samain

189.   "I Dream."
    a.   In *The Complete Poetry and Translations*, Volume 3 (A.73).
    Translation of an untitled poem. 10 lines.

190.   "[Myrtil and Palemone.]"
    a.   In *The Complete Poetry and Translations*, Volume 3 (A.73).
    Translation of "Myrtil et Palémone." In prose.

Fernand Severin

191.   "Sonnet."
    a.   In *The Complete Poetry and Translations*, Volume 3 (A.73).
    Translation of "Bois sacré." 12 lines (not a sonnet). CAS has translated only a part of the poem.

René François Armand Sully Prudhomme

192.   "Siesta."
    a.   In *The Complete Poetry and Translations*, Volume 3 (A.73).
    Translation of "Sieste." Sonnet.

Paul Verlaine

193. "IX (Ariettes Oubliées)."
    a.   In *Selected Poems* (A.27).
    b.   In *The Complete Poetry and Translations*, Volume 3 (A.73).
    Translation of "Ariettes Oubliées IX." 8 lines.

194. "Il Bacio."
    a.   In *The Complete Poetry and Translations*, Volume 3 (A.73).
    In prose.

195. "La Bonne Chanson" [nos. I, III, V, VI, and VII].
    a.   In *The Complete Poetry and Translations*, Volume 3 (A.73).
    20 lines (fragment), 18 lines, 10 lines, 20 lines, and 12 lines.

196. "Crimen Amoris."
   a. In *Selected Poems* (A.27).
   b. In *The Complete Poetry and Translations*, Volume 3 (A.73).
       96 lines. One stanza not translated by CAS.

197. "En Sourdine."
   a. In *Selected Poems* (A.27).
   b. In *The Complete Poetry and Translations*, Volume 3 (A.73).
       20 lines.

198. "The Faun."
   a. In *Selected Poems* (A.27).
   b. In *The Complete Poetry and Translations*, Volume 3 (A.73).
       Translation of "Le Faune." 8 lines.

199. "Green."
   a. In *The Complete Poetry and Translations*, Volume 3 (A.73).
       12 lines. Verlaine's poem is titled in English.

200. "Moonlight."
   a. *Weird Tales* 36, No. 6 (July 1942): 49 (as translated by "Timeus Gaylord").
   b. In *Selected Poems* (A.27).
   c. In *The Complete Poetry and Translations*, Volume 3 (A.73).
       Translation of "Claire de lune." 12 lines.

201. "Song from *Les Uns et les autres*."
   a. In *The Complete Poetry and Translations*, Volume 3 (A.73).
       Translation of [Song from] *Les Uns et les autres*. 12 lines.

202. "Spleen."
   a. In *The Complete Poetry and Translations*, Volume 3 (A.73).
       12 lines.

203. "To a Woman."
   a. In *The Complete Poetry and Translations*, Volume 3 (A.73).
       Translation of "A une Femme." Sonnet.

b. From Spanish

Gustavo Adolfo Béquer

1. "Invocation."
    a. In *The Complete Poetry and Translations*, Volume 3 (A.73).
    Translation of "Rimas LII." 16 lines.

2. "The Sower."
    a. *Asmodeus* No. 2 (Fall 1951): 9.
    b. In *The Complete Poetry and Translations*, Volume 3 (A.73).
    Translation of "Rimas LX." 5 lines.

3. "Where?"
    a. In *Spells and Philtres* (A.14) (as "Rimas XXXIII").
    b. In *Selected Poems* (A.27).
    c. In *The Complete Poetry and Translations*, Volume 3 (A.73).
    Translation of "Rimas XXXVIII." 4 lines.

4. "The World Rolls On."
    a. In *The Complete Poetry and Translations*, Volume 3 (A.73).
    Translation of "Rimas I (Libro de los gorriones)." 8 lines.

José A. Calcaño

5. "The Cypress."
    a. *Spearhead* 2, No. 1 (Summer 1950): [12].
    b. In *The Dark Chateau* (A.13).
    c. In *Selected Poems* (A.27).
    d. In *The Complete Poetry and Translations*, Volume 3 (A.73).
    Translation of "El ciprés." 32 lines.

José Santos Chocaño

6. "The Sleep of the Cayman."
    a. *Asmodeus* No. 2 (Fall 1951): 22.
    b. In *The Complete Poetry and Translations*, Volume 3 (A.73).
    Translation of "El sueño del calmán." Sonnet.

Rubén Darío

7.   "The Song of Songs."
   a.   In *The Complete Poetry and Translations*, Volume 3 (A.73).
        Translation of "El Cantar de los Cantares." Sonnet.

Juana de Ibarbourou

8.   "Rustic Life."
   a.   In *The Complete Poetry and Translations*, Volume 3 (A.73).
        Translation of "Vida aldeana." Sonnet.

Jorge Isaacs

9.   "Luminary."
   a.   In *The Complete Poetry and Translations*, Volume 3 (A.73).
        Translation of "Luminar." Sonnet.

Juan Lozano y Lozano

10. "Rhythm."
   a.   In *The Complete Poetry and Translations*, Volume 3 (A.73).
        Translation of "Ritmo." Sonnet.

Amado Nervo

11. "Night."
   a.   In *The Complete Poetry and Translations*, Volume 3 (A.73).
        Translation of "Noche." 13 lines.

iv. Poems in Prose

1. "The Abomination of Desolation."
    a. *Fantasmagoria* 1, No. 4 (November 1938): 11.
    b. In *Poems in Prose* (A.23).
    c. In *Hyperborea* (A.29) (as "The Desolation of Soom").
    d. In *Nostalgia of the Unknown* (A.49).
    e. In *The Dark Eidolon and Other Fantasies* (A.84).
    f. In *In the Realms of Mystery and Wonder* (A.87).

    Written 16 December 1929.

2. "The Black Lake."
    a. In *Ebony and Crystal* (A.3).
    b. In *Poems in Prose* (A.23).
    c. In *Nostalgia of the Unknown* (A.49).
    d. In *A Phantasy and Other Prose Poems* (A.77).
    e. In *In the Realms of Mystery and Wonder* (A.87).

3. "The Caravan."
    a. In *Ebony and Crystal* (A.3).
    b. In *Poems in Prose* (A.23).
    c. In *Nostalgia of the Unknown* (A.49).
    d. In *A Phantasy and Other Prose Poems* (A.77).
    e. In *In the Realms of Mystery and Wonder* (A.87).

4. "A Chinese Fable."
    a. *Lost Worlds* No. 2 (2004): 2.
    b. In *The Red World of Polaris* (A.62) (lettered edition only).
    c. In *In the Realms of Mystery and Wonder* (A.87).

5. "Chinoiserie."
    a. *Philippine Magazine* 27, No. 12 (November 1931): 728, 752, 756.
    b. *Fantasy Fan* 1, No. 8 (April 1934): 116 (as "Prose Pastels 1").
    c. *Acolyte* 1, No. 4 (Summer 1943): 3.
    d. In *The Abominations of Yondo* (A.15).
    e. In *Poems in Prose* (A.23).
    f. In *Nostalgia of the Unknown* (A.49).
    g. In *The White Sybil* (A.68).

326 I. Works by Smith in English I.B.iv.6

h. In Charles D. Hornig, ed. *The Fantasy Fan: September, 1933–February, 1935.* [n.p.: Lance Thingmaker, 2010.] 116 (as "Prose Pastels 1"; facsimile of b.).

i. In *In the Realms of Mystery and Wonder* (A.87).

Written December 1929.

6. "The City of Destruction."
   a. In *Nostalgia of the Unknown* (A.49).
   b. In *Strange Shadows* (A.52).
   c. In *In the Realms of Mystery and Wonder* (A.87).

   Fragment.

7. "The Corpse and the Skeleton."
   a. In *Poems in Prose* (A.23).
   b. In *Nostalgia of the Unknown* (A.49).
   c. *Fungi* No. 20 (Spring 2011): 112.
   d. In *The Dark Eidolon and Other Fantasies* (A.84).
   e. In *In the Realms of Mystery and Wonder* (A.87).

   Written 5 April 1915.

8. "The Crystals."
   a. In *Poems in Prose* (A.23).
   b. In *Nostalgia of the Unknown* (A.49).
   c. In *The Hashish-Eater* (A.55).
   d. In *The Hashish-Eater* (A.75).
   e. In *In the Realms of Mystery and Wonder* (A.87).

   Written 27 July 1914.

9. "The Days."
   a. In *Grotesques and Fantastiques* (A.32).
   b. In *Nostalgia of the Unknown* (A.49).
   c. In *Strange Shadows* (A.52).
   d. In *In the Realms of Mystery and Wonder* (A.87).

10. "The Demon, the Angel, and Beauty."
    a. In *Ebony and Crystal* (A.3).
    b. In *Poems in Prose* (A.23).
    c. In *Nostalgia of the Unknown* (A.49).
    d. In *A Phantasy and Other Prose Poems* (A.77).
    e. In *The Dark Eidolon and Other Fantasies* (A.84).

     f.   In *In the Realms of Mystery and Wonder* (A.87).

11. "A Dream of Lethe."
     a.   In *Ebony and Crystal* (A.3).
     b.   In *Poems in Prose* (A.23).
     c.   In *Nostalgia of the Unknown* (A.49).
     d.   In *A Phantasy and Other Prose Poems* (A.77).
     e.   In *The Dark Eidolon and Other Fantasies* (A.84).
     f.   In *In the Realms of Mystery and Wonder* (A.87).

12. "Ennui."
     a.   *Smart Set* 56, No. 1 (September 1918): 32.
     b.   In *Ebony and Crystal* (A.3).
     c.   In *Poems in Prose* (A.23).
     d.   In *Nostalgia of the Unknown* (A.49).
     e.   In *A Phantasy and Other Prose Poems* (A.77).
     f.   In *The Dark Eidolon and Other Fantasies* (A.84).
     g.   In *In the Realms of Mystery and Wonder* (A.87).

13. "The Flower-Devil."
     a.   In *Ebony and Crystal* (A.3).
     b.   In *Poems in Prose* (A.23).
     c.   In *Nostalgia of the Unknown* (A.49).
     d.   In *Collected Fantasies,* Volume 3 (A.70).
     e.   In *A Phantasy and Other Prose Poems* (A.77).
     f.   *Dark Discoveries* No. 20 (Spring 2012): 47.
     g.   In *The Dark Eidolon and Other Fantasies* (A.84).
     h.   In *In the Realms of Mystery and Wonder* (A.87).
     i.   In *Clark Ashton Smith's Works* (A.90).

     Written before 29 September 1920. The nucleus of the tale "The Demon of the Flower" (B.i.26).

14. "The Forbidden Forest."
     a.   *Acolyte* 2, No. 1 (Fall 1943): 3.
     b.   In *Poems in Prose* (A.23).
     c.   *Nyctalops* No. 7 (August 1972): 85 (under heading "Prose Pastels").
     d.   In *Nostalgia of the Unknown* (A.49).
     e.   In *In the Realms of Mystery and Wonder* (A.87).

     Written 20 December 1929.

15.   "From a Letter."
     a.   In *Ebony and Crystal* (A.3).
     b.   In *Poems in Prose* (A.23).
     c.   In *Poseidonis* (A.34) (as "The Muse of Atlantis").
     d.   In *Nostalgia of the Unknown* (A.49).
     e.   In *A Phantasy and Other Prose Poems* (A.77).
     f.   In *Mondes premiers* (II.A.iii.14) (as "The Muse of Atlantis").
     g.   In *In the Realms of Mystery and Wonder* (A.87).

16.   "From the Crypts of Memory."
     a.   *Bohemia* 2, No. 3 (April 1917): 27.
     b.   In *Ebony and Crystal* (A.3).
     c.   In *Out of Space and Time* (A.9).
     d.   *Fantasy Sampler* No. 4 (June 1956): 12–13.
     e.   In *Poems in Prose* (A.23).
     f.   In *Xiccarph* (A.30).
     g.   A.35.
     h.   In Lin Carter, ed. *Kingdoms of Sorcery.* Garden City, NY: Double-day, 1976. 115–16 (as "Fables from the Edge of Night," Part III).
     i.   In *Nostalgia of the Unknown* (A.49) (two different texts).
     j.   In *Collected Fantasies*, Volume 1 (A.70).
     k.   In *A Phantasy and Other Prose Poems* (A.77).
     l.   In *The Dark Eidolon and Other Fantasies* (A.84).
     m.   In *Autres mondes* (II.A.iii.16).
     n.   In *In the Realms of Mystery and Wonder* (A.87).

     The nucleus of the tale "The Planet of the Dead" (B.i.115).

17.   "The Frozen Waterfall."
     a.   In *Nostalgia of the Unknown* (A.49).
     b.   In *Strange Shadows* (A.52).
     c.   In *In the Realms of Mystery and Wonder* (A.87).

18.   "The Garden and the Tomb."
     a.   In *Ebony and Crystal* (A.3).
     b.   *Phantagraph* 4, No. 3 (February 1936): 12.
     c.   In *Poems in Prose* (A.23).
     d.   In *Nostalgia of the Unknown* (A.49).
     e.   In *A Phantasy and Other Prose Poems* (A.77).
     f.   In *In the Realms of Mystery and Wonder* (A.87).

     Written 9 June 1915.

19.   "The Image of Bronze and the Image of Iron."
      a.   In *Poems in Prose* (A.23).
      b.   In *Nostalgia of the Unknown* (A.49).
      c.   In *The Dark Eidolon and Other Fantasies* (A.84).
      d.   In *In the Realms of Mystery and Wonder* (A.87).

      Fragment. Written 1914 or earlier.

20.   "Images."
      a.   In *Ebony and Crystal* (A.3).
      b.   In *Poems in Prose* (A.23).
      c.   In *Nostalgia of the Unknown* (A.49).
      d.   In *In the Realms of Mystery and Wonder* (A.87).

      Includes "Tears," "The Secret Rose," "The Wind and the Garden,"
      "Offerings," and "A Coronal."

21.   "In Cocaigne."
      a.   In *Ebony and Crystal* (A.3).
      b.   In *Poems in Prose* (A.23).
      c.   In *Poseidonis* (A.34).
      d.   In *Nostalgia of the Unknown* (A.49).
      e.   In *A Phantasy and Other Prose Poems* (A.77).
      f.   In *The Dark Eidolon and Other Fantasies* (A.84).
      g.   In *The Averoigne Chronicles* (A.85).
      h.   In *In the Realms of Mystery and Wonder* (A.87).

      Written before 5 September 1921.

22.   "The Lake of Enchanted Silence."
      a.   *Crypt of Cthulhu* No. 20 (Eastertide 1984): 52.
      b.   In *Nostalgia of the Unknown* (A.49).
      c.   In *Strange Shadows* (A.52).
      d.   In *A Phantasy and Other Prose Poems* (A.77).
      e.   In *In the Realms of Mystery and Wonder* (A.87).

23.   "The Litany of the Seven Kisses."
      a.   In *Ebony and Crystal* (A.3).
      b.   *Laughing Horse* No. 6 (1923): [19].
      c.   In *Poems in Prose* (A.23).
      d.   In *Nostalgia of the Unknown* (A.49).
      e.   In *A Phantasy and Other Prose Poems* (A.77).
      f.   In *The Dark Eidolon and Other Fantasies* (A.84).

    g.   In *In the Realms of Mystery and Wonder* (A.87).

    Written Spring 1921.

24.   "The Lotus and the Moon."
    a.   *Fantasy Fan* 2, No. 1 (September 1934): 7 (as "Prose Pastels IV").
    b.   *Acolyte* 1, No. 4 (Summer 1943): 3.
    c.   *Eldritch Dream Quest* 1, No. 3 (April 1963): 72.
    d.   In *Poems in Prose* (A.23).
    e.   In *Nostalgia of the Unknown* (A.49).
    f.   In Charles D. Hornig, ed. *The Fantasy Fan: September, 1933– February, 1935.* [n.p.: Lance Thingmaker, 2010.] [Part 2,] 7 (as "Prose Pastels IV"; facsimile of a.).
    g.   In *In the Realms of Mystery and Wonder* (A.87).

    Written 18 December 1929.

25.   "The Memnons of the Night."
    a.   *Bohemia* 2, No. 1 (1 February 1917): 27 (as "Memnons of the Night").
    b.   In *Ebony and Crystal* (A.3).
    c.   *Phantagraph* 4, No. 2 (November–December 1935): [9].
    d.   In *Poems in Prose* (A.23).
    e.   In Donald A. Wollheim, ed. *Operation Phantasy.* Rego Park, NY: Phantagraph Press, 1967. 46–47.
    f.   In *Hyperborea* (A.29).
    g.   In *Nostalgia of the Unknown* (A.49).
    h.   In *A Phantasy and Other Prose Poems* (A.77).
    i.   In *The Dark Eidolon and Other Fantasies* (A.84).
    j.   In *In the Realms of Mystery and Wonder* (A.87).
    k.   In *Clark Ashton Smith's Works* (A.90).

    Written 18 December 1915.

26.   "The Mirror in the Hall of Ebony."
    a.   *Fantasy Fan* 1, No. 9 (May 1934): 140, 144 (as "Prose Pastels 2").
    b.   *Acolyte* 1, No. 4 (Summer 1943): 3–4.
    c.   In *The Abominations of Yondo* (A.15).
    d.   In *Poems in Prose* (A.23).
    e.   In *Nostalgia of the Unknown* (A.49).
    f.   In *The White Sybil* (A.68).
    g.   In *The Dark Eidolon and Other Fantasies* (A.84).

h. In Charles D. Hornig, ed. *The Fantasy Fan: September, 1933–February, 1935.* [n.p.: Lance Thingmaker, 2010.] 140, 144 (as "Prose Pastels 2"; facsimile of a.).
i. In *In the Realms of Mystery and Wonder* (A.87).

Written 17 December 1929.

27. "The Mithridate."
a. *Acolyte* 2, No. 1 (Fall 1943): 4.
b. In *Poems in Prose* (A.23).
c. *Nyctalops* No. 7 (August 1972): 85 (under heading "Prose Pastels").
d. In *Nostalgia of the Unknown* (A.49).
e. In *In the Realms of Mystery and Wonder* (A.87).

Written 21 December 1929.

28. "The Mortuary."
a. A.28.
b. In Jonathan Bacon and Steve Troyanovich, ed. *Omniumgathum: An Anthology of Verse by Top Authors in the Field of Fantasy.* Lamoni, IA: Stygian Isle Press, 1976. 30.
c. In *Nostalgia of the Unknown* (A.49).
d. In *Strange Shadows* (A.52).
e. In *The Emperor of Dreams* (A.59).
f. In *In the Realms of Mystery and Wonder* (A.87).

29. "The Muse of Hyperborea."
a. *Fantasy Fan* 1, No. 10 (June 1934): 154 (as "Prose Pastels III").
b. *Acolyte* 1, No. 4 (Summer 1943): 4.
c. In *Poems in Prose* (A.23).
d. In *Hyperborea* (A.29).
e. In *Nostalgia of the Unknown* (A.49).
f. In *The Book of Hyperborea* (A.58).
g. In *Collected Fantasies,* Volume 4 (A.70).
h. In Charles D. Hornig, ed. *The Fantasy Fan: September, 1933–February, 1935.* [n.p.: Lance Thingmaker, 2010.] 154 (as "Prose Pastels III"; facsimile of a.).
i. In *The Dark Eidolon and Other Fantasies* (A.84).
j. In *Mondes premiers* (II.A.iii.15).
k. In *In the Realms of Mystery and Wonder* (A.87).

Written 22 December 1929.

30. "Narcissus."
    a. *Acolyte* 3, No. 1 (Winter 1945): 4.
    b. In *Poems in Prose* (A.23).
    c. In *Nostalgia of the Unknown* (A.49).
    d. In *In the Realms of Mystery and Wonder* (A.87).

31. "Offering."
    a. In *Grotesques and Fantastiques* (A.32).
    b. In *Nostalgia of the Unknown* (A.49).
    c. In *Strange Shadows* (A.52).
    d. In *In the Realms of Mystery and Wonder* (A.87).

32. "The Osprey and the Shark."
    a. In *Nostalgia of the Unknown* (A.49).
    b. In *Strange Shadows* (A.52).
    c. In *In the Realms of Mystery and Wonder* (A.87) (as "The Shark and the Osprey").

33. "The Passing of Aphrodite."
    a. *Fantasy Fan* 2, No. 4 (December 1934): 59–60 (as "Prose Pastels 5").
    b. *Acolyte* 1, No. 4 (Summer 1943): 4–6.
    c. In *The Abominations of Yondo* (A.15).
    d. In *Poems in Prose* (A.23).
    e. In *Hyperborea* (A.29).
    f. In Lin Carter, ed. *Kingdoms of Sorcery.* Garden City, NY: Doubleday, 1976. 113–15 (as "Fables from the Edge of Night," Part II).
    g. In *Nostalgia of the Unknown* (A.49).
    h. In *The White Sybil* (A.68).
    i. In Charles D. Hornig, ed. *The Fantasy Fan: September, 1933–February, 1935.* [n.p.: Lance Thingmaker, 2010.] 59–60 (as "Prose Pastels 5"; facsimile of a.).
    j. In *The Dark Eidolon and Other Fantasies* (A.84).
    k. In *In the Realms of Mystery and Wonder* (A.87).

    Written 26 February 1925.

34. "The Peril That Lurks among Ruins."
    a. *Acolyte* 3, No. 1 (Winter 1945): 3.
    b. In *Poems in Prose* (A.23).
    c. In *Nostalgia of the Unknown* (A.49) (two different texts).
    d. In *In the Realms of Mystery and Wonder* (A.87).

35. "A Phantasy."
  a. *Bohemia* 1, No. 5 (15 November 1916): 157.
  b. In *Ebony and Crystal* (A.3).
  c. In *Poems in Prose* (A.23).
  d. In *Nostalgia of the Unknown* (A.49).
  e. In *A Phantasy and Other Prose Poems* (A.77).
  f. *Fungi* No. 20 (Spring 2011): 171.
  g. In *In the Realms of Mystery and Wonder* (A.87).

36. "Preference."
  a. *Crypt of Cthulhu* No. 20 (Eastertide 1984): 11.
  b. In *Nostalgia of the Unknown* (A.49).
  c. In *Strange Shadows* (A.52).
  d. In *In the Realms of Mystery and Wonder* (A.87).

37. "The Princess Almeena."
  a. *Smart Set* 61, No. 2 (February 1920): 1.
  b. In *Ebony and Crystal* (A.3).
  c. In *Poems in Prose* (A.23).
  d. In *Nostalgia of the Unknown* (A.49).
  e. In *A Phantasy and Other Prose Poems* (A.77).
  f. In *In the Realms of Mystery and Wonder* (A.87).

38. "Remoteness."
  a. In *Ebony and Crystal* (A.3).
  b. In *Poems in Prose* (A.23).
  c. In *Nostalgia of the Unknown* (A.49).
  d. In *A Phantasy and Other Prose Poems* (A.77).
  e. In *In the Realms of Mystery and Wonder* (A.87).

39. "The Shadows."
  a. In *Ebony and Crystal* (A.3).
  b. In *Out of Space and Time* (A.9).
  c. In *Poems in Prose* (A.23).
  d. In *Poseidonis* (A.34).
  e. In *Nostalgia of the Unknown* (A.49).
  f. In *A Phantasy and Other Prose Poems* (A.77).
  g. *Dark Discoveries* No. 20 (Spring 2012): 48.
  h. In *The Dark Eidolon and Other Fantasies* (A.84).
  i. In *In the Realms of Mystery and Wonder* (A.87).
  j. In *Clark Ashton Smith's Works* (A.90).

40. "The Statue of Silence."
  a. In *Ebony and Crystal* (A.3).
  b. In *Poems in Prose* (A.23).
  c. In *Nostalgia of the Unknown* (A.49).
  d. In *A Phantasy and Other Prose Poems* (A.77).
  e. In *In the Realms of Mystery and Wonder* (A.87).

   Written before 20 August 1915.

41. "The Sun and the Sepulchre."
  a. In *Poems in Prose* (A.23).
  b. In *Nostalgia of the Unknown* (A.49).
  c. In *In the Realms of Mystery and Wonder* (A.87).

   Written before 10 January 1926.

42. "To the Daemon."
  a. *Acolyte* 2, No. 1 (Fall 1943): 3.
  b. In *Poems in Prose* (A.23).
  c. In *Xiccarph* (A.30).
  d. *Nyctalops* No. 7 (August 1972): 85 (under heading "Prose Pastels").
  e. In *Nostalgia of the Unknown* (A.49).
  f. In *Collected Fantasies*, Volume 1 (A.70).
  g. In *A Phantasy and Other Prose Poems* (A.77).
  h. In *The Dark Eidolon and Other Fantasies* (A.84).
  i. In *Autres mondes* (II.A.iii.16).
  j. In *In the Realms of Mystery and Wonder* (A.87).

43. "The Touch-Stone."
  a. In *Poems in Prose* (A.23).
  b. In *Nostalgia of the Unknown* (A.49).
  c. In *The Dark Eidolon and Other Fantasies* (A.84).
  d. In *In the Realms of Mystery and Wonder* (A.87).

   Written 18 December 1929.

44. "The Traveller."
  a. In *Ebony and Crystal* (A.3).
  b. In *Poems in Prose* (A.23).
  c. In *Nostalgia of the Unknown* (A.49).
  d. In *Collected Fantasies*, vol. 5 (A.70).
  e. In *A Phantasy and Other Prose Poems* (A.77).

    f. In *In the Realms of Mystery and Wonder* (A.87).

    g. In *Clark Ashton Smith's Works* (A.90).

45. "Vignettes."

    a. In *Ebony and Crystal* (A.3).

    b. In *Poems in Prose* (A.23).

    c. In *Nostalgia of the Unknown* (A.49).

    d. In *The Averoigne Chronicles* (A.85) ("The Broken Lute" only).

    e. In *In the Realms of Mystery and Wonder* (A.87).

Includes "Beyond the Mountains," "The Broken Lute," "Nostalgia of the Unknown," "Grey Sorrow," "The Hair of Circe," and "The Eyes of Circe."

46. [Untitled.]

    a. *Crypt of Cthulhu* No. 20 (Eastertide 1984): 50.

    b. In *Strange Shadows* (A.52) (as "[The Land of Fruitful Palms]").

    c. In *Nostalgia of the Unknown* (A.49).

    d. In *In the Realms of Mystery and Wonder* (A.87).

Written 16 April 1960.

v. Nonfiction

1.   "Argument of 'The Hashish-Eater.'"
     a.   In *Strange Shadows* (A.52).
     b.   In *The Hashish-Eater* (A.55).
     c.   In *The Hashish-Eater* (A.75).

2.   "Atmosphere in Weird Fiction."
     a.   *Amateur Correspondent* 2, No. 3 (November–December 1937):
          6–7.
     b.   In *Planets and Dimensions* (A.33).

3.   "An Autobiography of Clark Ashton Smith."
     a.   *Science Fiction Fan* 1, No. 2 (August 1936): 2–3.
     b.   *In Memoriam: Clark Ashton Smith* (III.D.4) (as "Autobiog-
          raphy").
     c.   In *Planets and Dimensions* (A.33).
     d.   In *Shadows Seen and Unseen* (A.71).

4.   "Checklist: The Carvings of Clark Ashton Smith."
     a.   *Arkham Sampler* 1, No. 1 (Winter 1948): 43–48.

5.   "Clark Ashton Smith—An Autobiographette."
     a.   *Fantasy Fan* 2, No. 3 (November 1934): 34.
     b.   In *Planets and Dimensions* (A.33).
     c.   In Charles D. Hornig, ed. *The Fantasy Fan: September,
          1933–February, 1935.* [n.p.: Lance Thingmaker, 2010.] [Part
          2,] 34 (facsimile of a.).

6.   "Clark Ashton Smith's Column."
     a.   *Auburn Journal* 23, No. 51 (4 October 1923): 6 (subtitled
          "Epigrams").

7.   "Clark Ashton Smith's Column."
     a.   *Auburn Journal* 23, No. 52 (11 October 1923): 6 (subtitled
          "Cocktails and Creme de Menthe").
     b.   In *The Devil's Notebook* (A.54).

8.   "Clark Ashton Smith's Column."
     a.   *Auburn Journal* 24, No. 1 (18 October 1923): 6 (subtitled
          "Cocktails and Creme de Menthe").

b. In *The Devil's Notebook* (A.54).

9.   "Clark Ashton Smith's Column."
a. *Auburn Journal* 24, No. 2 (25 October 1923): 6 (subtitled "Cocktails and Creme de Menthe").
b. In *The Devil's Notebook* (A.54).

10. "Clark Ashton Smith's Column."
a. *Auburn Journal* 24, No. 3 (1 November 1923): 6 (subtitled "Points for the Pious").
b. In *The Devil's Notebook* (A.54).

11. "Clark Ashton Smith's Column."
a. *Auburn Journal* 24, No. 4 (8 November 1923): 6 (subtitled "Cocktails and Creme de Menthe").
b. In *The Devil's Notebook* (A.54).

12. "Clark Ashton Smith's Column."
a. *Auburn Journal* 24, No. 5 (15 November 1923): 6 (subtitled "Points for the Pious").
b. In *The Devil's Notebook* (A.54).

13. "Clark Ashton Smith's Column."
a. *Auburn Journal* 24, No. 6 (22 November 1923): 6 (subtitled "Cocktails and Creme de Menthe").
b. In *The Devil's Notebook* (A.54).

14. "Clark Ashton Smith's Column."
a. *Auburn Journal* 24, No. 7 (29 November 1923): 6 (subtitled "Cocktails and Creme de Menthe").
b. In *The Devil's Notebook* (A.54).

15. "Clark Ashton Smith's Column."
a. *Auburn Journal* 24, No. 8 (6 December 1923): 6 (subtitled "Cocktails and Creme de Menthe").
b. In *The Devil's Notebook* (A.54).

16. "Clark Ashton Smith's Column."
a. *Auburn Journal* 24, No. 9 (13 December 1923): 6 (subtitled "Cocktails and Creme de Menthe").
b. In *The Devil's Notebook* (A.54).

17. "Clark Ashton Smith's Column."
    a. *Auburn Journal* 24, No. 10 (20 December 1923): 6 (subtitled "Cocktails and Creme de Menthe").
    b. In *The Devil's Notebook* (A.54).

18. "Clark Ashton Smith's Column."
    a. *Auburn Journal* 24, No. 11 (27 December 1923): 6 (no subtitle).

19. "Clark Ashton Smith's Column."
    a. *Auburn Journal* 24, No. 13 (10 January 1924): 13 (subtitled "Cocktails and Creme de Menthe").
    b. In *The Devil's Notebook* (A.54).

20. "Clark Ashton Smith's Column."
    a. *Auburn Journal* 24, No. 14 (17 January 1924): 6 (subtitled "Cocktails and Creme de Menthe").
    b. In *The Devil's Notebook* (A.54).

21. "Clark Ashton Smith's Column."
    a. *Auburn Journal* 24, No. 15 (24 January 1924): 6 (subtitled "Cocktails and Creme de Menthe").
    b. In *The Devil's Notebook* (A.54).

22. "Clark Ashton Smith's Column."
    a. *Auburn Journal* 24, No. 16 (31 January 1924): 6 (subtitled "Cocktails and Creme de Menthe").
    b. In *The Devil's Notebook* (A.54).

23. "Clark Ashton Smith's Column."
    a. *Auburn Journal* 24, No. 17 (7 February 1924): 6 (subtitled "Points for the Pious").
    b. In *The Devil's Notebook* (A.54).

24. "Clark Ashton Smith's Column."
    a. *Auburn Journal* 24, No. 19 (21 February 1924): 6 (subtitled "Unpopular Sayings").
    b. In *The Devil's Notebook* (A.54).

25. "Clark Ashton Smith's Column."
    a. *Auburn Journal* 24, No. 20 (28 February 1924): 6 (subtitled "New Teeth for Old Saws").
    b. In *The Devil's Notebook* (A.54).

26. "Clark Ashton Smith's Column."
    a. *Auburn Journal* 24, No. 21 (6 March 1924): 6 (subtitled "The Devil's Note-Book").
    b. In *The Devil's Notebook* (A.54).

27. "Clark Ashton Smith's Column."
    a. *Auburn Journal* 24, No. 22 (13 March 1924): 6 (subtitled "The Devil's Note-Book").
    b. In *The Devil's Notebook* (A.54).

28. "Clark Ashton Smith's Column."
    a. *Auburn Journal* 24, No. 27 (17 April 1924): 6 (subtitled "The Devil's Note-Book").
    b. In *The Devil's Notebook* (A.54).

29. "Clark Ashton Smith's Column."
    a. *Auburn Journal* 24, No. 28 (24 April 1924): 6 (subtitled "The Devil's Note-Book").
    b. In *The Devil's Notebook* (A.54).

30. "Clark Ashton Smith's Column."
    a. *Auburn Journal* 24, No. 29 (1 May 1924): 6 (subtitled "The Devil's Note-Book").
    b. In *The Devil's Notebook* (A.54).

31. "Clark Ashton Smith's Column."
    a. *Auburn Journal* 24, No. 30 (8 May 1924): 6 (subtitled "The Devil's Note-Book").
    b. In *The Devil's Notebook* (A.54).

32. "Clark Ashton Smith's Column."
    a. *Auburn Journal* 24, No. 31 (15 May 1924): 6 (no subtitle).

33. "Clark Ashton Smith's Column."
    a. *Auburn Journal* 24, No. 34 (5 June 1924): 4 (no subtitle).

34. "Clark Ashton Smith's Column."
    a. *Auburn Journal* 24, No. 37 (26 June 1924): 6 (subtitled "The Devil's Note-Book").
    b. In *The Devil's Notebook* (A.54).

35. "Clark Ashton Smith's Column."
    a. *Auburn Journal* 24, No. 38 (3 July 1924): 6 (subtitled "The Devil's Note-Book").
    b. In *The Devil's Notebook* (A.54).

36. "Clark Ashton Smith's Column."
    a. *Auburn Journal* 24, No. 51 (2 October 1924): 6 (subtitled "Paradox and Persiflage").
    b. In *The Devil's Notebook* (A.54).

37. "Clark Ashton Smith's Column."
    a. *Auburn Journal* (6 November 1924): 2 (subtitled "Paradox and Persiflage").

38. "Clark Ashton Smith's Column."
    a. *Auburn Journal* (11 December 1924): 4 (subtitled "Paradox and Persiflage").
    b. In *The Devil's Notebook* (A.54).

39. "Clark Ashton Smith's Column."
    a. *Auburn Journal* (18 December 1924): 14 (subtitled "Selected Epigrams").
    b. In *The Devil's Notebook* (A.54).

40. "Clark Ashton Smith's Column."
    a. *Auburn Journal* 25, No. 13 (8 January 1925): 4 (subtitled "Paradox and Persiflage" and "Selected Paragraphs").
    b. In *The Devil's Notebook* (A.54).

41. "Clark Ashton Smith's Column."
    a. *Auburn Journal* 25, No. 17 (5 February 1925): 4 (subtitled "Paradox and Persiflage").
    b. In *The Devil's Notebook* (A.54).

42. "Clark Ashton Smith's Column."
    a. *Auburn Journal* 25, No. 18 (12 February 1925): 4 (subtitled "Selected Paragraphs").

43. "Clark Ashton Smith's Column."
    a. *Auburn Journal* 25, No. 20 (26 February 1925): 4 (subtitled "Paradox and Persiflage").
    b. In *The Devil's Notebook* (A.54).

44. "Clark Ashton Smith's Column."
   a. *Auburn Journal* 25, No. 21 (5 March 1925): 8 (subtitled "Paradox and Persiflage").
   b. In *The Devil's Notebook* (A.54).

45. "Clark Ashton Smith's Column."
   a. *Auburn Journal* 25, No. 23 (19 March 1925): 4 (no subtitle).

46. "Clark Ashton Smith's Column."
   a. *Auburn Journal* 25, No. 32 (21 May 1925): 7 (subtitled "Paradox and Persiflage" and "Selections").
   b. In *The Devil's Notebook* (A.54).

47. "Clark Ashton Smith's Column."
   a. *Auburn Journal* 25, No. 35 (11 June 1925): 4 (subtitled "Paradox and Persiflage").
   b. In *The Devil's Notebook* (A.54).

48. "A Cosmic Novel."
   a. *Arkham Sampler* 1, No. 4 (Autumn 1948): 88–89.
   b. In *Planets and Dimensions* (A.33).

   Review of Donald Wandrei's *The Web of Easter Island*.

49. "The Decline of Civilization."
   a. *Thrilling Wonder Stories* 11, No. 2 (April 1938): 126.
   b. In *Planets and Dimensions* (A.33).

   A comment on the writing of "The Dark Age."

50. "The Demonian Face."
   a. *Fantasy Fan* 2, No. 3 (November 1934): 39.
   b. In *Planets and Dimensions* (A.33).
   c. In Charles D. Hornig, ed. *The Fantasy Fan: September, 1933–February, 1935*. [n.p.: Lance Thingmaker, 2010.] [Part 2,] 39 (facsimile of a.).

51. "Epigrams."
   a. In *Grotesques and Fantastiques* (A.32).

52. "Epigrams and Apothegms."
   a. In *Spells and Philtres* (A.14).
   b. In *The Devil's Notebook* (A.54).

53.   "The Epigrams of Alastor."
      a.   *Dragon Fly* No. 1 (15 October 1935): [10].
      b.   *International Observer* 2, No. 7 (January 1937): 8.
      c.   In *The Devil's Notebook* (A.54).

54.   "Excerpts from 'The Black Book' of Clark Ashton Smith."
      a.   *Acolyte* 2, No. 2 (Spring 1944): 15–16.
      b.   *Nyctalops* No. 7 (August 1972): 82.
      c.   In *The Black Book of Clark Ashton Smith* (A.39).

55.   "The Favorite Weird Stories of Clark Ashton Smith."
      a.   *Fantasy Fan* 2, No. 4 (December 1934): 55.
      b.   In *Planets and Dimensions* (A.33) (as "The Favorite Weird Sto-
           ries of C. A. Smith").
      c.   In Charles D. Hornig, ed. *The Fantasy Fan: September, 1933–
           February, 1935.* [n.p.: Lance Thingmaker, 2010.] [Part 2,] 55
           (facsimile of a.).

56.   [Fragment of an essay.]
      a.   In *The Sword of Zagan and Other Writings* (A.64).

57.   "George Sterling—An Appreciation."
      a.   *Overland Monthly* 85, No. 3 (March 1927): 79–80.
      b.   In *Planets and Dimensions* (A.33).
      c.   In George Sterling. *The Thirst of Satan: Poems of Fantasy and
           Terror.* New York: Hippocampus Press, 2003. 195–200.
      d.   In *The Shadow of the Unattained* (A.69).

58.   "George Sterling: Poet and Friend."
      a.   *Mirage* 1, No. 6 (Winter 1963–64): 19–24.
      b.   In *Planets and Dimensions* (A.33).
      c.   In *The Shadow of the Unattained* (A.69).

59.   "In Appreciation of William Hope Hodgson."
      a.   *Phantagraph* 5, No. 6 (March–April 1937): 7–8 (abridged).
      b.   *Reader and Collector* 3, No. 3 (June 1944): 7.
      c.   In *Planets and Dimensions* (A.33).
      d.   In John Pelan and Jerad Walters, ed. *Conversations with the
           Weird Tales Circle.* Lakewood, CO: Centipede Press, 2009, 2011.
           63–64.

60. "In Memoriam: H. P. Lovecraft."
    a. *Tesseract* 2, No. 4 (April 1937): 5.
    b. In *Planets and Dimensions* (A.33).
    c. In John Pelan and Jerad Walters, ed. *Conversations with the Weird Tales Circle*. Lakewood, CO: Centipede Press, 2009, 2011. 62 (as part of "On H. P. Lovecraft").

61. "Introduction."
    a. In Susan Myra Gregory. *Shadows of Wings*. San Diego: Troubadour Press, 1930. 7.
    b. In *Strange Shadows* (A.52) (as "Introduction to *Shadows of Wings*").

62. "Introduction to 'The Plutonian Drug.'"
    a. In August Derleth, ed. *The Outer Reaches: Favorite Science-Fiction Stories Chosen by Their Authors*. New York: Pellegrini & Cudahy, 1951. 240.
    a. In *Planets and Dimensions* (A.33) (as "About 'The Plutonian Drug'").

63. "Introduction."
    a. In Lilith Lorraine. *Wine of Wonder*. Dallas: Bookcraft, 1952, dust jacket.
    b. *Avalonian* (Anthology of 1952): 41.
    c. In *Strange Shadows* (A.52) (as "Introduction to *Wine of Wonder*"),

64. "The Kingdom of the Worm: For[e]word."
    a. *Fantasy Fan* 1, No. 2 (October 1933): 17.
    b. In Charles D. Hornig, ed. *The Fantasy Fan: September, 1933–February, 1935*. [n.p.: Lance Thingmaker, 2010.] 17 (facsimile of a.).

65. "Local Boy Makes Good."
    a. *Auburn Journal* (3 November 1941): 1, 4 (unsigned).
    b. *Weird Tales* 36, No. 4 (March 1942): 119–21 (under heading "The Eyrie"; as "Clark Ashton Smith—His Life and Letters").

66. "On Fantasy."
    a. *Fantasy Fan* 2, No. 3 (November 1934): 37, 45.
    b. In *Planets and Dimensions* (A.33).
    c. In *The Emperor of Dreams* (A.59).

d. In Charles D. Hornig, ed. *The Fantasy Fan: September, 1933–February, 1935.* [n.p.: Lance Thingmaker, 2010.] [Part 2,] 37, 45 (facsimile of a.).

67. "[On the Art of Ephraim Doner.]"
   a. In *Strange Shadows* (A.52).

68. "Pertinence and Impertinence."
   a. *Dragon Fly* No. 2 (15 May 1936): 61.
   b. In *The Devil's Notebook* (A.54).

   In b. the two epigrams are scattered without the title from a.

69. "The Philosophy of the Weird Tale."
   a. *Acolyte* 2, No. 4 (Fall 1944): 19.
   b. *Nyctalops* No. 7 (August 1972): 81.
   c. In *Planets and Dimensions* (A.33).

70. "Planets and Dimensions."
   a. *Tales of Wonder* No. 11 (Summer 1940): 95.
   b. In *Planets and Dimensions* (A.33).

71. [Review of Marianne Moore's *Nevertheless.*]
   a. *Wings* 7, No. 1 (Spring 1945): 26.
   b. In *Planets and Dimensions* (A.33).

72. "The Weird Works of M. R. James."
   a. *Fantasy Fan* 1, No. 6 (February 1934): 89–90.
   b. In *Planets and Dimensions* (A.33).
   c. In Charles D. Hornig, ed. *The Fantasy Fan: September, 1933–February, 1935.* [n.p.: Lance Thingmaker, 2010.] 89–90 (facsimile of a.).

73. "Why I Selected—'The Uncharted Isle.'"
   a. In Leo Margulies and Oscar J. Friend, ed. *My Best Science Fiction Story.* New York: Merlin Press, 1949. 402.
   b. In *Planets and Dimensions* (A.33).

vi. Published Letters

a. Multiple Publications

1. "My Dear Friend: Letters of Clark Ashton Smith to George Sterling."
    a. *Mirage* No. 10 (1971): 63–70.

    Contains: Letters to George Sterling, 6 October 1911 (63–65); 12 April 1912 (65–66); 28 April 1912 (66–67); 26 May 1912 (68–69); 9 June 1912 (69–70).

2. "'Dear Éch-Pi-El': Unpublished Letters to H. P. Lovecraft."
    a. *Kadath* No. 1 (1974): 16–19.

    Contains: Extracts of letters to H. P. Lovecraft, "early 1934" (i.e., mid-March 1932) and "June 1934" (i.e., late June 1935).

    The issue was printed but not officially distributed; the editor, Lin Carter, provided copies to a few friends.

3. "Letters from Auburn."
    a. *Klarkash-Ton* No. 1 (June 1988): 16–25.

    Contains: Letters to R. H. Barlow, 16 May 1937 (16–18); to Samuel J. Sackett, 30 June 1949 (18–21); To Samuel J. Sackett, 11 July 1950 (21–23); to L. Sprague de Camp, 21 October 1952 (23–25).

4. "Letters from Auburn."
    a. *Dark Eidolon* No. 2 (July 1989): 28–32.

    Contains: Letters to R. H. Barlow, 16 June 1934 (28–29), 10 September 1934 (29–31), 5 July 1938 (31–32).

b. Individual Publications

1. [To *Munsey's* (c. 1910).]
    a. In *The Sword of Zagan and Other Writings* (A.64).

2. [To the Editor.]
    a. *Sacramento Bee* (21 December 1911): 4 (as "Calls Attacks Unwarranted. An Adrian Apologist Believes He Has Not Been Treated Fairly").

Defends H. A. Adrian of Santa Barbara schools against criticism for his defense of the British Empire during the American Revolution.

3.   [To Edward F. O'Day.]
   a. *Oakland Inquirer* (10 January 1920): 8 (under the heading "Men and Women in the Mirror").

   On George Sterling's dramatic poem *Lilith*.

4.   [To Farnsworth Wright.]
   a. *Weird Tales* 16, No. 1 (July 1930): 10 (under heading "The Eyrie").

5.   [To Farnsworth Wright.]
   a. *Weird Tales* 16, No. 3 (September 1930): 423 (under heading "The Eyrie").

6.   [To Farnsworth Wright.]
   a. *Weird Tales* 16, no. 6 (December 1930): 726, 852 (under heading "The Eyrie").

7.   [To Farnsworth Wright.]
   a. *Weird Tales* 17, No. 2 (February–March 1931): 154 (under heading "The Eyrie").

8.   [To Farnsworth Wright.]
   a. *Weird Tales* 17, No. 3 (April–May 1931): 296, 298 (under heading "The Eyrie").

9.   [To Farnsworth Wright.]
   a. *Oriental Stories* (Spring 1931): 574 (under heading "The Souk").

10.   [To the Editor.]
   a. *Astounding Stories* 7, No. 1 (July 1931): 131–32 (as "Where Fantasy Meets Science Fiction"; under heading "The Reader's Corner").
   b. *Nyctalops* No. 7 (August 1972): 22.
   c. In *Planets and Dimensions* (A.33) (as "[Where Fantasy Meets Science Fiction]").

11.   [To Farnsworth Wright.]
   a. *Weird Tales* 18, No. 3 (October 1931): 298 (under heading "The Eyrie").

12. [To Hugo Gernsback.]
  a. *Wonder Stories* 4, No. 3 (August 1932): 281 (as "C. A. Smith on 'Garbage-Mongering'").
  b. In *Planets and Dimensions* (A.33) (as "[On Garbage-Mongering]").
  c. In *Dawnward Spire, Lonely Hill* (A.86) (as "[On Garbage-Mongering]").

13. [To the Editor.]
  a. *Amazing Stories* 7, No. 7 (October 1932): 670–71 (as "An Answer to Mr. Julian Gray's Recent Criticism in Our Discussions Column").
  b. In *Planets and Dimensions* (A.33) (as "[Fantasy and Human Experience]").
  c. In *Dawnward Spire, Lonely Hill* (A.86) (as "[Fantasy and Human Experience]").

14. [To Harry Bates.]
  a. *Strange Tales of Mystery and Terror* 3, No. 1 (January 1933): 137–38 (as "The Tale of Macrocosmic Horror").
  b. In *Planets and Dimensions* (A.33) (as "[The Tale of Macrocosmic Horror]").
  c. In *Dawnward Spire, Lonely Hill* (A.86) (as "[The Tale of Macrocosmic Horror]").

15. [To Farnsworth Wright.]
  a. *Weird Tales* 21, No. 2 (February 1933): 262 (under heading "The Eyrie").
  b. In *Planets and Dimensions* (A.33) (as "[The Validity of Weird Stories]").
  c. In John Pelan and Jerad Walters, ed. *Conversations with the Weird Tales Circle*. Lakewood, CO: Centipede Press, 2009, 2011. 60 (as "The Validity of Weird Stories").

16. [To Hugo Gernsback.]
  a. *Wonder Stories* 4, No. 9 (February 1933): 735–36 (as "Mr. Smith to Mr. Miller").
  b. In *Planets and Dimensions* (A.33) (as "[Realism and Fantasy]").
  c. In *Dawnward Spire, Lonely Hill* (A.86) (as "[Realism and Fantasy]").

17. [To Farnsworth Wright.]
  a. *Weird Tales* 21, No. 4 (April 1933): 536, 538 (under heading "The Eyrie").

18. [To the Editor.]
   a. *Science Fiction Digest* 2, No. 1 (September 1933) (under heading "The Editor Broadcasts"): 20–21, 23.

19. [To Charles D. Hornig.]
   a. *Fantasy Fan* 1, No. 1 (September 1933): 2 (under heading "Well Wishes").
   b. In Charles D. Hornig, ed. *The Fantasy Fan: September, 1933–February, 1935.* [n.p.: Lance Thingmaker, 2010.] 2 (under heading "Well Wishes"; facsimile of a.).

20. [To the Editor.]
   a. *San Francisco Chronicle* (25 September 1933): 8 (as "In Such Cases We Are All Jurors").

21. [To Charles D. Hornig.]
   a. *Fantasy Fan* 1, No. 2 (October 1933): 14 (under heading "Our Readers Say").
   b. In Charles D. Hornig, ed. *The Fantasy Fan: September, 1933–February, 1935.* [n.p.: Lance Thingmaker, 2010.] 14 (under heading "Our Readers Say"; facsimile of a.).

22. [To Charles D. Hornig.]
   a. *Fantasy Fan* 1, No. 2 (October 1933): 27 (under heading "The Boiling Point").
   b. In *Planets and Dimensions* (A.33) (as part of "Horror, Fantasy, and Science").
   c. In [Marc A. Michaud, ed.] *The Boiling Point.* West Warwick, RI: Necronomicon Press, 1985. [4].
   d. In Charles D. Hornig, ed. *The Fantasy Fan: September, 1933–February, 1935.* [n.p.: Lance Thingmaker, 2010.] [Part 2,] 27 (under heading "The Boiling Point"; facsimile of a.).
   e. In *Dawnward Spire, Lonely Hill* (A.86).

23. [To Charles D. Hornig.]
   a. *Fantasy Fan* 1, No. 3 (November 1933): 33 (under heading "Our Readers Say").
   b. In Charles D. Hornig, ed. *The Fantasy Fan: September, 1933–February, 1935.* [n.p.: Lance Thingmaker, 2010.] 33 (under heading "Our Readers Say"; facsimile of a.).

24. [To Charles D. Hornig.]
   a. *Fantasy Fan* 1, No. 3 (November 1933): 38 (under heading "Startling Fact").
   b. In *Planets and Dimensions* (A.33) (as "[On the Forbidden Books]").
   c. *Dark Eidolon* No. 2 (July 1989): 20 (as "Startling Fact").
   d. In Charles D. Hornig, ed. *The Fantasy Fan: September, 1933–February, 1935.* [n.p.: Lance Thingmaker, 2010.] 38 (under heading "Startling Fact"; facsimile of a.).
   e. In *Dawnward Spire, Lonely Hill* (A.86) (as "[On the Forbidden Books]").

25. [To Charles D. Hornig.]
   a. *Fantasy Fan* 1, No. 5 (January 1934): 78 (under heading "Our Readers Say").
   b. In Charles D. Hornig, ed. *The Fantasy Fan: September, 1933–February, 1935.* [n.p.: Lance Thingmaker, 2010.] 78 (under heading "Our Readers Say"; facsimile of a.).

26. [To Charles D. Hornig.]
   a. *Fantasy Fan* 1, No. 6 (February 1934): 81–82 (under heading "Our Readers Say").
   b. In Charles D. Hornig, ed. *The Fantasy Fan: September, 1933–February, 1935.* [n.p.: Lance Thingmaker, 2010.] 81–82 (under heading "Our Readers Say"; facsimile of a.).

27. [To Charles D. Hornig.]
   a. *Fantasy Fan* 1, No. 6 (February 1934): 93 (under heading "The Boiling Point").
   b. In *Planets and Dimensions* (A.33) (as part of "Horror, Fantasy, and Science").
   c. In [Marc A. Michaud, ed.] *The Boiling Point.* West Warwick, RI: Necronomicon Press, 1985. [10].
   d. In Charles D. Hornig, ed. *The Fantasy Fan: September, 1933–February, 1935.* [n.p.: Lance Thingmaker, 2010.] 93 (under heading "The Boiling Point"; facsimile of a.).
   e. In *Dawnward Spire, Lonely Hill* (A.86).

28. [To Charles D. Hornig.]
   a. *Fantasy Fan* 1, No. 7 (March 1934): 97 (under heading "Our Readers Say").

b. In Charles D. Hornig, ed. *The Fantasy Fan: September, 1933–February, 1935.* [n.p.: Lance Thingmaker, 2010.] 97 (under heading "Our Readers Say"; facsimile of a.).

29. [To Charles D. Hornig.]
a. *Fantasy Fan* 1, No. 8 (April 1934): 113 (under heading "Our Readers Say").
b. In Charles D. Hornig, ed. *The Fantasy Fan: September, 1933–February, 1935.* [n.p.: Lance Thingmaker, 2010.] 113 (under heading "Our Readers Say"; facsimile of a.).

30. [To Charles D. Hornig.]
a. *Fantasy Fan* 1, No. 9 (May 1934): 127–28 (under heading "Our Readers Say").
b. In *Planets and Dimensions* (A.33) (as "[The Psychology of the Horror Story]").
c. In Charles D. Hornig, ed. *The Fantasy Fan: September, 1933–February, 1935.* [n.p.: Lance Thingmaker, 2010.] 127–28 (under heading "Our Readers Say"; facsimile of a.).

31. [To Charles D. Hornig.]
a. *Fantasy Fan* 1, No. 10 (June 1934): 145 (under heading "Our Readers Say").
b. In Charles D. Hornig, ed. *The Fantasy Fan: September, 1933–February, 1935.* [n.p.: Lance Thingmaker, 2010.] 145 (under heading "Our Readers Say"; facsimile of a.).

32. [To Charles D. Hornig.]
a. *Fantasy Fan* 1, No. 11 (July 1934): 162 (under heading "Our Readers Say").
b. In Charles D. Hornig, ed. *The Fantasy Fan: September, 1933–February, 1935.* [n.p.: Lance Thingmaker, 2010.] 162 (under heading "Our Readers Say"; facsimile of a.).

33. [To Charles D. Hornig.]
a. *Fantasy Fan* 1, No. 12 (August 1934): 178 (under heading "Our Readers Say").
b. In Charles D. Hornig, ed. *The Fantasy Fan: September, 1933–February, 1935.* [n.p.: Lance Thingmaker, 2010.] 178 (under heading "Our Readers Say"; facsimile of a.).

34. [To Duane W. Rimel (13 September 1934).]
    a. In H. P. Lovecraft and Divers Hands. *Something about Cats and Other Pieces*. Ed. August Derleth. Sauk City, WI: Arkham House, 1949; Freeport, NY: Books for Libraries Press, 1971. 169.

    A comment on "The Battle That Ended the Century," by H. P. Lovecraft and R. H. Barlow.

35. [To Charles D. Hornig.]
    a. *Fantasy Fan* 2, No. 3 (November 1934): 35 (under heading "Our Readers Say").
    b. In Charles D. Hornig, ed. *The Fantasy Fan: September 1933–February 1935*. [n.p.: Lance Thingmaker, 2010.] [Part 2,] 35 (under heading "Our Readers Say"; facsimile of a.).

36. [To Farnsworth Wright.]
    a. *Weird Tales* 25, No. 5 (May 1935): 656 (under heading "The Eyrie").

37. [To Farnsworth Wright.]
    a. *Weird Tales* 28, No. 5 (December 1936): 638 (under heading "The Eyrie").
    b. *Tales from the Pulps* No. 5 (15 May 2016): 126 (facsimile of a.).

38. [To Claire Beck.]
    a. *Science-Fiction Critic* No. 9 (May 1937): 1–2 (under heading "A Note from the Editor").
    b. In *Planets and Dimensions* (A.33) (as "[On H. P. Lovecraft—II]").
    c. In John Pelan and Jerad Walters, ed. *Conversations with the Weird Tales Circle*. Lakewood, CO: Centipede Press, 2009, 2011. 61–62 (as part of "On H. P. Lovecraft").

39. [To Farnsworth Wright.]
    a. *Weird Tales* 30, No. 1 (July 1937): 122 (under heading "The Eyrie").
    b. *Golden Atom* 1, No. 9 (December 1940): 15 (as "From Clark Ashton Smith").
    c. In *Planets and Dimensions* (A.33) (as "[On H. P. Lovecraft—I]").
    d. In Peter Cannon, ed. *Lovecraft Remembered*. Sauk City, WI: Arkham House, 1998. 284 (as "Letter to *Weird Tales*").

    e. In John Pelan and Jerad Walters, ed. *Conversations with the Weird Tales Circle.* Lakewood, CO: Centipede Press, 2009, 2011. 61 (as part of "On H. P. Lovecraft").

40. [To the Editor.]
    a. *Sacramento Bee* (19 May 1938): 26 (as "Deplores Harsh Criticism of Symphony Concert").

41. [To Farnsworth Wright.]
    a. *Weird Tales* 33, No. 5 (May 1939): 154 (under heading "The Eyrie").

42. [To Farnsworth Wright.]
    a. *Weird Tales* 34, No. 5 (November 1939): 129 (under heading "The Eyrie").

43. [To Farnsworth Wright.]
    a. *Weird Tales* 35, No. 1 (January 1940): 127 (under heading "The Eyrie").

44. [To Larry Farsaci.]
    a. *Golden Atom* 1, No. 5 (February 1940): 28.

45. [To Larry Farsaci.]
    a. *Golden Atom* 1, No. 8 (May 1940): 3

46. [To Francis T. Laney.]
    a. *Acolyte* 1, No. 3 (Spring 1943): 28 (in column "Cracks—Wise and Otherwise").

47. [To the Editor.]
    a. *Diablerie* (February 1944): 17.

48. [To R. H. Barlow.]
    a. *Acolyte* 2, No. 3 (Summer 1944): 9–10 (as "The Family Tree of the Gods").
    b. In H. P. Lovecraft and Divers Hands. *The Shuttered Room and Other Pieces.* Ed. August Derleth. Sauk City, WI: Arkham House, 1959. 274–76 (without title; in T. G. L. Cockcroft's "Addendum: Some Observations on the Carter Glossary").
    c. In *Planets and Dimensions* (A.33) (as "The Family Tree of the Gods").

49. [To R. A. Hoffman.]
   a. *Acolyte* 3, No. 1 (Winter 1945): 28 (in column "Fantasy Forum").

50. [To August Derleth.]
   a. *Arkham Sampler* 1, No. 2 (Spring 1948): 50–51 (as "From a Letter").
   b. In *Planets and Dimensions* (A.33) (as "[On Grotesque Carvings]").

51. [To August Derleth.]
   a. *Arkham Sampler* 2, No. 2 (Spring 1949): 96–97 (under heading "Letters to the Editor").
   b. In *Planets and Dimensions* (A.33) (as "[On Science Fiction History]").

52. [To Robert E. Briney.]
   a. In Robert E. Briney. "Professionally Published Works." *The Lovecraft Collectors Library, Volume VII: Bibliographies,* ed. George T. Wetzel. North Tonawanda, NY: SSR Publications, 1955. 36–37.
   b. In Robert E. Briney. "Professionally Published Works." *Howard Phillips Lovecraft: Memoirs, Critiques, Bibliographies,* ed. George T. Wetzel. North Tonawanda, NY: SSR Publications, 1955. 77–78.
   c. In *Planets and Dimensions* (A.33) (as "[On Tales about the Cthulhu Mythos]").

53. [To the Editor.]
   a. *Epos* 8, No. 1 (Fall 1956): 27 (as "The Poet Speaks").

vii. Published Artwork

1. "An Afreet" [drawing].
    a. In *The Last Oblivion* (A.61) (p. 3).

2. "The Basilisk" [painting].
    a. In *Shadows Seen and Unseen* (A.71) (p. 61).

3. "CAS Self-Portrait."
    a. In Robert Weinberg. *The Weird Tales Story* West Linn, OR: FAX Collector's Editions; 1977; Holicong, PA: Wildside Press, 1999. 31.

4. [Carvings.]
    a. In H. P. Lovecraft. *Beyond the Wall of Sleep.* Sauk City, WI: Arkham House, 1943. Front cover of dust jacket.
    b. In Randy Broeker, Robert Weinberg, and Frank Robinson. *Art of Imagination: 20th Century Visions of Science Fiction, Horror, and Fantasy.* Portland, OR: Collectors Press, 2002. 377.
    c. In Richard Gilliam, ed. *Architecture of Fantasy and Horror.* n.p.: World Fantasy Convention, 2005. 80.
    d. *Windy City Pulp Stories* No. 15 (2015): 34.

    The photograph of the carvings is by Burt Trimpey.

5. [Carvings.]
    a. In *Lost Worlds* (A.10). Front cover of dust jacket.
    b. In Richard Gilliam, ed. *Architecture of Fantasy and Horror.* n.p.: World Fantasy Convention, 2005. 86.

    The photograph of the carvings is by Burt Trimpey of carvings.

6. [Carvings.]
    a. In *The Selected Letters of Clark Ashton Smith* (A.63). Front cover of dust jacket.

7. "The Charnel God" [interior artwork].
    a. *Weird Tales* 23, No. 3 (March 1934): 316–30.
    b. In *Tales of Zothique* (A.56) (p. 41).
    c. In *In the Realms of Mystery and Wonder* (A.87) (p. 229).

8. "The Colossus of Ylourgne" [interior artwork].
    a. *Weird Tales* 23, No. 6 (June 1934): 696–720.
    b. *Magazine of Horror* 4, No. 2 (January 1969): 80–113.
    c. In *In the Realms of Mystery and Wonder* (A.87) (p. 230).

9. "The Dark Eidolon" [interior artwork].
    a. *Weird Tales* 25, No. 1 (January 1935): 93–111.
    b. In *Tales of Zothique* (A.56) (p. 56).
    c. In *In the Realms of Mystery and Wonder* (A.87) (p. 231).

10. "The Death of Malygris" [interior artwork].
    a. *Weird Tales* 30, No. 3 (April 1934): 488–96.
    b. In Robert Weinberg. *The Weird Tales Story*. West Linn, OR: FAX Collector's Editions, 1977; Holicong, PA: Wildside Press, 1999. 88.
    c. In Farnsworth Wright, ed. *Weird Tales, Volume 30, Number 3 (April 1934)*. Mississauga, ON: Girasol Collectables, 2014. 488–95 (facsimile of a.).
    d. In *In the Realms of Mystery and Wonder* (A.87) (p. 232).

11. "Entity from Algol" [painting?].
    a. In Emil Petaja, ed. *The Hannes Bok Memorial Showcase of Fantasy Art*. San Francisco: SISU, 1974. 76.

12. "Estuary" [painting].
    a. *Lost Worlds* No. 2 (2004): front cover.

13. "Lilith."
    a. In "Pro/Fan Art Portfolio: Robert E. Howard's Women Characters." *Fantasy Crossroads* No. 3 (May 1975): 10.

    The drawing dates to 1920.

14. "The Lurking Fear" by H. P. Lovecraft [interior illustrations].
    a. *Home Brew* 2, No. 6 (January 1923): 4–10; 3, No. 1 (February 1923): 18–23; 3, No. 2 (March 1923): 31–37, 44, 48; 3, No. 3 (April 1923): 35–42.
    b. In John E. Vetter. "Lovecraft's Illustrators." In H. P. Lovecraft et al. *The Dark Brotherhood and Other Pieces*. Sauk City, WI: Arkham House, 1966. Facing p. 274 (2 illustrations only).
    c. In H. P. Lovecraft. *The Lurking Fear*. West Warwick, RI: Necronomicon Press, 1977 (facsimile of a.).

  d. In *In the Realms of Mystery and Wonder* (A.87) (p. 234) [one illustration ("Gryphon Gazing upon the Gulf") only].

15. "Moonlight on Boulder Ridge" [painting].
  a. *Lost Worlds* No. 1 (2004): front cover.
  b. In *Shadows Seen and Unseen* (A.71) (p. 82).

16. "Plants" [painting].
  a. In *Shadows Seen and Unseen* (A.71) (p. 30).

17. "The Seven Geases" [interior artwork].
  a. *Weird Tales* 24, No. 4 (October 1934): 422–35.
  b. In *The Book of Hyperborea* (A.58) [back cover].
  c. In Farnsworth Wright, ed. *Weird Tales, Volume 24, Number 4 (October 1934)*. Mississauga, ON: Girasol Collectables, 2014. 422–35 (facsimile of a.).
  d. In *In the Realms of Mystery and Wonder* (A.87) (p. 201).

18. [Self-portrait.]
  a. Artwork on back panel of dust jacket of *Other Dimensions* (A.24).

19. "Spring Clouds" [painting].
  a. In *Shadows Seen and Unseen* (A.71) (p. 10).

20. "The Spy" [painting].
  a. In *Shadows Seen and Unseen* (A.71) (p. 17).
  a. In *The Dark Eidolon and Other Fantasies* (A.84). Front cover.

21. "Uranus" [painting].
  a. *Lost Worlds* No. 3 (2006): front cover (abridged), 1.

  Reprinted from *Grotesques and Fantastiques* (A.32).

22. "Venusian Landscape" [painting].
  a. *Lost Worlds* No. 5 (2008): front cover (abridged), 47.

23. "The Weaver in the Vault" [interior artwork].
  a. *Weird Tales* 23, No. 1 (January 1934): 85–93.
  b. In *Tales of Zothique* (A.56) (p. 95).
  c. In *In the Realms of Mystery and Wonder* (A.87) (p. 233).

24. "Xeethra" [interior artwork].
  a. *Weird Tales* 24, No. 6 (December 1934): 726–38.

  b. In *Tales of Zothique* (A.56) (p. 114).
  c. In Farnsworth Wright, ed. *Weird Tales, Volume 24, Number 6 (December 1934)*. Mississauga, ON: Girasol Collectables, 2013. 726–38 (facsimile of a.).
  d. In *In the Realms of Mystery and Wonder* (A.87) (p. 234).

25. "Young Ghoul" [carving].
  a. In *Shadows Seen and Unseen* (A.71).

26. [Untitled drawing.]
  a. In Lin Carter. *History & Chronology of the Book of Eibon*. New York: Charnel House, 1984. Front cover.

27. [Untitled drawing.]
  a. In Les Daniels. *Living in Fear: A History of Horror in the Mass Media*. New York: Scribner's, 1975; New York: Da Capo Press, 1983. 124.

  Not included in the British reprint (London: Paladin, 1977).

28. [Untitled drawings.]
  a. *Nyctalops* No. 7 (August 1972): 22, 70 [self-portrait], 71, 73 [two drawings], 74 [two drawings], 75 [two drawings], 78, 80 [two drawings], 83, outside back cover ["C A S"].

29. [Untitled drawings.]
  a. *Lost Worlds* No. 3 (2006): 12, 13, 18, 21, 25, 28, 31, 35, 39.

  Reprinted from *Grotesques and Fantastiques* (A.32).

30. [Untitled drawings?]
  a. In Gerry de la Ree, ed. *The Art of the Fantastic*. Saddle River, NJ: Gerry de la Ree, 1978. 124–26.

  A portfolio of 10 drawings.

31. [Untitled paintings.]
  a. In *The Last Oblivion* (A.61). Front cover and two paintings between pp. 128–29.

32. [Untitled painting.]
  a. *Lost Worlds* No. 4 (2006): front cover (abridgd), 1.

  Reprinted from *Grotesques and Fantastiques* (A.32).

viii. Miscellany

1.   [Advertisement for *Ebony and Crystal.*]
     a.   *Auburn Journal* (20 November 1924): 4.

2.   [Advertisement for carvings.]
     a.   *Science-Fiction Critic* 1, No. 8 (March 1937): 8–9 (as "Clark Ashton Smith's Carvings: Available as Replics").
     b.   *Science-Fiction Critic* 1, No. 9 (May 1937): 8.

3.   [Advertisement for *The Double Shadow and Other Fantasies.*]
     a.   Separate flyer. [1933], 1 page.

     Advertises *The Double Shadow* for 25¢ and also offering remaining copies of *Ebony and Crystal* for $1.00

4.   [Advertisement for *The Double Shadow and Other Fantasies.*]
     a.   *Weird Tales* 22, No. 1 (July 1933): 141.
     b.   *Weird Tales* 22, No. 5 (November 1933): 655.
     c.   *Weird Tales* 22, No. 6 (December 1933): 783.
     d.   *Weird Tales* 23, No. 1 (January 1934): 143.

5.   [Advertisement for *The Double Shadow and Other Fantasies* and *Ebony and Crystal.*].]
     a.   *Science Fiction Digest* 2, No. 1 (September 1933): 25.
     b.   *Science Fiction Digest* 2, No. 2 (October 1933): [25].
     c.   *Fantasy Fan* 1, No. 2 (October 1933): 32 (repeated until the February 1935 issue).
     d.   In Charles D. Hornig, ed. *The Fantasy Fan: September, 1933–February, 1935.* [n.p.: Lance Thingmaker, 2010.] 32 (facsimile of c.).

6.   [Advertisement for *The Double Shadow and Other Fantasies.*]
     a.   *Acolyte* 2, No. 2 (Spring 1944): 29.

7.   [Advertisement for piece work typing.]
     a.   *Auburn Journal* (23 April 1925): 3.
     b.   *Auburn Journal* (7 May 1925): 12.
     c.   *Auburn Journal* (14 May 1925): 12.
     d.   *Auburn Journal* (21 May 1925): 14.
     e.   *Auburn Journal* (28 May 1925): 12.

    f. *Auburn Journal* (4 June 1925): 12.
    g. *Auburn Journal* (11 June 1925): 12.

8.   [Advertisement for "typing done at regular rates."]
    a. *Auburn Journal* (25 October 1928): 8.

9.   [Advertisement reducing *Ebony and Crystal* to $1.50.]
    a. *Auburn Journal* (25 December 1924): 6.
    b. *Auburn Journal* (1 January 1925): 2.

10.   [Crossword puzzles.]
    a. In *Dawnward Spire, Lonely Hill* (A.86).

II. Works by Smith in Translation

A. Books and Pamphlets

i. Dutch

1. *De kolos van Ylourgne.* Edited by Aart C. Prins.
   a. Utrecht: A. W. Bruna & zoon, 1971. 192 pp.

   Contents: "De soriijjes van klarkash-ton" by Aart C. Prins (5–7); "De priesters van mordiggian"("The Charnel God" [tr. Henk J. Bouwman]) (8–35); "Moeder per padden" ("Mother of Toads" [tr. F. Lancel]) (36–45); "De dubbele schaduw" ("The Double Shadow" [tr. F. Lancel]) (46–60); "Het rijk van de dodenbezweerders" ("The Empire of the Necromancers" [tr. J. B. de Mare]) (61–71); "Het zaad uit het graf" ("The Seed from the Sepulcher" [tr. R. Germeraad]) (72–86); "De wever in de catacomben" ("The Weaver in the Vault" [tr. R. Germeraad]) (87–102); "De openbaring van de dood" ("The Epiphany of Death" [tr. J. B. de Mare]) (103–9); "De verschrikkingen van Yondo" ("The Abominations of Yondo" [tr. M. Slagt-Prins]) (110–18); "De zwarte abt van Puthuum" ("The Black Abbot of Puthuum" [tr. M. Slagt-Prins]) (119–45); "De kolos van Ylourgne" ("The Colossus of Ylourgne" [tr. W. G. Voges]) (146–92).
   Notes. Bound in paper. Cover artwork by Bob van Bloomestein.

2. *De gewelven van Yoh-Vombis.* Edited by Aart C. Prins.
   a. Utrecht: A. W. Bruna & Zoon, 1975. 302 pp.

   Contents: "Genius Loci" ("Genius Loci" [tr. Lon Falger]) (7–26); "Het testament van Athammaus" ("The Testament of Athammaus") (27–48); "De laatste bezwering" ("The Last Incantation") (49–54); "De terugkeer van de magiër" ("The Return of the Sorcerer") (55–72); "De wortel van Ampoi" ("The Root of Ampoi" [tr. W. G. Voges]) (73–90); "De heiligheid van Azédarac" ("The Holiness of Azédarac") (91–113); "Xeethra" (114–35); "De doolhof van Maal Dweb" ("The Maze of Maal Dweb") (136–50); "De verschrikking van Venus" ("The Disinterment of Venus" [tr. M. Slagt-Prins]) (151–68); "Het licht op de heuvel" ("The Secret of the Cairn") (169–91); "Het zwarte afgodsbeeld" ("The Dark Eidolon") (192–222); "De zeven betoveringen" ("The Seven Geases") (223–45); "De reis van de koning Euvoran" ("The Voyage of King Euvoran" [tr. Ef Leonard]) (246–72); "De glijider in het stof" ("The Treader of the Dust") (273–81); "De

gewelven van Yoh-Vombis" ("The Vaults of Yoh-Vombis'")
(282–300); "Naschrift" (final part of "The Vaults of Yoh-Vombis"
erroneously set apart from the main text, 301–2).

> Notes. Bound in paper. Translated by Heleen ten Holt save
> where indicated. Cover artwork by Bob van Bloomestein.

3. *Zothique en andere verlorn werelden.* Edited by E. L. de Marigny
    [*pseud.*].
    a. Amsterdam: Meulenhoff, 1983. 215 pp.

> *Contents: Zothique:* "Het eukand der folteraars" ("The Isle of the
> Torturers") (9–27); "De tuin van Adompha" ("The Garden of
> Adompha") (28–39); "De gebieder der krabben" ("The Master of
> the Crabs") (40–55); "Morthylla" (56–67); "Het grafgebroed"
> ("The Tomb-Spawn") (68–79); "De hekserij van Ulua" ("The
> Witchcraft of Ulua") (80–91); *Xiccarph:* "De bloemvrouwen"
> ("The Flower-Women") (95–108); *Poseidonis:* "De dood van
> Malygris" ("The Death of Malygris") (111–25); *Hyperborea:* "De
> deur tot Saturnus" ("The Door to Saturn") (129–51); "Het noo-
> dlot van Avoosl Wuthoqquan" ("The Weird of Avoosl Wuth-
> oqquan") (152–61); "De witte Sibylle" ("The White Sybil")
> (162–72); "De duefstal van dertig-en-negen gordels" ("The Theft
> of the Thirty-nine Girdles") (173–85); "Het relaas van Satampra
> Zeiros" ("The Tale of Satampra Zeiros") (186–200); "De komst
> van de Witte Worm" ("The Coming of the White Worm")
> (201–15).

> *Notes.* Bound in paper. Translated by Jaime Martijn. Cover
> artwork by Eric Ladd. "E. L. de Marigny" is a pseudonym derived
> from a character in "Through the Gates of the Silver Key," by
> H. P. Lovecraft and E. Hoffmann Price.

ii. Finnish

1. *Viimeinen hieroglyfi.* Edited by Markku Sadelehto.
    a. Helsinki: Werner Söderström, 1994. 305 pp.

> *Contents:* "Esipuhe" by Markku Sadelehto (7–12); "Laulavan
> liekin kaupunki" ("The City of the Singing Flame") (13–34);
> "Saturnuksen portti" ("The Door to Saturn") (34–54); "Valkoi-
> nen mato" ("The Coming of the White Worm") (55–68); "Jä-
> ädemoni" ("The Ice-Demon") (69–85); "Viimeinen loitsu" ("The
> Last Incantation") (86–91); "Malygriksen kuolema" ("The Death
> of Malygris") (92–106); "Kaksoisvarjo" ("The Double Shadow")

(107–20); "Xeethra" (121–42); "Kuolleiden jumala" ("The Charnel God") (143–68); "Musta seitti" ("The Dark Eidolon") (169–97); "Viimeinen hieroglyfi" ("The Last Hieroglyph") (198–215); "Noitien Naat" ("Necromancy in Naat") (216–36); "Adomphan puutarha" ("The Garden of Adompha") (237–47); "Kiduttajien saari" ("The Isle of the Torturers") (248–65); "Ennustuksen hirviö" ("The Monster of the Prophecy") (266–305).

Notes. Bound in paper. Translated by Ilkka Äärelä. Cover art by Jukka Murtosaari.

iii. French

1. *Autres Dimensions.*
   a. Paris: Christian Bourgois, June 1974. 383 pp.

   Contents: "Abandonnés dans l'Andromède" ("Marooned in Andromeda") (7–39); "L'Étonnante Planète" ("The Amazing Planet") (41–86); "Une Aventure dans le futur" ("An Adventure in Futurity") (87–125); "L'Incommensurable Horreur" ("The Immeasurable Horror") (127–42); "La Ville invisible" ("The Invisible City") (143–65); "La Dimension du hasard" ("The Dimension of Chance") (167–92); "La Métamorphose de la terre" ("The Metamorphosis of the World") (193–223); "Tel phénix" ("Phoenix") (225–35); "Le Conte de nécromancie" ("The Necromantic Tale") (237–48); "La Vénus d'Azombeii" ("The Venus of Azombeii") (249–75); "La Résurrection du serpent à sonnette" ("The Resurrection of the Rattlesnake") (277–82); "Le Cadavre en trop" ("The Supernumerary Corpse") (283–91); "Les Mandragores" ("The Mandrakes") (293–300); "Treize fantasmes" ("Thirteen Phantasms") (301–4); "Une Offrande à la lune" ("An Offering to the Moon") (305–16); "Les Monstres de la nuit" ("Monsters in the Night") (317–20); "Le Kriss malais" ("The Malay Krise") (321–23); "Le Fantôme de Mohammed Din" ("The Ghost of Mohammed Din") (325–31); "Le Cornac" ("The Mahout") (333–39); "Le Rajah et le tigre" ("The Raja and the Tiger") (341–47); "Quelque chose de nouveau" ("Something New") (349–51); "La Justice de l'éléphant" ("The Justice of the Elephant") (353–56); "Le Baiser de Zoraida" ("The Kiss of Zoraida") (357–62); "Un Conte de Sir John Maundeville" ("A Tale of Sir John Maundeville") (363–70); "La Goule" ("The Ghoul") (371–76); "Conte du désert" ("Told in the Desert") (377–83).

Notes. Bound in paper. Translation of *Other Dimensions* (I.A.24). Translated by Gloria de Cherisey.

2.   *Zothique.*
   a.   Paris: Librairie des Champs-Élysées, 1978. 254 pp.

   Contents: "Avant-propos" by Jean-Baptiste Baronian; "Les Nécromanciens de Naat" ("Necromancy in Naat") (7–32); "Morthylla" (33–45); "Le Dieu carnivore" ("The Charnel God") (46–73); "La Fileuse de momies" ("The Weaver in the Vault") (74–89); "Le Maître des crabes" ("The Master of the Crabs") (90–107); "Les Charmes d'Ulua" ("The Witchcraft of Ulua") (108–21); "Le Supérieur noire de Puthuum" ("The Black Abbot of Puthuum") (122–50); "Le Frai de la tombe" ("The Tomb Spawn") (151–64); "Le Dernier Hiéroglyphe" ("The Last Hieroglyph") (165–85); "Le Jardin d'Adompha" ("The Garden of Adompha") (186–98); "L'Île des tortionnaires" ("The Isle of the Torturers") (199–218); "L'Idole noire" ("The Dark Eidolon") (219–54).

   Notes. Bound in paper. Translated by Françoise Levie. Cover artwork by Tibor Csernus.

3.   *Poséidonis.*
   a.   Paris: Librairie des Champs-Élysées, March 1981. 245 pp.

   Contents: "La Magie de l'Atlantide" by Lin Carter; *Poséidonis:* "La Muse de l'Atlantide" ("The Muse of Atlantis") (21–22); "La Dernière Incantation" ("The Last Incantation") (23–30); "La Mort de Malygris" ("The Death of Malygris") (31–50); "L'Ombre double" ("The Double Shadow") (51–70); "Cap sur Sfanomoë" ("A Voyage to Sfanomoë") (71–83); "Un Grand Cru d'Atlantide" ("A Vintage from Atlantis") (85–95); *La Lémurie:* "Offrande à la lune" ("An Offering to the Moon") (101–17); "L'Île inconnue" ("The Uncharted Isle") (119–35); *Ptolémides:* "L'Epiphanie de la mort" ("The Epiphany of Death") (141–48); *Autres Royaumes:* "Au pays de Cocagne" ("In Cocaigne") (153–54); "Le Festin de la Gorgone" ("Symposium of the Gorgon") (155–68); "La Vénus d'Azombéii" ("The Venus of Azombeii") (169–208); "La Racine d'Ampoï" ("The Root of Ampoi") (209–31); "Le Paysage aux saules" ("The Willow Landscape") (233–40); "Les Ombres" ("The Shadows") (241–43).

   Notes. Bound in paper. Translation of *Poseidonis* (I.A.34). Translated by Dominique Mols.

4. *L'Île inconnue.*
   a. Paris: Nouvelles Éditions Oswald, 1985. 181 pp.

   Contents: "Introduction: Pour saluer Clark Ashton Smith maître des rêves et des cauchemars, des dêmons et des merveilles, guide initiatique et génie visionnaire, créateur de mondes fabuleux . . ." by François Truchaud (5–10); *Récis venus de l'espace et du temps:* "La Fin de l'histoire" ("The End of the Story" [tr. Dominique Mols]) (15–33); "Un Rendez-vous en Averoigne" ("A Rendez-vous in Averoigne" [tr. Xavier Perret]) (34–48); "Une Nuit à Malnéant" ("A Night in Malnéant" [tr. Xavier Perret]) (49–55); "La Cité de la flamme chantante" ("The City of the Singing Flame" [tr. France-Marie Watkins]) (56–96); "L'Île inconnue" ("The Uncharted Isle" [tr. Dominique Mols]) (97–108); *Histoires de jugements et de condamnations:* "Les Funérailles de Sir Magbane" ("The Second Interment" [tr. Xavier Perret]) (111–22); "L'Ombre double" ("The Double Shadow" [tr. Dominique Mols]) (123–37); "Les Chaînes de feu" ("The Chain of Aforgomon" [tr. Xavier Perret]) (138–55); "L'Idole noire" ("The Dark Eidolon" [tr. Françoise Levie]) (156–81); "Bibliographie" (183).
   Notes. Bound in paper. Cover art by Jean-Michel Nicollet. Translation of the first half of *Out of Space and Time* (I.A.9). The ending of "L'Idole noire" was accidentally omitted and was included in item 5.

5. *Ubbo-Sathla.*
   a. Paris: Nouvelles Éditions Oswald, 1985. 180 pp.

   Contents: "Introduction: Décadence et romantisme" by Xavier Perret (5–9); *Histoires de jugements et de condamnations:* "L'Idole noire (la véritable fin)" ("The Dark Eidolon" [true ending] [tr. Xavier Perret]) (13–14); "Le Dernier Hiéroglyphe" ("The Last Hieroglyph" [tr. Françoise Levie]) (15–31); "Sadastor" (tr. Xavier Perret) (32–36); "La Mort d'Ilalotha" ("The Death of Ilalotha" [tr. France-Marie Watkins]) (37–48); "Le Retour du sorcier" ("The Return of the Sorcerer" [tr. Jacques Parsons]) (49–66); *Visions grotesques d'Hyperborée;* "Le Témoignage d'Athammaus" ("The Testament of Athammaus" [tr. Xavier Perret]) (69–89); "Le Destin d'Avoosl Wuthoqquan" ("The Weird of Avoosl Wuthoqquan" [tr. Xavier Perret]) (90–99); "Ubbo-Sathla" (tr. Claude Gilbert) (100–109); *Récits interplanétaires:* "Le Monstre de la prophétie" ("The Monster of the Prophecy" [tr. Xavier Perret]) (113–51); "Les Caveaux de Yoh-Vombis" ("The Vaults of

Yoh-Vombis" [tr. Xavier Perret]) (152–71); "Dans les cryptes du souvenir" ("From the Crypts of Memory" [tr. Xavier Perret]) (172–74); "Les ombres" ("The Shadows" [tr. Dominique Mols]) (175–77); "Bibliographie" (179).

Notes. Bound in paper. Cover art by Jean-Michel Nicollet. Translation of the second half of *Out of Space and Time* (I.A.9).

6.   *L'empire des nécromants.*
a.   Paris: Nouvelles Éditions Oswald, 1986. 213 pp.
b.   Paris: Société d'Édition des Belles Lettres, September 1998. 271 pp.

Contents: "Introduction: Les Cycles d'un magicien du langage" by Jean-Luc Buard (5–9); *Hyperborée:* "L'Histoire de Satampra Zeiros" ("The Tale of Satampra Zeiros" [tr. Yves Le Brun]) (15–27); "La Porte sur Saturne" ("The Door to Saturn" [tr. Yves Le Brun]) (28–46); "Les Sept Sortilèges" ("The Seven Geases" [tr. Yves Le Brun]) (47–67); "La Venue du ver blanc" ("The Coming of the White Worm" [tr. Yves Le Brun]) (68–81); *Atlantide:* "La Dernière Incantation" ("The Last Incantation" [tr. Dominique Mols]) (85–90); "Cap sur Sfanomoë" ("A Voyage to Sfanomoë" [tr. Dominique Mols]) (91–99); "La Mort de Malygris" ("The Death of Malygris" [tr. Dominique Mols]) (100–112); *Averoigne:* "La Sainteté d'Azédarac" ("The Holiness of Azédarac" [tr. Yves Le Brun]) (115–34); "La Bête d'Averoigne" ("The Beast of Averoigne" [tr. Yves Le Brun]) (135–45); *Zothique:* "L'Empire des nécromants" ("The Empire of the Necromancers" [tr. France-Marie Watkins]) (149–57); "L'Île des tortionnaires" ("The Isle of the Torturers" [tr. Françoise Levie]) (158–71); "Les Nécromanciens de Naat" ("Necromancy in Naat" [tr. Françoise Levie]) (172–89); "Xeethra" (tr. Jean Marigny) (190–209); "Bibliographie" (211).

Notes. Translation of the first half of *Lost Worlds* (I.A.10). The NeO edition is bound in paper, with cover artwork by Jean-Michel Nicollet. The Belles Lettres edition is bound in paper, omits the introduction by Jean-Luc Buard, and includes an afterword, "Le Journal du Cabinet Noir," which discusses CAS and his publication history in France; it includes lengthy quotations from François Truchaud's introduction to *L'Île inconnu* (item 4 above). The Belles Lettres edition is part of the Collection "Le Cabinet Noir."

7. *La Gorgone.*
   a. Paris: Nouvelles Éditions Oswald, 1986. 169 pp.

   Contents: "Introduction: Les Visions vertineuses de Clark Ashton Smith" by Jean-Luc Buard (5–9); *Xiccarph:* "Le Labyrinthe de Maal Dweb" ("The Maze of Maal Dweb") (13–26); "Les Femmes-fleurs" ("The Flower-Women") (27–38); *Autres Mondes:* "Le Démon de la fleur" ("The Demon of the Flower") (41–50); "La Drogue de Pluton" ("The Plutonian Drug") (51–61); "La Planète des morts" ("The Planet of the Dead") (62–74); "La Gorgone" ("The Gorgon") (75–86); "La Lettre de Mohaun Los" ("The Letter from Mohaun Los") (87–120); "La Lumière de l'au-delà" ("The Secret of the Cairn") (121–41); "Les Chasseurs de l'au-delà" ("The Hunters from Beyond") (142–58); "Celui qui marchait dans la poussière" ("The Treader of the Dust") (159–67).
   Notes. Bound in paper. Cover art by Jean-Michel Nicollet. Translation of the second half of *Lost Worlds* (I.A.10). Translated by Yves Le Brun.

8. *Le Dieu carnivore.*
   a. Paris: Nouvelles Éditions Oswald, 1987. 2 vols. (139 pp. and 153 pp.).

   Contents:

   Volume 1: "Introduction: Un Talent universel" by Jean Marigny (5–13); "Genius Loci" (tr. Jean Marigny) (14–35); "Le Paysage aux saules" ("The Willow Landscape" [tr. Dominique Mols]) (36–42); "Le Neuvième Squelette" ("The Ninth Skeleton") (43–49); "Les Cendres du passé" ("The Phantoms of the Fire") (50–56); "Le Monde éternel" ("The Eternal World") (57–81); "Vulthoom" (82–113); "Mutation cosmique" ("A Star-Change") (114–37); "Bibliographie" (138).

   Volume 2: "La Cité première" ("The Primal City") (5–14); "La Vénus de Périgon" ("The Disinterment of Venus") (15–24); "Le Colosse d'Ylourgne" ("The Colossus of Ylourgne") (25–68); "Le Satyre" ("The Satyr") (69–76); "Le Jardin d'Adompha" ("The Garden of Adompha" [tr. France-Marie Watkins]) (77–88); "Le Dieu carnivore" ("The Charnel God" [tr. Françoise Levie]) (89–112); "Le Supérieur noire de Puthuum" ("The Black Abbot of Puthuum" [tr. Françoise Levie]) (113–36); "La Fileuse de momies" ("The Weaver in the Vault" [tr. Françoise Levie]) (137–49); "Bibliographie" (151).

Notes. Bound in paper. Cover art by Jean-Michel Nicollet. Translation of *Genius Loci and Other Tales* (I.A.11). Translated by Gérard Coisne save where indicated.

9.   *Les Abominations de Yondo.*
    a.   Paris: Nouvelles Éditions Oswald, 1988. 285 pp.

     Contents: "Introduction: Un Grand Cru" by Bernard Malerne [pseud. of Jean-Luc Buard] (5–9); "L'Héritier des ténèbres" ("The Nameless Offspring" [tr. Gérard Coisne]) (11–33); "Les Charmes d'Ulua" ("The Witchcraft of Ulua" [tr. Françoise Levie]) (34–45); "L'Adepte du mal" ("The Devotee of Evil" [tr. Gérard Coisne]) (46–60); "L'Epiphanie de la mort" [tr. Dominique Mols]) (61–67); "Un Grande Cru d'Atlantide" ("A Vintage from Atlantis" [tr. Dominique Mols]) (68–77); "Les Abominations de Yondo" ("The Abominations of Yondo" [tr. Alain Garsault]) (78–86); "La Sibylle blanche" ("The White Sybil" [tr. Gérard Coisne]) (87–98); "Le Démon des glaces" ("The Ice-Demon" [tr. Gérard Coisne]) (99–118); "Le Voyage du roi Euvoran" ("The Voyage of King Euvoran" [tr. Alain Garsault]) (119–44); "Le Maître des crabes" ("The Master of the Crabs" [tr. Françoise Levie]) (145–60); "L'Enchanteresse de Sylaire" ("The Enchantress of Sylaire" [tr. Dominique Mols]) (161–80); "L'Habitant des gouffres" ("The Dweller in the Gulf" [tr. Gérard Coisne]) (181–204); "Les Âges sombres" ("The Dark Age" [tr. Gérard Coisne]) (205–23); "Le Troisième Épisode de Vathek" ("The Third Episode of Vathek" [tr. Gérard Coisne]) (224–74); "Chinoiserie" ("Chinoiserie" [tr. Xavier Perret]) (275–76); "Le Miroir dans le couloir d'ébène" ("The Mirror in the Hall of Ebony" [tr. Xavier Perret]) (277–78); "L'Apparition d'Aphrodite" ("The Passing of Aphrodite" [tr. Xavier Perret]) (279–81); "Bibliographie" (282–83).

     Notes. Bound in paper. Cover art by Jean-Michel Nicollet. Translation of *The Abominations of Yondo* (I.A.15).

10.   *Morthylla.*
    a.   Paris: Nouvelles Éditions Oswald, 1989. 249 pp.

     Contents: "Evocation de Clark Ashton Smith" ("Clark Ashton Smith: A Memoir") by E. Hoffmann Price (tr. Yves Le Brun) (5–18); "Le Maître de l'astéroïde" ("Master of the Asteroid" [tr. Yves Le Brun]) (19–37); "Semences de mort" ("The Seed from the Sepulcher" [tr. Jacques Papy]) (39–51); "La Racine d'Ampoï" ("The Root of Ampoi" [tr. Dominique Mols]) (53–68); "Les

Immortels de Mercure" ("The Immortals of Mercury" [tr. Yves Le Brun]) (69–106); "Meurtre dans la quatrième dimension" ("Murder in the Fourth Dimension" [tr. Yves Le Brun]) (107–17); "La Semence de Mars" ("Seedling of Mars" [tr. Yves Le Brun]) (119–63); "Le Sculpteur de gargouilles" ("The Maker of Gargoyles" [tr. Yves Le Brun]) (165–80); "Le Grand Dieu Awto" ("The Great God Awto" [tr. France-Marie Watkins]) (181–86); "Mère des Crapauds" ("Mother of Toads" [tr. Yves Le Brun]) (187–96); "Le Frai de la tombe" ("The Tomb-Spawn" [tr. Françoise Levie]) (197–206); "Quand le diable y serait . . ." ("Schizoid Creator" [tr. Jacques Papy]) (207–14); "Le Festin de la Gorgone" ("Symposium of the Gorgon" [tr. Dominique Mols]) (215–24); "Le Vol des trente-neuf ceintures" ("The Theft of the Thirty-nine Girdles" [tr. Yves Le Brun]) (225–38); "Morthylla" (tr. Françoise Levie) (239–47); "Bibliographie" (249).

Notes. Bound in paper. Cover art by Jean-Michel Nicollet. Translation of *Tales of Science and Sorcery* (I.A.22).

11. *Le Mangeur de hachisch ou L'Apocalypse du Mal.*
   a. Dole: La Clef d'Argent, 2000. 24 pp.

   Contents: "Introduction" by Philippe Gindre (5–7); *Le Mangeur de hachisch ou L'Apocalypse du Mal* (*The Hashish-Eater; or, The Apocalypse of Evil*) (8–23).

   Notes. Pamphlet, saddle-stitched. Cover art by Philippe Dougnier. Translated by Philippe Gindre from a text prepared by David E. Schultz. 500 copies printed.

12. *Nostalgie de l'inconnu.*
   a. Dole: La Clef d'Argent, 2002. 80 pp.

   Contents: "Klarkash-Ton mythe" by Christian Hibon (7–9); *Textes tirés de* Ebony and Crystal: "Le Voyageur" ("The Traveller") (11–12); "La Fleur-diable" ("The Flower-Devil") (13–14); "Images" ("Larmes" ["Tears"], "La Rose secrète" ["The Secret Rose"], "Le Vent et le jardin" ["The Wind and the Garden"], "Offrandes" ["Offerings"], "Une Couronne" ["A Coronal"]) (14–15); "Le Lac noir" ("The Black Lake") (16–17); "Vignettes" ("Au-delà des montagnes" ["Beyond the Mountains"], "Le Luth brisé" ["The Broken Lute"], "Nostalgie de l'inconnu" ["Nostalgia of the Unknown"], "Tristesse grise" ["Grey Sorrow"], "La Chevelure de Circé" ["The Hair of Circe"], "Les Yeux de Circé" ["The Eyes of Circe"]) (17–19); "Une Vision du Lethé" ("A Dream of Lethe") (19–20); "La Caravane" ("The Caravan") (20–21); "La Princesse

Almina" ("The Princess Almeena") (21–22); "Ennui" (22–23); "La Statue du silence" ("The Statue of Silence") (24); "Éloigne- ment" ("Remoteness") (24–25); "Les Memnons de la nuit" ("The Memnons of the Night") (25–26); "Le Jardin et la tombe" ("The Garden and the Tomb") (26); "Au pays de Cocaigne" ("In Co- caigne") (27); "La Litanie des sept baisers" ("The Litany of the Seven Kisses") (29); "Extrait d'une lettre" ("From a Letter") (29–30); "Dans les cryptes du souvenir" ("From the Crypts of Memory") (30–32); "Vision fantastique" ("A Phantasy") (32–33); "Le Démon, l'ange et la beauté" ("The Demon, the Angel, and Beauty") (33–35); "Les Ombres" ("The Shadows") (35–37); *Décembre 1929:* "Le Miroir dans le couloir d'ébène" ("The Mirror in the Hall of Ebony") (38–39); "Au démon" ("To the Daemon") (39–40); "L'Abomination de la désolation" ("The Abomination of Desolation") (40–41); "La Pierre de touche" ("The Touchstone") (41–43); "Le Lotus et la lune" ("The Lotus and the Moon") (43); "L'Orfraie et le requin" ("The Osprey and the Shark") (44); "La Forêt interdite" ("The Forbidden Forest") (44–46); "Le Mithridate" ("The Mithridate") (46–47); "La Muse d'Hyperborée" ("The Muse of Hyperborea") (47–48); "Chinoiserie" (48–49); *Autres Poèmes et fragments retrouvés:* "La Cité de la destruction" ("The City of De- struction") (50–51); "L'Effigie de bronze et l'effigie de fer" ("The Image of Bronze and the Image of Iron") (51–52); "Les Cristaux" ("The Crystals") (53–54); "Le Lac du silence enchanté" ("The Lake of Enchanted Silence") (54); "L'Enclos funèbre" ("The Mortuary") (54–56); "Le Cadavre et le squelette" ("The Corpse and the Skeleton") (56–58); "Le Soleil et le sépulcre" ("The Sun and the Sepulchre") (58–59); "La Cascatelle gelée" ("The Frozen Waterfall") (59); "Préference" ("Preference") (59–60); "L'Apparition d'Aphrodite" ("The Passing of Aphrodite") (60–63); "Les Jours" ("The Days") (63); "Offrande" ("Offering") (63–64); "Narcisse" ("Narcissus") (64–65); "Le Péril tapi au sein des ruines" ("The Peril That Lurks among Ruins") (65–66); "Sans titre" ([Untitled]) (66); "Glossaire smithien sélectif" (67–75).

Notes. Bound in paper. Translation of *Nostalgia of the Unknown* (I.A.49). Translated by Philippe Gindre after a preliminary reading by Christian Hibon. Cover art by Philippe Dougnier. 571 copies printed, of which 71 copies were laid into a special case, designed by Jean-Claude Gauthier, that mimics the appearance of the 1922 edition of *Ebony and Crystal*. This edition was also accompanied by a number of facsimiles of the prose poems' original appearances, as well as related photographs and artwork by CAS. 54 numbered copies were offered for sale, while seventeen copies numbered in Roman numerals were reserved for the press.

13.   *La Flamme chantante.*
   a.   Arles: Actes Sud Éditions, 2013. 107 pp.

   Contents: "The City of the Singing Flame" (English); "La Flamme chantante."
       Notes. Bilingual edition. Translated by Joachim Zemmour.

14.   *Mondes derniers.*
   a.   Saint-Laurent d'Oings, France: Les Éditions Mnémos, June 2017.

   Contents: "Préface" ("Preface") by Scott Connors (5–16); *Zothique:* "Zothique" (English and French) (22–23); "L'Empire des nécroomants" ("The Empire of the Necromancers") (24–33); "L'Ile des tortionnaires" ("The Isle of the Torturers") (34–47); "Le Dieu nécrophage" ("The Charnel God") (48–67); "Le Sombre Eidolon" ("The Dark Eidolon") (68–89); "Le Voyage du roi Euvoran" ("The Voyage of King Euvoran") (90–109); "Le Tisseur dans la tombe" ("The Weaver in the Vault") (110–22); "Le Fruit de la tombe" ("The Tomb-Spawn") (124–32); "Les Charmes d'Ulua" ("The Witchcraft of Ulua") (134–45); "Xeethra" (146–62); "Le Dernier Hiéroglyphe" ("The Last Hieroglyph") (164–77); "Les Nécromants de Naat" ("Necromancy in Naat") (178–97); "L'Abbé noir de Puthuum" ("The Black Abbot of Puthuum") (198–215); "La Mort d'Ilalotha" ("The Death of Ilalotha") (216–25); "Le Jardin d'Adompha" ("The Garden of Adompha") (226–35); "Le Maître des crabes" ("The Master of the Crabs") (236–47); "Morthylla" (248–55); *Des Morts tu subiras l'adultère* (*The Dead Will Cuckold You*) (256–79); "Fragments & Synopsis" (280–83); *Averoigne:* "Averoigne" (English and French) (288–89); "La Fin de l'histoire" ("The End of the Story") (290–305); "Le Satyre" ("The Satyr") (306–11); "Un Rendez-vous en Averoigne" ("A Rendezvous in Averoigne") (312–25); "Le Faiseur de gargouilles" ("The Maker of Gargoyles") (326–37); "Saint Azédarac" ("The Holiness of Azédarac") (338–54); "Le Colosse d'Ylourgne" ("The Colossus of Ylourgne") (356–85); "Les Mandragores" ("The Mandrakes") (386–93); "La Bête d'Averoigne" ("The Beast of Averoigne") (395–406); "La Vénus exhumée" ("The Disinterment of Venus") (408–16); "La Mère des crapauds" ("Mother of Toads") (418–25); "L'Enchanteresse de Sylaire" ("The Enchantress of Sylaire") (426–38); "Fragments & Synopsis" (440–46);

"Postface" ("Afterword") by S. T. Joshi (448–57); "Note d'intention" by Julien Bétan (458–59).

Notes. Bound in black cloth; spine stamped in gold. No dust jacket; front cover features an illustration by Santiago Caruso (more illustrations by Caruso in the text). Front endpapers feature a map of Zothique, back endpapers a map of Averoigne, both by Zdzislaw Beksinski. Texts translated by Alex Nikolavitch. Clark Ashton Smith Intégrale, Volume 1.

15. *Mondes premiers.*

a. Saint-Laurent d'Oings, France: Les Éditions Mnémos, June 2017.

Contents: "Préface" ("Preface") by Scott Connors (4–16); *Hyperborée:* "La Muse d'Hyperborée" ("The Muse of Hyperborea") (English and French) (22–23); "L'Histoire de Satampra Zeiros" ("The Tale of Satampra Zeiros") (24–37); "La Porte vers Saturne" ("The Door to Saturn") (38–55); "Le Testament d'Athammaus" ("The Testament of Athammaus") (56–73); "L'Infortune d'A- voosl Wuthoqquan" ("The Weird of Avoosl Wuthoqquan") (74–82); "Ubbo-Sathla" (84–91); "Le Démon de glace" ("The Ice-Demon") (92–107); "La Sibylle blanche" ("The White Sybil") (108–17); "L'Avènement du ver blanc" ("The Coming of the White Worm") (118–34); "Les Sept Geasa" ("The Seven Geases") (136–55); "Le Vol des trente-neuf ceintures" ("The Theft of the Thirty-nine Girdles") (156–66); "Fragment: La Maison d'Haon-Dor" ("The House of Haon-Dor") (168–72); *Poseidonis:* "L'Atlantide" ("Atlantis") (English and French) (178–79); "La Muse d'Atlantide" ("The Muse of Atlantis") (English and French) (180–81); "La Dernière Incantation" ("The Last Incantation") (182–86); "Voyage pour Sfanomoë" ("The Voyage to Sna- fomoë") (188–96); "Un Grand Cru d'Atlantide" ("A Vintage from Atlantis") (198–205); "L'Ombre double" ("The Double Shad- ow") (206–17); "La Mort de Malygris" ("The Death of Malygris") (220–32); "Tolometh" (English and French) (234–37); "Postface" ("Afterword") by S. T. Joshi (240–49); "Note d'in- tention" by Julien Bétan (250–51).

Notes. Bound in black cloth; spine stamped in gold. No dust jacket; front cover features an illustration by Santiago Caruso (more illustrations by Caruso in the text). Front endpapers feature a map of Hyperborea, back endpapers a map of Poseidonis, both by Zdzislaw Beksinski. Texts translated by Alex Nikolavitch. Clark Ashton Smith Intégrale, Volume 2.

16. *Autres mondes.*
   a. Saint-Laurent d'Oings, France: Les Éditions Mnémos, June 2017.

   Contents: "Préface" ("Preface") by Scott Connors (4–12); *Mars:* "Les Caveaux de Yoh-Vombis" ("The Vaults of Yoh-Vombis") (14–32); "L'Habitant du gouffre" ("The Dweller in the Gulf") (34–49); "Vulthoom" (50–72); *Xiccarph:* "Le Dédale de Maal Dweb" ("The Maze of Maal Dweb") (74–87); "Les Femmes-fleurs" ("The Flower-Women") (88–98); *Autres mondes:* "Les Abominations de Yondo" ("The Abominations of Yondo") (102–9); "Une Nuit en Malnéant" ("A Night in Malnéant") (110–17); "Le Monstre de la prophétie" ("The Monster of the Prophecy") (118–50); "Le Démon de la fleur" ("The Demon of the Flower") (152–62); "La Planète défunte" ("The Planet of the Dead") (164–74); *Poèmes:* "Ombres" ("Shadows") (English and French) (180–83); "Depuis les crypts du souvenir" ("From the Crypts of Memory") (English and French) (186–89); "Sadastor" (English and French) (192–97); "Au Démon" ("To the Daemon") (English and French) (200–201); "Postface" ("Afterword") by S. T. Joshi (202–10); "Note d'intention" by Julien Bétan (212–13); "Glossaire" ("Glossary") (216–33).

   Notes. Bound in black cloth; spine stamped in gold. No dust jacket; front cover features an illustration by Zdzislaw Beksinski. Additional interior illustrations by various artists. Texts translated by Alex Nikolavitch. Clark Ashton Smith Intégrale, Volume 3.

17. *Celui qui marchait parmi les étoiles: Choix de poèmes cosmiques.*
   a. Paris: Éditions de L'Oeil du Sphinx, August 2017. 319 pp.

   Contents: "Avant-propos" by Jean Hautepierre (5–18); *Le Mangeur de haschisch, ou l'Apocalypse de mal (The Hashish-Eater; or, The Apocalypse of Evil)* (19–54); "Celui qui marchait parmi les étoiles" ("The Star-Treader") (55–63); "Le Château sombre" ("The Dark Chateau") (64–67); "Le Royaume des ombres" ("The Kingdom of Shadows") (68–71); "Ougabalys" (72–73); "La Momie" ("The Mummy") (74–75); "Mors" (76–77); "Laus Mortis" (78–79); "L'Espoir en l'infini" ("The Hope of the Infinite") (80–81); "La Quête immemoriale" ("The Infinite Quest") (82–83); "À l'Obscurité" ("To the Darkness") (84–87); "Ode à l'abîme" ("Ode to the Abyss") (88–93); "Ode à la matière" ("Ode to Matter") (94–97); "Les Atomes" ("The Motes") (98–99); "Triple Aspect" (100–101); "Les Étranges Ténèbres" ("The Eldritch Dark") (102–3);

"Les Ombres" ("Shadows") (104–5); "Ode à la imagination" ("Ode on Imagination") (106–11); "L'Imagination" ("Imagination") (112–20); "Pour chercher du nouveau" (121–24); "Saturne" ("Saturn") (125–40); "Les Titans en Tartare" ("The Titans in Tartarus") (141–46); "Chant de l'Enfer" ("A Song from Hell") (147–50); "La Révolte de Satan" ("Satan Unrepentant") (151–57); "Dissonance" (158–59); "Transcendance" ("Transcendence") (160–61); "Le Pont de Rêve" ("The Dream- Bridge") (162–63); "Les Îles de nuages" ("The Cloud-Islands") (164–65); "Le Fantôme sans nom" ("The Nameless Wraith") (166–67); "Rêve de beauté" ("A Dream of Beauty") (168–69); "Au désert" ("Psalm to the Desert") (170–73); "Désolation" ("Desolation") (174–75); "Après le Grand Muraille" ("Beyond the Great Wall") (176–77); "Echo de Memnon" ("Echo of Memnon") (178–79); "Memnon à minuit" ("Memnon at Midnight") (180–81); "Méduse" ("Medusa") (182–85); "Néron" ("Nero") (186–93); "La Cité des Titans" ("The City of the Titans") (194–95); "La Cité de la destruction" ("The City of Destruction") (196–99); "La Dernière Nuit" ("The Last Night") (200–201); "Rêve de néant" ("A Dream of Oblivion") (202–3); "L'Envol d'Azraël" ("The Flight of Azrael") (204–7); "La Goule et la séraphine" ("The Ghoul and the Seraph") (208–17); "Le Hasard" ("Chance") (218–19); "La Néréide" ("The Nereid") (220–23); "La Lamie" ("Lamia") (224–25); "L'Atlantide" ("Atlantis") (226–27); "Zothique" (228–29); "Le Santal" ("Sandalwood") (230–31); "Cléopâtre" ("Cleopatra") (232–33); "Le Lac du cauchemar" ("The Nightmare Tarn") (234–37); "Connaissance" (238–39); "Cantique" ("Canticle") (240–42); "Résurrection" ("Resurrection") (243–45); "Aliénation" ("Alienage") (246–49); "Le Suprème Oubli" ("Forgetfulness") (250–51); "Rosa mystica" (252–53); "La Colline de Dionysos" ("The Hill of Dionysus" (254–57); "Le Château de mes rêves" ("The Dream-God's Realm") (258–59); "Soliloque dans un tour ébène" ("Soliloquy in an Ebon Tower") (260–67); "Les Envoyés" ("The Envoys") (268–71); "À Omar Khayyam" ("To Omar Khayyam") (272–77);

"À Nora May French" ("To Nora May French") (278–84); "À George Sterling: Discourse d'adieu" ("To George Sterling: A Valediction") (285–91); "À Howard Phillips Lovecraft" ("To Howard Phillips Lovecraft") (292–95); "H.P.L." (296–97); "Le Chant de nécromant" ("Song of the Necromancer") (298–301); "Cycles" (302–4); "Notes du traducteur" by Jean Hautepierre (305–14); "Sources bibliographiques" (315–16).

Notes. Bound in hardcover (no dust jacket). Bilingual edition. Photograph of CAS on the front cover. Translated by Jean Hautepierre. Interior illustrations by El Jicé.

iv. *German*

1. *Saat aus dem Grabe.*
   a. Frankfurt am Main: Insel Verlag, 1970. 217 pp.
   b. Frankfurt am Main: Suhrkamp, 1982. 250 pp.

   Contents: "Saat aus dem Grabe" ("The Seed from the Sepulcher") (5–21); "Des Magiers Wiederkehr" ("The Return of the Sorcerer") (22–41); "Adomphas Garten" ("The Garden of Adompha") (42–56); "Das befremdliche Los des Ejwuusl Wessahqquan" ("The Weird of Avoosl Wuthoqquan") (57–69); "Die Stadt der singenden Flamme" ("The City of the Singing Flame") (70–123 [includes "Beyond the Singing Flame"]); "Teichlandschaft mit Erlen und Weide" ("Genius Loci") (124–47); "Der fremde Gott" ("Vulthoom") (148–81); "Das Reich der Toten" ("The Empire of the Necromancers") (182–94); "Die Grabgewölbe von Yoh-Vombis" ("The Vaults of Yoh-Vombis") (195–217).

   Notes. The Insel edition is bound in black cloth with a dust jacket designed by Hans Ulrich and Ute Osterwalder. It is part of the series "Bibliothek des Hauses Usher," edited by Kalju Kirde. Translated by Friedrich Polakovics. The Suhrkamp edition is bound in paper.

2. *Der Planet der Toten.*
   a. Frankfurt am Main: Insel Verlag, 1971. 252 pp.
   b. Frankfurt am Main: Suhrkamp, 1972. 280 pp.

   Contents: "Der Planet der Toten" ("The Planet of the Dead") (5–20); "Der Herr der Tiefen" ("The Dweller in the Gulf") (21–45); "Der Irrgarten des Maal Dweb" ("The Maze of Maal Dweb") (46–64); "Aforgomons Kette" ("The Chain of Aforgomon") (65–88); "Schrecken ohne Mass" ("The Immeasurable Horror") (89–108); "Der fremde Schatten" ("The Double Shadow") (109–24); "Rendezvous in Averoigne" ("A Rendezvous in Averoigne") (125–42); "Der Koloss von Ylourgne" ("The Colossus of Ylourgne") (143–87); "Ilalothas Tod" ("The Death of Ilalotha") (188–200); "Das dunkle Idol" ("The Dark Eidolon") (201–31); "Die Folterer-Insel" ("The Isle of the Torturers") (232–50).

Notes. Insel edition bound in black cloth with a dust jacket designed by Hans Ulrich and Ute Osterwalder. It is part of the series "Bibliothek des Hauses Usher," edited by Kalju Kirde. Translated by Friedrich Polakovics. The Suhrkamp edition is bound in paper.

3. *Poseidonis.*
    a. Rastatt: Arthur Moewig Verlag, 1985. 159 pp.

    Contents: Poseidonis: "Die Muse von Atlantis" ("The Muse of Atlantis") (8); "Die letzte Beschwörung" ("The Last Incantation") (9–13); "Der Tod des Malygris" ("The Death of Malygris") (14–26); "Tolometh" (27); "Der doppelte Schatten" ("The Double Shadow") (28–41); "Eine Reise nach Sfanomoë" ("A Voyage to Sfanomoë") (41–49); "Ein guter Wein von Atlantis" ("A Vintage from Atlantis") (49–56); *Lemuria:* "In Lemuria" ("In Lemuria") (58); "Eine Opfergabe an den Mond" ("An Offering to the Moon") (58–69); "Die unentdeckte Insel" ("The Uncharted Isle") (69–80); "Lemurienne" (80); *Ptolemides:* "Die Epiphanie des Todes" ("The Epiphany of Death") (82–86); *Andere Reiche:* "Das Gastmahl der Gorgo" ("Symposium of the Gorgon") (88–96); "Die Venus von Azombeii" ("The Venus of Azombeii") (89–123); "Die Wurzel der Ampoi" ("The Root of Ampoi") (123–37); "Die unsichtbare Stadt" ("The Invisible City") (137–59).
    Notes. Bound in paper. Cover art by Franz Berthold. Translated by Martin Eisele.

4. *Der Haupt der Medusa.* Edited by Kalju Kirde.
    a.1. Frankfurt am Main: Suhrkamp, 1988. 211 pp.
    a.2. Frankfurt am Main: Suhrkamp, 1996.

    Contents: "Dem Bösen verfallen" ("The Devotee of Evil") (7–21); "Die Landschaft aus den Weiden" ("The Willow Landscape") (22–27); "Das Tor zum Saturn" ("The Door to Saturn") (28–48); "Verfolger von Drüben" ("The Hunters from Beyond") (48–65); "Die Heiligkeit des Azédarac" ("The Holiness of Azédarac") (88–109); "Licht aus der Gegenwelt" ("The Secret of the Cairn") (110–30); "Die Insel der lebenden Toten" ("Necromancy in Naat") (131–51); "Die Blume des Dämons" ("The Demon of the Flower") (152–62); "Das Haupt der Medusa" ("The Gorgon") (163–74); "Der Zertreter des Staubes" ("The Treader of the Dust") (175–82); "Die Blumenvampire" ("The Flower-Women") (183–94); "Die letzte Hieroglyphe" ("The Last Hieroglyph") (195–210).
    Notes. Bound in paper. Translated by Friedrich Polakovics.

5. *Necropolis.*
   a. Almersbach: Festa Verlag, May 2001. 254 pp.

   Contents: "Clark Ashton Smiths Leben" by [Unsigned] (7–13);
   "Für Clark Ashton Smith" ("To Clark Ashton Smith") by H. P.
   Lovecraft (14); *Sieben Geschichten aus Zothique:* "Necropolis—Das
   Reich der Toten" ("The Empire of the Necromancers" [tr. Heiko
   Langhans]) (19–27); "Der Leichengott" ("The Charnel God" [tr.
   Heiko Langhans]) (28–49); "Ilalothas Tod" ("The Death of Ila-
   lotha" [tr. Heiko Langhans]) (50–60); "Der schwarze Abt von
   Puthuum" ("The Black Abbot of Puthuum" [tr. Andreas Diesel])
   (61–80); "Xeethra" (tr. Andreas Diesel) (81–98); "Morthylla" (tr.
   Frank Festa) (99–107); "Die Seereise des König Euvoran" ("The
   Voyage of King Euvoran" [tr. Andreas Diesel]) (108–29); *Ges-
   chichten aus dieser und jener Welt:* "Genius Loci" (tr. Heiko Lan-
   ghans) (135–52); "Das Gorgonhaupt" ("The Gorgon" [tr. Heiko
   Langhans]) (153–63); "Die Rückkehr des Hexers" ("The Return
   of the Sorcerer" [tr. Heiko Langhans]) (164–78); "Die Venus von
   Azombeii" ("The Venus of Azombeii" [tr. Martin Eisele])
   (179–204); "Die Wurzel der Ampoi" ("The Root of Ampoi" [tr.
   Martin Eisele]) (205–19); "Die unentdeckte Insel" ("The Uncharted Isle" [tr. Martin Eisele]) (220–30); "Mutter Kröte"
   ("Mother of Toads" [tr. Heiko Langhans]) (231–38); "Die
   Ankunft des Weissen Wurms" ("The Coming of the White Worm"
   [tr. Andreas Diesel]) (239–54).

   Notes. Bound in black cloth. Dust jacket by www.babbarammdass.de.

6. *Der Haschisch-esser oder die apokalypse des bösen.*
   a. Bremen: Rough Art Verlag, December 2001. [34 pp.]

   Contents: Excerpt from "Supernatural Horror in Literature" by H.
   P. Lovecraft ([5]); *Der Haschisch-esser oder die apokalypse des bösen*
   (*The Hashish-Eater; or, The Apocalypse of Evil*) ([7–33]).

   Notes. Pamphlet, saddle-bound with paper covers. Translated
   and illustrated by Denis Verdinski. Limited to 100 numbered
   copies.

7. *Die Sehnsucht nach dem Unbekannten: Prosegedichte.*
   a. Bremen and Hamburg: Rough Art Verlag, June 2002. 47 pp.

   Contents: "Entlegenheit" ("Remoteness") (7); "Das Land von
   Fruchtbar Palmen" ("Untitled") (8); "Graue Trauer" ("Grey
   Sorrow") (9); "Eine Krönung" ("A Coronal") (11); "Die Mem-
   monen der Nacht" ("The Memnons of the Night") (12–13); "Die

Muse von Hyperborea" ("The Muse of Hyperborea") (14–15); "Tränen" ("Tears") (16); "Die Kristalle" ("The Crystals") (18–19); "Der Lotus und der Mond" ("The Lotus and the Moon") (20); "Das Haar der Circe" ("The Hair of Circe") (21); "Die Augen der Circe" ("The Eyes of Circe") (22); "Der See von Bezaubernd Stille" ("The Lake of Enchanted Silence") (23); "Darbietungen" ("Offerings") (24); "Die Verborgene Rose" ("The Secret Rose") (26); "Die Litanei der Sieben Küsse" ("The Litany of the Seven Kisses") (27–28); "Die Sehnsucht nach dem Unbekannten" ("Nostalgia of the Unknown") (29); "Eine Phantasie" ("A Phantasy") (30); "Der Wund und der Garten" ("The Wind and the Garden") (32); "Die zerbrichene Laute" ("The Broken Lute") (33); "Aus einem Brief" ("From a Letter") (34–35); "Der Garten und das Grab" ("The Garden and the Tomb") (36); "Die Abscheulichkeit der Verlassenheit" ("The Abomination of Desolation") (37); "Jenseits der Berge" ("Beyond the Mountains") (40); "Der schwarze See" ("The Black Lake") (41–42); "In Cocaigne" (43–44); "Die Sonne und das Grab" ("The Sun and the Sepulchre") (45). Translated by Denis Verdinski.

Notes. Pamphlet, saddle-bound with paper covers. Translated and illustrated by Denis Verdinski. Limited to 50 numbered copies.

8.   *Gesammelte Erzählungen.*

    a.   Leipzig: Festa Verlag, 2011–17. 6 vols.

    Contents:

    Volume 1: *Die Stadt der Singenden Flamme* (2011): "Die vergessenen Welten des Klarkash-Ton" ("The Lost Worlds of Klarkash-Ton") by Stephen Jones (7–44); "Über Fantasy" ("On Fantasy") (45–48); "Die Stadt der Singenden Flamme" ("The City of the Singing Flame") (49–72); "Jenseits der Singenden Flamme" ("Beyond the Singing Flame") (73–102); "Das neunte Skelett" ("The Ninth Skeleton") (103–8); "Der malaiische Kris" ("The Malay Krise") (109–11); "Die Abscheulichkeiten von Yondo" ("The Abominations of Yondo") (112–21); "Die Auferweckung der Klapperschlange" ("The Resurrection of the Rattlesnake") (122–29); "Die Schrecken der Venus" ("The Immeasurable Horror") (13—49); "Aus den Grüften der Erinnerung" ("From the Crypts of Memory") (150–54); "Das Hyperborea von Clark Ashton Smith" (introduction to *The Book of Hyperborea*) by Will Murray (155–68); "Die Geschichte des Satampra Zeiros" ("The Tale of Satampra Zeiros") (169–85); "Die Muse von Hyperborea" ("The Muse of Hyperborea") (186); "Das Tor zum Saturn" ("The

Door to Saturn") (187–213); "Das Manuskript des Athammaus" ("The Testament of Athammaus") (214–39); "Das wunderliche Schicksal des Avoosl Wuthoqquan" ("The Weird of Avoosl Wuthoqquan") (240–51); "Ubbo-Sathla" (252–61); "Der Eisdämen" ("The Ice-Demon") (262–83); "Die seben Banngelübde" ("The Seven Geases"); "Die weisse Seherin" ("The White Sybil") (312–24); "Die Ankunft des Weissen Wurms" ("The Coming of the White Worm") (325–45); "Der Raub der neununddreissig Keuschheitsgürtel" ("The Theft of the Thirty-nine Girdles") (346–60); "Anmerkungen zu den Erzählungen" (story notes) by Scott Connors and Ron Hilger (361–96).

Volume 2: *Die Grabgewölbe von Yoh-Vombis* (2012): "Die unentdeckte Insel" ("The Uncharted Isle") (7–21); "Das Ungeheuer aus der Prophezeiung" ("The Monster of the Prophecy") (22–68); "Der Brief aus Mohaun Los" ("The Letter from Mohaun Los") (69–113); "Die Epiphanie des Todes" ("The Epiphany of Death") (129–35); "Eine nekromantische Geschichte" ("The Necromantic Tale") (136–52); "Die Unsterblichen des Merkur" ("The Immortals of Mercury") (153–97); "Ein Leichnam zu viel" ("The Supernumerary Corpse") (198–208); "Die namenlose Ausgeburt" ("The Nameless Offspring") (209–34); "Die Knospen des Grabes" ("The Seed from the Sepulcher") (235–56); "Der Mars-Zyklus von Clark Ashton Smith" by Will Murray (257–66); "Die Grabgewölbe von Yoh-Vombis" ("The Vaults of Yoh-Vombis") (267–96); "Der Herrscher der Tiefe" ("The Dweller in the Gulf") (297–321); "Vulthoom" (322–62); "Erinnerungen an Klarkash-Ton" ("Clark Ashton Smith: A Memoir") by E. Hoffmann Price (363–82); "Anmerkungen zu den Erzählungen" (story notes) by Scott Connors and Ron Hilger (383–415).

Volume 3: *Das Labyrinth des Maal Dweb* (2013): "Die Kette des Aforgomon" ("The Chain of Aforgomon") (7–32); "Ein Trank für die Mondgöttin" ("An Offering to the Moon") (33–48); "Prinz Alcouz und der Magier" ("Prince Alcouz and the Magician") (49–51); "Ein Abenteuer in der Zukunft" ("An Adventure in Futurity") (51–104); "Die Venus von Azombeii" ("The Venus of Azombeii") (105–40); "Der Allmächtige des Mars" ("Seedling of Mars") (141–96); "Der Flirt" ("The Flirt") (218–19); "Genius Loci" (220–43); "Etwas Neues" ("Something New") (244–47); "Die Dimension des Zufalls" ("The Dimension of Chance") (248–82); "Ein Gedichtband von Burns" ("A Copy of Burns") (283–86); "Invasion von der Venus" ("The Metamorphosis of the

World") (287–328); "Sadastor" (329–33); "Maal Dweb, Herrscher über Xiccarph" by Will Murray (334–39); "Das Labyrinth des Maal Dweb" ("The Maze of Maal Dweb") (340–62); "Das Vagnis des Maal Dweb" ("The Flower-Women") (363–80); "Anmerkungen zu den Erzählungen" (story notes) by Scott Connors and Ron Hilger (381–411).

Volume 4: *Die Bestie von Averoigne* (2015): "Ein Mord in der vierten Dimension" ("Murder in the Fourth Dimension") (7–18); "Lebendig begraben" ("The Second Interment") (19–34); "Im Banne des Bösen" ("The Devotee of Evil") (35–52); "Die Jäger aus der Tiefe" ("The Hunters from Beyond") (53–76); "Ein Nacht in Malnéant" ("A Night in Malnéant") (77–85); "Der Planet der Toden" ("The Planet of the Dead") (86–103); "Die Wurzel der Ampoi" ("The Root of Ampoi") (104–23); "Der Gott des Asteroiden" ("Master of the Asteroid") (124–45); "Die plutonische Droge" ("The Plutonian Drug") (146–59); "Der Radschah und der Tiger" ("The Raja and the Tiger") (160–68); "Der grosse Gott Awto" ("The Great God Awto") (169–76); "Die Chroniken von Averoigne" by Will Murray (177–87); "Wie die Geschichte endet" ("The End of the Story") (188–213); "Die Satyr" ("The Satyr") (214–21); "Ein Rendezvous in Averoigne" ("A Rendezvous in Averoigne") (222–42); "Die Heiligkeit des Azédarac" ("The Holiness of Azédarac") (243–71); "Der Steinmetz und die Wasserspeier" ("The Maker of Gargoyles") (272–92); "Die Bestie von Averoigne" ("The Beast of Averoigne") (293–314); "Der Koloss von Ylourgne" ("The Colossus of Ylourgne") (315–68); "Die Alraunen" ("The Mandrakes") (369–78); "Die Venus von Périgon" ("The Disinterment of Venus") (379–92); "Mutter von Kröte" ("Mother of Toads") (393–404); "Die Zauberin von Sylaire" ("The Enchantress of Sylaire") (405–26); "Anmerkungen zu den Erzählungen" (story notes) by Scott Connors and Ron Hilger (427–62).

Volume 5: *Die Totenbeschwörer von Naat* (2016): "Der Zotique-Zyklus von Clark Ashton Smith" (introduction to *Tales of Zothique*) by Will Murray (7–17); "Necropolis—Das Reich der Toten" ("The Empire of the Necromancers") (18–29); "Die Seereise des König Euvoran" ("The Voyage of King Euvoran") (30–59); "Die Insel der Folterer" ("The Isle of the Torturers") (60–82); "Zeethra" (83–107); "Die Zauber-Ränke der Prinzessin Ulua" ("The Witchcraft of Ulua") (108–21); "Der Zehrer in der Gruft" ("The Weaver in the Vault") (122–39); "Die Grabesbrut"

("The Tomb-Spawn") (140–52); "Der Leichengott" ("The Charnel God") (153–81); "Ilalothas Tod" ("The Death of Ilalotha") (182–96); "Das dunkle Götzenbild" ("The Dark Eidolon") (197–235); "Die letzte Hieryglyphe" ("The Last Hieroglyph") (236–59); "Die Totenbeschwörer von Naat" ("Necromancy in Naat") (260–91); "Der schwarze Abt von Puthuum" ("The Black Abbot of Puthuum") (292–318); "Adomphas Garten" ("The Garden of Adompha") (319–32); "Der Herr der Krabben" ("The Master of the Crabs") (333–51); *Die Toten werden dich zum Hahnrei machen* (*The Dead Will Cuckold You*) (352–80); "Morthylla" (381–93); "Chinoiserie" (394–95); "Die dritte Episode des Vathek" ("The Third Episode of Vathek" [with William Beckford]) (396–455); "Schizophrener Schöpfer" ("Schizoid Creator") (456–65); "Der Spiegel im Ebenholzsaal" ("The Mirror in the Hall of Ebony") (466–67); "Der Ghoul" ("The Ghoul") (468–75); "Das Geheimnis des Steinhügels" ("The Light from Beyond") (476–502); "Eine Sternenwandlung" ("A Star-Change") (503–28); "Anmerkungen zu den Erzählungen" (story notes) by Scott Connors and Ron Hilger (529–74).

Volume 6: *Der doppelte Schatten* (2017): "Die letzte Beschwörung" ("The Last Incantation") (9–15); "Eine Reise nach Sfanomoë" ("A Voyage to Snafomoë") (16–26); "Der doppelte Schatten" ("The Double Shadow") (27–44); "Ein edler Tropfen aus Atlantis" ("A Vintage from Atlantis") (45–54); "Der Tod des Malygris" ("The Death of Malygris") (55–71); "Der Kuss der Zoraida" ("The Kiss of Zoraida") (71–80); "Das dunkle Zeitalter" ("The Dark Age") (81–101); "Das Phantome des Feuers" ("The Phantoms of the Fire") (102–9); "Der Mahut" ("The Mahout") (110–18); "Die ewige Welt" ("The Eternal World") (119–44); "Der Geist des Mohammed Din" ("The Ghost of Mohammed Din") (145–54); "Gestrandet auf Andromeda" ("Marooned on Andromeda") (155–96); "Gefangen im Sternbild der Schlange" ("A Captivity in Serpens") (197–256); "Landschaft mit Weiden" ("The Willow Landscape") (257–63); "Der in den Staub tritt" ("The Treader of the Dust") (264–74); "Phönix" ("Phoenix") (275–89); "Der Dämon der Blume" ("The Demon of the Flower") (290–304); "Die unsichtbare Stadt" ("The Invisible City") (305–43); "Die Gerechtigkeit des Elefanten" ("The Justice of the Eelphant") (334–38); "Das Königreich des Wurms" ("The Kingdom of the Worm"); "Die urweltliche Stadt" ("The Primal City") (349–58); "13 Phantasmen" ("Thirteen Phantasms") (359–64); "Der Abschied der Aphrodite" ("The Passing of Aphrodite") (364–66); "Das Symposium der Gorgone" ("Symposium of the Gorgon") (367–79); "Anmerkungen zu den Erzählungen" (story notes) by Scott Connors and Ron Hilger (380–408).

> *Notes.* Bound in cloth. Translations by Alexander Amberg, Andreas Diesel, Malte S. Sembten, and others. The essay by Stephen Jones in volume 1 is taken from the afterword to *The Emperor of Dreams* (I.A.59). The story notes in each volume are taken from *Collected Fantasies* (I.A.70), although otherwise this edition is not a direct translation of the *Collected Fantasies*. The volumes are part of the publishers H. P. Lovecrafts Bibliothek des Schreckens.

v. Greek

1. *Ē polē tēs tragoudistēs flogas.* Edited by Makis Panorios.
    a. Athens: Eolos, 1995. 227 pp.

> *Contents:* "Prologos: Clark Ashton Smith" by Arēs Sfakianakēs (9–24); "Ē istoria tou Satampra Zeiros" ("The Tale of Satampra Zeiros") (25–38); "Ē pulē gia ton Krono" ("The Door to Saturn") (39–60); "O erchomos tou asprou skoulēkiou" ("The Coming of the White Worm") (61–76); "To teleutaio zorki" ("The Last Incantation") (77–82); "Ē diplē skia" ("The Double Shadow") (83–96); "O panagiotatos Azédarac" ("The Holiness of Azédarac") (97–120); "Pantebou stēn Averoigne" ("A Rendezvous in Averoigne") (121–38); "To nēsi tōn basanistōn" ("The Isle of the Torturers") (139–56); "O labyrinthos tou Maal Dweb" ("The Maze of Maal Dweb") (157–72); "Ē polē tēs tragoudistēs flogas" ("The City of the Singing Flame") (173–220); "Mia nyxta stē Malnéant" ("A Night in Malnéant") (221–27).
>
> *Notes.* Bound in paper. Cover artwork by Bruce Pennington. Translated by Arēs Sfakianakēs.

2. *Ta magika taksidia.*
    a. Thessaloniki: Terranova, December 2000. 365 pp.

> *Contents:* "Clark Ashton Smith: O poiētēs magos" by Kostantina Pegiou (9–22); "O planētēs tōn nekrōn" ("The Planet of the Dead") (23–41); "O ktēnos tēs Averoigne" ("The Beast of Averoigne") (43–58); "Ena taxidi pros tē Sfanomoë" ("A Voyage to Sfanomoë") (61–72); "To narkōtiko apo ton Ploutōna" ("The Plutonian Drug") (75–92); "To gramma apo to Mohaun Los" ("The Letter from Mohaun Los") (93–143); "Ē autokratopia tōn nekromantōn" ("The Empire of the Necromancers") (145–59); "O

daimonas tou louloudiou" ("The Demon of the Flower")
(161–75); "O thanatos tou Malygris" ("The Death of Malygris")
(177–95); "Xeethra" (197–225); "Ta epta gkēs" ("The Seven
Geases") (227–57); "Oi gunaikes-louloudia" ("The Flower-
Women") (259–77); "To phos apo to uperperan" ("The Secret of
the Cairn") (279–309); "Ē gorgō" ("The Gorgon") (311–27); "Oi
kynēgoi apo to uperperan" ("The Hunters from Beyond")
(329–51); "O peripatētēs tēs skonēs" ("The Treader of the Dust")
(353–65).

Notes. Bound in paper. Translated by Kostantina Pegiou.

3.   *Istories apo tē Zothik.*
   a.   Athens: Locus-7, 2002. 228 pp.

   Contents: "Prologo" by Giorgos Mialanos (7–10); "Ē autokratoria
tōn nekromanteōn" ("The Empire of the Necromancers")
(11–26); "O kēpos tou Adompha" ("The Garden of Adompha")
(27–42); "Ē mageia tēs Ulua" ("The Witchcraft of Ulua")
(43–58); "To taxidi tou basilia Euvoran" ("The Voyage of King
Euvoran") (59–98); "O theos tōn nekrōn" ("The Charnel God")
(99–134); "Xeethra" (135–66); "To mauros ēgoumenos tou Puthuum" ("The Black Abbot of Puthuum") (167–202); "To nēsi
tōn basanistōn" ("The Isle of the Torturers") (203–28).

   Notes. Bound in paper. Translated by Giorgos Mialanos.

vi. Italian

1.   *Zothique.*
   a.1.Milan: Editrice Nord, 1977. ix, 257 pp.
   a.2.Milan: Editrice Nord, 1992 (as *L'universo Zothique*).

   Contents: "Introduzione: Quando il mondo invecchia" by Lin
Carter (v–ix); "Zothique" (1); "Xeethra" (3–21); "I negromanti di
Naat" ("Necromancy in Naat") (23–41); "L'impero dei negro-
manti" ("The Empire of the Necromancers") (43–51); "Il signore
dei granchi" ("The Master of the Crabs") (53–66); "La morte di
Ilalotha" ("The Death of Ilalotha") (67–77); "Il tessitore della
cripta" ("The Weaver in the Vault") (79–90); "La stregoneria di
Ulua" ("The Witchcraft of Ulua") (91–100); Il dio dei morti"
("The Charnel God") (101–21); "L'idolo tenebroso" ("The Dark
Eidolon") (123–48); "Morthylla" (149–57); "L'abate nero di
Puthuum" ("The Black Abbot of Puthuum") (159–79); "Nato
nella tomba" ("The Tomb-Spawn") (181–90); "L'ultimo gerogli-

fico" ("The Last Hieroglyph") (191–206); "L'isola dei torturatori" ("The Isle of the Torturers") (207–21); "Il giardino di Adompha" ("The Garden of Adompha") (223–22); "Il viaggio di re Euvoran" ("The Voyage of King Euvoran") (233–54); "Epilogo: La sequenza dei racconti di Zothique," by Lin Carter (255–57).

Notes. Bound in paper. Cover artwork by Karel Thole. Translation of *Zothique* (I.A.25). Translated by Roberta Rambelli.

2.   *Genius loci e altri racconti.*
   a.   Torino: Casa Editrice MEB, 1978. 180 pp.

     Contents: "Nota introduttiva" by Teobaldo del Tanaro (7–8); "Genius loci" (9–26); "Il paesaggio dei salici" ("The Willow Landscape") (27–32); "Il nono scheletro" ("The Ninth Skeleton") (33–37); "I fantasmi del fuoco" ("The Phantoms of the Fire") (38–43); "La città fantasma" ("The Invisible City") (44–50); "La gorgone" ("The Gorgon") (51–61); "La santità di Azédarac" ("The Holiness of Azédarac") (62–81); "Il monstro dell'Averoigne" ("The Beast of Averoigne") (82–92); "Il ritrovamento di Venere" ("The Disinterment of Venus") (93–100); "Il colosso di Ylourgne" ("The Colossus of Ylourgne") (101–40); "Il satiro" ("The Satyr") (141–46); "Il giardino di Adompha" ("The Garden of Adompha") (147–57); "Il dio dei morti" ("The Charnel God") (158–80).

     Notes. Bound in paper. Cover artwork by Macc Ross. Translated by Teobaldo Del Tanaro.

3.   *Mondi perduti e altri racconti.*
   a.   Torino: MEB, 1979. 232 pp.

     Contents: [Biography of CAS] (5–6); "Le sette fatiche" ("The Seven Geases") (7–25); "L'ultimo incantesimo" ("The Last Incantation") (26–31); "Viaggio a Sfanomoë" ("A Voyage to Sfanomoë") (32–39); "La morte di Malygris" ("The Death of Malygris") (40–52); "Il labirinto di Maal Dweb" ("The Maze of Maal Dweb") (53–65); "Sirene floreali" ("The Flower-Women") (66–77); "Il demone del fiore" ("The Demon of the Flower") (78–87); "La droga plutoniana" ("The Plutonian Drug") (88–98); "Il pianeta della morte" ("The Planet of the Dead") (99–110); "La lettera da Mohaun Los" ("The Letter from Mohaun Los" (111–42); "La luce dell'aldilà" ("The Secret of the Cairn") (143–61); "Il mondo senza tempo" ("The Eternal World") (162–82); "Vulthoom" (183–208); "Da stella a stella" ("A Star-Change") (209–28); "Titoli e fonti" (bibliography) (229–30).

Notes. Bound in paper. Cover artwork by Walter Falciatore. Translated by Teobaldo Del Tanaro.

4.   *Gli orrori di Yondo e altri racconti.*
   a.   Torino: MEB, 1979. 220 pp.

Contents: "La progenie senza nome" ("The Nameless Offspring") (7–24); "L'adoratore del demonio" ("The Devotee of Evil") (25–36); "Epifania di morte" ("The Epiphany of Death") (37–41); "Il vino dell'Atlantide" ("A Vintage from Atlantis") (42–48); "Gli orrori di Yondo" ("The Abominations of Yondo") (49–56); "La sibilla bianca" ("The White Sybil") (57–66); "Il demone di ghiaccio" ("The Ice-Demon") (67–82); "L'incantatrice di Sylaire" ("The Enchantress of Sylaire") (83–98); "I figli dell'abisso" ("The Dweller in the Gulf") (99–117); "Medio evo" ("The Dark Age") (118–32); "Il terzo racconto di Vathek" ("The Third Episode of Vathek") (133–76); "L'avvento del verme bianco" ("The Coming of the White Worm") (177–90); "I cacciatori dell'aldilà" ("The Hunters from Beyond") (191–205); "Il dio della polvere" ("The Treader of the Dust") (206–13); "Cineserie" ("Chinoiserie") (214); "Lo specchio nella sala d'ebano" ("The Mirror in the Hall of Ebony") (215); "La partenza di Afrodite" ("The Passing of Aphrodite") (216–18).
Notes. Bound in paper. Cover artwork by Walter Falciatore. Translated by Teobaldo Del Tanaro.

5.   *Al di là tempo e dello spazio.*
   a.   Torino: MEB, 1979. 260 pp.

Contents: "La fine della storia" ("The End of the Story") (7–22); "Un rendezvous in Averoigne" ("A Rendezvous in Averoigne") (23–35); "Una notte a Malneant" ("A Night in Malnéant") (36–41); "La città della fiamma musicale" ("The City of the Singing Flame") (42–77); "L'isola senza nome" ("The Uncharted Isle") (78–87); "La seconda sepoltura" ("The Second Interment") (88–97); "La doppia ombra" ("The Double Shadow") (98–108); "La centena di Aforgomon" ("The Chain of Aforgomon") (109–24); "Sadastor" (125–28); "Il ritorno dello stregone" ("The Return of the Sorcerer") (129–43); "Il testamento di Athammaus" ("The Testament of Athammaus") (144–60); "Il destino di Avoosl Wuthoqquan" ("The Weird of Avoosl Wuthoqquan") (161–69); "Ubbo-Sathla" (170–77); "Il racconto di Satampra Zeiros" ("The Tale of Satampra Zeiros") (178–90); "Il mostro della profezia" ("The Monster of the Prophecy") (191–222); "La porta di

Saturno" ("The Door to Saturn") (223–40); "Le cripte di Yoh Vombis" ("The Vaults of Yoh-Vombis") (241–54); "Dalle cripte della memoria" ("From the Crypts of Memory") (255–56); "Le ombre" ("The Shadows") (257–58).

Notes. Bound in paper. Cover artwork by Walter Falciatore. Translated by Teobaldo Del Tanaro and Ina Paparella Morata.

6. *Il destino di Antarion.*
   a. Rome: Fanucci, 1986. 209 pp.

   Contents: "Altre stelle . . . altri cieli . . . lo stesso esotismo" by Gianni Pilo (5–8); "Il destino di Antarion" ("The Planet of the Dead") (11–26); "Il fabbricante di gronde" ("The Maker of Gargoyles") (27–42); "La pianta di Marte" ("Seedling of Mars") (43–56); "La dezolazione di Soom" ("The Abomination of Desolation") (87–88); "Omicidio nella quarta dimensione" ("A Murder in the Fourth Dimension") (89–99); "Dio lunare" ("The God of the Asteroid") (101–17); "La radice di Ampoi" ("The Root of Ampoi") (119–35); "I memnon della notte" ("Memnons of the Night") (137); "Il simposio della gorgone" ("Symposium of the Gorgon") (139–48); "Il furto delle 39 cinture" ("The Theft of the Thirty-nine Girdles") (149–60); "Madre di rospi" ("Mother of Toads") (161–69); "Clark Ashton CAS: Ricordi" ("Clark Ashton CAS: A Memoir") by E. Hoffmann Price (173–87); "L'ultimo dei decadenti: Clark Ashton Smith" by Domenico Cammarota (189–208).

   Notes. Bound in paper. Cover artwork by Boris Vallejo. Translated by Daniela Galdo. I miti di Cthulhu 6.

7. *La Venere di Azombeii.*
   a. Rome: Fannuci, 1987. 211 pp.

   Contents: "Clark Ashton Smith e Iperborea" by Gianni Pilo (5–10); "Il vagabondo nel deserto" ("Told in the Desert") (13–19); "L'avo" ("The Necromantic Tale") (21–33); "Il pugnale malese" ("The Malay Krise") (35–37); "Il cadavere in eccesso" ("The Supernumerary Corpse") (39–47); "Il serpente a sonagli" ("The Resurrection of the Rattlesnake") (49–55); "Il bacio di Zoraida" ("The Kiss of Zoraida") (57–62); "La mandragora" ("The Mandrakes") (63–70); "La giustizia dell'elefante" ("The Justice of the Elephant") (71–74); "Un'avventura nel futuro" ("An Adventure in Futurity") (75–114); "I tredici fantasmi" ("Thirteen Phantasms") (115–18); "Il fantasma di Mohammed Din" ("The Ghost of Mohammed Din") (119–26); "Il confucente di elefanti" ("The

Mahout") (127–33); "La fenice" ("Phoenix") (135–46); "Qualcosa di nuovo" ("Something New") (147–49); "Mostri nella notte" ("Monsters in the Night") (151–54); "Un racconto di Sir John Maundeville" ("A Tale of Sir John Maundeville") (155–63); "L'incommensurabile orrore" ("The Immeasurable Horror") (165–80); "La Venere di Azombeii" ("The Venus of Azombeii") (181–209).

Notes. Bound in paper. Cover artwork by Boris Vallejo. Translated by Maria Teresa Tenore. I miti di Cthulhu 12.

8.   *Le Metamorfosi della terra.*
    a.   Rome: Fanucci, 1987. 213 pp.

     Contents: "Le metamorfosi della terra" ("The Metamorphosis of the World") (5–40); "Il pianeta stupefacente" ("A Captivity in Serpens") (41–88); "La dimensione del caso" ("The Dimension of Chance") (89–114); "Un'offerta alla luna" ("An Offering to the Moon") (115–26); "Il rajah e la tigre" ("The Raja and the Tiger") (127–34); "Abbandonati su Andromeda" ("Marooned in Andromeda") (135–70); "Invito alla lettura di C. A. Smith" by Giorgio Giorgi (171–86); "Il fauno inginocchiato: Agostino John Sinadinò" by Domenico Cammarota (187–204); "Bibliografia generale" (205–12).

     Notes. Bound in paper. Cover artwork by Boris Vallejo (uncredited). Transalted by Gianni Pilo. I miti di Cthulhu 18.

9.   *Hyperborea.*
    a.   Rome: Fanucci, 1989. 215 pp.

     Contents: "Hyperborea e il ciclo di Commorion" (unsigned) (5–11); "Le sette fatiche" ("The Seven Geases") (15–37); "Il destino di Avoosl Wuthoqquan" ("The Weird of Avoosl Wuthoqquan") (39–48); "La sibilla bianca" ("The White Sybil") (49–60); "Il testamento di Athammaus" ("The Testament of Athammaus") (61–80); "L'avvento del verme bianco" ("The Coming of the White Worm") (81–96); "Ubbo-Sathla" (97–105); "La porta di Saturno" ("The Door to Saturn") (107–28); "Il demone di ghiaccio" ("The Ice-Demon") (129–48); "Il racconto di Satampra Zeiros" ("The Tale of Satampra Zeiros") (149–63); "Gli orrori di Yondo" ("The Abominations of Yondo") (167–75); "La partenza di Afrodite" ("The Passing of Aphrodite") (177–80); "Il castello" by Angelo R. Mazzarese (183–94); "Plenilunio" by Angelo R. Mazzarese (195–206); "Homme Garou" by Bernardo Cicchetti (207–13).

Notes. Bound in paper. Cover artwork by Chris Achilleos (un-credited). Translated by Marta Simonetti. This book includes three original Italian-language short stories. I miti di Cthulhu 32.

10. *Xiccarph.*
   a. Rome: Fanucci, 1989. 208 pp.

   Contents: "Al demonio" ("To the Daemon") (5–6); "Il labirinto di Maal Dweb" ("The Maze of Maal Dweb") (9–24); "Sirene floreali" ("The Flower-Women") (25–40); "Vulthoom" (41–70); "I figli dell'abisso" ("The Dweller in the Gulf") (71–94); "Le cripte di Yoh-Vombis" ("The Vaults of Yoh-Vombis") (96–114); "Il demone del fiore" ("The Demon of the Flower") (115–28); "Il mostro della profezia" ("The Monster of the Prophecy") (129–68); "La città fantasma" ("The Invisible City") (169–78); "Il paesaggio dei salici" ("The Willow Landscape") (179–84); "La gorgone" ("The Gorgon") (185–198); "Sadastor" (201–4); "Dalle cripte della memoria" ("From the Crypts of Memory") (205–6).
   Notes. Bound in paper. Cover artwork by Chris Achilleos (un-credited). Translated by Marta Simonetti. I miti di Cthulhu 33.

11. *Averoigne.*
   a. Rome: Fanucci, 1989. 231 pp.

   Contents: "Il poeta della fiamma cantante" (unsigned) (5–9); "Il satiro" ("The Satyr") (13–19); "Il mostro dell'Averoigne" ("The Beast of Averoigne") (21–33); "La santità di Azédarac" ("The Holiness of Azédarac") (35–59); "La fine della storia" ("The End of the Story") (61–79); "Un rendezvous in Averoigne" ("A Ren-dezvous in Averoigne") (81–95); "L'incantatrice di Sylaire" ("The Enchantress of Sylaire") (97–114); "Il ritrovamento di Venere" ("The Disinterment of Venus") (115–23); "Il colosso di Yl-ourgne" ("The Colossus of Ylourgne") (125–72); "La città della fiamma cantante" ("The City of the Singing Flame") (175–219); "Cineserie" ("Chinoiserie") (221–22); "Il nono scheletro" ("The Ninth Skeleton") (223–28); "Lo specchio nella sala d'ebano" ("The Mirror in the Hall of Ebony") (229).
   Notes. Bound in paper. Cover artwork by Chris Achilleos (un-credited). Translated by Marta Simonetti. I miti di Cthulhu 34.

12. *Malneant.*
   a. Rome: Fanucci, 1990. 221 pp.

Contents: "Una notte a Malneant" ("A Night in Malnéant") (5–11); "La progenie senza nome" ("The Nameless Offspring") (13–33); "L'adoratore del demonio" ("The Devotee of Evil") (35–48); "I cacciatori dell'aldilà" ("The Hunters from Beyond") (49–66); "Genius Loci" (67–87); "Il dio della polvere" ("The Treader of the Dust") (89–97); "La drogas plutoniana" ("The Plutonian Drug") (99–110); "La lettera di Mohaun Los" ("The Letter from Mohaun Los") (111–48); "La luce dell'aldilà" ("The Secret of the Cairn") (149–71); "Il mondo senza tempo" ("The Eternal World") (173–96); "Medio evo" ("The Dark Age") (197–213); "I fantasmi del fucco" ("The Phantoms of the Fire") (215–21).

Notes. Bound in paper. Cover artwork by Chris Achilleos (uncredited). Translated by Marta Simonetti. I miti di Cthulhu 36.

13. *Atlantide e i mondi perduti.* xvi, 600 pp.

    a.   Milan: Mondadori, [November] 2017.

Contents: "Introduzione: Alla ricerca dei mondi perduti" by Giuseppe Lippi; *Parte prima: Atlantide:* "Da una lettera" ("From a Letter"); "L'ultimo incantesimo" ("The Last Incantation"); "Viaggio a Sfanomoë" ("A Voyage to Snafomoe"); "La doppia ombra" ("The Double Shadow"); "Un vino di Atlantide" ("A Vintage from Atlantis"); "La morte di Malygris" ("The Death of Malygris"); "Tolometh" (English and Italian); "Atlantis" (English and Italian); *Parte seconda: Averoigne:* "La fine della storia" ("The End of the Story"); "Il satiro" ("The Satyr"); "Appuntamento in Averoigne" ("A Rendezvous in Averoigne"); "Lo scultore di mostri" ("The Maker of Gargoyles"); "Le mandragore" ("The Mandrakes"); "La Bestia di Averoigne" ("The Beast of Averoigne"); "La santità di Azédarac" ("The Holiness of Azédarac"); "Il colosso di Ylourgne" ("The Colossus of Ylourgne"); "La scoperta di Venere" ("The Disinterment of Venus"); "La madre dei rospi" ("Mother of Toads"); "L'incatatrice di Sylaire" ("The Enchantress of Sylaire"); "Averoigne" (English and Italian); *Parte terza: Zothique:* "Zothique" (English and Italian); "L'impero dei negromanti" ("The Empire of the Necromancers"); "L'isola dei torturatori" ("The Isle of the Torturers"); "Il viaggio di re Euvoran" ("The Voyage of King Euvoran"); "Il tessitore nella cripta" ("The Weaver in the Vault"); "Il frutto della tumba" ("The Tomb-Spawn"); "Le stregonerie di Ulua" ("The Witchcraft of Ulua"); "Il dio dei cadaveri" ("The Charnel God"); "Xeethra"; "L'idolo oscuro" ("The Dark Eidolon"); "L'ultimo geroglifico" ("The Last Hieroglyph"); "L'abate nero di Puthuum" ("The Black

Abbot of Puthuum"); I negromanti di Naat" ("Necromancy in Naat"); "La morte di Ilalotha" ("The Death of Ilalotha"); "Il giardino di Adompha" ("The Garden of Adompha"); "Il signore dei granchi" ("The Master of the Crabs"); "Morthylla"; *I morti di faran cornuto* (*The Dead Will Cuckold You*); "Forme di pietra" ("Shapes of Adamant"); "Il nemico di Mandor" ("Mandor's Enemy"); *Parte quarta: Xiccarph:* "Il labirinto dell'incantatore" ("The Maze of Maal Dweb"); "Le donne-fiore" ("The Flower-Women"); "Bibliografia"; "Copyright."

Notes. Bound in cloth (no dust jacket). Cover art by Greta Grendel. Translated by Giuseppe Lippi.

vii. Japanese

1. *Majutsushi no teikoku.*
    a. Tokyo: Sodosha, 1974. 498 pp.
    b, Tokyo: Shoenshinsha, Atelier Third, 2017 (2 vols.).

    Contents: "Zoshīku" ("Zothique"); "Jīsura" ("Xeethra"); "Yomi no shima" ("Necromancy in Naat"); "Majutsushi no teikoku" ("The Empire of the Necromancers"); "Urua no majutsu" ("The Witchcraft of Ulua"); "Ankoku no gūzō" ("The Dark Eidolon"); "Bōkyaku no funbo" ("The Tomb-Spawn"); "Saigo no moji" ("The Last Hieroglyph"); "Adonfa no sono" ("The Garden of Adompha"); "Haipāboria no myūzu" ("The Muse of Hyperborea"); "Nanatsu no noroi" ("The Seven Geases"); "Abūsuru Utokan no hisan na unmei" ("The Weird of Avoosl Wuthoqquan"); "Shiroi miko" ("The White Sybil"); "Ubo-Satura" ("Ubbo-Sathla"); "Kioku no fuchi yori" ("From the Crypts of Memory"); "Hana no otometachi" ("The Flower-Women"); "Yō Bomubisu no chikabochi" ("The Vaults of Yoh-Vombis"); "Yogen no mamono" ("The Monster of Prophecy"); "Kanashimi no hoshi" ("Sadastor"); "Nijū no kage" ("The Double Shadow"); "Yondo no mamonotachi" ("The Abominations of Yondo"); "Sūmu no sabaku" ("The Abomination of Desolation"); "Yoru no Memunon" ("The Memnons of the Night"); *Taima Kyūinsha* (*The Hashish-Eater*).

    Notes. Translated by Akio Hachiya, Hiroshi Aramata, Hitoshi Yasuda, Akira Kagami, Kozo Hirota, Morihiro Yoneda, Osamu Yamada, and Kozo Watanabe. The 2017 reprint omits *The Hashish-Eater*.

2. *Makai ōkoku.*
    a. Tokyo: Asahi Sonorama, 1985.

    Contents: "Kani no Ō" ("Master of Crabs"); "Bosho e no sasoi" ("The Death of Ilalotha"); "Gōmontō" ("The Isle of the Torturers"); "Kyūketsuki" ("Morthylla"); "Hyōma" ("The Ice-Demon"); "Shinden no tōzoku" ("The Theft of Thirty-nine Girdles"); "Mū dairiku no tsuki" ("An Offering to the Moon"); "Saigo no majutsu" ("The Last Incantation"); "Atorantisu no bishu" ("A Vintage from Atlantis"); "Kurayami ni kaeru" ("The Epiphany of Death"); "Hikyō no Vīnasu" ("The Venus of Azombeii").
    Notes. Translated by Eiko Kakinuma.

3. *Atorantisu no noroi.*
    a. Tokyo: Kokusho Kankokai, 1986.

    Contents: "Shinigami no miyako" ("The Charnel God"); "Kōri no maō" ("The Ice-Demon"); "Kaitō nigashimu jaumu no kubi" ("The Testament of Athammaus"); "Futatsu no emerarudo" ("The Weird of Avoosl Wuthoqquan"); "Iseki no himitsu" ("The Vaults of Yoh-Vombis"); "Atorantisu no noroi" ("A Vintage from Atlantis").
    Notes. Children's book. Illustrated by Miho Satake. Translated by Satoru Enokibayashi.

4. *Norowareshi roki.*
    a. Tokyo: Kokusho Kankokai, 1986.

    Contents: "Chirei" ("Genius Loci"); "Yanagi no aru fūkei" ("The Willow Landscape"); "Kokonotsume no gaikotsu" ("The Ninth Skeleton"); "Kaji no Gen'ei" ("The Phantoms of the Fire"); "Eien no sekai" ("The Eternal World"); "Vurutūmu" ("Vulthoom"); "Ijigen no wakusei" ("A Star-Change"); "Ōmukashi no machi" ("The Primal City"); "Vīnasu no kaihō" ("The Disinterment of Venus"); "Irūrunyu no kyozō" ("The Colossus of Ylourgne"); "Mori no kami satyurosu" ("The Satyr"); "Adonpa no teien" ("The Garden of Adompha"); "Shokushiki no kami" ("The Charnel God"); "Putūmu no kuroi sōinchō" ("The Black Abbot of Puthuum"); "Chikamaisōshitsu ni su wo haru mono" ("The Weaver in the Vault").
    Notes. Translated by Takashi Ogura.

5. *Irūnyu no kyojin.*
    a. Tokyo: Sogensha, 1986. 403 pp.

    Contents: "Marunean no yoru" ("A Night in Malnéant") (10–19); "Atamausu no yuigon" ("The Testament of Athammaus") (22–47);

"Seijin Azedaraku" ("The Holiness of Azédarac") (50–79); "Averowānyu no kemono" ("The Beast of Averoigne") (82–96); "Kanata kara no hikari" ("The Secret of the Cairn") (98–126); "Shi no kengen" ("The Epiphany of Death") (128–35); "Kōri no mamono" ("The Ice-Demon") (138–59); "Shirēru no onna-mahōtsukai" ("The Enchantress of Sylaire") (162–84); "Tochi-gami" ("Genius Loci") (186–210); "Yanagi no aru fūkei" ("The Willow Landscape") (212–18); "Kyūbanme no gaikotsu" ("The Ninth Skeleton") (220–26); "Irūnyu no kyojin" ("The Colossus of Ylourgne") (228–79); "Hikigaeru obasan" ("Mother of Toads") (282–92); "Hakarigatai kyōfu" ("The Immeasurable Horror") (294–314); "Mienai machi" ("The Invisible City") (316–46); "Yo-bun na shitai" ("The Supernumerary Corpse") (348–60); "Yoru no kaibutsutachi" ("Monsters in the Night") (362–66); "Yūvo-ran-Ō no funatabi" ("The Voyage of King Euvoran") (368–401).

Notes. Bound in paper with dust jacket. Translated by Akemi Itsuji.

6. *Zotīku gen'yō kaiitan.*
   a. Tokyo : Sogensha, 2009. 453 pp.

   Contents: "Zotīku" ("Zothique"); "Kōreijutsushi no teikoku" ("The Empire of the Necromancers"); "Gōmonsha no shima" ("The Isle of the Torturers"); "Shitai anchisho no kami" ("The Charnel God"); "Ankoku no mazō" ("The Dark Eidolon"); "Euworan-Ō no koukai" ("The Voyage of King Euvoran"); "Chikabunkotsusho ni su wo haru mono" ("The Weaver in the Vault"); "Haka no otoshigo" ("The Tomb-Spawn"); "Urua no yōjutsu" ("The Witchcraft of Ulua"); "Kusētura" ("Xeethra"); "Saigo no shōkeimoji" ("The Last Hiero-glyph"); "Nāto no kōreijutsu" ("Necromancy in Naat"); "Putūmu no kokujin no daishūdōinchō" ("The Black Abbot of Puthuum"); "Ira-rota no shi" ("The Death of Ilalotha"); "Adomufa no teien" ("The Garden of Adompha"); "Kani no shihaisha" ("Master of Crabs"); "Morutyurra" ("Morthylla").

   Notes. Translated by Keisuke Ôtaki.

7. *Averowānyu yōmi rōmantan.*
   a. Tokyo: Sogensha, 2011. 424 pp.

   Contents: "Averowānyu" ("Averoigne"); "Kaibutsuzou wo tsukuru mono" ("The Maker of Gargoyles"); "Azedaraku no seisei" ("The Holiness of Azedarac"); "Iruurunyu-jō no kyozō" ("The Colossus of Ylourgne"); "Averowānyu no aibiki" ("A Rendezvous in Aver-oigne"); "Averowānyu no kemono" ("The Beast of Averoigne");

"Mandoragora" ("The Mandrakes"); "Wenusu no hakkutsu" ("The Disinterment of Venus"); "Satyurosu" ("The Satyr"); "Shirēru no majo" ("The Enchantress of Sylaire"); "Monogatari no ketsumatsu" ("The End of the Story"); "Senjo no obasan" ("Mother of Toads"); "Afōgomon no kusari" ("The Chain of Aforgomon"); "Maryoku no aru monogatari" ("The Necromantic Tale"); "Yōjutsushi no kikan" ("The Return of the Sorcerer"); "Bunretsubyō no zōbutsushu" ("Schizoid Creator"); "Kanata kara karitateru mono" ("The Hunters from Beyond"); "Jin'ai wo fumiaruku mono" ("The Treader of the Dust").
Notes. Translated by Keisuke Ôtaki.

8. *Hyuperuboreosu kyokuhoku shinkaitan.*
    a. Tokyo: Sogensha, 2011. 446 pp.

    Contents: "Hyuperuboreosu no mūsa" ("The Muse of Hyperborea"); "Nanatsu no noroi" ("The Seven Geases"); "Aūsuru Utokkuan no fuun" ("The Weird of Avoosl Wuthoqquan"); "Atamumausu no isho" ("The Testament of Athammaus"); "Byakushu no shūrai" ("The Coming of the White Worm"); "Dosei e no tobira" ("The Door to Saturn"); "Kōhaku no miko" ("The White Sybil"); "Kōri no mamono" ("The Ice-Demon"); "Satamupura Zeirosu no hanashi" ("The Tale of Satampra Zeiros"); "Sanjūkyū no shokutainusumi" ("The Theft of Thirty-nine Girdles"); "Ubbo-Satura" ("Ubbo-Sathla"); "Saigo no jumon" ("The Last Incantation"); "Maryugurisu no shi" ("The Death of Malygris"); "Nijū no kage" ("The Double Shadow"); "Sufanomoē e no tabi" ("A Voyage to Sfanomoë"); "Atorantisu no bishu" ("A Vintage from Atlantis"); "Shigen no toshi" ("The Primal City"); "Tsuki e no sonaemono" ("An Offering to the Moon"); "Chizu ni nai shima" ("The Uncharted Isle"); "Utau Honou no toshi" ("The City of the Singing Flame"); "Marunean de no ichiya" ("A Night in Malneant"); "Sadasutoru" ("Sadastor"); "Yanagi no aru sansuiga" ("The Willow Landscape").
    Notes. Translated by Keisuke Ôtaki.

viii. Polish

1. *Miasto śpiewającego płomienia.* Edited by Joanna Egert.
    a. Warsaw: Wydawnictwo Alfa, 1994. 202 pp.

    Contents: "Potwór z przepowiedni Abbolechiolora" ("The Monster of the Prophecy" [tr. Andrzej Polkowski]) (9–54); "Miasto śpiewającego płomienia" ("The City of the Singing Flame" [tr.

Jacek Manicki]) (57–112 [includes "Beyond the Singing Flame"]); "Pan otchłani" ("The Dweller in the Gulf" [tr. Iwona Żółtowska]) (115–42); "Los Antariona" ("The Planet of the Dead" [tr. Iwona Żółtowska]) (145–61); "Kobiety-kwiaty" ("The Flower-Women" [tr. Iwona Żółtowska]) (165–80); "Przeklęty kwiat" ("The Demon of the Flower" [tr. Iwona Żółtowska]) (181–96); "Posłowie" by Iwona Żółtowska (197–202).

Notes. Bound in paper. Cover artwork by Lang.

ix. Spanish

1. *Zothique.*
    a.1. Madrid: Edaf, 1977. 378 pp.
    a.2. Madrid: Edaf, 1990.

    Contents: "Cuando el mundo envejezca" by Lin Carter (11–18); "Zothique" (19); "Xeethra" (21–48); "Nigromancia en Naat" ("Necromancy in Naat") (49–76); "El imperio de los nigroman-tes" ("The Empire of the Necromancers") (77–90); "El amo de los cangrejos" ("The Master of the Crabs") (91–110); "La muerte de Ilalotha" ("The Death of Ilalotha") (111–26); "El tejedor de la tumba" ("The Weaver in the Vault") (127–44); "La magia de Ulúa" ("The Witchcraft of Ulua") (145–58); "El dios de los muertos" ("The Charnel God") (159–88); "El ídolo oscuro" ("The Dark Eidolon") (189–226); "Morthylla" (227–40); "El abad ne-gro de Puthuum" ("The Black Abbot of Puthuum") (241–70); "El fruto de la tumba" ("The Tomb-Spawn") (271–84); "El último jeroglífico" ("The Last Hieroglyph") (285–306); "El jardín de Adompha" ("The Garden of Adompha") (329–42); "El viaje del rey Euvorán" ("The Voyage of King Euvoran") (343–74); "Epilogo: La secuencia de los cuentos de Zothique" by Lin Carter (375–78).

    Notes. Bound in paper. Cover artwork by George Barr. Trans-lation of *Zothique* (I.A.25). Translated by Inmaculada de Dios.

2. *Hyperbórea.*
    a. Madrid: Edaf, 1978. 285 pp.

    Contents: "Introducción: Detrás del viento del norte" by Lin Carter (11–22); "La musa de Hyperbórea" ("The Muse of Hyperborea") (23–24); "Las siete pruebas" ("The Seven Geases") (25–57); "El extraño caso de Avoosl Wuthoqquan" ("The Weird of Avoosl Wuthoqquan") (58–71); "La sibila blanca" ("The White Sybil")

(72–87); "El testamento de Athammaus" ("The Testament of Athammaus") (88–117); "La llegada del gusano blanco" ("The Coming of the White Worm") (118–39); "Ubbo-Sathla" (140–53); "La puerta de Saturno" ("The Door to Saturn") (154–84); "El demonio de hielo" ("The Ice-Demon") (185–211); "El relato de Satampra Zeiros" ("The Tale of Satampra Zeiros") (212–32); "El robo de los treinta y nueve cinturones" ("The Theft of the Thirty-nine Girdles") (233–52); "Las abominaciones de Yondo" ("The Abominations of Yondo") (253–64); "La desolación de Soom" ("The Desolation of Soom") (265–66); "La marcha de Afrodita" ("The Passing of Aphrodite") (267–71); "Las estatuas de la noche" ("The Memnons of the Night") (272–73); "Notas al ciclo mítico de Commorión" by Lin Carter (274–85).

Notes. Bound in paper. Cover art by Bill Martin. Translation of *Hyperborea* (I.A.29). Translated by Guadalupe Rubio de Urquía.

3. *Los mundos perdidos y otros relatos.* Edited by Alberto Santos Castillo.
a. Madrid: Edaf, 1991. 547 pp.

Contents: "Introducción a la edición española" by Alberto Santos Castillo (9–14); "Introducción a la edición americana" by Ray Bradbury [from *A Rendezvous in Averoigne* (I.A.47)] (15–16); "La santidad de Azédarac" ("The Holiness of Azédarac") (19–47); "El coloso de Ylourgne" ("The Colossus of Ylourgne") (49–104); "El final de la historia" ("The End of the Story") (105–131); "Una cita en Averoigne" ("A Rendezvous in Averoigne") (133–54); "El último hechizo" ("The Last Incantation") (157–64); "La muerte de Malygris" ("The Death of Malygris") (165–82); "Un viaje a Sfanomoë" ("A Voyage to Sfanomoë") (183–94); "La sombra doble" ("The Double Shadow") (195–213); "El habitante de la sima" ("The Dweller in the Gulf") (214–45); "Las criptas de Yoh-Vombis" ("The Vaults of Yoh-Vombis") (247–71); "Señor del asteroide" ("Master of the Asteroid" 273–95); "Siembra de Marte" ("Seedling of Mars") (297–354); "La ciudad de la llama que canta" ("The City of the Singing Flame") (355–81); "El laberinto de Maal Dweb" ("The Maze of Maal Dweb") (383–402); "La cadena de Aforgomon" ("The Chain of Aforgomon") (403–28); "Genius Loci" (428–54); "El planeta de los muertos" ("The Planet of the Dead") (455–73); "La droga plutoniana" ("The Plutonian Drug") (475–90); "El devoto del mal" ("The Devotee of Evil") (491–508); "La raíz de Ampoi" ("The Root of Ampoi") (509–29); "La isla que no estaba en los mapas" ("The Uncharted Isle") (531–47).

Notes. Bound in paper. Cover artwork by Frank Frazetta. Translated by Arturo Villarrubia.

4. *Historia de la princesa Zulkaïs y el principe Kalilah: El tercer episodio de Vathek* (with William Beckford)
   a. Madrid: Valdemar (El Club Dumas), February 1999. 119 pp.

      Contents: "Prologo" (9–16); "El tercer episodio de Vathek" ("The Third Episode of Vathek") (17–119).

      Notes. Bound in paper. Cover artwork from a watercolor by Sir John Gardner Wilkonson. Translated by José María Nebreda.

5. *Averoigne.*
   a. Madrid: Río Henares Prodduciones Gráficas, September 2003. 285 pp.

      Contents: "Klarkash-Ton, sacerdote de la Atlántida" by José Miguel Pallarés (5–23); "Introducción a la ediciòn nortemerica" [from *A Rendezvous in Averoigne* (I.A.47)] by Ray Bradbury (25–26); *Averoigne:* "El escultor de gárgolas" ("The Maker of Gargoyles") (29–42); "La santidad de Azedarac" ("The Holiness of Azédarac") (43–62); "El coloso de Ylourgne" ("The Colossus of Ylourgne") (63–100); "La madre de los sapos" ("Mother of Toads") (101–10); "La hechicera de Sylaire, o La torre de Istarelle" ("The Enchantress of Sylaire") (111–24); "La bestia de Averoigne" ("The Beast of Averoigne") (125–36); "Las mandrágoras" ("The Mandrakes") (137–44); "La exhumación de Venus" ("The Disinterment of Venus") (145–52); "Una cita en Averoigne" ("A Rendezvous in Averoigne") (153–68); "El sátiro" ("The Satyr") (169–76); "El final de la historia" ("The End of the Story") (177–94); *California:* "El devoto del mal" ("The Devotee of Evil") (197–208); "La raíz de Ampoi" ("The Root of Ampoi") (209–24); "Genius Loci" (225–42); "La ciudad de la llama cantarina" ("The City of the Singing Flame") (243–83 [includes "Beyond the Singing Flame"]).

      Notes. Bound in paper. Cover artwork by Amadeo Garrigós. Translated by Román Goicoechea.

6. *Zothique, el ultimo continente.*
   a. Madrid: Valdemar, 2011. 317 pp.

      Contents: "Zothique" (9); map of Zothique by G. R. Hager; "Xeethra" (11–36); "Nigromancia en Naat" ("Necromancy in Naat" (37–60); "El imperio de los nigromantes" ("The Empire of the Necromancers") (61–71); "El señor de los cangrejos" ("The Master of the Crabs") (73–88); "La muerte de Ilalotha" ("The Death of Ilalotha") (89–101); "El tejedor de la cripta" ("The Weaver in the Vault") (103–17); "La brujera de Ulua" ("The Witchcraft of Ulua") (119–29); "El dios carroñeos" ("The Charnel God") (131–56); "El oscuro eidolon" ("The Dark Eidolon") (157–88); "Morthylla" (189–200); "El abad negro de Puthuum" ("The Black Abbot of Puthuum") (201–26); "El engendro de la tumba" ("The Tomb-Spawn") (227–38); "El ultimo jeroglifico" ("The Last Hieroglyph") (239–57); "La isla de los torturadoros") ("The Isle of the Torturers") (259–77); "El jardin de Adompha" ("The Garden of Adompha") (277–88); "El viaje del rey Euvoran" ("The Voyage of King Euvoran") (289–316).

    Notes. Bound in black pictorial boards. Translated by Marta Lila Murillo.

7.   *Hiperbórea y otros mundos perdidos.*
   a. Madrid: Valdemar, 2014. 308 pp.

    Contents: "Flores extrañas" (introduction), by Jesús Palacios (9–21); HIPERBÓREA: "La musa de Hiperbórea" ("The Muse of Hyperborea") (25); "Los siete *Geases*" ("The Seven Geases" (27–50); "El sino de Avoosl Wuthoqquan" ("The Weird of Avoosl Wuthoqquan") (51–61); "La sibila blanca" ("The White Sybil") (63–74); "El testamento de Athammaus" ("The Testament of Athammaus") (75–97); "La llegada del gusano blanco") ("The Coming of the White Worm") (99–114); "Ubbo-Sathla" (115–24); "La puerta a Satuno" ("The Door to Saturn") (125–46); "La historia de Satampra Zeiros" ("The Tale of Satampra Zeiros") (147–61); "El demonio de hielo" ("The Ice-Demon") (163–81); "El robo de los treinta y nueve cinturones" ("The Theft of the Thirty-nine Girdles") (183–95); AIHAI (MARTE): "Vulthoom" (199–229); "El morador del abismo" ("The Dweller in the Gulf") (231–54); "Las criptas de Yoh-Vombis" ("The Vaults of Yoh-Vombis") (255–74); XIC-CARPH: "El laberinto de Maal Dweb" ("The Maze of Maal Dweb") (277–94); "Las mujeres flor" ("The Flower-Women") (295–308).

    Notes. Bound in cloth (no dust jacket). Cover art by Juan Serrano. Translated by Marta Lila Murillo.

8.   *El libro di Hiperbórea.*
   a. Madrid: Ediciones Cátedra, 2015. 285 pp.

Contents: "Introducción"; "La historia de Satampra Zeiros" ("The Tale of Satampra Zeiros"); "La puerta a Saturno" ("The Door to Saturn"); "El testamento de Athammaus" ("The Testament of Athammaus"); "El sino de Avoosl Wuthoqquan" ("The Weird of Avoosl Wuthoqquan"); "Ubbo-Sathla"; "La sibila blanca" ("The White Sybil"); "El demonio de hielo" ("The Ice-Demon"); "La venida de gusano blanco" ("The Coming of the White Worm"); "La siete geas" ("The Seven Geases"); "El robo de los treinta y nueves cinturones" ("The Theft of the Thirty-nine Girdles"); "La casa de Haon-Dor" ("The House of Haon-Dor"); "final alternativo de 'La sibila blanca'" (variant ending of "The White Sibyl"); "La Musa de Hiperbórea" ("The Muse of Hyperborea"); "La sombra antigua/La sombra del sarcófago" ("The Ancient Shadow/The Shadow from the Sarcophagus"); "La ciudad hiperbórea" ("The Hyperborean City" [synopsis]).

Notes. Bound in paper. Cover design (incorporating a map by Gerardus Mercator) by Plurabelle. Translated by Luis Gámez. Apparently a partial translation of *The Book of Hyperborea* (I.A.58). The last two items were taken from Will Murray's "Postscript" to that volume.

x. *Turkish*

1. *Dusler imparatoru.*
   a. Istanbul: Ithaki Publications, 2003. 201 pp.

   Contents: "Ölüler büyücüsünün şarkisi" ("Song of the Necromancer") (9–10); "Yondo'nun tiksinçleri" ("The Abominations of Yondo") (11–18); "Dokuzuncu ìskelet" ("The Ninth Skeleton") (19–24); "Son büyü" ("The Last Incantation") (25–30); "Gorgon" ("The Gorgon") (31–42); "Satürn Kapisi" ("The Door to Saturn") (43–62); "Büyücü'nün dönüşşü" ("The Return of the Sorcerer") (63–78); "Ubbo-Sathla" (79–88); "Satampra Zeiros'un öyküsü" ("The Tale of Satampra Zeiros") (87–100); "Işkenceciler adasi" ("The Isle of the Torturers") (101–16); "Öteden gelen avcilar" ("The Hunters from Beyond" [tr. Bariş Emre Alkim]) (117–34); "Züreyda'nin öpücüşü" ("The Kiss of Zoraida") (135–40); "Ölü büyücülerinin imparatorluşu" ("The Empire of the Necromancers") (141–50); "Leş yiyen" ("The Ghoul") (151–56); "Averoigne'da randevu" ("A Rendezvous in Averoigne") (157–72); "Averoigne canavari" ("The Beast of Averoigne") (173–85); "Mezardaki tohum" ("The Seed from the Sepulcher") (187–201).

Notes. Bound in paper. Cover design by Kitap Matbaacilik. Translated by Sönmez Güven save where noted.

xi. *Galician*

1. *O escultor de gárgolas e outras historias de Averoigne.*
   a. Santiago de Compostela, Spain: Urco Editora, 2016. 191 pp.

   Contents: "O remate de histora" ("The End of the Story"); "Un encontro en Averoigne" ("A Rendezvous in Averoigne"); "O escultor de gárgolas" ("The Maker of Gargoyles"); "As mandrágoras" ("The Mandrakes"); "A besta de Averoigne" ("The Beast of Averoigne"); "A santitade de Azédarac" ("The Holiness of Azédarac"); "O coloso de Ylourgne" ("The Colossus of Ylourgne"); "A exhumación de Venmus" ("The Disinterment of Venus"); "Nai dos sapos" ("Mother of Toads"); "O sátiro" ("The Satyr").

   Notes. Bound in paper. Translated by Tomás González Ahola.

B. Contributions to Books and Periodicals

i. Fiction

1. "The Abominations of Yondo."
    a. *Ganymed Horror* Nos. 10/11/12 (September 1974): 91–97 (tr. Uwe Anton; under heading "Am Rande die Welt").
    b. In Jacques Goimard, ed. *L'Année 1978–1979 de la science-fiction et du fantastique.* Paris: Julliard, 1979. 142–47 (as "Yondo"; tr. Alain Garsault).
    c. In Marc Duveau, ed. *La Citadelle écarlate.* Paris: Presses Pocket, 1979, 1988. 29–38 (as "Yondo"; tr. Alain Garsault).
    d. *Fikcje* No. 12 (February 1984): 5–12 (as "Okropności Yondo"; tr. Piotr W. Cholewa).
    e. In Antonia Gasquez and Edith Heintzmann, ed. *La Science-Fiction.* Paris: Nathan, 1999. 79–89 (as "Yondo"; tr. Alain Garsault).
    f. In Marc Duveau, ed. *La Grande Anthologie de la fantasy.* Paris: Omnibus, 2003. 29–48 (as "Yondo"; tr. Alain Garsault).

2. "Beyond the Singing Flame."
    a. *Jules Verne-Magasinet/Veckans Äventyr* No. 48 (1945): 6–9, 44–49 (as "Bortom den sjungande lågan"; tr. unknown).
    b. In Sam J. Lundwall, ed. *Första stora monsterboken.* Bromma: Sam J. Lundwall Fakta & Fantasi, 1991. 140–57 (as "Bortom den sjungande lågan"; tr. Sam J. Lundwall).
    c. In H. P. Lovecraft [et al.]. *Il vento delle stelle: Storie in versi e no.* Ed. Sebastiano Fusco. Rome: Agpha Press, 1979. 290–304 (as "Al di là della fiamma"; tr. Sebastiano Fusco).

3. "The Black Abbot of Puthuum."
    a. In [Unsigned, ed.] *Horror 1.* Milan: Sugar, 1965. 13–44 (as "L'abate nero di Puthuum"; tr. Carlo Masi).
    b. *Stampe Sera* (Turin) (21/26 November 1977) (as "L'abate nero"; tr. Roberta Rambelli). [Published in six installments.]

4. "The Charnel God."
    a. In Michael Görden, ed. *Dämonengeschenk.* Bergisch Gladbach: Bastei Lübbe, 1985. 277–97 (as "Dämongeschenk"; tr. Brigitte Peterka).

5.   "The City of the Singing Flame."
   a. In Jacques Sadoul, ed. *Les Meilleurs Récits de WONDER STO-RIES*. Paris: J'ai Lu, 1978. 9–67 (as "La cité de la flamme chantante"; tr. France-Marie Watkins; incorporates "Beyond the Singing Flame").
   b. In John Brunner. *Abominazione atlantica*. Milan: Mondadori, 1983. 123–56 (as "Titan City"; tr. Delio Zinoni).
   c. In H. P. Lovecraft [et al.]. *Il vento delle stelle: Storie in versi e no.* Ed. Sebastiano Fusco. Rome: Agpha Press, 1998. 277–89 (as "La città della fiamma che canta"; tr. Sebastiano Fusco).

6.   "The Colossus of Ylourgne."
   a. In Michel Parry, ed. *I rivali di Frankenstein*. Milan: SIAD, 1979. 17–62 (as "Il colosso di Ylourgne"; tr. Marika Boni Grandi). [Translation of *The Rivals of Frankenstein* (I.B.i.18.d).]
   b. In Isaac Asimov, Martin H. Greenberg, and Charles G. Waugh, ed. *Giganti*. Rome: Fanucci, 1987. 287–334 (as "Il colosso di Ylourgne"; tr. Iva Guglielmi and Gianni Pilo). [Translation of *Isaac Asimov's Magical Worlds of Fantasy #5: Giants* (I.B.i.18.f).]
   c. In Gianni Pilo, ed. *Storie di streghe*. Rome: Newton Compton, 1996. 449–78 (as "Il colosso di Ylourgne"; tr. Gianni Pilo).

7.   "The Coming of the White Worm."
   a. In Sandro Pergameno, ed. *Fantasy*. Milan: Editrice Nord, 1985, 1996. 119–32 (as "L'avvento del verme bianco"; tr. Roberta Rambelli).
   b. In [Unsigned, ed.] *Fantasy*. Bergamo: Euroclub, 1989. 85–92 (as "L'avvento del verme bianco"; tr. Robert Rambelli).
   c. In Robert M. Price, ed. *Eibon no sho*. Tokyo: Shin Kigensha, 2008. 107–24 (as "Shirouji no shuurai"). [Translation of *The Book of Eibon* (I.B.i.18.k).]

8.   "The Dark Eidolon."
   a. In Alex Voglino, ed. *Il grande libro della heroic fantasy*. Milan: Editrice Nord, 1998. 217–54 (as "L'idolo tenebroso"; tr. Viviana Viviani).

9.   "The Dart of Rasasfa."
   a. *Yorick* Nos. 20/21 (December 1995/May 1996): 4–5 (as "Gli uomini-rettile di Rasasfa"; tr. Pietro Guarriello).

10. "The Death of Ilalotha."
   a. In [James Dickie, ed.] *14 Horror Stories*. Munich: Wilhelm Heyne, 1973. 171–83 (as "Der Tod der Ilalotha"; tr. Maikell Michael). [Translation of *The Undead* (I.B.i.25.d).]
   b. In Jacques Sadoul, ed. *Les Meilleurs Récits de WEIRD TALES 2: Période 1933/37*. Paris: J'ai Lu, 1975. 11–25 (as "La Mort d'Ilalotha"; tr. France-Marie Watkins).
   c. In Jacques Sadoul, ed. *Anthologie de la littérature de science-fiction*. Paris: Ramsay, 1981. 63–71 (as "La Mort d'Ilalotha"; tr. France-Marie Watkins).
   d. In Jacques Sadoul, ed. *Les Meilleurs Récits de WEIRD TALES*. Paris: J'ai Lu, 1989. 243–57 (as "La Mort d'Ilalotha"; tr. France-Marie Watkins).
   e. In Jacques Sadoul, ed. *Une Histoire de la science-fiction 1: 1901– 1937 Les Premiers Maîtres*. Paris: Librio, 2000. 100–110 (as "La Mort d'Ilalotha"; tr. France-Marie Watkins).
   f. In Frank Festa, ed. *Denn das Blut ist Leben: Geschichten der Vampire*. Leipzig: Festa Verlag, 2007. 215–27 (as "Ilalothas Tod"; tr. Heiko Langhans).

11. "The Death of Malygris."
   a. In Lauric Guillaud, ed. *Atlantides: Les Îles englouties*. Paris: Omnibus, 1995. 900–911 (as "La Mort de Malygris"; tr. Dominique Mols).

12. "The Devotee of Evil."
   a. In Gianni Pilo, ed. *Storie di diavoli*. Rome: Newton Compton, 1997. 169–76 (as "L'adoratore del demonio": tr. Gianni Pilo).

13. "The Door to Saturn."
   a. In [Unsigned, ed.] *La puerta de Saturno*. Barcelona: Géminis, 1968. 173–203 (as "La puerta de Saturno"; tr. Leoncio Sureda Guytó).
   b. In Robert M. Price, ed. *Eibon no sho*. Tokyo: Shin Kigensha, 2008. 234–50 (as "Dosei e no tobira"). [Translation of *The Book of Eibon* (I.B.i.31.i).]

14. "The Double Shadow."
   a. In Lauric Guillaud, ed. *Atlantides: Les Îles englouties*. Paris: Omnibus, 1995. 912–24 (as "L'Ombre double"; tr. Dominique Mols).

b. In Stephen Jones and Dave Carson, ed. *L'horrore secondo Love-craft*. Milan: Mondadori, 1995. 417–32 (as "La duplice ombra"; tr. Diego Pastorino). [Translation of *H. P. Lovecraft's Book of Horror* (I.B.i.34.h).]

c. In Mike Ashley, ed. *Wielka księga opowieści o czarodziejach. Tom 1.* Lublin: Fabryka Słów, 2010. 259–80 (as "Drugi cień"; tr. Marcin Mortka). [Translation of *The Mammoth Book of Sorcerers' Tales.*]

15. "The Dweller in the Gulf."
   a. In Forrest J Ackerman, ed. *Las mejores historias de horror*. Barcelona: Bruguera, 1969, 1973. 571–92 (as "El habitante de las profundidades de Marte"; tr. Joaquín Llinás).
   b. *Lhork* No. 9 [*Lhork Extra 5 Especial Ciencia Ficción*] (1994): 35–42 (as "El habitante de las profundidades de Marte"; tr. anon.).

16. "The Empire of the Necromancers."
   a. In Jacques Sadoul, ed. *Les Meilleurs Récits de WEIRD TALES 1: Période 1925/32*. Paris: J'ai Lu, 1975. 11–23 (as "L'Empire des nécromants"; tr. France-Marie Watkins).
   b. In Giuseppe Lippi, ed. *Racconti fantastici del 900: Volume 1*. Milan: Mondadori, 1987. 179–90 (as "L'impiro dei negromanti"; tr. Giuseppe Lippi).
   c. In Jacques Sadoul, ed. *Les Meilleurs Récits de WEIRD TALES*. Paris: J'ai Lu, 1989. 9–21 (as "L'Empire des nécromants"; tr. France-Marie Watkins).
   d. In Juhani Hinkkanen, ed. *Velhojen valtakunta*. Helsinki: Jalava, 1989. 25–32 (as "Velhojen valtakunta"; tr. Ilkka Äärelä).
   e. In Frank Festa, ed. *Necrophobia 2: Meister der Angst*. Leipzig: Festa, 2008. 129–41 (as "Necropolis—Das Reich der Toten"; tr. Heiko Langhans).
   f. In Jesús Palacios, ed. *La plaga de los zombis y otras historias de muertos vivientes*. Madrid: Valdemar, 2010. 271–81 (as "El imperio de los nigromantes"; tr. Marta Lila Murillo).

17. "The Enchantress of Sylaire."
   a. In Jean Marigny, ed. *Histoires anglo-saxonnes de vampires*. Paris: Librairie des Champs-Elysées, 1978. 18–94 (as "L'Enchanteresse de Sylaire"; tr. Dominique Mols).
   b. In Gianni Pilo, ed. *Storie di streghe*. Rome: Newton Compton, 1996. 605–16 (as "La stregha di Sylaire"; tr. Gianni Pilo).

    c. In Barbara Sadoul, ed. *Fées, sorcières ou diablesses*. Paris: Librio, 2002. 27–40 (as "L'Enchanteresse de Sylaire"; tr. Dominique Mols).

    d. In Frank Festa, ed. *Und nachts der Werwolf.* Augsburg: Weltbild, 2009. 277–97 (as "Die Zauberin von Sylaire"; tr. Doris Hummel).

18. "The End of the Story."

    a. In [James Dickie, ed.] *14 Horror Stories*. Munich: Wilhelm Heyne Verlag, 1973. 149–69 (as "Die Ruinen von Schloss Faussesflammes"; tr. Maikell Michael). [Translation of *The Undead* (I.B.i.41.c).]

    b. In Jean Marigny, ed. *Histoires anglo-saxonnes de vampires.* Librairie des Champs-Elysées,, 1978. 165–80 (as "La Fin de l'histoire"; tr. Dominique Mols).

    c. In Juan Antonio Molina Foix, ed. *El horror según Lovecraft (Volumen 2)*. Madrid: Siruela, 1988. 385–411 (as "El final de la historia"; tr. José Luis López-Muñoz).

    d. In Gianni Pilo, ed. *Storie di vampiri*. Rome: Newton Compton, 1994, 2005. 547–57 (as "Nicea"; tr. [Teobaldo Del Tanaro and Ina Paparella Morata]).

    e. In Juan Antonio Molina Foix, ed. *El horror según Lovecraft*. Madrid: Siruela, 2003. 405–26 (as "El final de la historia"; tr. José Luis López-Muñoz).

19. "The Epiphany of Death."

    a. *C[ol]laps* No. 29 (1989): 6–8 (as "Epifania śmierci"; tr. unknown).

    b. In Frank Festa, ed. *Der Lovecraft-Zirkel*. Windeck: Blitz Verlag, 2000. 31–36. Leipzig: Festa Verlag, 2006. 38–45 (as "Die Epiphanie des Todes"; tr. Martin Eisele).

20. "The Flower-Women."

    a. *Nueva Dimensión* No. 76 (1976): 42–51 (as "Las mujeres-flor"; tr. Luis Vigil).

    b. In Gianni Pilo, ed. *Storie di streghe*. Rome: Newton Compton, 1996. 813–21 (as "Sirene floreali"; tr. Gianni Pilo).

21. "The Garden of Adompha."

    a. *Stampe Sera* (Turin) (15 July 1977): 21; (16 July 1977): 19 (as "Il giardino di Adompha"; tr. Roberta Rambelli).

    b. In Jacques Sadoul, ed. *Les Meilleurs Récits de WEIRD TALES 3: Période 1938/42*. Paris: J'ai Lu, 1979. 87–99 (as "Le Jardin d'Adompha"; tr. France-Marie Watkins).

    c. In Benoît Virot and Dominique Bordes, ed. *Perdus/Trouvés: Anthologie de littérature oubliée*. Toulouse: Monsieur Toussaint Louverture, 2007. 525–36 (as "Le Jardin d'Adompha"; tr. France-Marie Watkins).

    d. In [Unsigned, ed.] *Il giardino di Adompha e altre storie*. n.p.: Funfactory Edition, 2012 (as "Il giardino di Adompha"; tr. anon.).

22. "Genius Loci."

    a. In Gianni Montanari, ed. *Horroriana: 24 storia di paura*. Milan: Mondadori, 1979. 101–22 (as "Nella paluda"; tr. Giuseppe Lippi).

    b. In Markku Sadelehto, ed. *Outoja tarinoita 4*. Helsinki: Javala, 1992. 62–79 (as "Gorgo"; tr. Matti Rosvall).

23. "The Ghoul."

    a. In Gianni Pilo, ed. *La saga di Cthulhu*. Rome: Fanucci, 1986. 161–68 (as "Il ghoul"; tr. Daniela Galdo, Maria Teresa Tenore, and Gianni Pilo).

    b. *Barsoom* No. 3 (2007): 36–38 (as "El ghoul"; tr. Javier Jiménez Barco).

24. "The Gorgon."

    a. In Gianni Pilo, ed. *Sempre Weird Tales*. Rome: Fanucci, 1985. 345–56 (as "Lo sguardo di pietra"; tr. Gianluigi Zuddas).

    b. In Markku Sadelehto, ed. *Outoja tarinoita 1*. Helsinki: Javala, 1990. 53–66 (as "Gorgo"; tr. Leena Peltonen).

    c. In Gianni Pilo, ed. *Storie dell'orrore*. Rome: Newton Compton, 1999. 490–97 (as "Lo sguardo di pietra"; tr. Gianni Pilo).

25. "The Great God Awto."

    a. In Roberta Rambelli, ed. *Il grande dio Awto e altri racconti*. Turin: Editrice dell'Automobile, 1965. 187–96 (as "Il grande dio Awto"; tr. Luigi Cozzi).

    b. In [Unsigned, ed.] *Storie di fantamore*. Milan: Mondadori, 1967. 160–66 (as "Lezione di archeologia"; tr. Beata Della Frattina).

    c. In Jacques Sadoul, ed. *Les Meilleurs Récits de THRILLING WONDER STORIES*. Paris: J'ai Lu, 1978. 155–62 (as "Le Grand Dieu Awto"; tr. France-Marie Watkins).

26. "The Hunters from Beyond."
   a. *Historias para no dormi* 3, No. 4 (April 1974): 33–45 (as "Los cazadores del más allá"; tr. ?).
   b. *Robot* No. 39 (June 1979): 56–69 (as "I cacciatori dell'al di là"; tr. Stefano Negrini).
   c. *Los Diletantes de Lovecraft* No. 6 (1999): 4–18 (as "Los cazadores del más allá"; tr. ?).

27. "The Immortals of Mercury."
   a. In [Unsigned, ed.] *Margherite per Dorothy*. Milan: Mondadori, 1969. 25–58 (as "Gli immortali di Mercurio"; tr. Beata Della Frattina).

28. "The Invisible City."
   a. *Bibliothek der Unterhaltung und des Wissens* No. 9 (1933): 5–16 (as "Die unsichtbare Stadt"; tr. anon.; as by "A. C. Smith").

29. "The Justice of the Elephant."
   a. *Barsoom* No. 9 (2009): 24–25 (as "La justicia del elefante"; tr. Javier Jiménez Barco).

30. "The Kiss of Zoraida."
   a. *Weird Tales de Lhork* No. 29 (2008): 119–20 (as "El beso de Zoraida"; tr. Javier Jiménez Barco).

31. "The Last Hieroglyph."
   a. In Mike Ashley, ed. *Wielka księga fantasy, Tom 1*. Lublin: Fabryka Słów 2011. 188–209 (as "Ostatni hieroglif"; tr. Milena Wój-towicz). [Translation of *The Mammoth Book of Fantasy*.]

32. "The Last Incantation."
   a. In Lauric Guillaud, ed. *Atlantides: Les Îles englouties*. Paris: Omnibus, 1995. 895–900 (as "La Dernière Incantation"; tr. Dominique Mols).

33. "The Master of the Asteroid."
   a. *Bibliothek der Unterhaltung und des Wissens* No. 5 (1933): 5–22 (as "Das Geheimnis des Asteroiden"; tr. anon.).
   b. In [Unsigned, ed.] *Metà A, metà B*. Milan: Mondadori, 1967. 149–68 (as "Il padrone dell'asteroide"; tr. Beata Della Frattina).

34. "The Maze of the Enchanter."
    a. *Nueva Dimensión* No. 76 (1976): 29–41 (as "El laberinto de Maal Dweb"; tr. Luis Vigil).
    b. In Lin Carter, ed. *Die Zaubergärten*. Rastatt/Baden: Pabel Verlag, 1978. 74–91 (as "Der Irrgarten des Maal Dweb"; tr. Lore Strassl). [Translation of *The Young Magicians* (I.B.i.91.e).]

35. "Monsters in the Night."
    a. *El Grito* No. 3 (1990): 46–48 (as "Una profecía de monstruos"; tr. Carmen Asensio).

36. "Morthylla."
    a. *Luther's Grusel Magazin* No. 18 (n.d.): 56–67 (tr. ?).
    b. *Stampe Sera* (Turin) (22 July 1977): 19; (23 July 1977): 19 (as "Io sono Morthylla"; tr. Roberta Rambelli).
    c. In Jacques Goimard and Roland Stragliati, ed. *La grande anthologie du fantastique 3*. Paris: Omnibus, 1997. 296–305 (tr. Françoise Levie).

37. "Mother of Toads."
    a. *Bucanero* No. 5 (June 1997): 27–31 (as "La madre de los sapos"; tr. Esther Caballero).
    b. *Phantastisch!* No. 1 (2001): 30–36 (as "Mutter Kröte"; tr. anon.).
    c. In Scott Allie, ed. *Dark Horse: Il libro della stregoneria*. Città di Costello: Free Books, 2005. 23–35 (as "Madre di rospi"; tr. Dario Mattaliano). [Translation of *The Dark Horse Book of Witchcraft* (I.B.i.98.f).]

38. "The Nameless Offspring."
    a. In Rafael Llopis, ed. *Los mitos de Cthulhu*. Madrid: Alianza, 1969, 1970, 1997 (16th printing), 1999, 2000. 270–86 (as "Estirpe de la cripta"; tr. Francisco Torres Oliver).
    b. *Robot* No. 39 (June 1979): 105–20 (as "Il frutto della tomba"; tr. Stefano Negrini).
    c. In H. P. Lovecraft. *Oeuvres 1*. Paris: Robert Laffont, 1991. 687–702 (as "L'Héritier des ténèbres"; tr. Gérard Coisne).
    d. In Gianni Pilo, ed. *Storie di vampiri*. Rome: Newton Compton, 1994, 2005. 373–84 (as "Vampiro"; tr. [Teobaldo Del Tanaro]).

39. "Necromancy in Naat."
    a. *Narraciones Terroríficas* No. 8 (1939): 14–25 (as "Nigromancia en Naat"; tr. ?).

40. "A Night in Malnéant."
    a. *Robot* No. 40 (July–August 1979): 79–84 (as "Una notte a Malnéant"; tr. tr. Elvira Lippi).
    b. In Peter Haining, ed. *Ancora Weird Tales: Il secondo periodo 1939–1954*. Rome: Fanucci, 1984. 57–64 (as "Una notte a Malnéant"; tr. Roberta Rambelli).

41. "The Ninth Skeleton."
    a. In Leo Margulies and Oscar J. Friend, ed. *En el rincón obscuro*. Mexico City: La Prensa, 1956. 145–52 (as "El noveno esqueleto"; tr. Óscar Kaufmann Parra).

42. "An Offering to the Moon."
    a. In Lauric Guillaud, ed. *Atlantides: Les Îles englouties*. Paris: Omnibus, 1995. 941–50 (as "Offrande à la lune"; tr. Dominique Mols).

43. "Phoenix."
    a. In August Derleth, ed. *Tiempo por venir*. Buenos Aires: Vértice, 1968. 77–92 (as "Fénix"; tr. Fernando M. Sesén). [Translation of *Time to Come* (I.B.i.113.a).]
    b. In August Derleth, ed. *Paradies II*. Munich: Wilhelm Heyne, 1970. 134–44 (as "Prometheus"; tr. Wulf H. Bergner). [Abridged translation of *Time to Come* (I.B.i.113.a).]
    c. In Isaac Asimov, Martin H. Greenberg, and Charles G. Waugh, ed. *Catastrofi!* Milan: Mondadori, 1984. 109–20 (as "Fenice"; tr. Giuseppe Lippi). [Translation of *Catastrophes!* (I.B.i.114.d).]

44. "Prince Alcouz and the Magician."
    a. In Peter Ruber, ed. *Maestros del horror de Arkham House*. Madrid: Valdemar, 2003. 97–100 (as "El príncipe Alcouz y el hechicero"; tr. José María Nebreda). [Translation of *Arkham's Masters of Horror* (I.B.i.120.a).]

45. "The Raja and the Tiger."
    a. *Sable* No. 4 (2005): 41–44 (as "El rajá y el tigre"; tr. Fermín Moreno González).

b. *Barsoom* No. 2 (2007): 23–25 (as "El rajá y el tigre"; tr. Javier Jiménez Barco).

46. "A Rendezvous in Averoigne."
   a. *Narraciones Terroríficas* No. 12 (1939): 76–84 (as "Una cita en Averoigne"; tr. anon).
   b. In Juan Montoro, ed. *El misterio del hermano fantasma*. Barcelona: Molino, 1943. 104–12 (as "Una cita en Averoigne"; tr. anon).
   c. In [Unsigned, ed.] *Psycho: I racconti della paura 4*. Milan: Armenia, 1979. 34–49 (as "Un incontro in Averoigne"; tr. Elvira Lippi).
   d. In [Unsigned, ed.] *I classici del terrore: Raccolta psycho 2*. Milan: Armenia, 1979, [Part 2]. 34–49 (as "Un incontro in Averoigne"; tr. Elvira Lippi).
   e. In Gianni Pilo, ed. *Storie di vampiri*. Rome: Newton Compton, 1994. 894–902 (as "Il signore di Malinbois"; tr. [Teobaldo Del Tanaro and Ina Paparella Morata]).

47. "The Return of the Sorcerer."
   a. In Roland Stragliati, ed. *Les Miroirs de la peur*. Paris: Casterman, 1969. 113–32 (as "La Retour du sorcier"; tr. Jacques Parsons).
   b. In August Derleth, ed. *I miti di Cthulhu*. Rome: Fanucci, 1975. 145–58 (as "La vendetta dello stregone"; tr. Alfredo Pollini and Sebastiano Fusco). [Translation (with additions) of *Tales of the Cthulhu Mythos* (I.B.i.125.f).]
   c. In August Derleth, ed. *Légendes du mythe de Cthulhu*. Paris: Christian Bourgeois, 1975; Paris: Presses Pocket, 2000 (as *L'Appel de Cthulhu: Légendes du mythe de Cthulhu*). 55–73. Paris: J'ai Lu, 1981. 61–82. Paris: Presses Pocket, 1985. 61–81 (as "Talion"; tr. Claude Gilbert). [Translation of *Tales of the Cthulhu Mythos* (I.B.i.125.f).]
   d. In August Derleth, ed. *Légendes du mythe de Cthulhu 1*. Paris: France Loisirs, 1975. 55–73 (as "Talion"; tr. Claude Gilbert). [Abridged translation of *Tales of the Cthulhu Mythos* (I.B.i.125.f).]
   e. In Michel Parry, ed. *Acht Teufelseier*. Rastatt/Baden: Erich Pabel Verlag, 1976. 46–65 (as "Die Hand vor der Tür"; tr. Werner Maibohm). [Translation of *The 2nd Mayflower Book of Black Magic Stories* (I.B.i.126.h).]
   f. In August Derleth, ed. *Relatos de los mitos de Cthulhu 1*. Barcelona: Bruguera, 1977, 1978, 1981. 71–94 (as "El regreso del

brujo"; tr. Francisco Torres Oliver). [Translation of *Tales of the Cthulhu Mythos* (I.B.i.125.f).]

g. In Tomás Doreste, ed. *Antología del horror y el misterio: Volumen III.* Madrid: Grijalbo, 1990. 663–77 (as "El regreso del brujo"; tr. Tomás Doreste).

h. In H. P. Lovecraft. *Oeuvres 1.* Paris: Robert Laffont, 1991. 648–61 (as "Talion"; tr. Claude Gilbert).

i. *Magia i Miecz* No. 46 (October 1997): 50–54 (as "Powrót czarnoksiężnika"; tr. Witold Nowakowski).

j. In August Derleth and James Turner, ed. *Cthulhu: Una celebración de los mitos.* Madrid: Valdemar, 2001. 47–62 (as "El regreso del brujo"; tr. Francisco Torres Oliver). [Translation of *Tales of the Cthulhu Mythos,* rev. ed. (I.B.i.125.j).]

k. In August Derleth and James Turner, ed. *L'orrore di Cthulhu.* Rome: Newton Compton, 2001. 40–49 (as "La vendetta dello stregone"; tr. Gianni Pilo and Sebastiano Fusco). [Translation of *Tales of the Cthulhu Mythos,* rev. ed. (I.B.i.125.j).]

l. In Frank Festa, ed. *Necrophobia: Meister der Angst.* Leipzig: Festa, 2005. 239–60 (as "Die Rückkehr des Hexers"; tr. Heiko Langhans).

48. "Schizoid Creator."
   a. In [Unsigned, ed.] *Il bambino nel forno: 12 racconti di "Fantasy."* Milan: Mondadori, 1967. 36–44 (as "Doppio gioco"; tr. Beata Della Frattina).
   b. *Fiction* No. 205 (January 1971): 35–43 (as "Quand le diable y serait . . ."; tr. Jacques Papy).

49. "The Second Interment."
   a. In [Unsigned, ed.] *Psycho: I racconti della paura 3.* Milan: Armenia, 1978. 82–94 (as "La seconda sepoltura"; tr. Elvira Lippi).
   b. In [Unsigned, ed.] *I classici del terrore: Raccolta psycho 2.* Milan: Armenia, 1979 [Part 1]. 82–94 (as "La seconda sepoltura"; tr. Elvira Lippi).
   c. In Enrico Badellino, ed. *Sepolto vivo! Quindici racconti dalle tenebre.* Turin: Einaudi, 1999. 205–16 (as "La seconda sepoltura"; tr. [Teobaldo Del Tanaro and Ina Paparella Morata]).

50. "The Seed from the Sepulcher."
   a. In Jacques Papy, ed. *Nouvelles histoires d'outre-monde.* Paris: Casterman, 1967. 299–312 (as "Semences de mort"; tr. Jacques Papy).

b. In [Unsigned, ed.] *Il bambino nel forno: 12 racconti di "Fantasy."* Milan: Mondadori, 1967. 92–106 (as "Il seme nel sepolcro"; tr. Beata Della Frattina).

c. In Domingo Santos, Luis Vigil, and Sebastián Martínez, ed. *Antología de relatos de espanto y terror 3.* Barcelona: Dronte, 1972. 109–24 (as "La semilla del sepulcro"; tr. B. Samarbete).

d. In [Unsigned, ed.] *Omnibus fantascienza Mondadori.* Milan: Mondadori, 1974. 209–19 (as "Il seme nel sepolcro"; tr. Beata Della Frattina).

e. In Carlo Fruttero and Franco Lucentini, ed. *Scendendo: Romanzi e racconti di fantascienza sotterranea.* Milan: Omnibus, 1977. 209–19 (as "Il seme nel sepolcro"; tr. [Beata Della Frattina]).

f. *Robot* No. 36 (March 1979): 10–22 (as "Il seme nel sepolcro"; tr. Alex Voglino).

g. In Tomás Doreste, ed. *Antología del horror y el misterio: Volumen III.* Madrid: Grijalbo, 1990. 651–61 (as "Semillas de muerte"; tr. Tomás Doreste).

h. *Los Diletantes de Lovecraft* No. 1 (1997): 9–22 (as "La semilla del sepulcro"; tr. B. Samarbete).

51. "The Seven Geases."
a. In Robert M. Price, ed. *I miti di Lovecraft.* Milan: Mondadori, 2010. 45–68 (as "Le sette maledizioni"; tr. Silvia Castoldi). [Translation of *Tales of the Lovecraft Mythos* (I.B.i.134.f).]
b. In Massimo Spiga, ed. *Lovecraft Zero.* Cagliari: Arkadia Editore, 2014. 141–60 (as "Sette catene"; tr. Massimo Spiga).

52. "The Tale of Satampra Zeiros."
a. In Markku Sadelehto, ed. *Mustan jumalan suudekma.* Helsinki: Werner Söderström, 1993. 103–16 (as "Satampra Zeiroksen tarina"; tr. Ulla Selkälä).

53. "The Testament of Athammaus."
a. In L. Sprague de Camp, ed. *Schwerter und Magie.* Berlin: Ullstein Taschenbuchverlag, 1988. 171–91 (as "Das Testament des Athammaus"; tr. Ingrid Rothmann and Ronald M. Hahn). [Translation of *Swords and Sorcery* (I.B.i.145.c).]

54. "The Tomb-Spawn."
a. In Gianfranco Manfredi, ed. *Ultimo sangue.* Bologna: Editoriale Dardo, 1992. 28–33 (as "Nato nella tomba"; tr. Roberta Rambelli).

55.   "The Treader of the Dust."
   a.   In Gianni Pilo, ed. *Sempre Weird Tales*. Rome: Fanucci, 1985.
       329–38 (as "Colui che cammina nella polvere"; tr. Gianluigi
       Zuddas).
   b.   In Gianni Pilo, ed. *Storie dell'orrore*. Rome: Newton Compton,
       1999. 557–62 (as "Colui che cammina nella polvere"; tr. Gianni
       Pilo).

56.   "Ubbo-Sathla."
   a.   In August Derleth, ed. *Légendes du mythe de Cthulhu*. Paris:
       Christian Bourgeois, 1975. 75–84. Paris: J'ai Lu, 1981. 83–94.
       Paris: Presses Pocket, 1985. 83–93. Paris: Presses Pocket, 2000
       (as *L'Appel de Cthulhu: Légendes du mythe de Cthulhu*). 74–83
       (tr. Claude Gilbert). [Translation of *Tales of the Cthulhu Mythos*
       (I.B.i.152.d).]
   b.   In August Derleth, ed. *Légendes du mythe de Cthulhu 1*. Paris:
       France Loisirs, 1975. 75–84 (tr. Claude Gilbert). [Abridged
       translation of *Tales of the Cthulhu Mythos* (I.B.i.152.d).]
   c.   In August Derleth, ed. *I miti di Cthulhu*. Rome: Fanucci, 1975.
       177–84 (tr. Alfredo Pollini and Sebastiano Fusco). [Translation
       (with additions) of *Tales of the Cthulhu Mythos* (I.B.i.152.d).]
   d.   In August Derleth, ed. *Relatos de los mitos de Cthulhu 1*. Barcelona:
       Bruguera, 1977, 1978, 1981. 95–108 (tr. Francisco Torres Oli-
       ver). [Translation of *Tales of the Cthulhu Mythos* (I.B.i.152.d).]
   e.   In H. P. Lovecraft. *Oeuvres 1*. Paris: Robert Laffont, 1991.
       725–32 (tr. Gérard Coisne).
   f.   In Markku Sadelehto, ed. *Musta kivi*. Helsinki: Werner Söder-
       ström, 1995. 48–56 (tr. Ulla Selkälä and Ilkka Äärelä).
   g.   *Jules Verne-Magasinet* No. 478 (1996): 20–24 (tr. Sam J.
       Lundwall).
   h.   In August Derleth and James Turner, ed. *Cthulhu: Una cele-
       bración de los mitos*. Madrid: Valdemar, 2001. 63–72 (tr. Fran-
       cisco Torres Oliver). [Translation of *Tales of the Cthulhu Mythos*,
       rev. ed. (I.B.i.152.i).]
   i.   In August Derleth and James Turner, ed. *L'orrore di Cthulhu*.
       Rome: Newton Compton, 2001. 50–57 (tr. Gianni Pilo and
       Sebastiano Fusco). [Translation of *Tales of the Cthulhu Mythos*,
       rev. ed. (I.B.i.152.i).]
   j.   *Jules Verne-Magasinet* No. 530 (2006): 29–31 (tr. Sam J.
       Lundwall).

   k. In Sam J. Lundwall, ed. *Cthulhus arv*. Stockholm: Sam J. Lundwall Fakta & Fantasi, 1996. 21–29 (tr. Sam J. Lundwall).

   l. In Frank Festa, ed. *Der Cthulhu Mythos 1917–1975*. Leipzig: Festa Verlag, 2002. 110–19 (tr. Andreas Diesel).

57. " The Uncharted Isle."

   a. In Jacques Sadoul, ed. *Les Meilleurs Récits de WEIRD TALES 1: Période 1925/32*. Paris: J'ai Lu, 1975. 147–60 (as "L'Île inconnue"; tr. France-Marie Watkins).

   b. In Kurt Singer, ed. *El cinturón de Venus*. Barcelona: Caralt, 1977. 189–202 (as "La isla que faltaba en los mapas"; tr. Antonio-Prometeo Moya and Pablo Mañé Garzón).

   c. *Robot* No. 40 (July–August 1979): 102–11 (as "L'isola non segnata sulle carte"; tr. Elvira Lippi).

   d. In Jacques Sadoul, ed. *Les Meilleurs Récits de WEIRD TALES*. Paris: J'ai Lu, 1989. 142–55 (as "L'Île inconnue"; tr. France-Marie Watkins).

   e. In Lauric Guillaud, ed. *Atlantides: Les Îles englouties*. Paris: Omnibus, 1995. 951–60 (as "L'Île inconnue"; tr. Dominique Mols).

58. "The Venus of Azombeii."

   a. In Francisco Arellano, ed. *Weird Tales (1923–1932)*. Madrid: La Biblioteca del Laberinto, 2006. 203–23 ("La Venus de Azombeii"; tr. Francisco Arellano).

59. "A Vintage from Atlantis."

   a. In Lauric Guillaud, ed. *Atlantides: Les Îles englouties*. Paris: Omnibus, 1995. 931–38 (as "Un Grand Cru d'Atlantide"; tr. Dominique Mols).

   b. *Barsoom* No. 6 (2008): 55–57 (as "Un añejo de la Atlántida"; tr. Javier Jiménez Barco).

60. "The Voyage of King Euvoran."

   a. In Marc Duveau, ed. *Le Livre d'or de la science-fiction: Le Manoir des roses*. Paris: Presses Pocket, 1978, 1988 (as *High Fantasy 1: Le Manoir des roses*). 75–106 (as "Le Voyage du roi Euvoran"; tr. Alain Garsault).

   b. In Alex Voglino, ed. *Il grande libro della heroic fantasy*. Milan: Editrice Nord, 1998. 93–124 (as "Il viaggio di re Euvoran"; tr. Viviana Viviani).

II. Works by Smith in Translation II.B.i.61

    c.   In Marc Duveau, ed. *La Grande Anthologie de la Fantasy*. Paris: Omnibus, 2003. 29–48 (as "Le Voyage du roi Euvoran"; tr. Alain Garsault).

61.   "A Voyage to Sfanomoë."
    a.   In [Unsigned, ed.] *Grande enciclopedia della fantascienza*. Milan: Editoriale Del Drago, 1980. 64–72 (as "Un viaggio a Sfanomoë"; tr. Hilia Brinis).
    b.   In Lauric Guillaud, ed. *Atlantides: Les Îles englouties*. Paris: Omnibus, 1995. 924–31 (as "Cap sur Sfanomoë"; tr. Dominique Mols).

62.   "The Weird of Avoosl Wuthoqquan."
    a.   In Paolo Brizzi, ed. *Fantasy: Racconti di spade, magie e draghi*. Brescia: Editrice La Scuola, 1994. 249–64 (as "Il destino di Avoosl Wuthoqquan"; tr. anon.).

63.   "The White Sybil."
    a.   *Galaxia* No. 8 (2004): 16–20 (as "La sibila blanca"; tr. José Miguel Pallarés).

64.   "The Willow Landscape."
    a.   *Narraciones Terroríficas* No. 41 (May 1944): 92–95 (as "Pintura sobre seda"; tr. Molino).
    b.   In H. A. Livingston Hahn, ed. *Hastings y Doug, aventureros*. Barcelona: Molino, 1947. 77–80 (as "Pintura sobre seda"; tr. H. C. Granch).
    c.   In Leo Margulies and Oscar J. Friend, ed. *En el rincón obscuro*. Mexico City: La Prensa, 1956. 107–14 (as "Pintura sobre seda"; tr. Óscar Kaufmann Parra).

65.   "Xeethra."
    a.   *Zothique* No. 1 (1985): 20–29 (tr. Jean Marigny).

Synopses

66.   "The Feet of Sidaiva."
    a.   *Zothique* No. 1 (1985): 30 (as "Les Pieds de Sidaiva"; tr. Jean-Luc Buard).

67.   "The Madness of Chronomage."
    a.   *Zothique* No. 1 (1985): 30 (as "La Folie de Chronomage"; tr. Jean-Luc Buard).

68. "Mandor's Enemy."
   a. *Zothique* No. 1 (1985): 30 (as "L'Adversaire de Mandor"; tr. Jean-Luc Buard).

69. "Shapes of Adamant."
   a. *Zothique* No. 1 (1985): 29 (as "Formes noires"; tr. Jean-Luc Buard).

ii. Poems

1.   "Atlantis."
   a. In [Unsigned, ed.] *Delirio: Ciencia ficción y fantasía 4*. Madrid: La Biblioteca del Laberinto, 2009. 166 (tr. ?).

2.   "Beyond the Great Wall."
   a. *Novae Terrae* No. 1 (March 1979): [29] (as "Al di là della Grande Muraglia"; tr. Roldano Romanelli).

3.   "Chant of Autumn."
   a. *Novae Terrae* No. 1 (March 1979): [30] (as "Canto d'autunno"; tr. Roldano Romanelli).

4.   *The Dead Will Cuckold You.*
   a. *Alia: L'arcipelago del fantastico* No. 3 (November 2005): 349–72 (as *I morti ti faranno cornuto;* tr. Davide Mana).

5.   "Don Quixote on Market Street."
   a. *Fictionaire* No. 1 (October 1999): 74 (as "Don Chisciotte al supermarket"; tr. Sebastiano Fusco).
   b. *Mystero* No. 1 (June 2000): 65 (as "Don Chisciotte al supermarket"; tr. [Sebastiano Fusco]).

6.   "The Faun"
   a. *Coś na progu* No. 2 (May–June 2012): 31 (as "Faun"; tr. Jakub Wiśniewski).

7.   "Exotique."
   a. *L'en dehors* no 150 (January 1929): 3 (tr. unidentified).

8.   "Finis."
   a. *Antarès* No. 9 (1st Quarter 1983): 109–10 (as "Fin"; tr. Lyvie Gueret).

9. "The Funeral Urn"
   a. *Coś na progu* No. 2 (May–June 2012): 31 (as "Urna"; tr. Jakub Wiśniewski).

10. "H. P. L."
   a. *Coś na progu* No. 2 (May–June 2012): 31 (tr. Jakub Wiśniewski).

11. "The Last Night."
   a. *Antarès* No. 9 (1st Quarter 1983): 110 (as "La Dernière Nuit"; tr. Jean Raguseo).

12. "Luna Aeternalis."
   a. *Yorick* Nos. 32/33 (December 2001/January 2002): 67 (tr. Federica Daino).

13. "The Medusa of the Skies."
   a. *Antarès* No. 9 (1st Quarter 1983): 111 (as "La Méduse des cieux"; tr. Lyvie Gueret).

14. "The Mummy."
   a. In [Unsigned, ed.] *La maldición de la momia: Relatos de horror sobre el antiguo Egipto.* Madrid: Valdemar, 2006. 499–506 (as "La momia"; tr. José Luis Moreno-Ruiz).

15. "No Stranger Dream."
   a. *Yorick* Nos. 28/29 (December 1999/May 2000): 20 (as "Non c'è sogno più strano"; tr. Pietro Guarriello).

16. "Shadow of Nightmare."
   a. *Antarès* No. 7 (3rd Quarter 1982): 1 (as "Ombre de cauchemar"; tr. Jean Raguseo).

17. "The Sorcerer Departs."
   a. *Yorick* Nos. 24/25 (May 1997): 12 (as "Morte di uno stregone"; tr. Pietro Guarriello).

18. "The Star-Treader."
   a. *Tuli&Savu* No. 53 (3rd Quarter 2008): 44–45 (as "Tähtivaeltaja"; tr. Teemu Manninen).

19. "To Howard Phillips Lovecraft."
   a. *Karpath* No. 1 (4th Quarter 1989): 10–11 (as "À Howard Phillips Lovecraft"; tr. François Truchaud).

20. "To the Chimera."
   a. In Peter Haining, ed. *Ancora Weird Tales: Il secondo periodo 1939–1954*. Rome: Fanucci, 1984. 277–78 (as "Alla chimera"; tr. Roberta Rambelli).

21. "Two Myths and a Fable."
   a. *Vórtice en Línea* No. 3 (2005): 4 (as "Dos mitos y una fábula"; tr. Óscar Mariscal).
   b. *Los Diletantes de Lovecraft* No. 7 (2001): 8–9 (as "Dos mitos y una fábula"; tr. Óscar Mariscal).
   c. *Weird Tales de Lhork* No. 24 (2001): 88 (as "Dos mitos y una fábula"; tr. Óscar Mariscal).
   d. *Weird Tales de Lhork* No. 29 (2008): 18 (as "Dos mitos y una fábula"; tr. Óscar Mariscal).

22. "White Death."
   a. *Antarès* No. 9 (1st Quarter 1983): 111 (as "Mort blanche"; tr. Lyvie Gueret).

23. "The Witch with Eyes of Amber."
   a. *Yorick* Nos. 30/31 (December 2000): 79 (as "La strega degli occhi d'ambra"; tr. Pietro Guarriello).

24. "Zothique."
   a. *Zothique* No. 1 (1985): 3 (tr. Denis Bonnecase; with English text).
   b. *Zothique* No. 1 (Winter 2017): 5–6 (tr. Pietro Guarriello).

iii. Poems in Prose

1. "The Abomination of Desolation."
   a. In Marc Duveau, ed. *Le Livre d'or de la science-fiction: La Citadelle écarlate*. Paris: Presses Pocket, 1979, 1988 (as *Heroic Fantasy 2: La Citadelle écarlate*). 289–90 (as "Le Désert désolé de Soom"; tr. Alain Garsault).
   b. *Jules Verne-Magasinet* No. 477 (1996): 23 (as "Öknen"; tr. Sam J. Lundwall).
   c. *Fictionaire* No. 1 (October 1999): 72–73 (as "Il deserto del terrore"; tr. anon.).
   d. *Mystero* No. 1 (June 2000): 64 (as "Il deserto dell'incubo"; tr. anon.).

    e. In Marc Duveau, ed. *La Grande Anthologie de la Fantasy*. Paris: Omnibus, 2003. 378–79 (as "Le Désert désolé de Soom"; tr. Alain Garsault).

    f. *Galaxia* No. 1 (2003): 61 (as "La desolación de Soom"; tr. José Miguel Pallarés).

2. "A Dream of Lethe."

    a. *Fictionaire* No. 1 (October 1999): 66 (as "Le acque dell'oblio"; tr. anon.).

    b. *Mystero* No. 1 (June 2000): 65 (as "Il sogno e l'oblio"; tr. anon.).

3. "The Flower-Devil."

    a. *Le Codex Atlanticus* No. 3 (3rd Quarter 1995): 38–40 (as "La Fleur-Diable"; tr. Éric Dejaeger).

    b. In H. P. Lovecraft [et al.]. *Il vento delle stelle: Storie in versi e no.* Ed. Sebastiano Fusco. Rome: Agpha Press, 1998. 70–71 (as "Il dèmone del fiore"; tr. Sebastiano Fusco).

    c. *Sable* No. 6 (2008): 29 (as "La flor demonio"; tr. Fermín Moreno González).

4. "From the Crypts of Memory."

    a. *Antarès* No. 9 (1st Quarter 1983): 111–13 (as "Dans les cryptes du souvenir"; tr. Martine Blond).

5. "In Cocaigne."

    a. *In Memorie dal Buio* No. 1 (Spring 2004): 24 (tr. Bruno Aliotta and Francesco Bruni).

6. "The Lake of Enchanted Silence."

    a. *Vórtice en Línea* No. 3 (2005): 4–5 (as "El lago del silencio encantado"; tr. Óscar Mariscal).

    b. *Weird Tales de Lhork* No. 29 (2008): 18 (as "El lago del silencio encantado"; tr. Óscar Mariscal).

7. "Memnons of the Night."

    a. *Nova SF* No. 20 (September 1972): 183–85 (as "Signori della notte"; tr. Maurizio Cesari).

    b. In Marc Duveau, ed. *Le Livre d'or de la science-fiction: La Citadelle écarlate*. Presses Pocket, 1979, 1988 (as *Heroic Fantasy 2: La citadelle écarlate*). 77–78 (as "Memnons de la nuit"; tr. Alain Garsault).

    c.   In Marc Duveau, ed. *La Grande Anthologie de la Fantasy*. Paris: Omnibus, 2003. 229–30 (as "Memnons de la nuit"; tr. Alain Garsault).

8.   "The Mortuary."
    a.   *Le Codex Atlanticus* No. 4 (1st Quarter 1998): 56–59 (as "La Morgue"; tr. Philippe Gindre).

9.   "The Muse of Atlantis."
    a.   In Lauric Guillaud, ed. *Atlantides: Les Îles englouties*. Paris: Omnibus, 1995. 895 (as "La Muse de l'Atlantide"; tr. Dominique Mols).

10.   "Nostalgia of the Unknown."
    a.   In H. P. Lovecraft [et al.]. *Il vento delle stelle: Storie in versi e no*. Ed. Sebastiano Fusco. Rome: Agpha Press, 1998. 70 (as "La nostalgia di cose sconosciute"; tr. Sebastiano Fusco).

11.   "The Passing of Aphrodite."
    a.   *Stampe Sera* (Turin) (24 July 1980): 19 (as "La partenza di Afrodite"; tr. Teobaldo Del Tanaro).

12.   "The Shadows."
    a.   *Antarès* No. 9 (1st Quarter 1983): 106–9 (as "Les Ombres"; tr. Martine Blond).

iv. Nonfiction

1.   "The Oracle of Sadoqua."
    a.   *Barsoom* No. 8 (2009): 46 (as "El oráculo de Sadoqua"; tr. Javier Jiménez Barco).

    Item 48 from *The Black Book of Clark Ashton Smith* (A.39).

2.   [Untitled.]
    a.   *Zothique* No. 1 (1985): 59 (as "Aphorisme"; tr. Jean-Luc Buard).

    Item 134 from *The Black Book of Clark Ashton Smith* (A.39).

v. Published Letters

1.   [To H. P. Lovecraft (16 November 1930).]
    a.   *Barsoom* No. 3 (2007): 36 (tr. Javier Jiménez Barco).

2.   [To H. P. Lovecraft (18 November 1930).]
       a. *Barsoom* No. 3 (2007): 36 (tr. Javier Jiménez Barco).

3.   [To H. P. Lovecraft, late January 1934.]
       a. In H. P. Lovecraft et al. *Il libro dei gatti*. Ed. Gianfranco de
           Turris, Claudio De Nardi, and Pietro Guarriello. Rimini: Il
           Cerchio, 2012. 123 (tr. Pietro Guarriello).

4.   [To H. P. Lovecraft, late February/March 1934.]
       a. In H. P. Lovecraft et al. *Il libro dei gatti*. Ed. Gianfranco de
           Turris, Claudio De Nardi, and Pietro Guarriello. Rimini: Il
           Cerchio, 2012. 124–25 (tr. Pietro Guarriello).

5.   [To H. P. Lovecraft, c. June 1935.]
       a. In H. P. Lovecraft et al. *Il libro dei gatti*. Ed. Gianfranco de
           Turris, Claudio De Nardi, and Pietro Guarriello. Rimini: Il
           Cerchio, 2012. 126 (tr. Pietro Guarriello).

6.   [To R. H. Barlow.]
       a. *Delirio: Ciencia ficción y fantasía* No. 2 (2008): 153–56 (as "El
           árbol genealógico de los dioses"; tr. Óscar Mariscal). [Transla-
           tion of "The Family Tree of the Gods."]

III. Smith Criticism

A. News Items

1. Ackerman, Forrest J. "Clark Ashton Smith Dies at 68."
    a. *Science Fiction Times* 16, No. 16 (August 1961): 3.

2. [Allison, W. T.] "California Love Lyrics."
    a. *Winnipeg Tribune* (10 May 1927): 4 (as by "Ivanhoe").

    Review of the special CAS issue of the *Step Ladder* (G.i.7).

3. [Bonnet Theodore.] "The Spectator."
    a. *Town Talk* No. 973 (22 April 1911): 8.

4. [Bonnet, Theodore.] "The Spectator."
    a. *Town Talk* No. 1041 (3 August 1912): 9 (with subtitles "Auburn's Precocious Genius" and "The Abyss Triumphant").

5. [Bonnet, Theodore.] "The Spectator."
    a. *Town Talk* No. 1042 (10 August 1912): 10–11 (with subtitles "Discovering a Poet," "A Compliment to Town Talk," "The Real Discoverer," and "A Letter from Ambrose Bierce").

6. [Bonnet, Theodore.] "The Spectator."
    a. *Town Talk* No. 1156 (17 October 1914): 12.

7. [Bonnet, Theodore.] "The Spectator."
    a. *Town Talk* No. 1167 (2 January 1915): 12 (with subtitle "Clark Ashton Smith's Success").

8. [Bonnet, Theodore.] "The Spectator."
    a. *Town Talk* No. 1183 (24 April 1915): 12.

9. [Bonnet, Theodore.] "The Spectator."
    a. *Town Talk* No. 1213 (20 November 1915): 11 (with subtitle "A Poet Sees the Fair").

10. [Bonnet, Theodore.] "The Spectator."
    a. *Town Talk* No. 1342 (11 May 1918): 10–11.

11. [Bonnet, Theodore.] "The Spectator."
    a. *Town Talk* No. 1347 (15 June 1918): 10.

12. [Bonnet, Theodore.] "The Spectator."
     a. *Town Talk* No. 1361 (21 September 1918): 3.

13. [Bonnet, Theodore.] "The Spectator."
     a. *Town Talk* No. 1369 (16 November 1918): 9.

14. Connell, Sarah. "The State's Literary Output."
     a. *Town Talk* No. 1061 (21 December 1912): 14.

15. Couzens, Jean L. "The Book Corner."
     a. *Westart* (1 April 1966): 2.

16. Dare, Helen. "A Boy, a Woodpile and a Mountain."
     a. *San Francisco Chronicle* (11 August 1912): 26.

17. De Casseres, Benjamin. "Nehru, Gandhi May Recall John Bull as 'Easy Boss.'"
     a. *Detroit Times* (15 September 1942): 12.

     Includes review of *Out of Space and Time*.

18. Elder, Robert. "Clark Ashton Smith, Noted Writer and Poet, Dies at Pacific Grove."
     a. *Auburn Journal* (17 August 1961): 2.

19. F[ait], E[leanor]. "Auburn Artist–Poet Utilizes Native Rock in Sculptures."
     a. *Sacramento Union* (21 December 1941): 4C.
     b. *Dark Eidolon* No. 2 (July 1989): 26–27.

     Report of an exhibition of CAS's artwork to be shown at the Crocker Art Gallery.

20. F[ait], E[leanor]. "Wide Variety Marks Crocker Loan Exhibit for January."
     a. *Sacramento Union* (4 January 1942): 8.

21. Frankenstein, Alfred. "Around the Galleries."
     a. *San Francisco Chronicle* (8 May 1938): This World, p. 32.

22. "Geraldine." "Say It Pronto, Lovelorn Lad Told."
     a. *Oakland Tribune* (3 April 1937): 17.

     Discusses CAS's poetry in the context of precocious geniuses.

23. Gordan, John D. "New in the Berg Collection: 1957–1958: George Sterling and Clark Ashton Smith."
   a. *Bulletin of the New York Public Library* 63 (April 1959): 211–12.

   Brief account of the CAS–Sterling correspondence, acquired by the library.

24. Hailey, Gene. "Art News of the Week."
   a. *San Francisco Chronicle* (3 July 1927): D7.

   On an exhibition of CAS's paintings at the Hotel Claremont Art Gallery.

25. Hamilton, Mrs. G. K. [*sic*]. "A Poet and His Poetry"
   a. *Auburn Journal* (27 March 1915): 1.

   The author's name is Mrs. G. W. Hamilton.

26. [Hopkins, Ernest Jerome.] "Genius Flashes from the Sierras."
   a. *San Francisco Bulletin* (5 August 1912): 5.

27. Ingels, Beth. "Fun with Food: A Poet Concocts Mulligan, Chioppino."
   a. *Monterey Peninsula Herald* (5 May 1960): 23.

28. Jones, Pat. "Auburn's Awakening Pride in a Poet."
   a. *Colfax [CA] Record* (26 May 1977): 2.

29. Landis, Bob. "Creator of Fantasy."
   a. *Auburn Journal* (6 May 1948): 17.

   Brief biographical piece promoting *Genius Loci*.

30. McCarthy, Ryan. "Bard of Auburn: Turn-of-Century Author, Poet Gets Recognition."
   a. *Neighbors* [Placer County] (14 January 1933): 3, 10.

31. McCoy, Kathleen. "Auburn Remembers Clark Ashton Smith."
   a. *Auburn Journal* (16 May 1977): A6–7.

32. O'Day, Edward F. "Dr. Taylor as a Sonneteer."
   a. *Town Talk* No. 1306 (1 September 1917): 6–8.

   Quotes the entirety of CAS's sonnet "The Last Night" (p. 7).

33. O'Day, Edward F. "Varied Types: XVII.—George Sterling."
    a. *Town Talk* No. 972 (15 April 1911): 8.
    b. In Edward F. O'Day. *Varied Types*. San Francisco: Town Talk Press, 1915. 278–80.

    Sterling discusses his early relations with CAS and quotes the entirety of CAS's sonnet "The Last Night."

34. O'Day, Edward F. "Varied Types: XC.—Witter Bynner."
    a. *Town Talk* No. 1046 (7 September 1912): 7, 21.

35. Rubin, Hal. "Auburn's Hermit Poet: Young Readers Discover Old Horror Tales."
    a. *Sacramento Bee* (31 August 1975): E1–E2.

36. [Schofield, Ronald D.] "Shows at Crocker Gallery."
    a. *Sacramento Bee* (10 January 1942): 13.

    Review of an exhibition of CAS's artwork.

37. Shepard, W. A. "Verses Have Made Him Famous."
    a. *Sacramento Bee* (16 November 1912): 17, 19.

    Quotes the entirety of "The Night Forest," "A Live Oak Leaf," and "Pine Needles."

38. Thomson, Gus. "Cyber Revival: 1920s Sci-Fi Writer Clark Ashton Smith Enjoys Another 15-Minutes of Fame via the Internet."
    a. *Auburn Journal* (15 December 1996): B1, 7.

39. Thomson, Gus. "Glendale Man Hopes to Garner Unknown Writer a Bit of Fame."
    a. *Auburn Journal* (11 January 1993): A1, 8.

    Discusses efforts of CAS fan John Miller to have Auburn City Council proclaim the week of 10–16 January 1993 as "Clark Ashton Smith Week."

40. Thomson, Gus. "WordSmith Remembered: Devotees of Clark Ashton Smith Want to Keep the Late Auburn Author's Legacy Alive with Landmark in his Honor."
    a *Auburn Journal* (27 January 2002): B1, 2.

41. Wilson, Bill. "'Auburn's Hermit Poet.'"
    a. *Auburn Sentinel* (18 December 1992): 6, 10.

42. Woolley, Persia. "Clark Ashton Smith to Be Commemorated."
   a. *Auburn Sentinel* (10 January 2003): 1, 7.

43. "Yorick." "On the Margins: A Discussion on Poets: Their Use and Abuse."
   a. *San Diego Union* (18 August 1912): 17.

   The author objects to the extravagant claims made in the San Francisco papers about CAS and his first book.

44. [Unsigned.] "AAUW Art Show Ready to Open Friday Night."
   a. *Auburn Journal* (28 April 1949): 4.

   The art show includes some watercolors by CAS.

45. [Unsigned.] "Amusements."
   a. *Placer Herald* (2 December 1911): 5.

46. [Unsigned.] "Amusements."
   a. *Placer Herald* (30 March 1912): 5.

   On CAS's reading of a paper, "Philosophy of Literary Criticism."

47. [Unsigned.] "Asks Recognition of Young Placer Poet."
   a. *Sacramento Union* (1 April 1915): 5.

48. [Unsigned.] "Assembly Adjourns to Honor Gaylord."
   a. *Auburn Journal* (22 February 1940): 1.

   Mentions a proclamation given to CAS honoring his uncle.

49. [Unsigned.] "Auburn Boy Praised."
   a. *Placer Herald* (10 August 1912): 5.

50. [Unsigned.] "Auburn Has Big Boost in S. F. Examiner."
   a. *Auburn Journal* (14 July 1928): 2.

   Discusses CAS as part of Auburn's literary heritage.

51. [Unsigned.] "Auburn Personals."
   a. *Sacramento Bee* (19 November 1927): 14.

   CAS home after spending three weeks in San Francisco.

52. [Unsigned.] "Auburn Poet Featured."
   a. *Auburn Journal* (24 September 1942): 9.

Quotes in its entirety Benjamin De Casseres's review of *Out of Space and Time* (F.7.c).

53. [Unsigned.] "Auburn Poet to Appear on TV."
   a. *Auburn Journal* (8 May 1958): D6.

54. [Unsigned.] "Ballads of Clark Ashton Smith Receive Highly Favorable Comment: Among the Living He Stands Alone, Says Critic."
   a. *Auburn Journal* (4 September 1924): 5.

55. [Unsigned.] "Book of Poems By Local Poet."
   a. *Placer County Republican* (23 November 1912): 1.

56. [Unsigned.] "Books by Auburn Author Sought."
   a. *Auburn Journal* (31 October 1957): 26.

57. [Unsigned.] "Boy Is Poetic Genius."
   a. *San Francisco Call* (2 August 1912): 1–2.
   b. *Daily Capital Journal* (Salem, OR) (2 August 1912): 1 (as "Discovers a Literary Genius[:] Clark Ashton Smith, Age 19, Is It").
   c. *Oregon Daily Journal* (Portland, OR) (2 August 1912): 4 (as "Boy Poet of High Sierras Hailed as Great Genius").
   d. *Baltimore Sun* (3 August 1912): 6 (as (as "Lad of the High Sierras May be Child of Fame").
   e. *Santa Ana* [CA] *Register* (3 August 1912): 1.
   f. *Vancouver* [BC] *Daily World* (3 August 1912): 19 (as "Boy Hailed as One of World's Greatest Bards").
   g. *Arkansas Democrat* (Little Rock, AR) (10 August 1912): 1 (as "Boy Poetic Genius Discovered in Desert").
   h. *Saginaw* [MI] *Daily News* (12 August 1912): 7 (as "In the Public Eye").
   i. *Evansville* [IN] *Press* (14 August 1912): 2 (as "Boy Poetic Genius Has Lived All His Life in Wilds of Sierra").
   j. *Kentucky Post* (Covington, KY) (15 August 1912): 4 (as "Boy Poetic Genius Has Lived All His Life in Wilds of the Sierras")
   k. *Pittsburgh Press* (17 August 1912): 2 (as "Boy Poetic Genius Has Lived All His Life in Wilds of Sierra").
   l. *Allentown* [PA] *Leader* (19 August 1912): 3 (as "Youth a Poetic Genius").
   m. *Union Springs* [AL] *Herald* (21 August 1912): 6 (as "Youth a Poetic Genius").

n. *Fort Dodge* [IA] *Messenger* (24 August 1912): 14 (as "Boy Poet from a Farm").

o. *Daily Republican* (Monongahela, PA) (5 September 1912): 2 (as "Boy Poet from a Farm").

p. *Asbury Park* [NJ] *Press* (5 September 1912): 2 (as "Youth a Poetic Genius").

q. *Red Cloud* [NE] *Chief* (5 September 1912): 3 (as "Boy Poet from a Farm").

r. *Buffalo Sunday Morning News* (8 September 1912): 21 (as "Youth Is a Poetic Genius").

s. *Cape County Herald* (Cape Girardeau, MO) (20 September 1912): 7 (as "Boy Poet from a Farm").

t. *Lead* [SD] *Daily Call* (25 September 1912): 2 (as "Boy Poet from a arm").

u. *Perry County Democrat* (Bloomfield, PA) (16 October 1912): 1 (as "Boy Poet from a Farm").

v. *Richmond* [IN] *Item* (30 October 1912): 9 (as "Boy Poet from a Farm").

w. *Ness County News* (Ness City, KS) (30 November 1912): 8 (as "Boy Poet from a Farm").

x. *Steuben Republican* (Angola, IN) (22 January 1913): 4 (as "Boy Poet from a Farm").

y. *Winnipeg Tribune* (20 February 1913): 3 (as "Promising Young Versifier").

Quotes the entirety of "Nero" and "The Morning Pool." The article may be by Boutwell Dunlap, who claimed to have "discovered" CAS; at any rate, it was probably distributed by him in press packets to reporters. Many of the reprints of the article were abridged or rewritten.

58. [Unsigned.] "Boy Writes of Poems, Tells of Work."
a. *Oakland Tribune* (16 July 1913): 6.

59. [Unsigned.] "C. A. Smith Story in New Collection."
a. *Auburn Journal* (9 April 1959): 23.

On the inclusion of "The Hunters from Beyond" in *The Macabre Reader* (I.B.i.65.d).

60. [Unsigned.] "California Youth Is Hailed by Critics as Poetical Genius."
a. *San Francisco Chronicle* (2 August 1912): 6.

b. *Placer County Republican* (8 August 1912): 1 (as "Poet Will Help to Keep City on Map"; abridged and altered).

61. [Unsigned.] "Ceremony to Honor Smith."
a. *Auburn Journal* (16 August 1985): 14.

   On a plaque dedicated to CAS at the Placer County Library.

62. [Unsigned.] "Clark A. Smiths Visiting in Newcastle."
a. *Auburn Journal* (14 June 1956): 17.

63. [Unsigned.] "Clark Ashton Smith."
a. *Greensburg* [IN] *Weekly Democrat* (25 May 1916): 5.

64. [Unsigned.] "Clark Ashton Smith, Auburn Writer, Weds Mrs. C. Jones Dorman Here."
a. *Placer Herald* (18 November 1954): 4.

65. [Unsigned.] "Clark Ashton Smith Book Is Off Press."
a. *Auburn Journal* (8 June 1933): 1.

   Article announcing the publication of *The Double Shadow and Other Fantasies*.

66. [Unsigned.] "Clark Ashton Smith Books Are Published."
a. *Auburn Journal* (11 November 1965): B16.

67. [Unsigned.] "Clark Ashton Smith, Carolyn Dorman Married Here."
a. *Auburn Journal* (11 November 1954): 1.
b. *Monterey Peninsula Herald* (18 November 1954): 1.

68. [Unsigned.] "Clark Ashton Smith Dies at 68."
a. *Science-Fiction Times* (August 1961): 3.

69. [Unsigned.] "Clark Ashton Smith Drawings on Display."
a. *Auburn Journal* (25 March 1926): 1.

   On a display of CAS's drawings at a local optometrist.

70. [Unsigned.] "Clark Ashton Smith Has Art Display."
a. *Auburn Journal* (10 November 1941): 2.

   On exhibitions of CAS's carvings at the Auburn Public Library, the Crocker Art Gallery, and Gump's Department Store.

71. [Unsigned.] "Clark Ashton Smith Mystery Published."
    a. *Auburn Journal* (4 September 1930): 4.

    On the appearance of "Marooned in Andromeda" in *Wonder Stories*.

72. [Unsigned.] "Clark Ashton Smith Poem Wins Award."
    a. *Auburn Journal* (19 October 1967): 23.

73. [Unsigned.] "Clark Ashton Smith New Story Published."
    a. *Auburn Journal* (2 April 1931): 1.

    On the publication of "A Rendezvous in Averoigne" in *Weird Tales*.

74. [Unsigned.] "Clark Ashton Smith Writes Short Story."
    a. *Auburn Journal* (9 August 1928): 4.

    On the appearance of "The Ninth Skeleton" in *Weird Tales*.

75. [Unsigned.] "Clark Ashton Smith's New Book on Sale."
    a. *Auburn Journal* (8 July 1943): 1.

    On the availability of *Out of Space and Time* at a local store.

76. [Unsigned.] "Club News."
    a. *Berkeley Daily Gazette* (2 March 1927): 11.

    CAS's poetry is to be read at a meeting of the Berkeley League of American Pen Women, to be held at the home of Ina Coolbrith, California Poet Laureate.

77. [Unsigned.] "Collection Contains Smith Story."
    a. *Auburn Journal* (5 February 1959): D8.

    On the inclusion of "Phoenix" in *Time to Come* (I.B.i.113.a).

78. [Unsigned.] "Crocker Art Gallery to Show Work of Clark A. Smith."
    a. *Auburn Journal* (29 December 1941): 4.

79. [Unsigned.] "Death of Timeus Smith."
    a. *Placer Herald* (1 January 1938): 3.

80. [Unsigned.] [Editorial.]
    a. *Auburn Journal* (4 October 1923): 6.

81. [Unsigned.] "Father of Poet Is Deceased in Placer."
    a. *Sacramento Bee* (27 December 1937): 9.

82.   [Unsigned.] "Fire Destroys Clark Ashton Smith Home."
      a. *Auburn Journal* (12 September 1957): A1.

83.   [Unsigned.] "Former Auburnite Plans Exhibit of Works on Mon-
      terey."
      a. *Auburn Journal* (17 November 1955): 28.

      On an exhibition of CAS's carvings and books at the Monterey
      Public Library.

84.   [Unsigned.] "Funeral Services Are Held for Old Auburn Resident."
      a. *Auburn Journal* (30 December 1937): 7.

      Obituary of Timeus Smith.

85.   [Unsigned.] "George Work Is Local Visitor."
      a. *Bakersfield Californian* (15 April 1933): 5.

86.   [Unsigned.] "The Gossip Shop."
      a. *Bookman* (New York) 56, No. 3 (November 1922): 381.

      Quotes Witter Bynner on CAS as a disciple of George Sterling.

87.   [Unsigned.] "The Gossip Shop."
      a. *Bookman* (New York) 56, No. 4 (December 1922): 538.

      Quotes Laura Bell Everett praising CAS's poetry.

88.   "Library Shows Art, Books by Fantasy Writer."
      a. *Sacramento Bee* (12 July 1958): L-20 (58).

89.   [Unsigned.] "Library to Offer Special Program."
      a. *Auburn Journal* (18 May 1977): 15.

      On a program on CAS by Harold Rubin and Donald Sidney-Fryer.

90.   [Unsigned.] "Local and Personal."
      a. *Auburn Journal* (26 October 1922): 8.

91.   [Unsigned.] "Local and Personal."
      a. *Auburn Journal-Republican* (22 January 1925): 5.

92.   [Unsigned.] "Local and Personal."
      a. *Auburn Journal* (26 February 1925): 8.

      On CAS cutting his foot while chopping wood.

93. [Unsigned.] "Local and Personal."
    a. *Auburn Journal* (12 November 1925): 5.

    On CAS meeting with Mr. and Mrs. Emerson Myers of Medford, Oregon, along with his mother and Uncle Ed.

94. [Unsigned.] "Local and Personal."
    a. *Auburn Journal* (28 October 1926): 4.

95. [Unsigned.] "Local and Personal."
    a. *Auburn Journal* (7 July 1927): 5.

    Mrs. Timeus Smith is confined to home due to injured foot.

96. [Unsigned.] "Local and Personal."
    a. *Auburn Journal* (17 November 1928): 5.

    On CAS's return from a three-week visit to the Bay Area.

97. [Unsigned.] "Local and Personal."
    a. *Auburn Journal* (9 March 1939): 5.

    On CAS's return from visiting friends in Marin County.

98. [Unsigned.] "Local Poet Makes Pronounced Hit."
    a. *Placer County Republican* (16 November 1911): 1,

99. [Unsigned.] "Local Poet Praised by Noted Author."
    a. *Auburn Journal* (27 April 1933): 1.

    Discusses George Work's praise of CAS (see item 85).

100. [Unsigned.] "Makers of Books and Some Recent Works."
    a. *San Francisco Post* (10 August 1912): Magazine Section, p. 6.

101. [Unsigned.] "Monterey Library Exhibits Books by C. A. Smith."
    a. *Monterey Peninsula Herald* (25 November 1955): 12.

102. [Unsigned.] "More Anent Auburn Poet."
    a. *Auburn Journal* 69, No. 100 (13 November 1941): 5.

103. [Unsigned.] "Mrs. Dorman Is Bride of C. A. Smith, Poet-Writer."
    a. *Monterey Peninsula Herald* (13 November 1954): 8.

104. [Unsigned.] "Mrs. Jessie V. Cannon to Open New Studio."
    a. *Berkeley Daily Gazette* (13 September 1928): 5.

On the opening of a new art studio that will exhibit CAS's water-colors.

105. [Unsigned.] "Mrs. Timeus Smith Dead."
  a. *Placer Herald* (14 September 1935): 3.

106. [Unsigned.] "Mrs. Timeus Smith Ends Life's Journey."
  a. *Auburn Journal* (12 September 1935): 4.

107. [Unsigned.] "New Book for Poet Smith."
  a. *Monterey Peninsula Herald* (17 March 1958): 3.

108. [Unsigned.] "New Exhibitions at Crocker Art Gallery."
  a. *Oakland Tribune* (8 February 1942): 41.

109. [Unsigned.] "9[*sic*]-Year-Old Poet from Sierras."
  a. *Stockton Record* (5 August 1912): 2.

110. [Unsigned.] "Notes on Clark Ashton Smith."
  a. *Auburn Journal* (15 December 1941): 4.

111. [Unsigned.] "Obituary Notes."
  a. *Antiquarian Bookman* 28 (9 October 1961): 1265.

112. [Unsigned.] [Obituary of Clark Ashton Smith.]
  a. *Monterey Peninsula Herald* (15 August 1961): 1.

113. [Unsigned.] "Old Music Boxes Displayed at Library."
  a. *Auburn Journal* (17 November 1941): 4,

  Mentions a display of CAS's carvings and drawings at the library.

114. [Unsigned.] "Overland Monthly Boosts Poet Smith: Current Issue Dwells for Two Pages on His Work."
  a. *Auburn Journal-Republican* (17 February 1927): 7.

115. [Unsigned.] "Paintings Are Exhibited."
  a. *Sacramento Bee* (9 January 1942): 4.

  Exhibitions of paintings, carvings, and manuscripts at the Crocker Art Gallery.

116. [Unsigned.] "Paintings by Auburn Poet."
  a. *Auburn Journal* (20 November 1941): 4.

117. [Unsigned.] "Personal."
     a. *Auburn Journal* 8 March 1923): 5.

     On the convalescence of CAS's mother.

118. [Unsigned.] "Placer County Scribes and Artists Shine Brightly among the Stars of California's Literary Firmament."
     a. *Auburn Journal* (15 December 1921): 8.

119. [Unsigned.] "Placer Plans Big Day at Exhibition."
     a. *Sacramento Bee* (10 April 1915): 17.

     Placer County distributing souvenir postcards bearing CAS's poem "The Pines" [*sic*] at the Pan-American Exhibition. No poem of this title is known to exist. Perhaps "Pine Needles" was meant.

120. [Unsigned.] "Recital Benefit by Local Talent for Red Cross."
     a. *Red Bluff* [CA] *Daily News* (16 January 1918): 4.

     Mentions that CAS's poem "Pine Needles" was performed by Mrs. Herman P. Hatfield, with piano accompaniment by Emmet Pendleton.

121. [Unsigned.] "Reward Offered for Information on Fire."
     a. *Auburn Journal* (26 September 1957): A6.

122. [Unsigned.] "Roseville Women Entertain."
     a. *Sacramento Union* (14 October 1921); 3.

     Mention of CAS visiting Roseville along with his friend Drew (Andrew) Dewing.

123. [Unsigned.] "Sierra Teaches Poetry to Boy of Its Peaks."
     a. *San Francisco Examiner* (2 August 1912): 5.

124. [Unsigned.] "Smith Library Placed on Sale by Widow."
     a. *Auburn Journal* (11 January 1962): 28.

125. [Unsigned.] "Smith–Sterling Letters Sold."
     a. *Auburn Journal* (1 May 1958): 8.

126. [Unsigned.] "Smith to Publish New Volume."
     a. *Auburn Journal* (11 February 1960): 9.

     On the publication of *The Abominations of Yondo*.

127. [Unsigned.] "Smith's Latest Work at Public Library."
     a. *Auburn Journal* (21 December 1922): 7.

128. [Unsigned.] "Smith's Pictures on Display at Durfee's."
     a. *Auburn Journal* (25 October 1923): 1.

129. [Unsigned.] "Smith's Poems Are Selling Well."
     a. *Auburn Journal* (25 January 1923): 3.

130. [Unsigned.] "Smiths Feted at Birthday Party."
     a. *Auburn Journal* (16 January 1958): 27.

131. [Unsigned.] "Society."
     a. *Auburn Journal* (14 January 1925): 5.

     On a birthday party thrown for CAS.

132. [Unsigned.] "Society."
     a. *Auburn Journal* (16 April 1925); 5.

     CAS attends a birthday party for A. H. Gaylord.

133. [Unsigned.] "Society."
     a. *Auburn Journal* (14 January 1926): 5.

134. [Unsigned.] "State Birthday Celebration."
     a. *San Francisco Call* (4 August 1912): 36.

     CAS's name has been submitted for the Hall of Fame.

135. [Unsigned.] "Student's Songs to Furnish Program."
     a. *Oakland Tribune* (18 May 1919): 11.

     On Emmet Pendleton (one of the songs is a setting of CAS's "The Cherry-Snows").

136. [Unsigned.] "Three Exhibits Will Start at Crocker Friday."
     a. *Sacramento Bee* (27 December 1941): 11.

137. [Unsigned.] "Vandals Damage Smith Home."
     a. *Auburn Journal* (21 June 1956): 6.

138. [Unsigned.] "Will Publish Poems of Clark Ashton Smith."
     a. *Auburn Journal* (23 November 1922): 1.

139. [Unsigned.] "Works of Late Auburn Author Are Published."
   a. *Auburn Journal* (16 July 1970): C9.

140. [Unsigned.] "Young Composer of Half-Hour Program."
   a. *Oakland Tribune* (15 March 1919): 11.

   Discussion of the student composer Emmet Pendleton, who has set CAS's poems to music, among others.

141. [Unsigned.] "Young Composer Will Give Works."
   a. *Oakland Tribune* (11 May 1919): 59.

   Mention of CAS among California poets whose work Emmet Pendleton has set to music.

142. [Unsigned.] [Untitled.]
   a. *Auburn Journal* (14 April 1927): 8.

   Mentions that CAS plans to spend a week in Berkeley.

143. [Unsigned.] [Untitled.]
   a. *Auburn Journal* (18 November 1954): 6.

144. [Unsigned.] [Untitled.]
   a. *Time Traveller* 1, No. 4 (April–May 1932): 3.

   Briefly mentions CAS, Lovecraft's "The Whisperer in Darkness," and HPL's oblique mention of CAS in the story.

B. Encyclopedias

1. Bleiler, E. F. "Smith, Clark Ashton."
    a. In E. F. Bleiler. *Guide to Supernatural Fiction*. Kent, OH: Kent State University Press, 1983. 458–63.

    Plot summaries of CAS's stories in books from *The Double Shadow* (1933) to *Other Dimensions* (1970).

2. Bleiler, E. F., and Richard J. Bleiler. "Smith, Clark Ashton (1893–1961)."
    a. In E. F. Bleiler and Richard J. Bleiler. *Science Fiction: The Gernsback Years*. Kent, OH: Kent State University Press, 1998. 389–94.

    Plot summaries of selected science fiction tales by CAS.

3. Connors, Scott. "Smith, Clark Ashton."
    a. In S. T. Joshi and Stefan Dziemianowicz, ed. *Supernatural Literature of the World: An Encyclopedia*. Westport, CT: Greenwood Press, 2005. 1040–44 (Vol. 3).

    Overview of CAS's life and work, especially in terms of his contribution to supernatural fiction.

4. Dziemianowicz, Stefan. "Smith, Clark Ashton."
    a. In David Pringle, ed. *St. James Guide to Horror, Ghost & Gothic Writers*. Detroit: St. James Press, 1998. 549–51 (with bibliography).

    Brief overview of CAS's work.

5. Guillaud, Lauric. "Clark Ashton Smith."
    a. In Jean-Pierre Deloux and Lauric Guillaud, ed. *Atlantide et autres civilisations perdues de A à Z*. Paris: e-dite, 2001. 244–48.

6. Joshi, S. T., and David E. Schultz. "Smith, Clark Ashton."
    a. In S. T. Joshi and David E. Schultz. *An H. P. Lovecraft Encyclopedia*. Westport, CT: Greenwood Press, 2001; New York: Hippocampus Press, [2004]. 246–48.

    Overview of CAS's life and work, with emphasis on his relations with Lovecraft.

7.   Lawrence, A., ed. *Who's Who among North American Authors.*
     a.   Los Angeles: Golden Syndicate Publishing Co., 1927–28,
          1929, 1931, 1935, 1939. 795 (1927–28).

8.   Stableford, Brian. "Clark Ashton Smith."
     a.   In E. F. Bleiler, ed. *Science Fiction Writers*. New York: Scrib-
          ner's, 1982. 139–44.

9.   Stableford, Brian. "The Short Fiction of Smith."
     a.   In Frank N. Magill, ed. *Survey of Modern Fantasy Literature*, vol.
          4. Englewood Cliffs, NJ: Salem Press, 1983. 1692–97.

C. Bibliographies

1. Barrass, Glynn Owen, and Edward P. Berglund. "A Clark Ashton Smith Bibliography and Checklist."
    a. In *Anno Klarkash-Ton* (D.1).

2. Bell, Joseph, ed. *The Books of Clark Ashton Smith.* Toronto: Soft Books, 1987. 28 pp.
    Reviews.
    a. Dziemianowicz, Stefan. *Klarkash-Ton* No. 1 (June 1988): 35–36.

3. Berglund, E. P. "The Work of Clark Ashton Smith."
    a. *Xenophile* No. 18 (1975): 35–41.

4. Buard, Jean-Luc. "Bibliographie française de Clark Ashton Smith."
    a. *Zothique* No. 1 (1985): 10–19.

5. Cockcroft, T. G. L. *The Tales of Clark Ashton Smith: A Bibliography.* Lower Hutt, New Zealand: T. G. L. Cockcroft, 1951, 1959, v pp. (with 1-page addendum).
    Reviews.
    a. Stone, Graham B. *Stopgap* (January 1952): [4–5].

    The first bibliography of CAS.

6. Guarriello, Pietro. "Clark Ashton Smith: Bibliografia italiana."
    a. In *Ombre dal cosmo* (D.9).

7. Sidney-Fryer, Donald, et al. *Emperor of Dreams: A Clark Ashton Smith Bibliography.*
    a. West Kingston, RI: Donald M. Grant, 1978. 303 pp.

    Contents: "Introduction" (9–10); "Acknowledgments" (11–13); "Principal Facts of Biography" (15–25); "Collections" (list) (27); Eric Barker, "Clark Ashton Smith: In Memory of a Great Friendship" (29–31); "Poems" (33–102); Fritz Leiber, "Letter" (103); "Poems in French" (105–10); August Derleth, "Letter" (111–12); "Translations of Poems" (113–21); Stanton A. Coblentz, "Letter" (122); "Prose Translations of Verse" (123–25); Avram Davidson, "Letter" (126); "Contents of Poetry Collections" (127–42); H. Warner Munn, "Letter" (143); "Uncollected

Poems" (145–49); George F. Haas, "Letter" (150); "Appearances of Poems in Anthologies, etc." (151–52); Harlan Ellison, "Letter" (153); Madelynne Greene, "Letter" (154); "Poems in Prose" (155–58); "Collections of Poems in Prose" (159–60); E. Hoffman[n] Price, "Letter" (161); Sam Moskowitz, "Letter" (162); "Tales" (163–75); Ethel Heiple, "Letter" (176); "Addendum" (list of tales related by a common background, with supplementary chronology) (177–82); "Contents of Prose Collections" (183–89); Genevieve K. Sully, "Letter" (190); "Uncollected Tales" (191); Rah Hoffman, "Letter" (192–95); "Appearances of Tales in Anthologies, etc." (197–99); "Epigrams and Pensées" (201–3); "Miscellaneous Prose" (205–7); "Juvenilia" (208); "Periodicals" (209–10); "Published Letters" (211–13); *The Auburn Journal* and *Weird Tales*" (215–23); "About Clark Ashton Smith" (225–50); "Library Holdings of Smith Mss." (251–60); "Pseudonyms" (261); Marvin R. Hiemstra, "Five Approaches to the Achievements of Clark Ashton Smith—Cosmic Master Artist" (263–75); "Index to First Lines of Poems" (277–302); CAS, "The Sorcerer Departs" (303).

Reviews.
a.   Moran, John C. *Romantist* No. 3 (1979): 82–83.
b.   [Unsigned.] "New Library Volume Honors Auburn Poet." *Auburn Journal* (11 December 1978): 6.

Exhaustive bibliography of CAS's poetry, fiction, and other writings, with many significant memoirs and critical articles on CAS by various hands. On pp. 104, 196, 200, 204, 214, 224, and 262 are photographs of CAS or of locales relating to his life and work. On p. 276 is a portrait-caricature of CAS by Virgil Partch (E.223).

8.   Smith, Eldred. "C. A. Smith: A Bibliography."
a.   *Alien Culture* 1, No. 2 (April 1949): 3–6; 1, No. 3 (July 1949): 17–18.

9.   Tuck, Donald H. "Smith, Clark Ashton."
a.   In Donald H. Tuck. *Encycliopedia of Science Fiction and Fantasy through 1968.* Chicago: Advent, 1978. 2.396–97.

D. Books and Pamphlets about Smith

1. Barrass, Glynn, and Frederick J. Mayer, ed. *Anno Klarkash-Ton*.
    a. Calne, UK: Rainfall Books, 2017. 208 pp.

    Contents: Frederick J. Mayer, "Introduction" (ix–xx); *Poetry:* Leigh
    Blackmore, "To Clark Ashton Smith" (3); Leigh Blackmore,
    "Ubbo Sathla" (5); Christene Britton-Jones, "The Lore of Aver-
    oigne" (6); Ran Cartwright, "Ilaiyana" (7–8, 10; Perry M. Gray-
    son, "Emptiness: A Poem in Prose" (11); Wade German, "Night
    Vigil for the Necromancer" (13); W. H. Pugmire, "To Kiss Me-
    dusa" (15–16); Peter Rawlik, "Hyperborean Lament" (17); Peter
    Rawlik, "Amongst the Stars I Dream" (18–20); David Schembri,
    "The Lord That Reigns Alone" (21–23); David Schembri, "The
    Torturer's Oath" (24–26); Richard L. Tierney, "The Cave Wiz-
    ard" (27); Michael Fantina, "Inspired by Clark Ashton Smith"
    (includes "The Muse") [29]; "C. A. Smith Emperor of Dreams"
    [30]; "A Tribute to Clark Ashton Smith (1893–1961)" [31]; "For
    Clark Ashton Smith (1893–1961)" [32]; "Flame" [33]); Charles
    Lovecraft, "A Wreathe of Smithics Just for You, a Poppy Crown"
    (includes "The Wizard of the Auburn Hills" [35]; "Everything Is
    Broken" [36]; "CAS" [37]; "The Bibliotaph" [38]; "O Brother
    Spirit, Klarkash-Ton; or, The Hieroglypher out of Time" [39];
    "Lovecraft Was Right" [40]; "The Lost Worlds of Smith"
    [41–42]; "For Smith" [43]); *Fiction:* Steve Lines, "The Eyes of the
    Scorpion" (47–80); Frederick J. Mayer, "The Flight of the Tico"
    (81–92); *Artwork:* Frederick J. Mayer, "Kumiho" (95), "Shathak"
    (96), "Tcho Tcho Grand Queen" (97), "Shathak Masque" (98),
    "Tsathoggua Mood" (99), "Our Lady of Lamias" (100); Steve
    Lines, "Flower-Woman" (101), "Maal-Dweb" (102), "Malygris"
    (103), "Ghoul" (104); *Non-fiction:* Frank Belknap Long, "The
    Poetry of Clark Ashton Smith" (107–10); Robert M. Price,
    "Abhoth the Unclean" (111–17); Brian M. Sammons, "A Seven-
    ties Sorcerer on the Small Screen" (118–22); Scott Connors,
    "Clark Ashton Smith in Carmel" (123–29) [with appendix: "The
    Abalone Song" (130–32)]; Scott Connors, "A Machen Review of
    Clark Ashton Smith" (133–42); Donald Wandrei, "The Emperor
    of Dreams" (143–55); Clark Ashton Smith, "Postcards to H. P.
    Lovecraft" (156–73) [includes unsigned introduction (156–57);
    2 January 1932 (156); 14 May 1932 (156–57); 24 May 1932
    (158); 10 August 1933 (158–59); 17 August 1933 (159); 21

August 1933 (160); 28 August 1933 (160); 29 August 1933 (160); 14 September 1933 (161); 16 September 1933 (161–62); 2 October 1933 (162); 5[?] October 1933 (163); 10 October 1933 (163–64); 6 November [1933?] (164); 24 November 1933 (164–65); 6 December 1933 (165–66); 7 March 1934 (166); 23 March 1934 (167); 15 June 1934 (167); 23 July 1934 (168); 21 November 1934 (168); 5 April 1935 (168–69); 7 September 1935 (169); n.d. [c. November 1935–February 1936] (169–71); 5 February 1936 (171–72); 22 May 1936 (172); 13 October 1936 (172–73)]; Glynn Owen Barrass and Edward P. Berglund, "A Clark Ashton Smith Bibliography and Checklist" (174–98); "Biographies" (199–208).

Miscellaneous volume containing poetic tributes to CAS, stories imitating his style and themes, artwork based on CAS's stories, and some critical essays. The "Postcards to H. P. Lovecraft" were announced as being first published here; but because the book was so long in production, the postcards in fact first appeared in *Dawnward Spire, Lonely Hill* (I.A.86).

2.   Behrends, Steve. *Clark Ashton Smith.* (Starmont Reader's Guide 49.)
     a.   Mercer Island, WA: Starmont House, 1990. v, 112 pp.
     b.   San Bernardino, CA: Borgo Press, 2013 (as *Clark Ashton Smith: A Critical Guide to the Man and His Work*). 220 pp.
Reviews.
     a.   Dziemianowicz, Stefan. *Dark Eidolon* No. 3 (Winter 1993): 34–26.
     b.   Herron, Don. *Studies in Weird Fiction* No. 9 (Spring 1991): 41–43 (response by Behrends, 43).

Broad overview of CAS's life and work, with chapters on story cycles (Zothique, Hyperborea, Averoigne, Atlantis, Mars, etc.) and brief discussions of prose poems and poetry. With a primary and secondary bibliography and index. The 2013 edition is an exhaustively revised and expanded version.

3.   Carter, Lin. *History & Chronology of the Book of Eibon.*
     a.   New York: Charnel House, 1984. 8 pp.

History of the writing and publication of the *Book of Eibon* as revealed in CAS's stories. An Italian translation appears in *Ombre dal cosmo* (D.9).

4.   Chalker, Jack L., ed. *In Memoriam: Clark Ashton Smith*.

a.   Baltimore: "Anthem"/Jack L. Chalker and Associates, 1963. xiv, 98 pp.

Contents: Jack L. Chalker, "Foreword" (viii); Ray Bradbury, "Introduction" (ix); Theodore Sturgeon, "Clark Ashton Smith: 1893–1961" (poem) (xiv); Donald S. Fryer, "The Sorcerer Departs" (1–27); CAS, "Cycles" (27); CAS, "Autobiography" (28); George F. Haas, "As I Remember Klarkash-Ton" (29–48); CAS, "The Old Water-Wheel" (48); CAS, "Town Lights" (50); Litterio Farsaci, "Poet of Eternity" (51–56); CAS, "The Voice in the Pines" (57); "CAS, *Dominium in Excelsis*" (first six stanzas only) (58); Ethel Heiple, "Reminiscences" (59–62); CAS, "September" (63); CAS, "Ineffability" (64); L. Sprague de Camp, "The Prose Tales of Clark Ashton Smith" (65–68); CAS, "Neighboring Slaughterhouse" ("Cattle Salute the Psychopomp," "Slaughter-House in Spring," "Slaughter-House Pasture," "Behind the Abattoir") (69); CAS, "The Barrier" (70); Fritz Leiber, "Clark Ashton Smith: An Appreciation" (71–73); CAS, "The Weird of Avoosl Wuthoqquan" (74–80); CAS, *The Dead Will Cuckold You* (81–97).

Reviews.

a.   [Unsigned.] "Volume Pays Tribute to C. A. Smith." *Auburn Journal* (10 October 1963): 11.

Memorial volume compiled upon CAS's death; for notes on individual items, see Section E. Mimeographed, 8.5 × 11 inches, stapled. Illustrations by David Prosser and Harry Warren Douthwaite. Limited to 450 numbered copies, of which fifty were supposed to have been bound in black cloth.

5.   Connors, Scott, ed. *The Freedom of Fantastic Things: Selected Criticism of Clark Ashton Smith*.

a.   New York: Hippocampus Press, 2006. 376 pp.

Contents: Scott Connors, "Introduction" (7–10); CAS, "The Centaur" (11); Donald Sidney-Fryer, "Klarkash-Ton and 'Greek'" (13–33); "Contemporary Reviews of Clark Ashton Smith" [ed. Scott Connors] (35–70); James Blish, "Eblis in Bakelite" (71–73 [with addendum by Donald Sidney-Fryer, 73–75]); Donald Sidney-Fryer, "James Blish versus Clark Ashton Smith; to Wit, the Young Turk Syndrome" (76–84); S. J. Sackett, "The Last Romantic" (85–89); Fred Chappell, "Communicable Mysteries: The Last True Symbolist" (90–98); S. T. Joshi, "What Happens in *The Hashish-Eater*" (99–107); Dan Clore, "The Babel of Visions: The

Structuration of Clark Ashton Smith's *The Hashish-Eater*"
(108–23); Carl Jay Buchanan, "Clark Ashton Smith's 'Nero'"
(124–31); Phillip A. Ellis, "Satan Speaks: A Reading of 'Satan
Unrepentant'" (132–37); S. T. Joshi, "Lands Forgotten or Un-
found: The Prose Poetry of Clark Ashton Smith" (138–47); Brian
Stableford, "Outside the Human Aquarium: The Fantastic Im-
agination of Clark Ashton Smith" (148–67); John Kipling Hitz,
"Clark Ashton Smith: Master of the Macabre" (168–79); Scott
Connors, "Gesturing toward the Infinite: Clark Ashton Smith and
Modernism" (180–94); Charles K. Wolfe, "Clark Ashton Smith:
A Note on the Aesthetics of Fantasy" (195–99); Lauric Guillaud,
"Fantasy and Decadence in the Work of Clark Ashton Smith"
(200–220); John Kipling Hitz, "Humor in Hyperspace: Smith's
Uses of Satire" (221–28); Steve Behrends, "Song of the Necro-
mancer: 'Loss' in Clark Ashton Smith's Fiction" (229–39); [map
of Poseidonis by Tim Kirk] (238); Donald Sidney-Fryer, "Brave
World Old and New: The Atlantis Theme in the Poetry and Fic-
tion of Clark Ashton Smith" (239–58); [map of Hyperborea by
Tim Kirk] (260); Steven Tompkins, "Coming In from the Cold:
Incursions of 'Outsideness' in Hyperborea" (261–76); [map of
Zothique by Tim Kirk] (278); Jim Rockhill, "As Shadows Wait
upon the Sun: Clark Ashton Smith's Zothique" (279–92); [map of
Averoigne by Tim Kirk] (294); Stefan Dziemianowicz, "Into the
Woods: The Human Geography of Averoigne" (295–304); Peter
H. Goodrich, "Sorcerous Style: Clark Ashton Smith's *The Double
Shadow and Other Fantasies*" (305–17); Dan Clore, "Loss and Recuperation: A Model for Reading Clark Ashton Smith's 'Xeethra'"
(318–23); Scott Connors, "'Life, Love and the Clemency of Death':
A Reexamination of Clark Ashton Smith's 'The Isle of the Torturers'" (324–33); Ronald S. Hilger, "Regarding the Providence Point
of View" (334–37); Steve Behrends, "An Annotated Chronology of
the Fiction of Clark Ashton Smith" (338–45); "Bibliography"
(347–55);   "Contributors"   (357–60);   "Acknowledgements"
(361–62); "Index" (363–76).

Reviews.

a. Beatty, Greg. "Mapping the Unmappable." *Science-Fiction
    Studies* 36, No. 2 (July 2009): 356–58.

b. Dirda, Michael. "A Journey to the Fantastic Realms of Clark
    Ashton Smith." *Washington Post Book World* (18–24 February
    2007): 10.

    c. Schweitzer, Darrell. "Clark Ashton Smith: Inescapable, But Difficult to Love." *New York Review of Science Fiction* No. 235 (March 2008): 15–17.

    d. Taylor, John Alfred. *Lost Worlds* No. 4 (2006): 39–44.

    Exhaustive assemblage of CAS criticism, some reprints but largely original. For notes on individual items, see Section E.

6. De Casseres, Benjamin. *Clark Ashton Smith, Emperor of Shadows.*
    a. Lakeport, CT: Futile Press, 1937. 2 pp.
    b. Essex, MD: Union of Egoists/Underworld Amusements, 2017.

7. Dunais, David. *L'Art étrange de Clark Ashton Smith.*
    a. Paris: Les Éditions de L'Oeil du Sphinx, 2013. 251 pp.

    Contents: "Préface" by Donald Sidney-Fryer (5–7); "Introduction" (9–10); *Première partie: L'Art étrange de C. A. Smith* (11–34); *Deuxième partie: Le Mangeur de Haschisch: Le Mangeur de Haschisch, ou l'Apocalpyse du Mal* (the Hashish-Eater; or, The Apocalypse of Evil; tr. Jean Hautepierre) (37–55); "*The Hashish-Eater,* étude prosodique" (57–91); "Le *Hashish-Eater,* un héritage romantique" (93–126); *Troisième partie: C. A. Smith traduit Baudelaire:* "La traduction, forgerie poétique" (129–53); "Prosodie des traductions de Baudelaire par C. A. Smith" (155–65); "*Triste thuriféraire,* un tombeau de Baudelaire" (167–76); "Sept traductions de Baudelaire par C. A. Smith" ("Alchimie de la douleur" [French and English (178–84)]; "L'Aube spirituelle" [French and English (186–90)]; "La Béatrice" [French and English (192–99)]; "Brumes et pluies" [French and English (200–206)]; "Chant d'automne" [French and English (208–17)]; "Les Deux Bonnes Soeurs" [French and English (218–22)]; "Les Métamorphoses du vampire" [French and English (224–28)]; Postface: L'option fantastique chez C. A. Smith, une liberté libérante" by Emmanuel Thibault (231–42).

    Profound and wide-ranging study of CAS's poetry.

8. Gindre, Philippe. *Les Jardins de Klarkash-Ton: L'Horreur végétale selon Clark Ashton Smith.*
    a. Dole, France: La Clef d'Argent, 2008. 41 pp.

    On the use of flowers and plants in CAS's poetry and prose. A revision of E.116.a. For an English translation, see E.116.b.

9.   Guarriello, Pietro, ed. *Ombre dal cosmo: Fantasie di Clark Ashton Smith.*
     a.   Reggio Emilia: Yorick Fantasy Magazine, 1999. 152 pp.

> *Contents:* Donald Sidney-Fryer, "Introduzione" (11–16); S. T.
> Joshi, "Nota bio-bibliografica" (17–19); H. P. Lovecraft, "A Clark
> Ashton Smith, signore di Averoigne" ("To Clark Ashton Smith,
> Lord of Averoigne") (20); *Sezione I: Inediti:* CAS, "Universi par-
> alleli" ("Double Cosmos") (24–34); CAS, "Il buon imbalsama-
> tore" ("A Good Embalmer" [tr. Lorenzo Mussini and Massimo
> Tassi]) (35–39); CAS, "La foresta proibita" ("The Forbidden
> Forest") (40–42); CAS, "Il lago nero" ("The Blake Lake") (43);
> CAS, "L'impero delle ombre" ("The Kingdom of Shadows")
> (44–46); CAS, "Morte di un negromante" ("The Sorcerer De-
> parts") (47); *Sezione II: Saggi:* Jean Marigny, "L'universo fantas-
> tico di Clark Ashton Smith" ("L'Univers fantastique de Clark
> Ashton Smith") (51–61); Steve Behrends, "L'origine di Zothique"
> (excerpt from Chapter 2 of *Clark Ashton Smith* [D.2]) (62–67);
> Stefan Dziemianowicz, "All'interno della foresta: La geografia
> umana dell'Averoigne di Clark Ashton Smith" ("Into the Woods:
> The Human Geography of Clark Ashton Smith's Averoigne")
> (68–87); [Map of Averoigne by Ronald S. Hilger] (87); Pietro
> Guarriello, "From Auburn to the Stars: La fantascienza di Clark
> Ashton Smith" (88–99); Lin Carter, "Storia e cronologia del *Libro
> di Eibon*" ("History and Chronology of the *Book of Eibon*")
> (100–104); *Sezione III: Documenti:* "Clark Ashton Smith: Out-
> ward and Away" (excerpts from *Planets and Dimensions* and *The
> Black Book* edited and translated by Giuseppe Lippi) (107–14);
> "Lettere da Auburn: Selezione dall'epistolario" ("Letters from
> Auburn: A Selection" [To H. P. Lovecraft, October 1931,
> 117–18; to Lovecraft, c. October 21, 1930, 118–19; to Lovecraft,
> November 10, 1930, 119–20); to Harry Bates, c. June 1931,
> 120–21; to Farnsworth Wright, c. January 1933, 121–22); to
> Lovecraft, c. early November 1933, 122–24); to Charles D.
> Hornig, c. March 1934, 124–25); to Robert H. Barlow, Sep-
> tember 10, 1934, 125–27]); Eric Barker, "Clark Ashton Smith:
> Memoria di una grande amicizia" ("Clark Ashton Smith: In
> Memory of a Great Friendship") (132–36); Pietro Guarriello,
> "Clark Ashton Smith: Bibliografia italiana" (137–50).

> Translated by Pietro Guarriello save where indicated. Limited to
> 200 numbered copies.

10. Hilger, Ronald S., ed. *One Hundred Years of Klarkash-Ton: The Clark Ashton Smith Centennial Conference.* [Grass Valley, CA]: Averon Press, 1996. 42 pp.

> *Contents:* Donald Sidney-Fryer, "Introduction" (1); CAS, "O Golden-Tongued Romance" (2); Ronald S. Hilger, "Clark Ashton Smith: Forgotten Poet of Auburn" (3–5); CAS, "Cycles" (5); Henry J. Vester, "Strange Reflections: The Self-Image of Clark Ashton Smith" (6–10); Edgar Saltus, "Truth" (poem) (10); Jesse F. Knight, "Terrible Vistas: The Vision of Clark Ashton Smith and George Sterling" (11–16); George Sterling, "The Forty-Third Chapter of Job" (14–15); CAS, "Hyperborea" (painting) (18); photographs of sculptures by CAS (18); Violet Nelson Heyer, "Letter" (20–22); CAS, "The Old Water-Wheel" ; Marvin R. Hiemstra, "Clipped Wings: A Fable in Tribute to Clark Ashton Smith" (24–30); Ambrose Bierce, "Creation" (31); CAS, "The Motes" (31); CAS, "The Ghoul and the Seraph" (final dialogue only) (32–33); CAS, "Arabesque" (33); Robert B. Elder, "CAS—A Reminiscence"; Donald Sidney-Fryer, "A Clark Ashton Smith Roll of Honor" (40–42).

> Anthology of essays to commemorate the centennial of CAS's birth. Cover artwork by Gahan Wilson.

11. Marigny, Jean. *Les Mondes perdus de Clark Ashton Smith.*
     a.1. Dole, France: La Clef d'Argent, 2004. 22 pp.
     a.2. Dole, France: La Clef d'Argent, 2007.

12. Rickard, Dennis. *The Fantastic Art of Clark Ashton Smith.* Introduction by Gahan Wilson. 25[+35] pp.
     a. Baltimore: Mirage Press, 1973.

> Analysis of CAS's artwork, followed by reproductions of his paintings and carvings.

13. Sidney-Fryer, Donald. *Clark Ashton Smith: Poète en prose.* Trans. Philippe Gindre.
     a.1. Dole, France: La Clef d'Argent, 2001. 26 pp.
     a.2. Dole, France: La Clef d'Argent, 2008.

> Translation of a revised and updated version of Sidney-Fryer's introduction to *Poems in Prose* (E.285).

14. Sidney-Fryer, Donald. *Clark Ashton Smith: The Sorcerer Departs.*
     a. West Hills, CA: Tsathoggua Press, 1997. 37 pp.

b. Dole, France: Silver Key Press/La Clef d'Argent, 2007. 64 pp.

Contents (Tsathoggua Press edition): Perry M. Grayson, "Introduction: 'In Tsathoggua's Domain'" (5); CAS, "The Sorcerer Departs" (6); "1. A Biography of Clark Ashton Smith" (6–23); "2. Some General Remarks on Smith's Poetry and Prose" (23–34); CAS, "Cycles" (35); "Afterword" (36–37).

Reprint of E.300. The Silver Key Press edition contains: Philippe Gindre, "Foreword of the Publisher" (5–8); "A Biography of Clark Ashton Smith" (9–37); "Some General Remarks on Smith's Poetry and Prose" (38–56); CAS, "The Sorcerer Departs" (48); CAS, "Cycles" (57); "Afterword" (58); [Philippe Gindre], "Clark Ashton Smith: A Selective Bibliography" (60); "About Donald Sidney-Fryer" (61–63); "Donald Sidney-Fryer: A Bibliography" (64).

15. Sidney-Fryer, Donald. *The Last of the Great Romantic Poets.*
a. Albuquerque, NM: Silver Scarab Press, 1972. iv, 23[+4] pp. Illustrations by Herb Arnold.

Contents: George Sterling, "The Coming Singer" (i); "Caveat Lector" (ii); "The Last of the Great Romantic Poets" (1–23); "Addendum: Another Smith" (review of Franz Schmidt's Fourth Symphony in C Major) (1–4).

E. Criticism in Books and Periodicals

1. [Ackerman, Forrest J.] "Clark Ashton Smith—The Star Treader."
   a. *Famous Fantastic Mysteries* 10, No. 6 (August 1949): 109.

2. Ambrose, Michael E. "The Poetry of Clark Ashton Smith: An Introduction."
   a. *Dragonbane* No. 1 (Spring 1978): 48–51.

   Brief but cogent general essay on CAS as a poet.

3. Anderson, Douglas A. "On the Authorship of *As It Is Written*."
   a. *Klarkash-Ton* No. 1 (June 1988): 28–31.

   Refutes Will Murray's contention that De Lysle Ferrée Cass is CAS. See G.ii.2.

4. Anderson, Lester. "The Star Rover."
   a. *Science Fiction Digest* 1, No. 8 (April 1933): 7.

5. Andersson, Martin. "Clark Ashton Smith: Den okände mästaren."
   a. In Rickard Berghorn, ed. *Fantasins urskogar: Skräck, fantasy och science fiction i begynnelsen.* Bangkok: Aleph Bokförlag, 2017. 137–46.

   A biographical overview.

6. Ashley, Mike. "Evoking Wonder."
   a. *Lost Worlds* No. 3 (2006): 29–31.

   On "The Face by the River" and "The Red World of Polaris."

7. Ashley, Mike. "The Perils of Wonder: Clark Ashton Smith's Experiences with *Wonder Stories*."
   a. *Dark Eidolon* No. 2 (July 1989): 2–8.

   Biographical account of CAS's dealings with *Wonder Stories*.

8. Ashley, Mike, and Robert A. W. Lowndes. *The Gernsback Days: A Study of the Evolution of Modern Science Fiction from 1911 to 1936.*
   a. Holicong, PA: Wildside Press, 2004. 173–75, 200, 243, passim.

   Discussion of CAS's relations with Hugo Gernsback and his appearances in *Wonder Stories*.

9.   Austin, William N. "Clark Ashton Smith: A Deduction."
      a.   *Sinisterra* 1, No. 2 (Summer 1950): 4.

10.   Baldwin, F. Lee. "Within the Circle."
      a.   *Fantasy Fan* 1, No. 11 (July 1934): 164.
      b.   In Charles D. Hornig, ed. *The Fantasy Fan: September, 1933–February, 1935.* [n.p.: Lance Thingmaker, 2010.] 164. [Facsimile of a.]
      c.   In H. P. Lovecraft. *Letters to F. Lee Baldwin, Duane W. Rimel, and Nils Frome.* Ed. David E. Schultz and S. T. Joshi. New York: Hippocampus Press, 2016. 357.

      On CAS's recent stories in *Weird Tales.*

11.   Baldwin, F. Lee. "Within the Circle."
      a.   *Fantasy Fan* 2, No. 3 (November 1934): 36.
      b.   In Charles D. Hornig, ed. *The Fantasy Fan: September, 1933–February, 1935.* [n.p.: Lance Thingmaker, 2010.] [Part 2,] 36. [Facsimile of a.]
      c.   In H. P. Lovecraft. *Letters to F. Lee Baldwin, Duane W. Rimel, and Nils Frome.* Ed. David E. Schultz and S. T. Joshi. New York: Hippocampus Press, 2016. 359.

      On a fire near CAS's home and on his early fiction.

12.   Barker, Eric. "Clark Ashton Smith: In Memory of a Great Friendship."
      a.   In *Emperor of Dreams* (C.7).
      b.   In *In the Realms of Mystery and Wonder* (I.A.87).

      On the relations of Barker and his wife, Madelynne Greene, with CAS.

13.   Behrends, Steve. "An Annotated Chronology of the Fiction of Clark Ashton Smith."
      a.   *Crypt of Cthulhu* No. 26 (Hallowmas 1984): 17–23.
      b.   In *The Freedom of Fantastic Things* (D.5).

      Annotated listing of CAS's stories in chronological order.

14.   Behrends, Steve. "The Birth of Ubbo-Sathla: Smith, Wandrei, Alfred Kramer, and the Begotten Source."
      a.   *Crypt of Cthulhu* No. 45 (Candlemas 1987): 10–13.

      On the influence of Donald Wandrei's "The Lives of Alfred Kramer" on CAS's "Ubbo-Sathla."

15. Behrends, Steve. "CAS & Divers Hands: Ideas of Lovecraft and Others in Smith's Fiction."
    a. *Crypt of Cthulhu* No. 26 (Hallowmas 1984): 30–31.
    b. In Robert M. Price, ed. *The Horror of It All: Encrusted Gems from the 'Crypt of Cthulhu.'* Mercer Island, WA: Starmont, 1990. 65–67.

    On Lovecraft's influence on CAS's tales.

16. Behrends, Steve. "The Carter–Smith 'Collaborations.'"
    a. *Crypt of Cthulhu* No. 36 (Yuletide 1985): 25–31, 39.

    Discussion of the stories that Lin Carter wrote based on story notes by CAS. See also item 55.

17. Behrends, Steve. "Clark Ashton Smith: Cosmicist or Misanthrope?"
    a. *Dark Eidolon* No. 2 (July 1989): 12–14.

    CAS's cosmicism expresses itself as a "sense of distance and isolation from his fellow men."

18. Behrends, Steve. "Editorial."
    a. *Klarkash-Ton* No. 1 (June 1988): 2.

19. Behrends, Steve. "If Zothique Had Electrical Engineers: Some Thoughts on the New Two."
    a. *Lost Worlds* No. 3 (2006): 26–28.

    On "The Face by the River" and "The Red World of Polaris."

20. Behrends, Steve. "L'origine di Zothique."
    a. In *Ombre dal cosmo* (D.9).

    Excerpt from D.2.a.

21. Behrends, Steve. "Song of the Necromancer: 'Loss' in Clark Ashton Smith's Fiction."
    a. *Studies in Weird Fiction* No. 1 (Summer 1986): 3–12.
    b. In *The Freedom of Fantastic Things* (D.5).

    On the significance of the theme of loss in CAS's fiction.

22. Behrends, Steve, Donald Sidney-Fryer, and Rah Hoffman. "Errata to *Strange Shadows: The Uncollected Fiction and Essays of Clark Ashton Smith*."

   a. *Dark Eidolon* No. 3 (Winter 1993): 26–28.

23.   Bell, Ian. "Clark Ashton Smith."
   a. In Ian Bell. *Death's Dark Shadow: American Weird Fantasy of the Pulp Era.* Oxford: Oxford Polytechnic, 1982. 21–24.

   General overview of CAS's life and work.

24.   Benét, William Rose. "The Phoenix Nest."
   a. *Saturday Review of Literature* 25, No. 41 (10 October 1942): 14.

   Brief discussion of CAS as poet and fiction writer.

25.   Bennett, Raine. "Clark Ashton Smith, Virgin."
   a. *Studies in Weird Fiction* No. 18 (Winter 1996): 35–36 (introductory note by Steve Behrends, 34–35).

   A letter to H. L. Mencken (26 November 1950) in which Bennett recounts a plan by George Sterling to divest CAS of his virginity as a means of inspiring his poetry.

26.   Bierce, Ambrose. Letter to George Sterling (8 August 1911).
   a. In Ambrose Bierce. *The Letters of Ambrose Bierce.* Ed. Bertha Clark Pope. San Francisco: Book Club of California, 1922. 180–81.
   c. In *The Shadow of the Unattained* (I.A.69).

   Praise of CAS's "Ode to the Abyss."

27.   Bierce, Ambrose. Letter to *Town Talk* (6 August 1912).
   a. *Town Talk* No. 1042 (10 August 1912): 12.
   b. In Ambrose Bierce. *A Much Misunderstood Man: Selected Letters of Ambrose Bierce.* Ed. S. T. Joshi and David E. Schultz. Columbus: Ohio State University Press, 2003. 225.

   Bierce warns against making too much of his muted praise of CAS's poetry.

28.   [Blackbeard, Bill.] "Beardless, Brotherless, H. Allenless, a Mythic Smith Withal."
   a. *Los Angeles Science Fantasy Society Newsletter* No. 22 (February 1964): 2.

29.   [Blackbeard, Bill.] "CASus Belli."
   a. *Los Angeles Science Fantasy Society Newsletter* No. 22 (February 1964): 1.

30.   Bleiler, Richard. "Visionary Star-Treader: The Speculative Writings of Clark Ashton Smith."
   a.   In Gary Hoppenstand, ed. *Pulp Fiction of the 1920s and 1930s.* (Critical Insights.) Ipswich, MA: Salem Press, 2013. 66–83.

   Overview of CAS's fiction, focusing on his various cycles of fantasy tales as well as his science fiction.

31.   Blish, James. "Eblis in Bakelite."
   a.   *Tumbrils* No. 2 (June 1945): 12–13.
   b.   *Fantasy Aspects* No. 2 (November 1947): 13–14, 20.
   c.   *Lost Worlds* No. 1 (2004): 8–10 (with addendum by Donald Sidney-Fryer, 10–11).
   d.   In *The Freedom of Fantastic Things* (D.5).

   Maintains that CAS is overrated and that his poetry and prose are merely a tissue of literary influences.

32.   Bloch, Robert. "A Visitor from Averoigne."
   a.   *Nyctalops* No. 7 (August 1972): 75.

33.   Blond, Martine. "Clark Ashton Smith: Explorateur des mille et un univers de l'Heroic Fantasy."
   a.   *Crépuscule Galactique* No. 1 (1st Quarter 1979): 23–24.

34.   Boyd, Bill. "CAS Motif in Work of Jack Vance."
   a.   *Tales of Horror and Damnation* No. 6 (January 1985): 18–20, 24.

   On CAS's influence on the work of Jack Vance.

35.   Bradbury, Ray. "Introduction."
   a.   In *In Memoriam: Clark Ashton Smith* (D.4).
   b.   In *A Rendezvous in Averoigne* (I.A.47).

   Praise of CAS as a weaver of poetic prose.

36.   Brandenberger, Mary Ann. "Poetic Devices in 'The Empire of the Necromancers.'"
   a.   *Niekas* No. 45 (1998): 87–89.

37.   Brion, Florian. "Klarkash-Ton, l'empereur des nécromants."
   a.   *Karpath* No. 1 (4th Quarter 1989): 7–21.

38.   Bryant, Roger. "The Fading Red Sun of Zothique."
   a.   *Nyctalops* No. 7 (August 1972): 26–27.

39. Bryant, Roger. "The Return of the Sorcerer."
     a. *Nyctalops* No. 7 (August 1972): 18–19.

40. Buard, Jean-Luc. "L'Actualité de Clark Ashton Smith."
     a. *Zothique* No. 1 (1985): 4.

41. Buard, Jean-Luc. "Glossaire des noms de personnages, de lieux ainsi que divers autres. Suivi d'un index analytique."
     a. *Zothique* No. 1 (1985): 46–58.

42. Buard, Jean-Luc. "Introduction: Clark Ashton Smith ou le pouvoir des noms."
     a. *Zothique* No. 1 (1985): 3.

43. [Buard, Jean-Luc, et al.] "Le Cycle de Zothique: Étude."
     a. *Zothique* No. 1 (1985): 31–44.

     Includes: "Étude du corpus (avec bibliographie)," [by Jean-Luc Buard] (31–34); "Le Dernier Continent terrestre," [by Jean-Luc Buard] (35); "La Succession des contes de Zothique," by Lin Carter (36–37); "L'Univers de Zothique," [by Jean-Luc Buard] (40–44).

44. Buchanan, Carl Jay. "An Appreciation of Clark Ashton Smith's 'Ode to the Abyss.'"
     a. *Lost Worlds* No. 5 (2008): 15–18.

     "In the end, the poem expresses the insight that the aether, God's breath, is extinct rather than all-pervading . . ."

45. Buchanan, Carl Jay. "Clark Ashton Smith's 'Nero.'"
     a. *Central California Poetry Journal* (2001) [no longer online].
     b. In *The Freedom of Fantastic Things* (D.5).

     Analysis of the poem, with a discussion of early critics' assessment of it.

46. Cammarota, Domenico. "L'ultimo dei decadenti: Clark Ashton Smith."
     a. In *Il destino di Antarion* (II.A.vi.6). 189–208.

47. Campbell, Ramsey. "Introduction."
     a. In *Collected Fantasies,* Volume 1 (I.A.70).

     Appreciation of CAS's early tales of Averoigne and other realms.

48. Carter, Lin. "About Hyperborea, and Clark Ashton Smith: Behind the North Wind."
    a. In *Hyperborea* (I.A.29).

49. Carter, Lin. "About Poseidonis, and Clark Ashton Smith: The Mage of Atlantis."
    a. In *Poseidonis* (I.A.34).

50. Carter, Lin. "About Xiccarph, and Clark Ashton Smith: Other Stars and Skies."
    a. In *Xiccarph* (I.A.30).

51. Carter, Lin. "About Zothique, and Clark Ashton Smith: When the World Grows Old."
    a. In *Zothique* (I.A.25).

52. Carter, Lin. "Baleful Myths and Liturgies: Clark Ashton Smith's Contributions to the Cthulhu Mythos."
    a. *Dark Eidolon* No. 3 (Winter 1993): 9–12.

    On the books, gods, and other elements invented by CAS that were incorporated in Lovecraft's Cthulhu Mythos.

53. Carter, Lin. "The Emperor of Dreams: An Appreciation of Clark Ashton Smith."
    a. *Fantasy Advertiser* 3, No. 5 (November 1949): 12–14.

54. Carter, Lin. "Projected Clark Ashton Smith Collections."
    a. *Dark Eidolon* No. 3 (Winter 1993): 12–14.

    On five additional CAS collections planned by Carter for the Adult Fantasy Series.

55. Carter, Lin. "A Response."
    a. *Crypt of Cthulhu* No. 36 (Yuletide 1985): 32–34.

    Reply to Steve Behrends's article (item 16 above).

56. Carter, Lin. "Storia e cronologia del Libro di Eibon."
    a. In *Ombre dal cosmo* (D.9).

    Translation of D.3.

57. Cawthorn, James, and Michael Moorcock. "Clark Ashton Smith: *Zothique.*"
     a. In James Cawthorn and Michael Moorcock, ed. *Fantasy: The 100 Best Books.* London: Xanadu, 1988; New York: Carroll & Graf, 1988. 95–96.

     Brief overview of CAS's Zothique stories.

58. Chalker, Jack L. "Foreword."
     a. In *In Memoriam: Clark Ashton Smith* (D.4).

59. Chappell, Fred. "Communicable Mysteries: The Last True Symbolist."
     a. *Lost Worlds* No. 2 (2004): 3–11.
     b. In *The Freedom of Fantastic Things* (D.5).

     On the merits of CAS's poetry and its relation to French Symbolism.

60. Clore, Dan. "The Babel of Visions: The Structuration of Clark Ashton Smith's *The Hashish-Eater.*"
     a. *Studies in Weird Fiction* No. 18 (Winter 1996): 2–12.
     b. In *The Freedom of Fantastic Things* (D.5).

     On the sequence of scenes and images in CAS's poem.

61. Clore, Dan. "Loss and Recuperation: A Model for Reading Clark Ashton Smith's 'Xeethra.'"
     a. *Studies in Weird Fiction* No. 13 (Summer 1993): 15–18.
     b. In *The Freedom of Fantastic Things* (D.5).

     A structuralist analysis of the story.

62. Clore, Dan. "Satampra 'Lefty' Zeiros."
     a. *Lost Worlds* No. 3 (2006): 32–33.

     On the place of "The Tale of Satampra Zeiros" in the Hyperborea cycle.

63. Coblentz, Stanton A. "Letter."
     a. In *Emperor of Dreams* (C.7).

     Brief praise of CAS as an imaginative writer.

64. Cockcroft, T. G. L. "Pulp Cover Art on CAS: A Showcase."
     a. *Nyctalops* No. 7 (August 1972): 48–49.

65. Cockcroft, T. G. "The Reader Speaks: Reaction to Clark Ashton Smith in the Pulps."
     a. *Dark Eidolon* No. 2 (July 1989): 15–20.

     Provides extensive quotations from the letter columns of *Wonder Stories* and *Weird Tales* on CAS's work.

66. Cockcroft, T. G. L. "Some Bibliographic Notes on CAS."
     a. *Nyctalops* No. 7 (August 1972): 60–64.

     Miscellaneous bibliographic notes, including a chronological listing of stories in various magazines.

67. Comtois, Pierre. "Clark Ashton Smith and the French Romantics."
     a. *Dark Eidolon* No. 3 (Winter 1993): 28–33.

     On the influence of Baudelaire, Mallarmé, Rimbaud, Apollinaire, and others on CAS.

68. Connors, Scott. "An Arthur Machen Review of Clark Ashton Smith."
     a. *Faunus: The Journal of the Friends of Arthur Machen* No. 6 (Autumn 2000): 31–38.
     b. In *Anno Klarkash-Ton* (D.1) (as "A Machen Review of Clark Ashton Smith").

     Discussion of Machen's belated review of *The Star-Treader* (F.1.g).

69. Connors, Scott. "Averoigne and Zothique."
     a. *Crypt of Cthulhu* No. 108 (Hallowmas 2017): 24–31.

     English-language version of the preface to *Mondes derniers* (II.A.iii.14).

70. Connors, Scott. "Clark Ashton Smith Collections in the San Francisco Bay Area, Part 2: The Bancroft Library."
     a. *Lost Worlds* No. 5 (2008): 35–39.

     On CAS poetry and other mss. at the Bancroft Library. See also item 132.

71. Connors, Scott. "Clark Ashton Smith in Carmel."
     a. *Skelos* 1, No. 2 (Winter 2017): 27–30.
     b. In *Anno Klarkash-Ton* (D.1).

     On CAS's month-long stay with George Sterling in Carmel, May–June 1912.

72. Connors, Scott. "Dust and Atoms: The Influence of William Hope Hodgson on Clark Ashton Smith."
     a. *Sargasso: The Journal of William Hope Hodgson Studies* No. 2 (Fall 2014): 164–72.

     Traces the influence of *The House on the Borderland* and *The Night Land* on CAS's tales.

73. Connors, Scott. "The Editor Speaks: Lights, Camera, Inaction!"
     a. *Lost Worlds* No. 5 (2008): 2.

     On the lack of movie adaptations of CAS's work.

74. Connors, Scott. "The Face Behind the Mask."
     a. *Lost Worlds* No. 3 (2006): 15–18.

     On the discovery of "The Face by the River," with a brief analysis of the story.

75. [Connors, Scott.] "From the Vaults of Yoh-Vombis."
     a. *Lost Worlds* No. 3 (2006): 54.

76. Connors, Scott. "Gesturing toward the Infinite: Clark Ashton Smith and Modernism."
     a. *Studies in Weird Fiction* No. 25 (Summer 2001): 18–28.
     b. In *The Freedom of Fantastic Things* (D.5).

     On CAS's relations with the Modernist movement, including such writers as T. S. Eliot, C. S. Peirce, and Irving Babbitt.

77. Connors, "Introduction."
     a. In *In the Realms of Mystery and Wonder* (I.A.87).

     Detailed analysis of CAS's work as painter, sculptor, and prose-poet.

78. Connors, Scott. "Introduction" [to "Necromancy in Naat"].
     a. *Lost Worlds* No. 4 (2006): 2–4.

79. Connors, Scott. "Klarkash-Ton: The Emperor of Dreams."
     a. *Dark Discoveries* No. 20 (Spring 2012): 43–46.

80. Connors, Scott. "'Life, Love, and the Clemency of Death': A Reexamination of Clark Ashton Smith's 'The Isle of the Torturers.'"
     a. *Wormwood* No. 2 (Spring 2004): 37–47.
     b. In *The Freedom of Fantastic Things* (D.5).

Sees the influence of George Sterling's *Lilith* on the story.

81. Connors, Scott. "Pegasus Unbridled: Clark Ashton Smith and the Ghettoization of Fantasy."
    a. In Justin Everett and Jeffrey K. Shanks, ed. *The Unique Legacy of* Weird Tales. Lanham, MD: Rowman & Littlefield, 2015. 1512–71.

    On CAS's career as a pulp writer for *Weird Tales* and other weird and science fiction pulps of the period.

82. Connors, Scott. "Préface."
    a. In *Mondes derniers* (II.A.iii.14).

    Brief biography of CAS and overview of the Zothique and Averoigne cycles.

83. Connors, Scott. "Préface."
    a. In *Mondes premiers* (II.A.iii.15).

    Overview of the Hyperborea and Poseidonis cycles.

84. Connors, Scott. "Préface."
    a. In *Autres mondes* (II.A.iii.16).

    Overview of the Xiccarph, Mars, and othe cycles.

85. Connors, Scott. "The Return of the Sorcerer."
    a. *Lost Worlds* No. 1 (2004): 2.

    On the need for a journal of CAS studies.

86. [Connors, Scott.] "Scryings."
    a. *Lost Worlds* No. 1 (2004): 40.

87. Connors, Scott. "*Weird Tales* and the Great Depression."
    a. In Darrell Schweitzer, ed. *The Robert E. Howard Reader*. San Bernardino, CA: Borgo Press, 2010. 162–78,

    Discussion of the finances of pulp magazine publishing, using editor Farnsworth Wright's letters to CAS and August Derleth as primary sources.

88. Connors, Scott. "Who Discovered Clark Ashton Smith?"
    a. *Lost Worlds* No. 1 (2004): 25–34.

On whether George Sterling or Boutwell Dunlap deserves credit for promoting CAS's work in 1912.

89.   Connors, Scott, and Arinn Dembo. "*The Last Continent:* An Exchange."
     a.   *New York Review of Science Fiction* 14, No. 1 (September 2001): 157.

     A debate concerning *The Last Continent: New Tales of Zothique,* ed. John Pelan (ShadowLands Press, 1999), an anthology of new stories set in Zothique.

90.   [Connors, Scott, and Ronald S. Hilger.] "The Editors Speak."
     a.   *Lost Worlds* No. 3 (2006): 2–4.

     On the editing of the *Collected Fantasies* series (I.A.70).

91.   Connors, Scott, and Ron[ald S.] Hilger. "Introduction."
     a.   In *The Miscellaneous Writings of Clark Ashton Smith* (I.A.82).

     Analysis of CAS's juvenilia and other works included in the volume.

92.   Connors, Scott, and Ron[ald S.] Hilger. "Introduction: The Non-Human Equation."
     a.   In *Star Changes* (I.A.66).

     Overview of CAS's work as a science fiction writer.

93.   Connors, Scott, and David E. Schultz. "Introduction."
     a.   In *Selected Letters of Clark Ashton Smith* (I.A.63).

     On CAS's correspondence with George Sterling, H. P. Lovecraft, and others.

94.   Constantine, Storm. "*Lost Worlds* by Clark Ashton Smith."
     a.   In Stephen Jones and Kim Newman, ed. *Horror: Another 100 Best Books.* New York: Carroll & Graf, 2005. 95–98.

     Brief overview of the Arkham House volume.

95.   Davidson, Avram. "Letter."
     a.   In *Emperor of Dreams* (C.7).

     Davidson regrets that he never met CAS.

96.   Davin, Eric Leif. "The Age of Wonder."
     a.   *Fantasy Commentator* 4, No. 1 (Fall 1987): 4–25, 39–47.

b. In Eric Leif Davin. *Pioneers of Wonder: Conversations with the Founders of Science Fiction*. Amherst, NY: Prometheus Books, 1999. 78.

   Contains a brief passage by Charles D. Hornig talking about CAS.

97. de Camp, L. Sprague. *Lovecraft: A Biography*.
   a. Garden City, NY: Doubleday, 1975; London: New English Library, 1976; New York: Barnes & Noble, 1996. 112, 114, 172–74, 184, 241, 267, 301, 317–19, 321, 331–32, 358, 381, 385, 397, 408, 411, 431, 435, 448.
   b. New York: Ballantine, 1976. 122, 185–87, 197, 257, 283–84, 319, 336–38, 340, 351–52, 380, 405, 409, 423, 435, 438, 460, 465.

   Touches upon CAS's relations with Lovecraft. The Ballantine edition is slightly revised, abridged, and lacks notes and index.

98. de Camp, L. Sprague. "On 'The Alleged Influence of Lord Dunsany on Clark Ashton Smith.'"
   a. *Amra* No. 23 (January 1963): 23.

   A reply to Sidney-Fryer's essay (E.281).

99. de Camp, L. Sprague. "The Prose Tales of Clark Ashton Smith."
   a. In *In Memoriam: Clark Ashton Smith* (D.4).

100. de Camp, L. Sprague. "Sierran Shaman: Clark Ashton Smith."
   a. *Fantastic* 22, No. 1 (October 1972): 101–12.
   b. In L. Sprague de Camp. *Literary Swordsmen and Sorcerers: The Makers of Heroic Fantasy*. Sauk City, WI: Arkham House, 1976. 195–214.
   c. *Lhork* No. 9 [*Lhork Extra 5 Especial Ciencia Ficción*] (1994): 17–26 (as "Clark Ashton Smith: El brujo de las montañas"; tr. Colectivo Circulo de Lhork).

   General biocritical overview of CAS.

101. De Casseres, Benjamin. "Clark Ashton Smith, Emperor of Shadows."
   a. D.6.
   b. *Golden Atom* 1, No. 3 (16 December 1939): 3–4.
   c. *Portals* 1, No. 1 (November 1957): 10–14.
   d. In *Selected Poems* (I.A.27).

   Impressionistic account of CAS's poetry.

102. de la Ree, Gerry. "Clark Ashton Smith—Artist."
   a. In *Grotesques and Fantastiques* (I.A.32).

103. [DeAngelis, Michael.] "About C. A. Smith."
   a. *Asmodeus* No. 2 (Fall 1951): 10–13.

104. Dembo, Arinn. "Offering at the Tomb."
   a. *New York Review of Science Fiction* 13, No. 11 (July 2001): 1, 4.

   Review of *The Last Continent: New Tales of Zothique*, an anthology edited by John Pelan set in CAS's secondary world of Zothique. Dembo discusses her discovery of CAS and her impressions of his work.

   Derleth, August. "Contemporary Science Fiction."
   a. *English Journal* 41, No. 1 (January 1952): 1–8.

105. Derleth, August. "Letter."
   a. In *Emperor of Dreams* (C.7).

   General remarks on CAS's work.

106. Derleth, August, and Donald Wandrei. "Clark Ashton Smith: Master of Fantasy."
   a. In *Out of Space and Time* (I.A.9).

   Brief biocritical overview of CAS.

107. Dirda, Michael. "Introduction."
   a. In *Collected Fantasies,* Volume 3 (I.A.70).

   Appreciation of CAS's work as a fantasy writer.

108. Dziemianowicz, Stefan. "Into the Woods: The Human Geography of Clark Ashton Smith's Averoigne."
   a. *Dark Eidolon* No. 3 (Winter 1993): 2–9.
   b. In *Ombre dal cosmo* (D.9) (as "All'interno della foresta: La geografia umana dell'Averoigne di Clark Ashton Smith"; tr. Pietro Guarriello).
   c. In *The Freedom of Fantastic Things* (D.5).

   On the symbolism of the forest and other elements in CAS's Averoigne stories.

109. Elder, Robert B. "CAS: A Reminiscence."
   a. *Chronicles of the Cthulhu Codex* No. 5 (1989): 21–25.
   b. In *One Hundred Years of Klarkash-Ton* (D.10).

110. Ellis, Phillip A. "'Grown Together in Love': Theme and Image in 'Connaissance.'"
   a. *Lost Worlds* No. 5 (2008): 30–34.

   On the fusion of weirdness and love in the poem.

111. Ellis, Phillip A. "Satan Speaks: A Reading of 'Satan Unrepentant.'"
   a. In *The Freedom of Fantastic Things* (D.5).

   On CAS's creative adaptation of Miltonic themes in the poem.

112. Ellison, Harlan. "Letter."
   a. In *Emperor of Dreams* (C.7).

   On Ellison's response to CAS's writings.

113. Ellison, Harlan. "*Out of Space and Time* by Clark Ashton Smith."
   a. In Stephen Jones and Kim Newman, ed. *Horror: 100 Best Books.* London: Xanadu, 1988; New York: Carroll & Graf, 1988. 135–39.

114. Farsaci, Litterio [i.e., Larry B.]. "Poet of Eternity."
   a. In *In Memoriam: Clark Ashton Smith* (D.4).

115. Ferlinghetti, Lawrence, and Nancy Peters. *Literary San Francisco.* San Francisco: City Light Books/Harper & Row, 1980. 47, 116.

   General discussion of CAS as a California writer; includes two photos of CAS.

116. Gindre, Philippe. "Le Seigneur des parterres écarlates: L'Horreur végétale selon Clark Ashton Smith."
   a. *Le Boudoir des Gorgones* No. 9 (June 2004): 21–34.
   b. *Lost Worlds* No. 5 (2008): 19–29 (as "Lord of the Sultry, Red Parterres: Satanic Horror According to Clark Ashton Smith"; trans. Donald Sidney-Fryer).

   Translation of D.8.

117. Giorgi, Giorgio. "Invito alla lettura di C. A. Smith."
   a. In *Le metamorfosi della terra* (II.A.vi.8), pp. 171–86.

118. Glännhag, Martin. "Clark Ashton Smith."
   a. *Eskapix* 2 (2009): 15–20.

119. Glyer, Mike. "Through Time and Space with CAS."
     a. *Nyctalops* No. 7 (August 1972): 13–16.

     Discusses features common to the stories in *Out of Space and Time* and *Lost Worlds*.

120. Goodrich, Peter H. "Sorcerous Style: Clark Ashton Smith's *The Double Shadow and Other Fantasies.*"
     a. *Paradoxa* 5 (Nos. 13–14) (1999–2000): 213–25.
     a. In *The Freedom of Fantastic Things* (D.5).

     "The magical roots of words . . .—their ability to evoke correspondences between matter, spirit and human perception—are at the core of Smith's aesthetic."

121. Grabow, Jay. "Master of the Macabre."
     a. *California Highway Patrolman* 48, No. 11 (November 1984): 6–9.

122. Greene, Madelynne. "Letter."
     a. In *Emperor of Dreams* (C.7).

     Brief memoir of CAS.

123. Grose, Charles Richard. "Eros and the Ghoul: Necrophilia in the Prose and Poetry of Clark Ashton Smith."
     a. *Nyctalops* No. 7 (August 1972): 34–36.

124. Guillaud, Lauric. "C. A. Smith: De l'Heroic Fantasy à la 'Décadent Fantasy.'"
     a. *Phénix* No. 40 (April 1996): 143–62.

125. Guillaud, Lauric. "Fantasy and Decadence in the Work of Clark Ashton Smith."
     a. *Paradoxa* 5 (Nos. 13–14) (1999–2000): 189–212.
     a. In *The Freedom of Fantastic Things* (D.5).

     On CAS's "fascination with morbidity" in his poetry, prose poems, and tales.

126. Guillaud, Lauric. "Le Monde de C. A. Smith."
     a. In Lauric Guillaud. *L'Éternel déluge*. Paris: e-dite, 2001. 169–200.

127. Guillaud, Lauric. "La Thème de la décadence chez C. A. Smith et R. E. Howard."
   a. In Gilles Menegaldo, ed. *H. P. Lovecraft: Fantastique, mythe et modernité*. Paris: Dervy, 2002. 297–355.

128. Haas, George F. "As I Remember Klarkash-Ton."
   a. *Mirage* 1, No. 5 (Spring 1962): 22–37.
   b. In *In Memoriam: Clark Ashton Smith* (D.4).
   c. In *The Black Book of Clark Ashton Smith* (I.A.39).
   d. In John Pelan and Jerad Walters, ed. *Conversations with the Weird Tales Writers*. Lakewood, CO: Centipede Press, 2009, 2011. 67–92.
   e. In *In the Realms of Mystery and Wonder* (I.A.87).

   Extensive account of Haas's meetings with CAS, with much discussion of CAS's literary and artistic work and an evaluation of his character.

129. Haas, George F. "Letter."
   a. In *Emperor of Dreams* (C.7).

   Brief overview of CAS's writings and artwork.

130. Haas, George F. "Memories of Klarkash-Ton."
   a. *Nyctalops* No. 7 (August 1972): 70–74.
   b. In *The Black Book of Clark Ashton Smith* (I.A.39).
   c. In John Pelan and Jerad Walters, ed. *Conversations with the Weird Tales Circle*. Lakewood, CO: Centipede Press, 2009, 2011. 95–108.
   d. In *In the Realms of Mystery and Wonder* (I.A.87).

   Additional recollections of meeting CAS, especially in the latter days of his life.

131. Haefele, John D. "Far from Time: Clark Ashton Smith, August Derleth, and Arkham House."
   a. *Weird Fiction Review* No. 1 (Fall 2010): 154–89.

   Exhaustive essay discussing CAS's relations with Derleth and Arkham House; also includes a study of Derleth's opinions of CAS and his dealings with Carol Dorman Smith after CAS's death. Cites many primary documents.

132. Hall, Mark. "Clark Ashton Smith Collections in the San Francisco Bay Area, Part 1: Letters to Samuel Loveman."
    a. *Lost Worlds* No. 2 (2004): 31–38.

    On the acquisition of CAS's letters to Samuel Loveman by the Bancroft Library. For a continuation of the series, see item 70.

133. Hautepierre, Jean. "Avant-propos."
    a. In *Celui qui marchait parmi les étoiles* (II.A.iii.17).

134. Hawkins, Jim. "CAS & R. W. Chambers."
    a. *Tales of Horror and Damnation* No. 6 (January 1985): 25.

135. Heiple, Ethel. "Letter."
    a. In *Emperor of Dreams* (C.7).

    Memoir of CAS and his mother.

136. Heiple, Ethel. "Reminiscences."
    a. In *In Memoriam: Clark Ashton Smith* (D.4).
    b. In *In the Realms of Mystery and Wonder* (I.A.87).

    Recollections of meeting CAS from the late 1920s onward, with some account of his friends and colleagues.

137. Henseley, D. "Josephine, the Beloved."
    a. *Tales of Horror and Damnation* No. 6 (January 1985): 27.

138. Herron, Don. "Collecting Clark Ashton Smith."
    a. *Firsts* 10, No. 10 (October 2000): 26–37.

139. Herron, Don. "The Double Shadow: The Influence of Clark Ashton Smith."
    a. In Tim Underwood and Chuck Miller, ed. *Jack Vance*. New York: Taplinger, 1980. 87–102.

    On CAS's influence on Jack Vance.

140. Herron, Don. "The Mighty Ceewolf Has Fallen: A Personal Tribute."
    a. *Lost Worlds* No. 4 (2006): 23–25.

    Memoir of Charles K. Wolfe, editor of *Planets and Dimensions* (I.A.33).

141. Herron, Don. "Worlds Lost within Worlds."
    a. *Lost Worlds* No. 3 (2006): 22–25.

On "The Face by the River" and "The Red World of Polaris."

142. Heyer, Violet Nelson. "Letter."
    a. In *One Hundred Years of Klarkash-Ton* (D.10).

143. Hiemstra, Marvin R. "Clipped Wings: A Fable in Tribute to Clark Ashton Smith."
    a. In *One Hundred Years of Klarkash-Ton* (D.10).

144. Hiemstra, Marvin R. "Five Approaches to the Achievement of Clark Ashton Smith: Cosmic Master Artist."
    a. *Nyctalops* No. 7 (August 1972): 6–12.
    b. In *Emperor of Dreams* (C.7).

    Detailed analysis of the themes, imagery, and significance of CAS's prose and poetry.

145. Hilger, Ronald S. "Amithaigne."
    a. *Lost Worlds* No. 3 (2006): 34–35.

    On the draft of an unpublished poem, "Amithaigne" (an early draft of "Amithaine").

146. Hilger, Ronald S. "Clark Ashton Smith: Forgotten Poet of Auburn."
    a. In *One Hundred Years of Klarkash-Ton* (D.10).

147. Hilger, Ron[ald S.] "The Phosphor Lamps of Clark Ashton Smith."
    a. *Chronicles of the Cthulhu Codex* No. 17 (Winter 2000): 43–46 (with afterword by Donald Sidney-Fryer, 50–51).

148. Hilger, Ronald S. "Regarding the Providence Point of View."
    a. *Crypt of Cthulhu* No. 102 (Lammas 1999): 25–28.
    b. In *The Freedom of Fantastic Things* (D.5).

    Objects to seeing CAS's work through the prism of Lovecraft's thought and writings.

149. Hilger, Ron[ald S.]. "Something about Cats (and CAS!)."
    a. *Lost Worlds* No. 5 (2008): 3–4.

    On cats in CAS's life and work.

150. Hilger, Ron[ald S.]. "A Wind from the Unknown."
    a. In *The Hashish-Eater* (A.75).

151. Hilger, Ron[ald S.], and Henry J. Vester, III. "The Muse of Aver-
    oigne."
    a. *Fungi* No. No. 14 (Fall 1996): 4–6.

152. Hillman, Arthur F. "The Poet of Science Fiction."
    a. *Fantasy Review* 3, No. 14 (April–May 1949): 14–16.
    b. *Yawning Vortex* 3, No. 1 (October–November 1996): 35–37
       (as "Clark Ashton Smith: The Poet of Science Fiction").

    On the prose-poetic quality of CAS's tales of science fiction and
    fantasy.

153. Hitz, John Kipling. "Clark Aston Smith: Master of the Macabre."
    a. *Studies in Weird Fiction* No. 19 (Summer 1996): 8–15.
    b. In *The Freedom of Fantastic Things* (D.5).

    General discussion of the imagery in CAS's tales, with a focus on
    Poe's influence on his work.

154. Hitz, John Kipling. "Humor in Hyperspace: Smith's Uses of Satire."
    a. In *The Freedom of Fantastic Things* (D.5).

    On satire and black humor in CAS's tales.

155. Hoffman, R. A. "The Arcana of Arkham-Auburn."
    a. *Acolyte* 2, No. 2 (Spring 1944): 8–12.
    b. *Nyctalops* No. 7 (August 1972): 77–80.

    Discusses a pilgrimage made to see CAS on 27 December 1941 by
    Hoffman, Henry Hasse, Emil Petaja, and Paul Freehafer.

156. Hoffman, Rah. "Letter."
    a. In *Emperor of Dreams* (C.7).
    b. In *In the Realms of Mystery and Wonder* (I.A.87) (as "A Letter").

    Substantial letter telling of Hoffman's meetings with CAS.

157. Hoffman, Rah, and Donald Sidney-Fryer. "'Klarkash-Ton' versus
    'Clark Ashton': A Minor Issue for Controversy."
    a. *Dark Eidolon* No. 2 (July 1989): 25.
    b. In *The Golden State Phantasticks* (287).

    On the pronunciation of CAS's invented names.

158. Howard, Robert E. "Correspondence from Robert E. Howard to Clark Ashton Smith."
    a. *Nyctalops* No. 7 (August 1972): 96.

159. Hussey, Derrick. "Clark Ashton Smith and the Bohemian Club."
    a. *Underworlds* No. 1 (December 2002): 91–92.

160. J., J. "Common Themes and Thoughts for CAS, ERB and de Camp."
    a. *Tales of Horror and Damnation* No. 6 (January 1985): 28.

161. Jenkins, Lowell. "Reptile Fascination: Studies in Howard, Smith and de Camp."
    a. *Tales of Horror and Damnation* No. 6 (January 1985): 4–5, 24.

162. Jones, Stephen. "Afterword: The Lost Worlds of Klarkash-Ton."
    a. In *The Emperor of Dreams* (I.A.59).
    b. In *Gesammelte Erzählungen*, Volume 1 (II.A.iv.8) (as "Die vergessenen Welten des Klarkash-Ton").

    In b. the article is the introduction.

163. Joshi, S. T. "Clark Ashton Smith: Nota bio-bibliografica."
    a. In *Ombre dal cosmo* (D.9).

164. Joshi, S. T. *A Dreamer and a Visionary: H. P. Lovecraft in His Time.*
    a. Liverpool: Liverpool University Press, 2001. 117, 146, 157–59, 160, 166, 177–78, 257, 259, 281–82, 303, 309, 311, 333, 337, 345, 365, 390.

    Touches upon CAS's relations with Lovecraft.

165. Joshi, S. T. *H. P. Lovecraft: A Life.*
    a. West Warwick, RI: Necronomicon Press, 1996, 2003. 184, 280–82, 288, 296, 312, 326, 343, 374, 426, 427, 463, 493, 501, 504–5, 507, 537, 542, 555, 562, 592, 595, 622, 633, 638–39.

    Touches upon CAS's relations with Lovecraft.

166. Joshi, S. T. *I Am Providence: The Life and Times of H. P. Lovecraft.*
    a. New York: Hippocampus Press, 2010. 252, 289, 290, 397, 427–29, 433, 434, 438, 451, 453, 454, 475, 494, 519, 586, 591, 602, 676, 678, 681–82, 683, 698, 721, 740, 787, 790, 799, 803–5, 807, 825, 830, 832, 849, 857, 858, 859, 864, 866, 868, 869–70, 872, 873, 875, 887, 889, 892, 894, 900, 929,

944, 946, 949, 968, 970, 974, 993, 998, 1009, 1010, 1012, 1014, 1015, 1021, 1022 (2 vols.; numbered consecutively).

More extensive discussion of CAS's relations with Lovecraft.

167. Joshi, S. T. "Introduction."
    a. In *The Dark Eidolon and Other Fantasy Tales* (I.A.84).

168. Joshi, S. T. "Lands Forgotten or Unfound: The Prose Poetry of Clark Ashton Smith."
    a. In *The Freedom of Fantastic Things* (D.5).

    On major themes in CAS's prose poems.

169. Joshi, S. T. "Postface."
    a. In *Mondes derniers* (II.A.iii.14).

    Analysis of CAS's tales of Zothique and Averoigne.

170. Joshi, S. T. "Postface."
    a. In *Mondes premiers* (II.A.iii.15).

    Analysis of CAS's tales of Hyperborea and Atlantis, with a discussion of the influence of Lovecraft and Lord Dunsany on the former cycle.

171. Joshi, S. T. "Postface."
    a. In *Autres mondes* (II.A.iii.16).

172. Joshi, S. T. *The Rise and Fall of the Cthulhu Mythos.*
    a. Poplar Bluff, MO: Mythos Books, 2008. 20, 21, 22, 75, 84, 92, 99, 113, 114, 116, 123–30, 132, 139, 187, 190–92, 194, 227.
    b. New York: Hippocampus Press, 2015 (rev. ed.; as *The Rise, Fall, and Rise of the Cthulhu Mythos*). 22, 23, 69, 84, 95, 104, 105, 114, 130, 133, 142–49, 152, 153, 160, 195, 216, 220–22, 224, 264, 274.

    Touches upon CAS's relations with Lovecraft, with an analysis of his Cthulhu Mythos tales.

173. Joshi, S. T. *A Subtler Magick: The Writings and Philosophy of H. P. Lovecraft.*
    a. San Bernardino, CA: Borgo Press, 1996. 9, 28, 79, 141–42, 173–74, 179, 192, 222, 234, 236, 239–40, 248, 268.

    Touches upon CAS's relations with Lovecraft.

174. Joshi, S. T. "A Triumvirate of Fantastic Poets: Ambrose Bierce, George Sterling, and Clark Ashton Smith."
   a. *Extrapolation* 54, No. 2 (Summer 2013): 147–61.
   b. In S. T. Joshi. *Varieties of the Weird Tale*. New York: Hippocampus Press, 2017. 79–96.

   Examination of Bierce's mentorship of Sterling and Sterling's mentorship of CAS.

175. Joshi, S. T. *Unutterable Horror: A History of Supernatural Fiction*. Hornsea, UK: PS Publishing, 2012. New York: Hippocampus Press, 2014. 368, 488, 512, 513, 517–20, 527, 530–31, 534, 562, 595.

176. Joshi, S. T. "What Happens in *The Hashish-Eater*."
   a. *Dark Eidolon* No. 3 (Winter 1993): 16–20.
   b. In *The Freedom of Fantastic Things* (D.5).

   The Hashish-Eater has a recognizable plot and is not merely an unrelated series of cosmic images.

177. Joshi, S. T., ed. *H. P. Lovecraft: Four Decades of Criticism*.
   a. Athens: Ohio University Press, 1980. 14–15, 22, 25, 45n4, 96, 121, 127–28, 150, 160n2, 193, 202, 206, 216n12.

   Touches upon CAS's relations with Lovecraft.

178. Joshi, Sunand T., and Marc A. Michaud. "The Prose and Poetry of Clark Ashton Smith."
   a. *Books at Brown* 27 (1979): 81–87.

   General overview of CAS's life and work, based on the recently acquired CAS Papers.

179. Joshi, S. T., and David E. Schultz. "Introduction."
   a. In *Complete Poetry and Translations,* Volume 1 (I.A.73).

180. Joshi, S. T., and David E. Schultz. "Introduction."
   a. In *Complete Poetry and Translations,* Volume 3 (I.A.73).

181. Knight, Jesse F. "Terrible Vistas: The Vision of Clark Ashton Smith and George Sterling."
   a. *Yawning Vortex* 2, No. 3 (January 1996): 45–48.
   b. In *One Hundred Years of Klarkash-Ton* (D.10).

   On similarities and contrasts in the poetry of CAS and Sterling.

182. Kowcheck, Irene. "Survey Notes on the Classics of CAS Commentary."
    a. *Tales of Horror and Damnation* No. 6 (January 1985): 15–17.

183. Kuttner, Henry. "Exclusive Interviews: E. Hoffmann Price and Clark Ashton Smith."
    a. *Imagination!* 1, No. 3 (December 1937): 4.

184. Kuttner, Henry. [Letter to the Editor.]
    a. *Weird Tales* 32, No. 1 (July 1938): 127–28 (under heading "The Eyrie").

185. Lane, Joel. "Charnel Knowledge."
    a. *Crypt of Cthulhu* No. 30 (Eastertide 1985): 18–20.

    On "The Epiphany of Death" as a recasting of Lovecraft's "The Outsider."

186. Laney, Francis T. *Ah! Sweet Idiocy: The Fan Memoirs of Francis T. Laney.*
    a. Los Angeles: Francis T. Laney and Charles Burbee, 1948. 22–32.
    b. *Dark Eidolon* No. 2 (July 1989): 21–23 (extract; as "'The Weird Willys'").

    On Laney's meeting with CAS in 1943. The *Dark Eidolon* appearance includes several photographs of the visit.

187. Laney, Francis T. "Editorially Speaking."
    a. *Acolyte* 1, No. 3 (Spring 1943): 1–2.

    Contains a few paragraphs on CAS, among other topics.

188. Leiber, Fritz. "Clark Ashton Smith: An Appreciation."
    a. In *In Memoriam: Clark Ashton Smith* (D.4).
    b. In *In the Realms of Mystery and Wonder* (A.87).

    On a visit to CAS in 1944, with some discussion of his literary work.

189. Leiber, Fritz. "Letter."
    a. In *Emperor of Dreams* (C.7).

    "Smith is *sui generis,* one of the most uninfluenced and original writers I know of."

190. London, Debbie. "Geeting's TV Show Examines New Books."
    a. *Hornet* (Sacramento State College) (16 May 1958): 4.

Notice of CAS's appearance on a television show, *Reading for Pleasure,* hosted by Baxter M. Geeting.

191. Long, Frank Belknap. "The Poetry of Clark Ashton Smith."
    a. *Nyctalops* No. 7 (August 1972): 76.
    b. In *Anno Klarkash-Ton* (D.1).

    Brief overview of CAS's poetry, with some account of Long's association with CAS.

192. Lorraine, Lilith. "Tribute to Clark Ashton Smith."
    a. *Avalon News Digest* 1, No. 3 (Winter 1961): 12.

193. Lovecraft, H. P. Letter to Edwin Baird.
    a. *Weird Tales* 2, No. 3 (October 1923): 82 (under heading "The Eyrie").
    b. In S. T. Joshi and Marc A. Michaud, ed. *H. P. Lovecraft in "The Eyrie."* West Warwick, RI: Necronomicon Press, 1979. 16–18.

    Notes that CAS had sent the story "Dagon" to George Sterling.

194. Lovecraft, H. P. *Letters from New York.* Ed. S. T. Joshi and David E. Schultz.
    a. San Francisco: Night Shade Books, 2005. x, 19, 23, 31, 63, 105, 175, 195, 215, 242, 244, 253, 260, 276, 309.

    Random discussions of CAS.

195. Lovecraft, H. P. *Letters to Alfred Galpin.* Ed. S. T. Joshi and David E. Schultz.
    a. New York: Hippocampus Press, 2003. 10, 11, 135, 156, 160, 187, 193, 194, 217, 221, 229.

    Random discussions of CAS.

196. Lovecraft, H. P. *Letters to C. L. Moore and Others.* Ed. David E. Schultz and S. T. Joshi.
    a. New York: Hippocampus Press, 2017. 14, 25, 28, 31, 32, 33, 35, 38, 48, 54, 56, 69, 76, 212, 227, 234, 237, 240, 243, 246, 248, 261, 262, 301, 309, 320–21.

    Random discussions of CAS.

197. Lovecraft, H. P. *Letters to Elizabeth Toldridge and Anne Tillery Renshaw.* Ed. David E. Schultz and S. T. Joshi.

a. New York: Hippocampus Press, 2014. 26, 41, 135–36, 141, 162, 216, 245–46, 248, 249, 250, 251, 258, 261, 273, 281, 284, 289, 294, 314, 336, 348, 353.

Random discussions of CAS.

198. Lovecraft, H. P. *Letters to F. Lee Baldwin, Duane W. Rimel, and Nils Frome.* Ed. David E. Schultz and S. T. Joshi.
   a. New York: Hippocampus Press, 2016. 10, 16, 17, 25, 29, 30, 31, 32, 34, 39, 42, 47, 48, 50, 51–53, 77, 81, 85, 86, 88, 89, 91, 93, 97, 104, 113, 114, 115, 125, 128, 131, 133, 141–42, 143, 146, 147, 152, 155, 162, 164, 166, 168, 172, 173, 179, 180, 184, 192, 196, 197, 201, 202, 203, 205, 207, 208, 215, 224, 225, 228, 229, 232, 240, 248, 253, 255, 260–61, 264–65, 268, 270–71, 280, 287, 288, 289, 294, 302, 308, 312–13, 315n2, 316, 322, 327, 331, 333, 339, 345.

Extensive discussions of CAS.

199. Lovecraft, H. P. *Letters to J. Vernon Shea, Carl F. Strauch, and Lee McBride White.* Ed. S. T. Joshi and David E. Schultz.
   a. New York: Hippocampus Press, 2016. 18, 26, 30, 31, 33–34, 35, 38, 40, 41, 50, 53, 66, 67, 68, 75, 90, 111, 115, 124, 140, 141, 144, 148, 154, 163, 174, 212, 228, 236, 239, 245, 251, 252, 276, 285, 288, 289, 319, 323, 326, 329, 339, 341, 344, 346, 350–51, 353, 356–57, 363, 375.

Random discussions of CAS.

200. Lovecraft, H. P. *Letters to James F. Morton.* Ed. David E. Schultz and S. T. Joshi.
   a. New York: Hippocampus Press, 2011. 51, 63, 64, 86, 131n8, 144, 154, 184, 199, 280, 284, 287, 312, 317, 333, 360, 382, 398–99, 406n28, 444.

Random discussions of CAS.

201. Lovecraft, H. P. *Letters to Richard F. Searight.* Ed. David E. Schultz, S. T. Joshi, and Franklyn Searight.
   a. West Warwick, RI: Necronomicon Press, 1992. [9], 11–12, 13, 14, 18, 19, 20, 21, 22, 24, 25, 32, 33, 34, 36, 41, 46, 48, 57, 59, 60, 63, 65, 66, 68, 75, 78, 84, 86, 90.

Random discussions of CAS.

202. Lovecraft, H. P. *Letters to Robert Bloch.* Ed. David E. Schultz and S. T. Joshi.
  a. West Warwick, RI: Necronomicon Press, 1993. 9, 13, 15, 19, 20, 21, 22, 23, 24, 27, 28, 29, 30, 31, 33, 34, 35, 36, 37, 45, 47, 48, 49, 50, 51, 56, 59, 64, 67, 70, 73, 81.

  Random discussions of CAS.

203. Lovecraft, H. P. *Letters to Robert Bloch and Others.* Ed. David E. Schultz and S. T. Joshi.
  a. New York: Hippocampus Press, 2015. 11, 17, 23, 28, 29, 34–35, 37, 43, 46, 47, 48, 50–51, 54, 61, 63, 65, 66, 68, 72–73, 74, 76, 78, 79, 80, 93, 97, 100, 101, 102, 104, 105, 106, 110, 115, 125, 137, 138, 148, 155, 157, 161, 168, 174, 187, 192, 196, 202, 205, 206–7, 223, 224, 225, 226, 227, 228–29, 231, 232, 233, 237, 239, 240, 242, 243, 245, 249, 312, 315, 320, 321, 322, 332, 333, 334, 342, 358, 372–73, 377, 381, 384, 386, 389–90, 311, 413.

  Extensive discussions of CAS.

204. Lovecraft, H. P. *Lord of a Visible World: An Autobiography in Letters.* Ed. S. T. Joshi and David E. Schultz.
  a. Athens: Ohio University Press, 2000. 108, 207–8, 210, 222, 233, 252, 253–56, 273, 282, 297, 328, 348.

  Random discussions of CAS.

205. Lovecraft, H. P. *Mysteries of Time and Spirit: The Letters of H. P. Lovecraft and Donald Wandrei.* Ed. S. T. Joshi and David E. Schultz.
  a. San Francisco: Night Shade Books, 2002. ix, x, xiii, xiv, xviii, 1, 2, 3, 4, 6, 9–10, 11, 29, 31, 56, 57, 58, 61, 68, 71, 72, 83, 78, 85, 92, 94, 97, 98, 99, 101, 108, 110, 112, 115, 129–30, 132, 134, 138, 140, 145, 149, 150, 157–58, 159, 160–61, 163, 165, 167, 168, 171, 172–73, 186, 190, 192–93, 198, 201, 214, 215, 229, 230, 245, 249, 250, 252, 253, 254, 262, 264, 265, 273, 278, 279, 282, 283, 284, 286, 291, 292, 297, 298, 299, 301, 302, 303, 304, 307, 308, 318, 322, 324, 325, 326, 329, 330, 335, 338, 341, 343, 352, 353, 355, 363, 364, 369, 372, 376, 376, 378, 380, 381.

  Extensive discussions of CAS, especially his relations with Wandrei.

206. Lovecraft, H. P. *O Fortunate Floridian: H. P. Lovecraft's Letters to R. H. Barlow.* Ed. S. T. Joshi and David E. Schultz.
  a. Tampa, FL: University of Tampa Press, 2007. x, xix, xx, xxi, 4, 6–7, 10, 13, 14, 15, 17, 29, 30, 34, 35, 36, 37, 39, 40, 41–42, 43, 44, 50, 54, 55, 56, 59, 60, 67, 71, 73, 76, 78, 82, 85, 87, 89, 95, 101, 105, 106, 110, 112, 113, 120, 128, 129, 131, 142, 144, 150, 153, 155, 157, 158, 160, 161, 162, 164, 167, 168, 172, 175, 178, 180, 183, 184, 187, 191, 192, 193, 195, 203, 207, 218, 221, 224, 229, 230, 234, 249, 252, 255, 258, 260, 261, 265, 274, 277, 280, 281, 293, 294, 295, 297, 299, 305, 315, 318, 319, 321, 323, 328–29, 331, 338, 340, 343, 351, 363, 367, 373, 382–83, 395, 404, 406, 410, 415n23.

  Extensive discussions of CAS.

207. Lovecraft, H. P. *Selected Letters 1911–1924.* Ed. August Derleth and Donald Wandrei.
  a. Sauk City, WI: Arkham House, 1965. 162–63, 192, 195, 233, 259–60, 292–93, 315.

  Random discussions of CAS.

208. Lovecraft, H. P. *Selected Letters 1925–1929.* Ed. August Derleth and Donald Wandrei.
  a. Sauk City, WI: Arkham House, 1968. 22, 45, 163, 171, 178, 275–76, 321.

  Random discussions of CAS.

209. Lovecraft, H. P. *Selected Letters: 1929–1931.* Ed. August Derleth and Donald Wandrei.
  a. Sauk City, WI: Arkham House, 1971. 35, 55, 90, 131, 149–50, 156, 198, 220–21, 226, 275, 279, 284, 400, 416, 439.

  Random discussions of CAS.

210. Lovecraft, H. P. *Selected Letters: 1932–1934.* Ed. August Derleth and James Turner.
  a. Sauk City, WI: Arkham House, 1976. 28, 54, 91, 122, 153, 155, 183, 213–14, 236, 238, 297, 322, 340, 343, 346, 350, 381–82, 387–88, 399, 410–12, 417.

  Random discussions of CAS.

211. Lovecraft, H. P. *Selected Letters: 1934–1937.* Ed. August Derleth and James Turner.
   a. Sauk City, WI: Arkham House, 1976. 8, 14, 16, 83, 91, 109, 120, 132, 140, 151, 155–56, 158, 173, 183, 185, 194–95, 200, 219, 221, 226, 285, 291, 327, 368, 386–87, 401, 421, 430.

   Random discussions of CAS.

212. Lovecraft, H. P. "Supernatural Horror in Literature."
   a. *Recluse* 1 (1927): 48.
   b. In H. P. Lovecraft. *The Outsider and Others.* Ed. August Derleth and Donald Wandrei. Sauk City, WI: Arkham House, 1939. 538.
   c. New York: Ben Abramson, 1945; New York: Dover, 1973. 74–75. Pawtucket, RI: Montilla Publications, 1992. 81.
   d. In H. P. Lovecraft. *Dagon and Other Macabre Tales.* Ed. August Derleth. Sauk City, WI: Arkham House, 1965. 390–91. Rev. ed. (by S. T. Joshi), 1986. 412.
   e. In H. P. Lovecraft. *The Annotated Supernatural Horror in Literature.* Ed. S. T. Joshi. New York: Hippocampus Press, 2000. 54–55. Rev. ed. 2012. 72 (other discussions of CAS in editor's notes).
   f. In *Dawnward Spire, Lonely Hill* (I.A.86).

   Celebrated if brief discussion of CAS as a weird poet and fictionist. The passage on CAS (expanded in items b–e) did not appear in the incomplete serialization of the essay in the *Fantasy Fan* (October 1933–February 1935).

213. Lovecraft, H. P., and Willis Conover. *Lovecraft at Last.*
   a. Arlington, VA: Carrollton-Clark, 1975. xix, 42–43, 51, 57, 61, 86, 88, 115, 116, 184.

   Random discussions of CAS.

214. Lovecraft, H. P., and August Derleth. *Essential Solitude: The Letters of H. P. Lovecraft and August Derleth.* Ed. David E. Schultz and S. T. Joshi.
   a. New York: Hippocampus Press, 2008. 21, 51, 52, 55, 56, 58, 77, 124n1, 189, 211, 222, 230, 236, 247, 252, 255, 259, 274, 277–78, 280, 281, 282–83, 284, 286, 288, 290, 293, 299, 303, 316, 317, 319, 321, 323, 327, 334, 336, 337, 344, 353, 356, 358, 359, 360, 363, 366, 368, 369, 381, 388, 392, 393, 398, 400, 402, 403, 408, 433, 441, 443, 446, 447, 448, 451, 454,

455, 456, 458, 466, 471, 477, 478, 483, 486, 489, 491, 493, 503, 505, 524, 525, 527, 529, 532, 544, 545, 547, 552, 559, 560, 563, 564, 565, 567, 594, 595, 599, 608, 610, 613, 615, 616, 626, 628, 629, 632, 636–37, 642, 650, 661, 663, 664, 666, 669, 670, 671, 676, 677, 703, 704, 710, 712, 719, 729, 780 (2 vols.—numbered consecutively).

Extensive discussions of CAS.

215. Lovecraft, H. P., and Robert E. Howard. *A Means to Freedom: The Letters of H. P. Lovecraft and Robert E. Howard.* Ed. S. T. Joshi, David E. Schultz, and Rusty Burke.
   a.   New York: Hippocampus Press, 2009. 8, 31, 32, 40, 144, 279, 287, 307, 327, 375, 400, 429, 431, 462, 486, 618, 619, 620, 634, 655, 719, 727–28, 801, 857, 882 (2 vols.—numbered consecutively).

   Random discussions of CAS.

216. Lowndes, Robert A. W. "The Editor's Page."
   a.   *Bizarre Fantasy Tales* 1, No. 2 (March 1971): 4–9, 126, 128.

217. Lowndes, Robert A. W. "The Editor's Page."
   a.   *Magazine of Horror* 5, No. 1 (January 1969): 4–5, 127.

218. [Lowndes, Robert A. W.] "In Re: Clark Ashton Smith."
   a.   *Magazine of Horror* 1, No. 1 (August 1963): 106.

219. Lowndes, Robert A. W. "Why 'Famous'?"
   a.   *Famous Science Fiction* 1, No. 1 (Winter 1966/67): 6–7, 9, 116–22.

220. Lupoff, Richard A. "Introduction."
   a.   In *Collected Fantasies,* Volume 5 (I.A.70).

   General appreciation of CAS's work as a fantasist.

221. Luserke, Uwe. "Klarkash-Ton: Poet des Monströsen: Leben und Werk des Clark Ashton Smith."
   a.   *Science Fiction Times* (Germany) 27, No. 3 (March 1985): 3–7.

222. Lyman, William Whittingham. "Clark Ashton Smith."
   a.   *Lost Worlds* No. 3 (2006): 9–14.
   b.   In *In the Realms of Mystery and Wonder* (A.87).

Memoir of Lyman's encounters with CAS.

223. "Maliano." "Of Corsets and Flea-Traps."
   a. *Diablerie* (May [1945]): [27].

   Includes caricature of CAS by Virgil Partch.

224. Marigny, Jean. "Les Atlantides de Clark Ashton Smith."
   a. In Chantal Foucrier and Lauric Guillaud, ed. *Atlantides imagi-naires: Réécritures d'un mythe*. Paris: Michel Houdiard, 2005. 307–16.

225. Marigny, Jean. "L'Univers fantastique de Clark Ashton Smith."
   a. *Caliban* 16 (1979): 77–85.
   b. *Crypt of Cthulhu* No. 26 (Hallowmas 1984): 3–12 (as "Clark Ashton Smith and His World of Fantasy"; tr. S. T. Joshi).
   c. *Zothique* No. 1 (1985): 5–9.
   d. In *Ombre dal cosmo* (D.9) (as "L'universo fantastico di Clark Ashton Smith"; tr. Pietro Guarriello).

   General overview of themes in CAS's fiction, with a discussion of his "personal mythology" and his creative imaginaton.

226. Markham, Edwin. "Gossip on Parnassus."
   a. In Edwin Markham. *California the Beautiful*. New York: Edwin Markham Press, 1923. 360.
   b. In *The Freedom of Fantastic Things* (D.5). 63.

   Brief evaluation of CAS as a poet.

227. Markham, Edwin. "The Judgment of Mr. Markham."
   a. *Literary Review (New York Evening Post)* (12 September 1925): 6.
   b. In *The Freedom of Fantastic Things* (D.5). 64.

   Quotes some lines of CAS's poetry as "one of the highest reaches of the wing of the imagination."

228. Mayer, F. J. "Clark Ashton Smith, Artist and Sculptor."
   a. *Fantasy: A Forum for Science Fiction and Fantasy Artists* 2, No. 4 (Winter 1980): 8–11.

229. [Miske, J. Chapman.] "Stardust."
   a. *Spaceways* (May 1939): 17–18, 22 (as by "The Star-Treader").

230. Mitchell, Steve. "The Weird Fiction of Clark Ashton Smith."
  a. *Paperback Parade* no. 34 (June 1993): 65–84.

231. Mitchell, Steve. "The Weird Corner."
  a. *Echoes* (December 1991): 20–25.

232. Montal-Faubelle, Henri de. "Clarke [*sic*] Ashton Smith."
  a. *Les Artistes d'Aujourd'hui* (4 August 1928): 28.

233. Montejo, Gregorio. "Beyond the Clouds Lie the Pastures of the Sun: Clark Ashton Smith."
  a. *Fungi* 1, No. 6 (Summer 1985): 21–22.

234. Morris, Harry O., Jr. "Invocation."
  a. *Nyctalops* No. 7 (August 1972): 19.

    Brief essay on CAS and a discussion of the appropriateness of a theme issue on him.

235. Morris, Harry O., Jr. "The Strange Lands of Clark Ashton Smith."
  a. *Nyctalops* No. 1 (May 1970): [5–6].

    A general overview of CAS's fiction and poetry.

236. Moskowitz, Sam. "Letter."
  a. In *Emperor of Dreams* (C.7).

    On CAS's place in fantasy literature.

237. Mullen, Stanley. "Cartouche: Clark Ashton Smith."
  a. *Gorgon* 1, No. 3 (July 1947): 54–58.

238. Munn, H. Warner. "Letter."
  a. In *Emperor of Dreams* (C.7).

    Memoir of Munn's correspondence with CAS.

239. Murray, Will. "As It Was *Not* Written; or, The Curious Conundrum of De Lysle Ferrée Cass."
  a. *Studies in Weird Fiction* No. 4 (Fall 1988): 3–12.

    Extensive discussion of how Murray came to his erroneous view that De Lysle Ferrée Cass was CAS. See also G.ii.2.

240. Murray, Will. "The Clark Ashton Smythos."
  a. *Crypt of Cthulhu* No. 26 (Hallowmas 1984): 13–15.

b. In Robert M. Price, ed. *The Horror of It All: Encrusted Gems from the 'Crypt of Cthulhu.'* Mercer Island, WA: Starmont House, 1990. 68–70.

On the nature of CAS's tales of the Cthulhu Mythos.

241. Murray, Will. "Clark Ashton Smith's Last Sonnet."
a. *Studies in Weird Fiction* No. 2 (Summer 1987): 27–29.

Asserts erroneously that the sonnet, "The Love That Stirs Me So" (as by "Carl Buxton"), published in the *Thrill Book* (15 September 1919), is by CAS. Buxton was a pseudonym of Harold Hersey.

242. Murray, Will. "Introduction."
a. In *Tales of Zothique* (I.A.56).

243. Murray, Will. "Introduction."
a. In *The Book of Hyperborea* (I.A.58).

244. Murray, Will. "The Price–Smith Collaborations."
a. *Crypt of Cthulhu* No. 26 (Hallowmas 1984): 32–34.

Brief discussion of the stories that E. Hoffmann Price wrote with CAS.

245. Murray, Will. "Who Was Klarkash Kenton?"
a. *Dark Eidolon* No. 3 (Winter 1993): 14–15.

On the possibility that Superman's human name, Clark Kent, comes from CAS's name.

246. Norton, H. P. "The Caliph of Auburn: A Dissertation upon the Phantastic Tales of Clark Ashton Smith (1893–1961)."
a. *Xero* No. 8 (May 1962): 52–57.
b. In Pat and Dick Lupoff, ed. *The Best of Xero*. San Francisco: Tachyon, 2004. 157–64.

247. O'Day, Bob. "Two Points on Lovecraft."
a. *Tales of Horror and Damnation* No. 6 (January 1985): 14.

248. Parker, Robert Allerton. "Such Pulps as Dreams Are Made On (H. P. Lovecraft and Clark Ashton Smith)."
a. *VVV* 2/3 (March 1943): 62–66.
b. *Radical America*, Special Issue (January 1970): 70–77.

c. In S. T. Joshi, ed. *A Weird Writer in Our Midst: Early Criticism of H. P. Lovecraft.* New York: Hippocampus Press, 2010. 184–92.

General overview of CAS's work in the context of socioeconomic changes of the time.

249. Peeters, Bruno. "Un Magicien de l'imaginaire: Clark Ashton Smith."
a. In Marc Bailly, ed. *Lovecraft, le maître de Providence.* Paris: Naturellement, 1999. 369–78.

250. Petaja, Emil. "The Man in the Mist."
a. *Mirage* No. 10 (1971): 21–25.
b. In *In the Realms of Mystery and Wonder* (I.A.87).

Recollections of a visit to CAS in the early 1940s.

251. Powers, Tim. "Introduction."
a. In *Collected Fantasies,* Volume 2 (I.A.70).

Brief appreciation of CAS's writings.

252. Pratt, Harry Noyes. "Inspiration in Work of Clarke [*sic*] Ashton Smith."
a. *Courier* (Berkeley, CA) (9 July 1927): 16–17.
b. *Mill Valley Record* (16 July 1927): 1 (as "Poetic Intuition as Found in Art: Clarke [*sic*] Ashton Smith at Claremont").
c. *Auburn Journal* (28 July 1927): 21 (as "Mill Valley Paper Recognizes Auburn Poet as Artist").

253. Price, E. Hoffmann. "Clark Ashton Smith: A Memoir."
a. In *Tales of Science and Sorcery* (I.A.22).
b. In E. Hoffmann Price. *Book of the Dead: Friends of Yesteryear: Fictioneers & Others.* Ed. Peter Ruber. Sauk City, WI: Arkham House, 2004. 94–125 (revised; as "Clark Ashton Smith").

Lively account of Price's meetings with CAS.

254. Price, E. Hoffmann. "Clark Ashton Smith: Natal Horoscope."
a. *Nyctalops* No. 7 (August 1972): 28–30.

255. Price, E. Hoffman[n]. "Letter."
a. In *Emperor of Dreams* (C.7).

Brief memoir of CAS.

256. Price, E. Hoffmann. "The Story Tellers' Circle."
   a. *Short Stories* (25 May 1947): 4.

257. Price, Robert M. "Abhoth the Unclean."
   a. In *Anno Klarkash-Ton* (D.1).

   On the biblical significance of the phrase "Abhoth the Unclean" in "The Seven Geases."

258. Reiter, Geoffrey. "'A Round Cipher': Word-Building and World-Building in the Weird Works of Clark Ashton Smith."
   a. In Justin Everett and Jeffrey K. Shanks, ed. *The Unique Legacy of* Weird Tales. Lanham, MD: Rowman & Littlefield, 2015. 173–86.

   On the role of the artist and the wizard in CAS's poetry and fiction.

259. Reiter, Geoffrey. "'A Thoroughly Modern Disdain': The Materialist's Descent into Hell in 'The Seven Geases.'"
   a. *Lost Worlds* No. 5 (2008): 5–14.

   On the symbolism of the underworld adventures of the protagonist of "The Seven Geases."

260. Rickard, Dennis. "Drugs and Clark Ashton Smith."
   a. *Nyctalops* No. 7 (August 1972): 31–32.

   Discusses the mention of narcotic and hallucinogenic drugs in CAS's work.

261. Rockhill, Jim. "As Shadows Wait upon the Sun: Clark Ashton Smith's Zothique."
   a. In *The Freedom of Fantastic Things* (D.5).

   Study of the imagery and symbolism of CAS's Zothique tales.

262. Rockhill, Jim. "The Poetics of Morbidity: The Original Text of Clark Ashton Smith's 'The Maze of Maal Dweb' and Other Works First Published in *The Double Shadow and Other Fantasies.*"
   a. *Lost Worlds* No. 1 (2004): 20–25.

   On significant textual differences between the first publication of stories in *The Double Shadow* and subsequent appearances.

263. Rosenthal, Joe. "De Camp through CAS and Dunsany."
    a. *Tales of Horror and Damnation* No. 6 (January 1985): 22–23.

264. Ruber, Peter. "Clark Ashton Smith (1893–1961)."
    a. In Peter Ruber, ed. *Arkham's Masters of Horror*. Sauk City, WI: Arkham House, 2000. 53–61.

    General discussion of CAS's life and work.

265. Rubin, Hal. "Clark Ashton Smith: Ill-Fated Master of Fantasy."
    a. *Sierra Heritage* 5, No. 1 (June 1985): 34–38.

266. Ryder, David Warren. "The Price of Poetry."
    a. *Controversy* 1, No. 7 (7 December 1934): 86.
    b. In *Nero and Other Poems* (I.A.8).

    In b., the essay was printed on three loose sheets and laid into most, but not all, copies of the book. It was printed one month after the book proper.

267. Sackett, S[amuel] J. "The Last Romantic."
    a. *Fantasy Sampler* No. 4 (June 1956): 6–11.
    b. *Nyctalops* No. 7 (August 1972): 23–25.
    c. In *The Freedom of Fantastic Things* (D.5).

    General evaluation of CAS as a poet and fiction writer.

268. Sackett, Samuel J. "Recollections of Clark Ashton Smith."
    a. In *In the Realms of Mystery and Wonder* (I.A.87).

    On a visit by Sackett and George Modell to CAS in 1948.

269. Sammons, Brian M. "A Seventies Sorcerer on the Small Screen."
    a. In *Anno Klarkash-Ton* (D.1).

    Study of the adaptation of "The Return of the Sorcerer" on *Rod Serling's Night Gallery*.

270. Sanahujas, Simon, and Denis Labbé. "Clark Ashton Smith."
    a. *Faeries* No. 7 (May 2002): 60–80.

    Includes: Simon Sanahujas, "Clark Ashton Smith" (60–61); Simon Sanahujas, "Hyperborée" (62–64); Denis Labbé, "Zothique" (65–67); Denis Labbé, "Autres cycles" (68–71); Denis Labbé, "Un Pont entre le passé et l'avenir" (72–75); Denis Labbé, "Portrait d'un poète" (76–80).

271. Schiff, Stuart David. "In Search of a Smith Library."
    a. *Nyctalops* No. 7 (August 1972): 68–69.

272. Schultz, David E., and S. T. Joshi. "Introduction."
    a. In *Dawnward Spire, Lonely Hill* (I.A.86).

    Extensive discussion of Lovecraft's relations to CAS.

273. Schultz, David E., and S. T. Joshi, ed. *An Epicure in the Terrible: A Centennial Anthology of Essays in Honor of H. P. Lovecraft.*
    a. Rutherford, NJ: Fairleigh Dickinson University Press, 1991. 20, 37, 106, 107, 113, 117, 121, 122, 128, 218, 237, 252–53, 254, 309, 315, 318.
    b. New York: Hippocampus Press, 2011. 34, 106, 107, 114, 117, 118, 124, 131, 228, 247, 265, 267, 331, 335.

    Touches upon CAS's relations with Lovecraft.

274. Schwartz, [Julius], and [Mort] Weisinger. "Weird Whisperings."
    a. *Fantasy Fan* 1, No. 9 (May 1934): 137.
    b. In Charles D. Hornig, ed. *The Fantasy Fan: September, 1933–February, 1935.* [n.p.: Lance Thingmaker, 2010.] 137. [Facsimile of a.]

    Brief discussion of the friendship of CAS and Lovecraft.

275. Schwartz, [Julius], and [Mort] Weisinger. "Weird Whisperings."
    a. *Fantasy Fan* 1, No. 12 (August 1934): 179.
    b. In Charles D. Hornig, ed. *The Fantasy Fan: September, 1933–February, 1935.* [n.p.: Lance Thingmaker, 2010.] 179. [Facsimile of a.]

    Brief discussion of CAS's recent works of fiction.

276. Schwartz, Robert. "Clark Ashton Smith: Dunsanian Temporality, Visions and Literary Concepts."
    a. *Tales of Horror and Damnation* No. 6 (January 1985): 6–13, 17.

277. Schwartz, Robert. "Introduction."
    a. *Tales of Horror and Damnation* No. 6 (January 1985): 3.

278. Schwartz, Robert. "Return of the Golden Calf."
    a. *Tales of Horror and Damnation* No. 6 (January 1985): 26.

279. Schweitzer, Darrell. "Low Point X. Clark Ashton Smith: Master of Fantastic Worlds and Muddy Prose."
   a. *Space & Time* No. 18 (May 1973): 28–31.

280. Sidney-Fryer, Donald. "About Clark Ashton Smith and *The Hashish-Eater*."
   a. In *The Hashish-Eater* (I,A.55).
   b. In *The Hashish-Eater* (I.A.75).

281. Sidney-Fryer, Donald. "The Alleged Influence of Lord Dunsany on Clark Ashton Smith."
   a. *Amra* No. 23 (January 1963): 17–28 (as by "Donald S. Fryer").
   b. *Klarkash-Ton* No. 1 (June 1988): 9–13, 15 (as "On the Alleged Influence of Lord Dunsany on Clark Ashton Smith").
   c. In 287.

   "The superficial similarity of Dunsany and Smith forms an example of independent and (almost) parallel evolution."

282. Sidney-Fryer, Donald. "Averoigne: An Afterword."
   a. In *The Averoigne Chronicles* (I.A.85).

283. Sidney-Fryer, Donald. "Brave World Old and New: The Atlantis Theme in the Poetry and Fiction of Clark Ashton Smith."
   a. *Lost Worlds* No. 2 (2004): 11–30.
   b. In *The Freedom of Fantastic Things* (D.5).

   On the prevalence of Atlantis as a theme in CAS's poetry and prose.

284. Sidney-Fryer, Donald. "Clark Ashton Smith: A Chronology."
   a. *Mirage* No. 8 (June 1966): 13–24 (as by "Donald S. Fryer").

285. Sidney-Fryer, Donald. "Clark Ashton Smith, Poet in Prose."
   a. In *Poems in Prose* (I.A.23) (as by "Donald S. Fryer").
   b. D.13 (French translation).
   c. In 287.
   d. In *In the Realms of Mystery and Wonder* (I.A.87).

   Extensive essay on CAS as prose-poet, tracing the influence of such writers as Aloysius Bertrand, Baudelaire, and Poe on his work.

286. Sidney-Fryer, Donald. "A Clark Ashton Smith Roll of Honor."
   a. In *One Hundred Years of Klarkash-Ton* (D.10).

287. Sidney-Fryer, Donald. *The Golden State Phantasticks: The California Romantics and Related Subjects—Collected Essays and Reviews*. Ed. Leo Grin and Alan Gullette.
    a.   Los Angeles: Phosphor Lantern Press, 2011.
    b.   New York: Hippocampus Press, 2011.

> *Contains* (Phosphor Lantern/Hippocampus): "The Sorcerer Departs" (9–51/9–49); "Clark Ashton Smith, Poet in Prose" (53–67/50–63); "A Memoir of Timeus Gaylord: Reminiscences of Two Visits with Clark Ashton Smith, &c." (123–63/117–69); "Clark Ashton Smith: The Last of the Great Romantic Poets" (181–228/170–215); "A Statement for Imagination: George Sterling and Clark Ashton Smith" (229–47/216–32); "The Alleged Influence of Lord Dunsany on Clark Ashton Smith" (317–24/292–99); "Klarkash-Ton and E'ch-Pi-El: On the Alleged Influence of H. P. Lovecraft on Clark Ashton Smith" (325–33/300–307); "Clark Ashton Smith. *The City of the Singing Flame* (Introduction)" (403–6/372–75); "Clark Ashton Smith. *The Last Incantation* (Introduction)" (407–10/376–78); "Clark Ashton Smith. *The Monster of the Prophecy* (Introduction)" (411–14/379–82); "'Klarkash-Ton' versus 'Clark Ashton': A Minor Issue for Controversy" (with Rah Hoffman) (423–24/389–90); "*O Amor atque Realitas!* Clark Ashton Smith's First Adult Fiction" (427–34/393–400).

288. Sidney-Fryer, Donald. *Hobgoblin Apollo: The Autobiography of Donald Sidney-Fryer*. New York: Hippocampus Press, 2016, passim.

289. Sidney-Fryer, Donald. "Introduction."
    a.   In *One Hundred Years of Klarkash-Ton* (D.10).

290. Sidney-Fryer, Donald. "Introduzione."
    a.   In *Ombre dal cosmo* (D.9).

291. Sidney-Fryer, Donald. "James Blish versus Ashton Smith: To Wit, the Young Turk Syndrome, a Riposte."
    a.   *Lost Worlds* No. 1 (2004): 12–19.
    b.   In *The Freedom of Fantastic Things* (D.5).

> Rebuts James Blish's article (item 31 above), asserting that CAS creatively assimilated his literary influences and produced work of lasting aesthetic value.

292. Sidney-Fryer, Donald. "Klarkash-Ton and 'Greek.'"
  a. In *The Freedom of Fantastic Things* (D.5).

  Extensive discussion of CAS's relations with George Sterling
  (nicknamed "Greek" by Jack London), especially in regard to
  CAS's early poetry.

293. Sidney-Fryer, Donald. "Klarkash-Ton and Ech-Pi-El: On the Alleged Influence of H. P. Lovecraft on Clark Ashton Smith."
  a. *Mirage* 1, No. 6 (Winter 1963–64): 30–33 (as by "Donald S.
  Fryer").
  b. In 287.

294. Sidney-Fryer, Donald. "The Last of the Great Romantic Poets."
  a. D.15.
  b. In 287 (as "Clark Ashton Smith: The Last of the Great Romantic Poets").

295. Sidney-Fryer, Donald. "A Memoir of Timeus Gaylord: Reminiscences of Two Visits with Clark Ashton Smith, &c."
  a. *Romantist* 2 (1978): 1–19.
  b. In 287.

296. Sidney-Fryer, D[onald]. "*O Amor atque Realitas!* Clark Ashton
  Smith's First Adult Fiction."
  a. *Dark Eidolon* No. 3 (Winter 1993): 22–25.
  b. In I.A.82.
  c. In 287.

  On CAS's mainstream stories of the early to mid-1920s.

297. Sidney-Fryer, Donald. "On the Authorship of a Review of *Ebony
  and Crystal.*"
  a. *Lost Worlds* No. 3 (2006): 36–39.

  On George Sterling's authorship of a review published under the
  name George Douglas (see F.3.f).

298. Sidney-Fryer, Donald. "Principal Facts of Biography."
  a. In *Emperor of Dreams* (C.7).

  Basic biographical facts on CAS, with a note on his family background.

299. Sidney-Fryer, Donald. "A Report from Clark Ashton Smith Country."
  a. *Nyctalops* 2, No. 1 (April 1973): 38–39.

300. Sidney-Fryer, Donald. "The Sorcerer Departs."
  a. In *In Memoriam: Clark Ashton Smith* (D.4) (as by "Donald S. Fryer").
  b. D.14 (as *Clark Ashton Smith: The Sorcerer Departs*).
  c. In I.A.82.
  d. In 287.

  Lengthy essay recounting CAS's life, with some discussion of his poetry and fiction and a study of the reasons for his relative lack of critical success.

301. Sidney-Fryer, Donald. "A Statement for Imagination: George Sterling and Clark Ashton Smith."
  a. *Romantist* 6–7–8 (1982–83–84): 13–23.
  b. In 287.

302. Smith, Andrew. "*The Dead Will Cuckold You*, in Print and Manuscript, and an Additional Observation."
  a. *Dark Eidolon* No. 3 (Winter 1993): 20–22.

  On the history of the writing of CAS's play.

303. Smith, Eldred. "The Short Stories of Clark Ashton Smith."
  a. *Alien Culture* 1, No. 2 (April 1949): 3–6.

304. Smith, Peter. "Disciples of Dagon."
  a. In Peter Smith. *Nameless Aeons*. Mexborough, UK: Logos Press, 1999. 23–35.

305. Smith, Reginald. *Weird Tales in the Thirties*.
  a. Santa Ana, CA: Reginald Smith, 1966. 11–14, 34.

  Touches upon CAS's stories published in *Weird Tales*.

306. Squires, Roy A. "The Fiction of Clark Ashton Smith: When He Wrote It and What Remains Unpublished."
  a. *Nyctalops* No. 7 (August 1972): 65–67.

307. Stableford, Brian. "'Hyperborea.'"
    a. In T. A. Shippey and A. J. Sobczak, ed. *Magill's Guide to Science Fiction and Fantasy Literature*. Pasadena, CA: Salem Press, 1996. 2.451–52.
    b. In Gary Hoppenstand, ed. *Pulp Fiction of the 1920s and 1930s*. (Critical Insights.) Ipswich, MA: Salem Press, 2013. 192–95.

308. Stableford, Brian. "Outside the Human Aquarium: The Fantastic Imagination of Clark Ashton Smith."
    a. In Douglas Robillard, ed. *American Supernatural Fiction: From Edith Wharton to the* Weird Tales *Writers*. New York: Garland, 1996. 229–52.
    b. In *The Freedom of Fantastic Things* (D.5).

    Extensive overview of CAS's work, with a focus on his early poetry written under the aegis of George Sterling and his various story cycles.

309. Stableford, Brian. "The River and the Red World."
    a. *Lost Worlds* No. 3 (2006): 19–21.

    On "The Face by the River" and "The Red World of Polaris."

310. Stableford, Brian. "'Zothique.'"
    a. In T. A. Shippey and A. J. Sobczak, ed. *Magill's Guide to Science Fiction and Fantasy Literature*. Pasadena, CA: Salem Press, 1996. 4.1091–92.
    b. In Gary Hoppenstand, ed. *Pulp Fiction of the 1920s and 1930s*. (Critical Insights.) Ipswich, MA: Salem Press, 2013. 196–99.

311. Sterling, George. "The Poetry of the Pacific Coast—California."
    a. In William Stanley Braithwaite, ed. *Anthology of Magazine Verse for 1926*. Boston: Harold Vinal, 1926. 100.
    b. *Step Ladder* 13, No. 5 (May 1927): 129 (extract; as "The Poetry of Clark Ashton Smith").
    c. In *The Shadow of the Unattained* (I.A.69).

    Brief evaluation of CAS's poetry.

312. Sterling, George. "Preface."
    a. In *Odes and Sonnets* (I.A.2).
    b. In *The Shadow of the Unattained* (I.A.69).

". . . one will find in the sheer imagination of the succeeding pages evidence and proof of a precocity vast and sublime in its range, and quite unequalled in English verse."

313. Sterling, George. "Preface."
   a. In *Ebony and Crystal* (I.A.3).
   b. In *Selected Poems* (I.A.27).
   c. In *The Shadow of the Unattained* (I.A.69).

   Brief discussion of why CAS's poems will endure.

314. Stockton, Richard. "An Appreciation of the Prose Works of Clark Ashton Smith."
   a. *Acolyte* No. 14 (Spring 1946): 6–7.
   b. *Klarkash-Ton* No. 1 (June 1988): 14–15.

   Impressionistic discussion of CAS's work as a fount of imagination.

315. Sullivan, Shaun. "In Search of the Emperor of Dreams."
   a. *Fungi* No. 14 (Fall 1996): 14.

316. Sully, Genevieve K. "Letter."
   a. In *Emperor of Dreams* (C.7).

   Brief memoir of CAS.

317. Tierney, Richard L. "Richard L. Tierney: His Book."
   a. *Nyctalops* No. 7 (August 1972): 86–88.

   An account of his impressions of the Crater Ridge area.

318. Tierney, Richard L. "'The True Protest Is Beauty.'"
   a. *Nyctalops* No. 7 (August 1972): 33.

   Review of Donald Sidney-Fryer's *Songs and Sonnets Atlantean* (1971), with a discussion of CAS's influence on Sidney-Fryer.

319. Tompkins, Steven. "Coming In from the Cold: Incursions of 'Outsideness' in Hyperborea."
   a. *Studies in Fantasy Literature* No. 1 (2004): 12–28.
   a. In *The Freedom of Fantastic Things* (D.5).

   General discussion of the nature of the stories making up the Hyperborea cycle.

320. Triolo, Jean-Luc. "Le Magicien d'Hyperborée."
   a. *Planète à Vendre!* No. 10 (April 1992): 28–33.

321. Van Hise, James. "C. A. Smith—Emperor of Dreams."
   a. *Stardate* Nos. 5/6 (March–April 1985): 28–29
   b. *Etchings and Odysseys* No. 10 (1987): 19–21.

322. Vester, Henry J. III. "Strange Reflections: The Self-Image of Clark Ashton Smith."
   a. *Yawning Vortex* 2, No. 4 (July 1996): 13–6.
   b. In *One Hundred Years of Klarkash-Ton* (D.10).

323. Vetter, John E. "Lovecraft's Illustrators."
   a. In H. P. Lovecraft and Divers Hands. *The Dark Brotherhood and Other Pieces.* Ed. August Derleth. Sauk City, WI: Arkham House, 1966. 269.

   Briefly touches upon CAS's illustrations for Lovecraft's "The Lurking Fear" in *Home Brew.*

324. Wandrei, Donald A. "The Emperor of Dreams."
   a. *Overland Monthly* (December 1926): 380–81, 407.
   b. *Klarkash-Ton* No. 1 (June 1988): 3–8, 25.
   c. In *Anno Klarkash-Ton* (D.1).

   Important early article on CAS, stressing his work as a poet of cosmic imagination.

325. Weinberg, Robert. "A Note on Clark Ashton Smith by Edmond Hamilton."
   a. *Nyctalops* No. 7 (August 1972): 30.

326. Weinberg, Robert. *The Weird Tales Story.*
   a. West Linn, OR: FAX Collector's Editions, 1977. 21, 30–31, 32, 33, 34, 35, 36–37, 39, 42, 43, 46, 48, 49, 51, 53, 56, 59, 61, 76, 85, 88, 124, 126, 128.
   b. Holicong, PA: Wildside Press, 1999. 21, 30–31, 32, 33, 34, 35, 36–37, 39, 42, 43, 46, 48, 49, 51, 53, 56, 59, 61, 76, 85, 88, 124, 126, 128.
   Brief study of CAS's relations with *Weird Tales.*

327. Weisinger, Mortimer. "The Ether Vibrates."
   a. *Fantasy Magazine* 3, No. 4 (June 1934): 25–26.

328. Whitechapel, Simon. "Clark Ashton Smith: Fantasiste or Science Fictioneer?"
    a. *Chronicles of the Cthulhu Codex* No. 17 (Winter 2000): 27–36.

329. Wilson, Andrew J. "The Last Musketeer: Clark Ashton Smith and the Weird Marriage of Poetry and Pulp."
    a. In Gary Hoppenstand, ed. *Pulp Fiction of the 1920s and 1930s.* (Critical Insights.) Ipswich, MA: Salem Press, 2013. 36–51.

    Discussion of CAS's early career as a poet and his transition to fiction-writing in the late 1920s.

330. Wilson, Gahan. "Introduction."
    a. In *Collected Fantasies,* Volume 4 (I.A.70).

    Brief appreciation of CAS as fantasist.

331. Wilson, Gahan. "Introduction."
    a. In *The Averoigne Chronicles* (I.A.85).

    Brief evaluation of the Averoigne cycle.

332. Wolfe, Charles K. "CAS: A Note on the Aesthetics of Fantasy."
    a. *Nyctalops* No. 7 (August 1972): 20–22.
    b. *Dark Eidolon* No. 2 (July 1989): 9–11.
    c. In *The Freedom of Fantastic Things* (D.5).

    Study of CAS's theory of fantasy fiction and its application to his fantastic tales.

333. Wolfe, Gene. "Introduction."
    a. In *The Return of the Sorcerer* (I.A.76).

334. [Unsigned.] "Clark Ashton Smith, Master of Horror and Fantasy, Who Is Said to Even Surpass Poe."
    a. *Portals* 1, No. 1 (November 1957): 10–15.

335. [Unsigned.] "Clark Ashton Smith's Carvings Available as Replicas."
    a. *Science-Fiction Critic* 1, No. 8 (March 1937): 8–9.

336. [Unsigned.] "The Editor Broadcasts."
    a. *Science Fiction Digest* 1, No. 10 (June 1933): 16.

337. [Unsigned.] "Recent Poetry."
    a. *Current Literature* 53, No. 4 (October 1912): 473.

Brief note on CAS's celebrity in California.

338. [Unsigned.] "The Science Fiction Eye."
　　a. *Fantasy Magazine* 3, No. 1 (March 1934): 19.

339. [Unsigned.] "The Science Fiction Eye."
　　a. *Fantasy Magazine* 3, No. 5 (July 1934): 7.

340. [Unsigned.] "The Science Fiction Eye."
　　a. *Fantasy Magazine* 5, No. 1 (June 1935): 155.

341. [Unsigned.] [Untitled.]
　　a. *Auburn Journal* (5 April 1923): 1.

　　　Banner announcing forthcoming appearance of CAS's column, and also availability of *Ebony and Crystal*.

498   F. Book Reviews   III.F.1

F. Book Reviews

1. *The Star-Treader and Other Poems* (1912)

   a. Bashford, Herbert. "Clark Smith's Poems." *San Francisco Bulletin* (30 November 1912): 14.

   b. [Bonnet, Theodore.] "The Spectator." *Town Talk* No. 1056 (16 November 1912): 12–13.

   c. Braithwaite, William Stanley. "Our Modern Poets." *Boston Transcript* (2 April 1913): Part II, p. 24. In *The Freedom of Fantastic Things* (D.5). 51–53.

   d. [Galpin, Alfred.] "Echoes from Beyond Space." *United Amateur* (July 1925): 3–4. In H. P. Lovecraft. *Letters to Alfred Galpin.* Ed. S. T. Joshi and David E. Schultz. New York: Hippocampus Press, 2005. 273–75.

   e. Garnett, Porter. "A Young and True Poet." *San Francisco Call* (1 December 1912): 6. In *The Freedom of Fantastic Things* (D.5). 34–39.

   f. Jury, John. "The Star Treader: A Book of Verse by Clark Ashton Smith—A Review." *San Jose Mercury and Herald* (8 December 1912): Magazine Section, p. 2. In *The Freedom of Fantastic Things* (D.5). 46–50.

   g. Machen, Arthur. "Books of Today." *Evening News* (London) (12 February 1916): 1.

   h. O'Sheel, Shaemus. "A Young Poet." *New York Times Book Review* (26 January 1913): 38 (as "S. O'S."). In *The Freedom of Fantastic Things* (D.5). 50–51.

   i. [Phillips, Stephen.] "Voices from Overseas." *Poetry Review* 2, No. 4 (April 1913): 139–41 (esp. 141).

   j. Treadwell, Sophie. *San Francisco Evening Post* (23 November 1912): Magazine section, p. 2. In *The Freedom of Fantastic Things* (D.5). 43–46.

   *k. Y., G. R. "Clark Ashton Smith and His Book of Verse." Unidentified newspaper. In *The Freedom of Fantastic Things* (D.5). 40–42.

   l. [Unsigned.] "Junior Poet of the Sierras." *Placer Herald* (16 November 1912): 4.

   m. [Unsigned.] "The Latest Books." *Argonaut* (30 November 1912): 365.

n.   [Unsigned.] "The Last Poems of Mrs. Julia C. R. Dorr Have an Introduction by Her Daughter, Mrs. Steele, of Brooklyn—Verse by Other Singers." *Brooklyn Daily Eagle* (4 October 1913): 21.

o.   [Unsigned.] "Recent Poetry." *Current Opinion* 54, No. 2 (February 1913): 150.

p.   [Unsigned.] "Clark Ashton Smith." *Daily Palo Alto Times* (8 March 1915): 2.

q.   [Unsigned.] "Among Poets of the Day: Youthful Genius, West and East, Has Its Fling at Minstrelsy." *World* (New York) (7 December 1912): 9.

r.   [Unsigned.] "Book of Poems by Local Poet." *Placer County Republican* (28 November 1912): 1.

s.   [Unsigned.] *Poetry* 2, No. 2 (April 1913): 31–32.

t.   [Unsigned.] "C. A. Smith, Poet, For Whom Great Fame Is Forecast." *San Francisco Call* (13 November 1912): 10.

u.   [Unsigned.] "The Star-Treader and Other Poems: Collected Writings of Youthful Genius Published by A. M. Robertson." *San Francisco Chronicle* (13 November 1912): 9.

v.   [Unsigned.] "New Sierra Poet Gives Book to Public." *San Francisco Examiner* (13 November 1912): 7.

w.   [Unsigned.] "Books and Authors." *Wasp* (23 November 1912): 16. In *The Freedom of Fantastic Things* (D.5). 39–40.

A notice of the book by William T. Allison appeared c. 1919–20, but this has not been located.

2.   *Odes and Sonnets* (1918)

a.   [Bonnet, Theodore.] "The Spectator." *Town Talk* No. 1352 (20 July 1918): 10.

b.   Dare, Helen. "Book Club Garners Treasures Right Here from Home Field." *San Francisco Chronicle* (30 June 1918): 10.

c.   [Unsigned.] "Clark Ashton Smith of Auburn Lauded for His Latest Book of Poems." *Auburn Daily Journal* (1 July 1918): 1.

d.   [Unsigned.] "Auburn Poet Greater Than Chatterton." *Auburn Daily Journal* (19 September 1918): 4.

3. *Ebony and Crystal* (1922)

a.   [Allison, William T.] "Neither Kindergartens Nor Skyscrapers." *Winnipeg Tribune* (13 January 1923): 4 (as by "Ivanhoe").

b. [De Casseres, Benjamin.] "And a Little Book Shall Lead Them." *Arts and Decoration* 19, No. 4 (August 1923): 47, 50.

c. [Elliot, William Foster.] "A California Poet." *Sacramento Bee* (30 December 1922): 26. *Fresno Bee* (30 December 1922): 16. In *The Freedom of Fantastic Things* (D.5). 58–60.

d. [Galpin, Alfred.] "Echoes from Beyond Space." *United Amateur* (July 1925): 3–4. In H. P. Lovecraft. *Letters to Alfred Galpin.* Ed. S. T. Joshi and David E. Schultz. New York: Hippocampus Press, 2005. 273–75.

e. Lovecraft, H. P. *L'Alouette* 1, No. 1 (January 1924): 20–21. *Golden Atom* 1, No. 10 (Winter 1943): 22. *Different* 2, No. 6 (October 1964): [11]. In Lovecraft's *Uncollected Prose and Poetry.* Ed. S. T. Joshi and Marc A. Michaud. West Warwick, RI: Necronomicon Press, 1978. 35. In Lovecraft's *Collected Essays, Volume 2: Literary Criticism.* Ed. S. T. Joshi. New York: Hippocampus Press, 2004. 73–74. In *Dawnward Spire, Lonely Hill* (A.86).

f. [Sterling, George.] "Recent Books of Fact and Fiction." *San Francisco Bulletin* (19 December 1922): 8 (as by "George Douglas"). In *The Shadow of the Unattained* (I.A.69).

g. Todd, Morton. "Clark Ashton Smith's New Volume." *Argonaut* (16 December 1922): 387–88. In *The Freedom of Fantastic Things* (D.5). 53–58.

h. [Unsigned.] "Boy Publishes Poems." *San Francisco Examiner* (17 December 1922): 20.

i. [Unsigned.] "Clark Ashton Smith Publishes Poems." *Auburn Journal* (14 December 1922): 1.

j. [Unsigned.] "San Francisco Poet Treads New Worlds: Earth Fetters Cast Off by Star Rover." *San Francisco Chronicle* (10 December 1922): 59.

4. *Sandalwood* (1925)

a. Douglas, George. "A Gentle Bard." *San Francisco Bulletin* (14 November 1925): 10.

b. [Macomber, Ben.] "Clark Ashton Smith Soars High Again upon His Hippogriff." *San Francisco Chronicle* (10 January 1926): 4D.

c. Sterling, George. "Rhymes and Reactions." *Overland Monthly* 83, No. 11 (November 1925): 411.

d. [Todd, Morton] "The Bard of Auburn." *Argonaut* (14 November 1925): 9. In *The Freedom of Fantastic Things* (D.5). 60–61.

e. [Unsigned.] "Clark Ashton Smith Publishes New Book." *Auburn Journal* (5 November 1925): 3. In *The Freedom of Fantastic Things* (D.5). 64–65.

*f. [Unsigned.] "Debut Honors Sterling." Unidentified clipping.

5. *The Double Shadow and Other Fantasies* (1933)

a. Gagliani, William D. *Cemetery Dance* No. 51 (2005): 104.

b. Schweitzer, Darrell. "The Great Klarkash-Ton." *Flesh & Blood* No. 15 (2004): 33.

c. Wilson, Gahan. *Realms of Fantasy* 10, No. 4 (June 2004): 32.

6. *Nero and Other Poems* (1937)

a. [Coblentz, Stanton A.] *Wings* 3, No. 6 (Summer 1938): 27–28.

b. Derleth, August. "The Poets Sing Frontiers." *Voices* No. 51 (Autumn 1937): 45–46.

c. [Unsigned.] "Of C. A. Smith's Latest Poems." *Californian* (1 December 1937): 6.

7. *Out of Space and Time* (1942)

a. Boucher, Anthony. *San Francisco Chronicle* (15 November 1942): This World, p. 31. In *The Freedom of Fantastic Things* (D.5). 61–62. In *The Anthony Boucher Chronicles: Reviews and Commentary 1942–1947.* Ed. Francis M. Nevins. [Shreveport, LA:] Ramble House, 2009. 313–14.

b. Boucher, Anthony. *Unknown Worlds* 6, No. 6 (April 1943): 106.

c. De Casseres, Benjamin. "The March of Events." *San Francisco Examiner* (23 September 1942): 8.

d. Derleth, August. "The New Books: Things That Bump." *Capital Times* (Madison, WI) 50, No. 50 (2 August 1942): 8.

e. Dirda, Michael. "A Journey to the Fantastic Realms of Clark Ashton Smith." *Washington Post Book World* (18–24 February 2007): 10.

*f. Drake, Leah Bodine. *Evansville* [IN] *Courier.*

g. Field, Louise Maunsell. "Tales of Horror." *New York Times Book Review* (9 August 1942): 14.

h. Hays, Dan. *Statesman-Journal* (Salem, OR) (9 December 2006): 4E.

i. Jordan-Smith, Paul. "I'll Be Judge, You Be Jury." *Los Angeles Times* (23 August 1942): Sec. III, p. 6.

j. Lorraine, Lilith. *Raven* 1, No. 4 (Winter 1944): 43.

k.   Lowndes, Robert A. W. *Future Fantasy and Science Fiction* 3, No. 2 (December 1942): 71–72.

l.   Nye, Robert. "An Inside-Out and Upside-Down Utopia." *Guardian* (London) (16 September 1971): 9.

m.   Rockhill, Jim. *Lost Worlds* No. 5 (2008): 40–42.

n.   Rogers, Michael. *Library Journal* 131, No. 17 (15 October 2006): 97.

o.   Spencer, Paul. "Sayings of the Spence." *Banshee* No. 3 (December 1943): 3.

p.   Wollheim, Donald A. *Super Science Stories* 4, No. 3 (February 1943): 67.

q.   [Unsigned.] "The Eyrie." *Weird Tales* (November 1942): 121.

8. *Lost Worlds* (1944)

a.   Boucher, Anthony. *San Francisco Chronicle* (5 November 1944): This World, p. 9. In *The Anthony Boucher Chronicles: Reviews and Commentary 1942–1947*. Ed. Francis M. Nevins. [Shreveport, LA:] Ramble House, 2009. 36.

b.   Dirda, Michael. "A Journey to the Fantastic Realms of Clark Ashton Smith." *Washington Post Book World* (18–24 February 2007): 10.

c.   Farber, Marjorie. "Atlantis, Xiccarph." *New York Times Book Review* (19 November 1944): 18. *Klarkash-Ton* No. 1 (June 1988): 26–27.

d.   Hays, Dan. *Statesman-Journal* (Salem, OR) (9 December 2006): 4E.

e.   Nye, Robert. "An Inside-Out and Upside-Down Utopia." *Guardian* (London) (16 September 1971): 9.

f.   Rockhill, Jim. *Lost Worlds* No. 5 (2008): 40–42.

g.   Rogers, Michael. *Library Journal* 131, No. 17 (15 October 2006): 97.

9. *Genius Loci and Other Tales* (1949)

a.   Hillman, Arthur F. "The Lure of Clark Ashton Smith." *Fantasy Review* (February–March 1949): 25–26. In *The Freedom of Fantastic Things* (D.5). 62–63.

b.   Wagenknecht, Edward. "An Arkham Quartet." *Arkham Sampler* 2, No. 2 (Spring 1949): 89–91.

*c.   Lorraine, Lilith. [Not found.]

10. *The Dark Chateau* (1951)

a. Ferlinghetti, Lawrence. *San Francisco Chronicle* (3 February 1952): This World, p. 27.
b. [Unsigned.] "Clark A. Smith's New Volume of Poetry Published." *Auburn Journal* (20 March 1958): 7.
c. [Unsigned.] *Weird Tales* 44, No. 4 (May 1952): 94.

11. *The Abominations of Yondo* (1960)

a. de Camp, L. Sprague. *Amra* No. 13 (September 1960): 13.
b. Dewey, Violet. "Things That Go Bump." *Milwaukee Journal Sentinel* (24 April 1960): part 5, page 6 (86).
c. Starrett, Vincent. "Books Alive." *Chicago Tribune Magazine of Books* (22 May 1960): 6.

12. *The Hill of Dionysus* (1962)

a. Carter, Lin. *Spectrum, Three* (March–April 1963): 9–10.
b. Davidson, Avram. *Magazine of Fantasy and Science Fiction* 26, No. 6 (June 1964): 36–37.
c. [Lowndes, Robert A. W.] *Magazine of Horror* 1, No. 2 (November 1963): 48.
d. Schroyer, Frederick. *Los Angeles Herald-Examiner* (4 April 1965): C6.

13. *Tales of Science and Sorcery* (1964)

a. de Camp, L. Sprague. *Amra* No. 42 (September 1966): 6.
b. Lowndes, Robert A. W. *Magazine of Horror* 2, No. 4 (August 1965): 78, 84–85.
c. Simmonds, Henry K. *Insight* No. 2 (1965): 10.

14. *Poems in Prose* (1965)

a. Derleth, August. "Prose Poetry." *Capital Times* (Madison, WI) (22 July 1965): Sec. II, p. 12.
b. Leiber, Fritz. *Magazine of Fantasy and Science Fiction* 29, No. 6 (December 1965): 37.
c. Lowndes, Robert A. W. *Magazine of Horror* 2, No. 6 (Winter 1965–66): 80–82.
d. Shroyer, Frederick. *Los Angeles Herald-Examiner* (26 September 1965): B2.

15. *Other Dimensions* (1970)

 a. Lowndes, Robert A. W. "The Editor's Page." *Bizarre Fantay Tales* 1, No. 2 (March 1971): 72–75, 83, 114.
 b. Stephensen-Payne, Philip. *Paperback Parlour* 1, No. 2 (April 1977): 4.
 c. Wilson, Gahan. *Magazine of Fantasy and Science Fiction* 41, No. 2 (July 1971): 73–75.
 d. [Unsigned.] "Works of Late Auburn Author Are Published." *Auburn Journal* (16 July 1970): C4.

16. *Zothique* (1970)

 a. Brown, Charlie. *Locus* No. 59 (16 July 1970): 6.
 b. Cook, Glen. *Science Fiction Review* No. 41 (November 1970): 31.
 c. de Camp, L. Sprague. *Amra* No. 54 (April 1971): 16.
 d. Leiber, Fritz. *Fantastic* 1, No. 2 (February 1971): 107–9.
 e. Lowndes, Robert A. W. "The Editor's Page." *Bizarre Fantay Tales* 1, no. 2 (March 1971): 72–75, 83, 114.
 f. M[enville], D[ouglas]. "Calibrations." *Forgotten Fantasy* 1, No. 2 (December 1970): 33.
 g. Williams, Bill. "The Evil That Men Do." *Northwest Arkansas Times* (Fayetteville, AK) (11 September 1970): 7.
 h. Wilson, Gahan. *Magazine of Fantasy and Science Fiction* 41, No. 2 (July 1971): 75.
 i. [Unsigned.] "Works of Late Auburn Author Are Published." *Auburn Journal* (16 July 1970): C9.

17. *Selected Poems* (1971)

 a. de Camp, L. Sprague. *Amra* No. 56 (June 1972): 18–19.
 b. Wilson, Gahan. *Magazine of Fantasy and Science Fiction* 44, No. 5 (May 1973): 76.

18. *Hyperborea* (1971)

 a. de Camp, L. Sprague. *Amra* No. 55 (December 1971): 19.
 b. FitzOsbert, Robert. *Luna Monthly* No. 40 (September 1972): 23.
 c. Leiber, Fritz. *Whispers* 1, No. 2 (December 1973): 47.
 d. Williams, Bill. "Classic Tales Still Sparkle." *Northwest Arkansas Times* (Fayetteville, AK) (21 May 1971): 12.

19. *Xiccarph* **(1972)**

   a. Brown, Charlie. *Locus* No. 125 (27 October 1972): 7.

20. *Grotesques and Fantastiques* **(1973)**

   a. Burton, Bruce. *Fantastic* 23, No. 5 (Ju;y 1974): 105.
   b. de Camp, L. Sprague. *Amra* No. 60 (September 1973): 17.

21. *Planets and Dimensions* **(1973)**

   a. Miller, P. Schuyler. *Analog* 92, No. 2 (October 1973): 160.
   b. [Unsigned.] "Prof Writes on SF." *Tennessean* (Nashville) (15 July 1973): 10F.

22. *Klarkash-Ton and Monstro Ligriv* **(1974)**

   a. Schiff, Stuart David. *Whispers* No. 3 (March 1974): 45.

23. *The Black Book of Clark Ashton Smith* **(1979)**

   a. Eng, Steve. "The Sorcerer Arrives." *Romantist* 3 (1979): 77–79.
   b. Geis, Richard E. *Science Fiction Review* 9, No. 2 (May 1980): 44.
   c. Staicar, Tom. *Fantastic* 27, No. 10 (July 1980): 12.

24. *The City of the Singing Flame* **(1981)**

   a. Cerasini, Marc A. *Crypt of Cthulhu* No. 6 (St. John's Eve 1981): 35–36.
   b. Engebretson, Russell. *Science Fiction Review* 11, No. 2 (Summer 1982): 56.
   c. Searles, Baird. *Isaac Asimov's Science Fiction Magazine* 5, No. 10 (October 1981): 20.
   d. Staircar, Tom. *Amazing Stories* 55, No. 6 (March 1982): 20.
   e. Williams, Alma Jo. *Science Fiction Review* 11, N0. 4 (Winter 1982): 57.
   f. [Unsigned.] *Detroit Free Press* (27 September 1981): 21.
   g. [Unsigned.] *Muncie* [IN] *Evening Press* (3 October 1981): 26.

25. *The Last Incantation* **(1982)**

   a. Collins, Bill. *Science Fiction and Fantasy Book Review* No. 9 (November 1982): 22.
   b. Schlobin, Roger. *Fantasy Newsletter* No. 53 (November 1982): 37.
   c. Searles, Baird. *Isaac Asimov's Science Fiction Magazine* 6, No. 11 (November 1982): 20–21.

d. Williams, Alma Jo. *Science Fiction Review* 11, No. 4 (Winter 1982): 57.

26. *The Monster of the Prophecy* (1983)

a. Williams, Alma Jo. *Science Fiction Review* 12, No. 4 (November 1983): 44.

27. *L'Île inconnu* (1985)

a. Louvier, Frédéric. *Weird* No. 2 (December 1985): 47.

28. *Ubbo-Sathla* (1985)

a. Louvier, Frédéric. *Weird* No. 3 (February 1986): 49.

29. *L'Empire des nécromants* (1985)

a. Devaux, Claude-Éric. *Weird* No. 5 (June–July 1986): 55.

30. *The Dweller in the Gulf* (1987)

a. Dziemianowicz, Stefan. *Klarkash-Ton* No. 1 (June 1988): 33–35.
b. Price, Robert M. *Crypt of Cthulhu* No. 53 (Candlemas, 1988): 41–42.
c. Schultz, David E. *Studies in Weird Fiction* No. 3 (Fall 1988): 43–44, 34.

31. *Mother of Toads* (1987)

a. Dziemianowicz, Stefan. *Klarkash-Ton* No. 1 (June 1988): 33–35.
b. Price, Robert M. *Crypt of Cthulhu* No. 53 (Candlemas, 1988): 41–42.
c. Schultz, David E. *Studies in Weird Fiction* No. 3 (Fall 1988): 43–44, 34.

32. *Letters to H. P. Lovecraft* (1987)

a. Dziemianowicz, Stefan. *Crypt of Cthulhu* No. 52 (Yuletide, 1987): 45–46.
b. Joshi, S. T. *Lovecraft Studies* No. 15 (Fall 1987): 83–84, 64.
c. Schultz, David E. *Studies in Weird Fiction* No. 2 (Summer 1987): 38–39.

33. *A Rendezvous in Averoigne* (1988)

    a. Behrends, Steve. *Studies in Weird Fiction* No. 4 (Fall 1988): 35–36.

    b. Betancourt, John Gregory. *Weird Tales* No. 292 (Fall 1988): 13.

    c. Bryant, Edward. *Rod Serling's The Twilight Zone Magazine* 8, No. 5 (December 1988): 99.

    d. Chow, Dan. *Locus* 21, No. 7 (July 1988): 23–24.

    e. Dziemianowicz, Stefan. *Crypt of Cthulhu* No. 61½ (Yuletide 1988): 7–11.

    f. Hilger, Ronald S. *Lost Worlds* No. 1 (2004): 35–37.

    g. Searles, Baird. *Isaac Asimov's Science Fiction Magazine* 13, No. 4 (April 1989): 188–89.

34. *The Vaults of Yoh-Vombis* (1988)

    a. Dziemianowicz, Stefan. *Crypt of Cthulhu* No. 57 (St. John's Eve 1988): 43–44.

    b. Schultz, David E. *Studies in Weird Fiction* No. 4 (Fall 1988): 36–38.

35. *The Monster of the Prophecy* (1988)

    a. Dziemianowicz, Stefan. *Crypt of Cthulhu* No. 61½ (Yuletide 1988): 7–11.

    b. Schultz, David E. *Studies in Weird Fiction* No. 4 (Fall 1988): 36–38.

36. *Nostalgia of the Unknown* (1988)

    a. D'Ammassa, Don. *Science Fiction Chronicle* No. 164 (July 1993): 34.

    b. Dziemianowicz, Stefan. *Crypt of Cthulhu* No. 61½ (Yuletide 1988): 7–11.

    c. Ford, Carl T. *Dagon* No. 24 (January–March 1989): 52.

    d. Schultz, David E. *Studies in Weird Fiction* No. 4 (Fall 1988): 36–38.

37. *Xeethra* (1988)

    a. Dziemianowicz. Stefan. *Crypt of Cthulhu* No. 62 (Candlemas 1989): 66–67.

38. *The Witchcraft of Ulua* (1988)

    a. Dziemianowicz, Stefan. *Crypt of Cthulhu* No. 62 (Candlemas 1989): 66–67.

39. *The Hashish-Eater* (1989)

a. Ford, Carl T. *Dagon* No. 27 (June 1990): 54.

40. *Strange Shadows* (1989)

a. Dziemianowicz, Stefan. *Dark Eidolon* No. 2 (July 1989): 34–36.
b. Dziemianowicz, Stefan. *Crypt of Cthulhu* No. 68 (Hallowmas 1989): 50–52.
c. Herron, Don. *Romantist* 9–10 (1985–86): 99–100.
d. Leiber, Fritz. "Moons & Stars & Stuff." *Locus* 23, No. 1 (July 1989): 13, 49.
e. Michaud, Marc A. *Studies in Weird Fiction* No. 5 (Spring 1989): 31–32.
f. Schweitzer, Darrell. *Aboriginal Science Fiction* 3, No. 6 (November–December 1989): 25.

41. *The Devil's Notebook* (1990)

a. Behrends, Steve. *Studies in Weird Fiction* No. 9 (Spring 1991): 43–44.
b. Eng, Steve. "Persistence of the California Romantics." *Romantist* 9–10 (1985–86): 104–5.
c. Leiber, Fritz. *Locus* No. 364 (May 1991): 13–14.

42. *Tales of Zothique* (1995)

a. Stableford, Brian. "As in Ancient Days." *Necrofile* No. 22 (Fall 1996): 5–7.
b. Wilson, Gahan. *Realms of Fantasy* 2, No. 1 (October 1995): 12.

43. *The Book of Hyperborea* (1996)

a. Stableford, Brian. "As in Ancient Days." *Necrofile* No. 22 (Fall 1996): 5–7.
b. Wilson, Gahan. *Realms of Fantasy* 3, No. 2 (December 1996): 12.

44. *The Emperor of Dreams* (2002)

a. Gevers, Nick. *Locus* No. 497 (June 2002): 75.
b. Hilger, Ronald S. *Lost Worlds* No. 1 (2004): 35–37.
c. Wallace, Jon. *Vector* No. 224 (July/August 2002): 20.
d. Wilson, Gahan. *Realms of Fantasy* 9, No. 1 (October 2002): 12.
e. [Unsigned.] *Vector* No. 223 (May 2002): 34.

45. *The Black Diamonds* **(2002)**

   a. De Lint, Charles. *Magazine of Fantasy and Science Fiction* 104, No. 5 (May 2003): 34–35.

   b. Gullette, Alan. *Lost Worlds* No. 3 (2006): 41–46.

   c. [Schweitzer, Darrell.] *Weird Tales* No. 328 (Summer 2002): 10.

46. *The Last Oblivion* **(2002)**

   a. De Lint, Charles. *Magazine of Fantasy and Science Fiction* 104, No. 5 (May 2003): 33–35.

   b. Dirda, Michael. "A Journey to the Fantastic Realms of Clark Ashton Smith." *Washington Post Book World* (18–24 February 2007): 10.

   c. [Schweitzer, Darrell.] "The Eyrie." *Weird Tales* No. 331 (Spring 2003): 10–11.

47. *The Red World of Polaris* **(2003)**

   a. Dirda, Michael. "A Journey to the Fantastic Realms of Clark Ashton Smith." *Washington Post Book World* (18–24 February 2007): 10.

48. *Selected Letters* **(2003)**

   a. Bertonneau, Thomas F. "Red Mist: How Small Presses Rescue Classic Genre Writers from Oblivion." *University Bookman* 45, No. 1 (Winter 2007): 7.

   b. Betancourt, John Gregory. *Amazing Stories* 73, No. 1 (September 2004): 69.

   c. Bleiler, Richard. *Dime Novel Round-Up* 73, No. 3 (June 2004): 94–95.

   d. Dirda, Michael. "A Journey to the Fantastic Realms of Clark Ashton Smith." *Washington Post Book World* (18–24 February 2007): 10.

   e. Grin, Leo. "Howard in the Letters of Clark Ashton Smith." thecimmerian.com/2005/09/04/howard-in-the-letters-of-clark-ashton-smith/

   f. Hoffman, Barry. www.baryon-online.com/baryon96/slcas.html

   g. Joshi, S. T. "Clark Ashton Smith Redivivus." www.lsu.edu/necrofile/smith12

   h. Schweitzer, Darrell. "The Great Klarkash-Ton." *Flesh & Blood* No. 15 (2004): 33.

i.   Stableford, Brian. *Lost Worlds* No. 2 (2004): 39–40.
j.   Wilson, Gahan. "Contemporary Horror Fantasy Mirrors Our Troubled Times." *Realms of Fantasy* 10, No. 6 (August 2004): 32–34.
k.   [Unsigned.] "SF/Fantasy/Horror Notes." *Publishers Weekly* 250, No. 40 (6 October 2003): 67.

49. *The Sword of Zagan and Other Writings* (2004)

a.   Betancourt, John Gregory. *Weird Tales* No. 336 (December 2004): 20.
b.   Gullette, Alan. *Lost Worlds* No. 3 (2006): 41–46.
c.   Schweitzer, Darrell. "The Great Klarkash-Ton." *Flesh & Blood* No. 15 (2004): 33.
d.   [Unsigned.] *Lovecraft's Weird Mysteries* No. 8 (2004): 7.

50. *Star Changes* (2005)

a.   Schweitzer, Darrell. *New York Review of Science Fiction* 18, No. 12 (August 2006): 15–17.
b.   Wilson, Gahan. "Science Plays a Small Part in Science-Fiction, According to Clark Ashton Smith." *Realms of Fantasy* 12, No. 6 (August 2006): 28–30.

51. *The Shadow of the Unattained* (2005)

a.   Sidney-Fryer, Donald. *Lost Worlds* No. 4 (2006): 26–39.
b.   [Unsigned.] "SF/Fantasy/Horror Notes." *Publishers Weekly* 253, No. 3 (16 January 2006): 41.

52. *The Collected Fantasies of Clark Ashton Smith* (2006–10)

a.   Dirda, Michael. "A Journey to the Fantastic Realms of Clark Ashton Smith." *Washington Post Book World* (18–24 February 2007): 10.
b.   Grossman, Bruce. *Bookgasm* www.bookgasm.com/reviews/sci-fi/end-of-story-smith-vol-1/
c.   Guran, Paula. *Fantasy Magazine* 12 February 2007 www.darkfanta-sy.org/fantasy/2008/02/sam-enthoven-clark-ashton-smith/
d.   Hays, Carl. *Booklist* 103, No. 15 (1 April 2007): 36.
e.   Kleffel, Rick. "Beginning at the Beginning." The Agony Column. trashotron.com/agony/news/2007/01-15-07.htm
f.   Lupoff, Richard A. *Locus* No. 601 (February 2011): 25–26.

g. Schweitzer, Darrell. "Clark Ashton Smith: Inescapable, But Difficult to Love." *New York Review of Science Fiction* No. 235 (March 2008): 15–17.

h. Tompkins, Steve. *Dark Man* No. 6, Nos. 1 & 2 (November 2011): 99.

i. Van Calenbergh, Hubert. "The Ultimate Clark Ashton Smith." *Dead Reckonings* No. 2 (Fall 2007): 15–19.

j. Wilson, Gahan. "Night Shade Gives Readers Another Chance to Savor the Genius of Clark Ashton Smith." *Realms of Fantasy* No. 56 (June 2007): 32–34.

k. Witcover, Paul. *Realms of Fantasy* No. 59 (October 2007): 20–21.

l. [Unsigned.] *Publishers Weekly* 254, No. 8 (19 February 2007): 152.

53. *Shadows Seen and Unseen* (2006)

a. Herron, Don. *Lost Worlds* No. 5 (2008): 46–47.

b. Schweitzer, Darrell. "Clark Ashton Smith: Inescapable, But Difficult to Love." *New York Review of Science Fiction* No. 235 (March 2008): 15–17.

54. *The Complete Poetry and Translations* (2007–08)

a. Mariconda, Steven J. "Decadence in Verse and Prose." *Dead Reckonings* No. 2 (Fall 2007): 19–22.

b. Schweitzer, Darrell. *New York Review of Science Fiction* 26, No. 7 (March 2014): 21–23.

c. Stableford, Brian. *Lost Worlds* No. 5 (2008): 42–46 (Vol. 1).

55. *The Dark Eidolon and Other Fantasies* (2014)

a. Bebergal, Peter. "Weirdly." *Times Literary Supplement* (11 February 2015): 13.

b. Dziemianowicz, Stefan. *Locus* No. 642 (July 2014): 49.

c. Heck, Peter. *Asimov's Science Fiction* 39, No. 2 (February 2015): 1101–11.

56. *Dawnward Spire, Lonely Hill* (2017)

a. Dirda, Michael. "Boo! The Best Ghost Stories You Probably Haven't Heard Yet." *Washington Post* (19 October 2007). *New Journal* (Wilmington, DE) (24 October 2017): D2.

G. Special Periodicals and Miscellany

i. Special Periodicals

1. *Dark Eidolon*. Edited by Steve Behrends and Marc A. Michaud. No. 2 (July 1989), 36 pp.; No. 3 (Winter 1993), 36 pp.

   Continuation of *Klarkash-Ton* (item 4 below).

2. *Fantasy Fan*. Edited by Charles D. Hornig. 2, No. 3 (November 1934), 16 pp.

3. *Fantasy Sampler*. Edited by John W. Murdock. No. 4 (June 1956). 26 pp. Special CAS section, pp. 5–16.

4. *Klarkash-Ton*. Edited by Steve Behrends. No. 1 (June 1988), 36 pp.

5. *Lost Worlds: The Journal of Clark Ashton Smith Studies*. Edited by Scott Connors (Associate Editor: Ronald S. Hilger). No. 1 (2004), 40 pp.; No. 2 (2004), 40 pp.; No. 3 (2006), 54 pp.; No. 4 (2006), 50 pp.; No. 5 (2008), 48 pp.

6. *Nyctalops*. Edited by Harry O. Morris, Jr. No. 7 (August 1972), 99 pp.

7. *Step Ladder*. Edited by Flora Warren. 13, No. 5 (May 1927). 12 pp. (pp. 129–40; rest of issue not devoted to CAS).

8. *Tales of Horror and Damnation*. Edited by Robert Schwartz. No. 6 (January 1985), 28 pp. "Clark Ashton Smith" Tribute Issue.

9. *Zothique*. Edited by Jean-Luc Buard. No. 1 (1985), 58 pp.

ii. Miscellany

1. Allan, John. "To Clark Ashton Smith."
   a. *Mirage* No. 10 (1971): 47–53.

   Poem.

2. Cass, De Lysle Ferrée. *As It Is Written*. Edited by Will Murray.
   a. West Kingston, RI: Donald M. Grant, 1982.

Novella (scheduled for publication in *Thrill Book,* but not published there) falsely attributed to CAS.

3.   DeAngelis, Michael. "For Clark Ashton Smith."
     a. *Asmodeus* No. 2 (Fall 1951): 16.

     Poem.

4.   DeBill, Walter C., Jr. "The Oldest Dreamer."
     a. *Nyctalops* No. 7 (August 1972): 47.

     Poem about CAS.

5.   Farsaci, Larry B. "To Fantasy."
     a. *Helios* 1, No. 6 (March/April 1938): 32.
     b. *Golden Atom* 1, No. 3 (December 16, 1939): 4.

     Poem dedicated to CAS.

6.   Fryer, Donald S[idney-]. "To Clark Ashton Smith."
     a. *Flame Annual* ([February] 1965): 31–32 (as "One with the Stars").
     b. In Donald Sidney-Fryer. *Songs and Sonnets Atlantean.* Sauk City, WI: Arkham House, 1971. 10.
     c. *Nyctalops* No. 7 (August 1972): 99.
     d. In Donald Sidney-Fryer. *The Atlantis Fragments: The Trilogy of Songs and Sonnets Atlantean.* New York: Hippocampus Press, 2008. 51.
     e. In Donald Sidney-Fryer. *Not Quite Atlantis: A Selection of Poems.* Hornsea, UK: Stanza/PS Publishing, 2010. 5.

     Poem.

7.   Gullette, Alan. "The Artist: An Adulation."
     a. *Nyctalops* No. 7 (August 1972): 27.

     Poem about CAS.

8.   Lorraine, Lilith. "The Cup-Bearer."
     a. *Asmodeus* No. 2 (Fall 1951): 15.
     b. In Lilith Lorraine. *Wine of Wonder.* Dallas, TX: Bookcraft Publishing Co., 1952. 23.
     c. *Avalon News Digest* 1, No. 3 (Winter 1961): 12.

     Poem dedicated to CAS.

9.   Lovecraft, Charles, ed. *Avatars of Wizardry*.
     a.   Sydney, Australia: P'rea Press, 2012.

     Contents: S. T. Joshi, "Foreword" (9–11); Charles Lovecraft, "Publisher's Preface" (13–15); George Sterling, "A Wine of Wizardry" (19–25); CAS, *The Hashish-Eater* (27–43); Richard L. Tierney, "Visions of Golconda" (45–48); Leigh Blackmore, "Memoria: A Fragment from the Book of Wyvern" (49–53); Alan Gullette, "A Trip to the Hypnotist" (55–58); Bruce Boston, "Thirteen Ways of Looking At and Through Hashish" (59–76); Earl Livings, "The Mantle of Merlin" (77–81); Wade German, "The Necromantic Wine" (83–91); Michael Fantina, "Sandalwood" (93–97); Kyla Lee Ward, "Lucubration" (99–105); "Select Bibliography" (107); "About the Contributors" (109–14).

     A volume of poems inspired by CAS's *The Hashish-Eater* and George Sterling's "A Wine of Wizardry." Cover illustration by Gavin O'Keefe; frontispiece designed by David Schembri Studios.

10. Lovecraft, H. P. *Hail, Klarkash-Ton!*
     a.   [Glendale, CA: Roy A. Squires, 1971.]

     Collection of 9 postcards by Lovecraft to CAS.

11. Lovecraft, H. P. "To Clark Ashton Smith, Esq., upon His Phantastick Tales, Verses, Pictures, and Sculptures."
     a.   *Weird Tales* 31, No. 4 (April 1938): 392 (as "To Clark Ashton Smith").
     b.   In H. P. Lovecraft. *Beyond the Wall of Sleep*. Ed. August Derleth and Donald Wandrei. Sauk City, WI: Arkham House, 1943. 409.
     c.   *Asmodeus* No. 2 (Fall 1951): 30.
     d.   In H. P. Lovecraft. *Collected Poems*. [Ed. August Derleth.] Sauk City, WI: Arkham House, 1963. 92. New York: Ballantine, 1971 (as *Fungi from Yuggoth and Other Poems*). 91 (both as "To Klarkash-Ton, Lord of Averoigne").
     e.   In H. P. Lovecraft. *The Fantastic Poetry*. Ed. S. T. Joshi. West Warwick, RI: Necronomicon Press, 1990 (63), 1993 (59).
     f.   In *Ombre dal cosmo* (D.9) (as "A Clark Ashton Smith, signore di Averoigne"; tr. Pietro Guarriello).
     g.   In H. P. Lovecraft. *The Ancient Track: Complete Poetical Works*. Ed. S. T. Joshi. San Francisco: Night Shade, 2001. 80–81. Rev. ed. New York: Hippocampus Press, 2013. 96–97.

h. In *The Averoigne Chronicles* (I.A.85). [235] (as "To Klarkash-Ton, Lord of Averoigne").

Poem about CAS.

12. Morse, Richard Ely. "Dark Garden."
 a. *Californian* 4, No. 2 (Fall 1936): 27.
 b. *Phantagraph* 4, No. 6 (September 1936): [1].
 c. *Acolyte* 2, No. 3 (Summer 1944): 19.

Sonnet dedicated to CAS.

13. Squires, Roy A. *A Bibliographic Catalog of the Largest Collection Ever Offered for Sale of the Works of Clark Ashton Smith & H. P. Lovecraft.*
 a. Glendale, CA: Roy A. Squires, 1968. [12] pp.

14. Squires, Roy A. *Clark Ashton Smith/H. P. Lovecraft/R. H. Barlow: Catalog II.*
 a. Glendale, CA: Roy A. Squires, [1970]. [20] pp.

15. Sturgeon. Theodore. "Clark Ashton Smith: 1893–1961."
 a. In *In Memoriam: Clark Ashton Smith* (D.4).

Poem.

16. Thorne, Evelyn. "To Clark Ashton Smith."
 a. *Asmodeus* No. 2 (Fall 1951): 17.

Poem.

iii. Media Adaptations

a. Audio Recordings

1. *The Black Abbot of Puthuum.* Performed by Reg Green. 1 compact disc. Topanga, CA: Ziggurat Productions, 2003. 71 minutes.

Dramatic reading of the story, with music and sound effects by producer Bob E. Flick.

2. *The Charnel God.* Performed by Reg Green. 1 compact disc. Topanga, CA: Ziggurat Productions, 2003. 77 minutes.

Dramatic reading of the story, with music and sound effects by producer Bob E. Flick.

3. *Clark Ashton Smith—Live from Auburn: The Elder Tapes.*
    a. West Warwick, RI: Necronomicon Press, July 1995. Cassette tape.
    b. Syracuse, NY: Cadabra Records, 2016, 2017. 33⅓ rpm recording (LP).

    Contains readings by CAS of 11 of his poems, as recorded in the 1950s by Robert B. Elder. Includes "Desert Dweller," "Malediction," "Tired Gardener," "High Surf," "Seeker," "Don Quixote on Market Street," "Surrealist Sonnet," "Hesperian Fall," "Nada," "Ecclesiastes," and "Moly." The Necronomicon Press tape contains a cover by Gahan Wilson; produced by Wayne Haigh. The Cadabra recording contains art by Joe Keinberger.

4. *Collected Fantasies of Clark Ashton Smith.* [n.p.:] Audible Studios, 2013. 5 volumes.

    Contents:
    Book 1: The End of the Story.
    14 hours and 3 minutes (unabridged). Read by Fleet Cooper, Allan Robertson, Joe Knezevich, Bernard Setaro Clark, William Neenan, and Chris Kayser.

    Book 2: The Door to Saturn.
    14 hours and 9 minutes (unabridged). Read by William Neenan, Joe Knezevich, Bernard Setaro Clark, Allan Robertson, and Chris Kayser.

    Book 3: A Vintage from Atlantis.
    16 hours and 37 minutes (unabridged). Read by Fleet Cooper (Narrator), Daniel May (Narrator), Joe Knezevich, Bernard Setaro Clark, William Neenan, and Chris Kayser.

    Book 4: The Maze of the Enchanter.
    15 hours and 24 minutes (unabridged). Read by Gregory St. John, Bernard Setaro Clark, Chris Kayser, and Daniel May.

    Book 5: The Last Hieroglyph.
    14 hours and 53 minutes (unabridged). Read by Chris Kayser, Gregory St. John, William Neenan, Daniel May, Bernard Setaro Clark, and Fleet Cooper.

5. *The Double Shadow.* Read by Steve Cooper. 3 compact discs. [Chapel Hill, NC:] Audio Realms Productions, [2010]. Approximately 3.5 hours.

Contents: Disc 1,"The Double Shadow," "The Devotee of Evil." Disc 2, "A Night in Malnéant," "The Maze of the Enchanter," "The Willow Landscape." Disc 3, "The Voyage of King Euvoran."

6.   "The Face by the River." *Weird Tales Collection.* Read by Wayne June. 5 compact discs. [Chapel Hill, NC:] Audio Realms Productions, [2009].

7.   *The Flower-Women.* Performed by Reg Green. 1 compact disc. Topanga, CA: Ziggurat Productions, 2006. 38 minutes.

Dramatic reading of the story, with music and sound effects by producer Bob E. Flick.

8.   *The Hashish-Eater and Other Poems.* Performed by Donald Sidney-Fryer. 1 compact disc. Privately published, 2004. 65:58 minutes.

Contains readings of *The Hashish-Eater,* "Soliloquy in an Ebon Tower," "'O Golden-Tongued Romance,'" "Song of the Necromancer," "Cycles," and "The Sorcerer Departs," with introductory comments by Sidney-Fryer. The disc was produced by Philippe Gindre. See also A.75.
Review.
a.   Joshi, S. T. *Lost Worlds* No. 3 (2006): 40–41.

9.   *The Hashish–Eater.* Performed by Donald Sidney-Fryer. 1 compact disc. New York: Hippocampus Press, 2008. 48:40 minutes

Notes: Same recording as in item 8, laid into scholarly edition of the poem (see I.A.75).

10. *Inferno.* Read by S. T. Joshi. 45 rpm recording. [Syracuse, NY:] Cadabra Records, 2016.

Contains readings of "Inferno," "The Eldritch Dark," "Nyctalops," "Nightmare," and "To Howard Phillips Lovecraft." The liner notes contain an interview of Joshi about CAS. Sound by Theologian; art and design by Jonathan Dennison.

11. *The Isle of the Torturers.* Performed by Reg Green. 1 compact disc. Topanga, CA: Ziggurat Productions, 2003. 50 minutes.

Dramatic reading of the story, with music and sound effects by producer Bob E. Flick.

12. "The Master of the Crabs." *Anthology of Science Fiction, the Surreal, and the Other-Worldly*. Performed by Third Ear Radio Theatre. Topanga, CA: Ziggurat Productions [2002]

> Available only as a download from www.audible.com/pd/ref= sr_1_1?asin=B002UUKXZU&qid=1319856837&sr=1-1

13. *The Maze of Maal Dweb*. Performed by Reg Green. 1 compact disc. Topanga, CA: Ziggurat Productions, 2004. 72 minutes.

> Dramatic reading of the story, with music and sound effects by producer Bob E. Flick.

14. *The Muse of Hyperborea*. Read by S. T. Joshi. 33⅓ rpm recording (LP). [Syracuse, NY:] Cadabra Records, 2016.

> Contains recordings of "The Harlot of the World," "Nyctalops," "Ode to the Abyss," "A Dream of Lethe," "The Tears of Lilith," "Nero," "From the Crypts of Memory," "The Sorcerer Departs," "The Touch-Stone," "The Litany of the Seven Kisses," "To the Daemon," "The Nightmare Tarn," "Memnon at Midnight," "The Muse of Hyperborea," "The Mortuary," "The Traveller," and "Love Malevolent." Sound by Theologian; art by C. M. Kosemen.

15. "The Return of the Sorcerer." *Rod Serling's Night Gallery Reader, Volume 4*. Narrator unknown. 2 audio cassettes. Pharoah Audiobooks, 1993.

16. *Saat aus dem Grabe*. Read by Thomas Franke. 1 compact disc. Bonn: Ululation-Records, 2000. 40:10 minutes.
> *Contents*: "Saat aus dem Grabe" ("The Seed from the Sepulchre"). In German. Translator not identified.

17. *The Tale of Satampra Zeiros*. Performed by Jim Gallant. 2 compact discs. Topanga, CA: Ziggurat Productions, 2003. 39 minutes.

> Dramatic reading of the story, with music and sound effects by producer Bob E. Flick.

18. *Tales from Clark Ashton Smith's Atlantis*. Performed by Jim Gallant. 1 compact disc. Topanga, CA: Ziggurat Productions, 2004. 66 minutes.

> *Contents:* "Atlantis" [poem]; "The Last Incantation"; "The Death of Malygris." Dramatic readings, with music and sound effects by producer Bob E. Flick.

19. *The Weaver in the Vault*. Performed by Reg Green. 1 compact disc. Topanga, CA: Ziggurat Productions, 2003. 45 minutes.

> Dramatic reading of the story, with music and sound effects by producer Bob E. Flick.

20. "The Willow Landscape." Performed by Theodore. 33⅓ rpm recording (LP). *Coral Records Presents Theodore*. New York: Coral (Decca Records), 1959.

> CAS met the monologist, comedian, and actor Theodore Gottlieb (a.k.a. "Brother Theodore") sometime in the 1950s. Theodore performs a free adaptation of CAS's tale on side A of this LP recording.

b. Television

1. "The Return of the Sorcerer." *Rod Serling's Night Gallery* (NBC). Teleplay by Halsted Welles. Directed by Jeannot Szwarc. Starring Vincent Price, Bill Bixby, and Tisha Sterling. Narrated by Rod Serling. NBC, New York, 24 September 1972.
   a. *Rod Serling's Night Gallery: The Collector's Edition XIII*. Videocassette. Universal/Columbia House, 1999.
   b. *Night Gallery: The Complete First Season*. DVD. Universal, 2004. Included as a bonus on disc 3.

c. Film

1. *The Mother of Toads*. Screenplay by Richard Stanley, Scarlett Amaris, and Emiliano Ranzani. Directed by Richard Stanley. Starring Catriona MacColl, Shane Woodward, Victoria Maurette, Lisa Belle, and Amelie Salomon. A sergment of the portmanteau film *The Theatre Bizarre* (Severin Films, 2011).
   a. *The Theatre Bizarre*. DVD. Image Entertainment, 2011. Includes audio commentary by Richard Stanley, actress Victoria Maurette, and cinematographer Karim Hussain.

d. Graphic

1. "The Abominations of Yondo."
   a. *Conan the Adventurer* 1, No. 12 (May 1995).

Adapted by Roy Thomas. Drawn by Rafael Kayanan. CAS thought highly of Robert E. Howard's stories of Conan the Cimmerian, so he probably would be amused by the transformation of this story into one of his adventures.

2. "The Beast of Averoigne."
   a. *Horror Classics: Graphic Classics, Volume Ten.* Ed. Tom Pomplun. Mount Horeb, WI: Eureka Productions, 2004. 104–23.

   Script by Rod Lott. Art by Richard Jenkins.

3. "The Dream Bridge."
   a. *Fantasy Classics: Graphic Classics, Volume 15.* Ed. Tom Pomplun. Mount Horeb, WI: Eureka Productions, 2008. 95.

4. "The Last Incantation."
   a. *Karpath* No. 1 (fourth quarter 1989): 22–24 (as "La Derniere incantation").

   Adapted by Guillaume Sorel.

5. "Necromancy in Naat."
   a. *Conan the Savage* 1, No. 10 (May 1996): 1–48 (as "The Necromancers of Naat").

   Adapted by Roy Thomas (writer), John Buscema (artist), and Vickie Williams (letterer).

6. "Nightmare of the Lilliputian."
   a. *Aero into the Aether* (1979): 26–27.

   Adapted by Hal Rammel.

7. "The Ninth Skeleton."
   a. *Third Rail* 1, No. 1 (June 1981): 27–32.
   b. *Asylum* 1, No. 1 (1989): 20–24.

   Adapted by Tom Yeates and Job B. Bright. Art by Job B. Bright.

8. "The Return of the Sorcerer."
   a. *Densaga* No. 3 (1993): [17–26.]

   Adaptation and artwork by Richard Corben.

9. "The Seed from the Sepulcher."
   a. *Densaga* No. 1 (1992): [19–28].

   Adaptation and artwork by Richard Corben.

10. "The Tale of Satampra Zeiros."
    a. *Clark Ashton Smith's Hyperborea*. San Francisco, CA: Mock Man
        Press, Summer 2004. [24 pp.]

        Contents: "The Tale of Satampra Zeiros" (1–20); Map, by Adam
        Burns (21); "The Art of the Hyperboreans" (22); "Where Is
        Hyperborea?" by Jason Thompson.
            Adapted by Jason Thompson. Artwork by Jason Thompson.

11. "The Vaults of Yoh-Vombis."
    a. *Densaga* No. 2 (1993): [17–26.]

        Notes: Adaptation and artwork by Richard Corben.

12. "The Weird of Avoosl Wuthoqquan."
    a. *Conan the Adventurer* 1, No. 8 (January 1995).

        Adapted by Roy Thomas. Art by John Watkiss.

e. Musical Adaptations

1. "The Cherry-Snows." Set to music by Emmet Pendleton. Unpublished.

    CAS notes that "I believe that two lyrics from my first volume, for
    which melodies were written some years ago by a California
    composer, Emmet Pendleton, will appear presently both in sheet
    and book form" (CAS to August Derleth, 20 July 1937; ms.,
    Wisconsin Historical Society). In the unsigned article "A De-
    lightful Song Recital," *Pacific Coast Musical Review* 42, No. 7 (13
    May 1922): 8, it is noted that Pendleton's setting of CAS's "The
    Cherry-Snows" was performed by Martha Tinker Godbolt (mez-
    zo-soprano) and Pendleton (piano).

2. "The Dream Bridge." Set to music by Henry Cowell. September
    1915. Unpublished.

    Set for solo voice (soprano) and piano. Recorded on *The Songs of
    Henry Cowell*. Albany, NY: Albany, 1997. Mary Ann Hart, mez-
    zo-soprano; Jeanne Golan, piano.

3. "The Eldritch Dark." Set to music by Henry Cowell. October 1915.
    Unpublished.

    Set for solo voice and piano.

4. "Fairy Lanterns." Set to music by Henry Cowell. November 1915. Unpublished.

    Set for solo voice and piano.

5. "The Fugitives." Set to music by Henry Cowell. September 1915. Unpublished.

    Set for solo voice and piano.

6. "Impression." Set to music by Joseph W. Grant. New York: Carl Fischer, 1944. 4 pp.

    Set for women's voices with piano accompaniment.

7. "The Morning Pool." Set to music by Henry Cowell. February 1918. Unpublished.

    Set for solo voice (soprano) and piano. Recorded on *The Songs of Henry Cowell*. Albany, NY: Albany, 1997. Mary Ann Hart, mezzo-soprano; Jeanne Golan, piano.

8. "Pine Needles." Set to music by Kevin T. Padworski. n.p.: MusicSpoke, [2015]. 13 pp.

    Set for four voices (soprano, soprano, alto, alto), with piano accompaniment. A performance is available on YouTube (www.youtube.com/watch?v=z0IVFcncvVE).

9. "White Death." Set to music by Henry Cowell. September 1915. Unpublished.

    Set for voice and piano.

f. Dramatic Adaptations

1. *The Ghoul*. Frank Szelwach and Matt McGlade, puppeteers. 8mm Movie Matinee, 2012.

    Adaptation of "The Ghoul" by Mike Decay as a puppet show. Performed at Bar 82, 15 April 2012. facebook.com/events/s/8mm-movie-matinee/904685202924544/?ti=icl

iv. Online Sources

1.   "Clark Ashton Smith."
      a.   www.fantasticfiction.com/s/clark-ashton-smith

      Select bibliography of CAS's book publications as well as individual appearances of stories.

2.   "Clark Ashton Smith."
      a.   *Wikipedia* (en.wikipedia.org/wiki/Clark_Ashton_Smith).

      Extensive bio-critical article discussing the whole of CAS's life, with select bibliography and references.

3.   "The Double Shadow: A Clark Ashton Smith Podcast."
      a.   hppodcraft.com/forums/index.php?topic=1197.0

      Podcast that contains readings of CAS's stories (mostly from "The Eldritch Dark") and discussions of CAS. Operated by Philip Gelatt, Ruth Tillman, and Tim Mucci.

4.   "The Eldritch Dark: Clark Ashton Smith."
      a.   www.eldritchdark.com

      The most exhaustive online source for CAS material, containing texts of many of CAS's works; artwork by CAS or by others inspired by CAS's writings; critical and biographical articles on CAS; tributes to CAS (fiction, poetry, prose poetry); news on recent developments in CAS studies; and other matter. Site operated by Boyd Pearson.

5.   Ganderson, Adam. "The Last Warlock: A Brief History of Clark Ashton Smith and the Golden Age of Weird Fiction."
      a.   thefanzine.com/the-last-warlock-a-brief-history-of-clark-ashton-smith-and-the-golden-age-of-weird-fiction/

      Lengthy article on CAS's place in weird fiction and the recent rise in his reputation.

6.   Gioia, Ted. "Making a Case for Clark Ashton Smith."
      a.   www.conceptualfiction.com/the_dark_eidolon.html

      Article based on the publication of *The Dark Eidolon and Other Fantasies* (I.A.84), in which the author ponders the reasons for CAS's obscurity.

7.   Hickman, S. C. "Clark Ashton Smith: Visionary of the Fantastic."
      a.   socialecologies.wordpress.com/2016/09/18/clark-ashton-smith
           -visionary-of-the-dark-fantastic

      Substantial analysis of CAS as a writer of dark visionary fiction.

8.   Reiter, Geoffrey. "Dream Builder: Recognizing Clark Ashton
      Smith's Legacy in Fiction."
      a.   christandpopculture.com/dream-builder-recognizing-clark-ashton-
           smiths-legacy-fiction/

      CAS's work interpreted from a Christian perspective.

9.   Smith, Clark Ashton."
      a.   www.sf-encyclopedia.com/entry/smith_clark_ashton

      Biographical entry on CAS with extensive bibliography of CAS's
      book publications.

10.   "Summary Bibliography: Clark Ashton Smith."
      a.   www.isfdb.org/cgi-bin/ea.cgi?819

      Extensive bibliography of CAS's book publications as well as in-
      dividual publications of stories, poems, etc.

IV. Indexes

A. Names

Lorraine, Lilith I.B.ii.460n, v.63.a; III.E.192, F.7.j, 9.c, G.ii.8

Lott, Richard III.G.iii.d.2n

Louvrier, Frédéric III.F.27.a, 28.a

Lovecraft, Charles I.B.ii.356.k; III.D.1, G.ii.9

Lovecraft, H. P. I.A.37n, 43, 63, 71, 74n, 85, 86, B.i.42n, 65m, ii.350.a, 887.b, v.60, vi.a.2, b.34.a, 48.b, vii.14; II.A.i.3n, iv.5, 6, B.i.2.c, 5.c, 38.c, 45.h, 56.e, iii.3.b, 10.a, v.1–5, vii.4.a, 13; III.A.144n, D.1n, 9, E.10.c, 11.c, 15n, 46n, 52n, 93n, 97n, 148n, 164n, 165n, 166n, 170n, 172n, 173n, 177n, 185n, 193–215, 246n, 272n, 273n, 274n, 287n, 293n, 323n, F.3.d, e, G.ii.10, 11

Loveman, Samuel I.A.32n, 63, 65; III.E.132n

Lowndes, Robert A. W. III.E.8, 216–19, F.7.k, 12.c, 13.b, 14.c, 15.a, 16.e

Lozano y Lozano, Juan I.A.73, B.iii.a.b.10

Lubeck, Mrs. D. W. I.B.ii.761.b

Luce, Gregory I.B.i.125.q

Lucentini, Franco II.B.i.48.e

Lukens, Mrs. Earl I.B.ii.761.b

Lundwall, Sam J. II.B.i.2.b, 56.g, j, k, iii.1.b

Lupoff, Pat III.E.245.b, G.52.f

Lupoff, Richard A. I.A.70; III.E.220, 246.b

Luserke, Uwe III.E.221

Lyman, William Whittingham I.A.63, 87, B.i.90.b, ii.11.c, 155.d, 572.c, 741.d; III.E.222

MacCall, Catriona III.G.iii.c.1

McCarthy, Ryan III.A.30

McCoy, Kathleen III.A.31

Macdonald, Augustin S. I.B.ii.218.c

McDonald, T. Liam I.B.i.158.e

McGlade, Matt III.G.iii.f.1

Machen, Arthur III.E.68n, F.1.g

Mackail, J. W. I.B.ii.879n

McMurray, Jacob I.A.87n

Macomber, Ben III.F.4.b

McSherry, Frank D. I.B.i.158.d

McVicker, Terence I.A.3n, 72

Magill, Frank N. III.B.9

Maibohm, Werner II.B.i.47.e

Malerne, Bernard. See Buard, Jean-Luc

Maliano III.E.222

Mana, Davide II.B.ii.4.a

Manfredi, Gianfranco II.B.i.54.a

Manicki, Jacek II.A.viii.1

Manley, Seon I.B.i.153.d

Manninen, Teemu II.B.ii.18.a

Marbling, Ann Muir I.A.81n

Margulies, Leo I.B.i.6.f, 16.f, 97.c, 153.c, v.73.a; II.B.i.41.a, 64.c

Mariconda, Steven J. III.F.54.a

Marigny, E. L. de II.A.i.3

Marigny, Jean II.A.iii.6, 8, B.i.17.a, 18.b, 65.a; III.D.9, 11, E.224, 225

Mariscal, Óscar II.B.ii.21.a, b, c, d, iii.6.a, b, v.6.a

Markham, Edwin I.B.ii.63.e, 496.c, 546.d, 620.d; III.E.226, 227

Martijn, Jaime II.A.i.3

Martin, Bill I.A.29n; II.A.ix.2

Martínez, Sebastián II.B.i.48.c

Masi, Carlo I.B.i.3.a

Matbaacilik, Kitap II.A.x.1

Mattaliano, Dario II.B.i.37.c

Maurette, Victoria III.G.iii.c.1

May, Daniel III.G.iii.a.4n

Mayer, Frederick J. III.D.1, E.228

Mazzarese, Angelo R. II.A.vi.9

Mencken, H. L. III.E.25n

Menegaldo, Gilles III.E.127.a

Menville, Douglas III.F.16.f

Mercator, Gerardus II.A.ix.8n

Merrill, Stuart I.A.73, B.iii.a.185

Mialanos, Giorgos II.A.v.3

Michael, Maikell II.B.i.10.a, 18.a

Michaud, Marc A. I.A.49, B.vi.b.22.c, 27.c; III.E.178, 193.b, F.3.d, 40.e, G.i.1, a.1

Michaud, Susan I.A.49

Mighels, Ella Sterling I.B.ii.289.b, 662.b

Miller, Chuck III.E.136.a

Miller, Mamie Lowe I.B.ii.697n

Miller, John III.A.39n

Miller, P. Schuyler III.F.21.a

Miske, J. Chapman III.E.229

Mitchell, Steve III.E.230, 231

Modell, George III.E.269n

Molino II.B.i.64.a

Mols, Dominique II.A.iii.3, 4, 6, 8, 9, 10, B.i.11.a, 14.a, 17.a, c, 18.b, 32.a, 42.a, 57.e, 59.a, 61.b, iii.9.a

Montal-Faubelle, Henri de III.E.232

B. Titles by Smith

"Flower-Women, The" I.A.10, 30, 40, 59, 70, 89, B.i.48; II.A.i.3, iii.7, 16, iv.4, 8, v.2, vi.3, 10, 13, vii.1, viii.1, ix.7, B.i.20; III.G.iii.a.7
"Flower-Women, The" (synopsis) I.A.52
"Foggy Night" I.A.27, 73, B.ii.297
"Folie de Chronomage, La" II.B.i.66.a
"Folterer-Insel, Die" II.A.iv.2
"Fontaine de Sang, La" I.A.4, B.iii.a.61.a
"For a Wine-Jar" I.A.73, B.ii.298
"For an Antique Lyre" I.A.18, 27, 71, B.ii.299
"For Iris" I.A.73, B.ii.300
"For the Dance of Death" I.A.27, 73, B.ii.301
"Forbidden Forest, The" I.A.23, 49, 87, B.iv.14; II.A.iii.12; III.D.9
"Foreknowledge" I.B.ii.333n
"Foresta proibita, La" III.D.9
"Forêt interdite, La" II.A.iii.12
"Forgetfulness" I.A.3, 27, 73, B.ii.302; II.A.iii.17
"Forgotten Sorrow" I.A.4, 27, 61, 73, B.ii.303
"Formes noires" II.B.i.68.a
"Formi di pietra" II.A.vi.13
"Forteresse, La" I.A.73, B.ii.304, 305n
"Fortress, The" I.A.73, B.ii.304n, 305
"Fortune" I.A.73, B.ii.306
"Fountain, The" I.A.73, B.iii.a.60
"Fountain of Blood, The" I.A.27, 73, B.iii.a.61
"Fountain of Youth, The" I.A.73, B.ii.307
"Fragment" I.A.18, 27, 73, B.ii.308
"Fragment: La Maison d'Haon-Dor" II.A.iii.15
"Fragment, A" I.A.3, 27, 73, B.ii.309
"Fragment, A" [variant title] I.B.ii.442n
"[Fragment 1]" I.A.73, B.ii.310
"[Fragment 2]" I.A.73, B.ii.311
"[Fragment 3]" I.A.73, B.ii.312
"[Fragment 4]" I.A.73, B.ii.313
"[Fragment 5]" I.A.73, B.ii.314
"[Fragment 6]" I.A.73, B.ii.315
"[Fragment 7]" I.A.73, B.ii.316
"[Fragment of an Essay]" I.A.64, B.v.56
"Fragments & Synopsis" II.A.iii.14
"Frai de la tombe, Le" II.A.iii.2, 10

"Freedom of the Hills, The" I.A.73, B.ii.317
"Fremde Gott, Der" II.A.iv.1
"Fremde Schatten, Der" II.A.iv.2
"From a Letter" [letter] I.B.vi.b.48.a
"From a Letter" [prose poem] I.A.3, 23, 49, 77, 87, B.iv.15; II.A.iii.12, iv.7, vi.13
"From a Lost World" (synopsis) I.A.52
"From Arcady" I.A.27, 73, B.ii.318
"From Clark Ashton Smith" I.B.vi.b.38.b
"From 'Ludar's Litany to Thasaidon'" [I] I.A.73, B.ii.319
"From 'Ludar's Litany to Thasaidon'" [II] I.A.73, B.ii.320
"From Nero" I.B.ii.546.d
"From 'Ode to Antares'" I.A.73, B.ii.321
"From 'Song of King Hoaraph's Bow-men'" I.A.73, B.ii.322
"From 'Song of the Galley Slaves'" I.A.73, B.ii.323
"From the Crypts of Memory" I.A.3, 9, 23, 30, 35, 49, 70, 77, 84, 87, B.i.114n, iv.16; II.A.iii.5, 12, 16, iv.8, vi.5, 10, vii.1, B.iii.4; III.G.iii.a.14n
From the Crypts of Memory I.A.35
"From 'The Song of Xeethra'" I.A.73, B.ii.324
"From the Persian" [I read upon a gate . . .] I.A.73, B.ii.325
"From the Persian" [I stood amid the ruins . . .] I.A.73, B.ii.326
"From the Persian" [Out of the Great Bazaar . . .] I.A.73, B.ii.327
"Frozen Waterfall, The" I.A.49, 52, 87, B.iv.17; II.A.iii.12
"Fruit de la tombe, Le" II.A.iii.14
"Fruto de la tumba, El" II.A.ix.1
"Frutto della tomba, Il" II.A.vi.13, B.i.38.b
Fugitive Poems of Clark Ashton Smith, The I.A.26
Fugitive Poems of Clark Ashton Smith: Second Series, The I.A.38
"Fugitives, The" I.A.1, 73, 78, B.ii.328; III.G.iii.e.5
Fugitives, The I.A.52, 73, B.ii.329, 471n, 790n, 791n
"Fulfilled Prophecy, The" I.A.64, 89, B.i.49

C. Periodicals

www.ingramcontent.com/pod-product-compliance
Lightning Source LLC
Chambersburg PA
CBHW070616270326
41926CB00011B/1710